FEDERAL INCOME TAXATION

Tax Principles and Tax Planning

ROBERT S. HOLZMAN, Ph.D.

PROFESSOR OF TAXATION
GRADUATE SCHOOL OF BUSINESS ADMINISTRATION
NEW YORK UNIVERSITY

THE RONALD PRESS COMPANY · NEW YORK

2

Library of Congress Catalog Card Number: 60-6155
PRINTED IN THE UNITED STATES OF AMERICA

To

Carroll V. Newsom

For there is a man whose labour is in wisdom,
and in knowledge, and in equity . . .

——Ecclesiastes 2:21

PREFACE

A British judge declared, "Income-tax, if I may be pardoned for saying so, is a tax on income." *London County Council v. Attorney-General,* 4 T.C. 265 (1901). That is not very helpful.

An American judge stated in deathless prose, "Embellished with an erudition almost innocuous because almost obsolete, and expressed with a clarity characteristic of the dialectical tergiversations of the medieval theological controversialists, some of the objections to the indictment and the argument in their support involve processes of mental ratiocination not easily within the capacity of persons accustomed to deal with the law in its practical phases only." *Whitehead et al. v. United States,* 245 Fed. 385 (5th Cir., 1917). That is not very helpful, either.

The sole purpose of this book is to be helpful to the student of taxation. Unlike its predecessors in the textbook field, this book does not try to reach a variety of readers with specialized points of view so different that a compromise presentation results without full benefit to any party. This book does not try to list every possible facet of a particular proposition or exception; that can be handled adequately only by the huge, multivolumed loose-leaf tax services. This book is not intended to be a working manual for use by active tax practitioners or corporation tax executives with a definite problem to be researched; that is the function of specialized treatises and professional periodicals. This book does not seek to provide a specific citation for every statement made; the reader, instead, is directed to the applicable section of the Internal Revenue Code, from which point he may travel to a particular subsection, paragraph, subparagraph, or clause. This book is not an oversimplified checklist of what-to-do or how-to-save-x; the tax law is not simple, and it is dangerous to suggest otherwise.

Then, what is there left for this volume to do? There remains what should be the one objective of a student's textbook: instruction in how the Federal income tax works. There are the sources from which springs what is loosely referred to as the tax law. There is the theory of the tax law and of various portions of it. There are explanations of how the principal sections of the Internal Revenue Code operate, without effort to be so encyclopedic as to encompass the entire law in all its vastness. There are mathematical illustrations of those computations which are not self-evident. To each chapter there is a supplement, generally in three divisions: (A) *Suggested Reading Materials,* for students who wish to pursue a specific subject further; (B) *Leading Cases,* rather than a forbidding array of decisions that, in some texts, consist largely of highly individualized facts or relatively unimportant conclusions; (C) *Questions,* which are supplied in moderate quantity, so that the student does not allocate all of his available study time to working on solutions, at the expense of perusing the text.

The handling of tax questions does not consist merely of the preparation of tax returns. Transactions may be planned in advance, so that the consequences, when ultimately carried forward to the tax return, will result in lower taxes. One chapter is specifically entitled "Tax Planning," but there is considerable other material on the subject of how taxes may be reduced legitimately and also on the subject of seemingly routine transactions that may be "upset" by the Internal Revenue Service. Tax knowledge means more than awareness of what goes on Line 6 of Schedule H, and the reader is acquainted with techniques, alternatives, and procedures.

This book's organization differs materially from that of other textbooks. In actual practice, one does not start a tax return by computing the tax; that is almost the final step in preparing a return. This volume, as the tax return itself, follows the logical sequence of building up income; subtracting deductions and exemptions; applying credits; and only as a late step is tax computed. Nor is the student allowed to believe that when a return is filed on time, the taxpayer's responsibilities have been discharged. Considerable attention is paid to obligations of being a taxpayer; the need for and the form of workpapers; and the burden of proof. In short, computation of tax cannot be regarded as something that exists in a vacuum. Preparation of tax returns is only one phase of a process that has as integrated elements these factors: planning a transaction, weighing alternative courses of action, accumulation of data, mathematical computation, and justification of what appears on the tax return. Knowledge of what to do before and after the tax form is filed is just as important as familiarity with the return itself.

Robert S. Holzman

New York University
January, 1960

CONTENTS

FEDERAL INCOME TAXATION

Tax Principles and Tax Planning

1

GENERAL PRINCIPLES

Historical Background

Taxes and History. Taxes have meant far more to the American people than the mere payment of money. Taxes have had a very direct impact upon the history of this country.

It was a matter of taxation that precipitated the War of the Revolution. For long years, the American colonists submitted to what they regarded as unreasonable laws imposed by the British parliament; but a new tax upon tea was just too much. Samuel Adams in Massachusetts hotly demanded, "Now what liberty can there be, when property is taken away without consent?" "Taxation without reprcsentation is tyranny!" cried the colonists; and on the afternoon of December 16, 1773, a party of citizens disguised as Indians boarded an English ship and hurled the boxes of tea, tax stamps and all, into Boston harbor. There were reprisals, but the Americans resisted with the new rallying cry, "Taxation without representation is tyranny!" The war was fought and won.

During and after the Revolutionary War, the colonies operated under a vague and loose arrangement called the Articles of Confederation. Mindful of past experience, the colonists refused to give the national government certain powers that might be abused, such as the right of taxation. But every colony and state could, and in fact *did*, tax any shipment of goods that passed through it or its adjoining waters. It became prohibitively expensive to ship anything that had to pass through several states. To discuss reforms of the troublesome taxation upon interstate commerce by the states, desperate merchants called what is known as the Annapolis Convention in 1786. Actually this convention did nothing in itself, but it adjourned with a recommendation that a larger convention be held in Philadelphia the following May. As every schoolboy knows, the Constitution of the United States was the result of this Philadelphia convention. Had it not been for a question of taxation, we might never have drawn up this Constitution.

The United States of America was duly launched. But Government needed money (even at that time), and the Act of March, 1791, imposed a Federal excise tax upon the production of alcoholic spirits. "Is this freedom, when the Federal Government can interfere with our businesses?" demanded many liberty-loving persons. In 1794, when the United States attempted to enforce this tax, many people in western Pennsylvania refused to pay it. Revenue officers were tarred and feathered. In September, President Washington sent militia into that state to see that the tax was collected. It was. This was the first armed opposition to the Federal Government, and a tax created the issue. Collection of the tax showed that the Federal Government could use powers granted by Congress to enforce Federal laws within a state.

Another constitutional question quickly arose. The United States Supreme Court declared that it had the right to review the findings of lower courts when a substantial Federal question was involved. Jealous judges, and those who had won verdicts in lower courts, did not think that this was proper. But, in 1796, the Supreme Court definitely established that it *did* have the power of judicial review. The case in question[1] involved a tax issue: whether a tax upon carriages had to be levied in accordance with population.

As the nineteenth century dawned, democracy in practice was not so widespread as the printed word would indicate. Most of the state laws provided that no person could vote unless he were a property holder. But, in 1820, Massachusetts allowed the vote to all taxpayers: if someone paid taxes, he had as much interest in the Government as if he owned property, it was said at the time. This established the principle that a taxpayer is as good a citizen as a property holder is.

In the sensitive area where jealous Federal and state governments argued about sovereignty, it took a decision of the Supreme Court in a tax case to settle the issue. A state may not tax Federal functions, said Chief Justice John Marshall, for "the power to tax is the power to destroy." If Federal functions could be taxed by the states, these functions would be dependent upon the will of the states rather than of the national government, it was held.[2] There is some question as to the continued vitality of the words quoted. In a dissenting opinion, Mr. Justice Holmes declared, "The power to tax is not the power to destroy while this Court sits."[3]

[1] *Hylton v. United States,* 3 Dallas 171 (1796).
[2] *McCulloch v. Maryland,* 4 Wheaton 316 (1819).
[3] *Panhandle Oil Co. v. Mississippi ex rel. Knox,* 277 U.S. 218 (1928).

Early Taxes. The most common form of taxation in the American colonies was the property tax. But it did not take long before there were special taxes upon pride of possession. There were taxes on carriages, silver plate, hair powder, and armorial bearings, for an accumulation of the signs of wealth was a presumption of the ability to pay taxes. In colonial Virginia, it was provided that for all public "contributions," every unmarried man had to be assessed in church "according to his own apparel," while a married man was assessed "according to his own and his wife's apparel." Married men, at least, could not take active steps to become tax dodgers. But in Maryland, there was a special tax upon bachelors. Objection was made to this on the ground that it was a tax upon misfortune, although not everyone acquiesced.

The Income Tax. In 1646, Massachusetts imposed a tax upon certain types of income.[4] Mercantile profits were taxed by Rhode Island in 1673 and by New Jersey in 1684. Salaries of certain types were taxed in Pennsylvania, Delaware, and Maryland around the time of the Revolutionary War.

There was no Federal income tax until the Civil War. The constitutionality of these emergency measures was upheld long after the statutes themselves had lapsed.[5] But taxes which are tolerable in wartime are less acceptable in peacetime, and for long years little attention was paid to demands for a tax upon income. When an income tax was imposed in 1894, it was quickly challenged. In the following years the Supreme Court held that it was unconstitutional, as all direct taxes had to be levied upon the basis of proportionate population.[6] But much more was said by the justices, whose opinions required an even 200 pages in the printed record. An income tax, it was claimed, is an assault upon capital, and it makes for a war of the rich against the poor. But the advocates of the tax were no less angry, and one justice warned that if taxes were not based upon ability to pay, "the red specter of revolution would shake our institutions to their foundations."

The justices of the United States Supreme Court were not the only ones who could see the revolutionary aspects of an income tax. The Communist Manifesto enunciated in 1848 by Karl Marx and Friedrich Engels had warned: "The proletariat will use its polit-

[4] The authority for this paragraph is Eric L. Kohler, *Accounting Principles Underlying Federal Income Taxes 1925* (Chicago and New York: A. W. Shaw Co., 1925), p. 5.

[5] *Pacific Insurance Company v. Soule*, 74 U.S. 433 (1869).

[6] *Pollock v. Farmers' Loan and Trust Company*, 157 U.S. 429 (1895), *on rehearing*, 158 U.S. 601 (1895).

ical supremacy, to wrest, by degrees, all capital from the bourgeoisie. . . . These measures will of course be different in different countries. Nevertheless in the most advanced countries the following will be generally applicable. . . . A heavy progressive or graduated income tax." And Engels later wrote that the revolution would take the direction of: "1. Restriction of private property by progressive taxes." [7]

In 1909, there was passed what amounted to an income tax upon corporations. But this law was referred to as a corporation excise tax for the privilege of doing business, and an excise tax was not regarded as that type of direct tax which must be apportioned according to population. So the Supreme Court upheld the constitutionality of this act.[8]

By 1913, the Constitution had been amended to permit an income tax, and Representative Cordell Hull of Tennessee was primarily responsible for writing the Tariff Act of 1913, which imposed the first income tax under the authority of the Sixteenth Amendment. Said the St. Louis *Globe-Democrat,* "This is the most objectionable of all forms of tax." The Boston *Herald* feared that "the radical elements of the political community will repeat the experience of Turkey and Russia in taxing the life out of thrift and industry." The New York *Herald* found that the tax was "wrong in principle and un-American in spirit," and quoted a banker's opinion that "the Government, instead of taxing incomes, ought to pay premiums to men for achieving financial success." The Philadelphia *Public Ledger* commented, "Income taxes give rise to mendacity, to espionage, and to inquisitions that are vexatious, but they have one great virtue: direct taxes bring home to the taxed the meaning of taxation and of expensive governmental undertakings with certainty and power."

The constitutionality of a Federal income tax as enacted under the Sixteenth Amendment was upheld.[9] That did not completely settle the matter, however. Periodically, efforts are made to have the income tax law declared unconstitutional, with consequences too stupendous to imagine. One taxpayer vainly argued that the Sixteenth Amendment must fall as being contrary to the provisions of the Thirteenth Amendment, abolishing involuntary servitude, inasmuch as the tax laws and procedures "have compelled him to assume unreasonable duties, obligations and burdens in order to

[7] *Grundsätze des Kommunismus* (Buchhandlung Vorwärtz Paul Singer G.m.b.h., 1914), p. 24.

[8] *Flint v. Stone Tracy Company,* 220 U.S. 107 (1911).

[9] *Brushaber v. Union Pacific Railroad Company,* 240 U.S. 1 (1916).

make a just accounting of his income and pay the tax thereon." [10] Another taxpayer fruitlessly claimed that the Sixteenth Amendment was unconstitutional because the law was passed for motives other than the raising of revenue, and that an amendment should be defined as a change for the better and not for the worse.[11]

General Principles

What Is Taxed? The Sixteenth Amendment gave Congress the power to lay and collect taxes "on incomes, from whatever source derived . . ." That left it to revenue laws enacted under this general authorization to define what incomes are to be taxed, and to what extent. The Internal Revenue Code of 1954 imposes a tax on "taxable income." This will be defined in Chapter 5. It is sufficient to say at this point that taxable income, by definition, does not include every type of income. The tax will not reach items that are income by any other test: sound accounting principles, economic theory, or plain solid "cash on the barrel head."

What is taxed may be a question of *state* law, even where a Federal income tax statute is concerned. For example, property rights are determined customarily by state law. Thus a certain interest "was property under the laws of South Carolina. . . ." [12]

Who Is Taxed? The income tax is, in general, imposed upon that party who is entitled to the income. That may be an individual, corporation, estate, or trust. It does not include a partnership, for, as will be developed in Chapter 18, that entity only reports what income of various types it receives; the partners individually pay taxes upon their proportionate shares of this income. Under most circumstances, tax is imposed upon foreign income of citizens or residents of the United States; under certain conditions, tax is imposed upon income of foreign individuals, corporations, or other entities. See Chapter 22. Infants of tender age may be taxed upon their income which, in this age of the quiz show, may be considerable.

The tax law, the Internal Revenue Service, and the courts have created various safeguards to see that taxpayers do not shift income in order to have it taxed to a party other than the one entitled to it.

Transactions with Related Parties. Where there is common control, the Internal Revenue Service may re-allocate items of income

[10] *Porth v. Brodrick,* 214 F.2d 925 (10th Cir., 1954).
[11] *Lewis v. Commissioner,* D.C., Ill., 1954.
[12] *J. F. S. Crayton,* 11 B.T.A. 1375 (1928).

or expense in order to prevent the artificial channeling of taxes. Internal Revenue Code Section 482. See Chapter 27.

Constructive Receipt of Income. If a person is entitled to income, he may not by contract or otherwise provide that the income will be taxed to someone else. If a person performs services, he will not escape taxation by providing that the income is to be paid directly to someone else. "There is no doubt that the statute could tax salaries to those who earned them and provide that the tax could not be escaped by anticipatory arrangements and contracts however skillfully devised to prevent the salary when paid from vesting even for a second in the man who earned it. That seems to us the import of the statute before us and we think that no distinction can be taken according to the motives leading to the arrangement by which the fruits are attributed to a different tree from that on which they grew."[13] It is immaterial that the contract of assignment was irrevocable in character and was authorized by state law. If the terms of a contract require that the lessee make payments directly to the lessor's stockholders, it is the lessor that will be taxed.[14]

Under this same principle, the owner of stocks or bonds cannot escape income tax upon dividends or interest that are paid to another party. "[T]he import of the statute is that the fruit is not to be attributed to a different tree from that on which it grew."[15] An assignment, to be effective tax-wise, must embrace both tree and fruit.

Family Partnerships. An individual may not arrange to have his income taxed in part to a related party, by means of a partnership, if in reality there is no bona fide partnership. See Chapter 18.

Entities. If a taxpayer creates bona fide entities, each one will be regarded as separate for tax purposes, subject to the limitations in the next two paragraphs. Thus, if an individual creates a corporation which actually carries on activities in its own name and right, he cannot deny the separate tax existence of the corporation. "The facts, it seems to us, compel the conclusion that the taxpayer had a tax identity distinct from its stockholder."[16] If an individual elects to use a corporation to perform his business chores, he cannot claim that the corporation is really his alter ego and hence should not be taxed. But an exception often is made of realty companies.

[13] *Lucas v. Earl,* 281 U.S. 111 (1930).
[14] *United States v. Joliet & Chicago Railroad Company,* 315 U.S. 44 (1942).
[15] *Helvering v. Horst,* 311 U.S. 112 (1940).
[16] *Moline Properties, Inc. v. Commissioner,* 319 U.S. 436 (1943).

Where a corporation was formed solely to liquidate real estate and had no right, power, or discretion with respect to the disposition of income, it was held that the corporation was merely a conduit and not taxable; it had been formed for one purpose and had no control over income.[17] This rule often is extended to going corporations.

If there is created an entity for the primary purpose of tax avoidance or evasion, the Secretary may ignore what was done. "[T]he partnership served no business purpose."[18] The separate entity of a fully controlled subsidiary could be disregarded under the facts.[19]

Where multiple corporations are created primarily for tax purposes, the tax advantages of plural entities may be lost (*e.g.*, separate surtax exemptions). See Chapter 16.

When Is Tax Imposed? Tax is imposed upon taxable income, and the time of realization of that statutory term generally depends upon the accounting method used by the taxpayer. The two general methods of accounting are *cash* and *accrual*.

Cash Method. Income is deemed to be taxed when it is received, actually or constructively. It is immaterial whether receipt is in the form of cash or of property that may be valued in terms of cash. Income is received constructively when it is available to the person entitled to it without substantial restriction. An example is interest on a deposit in a savings bank. A person may not avoid the reporting of income by failing to collect his interest or by neglecting to have the interest notation entered in his bank book. The money was available to him without substantial limitation on, let us assume, December 31, and he will be taxed on it at that time. A person also constructively receives income when it is available to him, even though the payment actually is made in whole or in part to someone else. A man may work for $100 a week, and his check for one week is given to him on December 31. Actually, the check is for $74.25, because amounts were deducted by the employer for Federal withholding tax, Federal insurance contributions, Series E bond purchases, union dues, and company pension plan. Constructively, this individual received $100 on December 31, even though *physically* he did not. If a salesman earns a commission which he does not draw against until a later date, he will be deemed to have had income as of the time when he could have drawn upon

[17] *Silver Bluff Estates, Inc.*, T.C. Memo., Docket #12303, entered June 24, 1947.
[18] *Kocin v. United States*, 187 F.2d 707 (2d Cir., 1951).
[19] *Seattle Hardware Corp. v. Squire*, 83 F. Supp. 106 (D.C., Wash., 1948).

it. If he does not cash a check until sometime after he receives it, he is nonetheless taxed as of the date when he could have cashed it.

Similarly, deductions take place when payment actually is made, regardless of the period covered by the payments.

Accrual Method. Under this method, a person is deemed to have income whenever he has a *right* to it, regardless of the period covered by the payment and the time it actually is received. A seller would have to report sales income at the time he made the sale, regardless of when payment was received. As to deductions, the time would be the date when the *liability* to make payment arose, regardless of when the physical payment took place. An accrual-basis employer would claim a deduction for wages as of the time when the services were performed, without reference to the actual payment date.

Thus, a tax accrues in the year when all events have occurred which fix the amount of the tax and determine the liability of the taxpayer to pay it.[20] It is immaterial that the taxpayer did not know in the taxable year that the events had taken place, or that he did not know on the last day of the taxable year the extent of the liability. It is sufficient if the events setting his liability actually took place.

A taxpayer is required to be consistent in his use of one method or the other. A combination of both systems, known as a hybrid method, is generally not permitted except under special circumstances. "One such method, in the case of a small retail store, will be an accrual of items affecting gross income, such as purchases, sales of goods, accounts payable, and accounts receivable. In such a case items of deduction such as rent, interest, clerks' salaries, insurance and similar items may be accounted for on a cash basis. Any such hybrid method is, of course, subject to the requirements . . . that there be a clear reflection of income under the method." [21]

Actually, however, there are various instances where the tax law requires a person to be inconsistent. For example, individuals deduct charitable contributions when actually paid, regardless of whether a cash or accrual basis is used; the time of the obligation or liability is immaterial even for an accrual-basis individual. The same is true for medical expenses. Insurance premiums for a period of more than one year (for example, to take advantage of a savings when three years' premiums are paid at one time) must be prorated

[20] *United States v. Anderson et al.*, 269 U.S. 422 (1926).

[21] Ways and Means Committee Report Accompanying the 1954 Revenue Bill at Section 446.

over the period covered. Unrestricted advance payments are income at the time of receipt. Depreciation and amortization are handled by cash- and accrual-basis taxpayers in identical manner. An individual may be on the cash basis for all other purposes and yet report the increment on his Series E United States bonds on an accrual basis.

If an individual is engaged in several different businesses, he may use the cash basis for one or more and the accrual basis for others. The only requirement is that the method used be the one that properly reflects his taxable income.[22]

Claim of Right. Where a taxpayer receives income which he subsequently is obliged to return, there is no recomputation of tax for the original year. He received the income under a claim of right, and whatever happens in a later year does not affect his tax liability in the first instance.[23] Thus, where stockholders were obliged to refund dividends that a corporation had paid in error, the tax returns for the year of receipt were not re-opened.[24]

"There is a claim of right when funds are received and treated by a taxpayer as belonging to him. The fact that subsequently the claim is found to be invalid by a court does not change the fact that the claim did exist. A mistaken claim is nonetheless a claim."[25]

What Period Is Covered by the Tax Return? The general rule is that the return is filed for a period of twelve months. Inasmuch as tax rates are on a graduated scale, a person would profit if he could close his return before income mounted too high. In order to place all taxpayers upon the same basis, the year has been chosen as the standard. Thus, if a person changes his accounting period so that at some point his return will cover a period of fewer than twelve months, the income will have to be annualized; tax will be computed on that basis; and the resultant tax will be "de-annualized." This matter will be discussed in Chapter 3.

"The federal income tax system is based on an annual accounting. Under the law the question whether taxable profits have been made is determined annually by the result of the operations of that year."[26] "All the revenue acts which have been enacted since the adoption of the Sixteenth Amendment have uniformly assessed the tax on the basis of annual returns showing the net result of all the

[22] I.R.C. Section 446(d).
[23] *North American Oil Consolidated v. Burnet,* 286 U.S. 417 (1932).
[24] *Barnhardt v. United States,* 98 F. Supp. 552 (D.C., N.C., 1951).
[25] *Healy et al. v. Commissioner,* 325 U.S. 278 (1953).
[26] *Heiner v. Mellon,* 304 U.S. 271 (1938).

taxpayer's transactions during a fixed accounting period, either the calendar year, or, at the option of the taxpayer, the particular fiscal year which he may adopt."[27]

If a taxpayer has a year of fewer than twelve months because it is his first taxable year or his last (that is, he dies), the return may be filed on the basis of income that actually exists, without annualization.

The taxable year may be for a period of more than twelve months only in the case of a person using the 52–53 week method. This will be discussed in Chapter 3.

How Is Tax Imposed? "[T]he federal fiscal system is self-determined in the sense that the meaning of the terms does not depend upon the law of the state; nevertheless, when Congress imposes taxes based upon the existence of legal rights or duties, it must be understood to refer to such rights and duties as the state law creates, since there are no others."[28]

In a dissenting opinion, Mr. Justice Jackson declared that "The United States has a system of taxation by confession."[29]

What Records Must Be Kept? The basic requirement is that the taxpayer must be able to support every statement that he makes on the tax return. If he actually can meet this requirement, the precise form (or even existence) of his records is not important. This subject will be treated in Chapter 23.

"Taxable income shall be computed under the method of accounting on the basis of which the taxpayer regularly computes his income in keeping his books."[30] However, "If no method of accounting has been regularly used by the taxpayer, or if the method used does not clearly reflect income, the computation of taxable income shall be made under such method as, in the opinion of the Secretary or his delegate, does clearly reflect income."[31]

The Secretary of the Treasury or his delegate, the Commissioner, need not acquiesce in the method of accounting used by the taxpayer. He may insist that a change in accounting method be used if, in his judgment, taxable income is not being properly reflected. No court will interfere unless the Secretary is acting capriciously. "It is not the province of the court to weigh and determine the rela-

[27] *Burnet v. Sanford & Brooks Company,* 282 U.S. 359 (1931).
[28] *Johnston v. Helvering,* 141 F.2d 208 (2d Cir., 1944).
[29] *United States v. Kahringer,* 345 U.S. 22 (1953).
[30] I.R.C. Section 446(a).
[31] I.R.C. Section 446(b).

tive merits of systems of accounting."[32] The Secretary need not accept an accounting method required by another governmental agency.[33]

But if more than one method of accounting clearly reflects income, the taxpayer's choice may not be changed.[34] "The selection of a system of accounting is lodged exclusively in the taxpayer provided it is within the statutory limits of clearly reflecting income. . . . 'clearly,' as used in the statute, means plainly, honestly, straightforwardly and frankly, but that does not mean 'accurately' . . ."[35] Perhaps accuracy in taxation is impossible. "[R]easonable allowances cannot be ascertained with mathematical precision."[36]

Dramatis Personae

Who Is the Taxpayer? Etymologically, a taxpayer is one who pays taxes. In practice, everyone who files a tax return is generally referred to as a taxpayer. The term even is applied to a person who *should* have filed a tax return.

Who's Who in Taxation? Basically, there are only two parties: the taxpayer and the Government. But each of these parties appears in various guises.

In tax matters, the Government is personalized in the form of the Secretary of the Treasury or his delegate, the Commissioner of Internal Revenue. The Commissioner is the administrative head of the Internal Revenue Service, which issues tax forms and instructions, prepares rulings, receives payments of taxes, performs audits, collects deficiencies, makes refunds, and closes cases. On audit matters, the taxpayer customarily deals with a Revenue Agent. Chapter 26 deals with the problem of procedure.

When litigation is involved, the lowest tax tribunal is the Tax Court of the United States (which was known as the Board of Tax Appeals until 1942). Here the taxpayer is always bringing the action: specifically, he is petitioning the Tax Court to set aside a finding by the Internal Revenue Service. Reference to such a case generally bears only the name of the taxpayer, as it is understood that *"v. Commissioner of Internal Revenue"* is too obvious to repeat. Thus the case will appear in this manner: *"Michael F. McDonald,* 1 T.C. 738 (1942)"—that is, the case may be found in

[32] *Brown v. Helvering,* 291 U.S. 193 (1934).
[33] *National Airlines, Inc.,* 9 T.C. 159 (1947).
[34] *International Cigar Machinery Co.,* 36 B.T.A. 124 (1937).
[35] *Huntington Securities Corp. v. Busey,* 112 F.2d 368 (6th Cir., 1940).
[36] *Atlas Plaster & Fuel Co. v. Commissioner,* 55 F.2d 802 (6th Cir., 1932).

Volume 1 of the Tax Court reports at page 738, the decision having been delivered in 1942.

When a point of law is involved, the Tax Court decision generally will be a "regular" one, appearing as a Tax Court decision. When a point of fact is involved upon a matter where the law already has been interpreted, a "memorandum decision" may be issued by the Tax Court. In practice, it often is very difficult to determine why a particular decision was "regular" or "memorandum," but the standing of the two types of decision is identical. A citation of a memorandum decision would be:

Colonial Amusement Corp., T.C. Memo., Docket #13257, entered July 27, 1948.

The citation system for memorandum decisions has been simplified for cases decided since April 5, 1954:

Ralph Pate, T.C. Memo. 1957–59, filed March 29, 1957.

Citations of the opinions of the various other courts may be illustrated by the following:

McDonald v. Commissioner, 139 F.2d 400 (3d Cir., 1943). The taxpayer is appealing a decision in favor of the Government in the Third Court of Appeals. The text of the decision will be found in Volume 139 of the Federal Reporter (second series) at page 400.

United States v. Yuncker, 147 F. Supp. 97 (D.C., Ind., 1957). The Government is suing a taxpayer in the United States District Court in Indiana, and the text of the decision may be found in Volume 147 of the Federal Supplement at page 97.

Williams Investment Co. v. United States, 3 F. Supp. 225 (Ct. Cl., 1933). A taxpayer is suing the Government in the United States Court of Claims.

McDonald v. Commissioner, 323 U.S. 57 (1944). The taxpayer is appealing a decision in favor of the Government to the United States Supreme Court. The text of the decision may be found in Volume 323 of the United States Supreme Court reports at page 57.

In Tax Court cases, the Commissioner often is referred to as the respondent. In the other courts, someone is bringing action against someone; thus, either taxpayer or Government may be, respectively, plaintiff or defendant. On appeal, the one bringing the action is the appellant and the other party is the appellee.

Sometimes a case involves two parties, such as Damon and Pythias. The case may be cited as *Damon et al.;* that is, Damon and another (or others). When a man and his wife are the parties, Mr. and Mrs. Burke may be referred to as *Burke et ux.;* that is, Burke and spouse. Sometimes husband-and-wife cases also are listed as *et al.*

The Tax Law

According to Article I, Section 7 of the Constitution of the United States, "All bills for raising Revenue shall originate in the House of Representatives; but the Senate may propose or concur with amendments as on other bills."

The various revenue acts were first codified in 1939 in what is referred to today as the Internal Revenue Code of 1939. A new codification known as the Internal Revenue Code of 1954 is the source of the great bulk of the income tax law of today. The Code has been supplemented by subsequent legislation, such as the Act of February 11, 1958 (72 Stat. 4, P.L. 85-320 (H.R. 9035)), dealing with restricted stock options exercised after the death of an employee. In a number of instances, special tax treaties have been enacted with specific countries, to modify the tax treatment afforded in certain instances, such as dividends or interest in the case of a person who works in the United States but is a resident of another country, or vice versa; the purpose of the treaties is to eliminate double taxation or at least to mitigate it.

In a number of instances, tax law has, in effect, been written by the decision of a court. Although there is no authority for this "judge-made" law, it unquestionably exists. See the substantive tests on pages 1·14 and 1·15.

Regulations and Rulings

The Treasury Department issues rulings on many phases of the tax law. In some instances, the regulations attempt to clarify the law; elsewhere, the regulations give examples of the way in which the Treasury believes the Code should be applied. But the regulations, unlike the Code, are not the law of the land. "[A]lthough it is true that where an Act uses ambiguous terms or is of doubtful construction, a clarifying regulation or one indicating the method of an Act's application to specific cases is to be given weight by the courts, the interpretation of a statute always remains the function of the judiciary. The regulations cannot change what the Act originally meant."[37] "[T]he power of an administrative officer or board to administer a Federal statute and to prescribe rules and regulations to that end is not the power to make law . . . but the power to adopt regulations to carry into effect the will of Congress as expressed by the statute. A regulation which does not do this,

[37] *Saks v. Higgins,* 29 F. Supp. 996 (D.C., N.Y., 1939).

but operates to create a rule out of harmony with the statute, is a mere nullity." [38]

The income tax regulations appear as Chapter 26 in the Code of Federal Regulations (CFR). They are keyed into the section of the Internal Revenue Code to which they apply. Thus, a portion of Section 167 of the Code is discussed in the regulations in Section 1.167(a)–3.

At various times, the Internal Revenue Service (or the Treasury Department, of which it is a part) issued a large number of types of rulings: Income Tax Unit rulings (known as I.T.'s), General Counsel's Memoranda (G.C.M.'s), Office Decisions (O.D.'s), Internal Revenue Mimeographs (IR–Mim.'s), etc. Commencing in 1953, interpretations of substantive tax law became the scope of a unified series known as Revenue Rulings (Rev. Rul.'s). New regulations are generally issued in the form of Treasury Decisions (T.D.'s). All other statements of practices, procedures, or regulations, commencing in 1955, became the subject matter of Revenue Procedures (Rev. Proc.'s). See Revenue Procedures 1955–1, 1955–2 CB 879.

Each week, new Revenue Rulings, etc., are published in the *Internal Revenue Bulletin* (I.R.B.). Twice a year, these bulletins are published in clothbound form as *Cumulative Bulletin.* Thus the Revenue Procedure referred to in the last sentence of the previous paragraph was published on page 879 of the second *Cumulative Bulletin* of 1955.

Taxpayers or their counsel may write directly to the Commissioner of Internal Revenue for rulings on specific problems. As a rule, no ruling will be made on theoretical questions. Full names, dates, facts, and figures will be requested. These rulings (unless of wide general interest) are made by individual letters. Unfortunately, the Revenue Agents do not always see fit to abide by the letter rulings of the Commissioner, and the taxpayer, who thought that he had the best possible authority for his course of action, based upon the facts in his own particular circumstance, will have to litigate. Direct rulings made to taxpayers "have none of the force or effect of Treasury Rulings and do not commit the Department to any interpretation of the law." [39]

Substantive Tests

Form versus Substance. Even if a taxpayer plans a transaction so that what he does is word-for-word compliance with the Internal

[38] *Commissioner v. Winslow,* 113 F.2d 418 (1st Cir., 1940).
[39] *Helvering v. New York Trust Co.,* 292 U.S. 455 (1934).

Revenue Code, the Government or the court may find that the provisions of the law do not cover the case. "The legal right of a taxpayer to decrease the amount of what otherwise would be his taxes, or altogether avoid them, by means which the law permits, cannot be doubted. . . . But the question for determination is whether what was done, apart from the tax motive, was the thing which the statute intended. . . . The rule which excludes from consideration the motive of tax avoidance is not pertinent to the situation, because the transaction upon its face lies outside the plain intent of the statute. To hold otherwise would be to exalt artifice above reality and to deprive the statutory provision in question of all serious purpose." [40]

Net Economic Effect. Occasionally, the Government or the court will ignore the purpose of a transaction and assert tax in accordance with the economic effect of what has been done. Under this doctrine, "motive is immaterial. The decision must turn upon the effect of what was done." [41] "The statute is aimed at the result."[42] "A given result at the end of a straight path is not made a different result because reached by a devious path." [43]

Supplementary Material

A. Suggested Reading.

Marcel Klarman, "The Metamorphosis of the General Principles in Federal Taxation," *TAXES—The Tax Magazine*, March, 1958, Vol. XXXVI, #3, p. 179.

Everett C. Johnson, "Basic Principles Underlying Tax Laws," *TAXES—The Tax Magazine*, July, 1950, Vol. XXVIII, #7, p. 653.

William Raymond Green, *The Theory and Practice of Modern Taxation* (Chicago: Commerce Clearing House, Inc., 1938).

Joseph P. Crockett, *The Federal Tax System of the United States* (New York: Columbia University Press, 1954).

Randolph Paul, *Taxation in the United States* (Boston: Little, Brown & Co., 1954).

B. Leading Cases.

". . . the power to tax . . ." *McCulloch v. Maryland,* 4 Wheaton 316 (1819).

The income tax that was declared unconstitutional. *Pollock v. Farmers' Loan and Trust Company,* 157 U.S. 429 (1895), *on rehearing,* 158 U.S. 601 (1895).

The income tax is constitutional. *Brushaber v. Union Pacific Railroad Company,* 240 U.S. 1 (1916).

[40] *Gregory v. Helvering,* 293 U.S. 465 (1935).
[41] *Helvering v. Gordon,* 87 F.2d 663 (8th Cir., 1937).
[42] *Hirsch v. Commissioner,* 124 F.2d 24 (9th Cir., 1941).
[43] *Minnesota Tea Co. v. Helvering,* 302 U.S. 609 (1938).

Anticipatory assignment of income. *Lucas v. Earl,* 281 U.S. 111 (1930).
Entities. *Moline Properties, Inc. v. Commissioner,* 319 U.S. 436 (1943).
Reality of transaction. *Gregory v. Helvering,* 293 U.S. 465 (1935).

C. Questions.

1. A very eminent attorney, Benjamin F. Butler, once said: "The difficulty is we do not tax incomes at all—only the consciences of those who are supposed to have incomes." Discuss this point of view.
2. Assume that a certain Treasury Department regulation is contrary to a provision of the Internal Revenue Code; but this regulation is five years more recent and reflects later thinking on the subject. Which will prevail, new regulation or old statute?
3. An individual owned a pet boa constrictor, which was paid $1,000 for appearing on a television commercial. Is this income taxable in view of the fact that the Internal Revenue Code makes no reference to income earned by boa constrictors? If so, who is the taxpayer?
4. A taxpayer began business on December 15, 1960. He wants to report on a calendar year basis; but in order to avoid filing a tax return for a period of two weeks, he files a return for the period December 15, 1960–December 31, 1961. Is this permissible?
5. If a taxpayer plans a transaction to be, word for word, what the tax law permits as an exception to a general rule, may the tax consequences be foretold with mathematical exactitude?
6. Rudyard Waldo Jones, an author who was on the cash basis, was sent a royalty check by his publisher in the same city three days before the end of the taxable year. Because of a careless typist, the misaddressed envelope arrived a week later. The author had no knowledge that sales of his book had commenced as yet or that there were royalties due him. Is the income taxable to him in the taxable year (when the check was sent) or the following year (when the check was received)?
7. A businessman transacted his affairs as an individual. When he applied to a bank for a loan, he was told that a larger amount could be lent to a corporation than to an individual. Thereupon he formed a corporation, which obtained the bank loan. He claimed that the corporation did not have to file a tax return, as the company was a mere shell without real existence and the income was all taxable to him personally as the sole stockholder. Will the Internal Revenue Service agree with him?
8. A transaction had the same result as though a dividend had been declared. But the corporation involved had not declared a dividend; in fact, under the laws of the state of incorporation, no dividend could be declared except as a result of affirmative action by the majority of the directors at a meeting called specifically for the purpose, and no such meeting had been called. Is the Internal Revenue Service ever justified in labeling the transaction as a dividend under the circumstances?
9. An individual failed to make payments to the W.N.S. ("We Never Sleep") Finance Company upon the purchase of a car, and the company, by garnishee proceeding, collected $20 a week from his employer against his salary. The individual claimed that this $20 was not income to him, as it never had been available to him. Is he correct?

10. Under the Constitution, Congress writes the Federal tax laws. How then can it be said that judges sometimes write the tax laws?
11. "The power to tax is the power to destroy." How may the Treasury Department use the income tax law to combat crime?
12. Because of a mathematical error, a company paid a salesman a larger commission than was owing. The salesman included the full amount as income in that year. The following year, the employer discovered the error and demanded repayment by the salesman; he agreed. Is he justified in filing a refund claim for tax overpaid in the year the commission was received by him?
13. In what calendar year would the following types of income be shown by (a) a cash-basis taxpayer, Alpha, and (b) an accrual-basis taxpayer, Beta?
    (1) A dividend check dated December 15, 1962, which was cashed on January 3, 1963.
    (2) A salary check for December, 1962, services that was not drawn until January, 1963.
    (3) Savings bank interest for 1962, while the taxpayer was in prison until 1964 and could not possibly apply for the interest until that time.
    (4) Payment for sales where the merchandise was shipped in 1962 and paid for in 1963.

2

MANNER OF OPERATION

Although there is one Federal income tax law, it is not uniform in its application to all business or nonbusiness forms. Care should be given to the nontax as well as to the tax factors in deciding upon a method of operation. The change is not an irrevocable one. But it may be expensive. For example, if a business is operated as a corporation and it seems advisable to shift to the partnership form, there may be tax to be paid upon the liquidation of a corporation. *Any* change that seems to have no motivation other than the saving of taxes may be carefully scrutinized by the Secretary of the Treasury, who has broad powers to deny tax recognition for a transaction that is only for tax purposes.

Sole Proprietorships

If an individual does nothing about business forms but merely commences operations, he is deemed to be doing business as a sole proprietorship. This is pleasantly simple. As to Federal income tax, he will pay on a graduated scale ranging from 20% to 91% of his taxable income, which might be stated as gross income less certain permissible deductions, allowances, and credits. These tax rates are a composite of 3% normal tax and a mounting surtax that rises within brackets according to the amount of taxable income.[1] But regardless of the amount of a person's taxable income, he does not have to pay a total tax that amounts to more than 87% of his taxable income.

For most purposes, normal tax and surtax are applied to the same income, and the composite rates facilitate the problem of computation. But for certain purposes, income subject to normal tax is not the same as income subject to surtax; for example, interest on certain United States Government bonds is exempt from normal tax although subject to surtax.[2] This will be developed in Chapter 5. In

[1] I.R.C. Section 1.
[2] I.R.C. Section 103(b).

the case of a sale of an interest in oil or gas property where the principal value of the property has been demonstrated by prospecting, exploration, or discovery work done by the taxpayer, the portion of the surtax attributable to this sale may not exceed 30% of the selling price of the interest.[3]

Under certain circumstances, an individual's tax on capital gains may not exceed 25% of the gains; see Chapter 24.[4]

In the case of amounts (other than interest) received by a taxpayer from the United States by reason of a claim against the Government involving the acquisition of property, the tax upon this receipt may not exceed 30% of the amount (other than interest) that is received where this amount had remained unpaid for more than fifteen years.[5]

The President of the United States has the power to double the rates of citizens and corporations of foreign countries if citizens or corporations of the United States are subjected to discriminatory or extraterritorial taxes by these countries.[6]

If an individual is engaged in more than one business, the incomes of all of his enterprises are aggregated with his income from nonbusiness or personal sources. Thus the modest income of a small venture might be subjected to very high taxes if his income from other sources was substantial.

Tax Advantages. An individual has no tax to pay except that upon his income, whereas a corporation might be subjected to various other taxes as well. A multiplicity of returns is avoided if he actually is engaged in several lines of work. Certain income earned abroad is not taxed here, whereas corporation income would be. See Chapter 22.

Tax Disadvantages. The top tax brackets are considerably higher than the normal and surtaxes of corporations. The entire taxable income will be the basis of an individual's computation, whereas partnership income might actually be allocated to a number of individual taxpayers; for example, under certain circumstances an individual could properly arrange that his children pay taxes on income of his venture. See Chapter 18.

Nontax Aspects. An individual is liable only for his own obligations, whereas a partner might have to pay those of his partners.

[3] I.R.C. Section 632.
[4] I.R.C. Section 1201(b).
[5] I.R.C. Section 1347.
[6] I.R.C. Section 891.

The individual's resources, financial and personal, are presumably less than those of two or more partners. Comparing individual and corporate operation, one notes that a corporation is better insulation against personal liability, is more permanent, and provides a more simple way of transferring interests.

Partnerships

A partnership involves a joint venture of two or more persons. For tax purposes, the term may include a syndicate, pool, joint venture, or other unincorporated organization, through or by means of which any business, financial operation, or venture is carried out, if this organization is not deemed to be a trust, estate, or corporation.[7]

From the tax point of view, a partnership is only an income-reporting body; there is no tax to be paid by the partnership as such. Instead, each partner adds to his other income his proportionate share of the partnership profits each year, whether they are actually distributed to him or not. Thus it is not a simple matter to compare the tax cost of operating as a partnership as against a sole proprietorship or a corporation. An analysis must be made as to each partner individually.

Most of the tax cases involving partnerships are concerned with the problem of whether there is a bona fide partnership within the intendment of the Internal Revenue Code. What the articles of partnership or state laws declare is not decisive. This point will be developed in Chapter 18.

Tax Advantages. The income under proper circumstances may be spread among many taxpayers, all of whom may be members of the same family unit. There are no special penal taxes, as in the case of corporations.

Tax Disadvantages. A partner is not an employee, and thus he may not participate in pension and other compensation arrangements in the manner that a corporate executive could do. Death or other withdrawal of a partner could terminate the partnership, with the resultant realization of income under circumstances less than favorable; for example, unmatured installment obligations could produce several years' income at one time, with a resultant high tax.[8] Income is taxed to the partners, even though the partner-

[7] I.R.C. Section 7701(a)(2).
[8] I.R.C. Section 453(d)(1).

ship has good business reasons for not distributing this income, whereas shareholders in a corporation would not be taxed on their distributive shares of the profits if there was in fact no distribution. The various permissible elections permitted by the Internal Revenue Code generally must be made by the partnership as such, to the possible detriment of any particular partner. Many tax adjustments, primarily those involving basis, are very complex and are of such recent origin that there are few court decisions clarifying the ambiguities. See Chapter 19. Income from a partnership is taxed to the partners as self-employment income for purposes of the Federal Social Security Act, whereas salaries from a corporation are employment income. The tax on the former is one and a half times the tax on the latter.

Nontax Aspects. An individual may find that his financial situation is better by reason of his association with other persons; but the converse may also be true. He may become liable for debts incurred by them. He may find it very difficult to terminate his partnership interest, especially if the partnership articles provide that any sale must be to the other partners according to what might be an unfavorable formula; or the articles may provide that no one may purchase his interest without the approval of his partners, who may withhold approval on capricious or malicious grounds. A partner might not have the money to pay his tax on his distributive share of partnership profits, if the profits were not actually distributed.

Limited Partnerships

It may not be readily apparent what the tax status of a limited partnership actually is. A limited partnership, under the laws of most states, contains at least one general partner and at least one limited partner. The liability of the latter is limited to the amount of his investment, and generally it is required that the public at large be apprised of the individuals whose liability is limited. The difficulty of tax determination arises from the fact that a limited partnership *is* a partnership in many respects, but it also may have characteristics of a corporation; for example, the death of a limited partner may have no effect upon the life of the organization, and there may be that ease of transferability of interest that one associates with the corporate form. If a limited partner contributes services, he may find that he is treated as a general partner, with the consequent financial risk.

Association

Like the limited partnership, an association may be treated for tax purposes as a trust or as a corporation. In the ordinary situation, there is a quasi-corporate organization in which the beneficiaries have some voice in the management. But sometimes the trustees are a continuing body, with provisions for succession; and certificates of beneficial interest may be freely transferred in the manner of corporate stock. "The arrangement provided for centralized control, continuity, and limited liability, and the analogy to corporate organization was carried still further by the provisions for the issue of transferable certificates," it was said in one case where taxability as a corporation was found.[9]

Corporations

The term "corporation" includes associations, joint-stock companies, and insurance companies.[10] If an organization more nearly resembles a corporation than any other form, it will be taxed as a corporation.

For Federal income tax purposes, the term "domestic" when applied to a corporation means one with a charter from the United States or any state or territory.[11] (For state tax purposes, a corporation is regarded as a domestic corporation in the state that created it and as a foreign corporation in any other state.)

Numerically, the tax disadvantages of the corporate form outweigh the advantages; but most business operations of any size or complexity are carried on by corporations.

There is a normal tax of 30%. In addition, corporations pay a 22% surtax after the application of a $25,000 surtax exemption. See Chapter 24.

Tax Advantages. Under appropriate circumstances, a consolidated tax return may be filed with affiliated corporations, to the end that one company's deficit may reduce the group income, or intercompany items may be eliminated.[12] See Chapter 27. Shareholders will not be taxed on their shares of undistributed earnings.

Tax Disadvantages. There is a form of double tax, inasmuch as a corporation (except certain public utilities) does not get a deduc-

[9] *Morrissey v. Commissioner*, 296 U.S. 344 (1936).
[10] I.R.C. Section 7701(a)(3).
[11] I.R.C. Section 7701(a)(4).
[12] I.R.C. Section 1501.

tion for dividends paid, with the result that company and shareholder may be paying tax on precisely the same income. The corporation's income loses its characteristics when it is distributed, so that what is tax-exempt interest to the corporation will be fully taxable to the shareholders. With few exceptions (to be developed below), all income of United States corporations is taxed by the Internal Revenue Service, regardless of where the income was earned; there is no provision so favorable as those sections applicable to income earned outside of the country by individuals. A corporation may be subject to special taxes in addition to the income tax, whereas other entities are not so penalized. See Chapter 16. Instances are the accumulated earnings tax [13] and the personal holding company tax.[14] Losses of the shareholders should the corporation become insolvent are regarded as capital, subject to capital loss limitations. See Chapter 5.

Nontax Aspects. A corporation's chief nontax advantages are limitation of liability, permanency, and (as a rule) greater borrowing capacity than that possessed by other entities. Another advantage is ease of transfer of ownership. Shares of stock may be disposed of at any time to any party at any price (unless there is a by-law or restrictive agreement to the contrary). But the transfer of an interest in a partnership, for practical even if not legal reasons, requires the consent of the other parties, who might balk at the idea of a certain new partner. It is much easier for an individual to give stock in a corporation to his children than it would be for a proprietor or a partner to try to make his children participants in the enterprise, for the Internal Revenue Service might well regard as a profits diversion scheme any transfer of proprietary interest to a person who will not or cannot participate in the running of the venture.

A serious disadvantage is the greater degree of control exercised by Federal and state agencies, with a concomitant larger amount of paper work.

Not every organization may do business as a corporation. For example, groups of professional men might find it necessary to do business as partnerships. A businessmen's governing body, such as a stock exchange, might refuse members the right to function as a corporation, in order to provide the public greater financial protection in the case of an insolvency.

There is no special rule as to *closely held corporations;* but in

[13] I.R.C. Section 531.
[14] I.R.C. Section 541.

general, the Internal Revenue Service views transactions between such corporations and their stockholders, or between corporations with substantially identical shareholders, with considerable suspicion. A closely held corporation is one "the shares of which are owned by a relatively limited number of stockholders. Often the entire stock issue is held by one family." [15] "Executive salaries of closely held corporations are subject to the same requirements for deductibility as any executive's or employee's salary, except that they are subject to more careful examination. The burden of proving that the salaries are both reasonable and for services rendered is somewhat greater than in the case of executives, or employees, who have little or no stockholdings in the paying corporation." [16]

Western Hemisphere Trade Corporations

The term "Western Hemisphere Trade Corporation" means a domestic corporation all of the business of which (other than incidental purchases) is done in any country or countries in North, Central, or South America. The following conditions must be met:

(1) 95% or more of the gross income for the 3-year period immediately preceding the close of the taxable year must have been derived from sources without the United States. If the corporation was in existence for fewer than three years, the actual period of existence may be substituted for the three years mentioned.

(2) 90% or more of the gross income for that period must have been derived from the active conduct of a trade or business.[17]

For this purpose, a domestic corporation is one the charter of which was granted by the United States or by any of the states or territories or the District of Columbia.

If a corporation meets these requirements, the taxable income will be computed in the ordinary manner. To this will be applied a fraction, the numerator of which is 14% and the denominator of which is the total normal and surtax rate, which is 52% at the time of writing. The resultant figure will be taken as a special deduction in computing the corporation's tax.

The big practical difficulty is in seeing that at least 95% of the gross income is from sources outside the United States. In order to avoid problems, it is customary for a United States corporation that does business in the Western Hemisphere to create a special corpora-

[15] Revenue Ruling 54–77, 1954–1 CB 187.

[16] *Tax Guide for Small Business, Treasury Department Publication No. 34,* 1958 edition, p. 36.

[17] I.R.C. Section 921.

tion that does not do business anywhere else (including continental United States). A holding company would be ruled out by the second condition listed above.

A corporation which claims to qualify as a Western Hemisphere Trade Corporation must attach to its income tax return a statement showing: (1) that its entire business is done within the Western Hemisphere and, if any purchases are made outside that hemisphere, the amount of these purchases, the amount of its gross receipts from all sources, and any other pertinent information; and (2) for the 3-year period immediately preceding the close of the taxable year (or any shorter period that is permitted) (A) its total gross income from all sources, (B) the amount of this that is derived from the active conduct of a trade or business, (C) a description of the trade or business and the facts upon which the corporation relies to establish that the business was actively conducted by it, and (D) the amount of its gross income (if any) from sources within the United States.[18]

The special tax deduction will not be lost even if a domestic corporation creates a new corporation to carry on operations in the Western Hemisphere.[19]

Possessions of the United States

A domestic corporation (and, for that matter, a United States citizen) may avoid Federal income tax under certain circumstances upon that portion of the gross income which is derived from sources within possessions of the United States. "Possessions" means the Panama Canal Zone, Guam, American Samoa, Wake and the Midway Islands, and Puerto Rico "when used with respect to domestic corporations. The term does not include the Virgin Islands, nor does it include Puerto Rico when used with respect to citizens of the United States." [20]

If the following conditions can be met, gross income means only from sources within the United States, which might be zero:

(1) 80% or more of the gross income for the 3-year period immediately preceding the close of the taxable year must have been derived from sources within a possession of the United States. If there was a shorter period of existence, that time will be used.

(2) 50% or more of the gross income for that period was derived from the active conduct of a trade or business within a possession of

[18] Regulations Section 1.921-1(c).
[19] I.T. 3757, 1945 CB 200.
[20] Regulations Section 1.931-1(a)(1).

the United States. If the taxpayer is a citizen rather than a corporation, he may have conducted business either on his own account or as an employee or agent of another.[21]

Despite these provisions, there must be included in gross income all amounts received from sources within or without the United States.

In order to avoid arithmetical difficulties, it is usual for a United States corporation to use another corporation solely for the purpose of conducting business within possessions of the United States. The Federal tax result will then be zero, and double taxation is avoided.

China Trade Act Corporations

A China Trade Act Corporation is, under certain conditions, allowed a special deduction in computing taxable income. A China Trade Act Corporation is one organized under the provisions of the China Trade Act of 1922.[22]

This special deduction is an amount equal to the proportion of the taxable income derived from sources within Formosa and Hong Kong which the par value of the shares of stock of the corporation, owned on the last day of the taxable year by stipulated persons, bears to the par value of the whole number of shares of stock of the corporation outstanding on that date. The stipulated persons are (1) persons resident in Formosa, Hong Kong, the United States, or possessions of the United States and (2) individual citizens of the United States wherever resident.[23]

The reduction in corporate tax may not exceed the amount of the special dividend certified by the Secretary of Commerce to the Secretary of the Treasury. The term "special dividend" means the amount which is distributed as a dividend to or for the benefit of persons who on the last day of the taxable year were resident in Formosa, Hong Kong, the United States, or possessions of the United States or were individual citizens of the United States and owned shares of stock of the corporation. The dividend must be distributed not later than the filing date of the tax return (including extensions authorized). The special dividend does not include any other amounts payable to or for the benefit of these persons because of their interest in the corporation and must be made on a pro rata basis.[24]

[21] I.R.C. Section 931.
[22] 15 U.S.C., ch. 4, section 141 *et seq.*
[23] I.R.C. Section 941.
[24] Regulations Section 1.941–2(b).

Illustration. A China Trade Act Corporation has taxable income (without reference to the special deduction for corporations of this type) for the calendar year 1960 of $200,000 and receives no dividends from domestic corporations. All of its stock on December 31, 1960, is owned by persons resident in Formosa, Hong Kong, the United States, possessions of the United States, or individual citizens of the United States. It distributes a special dividend of $100,000 on February 16, 1961, which is duly certified by the Secretary of Commerce. For corporate tax purposes, it is necessary to make two computations, first, without allowing the special deduction and, second, allowing it.

(1)	Taxable income	$200,000
	Normal tax	60,000
	Surtax	38,500
	Total income tax	98,500
(2)	Taxable income	200,000
	(Per cent deductible, 100%, inasmuch as 100% of the stock was owned on the last day of the taxable year by residents of Formosa, etc.)	
	Special deduction from taxable income	200,000
	Amount of income subject to tax	None

A China Trade Act Corporation is not allowed the credits against the tax for taxes of foreign countries and possessions of the United States.[25] See Chapter 22.

The dividends received deduction does not apply to distributions from China Trade Act Corporations.[26] See Chapter 8.

Tax-exempt Organizations

The following organizations are exempt from Federal income tax, unless the exemption is forfeited for specific causes:

(1) Corporations organized under Act of Congress as instrumentalities of the United States not subject to tax.

(2) Corporations organized for the exclusive purpose of holding title to property, collecting income from it, and turning over the proceeds (less expenses) to a tax-exempt organization.

(3) Corporations, community chests, funds, or foundations organized and operated exclusively for religious, charitable, scientific, testing for public safety, literary, or educational purposes, or for the prevention of cruelty to children or animals. But no part of the net earnings of any such organization may inure to the benefit of any private shareholder or individual, no substantial part of the activities of which may be the carrying on of propaganda, or otherwise attempting to influence legislation, and no participation or intervention may be made in (including the publishing or distribut-

[25] I.R.C. Section 942.
[26] I.R.C. Section 246(a)(1).

ing of statements) any political campaign on behalf of any candidate for public office.

(4) Civic leagues or organizations not organized for profit but operated exclusively for the promotion of social welfare, or local associations of employees, the membership of which is limited to the employees of a designated person or persons in a particular municipality, and the net earnings of which are devoted exclusively to charitable, educational, or recreational purposes.

(5) Labor, agricultural, or horticultural organizations.

(6) Business leagues, chambers of commerce, real estate boards, or boards of trade, not organized for profit and no part of the net earnings of which inures to the benefit of any private shareholder or individual.

(7) Clubs organized and operated exclusively for pleasure, recreation, and other nonprofitable purposes, no part of the net earnings of which inures to the benefit of any private shareholder.

(8) Fraternal beneficiary societies, orders, or associations—

(A) Operating under the lodge system or for the exclusive benefit of the members of a fraternity itself operating under the lodge system and

(B) Providing for the payment of life, sick, accident, or other benefits to the members of such society, order, or association or their dependents.

(9) Voluntary employees' beneficiary associations providing for the payment of life, sick, accident, or other benefits to the members of such association or their dependents, if—

(A) No part of their net earnings inures (other than through these payments) to the benefit of any private shareholder or individual, and

(B) 85% or more of the income consists of amounts collected from members and amounts contributed to the association by the employer of the members for the sole purpose of making such payments and meeting expenses.

(10) Voluntary employees' beneficiary associations providing for the payment of life, sick, accident, or other benefits to the members of the association or their dependents or their designated beneficiaries, if—

(A) Admission to membership in the association is limited to individuals who are officers or employees of the United States Government, and

(B) No part of the net earnings of the association inures (other than through these payments) to the benefit of any private shareholder or individual.

(11) Teachers' retirement fund associations of a purely local character, if—

(A) No part of their net earnings inures (other than through payment of retirement benefits) to the benefit of any private shareholder or individual, and

(B) The income consists solely of amounts received from public taxation, amounts received from assessments on the teaching salaries of members, and income in respect of investments.

(12) Benevolent life insurance associations of a purely local character, mutual ditch or irrigation companies, mutual or cooperative telephone companies, or like organizations; but only if 85% or more of the income consists of amounts collected from members for the sole purpose of meeting losses and expenses.

(13) Cemetery companies owned and operated exclusively for the benefit of their members or which are not operated for profit; and any corporation chartered solely for burial purposes as a cemetery corporation and not permitted by its charter to engage in any business not necessarily incident to that purpose, no part of the net earnings of which inures to the benefit of any private shareholder or individual.

(14) Credit unions without capital stock organized and operated for mutual purposes and without profit; and corporations or associations without capital stock organized before September 1, 1951, and operated for mutual purposes and without profit for the purpose of providing reserve funds for, and insurance of, shares or deposits in—

(A) Domestic building and loan associations,

(B) Cooperative banks without capital stock organized and operated for mutual purposes and without profit, or

(C) Mutual savings banks not having capital stock represented by shares.

(15) Mutual insurance companies or associations other than life or marine (including interinsurers and reciprocal underwriters) if the gross amount received during the taxable year from gross investment income (other than capital gains) and premiums (including deposits and assessments) does not exceed $75,000.

(16) Corporations organized by farmers' cooperative associations (or their members) for the purpose of financing the ordinary crop operations of these members or other producers, and operated in conjunction with the association. Exemption will not be denied to such a corporation because it has capital stock, if the dividend rate of the stock is fixed at not to exceed the legal rate of interest in the state of incorporation or 8% per annum, whichever is greater, on

the value of the consideration for which the stock was issued and if substantially all this stock (other than nonvoting preferred stock, the owners of which are not entitled or permitted to participate, directly or indirectly, in the profits of the corporation, on dissolution or otherwise, beyond the fixed dividends) is owned by the association or its members. Furthermore, exemption will not be denied to such a corporation because there is accumulated and maintained by it a reserve required by state law or a reasonable reserve for any necessary purpose.[27]

Religious and Apostolic Organizations. Also exempt from Federal income tax are religious or apostolic associations or corporations, if they have a common or community treasury. These organizations even may engage in business for the common benefit of their members, but only if these members include on their own tax returns their entire pro rata shares, whether distributed or not, of the taxable income of the organization for that year. Amounts thus reported by the members are to be treated as a dividend received.[28]

Employee Trusts. Exemption extends to pension, profit-sharing, and stock bonus plans that are qualified under I.R.C. Section 401. These will be considered in Chapter 11.[29]

Proof of Tax Exemption. An organization is not exempt from tax merely because it is not organized and operated for profit. In order to establish its exemption, it is necessary to file with the district director of internal revenue for the district in which is located the principal place of business or principal office of the organization an application form as indicated in the next paragraph.

Numeral of Type of Organization as Listed Above	Application Form Number
(2), (9), (12), (13), (15)	1026
(3)	1023
(4), (5), (6), (8)	1024
(7)	1025
(14)	Letter showing state and date of incorporation, and proof that state credit union law is being complied with as to loans, investments, and dividends.

[27] I.R.C. Section 501(c).
[28] I.R.C. Section 501(d).
[29] I.R.C. Section 501(a).

Numeral of Type of Organization as Listed Above	Application Form Number
All others.	Letter showing character of the organization, purpose of organization, actual activities, sources of receipts and disposition thereof, all other relevant facts.

Annual returns must be filed by organizations claiming exemption, unless they are of the following types:

(1) Religious organizations as described in (3), above.

(2) Educational organizations of the type described in (3), above, if there is maintained a regular faculty and curriculum and there is normally a regular organized body of pupils or students in attendance at the place where educational activities regularly are carried on.

(3) Charitable organizations or organizations for the prevention of cruelty to children or animals as described in (3), above, if the organization is supported, in whole or in part, by funds contributed by the United States, or a state or political subdivision, or is primarily supported by contributions of the general public.

(4) Organizations described in (3), above, if operated, supervised, or controlled by or in connection with a religious organization as described in (3).

(5) Organizations of the type mentioned in (8), above.

(6) Organizations of the type mentioned in (1), above, if the organization is a corporation wholly owned by the United States, or any of its agencies or instrumentalities, or a wholly-owned subsidiary of such a corporation.[30]

Where annual returns are required, the necessary forms may be obtained from the district director of internal revenue, for filing not later than the fifteenth day of the fifth full calendar month following the close of the period for which the return is required.

Exemption is not available to subversive organizations registered under the Internal Security Act of 1950.[31]

Loss of Exemption. An organization will lose its exemption for any year in which it engaged in a "prohibited transaction." This includes (1) lending any part of its income or corpus, without adequate security or proper interest, (2) paying unreasonable personal compensation, (3) making services available at preferential terms, (4) selling at bargain rates, or (5) engaging in transactions that

[30] I.R.C. Section 6033(a).
[31] I.R.C. Section 501(e).

result in substantial diversion of income or corpus to one of the following: (A) the creator of the organization (if a trust); (B) a person who has made a substantial contribution to the organization; (C) a member of the family of an individual who is the creator of such trust or who has made a substantial contribution to such organization; (D) a corporation controlled by such creator or person through the ownership of 50% or more of the voting stock or 50% or more of the total value of all classes of stock of the corporation.[32] "Family" for this purpose means brothers and sisters (whether by the whole or half blood), spouse, ancestors, and lineal descendants.[33] But the loss of exemption may only be for the year in which the "prohibited transaction" took place.[34]

Unrelated Income. Some of the types of tax-exempt organization are not permitted to extend this exemption to *all* types of income. If such is the case, tax may be applied to the "unrelated income" of the organization.

The tax on unrelated income may be applied to the following types of organization:

(1) Any organization (other than a church, or a convention or association of churches) of the exempt types mentioned above as types (2), (3), (5), or (6).

(2) An exempt employees' trust.

(3) A college or university which is an agency or instrumentality of any government or political subdivision thereof, or which is owned or operated by a government or political subdivision. The tax also will apply in the case of any corporation wholly owned by such a college or university. But tax will not apply in the case of elementary and secondary schools operated by such governments.

The income of an exempt organization is subject to the tax on unrelated income only if two conditions are present: (1) the income must be from a trade or business which is regularly carried on by the organization and (2) the trade or business must not be substantially related (aside from the need of the organization for income or funds) to the exercise or performance by the organization in carrying on its function or purpose. For example, the operation of a wheat farm is substantially related to the exempt activity of an agricultural college if this farm is operated as part of the educational activity of the college and is not operated on a scale disproportionately large when compared with the educational program.

[32] I.R.C. Section 503(c).
[33] I.R.C. Section 267(c)(4).
[34] I.R.C. Section 503(d).

But the manufacture and sale of a product by an exempt college would not become substantially related merely because students as part of their educational program perform clerical or bookkeeping functions in the business.

Special Types of Corporations

Chapter 16 will treat with personal holding companies, foreign personal holding companies, banks, insurance companies, and regulated investment companies.

Special Types of Individuals

Chapter 15 covers the particular treatment afforded to farmers and to members of the armed forces.

Fiduciaries

Certain persons operate in a fiduciary capacity for others. Special tax treatment is applied in the case of a trust and an estate. The general pattern is that income will be taxed to the beneficiary; but if this income is not or cannot be earmarked for the beneficiary, then the fiduciary (the trustee or the executor) will be taxed. This subject will be discussed in Chapter 20.

Election To Be Taxed as a Corporation

Certain proprietorships and partnerships have the opportunity to elect to be taxed as a domestic corporation. The election must be made not later than 60 days after the close of the taxable year to which the election is first applicable by the proprietor or all of the partners having an interest in the enterprise at any time on or after the first day of that taxable year, up to and including the date of election. This requirement includes any owners of the enterprise who may have sold their interests prior to the date of the election. If in a year subsequent to the year of election there is a change of ownership requiring another election, then all persons owning an interest in the enterprise from the beginning of that year up to the date of election must make an election to continue to have the enterprise taxed as a corporation.[35]

Qualifications. The enterprise may not be owned by more than fifty individual taxpayers. If a partnership owns an interest in a

[35] I.R.C. Section 1361.

partnership for which an election is to be made, all of the partners of the owning partnership must be individuals and their number must be added to the other partners of the electing partnership in determining the number of its partners.

No proprietor or partner having more than a 10% interest in the electing enterprise can be an owner of another proprietorship or have more than a 10% interest in another partnership, either of which is taxable as a domestic corporation under Section 1361. For example, should an individual have an interest of 10% or less in a partnership taxed as a corporation, he may elect to have his proprietorship taxed as a corporation. If, however, he should own a proprietorship that is taxed as a corporation, he would be unable to make the election for another proprietorship, or for a partnership in which he had more than a 10% interest.

No proprietor or partner in an enterprise electing to be taxed as a corporation may be either a nonresident alien or a foreign partnership. These terms will be developed in Chapter 22.

The enterprise either must be one in which capital is a material income-producing factor, or one where 50% or more of the gross income consists of earnings derived from trading as a principal or from brokerage commissions derived from selling real property, securities, or commodities for others.

Income classified as personal holding company income under Section 543 (see Chapter 16) is excluded from the income of the enterprise. The amount so excluded is taxed directly to the proprietor or the partners, and any deductions attributable to this income will be allowed to the proprietor or partners rather than to the enterprise. Distributions of personal holding company includible in the income of individuals will not be taxed as a corporate distribution from the enterprise, inasmuch as this income is taxed whether or not distributed. Any undistributed personal holding company income will be considered as paid-in surplus, or as a contribution to the capital of the enterprise as of the close of the year in which it is earned. In this situation, the basis of the individual's interest in the enterprise would be accordingly increased. In determining whether rents and royalties are personal holding company income, all income earned by the enterprise will enter into the determination of the gross income of the enterprise for that year.

Binding Effect of Election. The election to be taxed as a corporation is binding on the enterprise and its owners as long as the original proprietor, or partners owning more than an 80% interest, continue to conduct the business in an unincorporated form. But the election will be considered to be revoked in any year in which the ownership of the proprietorship is changed, or the original electing partners no longer own more than 80% of the partnership, unless a new election is made. As to this 80% interest, the constructive ownership rules will apply; that is, a person will be deemed to own stock owned by his brothers and sisters (whether by the whole or half blood), spouse, ancestors, and lineal descendants. He will also own the proportionate part of those shares owned by a corporation or partnership in which he has an interest, and shares owned by a trust or estate of which he is a beneficiary.

What Is Not Covered. The enterprise will not be treated as a corporation for these purposes:

(1) A proprietor or partner may not participate as an employee in any qualified pension and profit-sharing plans of the business.

(2) Income derived from the enterprise will constitute self-employment income to the proprietor or individuals for Federal Social Security tax purposes. The tax rates are higher than for employees, which the proprietor or partners are not.

(3) The enterprise may not be treated as a corporation for the purpose of participating in a corporate reorganization (see Chapter 17), "except in the case where a proprietor or partner contributes property to the enterprise and gain or loss would be recognized on such contribution by applying the corporate rules."[36]

(4) The enterprise may not be included as a corporation in a consolidated income tax return.[37]

(5) Key personnel cannot be given the incentive of stock options, an attractiveness that is limited to corporations.

When Is Election Desirable? Election may be made whenever it is felt that taxation under the corporate rules would be more favorable. For example, individuals might be in higher tax brackets than the corporate rates. If the enterprise had business reasons for not paying distributions, the individuals could avoid the higher rates of tax.

But it has been indicated that not every type of proprietorship or partnership may make the election. And where there are plural partners, a dissident could refuse to participate in the election unless he received some sort of inducement. The opportunity for blackmail is present.

[36] *Senate Finance Committee Report on Internal Revenue Code of 1954,* Section 1361(m).

[37] I.R.C. Section 1504(b)(5).

Supplementary Material

A. Suggested Reading.

George E. Ray and Oliver W. Hammonds, "Corporation or Partnership: Tax Considerations," *TAXES—The Tax Magazine,* January, 1958, Vol. XXXV, #1, p. 9.

Herman T. Reiling, "Federal Taxation: What Is a Charitable Organization?" *The American Bar Association Journal,* June, 1958, Vol. XLIV, #6, p. 525.

Philmore H. Friedman, "Problems Involved in Qualifying as a Western Hemisphere Trade Corporation," *The Controller,* March, 1959, Vol. XXVII, #3, p. 125.

Carl Holzschuher, Jr., "Tax Problems and Consequences in Changing from Cash to Accrual Basis of Reporting," *Proceedings of the New York University Seventeenth Annual Institute on Federal Taxation* (Albany: Matthew Bender & Company, Inc., 1959), p. 249.

Carl L. Moore, "Should Your Business Be Taxed As A Corporation?" *TAXES—The Tax Magazine,* April, 1955, Vol. XXXIII, #4, p. 258.

B. Leading Cases.

What is a corporation? *Morrissey v. Commissioner,* 296 U.S. 344 (1936).
What is a partnership? *Commissioner v. Tower,* 327 U.S. 280 (1946).

C. Questions.

1. Are closely held corporations subject to different tax treatment from that afforded other corporations?
2. A certain tax-exempt organization is a trust set up by a corporation for the sole purpose of providing medical care and other benefits to employees of the corporation. The tax-exempt organization lends temporarily idle funds to the corporation at the prevailing interest rate, taking as security a like amount of marketable securities at market valuation. Does the organization lose its exempt status on the ground that it is engaged in a prohibited transaction?
3. (a) The Kavanaugh Korporation was inactive during the taxable year, and its only income was interest on City of Philadelphia bonds, which interest was at once distributed to the Korporation's shareholders. What is the tax status of the interest in their hands?
   (b) Would your answer be different if a partnership were involved rather than the Korporation? Assume that the distributions were made to the partners.
4. Why would an individual elect to be taxed as a corporation?
5. The All-purpose Association received a charter as an association from the state of Ohio. When a Revenue Agent sought to tax the organization as a corporation, he was shown the charter wherein the Secretary of state of Ohio proclaimed that the organization was an association. Is the Revenue Agent bound by this?
6. Inasmuch as an individual may file a joint income tax return with his wife, whereon tax is computed as if each party were entitled to half of the income, are there any reasons why husband and wife should operate a business as a partnership?

7. If a partnership elects to be taxed as a corporation, are the partners treated as corporate employees for tax purposes?
8. Why are there both normal tax and surtax? Are both applied to the same income?
9. Is the *permanency* of a particular taxpayer (such as a specified corporation) a tax advantage, or is this permanency purely of nontax advantage?
10. Why is it said frequently that corporate dividends are subject to double tax?
11. Why is a United States taxpayer given beneficial tax treatment (if the requirements can be met) in the case of income derived from sources within possessions of the United States? Is this treatment ever detrimental from the tax point of view?
12. Why are some organizations given the characterization of tax-exempt?
13. Why is "unrelated income" of certain tax-exempt organizations subject to tax, when the organization's income unquestionably will be devoted entirely to those objectives which gave the organization its tax-exempt status in the first place?
14. A corporation with a Delaware charter was formed to carry on a construction program in Jamaica, British West Indies. Its entire income since incorporation was derived from buildings erected in Jamaica. Federal income tax for the taxable year would be $104,000 if the corporation did not qualify as a Western Hemisphere Trade Corporation. What would the tax be if there were such qualification?

3

OBLIGATIONS OF BEING A TAXPAYER

A taxpayer has two general obligations: (1) he must file a tax return when the statute so requires, and (2) he must pay any tax indicated on this return, if it has not been paid previously by advance payments, withholding of tax by his employer, or the utilization of credits arising from some other taxable period.

Customarily, the first requirement is to file a tax return when one is due. "The rendering of a proper return should be regarded by every citizen as a vital part of his life equally with that of attention to his business." [1]

Structure of the Income Tax Return

General. An income tax form may serve one or both of two purposes: (1) it may be the basis for a tax payment or refund claim, or (2) it may serve as an information return so that the Internal Revenue Service may be directed to the tax return of some other party.

Most income tax returns are of the first type. Returns of individuals and of corporations accumulate and assemble various types of income and deductions to produce a figure that is referred to in the Internal Revenue Code as taxable income. The party who files the return then computes his tax on that figure. No one else is involved in the first instance, although failure to file supplementary reports as to certain payees may involve a penalty. See "Information Returns" later in this chapter.

A partnership, on the other hand, is not a taxpayer. The partnership income tax return is only an information return, so that the Internal Revenue Service may follow the various types of partnership income to the separate partners who will be taxed upon their respective shares. See Chapter 18.

A tax return that may either be the basis for a tax payment, or an information return, or both, is the fiduciary form that is filed for

[1] *Ned Wayburn,* 32 B.T.A. 813 (1935).

trusts and estates. Various types of income and deduction are accumulated on the tax return form, and *someone* will be taxed upon this income. *Who* will be taxed depends upon the instructions that the fiduciary had been given or the manner in which he exercised certain discretionary powers. In general, the fiduciary will be taxed unless the income was currently distributed or distributable to the beneficiaries, in which event they will be taxed. This subject will be dealt with in Chapter 20.

What Is Taxed? We have seen that a tax return may be a transmittal form or an information return or both. Another function of the form is to serve as a worksheet for the accumulation of data that are used for the determination of somebody's tax. Tax returns, depending upon their nature, contain varying assortments of schedules and itemized data. In the final analysis, they are all used to process figures so that there will result the statutory term "taxable income."

Income has many meanings to the accountant, economist, tax man, and man in the street. In the interest of uniformity and clarity, the Internal Revenue Code has produced a new term.[2] Tax is based on *taxable income*. The technical nature of this term will depend upon the type of taxpayer (individual, corporation, etc.); but the arriving at taxable income is the final step before tax may be computed.

Nature of the Return. The tax return is a systematic grouping of those data that are necessary to produce taxable income. In general, there are three types of data: (1) items of income, (2) items of deduction, and (3) items of information. Some of the information will fit on a specific line or place on the tax return. Other information may be built up on a schedule which is part of the form. Still other information has no place on the return, but the figures or facts must be supplied on supplementary returns or schedules, or on plain sheets of paper (usually referred to as riders).

Sometimes a taxpayer will be given a choice as to which return to use. For example, an individual, under certain circumstances, may file the regular return on Form 1040 or a simplified version on Form 1040A or Form 1040W. See Chapter 23.

It is impractical, if not impossible, for the Internal Revenue Service to determine the correct amount of tax liability if each taxpayer could submit his income tax return according to his own bookkeeping system or accounting records. Accordingly, despite the excellence or completeness of the taxpayer's records, the data may have to be

[2] I.R.C. Section 63.

regrouped or otherwise processed to produce the figures and schedules called for by the tax return form. Sometimes elaborate worksheets are necessary to transform book income into taxable income. See Chapter 23. This does not necessarily mean that book income is incorrect—for its purpose. But sound accounting practice and the computation of taxable income vary in many respects. When there is a conflict, the Internal Revenue Code prevails in tax matters.

Book Versus Taxable Income

Book income may differ from taxable income for many reasons, including the following. This list is intended to be exemplary rather than complete.

INCOME ITEMS

Type	*Example*
Items may not be taxed under the United States Constitution.	Items in foreign commerce. Interest on state bonds.
Items may not be taxed according to the Internal Revenue Code.	Life insurance proceeds. Income earned prior to March 1, 1913. Income on certain Federal bonds.
Taxpayer has election as to taxability.	Gains from involuntary conversions.
Income not realized in a tax sense.	Improvements by lessee.
Transaction not closed for tax purposes.	Tax-free reorganizations.
Internal Revenue Code limits the tax on gain.	Capital gains.
Internal Revenue Code mitigates the gain.	Bad debt recoveries. Spreading of income that requires more than 36 months to earn.
Taxation is by formula.	Annuity income.
Income may be spread.	Installment sales. Long-term contracts.
Income may not be spread.	Prepaid income.
Income is annualized.	Change of fiscal period.
Income is "presumed."	Constructive income. Constructive ownership of stock. Claim of right. Payment was "essentially equivalent to a dividend."

DEDUCTION ITEMS

Type	*Example*
Tax return deduction may exceed books.	Depletion allowance in excess of cost.
Taxpayer may accelerate deduction.	60-month amortization under Section 168.
Advantage may be taken of items of other years.	Carrybacks. Carryovers.
Deduction is limited.	Capital losses. Transactions with related parties. Certain items that are not paid within 75 days of close of year. Contributions.
Deduction is denied.	Wash sales. Federal income and estate taxes. Expenses allocable to exempt income. Most Federal excise taxes. Reserves. Fines and penalties. Not ordinary and necessary. Not reasonable in amount. Involuntary conversions. Insurance premiums on life of corporate officer. Corporate dividends. Proof is lacking.
Deduction must be spread.	Capital expenditures. Insurance premiums.
Deduction may not be spread.	Unrestricted advance payments.
Deduction may be spread.	Organization expense.
Time of deduction is largely at taxpayer's control.	Contested liabilities.
Deduction is subject to agreement between buyer and seller.	Real estate taxes.

Certain credits are recognized for tax purposes but not for book purposes: dividends received credit or deduction, Western Hemisphere Trade Corporation special deduction, etc.

The Internal Revenue Code or court decisions involving it recognize certain substantive bases for tax liability that are unknown to sound accounting principles; *e.g.*, sound business purpose, net economic effect, acquisitions made to evade or to avoid income tax.

For tax purposes, expenditures may be disallowed even though for accounting purposes they are legitimate; *e.g.*, entertainment expense.

Certain items are deliberately set up on different bases for tax and for book purposes. For example, depreciation per the tax return may be a figure arrived at after conferences with the Internal Revenue Service, while for book purposes a figure will be used that management honestly believes is reflective of actual wear and tear of the assets.

One of the most basic differences between sound accounting principles and tax accounting is philosophic. Ordinarily, an accountant is a pessimist; a Revenue Agent is an optimist. The accountant will set up reserves for every possible loss or contingency, but the Revenue Agent will not recognize them; the losses may never occur. The accountant will lean toward the writing off of a doubtful account, whereas the Revenue Agent will be inclined to feel that the debt is not yet hopeless. The United States Supreme Court sometimes feels that this latter attitude is not in order. "The taxing act does not require the taxpayer to be an incorrigible optimist." [3]

So many are the differences between sound accounting principles and tax accounting that some taxpayers keep two sets of books. This is not, as might appear to be the case at first flush, a matter of sly record-keeping.

Surplus Reconciliation Schedule. The corporation income tax return, Form 1120, contains a surplus reconciliation schedule. Nontaxable income items and unallowable deductions are listed in detail, so that a Revenue Agent may see at a glance what items were not treated in the same manner for tax and for book purposes.

Who Must File?

Individuals. A return must be filed by every individual who has for the taxable year a gross income of $600 or more. (Gross income is defined in Chapter 4. In brief, it means items that are not specifically excluded from the definition of gross income, such as interest on municipal bonds.) If the individual has attained the age of 65 before the close of his taxable year, no return need be filed unless he has a gross income of $1,200 or more.[4]

[3] *United States v. S. S. White Dental Manufacturing Co. of Pennsylvania*, 274 U.S. 398 (1927).

[4] I.R.C. Section 6012(a).

But the Internal Revenue Service has no jurisdiction over a person unless (1) he is a citizen or resident of the United States, or (2) he has derived income here. As to (2), a United States payor is obliged to withhold tax, and hence a nonresident alien may not be required to file a tax return; see Chapter 22. As to (1), it is immaterial where a citizen of the United States resides or what his nationality is should he be a resident; a return is required if the conditions of the previous paragraph are met.

This rule as to who must file embraces minors, members of the armed forces, and refugees. If a person otherwise subject should die during a taxable year, a return must be filed on his behalf (see Chapter 20, "Fiduciaries"). It is immaterial that a person knows that no tax will have to be paid because of his exemptions, deductions, or credits. Citizens of Puerto Rico, who are likewise citizens of the United States, and nonresident aliens who were bona fide residents of Puerto Rico during the entire taxable year must file United States income tax returns if they meet this gross income test.

If husband and wife are married on the last day of the taxable year (regardless of whether they actually are living together), a return must be filed if either spouse has a gross income of $600 or more. But no return is necessary where the aggregate gross income exceeds $600, if neither spouse had gross income in excess of that figure.

A return is not required from a nonresident alien individual with income of not more than $15,400, if his tax liability has been satisfied by the nonresident withholding tax. See Chapter 22. But a return is due, despite the adequacy of withholding tax, if his income exceeds $15,400. If a nonresident alien individual is engaged in trade or business in the United States, he must file a return, regardless of the amount of his income.

A person who previously has filed a tax return might be well advised to continue to file even though he is not obliged to do so in a particular year when his gross income is less than $600. The reason is that a Revenue Agent might investigate to ascertain *why* a return was not filed. Even if it can be shown that gross income actually was less than $600, it is advisable to avoid correspondence or even the psychological strain that even strong men experience when receiving an envelope marked "Internal Revenue Service."

If a person has had his income subject to withholding tax (for example, when a person works for an employer), a return should be filed even where gross income is less than $600. The return will then serve as a refund claim for recovery of the tax withheld, if no tax is shown to be due.

Partnerships. Every partnership must file an annual income tax return.[5] The nature or amount of the income is not a factor.

Corporations. Every corporation must file a return.[6] As long as a corporation has the privilege of acting in a corporate capacity, an annual return is due, regardless of whether the company is dormant or not.[7]

Whether an organization was perfected sufficiently to be a corporation may be a matter of state law. The same is true as to whether a corporation has expired because of failure to maintain annual requirements, such as the filing of state returns.

A nonresident foreign corporation is not required to file a return if its tax liability is satisfied by nonresident withholding tax. But a resident foreign corporation must file a return.

Estates. An estate must file a return if it has gross income for the taxable year of $600 or more.[8] A return must be filed if any beneficiary is a nonresident alien.[9]

Trusts. A trust must file a return if it has any taxable income, or if it has gross income of $600 or more, regardless of the amount of taxable income.[10] A return must be filed if any beneficiary is a nonresident alien.

What Must Be Submitted?

The basic requirements appear on the income tax forms. In addition, the taxpayer should submit in schedule or memorandum form anything that the Internal Revenue Service will have to have in order to audit the return. It may be wise to anticipate what the Revenue Agent is certain to request, for that can forestall a visit by the Agent or that ominous demand that the taxpayer report to the Director of Internal Revenue with all records.

Schedules on the tax return only need to be filled in if they are applicable; there is no reason to write "none" or "zero" next to "depletion" if the taxpayer has no assets that are depletable. But the information section is another matter entirely. *All* questions must be answered. If a return does not give the necessary information about inventories, for example, delinquency and negligence

[5] I.R.C. Section 6031.
[6] I.R.C. Section 6012 (a)(2).
[7] O.D. 882, 4 CB 307.
[8] I.R.C. Section 6012(a)(3).
[9] I.R.C. Section 6012(a)(5).
[10] I.R.C. Section 6012(a)(4).

penalties may be assessed.[11] The consequences of failing to answer a question may be even more severe. The tax return may be regarded as "no return," which means that the statute of limitations never runs, and the Internal Revenue Service may examine it at any time whatsoever. (The statute of limitations will be discussed in Chapter 26.)

In addition to the income tax return forms themselves, there may be separate schedules to supply if they are necessary for the computation of taxable income: Schedule C (Profit (or Loss) from Business or Profession), Schedule D (Gains and Losses from Sales or Exchanges of Property), Schedule F (Schedule of Farm Income and Expenses) may have to be filed by an individual, although these schedules are not part of the income tax form that he may obtain at his bank. Whether a supplementary form or schedule must be filed is sometimes a knotty problem. For example, a corporation must attach to its regular income tax return (Form 1120) a separate Form 1120PH, and there are penalties if this is not done. See Chapter 26. But this separate schedule is only due if the corporation is a personal holding company, and the officers may not realize that their company fits into this technical category.

How Must Tax Returns Be Submitted?

Where tax blanks are required, it is up to the taxpayer to obtain these forms and to use them. The fact that he has not been sent the forms or that they are not available is not a valid excuse for his failure to use them. Thus it is up to the taxpayer to ascertain what forms he requires well in advance of the filing date, so that he has opportunity to procure them. Under certain circumstances, he may have commercial printers reproduce tax forms for him.

The Secretary of the Treasury may permit the taxpayer to file a tax return in dollar amounts only, with cents being eliminated.[12]

When Are Returns Due?

Type of Return	*Not Later Than*
Corporation (but see "Foreign corporation . . .")	Fifteenth day of third month after year's close.
Estate.	Fifteenth day of fourth month after year's close.
Exempt cooperative association.	Fifteenth day of ninth month after year's close.

[11] *Carmichael Tile Co.*, T.C. Memo., Docket #22858, entered April 21, 1950.
[12] I.R.C. Section 6102.

Type of Return	*Not Later Than*
Foreign corporation not having office or place of business in the United States.	Fifteenth day of sixth month after year's close.
Individual (see "Nonresident alien . . .")	Fifteenth day of fourth month after year's close.
Nonresident alien individual whose wages are not subject to withholding.	Fifteenth day of sixth month after year's close.
Partnership.	Fifteenth day of fourth month after year's close.
Trust.	Fifteenth day of fourth month after year's close.[13]

If any of these dates falls on a Saturday, Sunday, or legal holiday, the return may be filed on the following day.[14]

The dates of declarations of estimated tax by individuals and by corporations are discussed in Chapter 25.

The penalties for late filing are given in Chapter 26.

Where Are Returns Filed?

Type of Return	*Internal Revenue District Where Is Located the Taxpayer's . . .*
Corporation.	Principal place of business or principal office or agency of the corporation.
Estate.	Domicile of decedent at time of death.
Individual (see next item).	Legal residence or principal place of business.
Nonresident alien individual.	Principal place of business in the United States.
Others.	Legal residence or principal place of business of the person making the return.[15]

Despite the above, the Secretary of the Treasury may permit a return to be filed in any internal revenue district. He may require the return of any officer or employee of the Treasury Department to be filed in a district selected by the Secretary.[16]

[13] I.R.C. Section 6072.
[14] I.R.C. Section 7503.
[15] I.R.C. Section 6091(b).
[16] I.R.C. Section 6091(b)(4).

In the absence of a legal residence or principal place of business in any internal revenue district (*e.g.*, nonresident foreign corporations), the return is to be filed with the District Director of Internal Revenue, Baltimore, Maryland.[17]

Information Returns

In certain instances, payors are obliged to report to the Internal Revenue Service the total of amounts paid to designated parties during the taxable year. These information returns are primarily for the purpose of enabling the Internal Revenue Service to check the tax returns of the payees. But the payor is held responsible for making the returns (penalties are discussed in Chapter 26). A question on the corporate income tax return (Form 1120) asks: "Did the corporation make a return of information on Forms 1096 and 1099 . . .?" An incorrect answer may constitute perjury; an omitted answer may have consequences previously discussed in this chapter.

All persons engaged in a trade or business who make payments resulting from this activity to another person of $600 or more in a taxable year are covered if the payments are of the following types: rent, salaries, wages, premiums, annuities, compensations, remunerations, emoluments, or other fixed or determinable gains, profits, and income (other than dividends).[18] Payments of corporate interest must be reported regardless of the amount.[19] Information as to dividend payments need only be furnished when specifically requested by the Secretary of the Treasury.[20] A report must be filed for patronage dividends of $100 or more to a single payee.[21]

Inasmuch as most wages are now reported to the Internal Revenue Service on Form W–2 in connection with the withholding tax (see Chapter 25), the information return on Form 1099 includes only items not reported as being wages; *e.g.*, reimbursement of expenses or the value of living quarters if they have not been included in the amount shown on Form W–2.

The following are not to be reported regardless of the amounts: payments of any type (other than patronage dividends, rebates, or refunds) to a corporation; payments to a nonresident alien reported on Form 1042; distributions or salaries to members of a partnership

[17] Revenue Ruling 55–171, 1955–1 CB 80.
[18] I.R.C. Section 6041(a).
[19] I.R.C. Section 6041(c).
[20] I.R.C. Section 6042(1).
[21] I.R.C. Section 6044.

reported on Form 1065; distributions to beneficiaries of trusts or estates reported on Form 1041; rent paid by a tenant to a real estate agent; payments made by a broker to his customers; interest on tax-free covenant bonds reported on Form 1012.

Payments of wages of 600 or more to a domestic or household employee by a housewife are not considered payments made in the course of a trade or business, and thus they are not reported on Form 1099. But reporting would be required if the services were rendered in a home used in the operation of a trade or business, such as a rooming house, tourist home, etc.[22]

All Forms 1099 of a single payor are to be submitted with a single transmittal Form 1099. The information returns show actual payments for the preceding calendar year and must be filed not later than February 28. They may be sent to Service Center, Internal Revenue Service, at any one of these three addresses:

1400 East 95 Street, Kansas City 14, Missouri
6 Lake Street, Lawrence, Massachusetts
Building 230, Utah General Supply Depot, Ogden, Utah

Certain specialized information returns are used in connection with corporate reorganizations. See Chapter 17.

Records

The obligation of being a taxpayer includes the maintenance of proper records to justify every item on the tax return. The problem of meeting the burden of proof will be treated in Chapter 23. It is not sufficient for a taxpayer to *be* right. He has to be in position to prove it. The point is being emphasized here in advance of the general discussion in Chapter 23 to alert the taxpayer to the fact that the groundwork for a later tax audit should be prepared before the tax return is even filed. Consequences of failure to keep records adequately may be loss of a deduction or credit, assignment of an item of income or expense to a less advantageous period, loss of a privilege or election, or a negligence penalty.

Reliance Upon an Advisor

A taxpayer has the obligation of knowing when to consult an advisor, what to tell him, and how much to rely on this advice. Penalties for failure to file a return, or to answer a question, or to perform an act will be waived where it may be shown that the tax-

[22] Revenue Ruling 56-46, 1956-1 CB 560.

payer made a full disclosure of all of the facts to an advisor competent to advise him, and where the advice was in fact followed.[23] But it is necessary for the taxpayer to have knowledge of what facts are necessary to furnish to an advisor. And who is competent to advise? If the taxpayer recognized that a question existed, he presumably would take steps to get the answer. But if he does not know, for example, that there is such a thing as a personal holding company, he will not know enough to ask an advisor whether such a state exists.

Formalities

Various technical advantages may be lost by the taxpayer if he does not comply with formalities required by the Internal Revenue Code or administrative requirements. "The statute clearly provides that the benefits of this paragraph shall not be allowed unless the taxpayer make application therefor in accordance with the regulations. The petitioner did not make application for the benefits . . . in accordance with the Commissioner's regulations or otherwise. . . . In any event, this Court is powerless to aid him. The filing of the application is condition precedent which we have no authority to waive." [24]

Excuses

"The only defense which the petitioners offer against the assessment of the proposed penalties is based upon the testimony of [the taxpayer], that he himself did not know of the requirements of the law for the filing of . . . returns. . . . However, as has often been pointed out, ignorance of the law alone is not a sufficient excuse." [25]

Choice of Accounting Period

The taxpayer has the responsibility of selecting the proper accounting period. The responsibility may be:

(1) To abide by the requirements of the Internal Revenue Code and the regulations; *e.g.,* to have a proper taxable year.

(2) To choose a period that is most satisfactory to the taxpayer himself; *e.g.,* to follow a natural business year, to close the books at

[23] *Burton Swartz Land Corporation v. Commissioner,* 198 F.2d 558 (5th Cir., 1952).

[24] *Louis Visintainer,* 13 T.C. 805 (1949), *aff'd,* 187 F.2d 519 (10th Cir., 1951).

[25] *Orient Investment & Finance Co., Inc. et al.,* T.C. Memo., Docket ##7003 and 7016, entered January 8, 1947.

the most convenient time, to align income and expenditures for the same transactions.

Taxable Year. Taxable income is computed and a return is filed for a period known as the taxable year.[26] The term "taxable year" means—

(1) The taxpayer's annual accounting period, if it is a calendar year or a fiscal year (that is, a year ending on the *last* day of any month other than December);

(2) The calendar year, if the taxpayer keeps no books or has no accounting period; or

(3) The period for which the return is made, if the return is for a period of less than twelve months, referred to as a "short period."

A taxable year may not cover a period of more than twelve calendar months except in the case of a 52–53 week taxable year.

A new taxpayer in his first return may adopt any taxable year which meets the above requirements without obtaining prior approval. This year must be followed in the future unless the Internal Revenue Service grants permission for a change to a different taxable year.

52–53 Week Year. A taxpayer may elect to compute his taxable income on the basis of a fiscal year which—

(1) Varies from 52 to 53 weeks.

(2) Ends always on the same day of the week, and

(3) Ends always on—

(A) Whatever date this same day of the week last occurs in a calendar month, or

(B) Whatever date this same day of the week falls which is nearest to the last day of the calendar month.

Illustration. If the taxpayer elects a taxable year ending always on the last Saturday in November, then for the year 1961 the taxable year would end on November 25. On the other hand, if he had elected a taxable year ending always on the Saturday nearest to the end of November, then for the year 1961 the taxable year would end on December 2. Thus, in the case of a taxable year described in (3)(A), the year will always end within the month and may end on the last day of the month, or as many as six days before the end of the month. In the case of a taxable year described in (3)(B), the year may end on the last day of the month, or as many as three days before or three days after the last day of the month.

A new taxpayer may adopt the 52–53 week taxable year for his first taxable year if he keeps his books and computes his income on that basis, or if he conforms his books accordingly in closing them. A taxpayer may change to a 52–53 week taxable year without the

[26] I.R.C. Section 441.

permission of the Commissioner if such a taxable year ends with reference to the end of the same calendar months as that in which the former taxable year ended, and if the taxpayer keeps his books and computes his income for the year of change on the basis of such a taxable year, or if he conforms his books accordingly in closing them.

Change of Accounting Period. If a taxpayer wishes to change his annual accounting period, he must first obtain approval from the Commissioner by filing an application on Form 1128. This must be filed on or before the last day of the month following the close of the short period for which a return is required to effect the change of accounting period.[27] In general, a change will be approved when the taxpayer establishes a substantial business purpose for making the change.

A corporation does not need to make an application if—

(1) The corporation has not changed its annual accounting period at any time within the ten calendar years ending with the calendar year which includes the beginning of the short period required to effect the change;

(2) The short period is not a taxable year in which there was a net operating loss;

(3) The taxable income for the short period is, if placed on an annual basis, 80% or more of the taxable income for the taxable year immediately preceding the short period; and

(4) If a corporation had a special status as described in the following sentence, it must have the same special status for both the short period and the taxable year. Special status includes only: a personal holding company, a foreign personal holding company, an exempt organization, a foreign corporation not engaged in trade or business within the United States, a Western Hemisphere Trade Corporation, and a China Trade Act Corporation.

Short Taxable Year. A return for a short period (that is, for a taxable year consisting of a period of less than twelve months) is made under any of the following circumstances:

(1) *Change of annual accounting period.* Where this takes place, a separate return must be filed for the short period of less than twelve months beginning with the day following the close of the old taxable year and ending with the day preceding the first day of the new taxable year.

(2) *The taxpayer was not in existence for the entire taxable year.* An individual may die before the end of his taxable year. A corpo-

[27] I.R.C. Section 442.

ration using a calendar year basis may be formed on April 21, or it may dissolve on November 22.

(3) *Termination of taxable year for jeopardy.* A return must be filed for a short period resulting from the termination by the Commissioner of a taxpayer's taxable year for jeopardy. See Chapter 26.

In the case of (1), income must be *annualized* on the short-period return. This is accomplished by a corporation by projecting its income to a full year; specifically, income is multiplied by a fraction, the numerator of which is twelve and the denominator is the number of months in the short period. Tax is computed and is then *de-annualized* by application of a fraction, the numerator of which is the number of months in the short period and the denominator of which is twelve.

Illustration. A corporation changes its accounting period. Taxable income for the short period of six months is $40,000.

Taxable income annualized ($40,000 × 12/6)		$80,000
Tax on annual basis: $80,000 at 52%............	$41,600	
Less: Allowance for surtax exemption..........	5,500	36,100
Tax for (6-month) short period ($36,100 × 6/12)		$18,050

In the case of a taxpayer other than a corporation, income for the short period is computed in this manner:

(1) Determine taxable income for the short period without taking into account any exemptions (see Chapter 24).

(2) Reduce exemptions to an amount which bears the same ratio to the total deduction for a full year as the number of months in the short period bears to twelve months.

(3) Deduct the amount in (2) from the amount in (1).

(4) Multiply the difference determined in (3) by twelve and divide by the number of months in the short period.

(5) Compute a tentative tax on the amount of the annualized income so determined.

(6) Multiply the amount of the tentative tax determined in (5) by the number of months in the short period and divide by twelve.

Illustration. An individual, for a 9-month period, has taxable income of $13,800 before considering his exemptions for himself, his wife, and two children. He has no income from dividends or partially tax-exempt interest. The computation will be:

(1) $13,800 (income for short period)
(2) $600 × 4 × 9/12 = $1,800
(3) $13,800 − $1,800 = $12,000
(4) $12,000 × 12/9 = $16,000 (annualized income)
(5) Tax on $16,000 = $3,920 (tentative tax)
(6) $3,920 × 9/12 = $2,940 (tax for short period)

A personal exemption must be reduced in computing the taxable income to be annualized. If the short period contains whole months, the deduction for exemptions must be reduced to an amount which bears the same ratio to the deduction for a full taxable year as the number of months in the short period bears to twelve.

The standard deduction (see Chapter 24) is not allowed when a short-period return is required because of a change in accounting period.

Credits for dividends received and for partially tax-exempt interest must be based on the annualized amount of these items in computing the tentative tax mentioned above.

Avoidance of Unfavorable Presumptions

A taxpayer has an obligation to himself to avoid additional tax and other unpleasant consequences of tax assessments. This means keeping his records in such a way that he can explain his personal and business finances. Unexplained wealth can bring about tax assessments on the theory of unreported income; that is, what is now bank accounts, securities, etc., may have been yesterday's earnings that never appeared on a tax return. Any increase in a taxpayer's net worth that cannot be explained may be treated as taxable income.[28] Unexplained bank deposits may be taxed as income.[29]

Supplementary Material

A. Suggested Reading.

Chester M. Edelmann, "Is Income Tax Accounting 'Good Accounting Practice'?" *TAXES—The Tax Magazine*, February, 1946, Vol. XXIV, #2, p. 116.

Dan Throop Smith and J. Keith Butters, *Taxable and Business Income* (Princeton: Princeton University Press, 1949).

Gerald A. Smith, "Methods of Determining Taxable Income Without Adequate Records," *Proceedings of the Tulane Seventh Annual Institute on Federal Taxation* (Indianapolis: The Bobbs-Merrill Company, 1958), p. 331.

Samuel Byer, "Net Worth and Civil Liability," *Proceedings of the New York University Seventeenth Annual Institute on Federal Taxation* (Albany: Matthew Bender & Co., Inc., 1959), p. 59.

Mark Richardson, "Accounting Methods and Changes Therein," *TAXES—The Tax Magazine*, December, 1957, Vol. XXXV, #12, p. 924.

T. T. Shaw, "Changes in Methods of Accounting," *The Journal of Accountancy*, November, 1957, Vol. CIV, #5, p. 50.

[28] *Holland et al. v. United States*, 348 U.S. 121 (1954).

[29] *Thaddeus G. Fibich et al.*, T.C. Memo., Docket #34362, entered April 27, 1953.

B. Leading Case.

Net worth. *Holland et al. v. United States,* 348 U.S. 121 (1954).

C. Questions.

1. The elder J. P. Morgan is alleged to have said that if the Government did not collect a man's tax, he would be a fool to do anything about it. Discuss this point of view.
2. If a payor fails to file an information return or other statement of a payment, is the payee justified in omitting the item likewise?
3. If a taxpayer carefully keeps his books in accordance with sound accounting principles, and a certified public accountant issues a statement to that effect, may this book income be used as the basis for tax computation?
4. Is it legally or morally wrong to keep two sets of books, one for accounting purposes and one for tax purposes?
5. An individual knows that because of the large number of his dependent children his personal exemptions will exceed his gross income, even without taking into consideration any deductions that might be questioned, such as contributions paid or business expenses. May he omit the filing of an income tax return on his $1,500 gross income since unquestionably there will be no tax liability?
6. Blaque and Whyte, a partnership, operated at a loss in the taxable year. Is a tax return required in view of the fact that there is no income to report? Would your answer be the same if the partnership were completely inactive during the taxable year?
7. The Internal Revenue Service failed to mail a tax form to a taxpayer for a particular year. Is he justified in deferring the filing of his return until the Government sends him a form? Would your answer be the same if he himself went to the local office of the Internal Revenue Service, which informed him that the available supply of forms was exhausted?
8. Mr. Smith lived in Los Angeles, California, and filed his returns with the Director of Internal Revenue in that city for many years. He moved to Boston, Massachusetts. Smith feels that the Los Angeles Revenue Agents are familiar with certain complex aspects of his business and that a tax audit would thus be less difficult in that office. May he continue to file his returns in California?
9. Officers of an organization believed that it was tax-exempt and filed no return. Subsequently a Revenue Agent discovered that the organization actually was not tax-exempt and that tax was due. Must interest and penalty be paid if it can be proved that the organization's officers had received a letter from their accountant stating that in his opinion no return had to be filed?
10. What is the tax significance of a natural business year?
11. For what reasons would a taxpayer elect to adopt a 52–53 week year?
12. What sufficient reasons could be given for requesting permission to change a taxpayer's accounting period?
13. Is the Internal Revenue Service justified in considering that a taxpayer's assets represent taxable income if he cannot trace the acquisition of his property? Why?
14. In case of honest doubt as to whether a return should be filed, is a taxpayer justified in resolving the doubt in his own favor?

15. Inasmuch as a tax return is a form for the submission of figures ultimating in taxable income and, perhaps, in tax, is an individual justified in omitting answers to factual questions when the information is difficult to obtain and seemingly irrelevant to a tax computation?
16. Methusalem Jones is not certain of his exact age, but he feels that he is at least 65. Must he file a tax return if his gross income is $1,000?
17. Husband had $500 in gross income; his wife had $400. Is a tax return necessary?

4

TYPES OF INCOME

The Internal Revenue Code refers to many types of income: gross income, adjusted gross income, taxable income, etc. But with few exceptions, the Federal income tax is levied upon *taxable income*.[1] In several instances (*e.g.*, capital gains), the tax arbitrarily may be limited. If the cost or other basis of an asset cannot be established, the full proceeds are taxable, as though there were a gross income tax. Yet in the vast majority of all situations, the basis for imposition is taxable income. This is the end result of what may be numerous and intricate computations. The starting point of an income tax return is *gross income.*

Gross Income

Gross income is not so all-inclusive a term as might at first appear to be the case. Two tests must be satisfied. First, is the item in question really income? And even if it is income, does Congress have the power to tax it?

First test. "'Income may be defined as the gain derived from capital, from labor, or from both combined,' provided it be understood to include profit gained through a sale or conversion of capital assets . . ."[2] Anything derived in other manner does not fit the concept of income. A gift, for example, is not income, because it does not come from capital, from labor, from both combined, or from a disposition of capital assets. This definition "was not meant to provide a touchstone to all future gross income questions."[3] But any modification of this durable definition involves highly specialized situations and seems to require litigation; *e.g.*, "insider profits" derived by a corporation's directors were includible in gross income because "The payments in controversy were neither capital contributions nor gifts."[4]

[1] I.R.C. Sections 1(a), 1(b), 11(a), 641(a).
[2] *Eisner v. Macomber*, 252 U.S. 189 (1920).
[3] *Commissioner v. Glenshaw Glass Co. et al.*, 348 U.S. 426 (1955).
[4] *General American Investors Co., Inc. v. Commissioner*, 348 U.S. 434 (1955).

Second test. Article I, Section 9, Clause 5 of the Constitution of the United States provides that "No tax or duty shall be laid on articles exported from any State." Tax could not be imposed upon the proceeds of an exporter's goods sold abroad, for "it cannot be applied to any income which Congress has no power to tax . . ." [5]

But even if an item *is* income and Congress has the *right* to tax it, the Congress may have specifically excluded this item from gross income.

"The consideration of the question whether the damages received for libel and slander are taxable as income must proceed not so much according to the refinements of economists . . . as according to such decisions of the Supreme Court as mark the course." [6]

The Statutory Definition. Unless specifically excluded by some other section of the Internal Revenue Code, gross income means all income from whatever source derived. As though this all-inclusive definition could be made even more all-inclusive, Section 61(a) enumerates as belonging in this catchall language the following:

(1) Compensation for services, including fees, commissions, and similar items.

(2) Gross income derived from business.
(3) Gains derived from dealings in property.
(4) Interest.
(5) Rents.
(6) Royalties.
(7) Dividends.
(8) Alimony and separate maintenance payments.
(9) Annuities.
(10) Income from life insurance and endowment contracts.
(11) Pensions.
(12) Income from discharge of indebtedness.
(13) Distributive share of partnership gross income.
(14) Income in respect of a decedent.
(15) Income from an interest in an estate or trust.

But "an item not named specifically in paragraphs (1) through (15) of section 61(a) will nevertheless constitute gross income if it falls within the general definition in section 61(a)." [7] Thus, the finder of treasure trove was deemed to have had gross income to the extent of the fair value.[8] A corporation that purchased and retired

[5] *William E. Peck and Co., Inc. v. Lowe,* 247 U.S. 165 (1918).
[6] *C. A. Hawkins,* 6 B.T.A. 1023 (1927).
[7] Ways and Means Report Accompanying the Internal Revenue Code of 1954 at Section 61.
[8] Revenue Ruling 61, 1953-1 CB 17.

its own bonds at less than their issue price derived income to the extent of this differential, as the corporation "has realized within the year an accession to income, if we take words in their plain popular meaning, as they should be taken here." [9]

Other sections of the Code specifically identify items as being includible (in whole or in part) in gross income. These include:

Prizes and awards.[10]

Damages for personal injury or sickness.[11]

Income taxes paid by lessee corporation.[12]

Scholarships and fellowship grants.[13]

Gross income also may include items of the following types:

Back pay.

Breach of contract damages.

Discounts on purchases.

Employees' awards.

Gambling winnings.

Jury fees.

Military pay.

Per diem allowances.

Recovered amounts (*e.g.*, bad debts previously written off).

Retirement pay.

Rewards.

Severance pay.

Strike benefits paid by union.

Tips and gratuities.

Travel allowance.

"The amount of all such items is required to be included in the gross income for the taxable year in which received by the taxpayer unless they may be properly accounted for on the accrual basis. . . ." [14] But it does not necessarily follow that all items includible in gross income must be picked up in their entirety. Even the fifteen types of item that the Code specifically lists as includible are subject to certain restrictions. Compensation may be spread under a deferral arrangement, so that some or all of it is included in gross income of subsequent years; the same may be true for pensions. See Chapter 11. Some income is exempt from gross income; some is partially exempt, as will be seen later in the present chapter. Alimony does not include all types of payment by divorced parents;

[9] *United States v. Kirby Lumber Co.*, 284 U.S. 1 (1931).

[10] I.R.C. Section 74.

[11] I.R.C. Section 104.

[12] I.R.C. Section 110.

[13] I.R.C. Section 117.

[14] *Burnet v. Sanford & Brooks Co.*, 282 U.S. 359 (1931).

see Chapter 15. Annuities may not be fully taxable, nor life insurance payments, nor interest from the discharge of indebtedness; these subjects are developed later in this chapter.

Gross income, then, means all items that are income and which are not specifically excluded by some law: the Constitution of the United States, a treaty with a foreign nation, the Internal Revenue Code, etc. The taxpayer has the burden of proof of showing that a particular form of income is covered by a specific exclusion.

Gross income is not confined to monetary receipts. It includes income realized in any form, whether in money, services, meals, accommodations, stock, or other property.[15]

The principal types of gross income will be examined in greater detail in the following pages.

Compensation for Services. Gross income includes wages, commissions, compensation for services on the basis of a percentage of profits, commissions on insurance premiums, tips, bonuses, Christmas "presents" from the employer if given in recognition of services, termination or severance pay, rewards, jury fees, marriage fees and other contributions received by a clergyman for services, pay of persons in the Armed Forces of the United States, retirement pay, pensions, and retirement allowances, *unless* covered by some specific exclusion in the law.[16] Under appropriate circumstances, the exceptions of primary concern are:

	I.R.C. Section
Distributions from employees' trusts. See Chapter 11.	402, 403
Compensation for child's services. See below.	73
Prizes and awards. See below.	74
Gifts. See below.	102
Compensation for injuries or sickness. See below.	104
Amounts received under accident and health plans. See below.	105
Scholarships and fellowship grants. See below.	117
Servicemen. See Chapter 15.	104, 113

An employee must include in gross income any compensation for his services. Thus if the employer makes payment to the employee's wife, creditors, or other persons, the employee will be deemed to have received the full amount constructively. If a taxpayer performs services to a person for the benefit of a charitable, religious, or

[15] Regulations Section 1.61–1(a).
[16] Regulations Section 1.61–2(a).

educational organization as defined in I.R.C. Section 170(c) pursuant to an understanding as to payment, the taxpayer will be deemed to have received taxable income.[17]

Illustration. A prominent society figure agrees that her picture may be used in the magazine advertisements of a cosmetic manufacturer on the condition that the manufacturer will give $5,000 to the American Red Cross. The society figure will be deemed to have received $5,000 in gross income.

Any economic benefit that a person receives from his employer because of the employer-employee relationship will be included in gross income. This includes bargain purchases, the value of living quarters or meals (unless furnished for the convenience of the employer), and stock options (unless restricted stock options, as discussed in Chapter 11). The employee must include in gross income any life insurance premiums paid on his life by the employer, if the proceeds are payable to the employee's beneficiaries, except in the case of group term life insurance. Group hospitalization premiums paid by the employer are not includible in the employee's income if the premiums are not deductible from wages. If the employer pays an employee's medical expenses, the latter has received gross income.[18]

A so-called gift by the employer to the employee will generally be treated as compensation; what was the purpose of it? Thus, an automobile given to a plant manager upon his completion of 25 years of service would be regarded as compensation, as would a diamond-encrusted watch given to a chemist by his employer upon the development of a new process. If the employer is a corporation, there is even less likelihood that a payment will be regarded as a gift, as a corporation may not make a gift.[19] This question always must be answered: Was there a *donative intent?* Or was the intent merely compensatory?

Vacation allowances paid to employees from a vacation fund established pursuant to a labor agreement are included in gross income where the allowances are based on services rendered.

The payment or reimbursement by an employer of the cost of moving an employee and his immediate family from one place of employment to another permanent place of employment is not compensation, if primarily for the benefit of the employer. But if all of the allowance or reimbursement is not spent by the employee as moving expenses, the excess is included in gross income. If the

[17] Regulations Section 1.61–2(c).
[18] *M. K. Kartsen Estate,* T.C. Memo. 1954–194, filed November 18, 1954.
[19] *Robert E. Binger,* 22 B.T.A. 111 (1930).

transfer is primarily for the benefit of the employee or at his request, the entire amount received is gross income.[20]

An employee's gross income includes his gross compensation, not the amount of the salary check that he receives. An employee constructively receives amounts which never reach him, such as the standard payroll deductions for withholding tax, Federal Insurance Contributions Act payments, Series E bond purchases, union dues check-offs, company credit union payments, garnishee of salary, contributions to company pension plan, etc.

Business Income. In a manufacturing, merchandising, or mining business, gross income means total sales, less the cost of goods sold, plus any income from investments and from incidental or outside operations or sources. Gross income is determined without subtraction of depletion allowances based on a percentage of income, and without subtraction of selling expenses, losses, or other items not ordinarily used in computing the cost of goods sold. The cost of goods sold should be determined in accordance with the method of accounting consistently used by the taxpayer.[21]

Farmers. This subject will be treated in Chapter 15.

Gains Derived from Dealings in Property. The general rule is that gain realized on the sale or exchange of property is included in gross income, unless excluded specifically by law. The exclusions may be of the following types:

	I.R.C. Section
Corporate reorganizations. See Chapter 17.	331, 333, 337, 351, 354, 355, 361
Partnership formations and distributions. See Chapters 18, 19.	721, 731
Tax-free exchanges. See Chapter 17.	1031, 1032, 1036
Involuntary conversions. See Chapter 5.	1033
Sale or exchange of residence. See Chapter 5.	1034
Sales or exchanges of insurance policies. See Chapter 5.	1035

Generally, the gain is the excess of the amount realized over the unrecovered cost or other basis of the property sold or exchanged.

Interest. As a general rule, interest received by or credited to the taxpayer is included in his gross income. This includes interest on bank deposits, coupon or registered bonds, open account, promissory

20 Revenue Ruling 54–429, 1954–2 CB 53.
21 Regulations Section 1.61–3(a).

notes, mortgages, G.I. insurance, life insurance proceeds held under an agreement to pay interest, and refunds on Federal taxes. It includes usurious interest, unless by state law it is automatically converted to a payment on the principal.[22] Interest on United States obligations issued on or after March 1,1941, is fully taxable.

Wholly tax-exempt interest is not included in gross income in the first instance; for tax purposes, it is *not* income of any type. This includes interest upon the obligations of a state, territory, or a possession of the United States, or any political subdivision of any of the foregoing, or of the District of Columbia. Covered are such bodies as the Port of New York Authority, the Indiana Toll Road Commission, State Industrial Development Boards, Oklahoma County Utility Services Authority, and various others of this general category, created for the furtherance of public functions. Interest is wholly exempt on obligations of the United States and its possessions issued not later than September 1, 1917. Interest on the first $5,000 principal amount of such bonds issued after September 1, 1917, and before March 1, 1941, is wholly tax-exempt. (The principal amount of the bond is the issue or purchase price and not the maturity value or the present sale price.) If husband and wife each own Treasury bonds issued prior to March 1, 1941, each may exclude from gross income the interest on up to $5,000 principal amount of these bonds, even though a joint income tax return is filed; but that is not the same as saying that on a joint return, interest on up to $10,000 principal amount of such bonds may be excluded, for separate ownership is required. Also excluded is interest on amounts deposited in a Postal Savings account before March 1, 1941.

Partially tax-exempt interest is the amount earned on United States obligations issued after September 1, 1917, and before March 1, 1941.

Illustration. An individual owned $12,000 principal amount of 3% bonds of the type mentioned in the previous sentence. Of the $360 received in a year, $150 is excluded from gross income entirely. The remaining $210 is included in gross income, subject to a credit under certain circumstances. The credit is illustrated in Chapter 24.

Rents and Royalties. Gross income includes rentals received or accrued for the occupancy of real estate or the use of personal property. Advance rentals must be included in gross income of the year of receipt, regardless of the period covered or the method of accounting used by the taxpayer. An amount received by a lessor from a

[22] Regulations Section 1.61–7(a).

lessee for canceling a lease constitutes gross income for the year in which it is received, as it is essentially a substitute for rental payments.[23]

Illustration. The owner of property enters into a 10-year lease, in 1961, for an annual rental of $5,000. In addition to $5,000 for the first year's rental, he also received, in 1961, $5,000 in advance as rent for the tenth and last year of the lease. Gross income from this transaction for 1961 is $10,000.

If the tenant pays any of the expenses of the landlord (*e.g.*, property taxes), the landlord must include these payments in his gross income, although he may be able to claim a deduction for expenses otherwise deductible.

Dividends. The general rule is that dividends are included in gross income. But such distributions must be from earnings accumulated since February 28, 1913. A return of capital, such as the complete or partial liquidation of a corporation, is not a dividend. But the shareholder has the burden of proof of showing that what he receives from a corporation is not a dividend, if the corporation has accumulated earnings large enough to support a dividend.

This subject will be treated in Chapter 8.

Alimony. Alimony and separation maintenance payments are included in gross income, except to the extent of permissible exclusions.[24] The income and deduction aspects of alimony will be treated in Chapter 15.

Pensions. Pensions and retirement allowances paid either by the Government or by private persons constitute gross income unless excluded by law. The principal exclusions refer to annuity and insurance payments, which are discussed in Chapter 12, and to payments under qualified employee benefit plans, which are considered in Chapter 11.

Cancellation of Indebtedness. There is no income if indebtedness is forgiven gratuitously. But if an individual gives anything in return for the cancellation or scaling down of indebtedness, he realizes income; for example, if the debtor performs services for the creditor, the debtor realizes income in the amount of the debt as compensation for his services.[25] Thus, if an individual is about to have a $12,000 debt canceled by his creditor, and in consideration for this act the debtor agrees to mow the creditor's lawn, the debtor

[23] Regulations Section 1.61–8(a), (b).
[24] Regulations Section 1.61–10.
[25] Regulations Section 1.61–12.

realizes $12,000 income as compensation for his services. Nothing should be done to mar the *gratuitous* character of the cancellation.

A taxpayer may realize income by the payment or purchase of his obligations at less than their face value.

If a taxpayer is discharged of his indebtedness as the result of an adjudication in bankruptcy under Section 14 of the Bankruptcy Act, or as the result of an agreement among his creditors not consummated under any provision of the Bankruptcy Act, he does not realize income if immediately thereafter his liabilities exceed the value of his assets. Furthermore, unless one of the principal purposes of seeking a confirmation under the Bankruptcy Act is the avoidance of income tax, income is not realized by a taxpayer in the case of a cancellation or reduction under (1) a plan of corporate reorganization confirmed under Chapter X of the Bankruptcy Act, (2) an "arrangement" or a "real property arrangement" under Chapter XI or XII of that act, or (3) a "wage earner's plan" confirmed under Chapter XIII of that act.[26]

Instead of realizing gross income as a result of a reduction or cancellation of indebtedness, a taxpayer may elect to exclude the amount from gross income.[27] This requires application of the reduction against the basis of assets.[28] This will be discussed in Chapter 5.

If a shareholder in a corporation which is indebted to him gratuitously forgives the debt, he does not derive gross income. This is regarded as a contribution to the corporation's capital to the extent of the principal of the debt.[29]

Distributive Share of Partnership Gross Income. A partner's distributive share of partnership gross income constitutes gross income to him.[30] See Chapter 19 for discussion on distributive shares of partnership gross income.

Income in Respect of a Decedent. Income in respect of a decedent constitutes gross income to the recipient. See Chapter 21.

Income from an Interest in an Estate or Trust. Income from an interest in an estate or trust constitutes gross income. A consideration of when this is income to the fiduciary and when to the beneficiary will be found in Chapter 20.

Sinking Fund. If a corporation, in order to secure the payment of indebtedness, places property in trust or sets aside certain

[26] Regulations Section 1.61–12(b).
[27] I.R.C. Section 108.
[28] I.R.C. Section 1017.
[29] Regulations Section 1.61–12(a).
[30] Regulations Section 1.61–13(a).

amounts in a sinking fund under the control of a trustee who may be authorized to invest and to reinvest the sums from time to time, the property or fund set aside by the corporation and held by the trustee is an asset of the corporation, and any gain must be included in the corporation's gross income.[31]

Prizes and Awards. Prizes and awards are, in general, to be included in gross income.[32] But there are special rules as to scholarships and fellowship grants. See the following paragraph. And prizes and awards are not included in gross income if (1) they were made primarily in recognition of past achievement of the recipient in religious, charitable, scientific, educational, artistic, literary, or civic fields; (2) the recipient was selected without any action on his part to enter the contest or proceeding; and (3) the recipient is not required to render substantial future services as a condition to receiving the prize or award. Thus, such awards as the Nobel prize or the Pulitzer prize would qualify for the exclusion, but not prizes or awards made by an employer to an employee in recognition of some achievement in connection with his employment.[33] Amounts received from radio and television giveaway shows, or as door prizes, or in any similar type of contest, would not qualify for the exclusion.[34]

Scholarships and Fellowship Grants. An individual does not report in his gross income any amount received as a scholarship at an educational institution, as defined in the following paragraph, or as a fellowship grant, including the value of contributed services and accommodations. Nor does he report any amount received to cover expenses for travel, research, clerical help, or equipment if he actually has expended the amount.[35]

For this purpose, "educational institution" means only an educational institution which normally maintains a regular faculty and curriculum and normally has a regularly organized body of students in attendance at the place where its educational activities are carried on.[36]

Individuals who are candidates for degrees. There will be no exclusion from gross income for that portion of any amount received as payment for teaching, research, or other services in the nature

[31] Regulations Section 1.61–13(b).
[32] I.R.C. Section 74(a).
[33] Regulations Section 1.74–1(b).
[34] Senate Finance Committee Report Accompanying the Internal Revenue Code of 1954 at Section 74.
[35] I.R.C. Section 117.
[36] I.R.C. Section 151(e)(4).

of part-time employment that are required as a condition to receiving the grant. Thus, if an individual is required as a condition of the grant to perform part-time teaching services, he must report in gross income what such teaching services ordinarily would command. Status reports as to his general progress are not regarded as performance of services.[37]

But if teaching, research, or other services are required of all candidates (whether or not recipients of grants) for a particular degree as a condition to obtaining it, then the services will not be treated as part-time employment. If all the candidates for a certain education degree are obliged to perform part-time practice teaching, the services would not have to be valued in the grantee's gross income.

Individuals who are not candidates for degrees. If an individual is not a candidate for a degree, the amount received as a scholarship or a fellowship grant which is excludable from gross income may not exceed an amount equal to $300 times the number of months for which the recipient received amounts under the grant during the taxable year. The exclusion may not exceed 36 months, whether utilized or not. If an individual received a fellowship grant of $7,200 for three years (which he elected to receive in 36 monthly installments of $200), his exclusion period would be exhausted even though he did not in any of the 36 months make use of the maximum exclusion.

The following payments or allowances are not considered to be amounts received as a scholarship or a fellowship grant for this purpose; educational and training allowances to veterans, allowances to members of the Armed Forces of the United States, amounts paid as compensation for services or primarily for the benefit of the grantor.[38]

Damages for Personal Injury or Sickness. Compensation for injuries or sickness is not included in gross income, except to the extent that these payments are attributable to (but not in excess of) medical expenses of a previous taxable year.[39] Excluded are (1) amounts received by an employee under a workman's compensation act, (2) damages received on account of personal injuries or sickness, (3) payments received through accident or health insurance for personal injuries or sickness, and (4) amounts received as pensions, etc., for certain personal injuries or sickness.

As to (1), the exclusion from gross income does not extend to a retirement pension or annuity to the extent that it is determined by

[37] Regulations Section 1.117–2(a).
[38] Regulations Section 1.117–4.
[39] I.R.C. Section 104.

reference to the employee's age or length of service, or the employee's prior contributions, even though the employee's retirement is occasioned by an occupational injury or sickness. Nor does the exclusion extend to amounts which are received as compensation for an occupational injury or sickness to the extent that they are in excess of the amounts provided for in the applicable workmen's compensation act.[40] As to (3), the exclusion from gross income does not extend to amounts received by an employee insofar as they are attributable to contributions of the employer which are not includible in the gross income of the employee, or which are paid by the employer. As to (4), any part of the disability retirement pay computed on the basis of years of active service which is in excess of the disability retirement pay that would be received if the disability pay were computed on the basis of percentage of disability will not be excluded.[41]

If a health or accident policy indemnifies a person against specified losses or bodily injuries, but does not provide reimbursement for medical expenses, amounts received under this policy are not gross income.[42]

Reimbursement for personal damages does not produce gross income but merely compensation for a loss. "One may be recompensed for an injury but it is a rare case in which one should have a profit out of it." [43] It was ruled that servicemen would not be taxed on payments by the Government in recognition of their not having received sufficient or proper food while prisoners of war. "*Held,* such amounts . . . are in the nature of reimbursements for the loss of personal rights and are not includible in the gross income of such individuals for Federal income tax purposes." [44] Claims paid by the West German Republic to citizens or residents of the United States as damages to body or health sustained while German citizens at the hands of the Nazis were not includible in gross income.[45]

An amount paid for the loss of life of a person traveling on the *Lusitania* was not gross income.[46]

Damages for Nonproperty Losses. Gross income does not include amounts that are but reimbursements. Examples are:

[40] Regulations Section 1.104–1(b).
[41] Revenue Ruling 55–88, 1955–1 CB 241.
[42] Revenue Ruling 55–331, 1955–1 CB 271.
[43] *Farmers and Merchants Bank of Catlettsburg, Kentucky v. Commissioner,* 59 F.2d 912 (6th Cir., 1932).
[44] Revenue Ruling 55-132, 1955–1 CB 213.
[45] Revenue Ruling 56-518, 1956–2 CB 25.
[46] I.T. 2420, VII–2 CB 123.

Breach of promise to marry.[47]

Award in compromise of an annulment action which had been based on fraud.[48]

Damages for wrongful death.[49]

Damages for personal libel.[50]

Damages for defamation of personal character.[51]

Payments by a state to a former employee to reimburse him for expenses that he sustained in an improper action initiated by the state.[52]

Amounts Received Under Accident and Health Plans. In general, amounts received by an employee through accident or health insurance for personal injuries or sickness are included in gross income to the extent that these amounts (1) are attributable to contributions by the employer which were not includible in the employee's gross income or (2) are paid by the employer. But the amount is not included in gross income if it is an amount actually expended for medical care, if it is a payment unrelated to absence from work, or if it conforms to the requirements of a wage continuation plan.[53]

For this purpose, "personal injury" means an externally caused sudden hurt or damage to the body brought about by an identifiable event. The term "sickness" means mental illnesses and all bodily infirmities and disorders other than "personal injuries." Diseases, whether resulting from the occupation or otherwise, are not considered personal injuries, but they are treated as a sickness.[54] Pregnancy is not within either of these definitions, although sickness resulting from pregnancy would be.[55]

These distinctions are important because of the required waiting period. If an employee is absent because of sickness, there will be no exclusion from gross income for amounts attributable to the first seven calendar days, unless he is hospitalized on account of sickness for at least one day during this period.

Illustration. If, on the tenth day of the period during which the employee is absent from work on account of sickness, he is admitted to a hospital on account of sickness, and is discharged from the hospital two days later, he may exclude (subject to the $100 weekly limitation) any amount of benefits received. Entry

[47] *Lyde McDonald*, 9 B.T.A. 1340 (1927).
[48] I.T. 1852, II-2 CB 66.
[49] Revenue Ruling 54-19, 1954-1 CB 179.
[50] *C. A. Hawkins*, 6 B.T.A. 1023 (1927).
[51] Sol. Op. 132, I-1 CB 92.
[52] *Cox v. Kraemer*, 88 F. Supp. 835 (D.C., Conn., 1948).
[53] I.R.C. Section 105.
[54] Regulations Section 1.105-4(b).
[55] Revenue Ruling 55-263, 1955-1 CB 16.

into a hospital as an in-and-out patient, or mere entry into the out-patient ward or the emergency ward of a hospital, does not constitute hospitalization. There is no waiting period in the case of absences from work on account of personal injury.

Absence under a quarantine because of someone else's sickness will not be the basis for a sick pay exclusion.

Reimbursements for amounts actually expended for medical care of the taxpayer, his spouse, and his dependents as defined in Chapter 24 are excluded from gross income. But there must be included in gross income amounts which are attributable to (and not in excess of) allowable medical expense deductions for any previous taxable year.[56]

Payments unrelated to absence from work are not gross income to the extent that these amounts (1) constitute payments for the permanent loss of use of a member or function of the body, or the permanent disfigurement of the taxpayer, his spouse, or a dependent and (2) are computed with reference to the nature of the injury without regard to the period the employee is absent from work.

A plan may be *noncontributory* or *contributory*. Under a noncontributory plan, the employer contributes the entire cost, by payment of premiums on an accident and health policy, contributions to a fund that will make payments, or direct payment of the benefits. All benefits received by an employee in such a case must be included in his gross income, unless exempted as being an amount expended for medical care, a payment unrelated to absence from work, or a payment under a wage continuation plan. Under a contributory plan, the employee pays for a part of the cost. The employee does not include in gross income that portion of the benefits that were provided by his own contribution.

If benefits are received by an employee under an individual accident or health policy paid for in part by the employer and in part by the employee, the portion of the benefits received which is attributable to the employer's contributions will be an amount which bears the same ratio to the amount received as the portion of the premiums paid by the employer for the current policy year bears to the total premiums paid for that year by employer and employee.

Illustration. Under a plan, the employer pays two-thirds of the annual premium cost on individual accident and health policies for his employees. The remainder of each employee's premium is paid by a payroll deduction from wages. The annual premium for a particular employee is $24, of which $16 is paid by the employer. Thus, 16/24 of all benefits received by this employee under the policy are attributable to the employer, and the remaining one-third is not included in the employee's gross income.[57]

[56] Regulations Section 1.105–2.

[57] Regulations Section 1.105–1(d).

If a group policy is paid for in part by employer and by employee, and the net premiums for a period of at least three policy years are known at the beginning of the calendar year, the portion of any amount received by an employee which is attributable to the employer's contribution will be an amount which bears the same ratio to the amount received as the portion of the net premiums contributed by the employer for the last three policy years which are known at the beginning of the calendar year bears to the total of the net premiums contributed by employer and employee for these policy years. If the net premiums for this coverage for a period of at least three policy years are not known at the beginning of the calendar year but are known for at least one policy year, this determination will be made by using the net premiums for this coverage which are known at the beginning of the calendar year. If the net premiums for this coverage are not known at the beginning of the calendar year for even one policy year, the determination will be made by using either (1) a reasonable estimate of the net premiums for the first policy year, or (2) if the net premiums for a policy year are ascertained during the calendar year, by using that net premium.

Illustration. An employer maintains a group accident and health policy of which a portion of the cost is paid for by the employees through payroll deductions. The net premium for the most recently completed policy year is not known on the first day of the taxable year because certain retroactive premium adjustments are not determinable until a subsequent date. Therefore, for purposes of this computation, the last three policy years are those immediately preceding the most recently completed policy year. Assume that in each of these three years, respectively, the net premiums were $8,000, $9,000, and $7,000 (or a total of $24,000), while the employer's contributions each year were, respectively, $3,000, $3,500, and $1,500 (or a total of $8,000). The portion of any amount received under the policy by an employee at any time during the taxable year which is attributable to the contributions of the employer is to be determined by using the ratio of $8,000 to $24,000. Thus, $\frac{\$8{,}000}{\$24{,}000}$ of the amounts received by an employee at any time during the taxable year is attributable to the employer's contribution.

If the benefits are a part of a noninsured plan to which both employer and employee contribute, and the plan has been in effect for at least three years before the beginning of the taxable year, the portion of the benefit received which is attributable to the employer's contribution will be an amount which bears the same ratio to the amount received as the contributions of the employer for the period of three years next preceding the year of receipt bear to the total contributions of employer and employee for that period. If, at the beginning of the year of receipt, the plan has not been in effect for at least three years but has been in effect for one year, the determination will be made during the 1-year or 2-year period during which the plan has been in effect. If the plan has not been in effect for one full year at the beginning of the year of receipt, the determination may be based upon the portion of the year of receipt preceding the time when the determination is made. Or the determination may be made periodically (such as monthly or quarterly) and used throughout the succeeding period.

Illustration. If an employee terminates his service on April 15, and that year is the first year the plan has been in effect, the determination may be based upon the contributions of employer and employees during the period beginning with January 1 and ending with April 15, or during the month of March, or during the quarter consisting of January, February, and March.[58]

A much more simple technique, if it is available to you, is to follow the suggestion of the Treasury Department's booklet *Your Income Tax:* "Your employer should be able to tell you the percentage of the benefits which are attributable to his contributions to the plan."

Benefit payments are not included in gross income if paid to an employee through a wage continuation plan as wages or payments in lieu of wages for a period during which the employee is absent from work on account of personal injuries or sickness. *Wage continuation plan* means an accident or health plan under which wages, or payments in lieu of wages, are paid to an employee for a period during which he is absent from work on account of a personal injury or sickness. This includes (1) plans under which payments are continued as long as the employee is absent from work on account of personal injury or sickness, as well as (2) plans under which there is a limitation on the period for which benefits will be paid, (3) plans under which benefits are continued until the employee either is able to return to work or reaches retirement age, and (4) plans under which wages or payments in lieu of wages are paid to an employee who is absent from work on account of personal injury or sickness, even though the plan also provides that these wages or payments may be paid to an employee who is absent from work for reasons other than a personal injury or sickness.

Amounts paid under a wage continuation plan are excluded only if attributable to periods during which the employee would be at work were it not for a personal injury or sickness. An employee is not absent from work if (1) he is not expected to work because he has reached retirement age or (2) he incurred the sickness or injury

[58] Regulations Section 1.105-1.

during his paid vacation. But if an employee who would otherwise be at work during a particular period is absent from work, and his absence is in fact due to a personal injury or sickness, a payment which he receives for that period under a wage continuation plan qualifies for the exclusion.

A period of absence from work commences the moment the employee first becomes absent from work and concludes the moment he first returns to work. Whether he is absent from work depends upon all the circumstances. An employee who is a farm hand and lives upon his employer's premises is deemed to be absent from work even though he is physically on his employer's premises. The employee is not absent from work when he performs substantial services for his employer, even though these services are performed at a place other than the usual place of employment. If an employee returns to his usual place of employment and performs any services for his employer, he has returned to work; but, if he merely holds occasional short conferences concerning his work with other employees or clients while hospitalized or at home recuperating, these conferences do not constitute a return to work.

The amount which is paid to an employee as wages or payments in lieu of wages will be determined by reference to the plan under which the amount is paid, and to the contract, statute, or regulation which provides the terms of the employment. But unless the governing instrument (contract, etc.) provides to the contrary, it will be presumed that no wages or plan benefits are attributable to days (or portions of days) which are not normal working days for the particular employee. Nor does the exclusion apply to amounts earned before or after the period of absence from work, even though received during that period.

Illustration. An employee receives regular wages of $70 a week and normally works five days a week, from Monday through Friday. He is injured and is absent from work Friday and the following Monday (two workdays). If he continues to receive his regular wages, he may exclude from gross income $28 (2/5 of $70). But if he were subject to call seven days a week, and the work arrangement provided for payment of wages on the basis of a 7-day week, the daily wage would be $10, and the exclusion would be $40 (4/7 of $70).

Illustration. An employee works from Monday through Friday, with Saturday and Sunday off. If he becomes ill at noon Friday and goes home, Friday is the first day of absence. But if he remains on the job until the end of his normal workday but failed to report for work Monday because of the illness, then Monday is the first day of his absence.

The pay period of a wage continuation plan is determined by the plan itself. If, in the usual operation of the plan, benefits are paid for the same periods as regular wages, then the pay period of the benefits will be the period for which a payment of wages is ordinarily made to the employee by the employer. If plan benefits are ordinarily paid for different periods from regular wages, then the pay period of these benefits will be the period for which payment of these benefits is ordinarily made.

The exclusion from gross income for payments under a wage continuation plan refers only to the first $100 of weekly wages, or the mathematical equivalent.

For the purpose of determining the $100 weekly limitation, all pay periods are geared to the weekly rate.

Pay Period	*To Get Weekly Rate,*
Biweekly.	Multiply rate in first column by 24, divide by 52.
Monthly.	Multiply rate in first column by 12, divide by 52.
Other pay periods.	Project the pay to an annual basis, divide by 52.

Illustration. If the salary is $520 per month, multiply this figure by 12 ($6,240). Divide by 52, and the result is $120, the weekly rate. If the compensation is $200 per pay period on the basis of a 10-day pay period, multiply $200 by 365 and divide by 10 to get an annual rate of $7,300. This is divided by 52 to get a weekly rate of $140.38.

If an employee receives amounts under two or more wage continuation plans (whether from the same employer or not), the weekly rate and the excludability of amounts received under each plan will be the sum of all the weekly rates.

Illustration. An employee whose weekly salary is $120 is covered by two wage continuation plans maintained by his employer. Plan A is a contributory insured plan to which the employee contributes 60% of the premiums and which provides a weekly payment of $30. Plan B is a salary continuation plan completely financed by the employer. Inasmuch as 60% of the cost of Plan A is contributed by the employee, 60% of the weekly payment of $30 ($18) is excluded from gross income. The remainder of each weekly payment ($12) is the weekly rate of Plan A. Inasmuch as the employer pays the entire cost of Plan B, the weekly rate of this plan is the total amount paid per week. The weekly rate for the employee for this purpose is $132 ($120 from Plan B plus $12 from Plan A).

Contributions by Employer to Health Plans. Amounts contributed by an employer to accident or health plans for the benefit of employees are not included in the gross income of the employees.[59] That is, amounts paid by the employer under such plans are not deemed to be constructive income to the employees. But if the plan provides for benefits in addition to accident and health, the exclusion from gross income refers only to that portion of the employer's cost that is allocable to the accident and health benefits.

[59] I.R.C. Section 106.

Rental Value of Parsonages. A minister of the gospel does not have to include in his gross income the rental value of a home furnished to him as part of his compensation, or the rental allowance paid to him as part of his compensation, to the extent used by him to provide a home.[60]

"Home" means a dwelling place and appurtenances, including furnishings and a garage. An allocation is necessary where a minister rents, purchases, or owns a farm or other business property in addition to a home.[61]

Chaplains in the armed forces, if regularly ordained ministers, are entitled to the exclusion.[62]

Improvements by Lessee. Gross income does not include income (other than rent) derived by a lessor of real property on the termination of a lease, where buildings or other improvements made by the lessee revert to the lessor.[63]

Illustration. OR Corporation leased to EE Corporation for a period of fifty years unimproved real estate, under a lease providing that EE Corporation would erect on the premises an office building costing $500,000, in addition to paying OR Corporation a lease rental of $10,000 per annum beginning on the date of completion of the improvements, the sum of $100,000 being placed in escrow for the payment of the rental. Five years later, the building was completed. The lease provided that all improvements made by the lessee would become the property of OR Corporation on the termination of the lease by forfeiture or otherwise, and that the lessor would become entitled upon this termination to any remaining sum in the escrow fund. Six years after the improvements were completed, EE Corporation forfeited the lease; at that time, the improvements had a value of $95,000. The $95,000 is excluded from the gross income of the OR Corporation. But any remaining amount in the escrow fund that was forfeited to OR Corporation is included in OR's gross income.[64]

Income Taxes Paid by Lessee Corporation. If two corporations had entered into a lease prior to 1954 under which the lessee was obligated to pay (or reimburse) the lessor for any part of the Federal income tax imposed upon the lessor on rents under this lease, the payment or reimbursement of the taxes will not be included in the lessor's gross income.[65]

A renewal or continuance after 1953 of an earlier lease will be treated as a lease made prior to 1954 if effected under an option existing prior to that date.[66]

[60] I.R.C. Section 107.
[61] Regulations Section 1.107–1.
[62] I.T. 1307, I–1 CB 110.
[63] I.R.C. Section 109.
[64] Regulations Section 1.109–1.
[65] I.R.C. Section 110.
[66] Regulations Section 1.110–1.

Recovery of Bad Debts, Prior Taxes, and Delinquency Amounts. The recovery of certain items previously deducted or credited in arriving at taxable income customarily must be included in gross income of the year of the recovery. This refers to bad debts, prior taxes, or delinquency amounts.[67] But the recovery may be excluded from gross income under certain circumstances if the original deduction or credit did not result in a tax benefit; for example, a debt was deducted as bad, but because the taxpayer had no taxable income in that year, the deduction provided no tax benefit.

The illustration of this rule as applied to bad debts (a typical application) will be developed in Chapter 13.

Combat Pay. Certain combat pay of members of the armed forces is excluded from gross income.[68] This subject is treated in Chapter 15.

At the present time, there are no combat areas within the meaning of the statute. Termination of combatant activities in Korea, the last such area, was announced in Executive Order 10585, January 1, 1955.

Mustering-out Payments for Members of the Armed Forces. This exclusion allowed by I.R.C. Section 113 will be considered in Chapter 15.

Sports Programs Conducted for the American National Red Cross. A corporation primarily engaged in the furnishing of sports programs may exclude from its gross income amounts received as proceeds from a sports program if (1) the corporation agrees in writing with the American National Red Cross to conduct such programs exclusively for the benefit of the A.N.R.C.; (2) the corporation turns over all proceeds from the program, less expenses, to the A.N.R.C.; and (3) the facilities of the corporation used in conducting such sports programs are not regularly used during the taxable year for the conduct of these sports programs.[69]

Section 114 does not apply in the case of a corporation organized or operated primarily to participate in one or more sports programs for the A.N.R.C.[70]

Income of States, Municipalities, Etc. Gross income does not include income derived from any public utility or the exercise of any essential governmental function that accrues (1) to a state or

[67] I.R.C. Section 111.
[68] I.R.C. Section 112.
[69] I.R.C. Section 114.
[70] Regulations Section 1.114–1.

territory, or political subdivision thereof, or the District of Columbia; or (2) to the government of any possession of the United States, or any political subdivision thereof.[71]

Contributions to the Capital of a Corporation. Contributions to the capital of a corporation are excluded from gross income.[72] This includes voluntary pro rata payments by the shareholders as well as contributions to capital made by persons other than shareholders. For example, the exclusion applies to the value of land or other property contributed to a corporation by a governmental unit or by a civic group for the purpose of inducing the corporation to locate its business in a particular locality. But the exclusion does not apply to any money or property transferred to the corporation in consideration for goods or services rendered, or to subsidies paid for the purpose of inducing the corporation to limit production.[73]

Meals or Lodgings Furnished for the Convenience of the Employer. An employee may exclude from his gross income the value of meals and lodgings furnished to him for the convenience of his employer, whether or not the meals or lodgings are furnished as compensation. In the case of meals, the exclusion is permitted only if the meals are furnished on the business premises of the employer. In the case of lodging, the exclusion is permitted only if the employee is required to accept the lodging on the business premises of the employer as a condition of his employment.[74]

The phrase "required as a condition of his employment" means "required in order for the employee properly to perform the duties of his employment."

Ordinarily, meals furnished to the employee during the working day will be deemed furnished for the convenience of the employer. Likewise, meals furnished immediately before or after the employee's working hours will be deemed to be for the convenience of the employer, if the furnishing of these meals serves a business purpose of the employer other than providing additional or indirect compensation to the employee. Meals furnished on nonworking days, or at times when the employee's presence does not serve a business purpose of the employer, do not qualify for the exclusion. If the employee is required to occupy living quarters on his employer's business premises as a condition of his employment, the exclusion applies to the value of meals furnished there. There is

[71] I.R.C. Section 115.
[72] I.R.C. Section 118.
[73] Regulations Section 1.118–1.
[74] I.R.C. Section 119.

no requirement that the employee accept such meals as a condition of employment to qualify for the exclusion.[75]

The value of lodging furnished to an employee by his employer is excluded from the employee's gross income if three tests are met: (1) the lodging is furnished on the business premises of the employer, (2) the lodging is furnished for the convenience of the employer, and (3) the employee is required to accept the lodging as a condition of his employment.[76]

This exclusion applies only to meals and lodging furnished in kind, without cost to the employee. If the employee has an option to receive additional compensation in lieu of meals or lodging in kind, or must pay for these items, there is no exclusion from gross income. But the mere fact that an employee, at his option, may decline to accept meals and lodging will not mean that they are includible in gross income.

Illustration. A waitress who works from 7 A.M. to 4 P.M. is furnished two meals a workday without charge. In order to insure that she will commence work on time, the employer encourages her to have her breakfast on his business premises before starting work, although she is not required to do so. But she is required to have lunch there. The waitress may exclude the value of both meals from gross income. But if she is permitted to have meals on the employer's premises on her days off, the value of the meals may not be excluded from her gross income.

Illustration. A Civil Service employee of a state is employed at an institution and is required by his employer to be available for duty at any time. Accordingly, the employer furnishes him with meals and lodging at the institution. Under state law, his meals and lodging are regarded as part of his compensation. He may exclude the value of meals and lodging from his gross income.

Illustration. An employee of an institution is given the choice of residing there free of charge, or of residing elsewhere and receiving a cash allowance in addition to his regular salary. If he elects to reside at the institution, the value of what the employer furnishes must be included in gross income. His residence at the institution is not required in order for him properly to perform his duties.

Statutory Subsistence Allowance Received by Police. A police official employed by a state, territory, or possession of the United States, by any of their political subdivisions, or by the District of Columbia may exclude from gross income any amount received as a statutory subsistence allowance to the extent that this allowance does not exceed $5 per day. To the extent that any such amounts are excludable from gross income, he may not take a deduction elsewhere for expenses in respect of which the statutory allowance is paid. But any expenses in excess of the allowance may be deducted under an appropriate provision of the tax law.[77]

[75] Regulations Section 1.119–1(a).
[76] Regulations Section 1.119–1(b).
[77] I.R.C. Section 120.

"Statutory subsistence allowance" means an established amount, apart from salary or other compensation, which is authorized under the laws of the employing body. The term "police official" includes an employee of any of the governmental units specified who has police duties, such as a sheriff, a detective, a policeman, or a state police trooper, regardless of what his designation may be.[78]

The exclusion is to be computed on a daily basis. If the statute providing the allowance does not specify the daily amount, the allowance must be converted to a daily basis.

Illustration. A state statute provides for a weekly subsistence allowance. The daily amount is to be determined by dividing the weekly amount by the number of days for which the allowance is paid. If one receives a weekly statutory subsistence of $40 for five days of the week, the daily amount would be $8 ($40 divided by 5). But only $5 per day may be excluded, or $25 on a weekly basis.

Other Examples. Under certain circumstances, a corporation will be deemed to have received income as a result of making a distribution of property. See Chapter 8.

The creator of a trust may be deemed to have income when the trust realizes it. See Chapter 21.

One party may be deemed to have income which ostensibly is attributed to another party. See Chapter 27.

A person may be deemed to have had gross income because he cannot satisfactorily explain his wealth, under the "net worth" theory. See Chapter 3.

Any economic benefit that a person received as a shareholder may be regarded as a dividend; any such benefit received as an employee may be regarded as compensation.

The fact that income arose from a transaction forbidden by law does not exclude the item from gross income. "Of course, Congress may tax what it also forbids." [79] Thus, income from bootlegging during the Prohibition era was includible.[80]

An individual may not exclude income on the ground that it did not come from services, if something was or was not done indirectly. Strike benefits paid by a union are includible in gross income.[81] So are lockout benefits.[82] Tips are not regarded as tax-free gifts; even if the payment is characterized as optional, it takes an unbelievably brave person to refuse.[83]

[78] Regulations Section 1.120–1.
[79] *United States v. Stafoff,* 260 U.S. 477 (1922).
[80] *United States v. Sullivan,* 274 U.S. 259 (1926).
[81] Revenue Ruling 57–1, I.R.B. 1957–1, 10.
[82] Revenue Ruling 58–139, I.R.B. 1958–14, 7.
[83] *Nazzareno D. Cesanelli et al.,* 8 T.C. 776 (1947); Revenue Ruling 57–403, I.R.B. 1957–36, 37.

Supplementary Material

A. Suggested Reading.

Roswell Magill, *Taxable Income* (New York: The Ronald Press Co., 1945).

H. Helmut Loring, "Some Tax Problems of Students and Scholars," *California Law Review,* May, 1957, Vol. XLV, p. 153.

Conrad J. Moss, "Taxation of Damages and Recoveries," *TAXES—The Tax Magazine,* April, 1958, Vol. XXXVI, #4, p. 273.

Robert S. Holzman, "Indemnity Payments to Nazi Victims," *TAXES—The Tax Magazine,* May, 1956, Vol. XXXIV, #5, p. 340.

P. J. Redford, "Gross Income Is Not Income," *TAXES—The Tax Magazine,* November, 1957, Vol. XXXV, #11, p. 851.

B. Leading Cases.

What is income? *Eisner v. Macomber,* 252 U.S. 189 (1920).

Income as related to use of the term in common speech. *United States v. Oregon-Washington Railroad & Navigation Co.,* 251 Fed. 211 (2d Cir., 1918).

Role of the books in determining income. *Doyle v. Mitchell Bros. Co.,* 247 U.S. 179 (1918).

Significance of realization. *Lucas v. American Code Co.,* 280 U.S. 445 (1930).

C. Questions.

1. A corporation made what was termed a gift to an employee because he had not been late for ten years. Is this income to him?
2. The Alumni Association of Gring College made an annual award of $1,000 to that professor who was voted by the students to be the best teacher on the campus. Is this taxable to the recipient?
3. A street cleaner, while at work, found $100 in a gutter. Although the newspapers printed the story, no one claimed the money. Is this income that he derived in the course of his employment, which included examination of gutters?
4. Mel Monolith, a college football player, was allowed $125 a month by the institution for unspecified expenses. No services were required of him in return, although he was expected to play football if the coach called upon him. Was the payment income to him?
5. A chef at a restaurant was given $20 by a customer for cooking "the best mushroom omelette I ever ate." Could this be considered as a gift?
6. A manufacturer sent Christmas gifts of substantial value to buyers at department stores. Was the value of such a gift income to the recipient?
7. What is donative intent?
8. Harry and Wilhelmina, husband and wife, filed a joint return. He owned $20,000 principal amount of United States bonds issued on April 21, 1938; she owned none. What is the amount that may be excluded from gross income?
9. A tenant paid her landlord $50 a month for the apartment, as well as supplying the landlord from her farm with all of the eggs, butter, and

cheese that he could use. How would the landlord calculate his rent income?

10. A retailer was in financial difficulties. A supplier agreed to cancel $5,000 of accounts receivable if the retailer promised to make all of his purchases from this supplier for the next five years. Was this cancellation of indebtedness "income" to the retailer?
11. Billy O. was convicted of a crime and was sent to prison. Three years later, the actual culprit confessed, and Billy was released. The state gave him $20,000 because of its mistake. Was this taxable to him?
12. An individual was obliged to stay away from his job for some days to tend to his critically ill wife, as no assistance could be obtained for the helpless woman. His employer paid him his full salary of $85 per week. Is there any sick pay exclusion?
13. What is the tax benefit rule?
14. An individual receives $39 in jury fees from the State of New Mexico. Is this exempt as derived from an essential governmental function?
15. A manufacturer offered its chief engineer the use of a company house next to its factory, in addition to his regular salary, if he agreed to be available for emergency repair work at any time of day or night. Is the value of this taxable to him?
16. Taxes sometimes are regarded as payments for protection by the state. May a person with illegal income argue that he owes no tax, as the state will not furnish him protection but, rather, would arrest him if he could be located?
17. A young man won a $10,000 quiz prize. This consisted of various lots of merchandise, worth $10,000 in aggregate at retail values. He sold the items and received $8,000. Is the prize income to him? If so, how much is taxable?
18. A boy broke a shopkeeper's window with a baseball. The youth agreed (reluctantly) to serve as a junior clerk without pay for four Saturdays to expiate his wrong. Does he have any income to report?
19. A taxpayer sold some securities for $15,000. Unquestionably he had paid *something* for them, but he had no records. Is the full $15,000 included in gross income?
20. Why is certain income from United States obligations nontaxable, while income from other United States obligations may be partially taxable, or completely taxable?
21. A private in the United States Army was assigned to protect piers during a waterfront strike. His platoon was engaged in hand-to-hand fighting with a mob, and tear gas was used. Could he exclude any part of his army salary as combat pay?

5

ORDINARY INCOME AND CAPITAL GAIN

Gain or loss for tax purposes will fall into one of two categories: ordinary or capital. The result of a transaction will be treated as ordinary income (or loss) or as capital gain (or loss). The classification may make a substantial distinction, although this is not always the case. As to gain, an individual might have to pay a tax as high as 91%, or a corporation as high as 52%, were the income ordinary. If capital gain resulted, however, an alternative tax rate of 25% would apply under appropriate circumstances. As to ordinary loss, it could be used as an offset to income, even if the result were a net loss that could be utilized in other years (see Chapter 14, "Carrybacks and Carryovers"). As to capital loss, it could be used only as an offset against capital gains and, in the case of noncorporate taxpayers, to a limited extent as an offset against ordinary income.

The basic rule is that transactions in capital assets beget capital gains or capital losses. But there are certain exceptions, which will be discussed in this chapter. All transactions in capital assets do not result in capital gains or losses; see page **5·27**. Various safeguards have been provided by the Internal Revenue Code to see that ordinary income is not converted into capital gain at will; for example, gains from sales of certain property between spouses or between an individual and a controlled corporation will be treated as ordinary rather than capital.[1] And some transactions result in capital gains even though capital assets are not involved; for example, I.R.C. Section 1231.

It has been held that capital gains are income for Federal income tax purposes.[2]

Theory of Special Treatment of Capital Gains and Losses

In theory, capital gains may be taxed at lower rates than ordinary income because the eventual profit was a-borning for several years,

[1] I.R.C. Section 1239.
[2] *Merchants Loan & Trust Co. v. Smietanka,* 255 U.S. 509 (1921).

and hence it is inequitable to tax this profit in full in a single year. That concept would be valid if all capital gains resulted from investments that had an increment over a number of taxable years, so that several years were required to produce the tax. The concept also ignores the fact that ordinary income often requires many years to produce. But the theory is far from valid in practical operation. An individual may purchase an asset and sell it within the same taxable year, reporting his profit at advantageous capital gains rates. But another individual may labor over a piece of handiwork for years, or he may hold inventory that constantly increases in value for a number of years; in such instances, the profit is nonetheless taxed as ordinary income, despite the time factor.

It also is argued that capital gains should be given preferential taxation (or even freedom from taxation) as an incentive for persons to invest in the stock or bonds of an enterprise. But it is no less desirable to provide incentive for persons to engage in other necessary activities, such as laboring, the income from which is fully taxable.

Thus, the theory of capital gains taxation does not explain the form of this tax. It is therefore necessary to understand *how* this type of taxation applies rather than *why*.

Definition of Capital Asset

A capital asset may best be defined by a process of subtraction. All assets held by a taxpayer are capital unless they are one of the five types specifically excluded by the Code.[3] The courts have somewhat broadened this list by various analogies. The statutory listing of items that are not capital is:

(1) Stock in trade of a taxpayer or other property of a kind which would properly be included in his inventory if on hand at the close of the taxable year, or property held by him primarily for sale to customers in the ordinary course of his trade or business.

(2) Depreciable property used in a taxpayer's trade or business, or real property so used.

(3) A copyright, a literary, musical, or artistic composition, or similar property, held by a taxpayer whose personal efforts created this property. Similarly treated is a copyright, etc., held by a taxpayer in whose hands (for the purpose of determining gain from a sale or exchange) the basis is the same as it was to the creator.

Illustration. A writes two plays. He gives the copyright of one to his son, B. He sells the copyright of the other play to an unrelated party, C. B has the

[3] I.R.C. Section 1221.

same basis for the copyright as A and hence the copyright is not a capital asset to him. C's basis is his cost, and the copyright is a capital asset to him.

"Similar property" includes a theatrical production, a radio program, a newspaper cartoon strip, or any other property eligible for copyright protection, but does not include a patent or an invention, or a design which may be protected only under the patent law and not under the copyright law.[4]

(4) Accounts or notes receivable acquired in the ordinary course of trade or business for services rendered or from the sale of property as described in (1), above.

Illustration. If a taxpayer acquires a note receivable for services rendered and reports the fair market value of the note as income, a subsequent sale of the note for less than the value previously reported would produce ordinary loss. But, if he later sells the note for more than the amount originally reported, the excess is treated as ordinary income.

The receivable in the hand of a purchaser is a capital asset.

(5) An obligation of the United States or any of its possessions, or of a state or territory, or any political subdivision thereof, or of the District of Columbia, issued on or after March 1, 1941, on a discount basis and payable without interest at a fixed maturity date not exceeding one year from the date of issue.

"Congress intended that profits and losses arising from the everyday operation of a business be considered as ordinary income or loss rather than capital gain or loss. The preferential treatment provided applies to transactions which are not the normal source of business income."[5] In order to remove the sale of an asset from the capital gains provisions of the Code, the taxpayer must be engaged in the trade or business of making such sales; he must have customers in the course of this business; he must hold the asset primarily for sale to these customers in the ordinary course of his business.

Whether assets are capital or noncapital depends upon various factors—such as the regularity and continuity of sales,[6] the nature of the acquisition of the property or the purpose of the acquisition,[7] the nature and extent of the taxpayer's "business,"[8] and the activity of the taxpayer in promoting the sales.[9] "No one of these facts is

[4] Regulations Section 1.1221–1(c).

[5] *Corn Products Refining Co. v. Commissioner,* 350 U.S. 46 (1955).

[6] *Brown v. Commissioner,* 143 F.2d 468 (5th Cir., 1944).

[7] *Kanawha Valley Bank,* 4 T.C. 242 (1944); *Three States Lumber Co. v. Commissioner,* 158 F.2d 61 (7th Cir., 1946).

[8] *Flint v. Stone Tracy Co.,* 220 U.S. 107 (1911).

[9] *W. D. Haden et al.,* T.C. Memo., Docket ##109477–80 and 110300–3, entered November 30, 1943.

decisive but the solution must depend upon all the pertinent facts and their relative importance in the case." [10]

Classification Dependent Upon Facts. The same asset may be a capital asset in the hands of one taxpayer and an ordinary asset in the hands of another. Thus, in the hands of most persons, a share of stock is a capital asset; but, in the hands of a securities dealer, the asset is not capital. It is excluded from the capital asset classification because it conforms to the statutory definition of inventory insofar as the dealer is concerned.

A wholesale liquor dealer who was unable to obtain whiskey during a national shortage made a purchase of stock in American Distilling Co., which offered rights to shareholders to buy specified amounts of whiskey. As soon as the rights were exercised, the liquor dealer sold the stock. The American Distilling shares were not capital assets in his hands; the acquisition was an incident in his obtaining inventory, and loss on the sale of the stock was deductible as ordinary.[11] But under similar facts, where the stock was retained after the rights were exercised, a subsequent sale of the shares resulted in capital loss.[12]

Bonds are generally regarded as a capital asset. But ordinary loss resulted where a corporation sold bonds it had acquired in the past solely to serve as a deposit of faithful performance under a manufacturing contract.[13] Ordinary loss resulted on a sale of bonds of a supplier which had been purchased in order to assure the taxpayer a reliable source of supply.[14]

Realization Is Necessary. "As applied to income derived from the sale or exchange of capital assets, it would be observed that the definition contains two elements: (1) a gain produced by or derived from capital, (2) a severance of such gain from the capital and receipt thereof by the taxpayer for his separate use, benefit and disposal." [15] As commission-hungry customer's brokers frequently tell their clients, "You can't make money on a paper profit." Nor do they derive taxable gains from a paper profit. See Chapter 6, "Recognition of Gain and Loss."

Limitations. Loss is not recognized upon the disposition of a capital asset, the use of which was personal as opposed to business or

[10] *M. E. Trapp v. United States,* 79 F. Supp. 320 (D.C., Okla., 1947), *aff'd,* 177 F.2d 1 (10th Cir., 1949).
[11] *Western Wine & Liquor Co.,* 18 T.C. 1090 (1952).
[12] *Gulftex Drug Co., Inc.,* 29 T.C. 118 (1958).
[13] *Commissioner v. Bagley & Sewall Co.,* 221 F.2d 944 (2d Cir., 1955).
[14] *Tulane Hardware Co.,* 24 T.C. 1146 (1955).
[15] *O'Meara v. Commissioner,* 34 F.2d 390 (10th Cir., 1929).

nonbusiness (*i.e.,* the production of income). Thus, an individual's home is a capital asset, and gain from its disposition would be reported as capital gain (unless the proceeds were fully reinvested in similar property, under the circumstances described in Chapter 6). But a loss on the disposition of a personal residence would not be recognized for tax purposes.[16]

Certain governmental bonds are regarded as tax-exempt. But this exemption refers only to taxability of interest. Thus, the disposition of a tax-exempt bond at a profit would result in capital gain that is taxed in the regular manner.[17]

Small Business Investment Companies

Ordinary loss rather than capital loss treatment is obtained under certain circumstances on convertible debentures of small investment companies, as well as the stock into which the debentures are converted.[18] This subject is treated in Chapter 16.

Long-term and Short-term Capital Transactions

Capital gains and losses are divided into two classifications according to the length of time during which the asset was deemed to have been held. A short-term capital gain means gain from the sale or exchange of a capital asset held for *not more than* six months, if and to the extent that this gain is taken into account in computing gross income. A short-term capital loss means loss from the sale or exchange of a capital asset held for not more than six months, if and to the extent that this loss is taken into account in computing taxable income. Where *more than* six months was involved in the holding period, the capital gain or loss is long-term.[19]

Net short-term capital gain means the excess of short-term capital gains for the taxable year over the short-term capital losses for that year. Net long-term capital gain is a similar computation for assets held more more than six months. The net short-term or net long-term transactions can, of course, result in loss as well as gain.

In the case of a corporation, net capital gain means the excess of the gains from sales or exchanges of capital assets over the losses from such sales or exchanges.

In the case of taxpayers other than corporations, net capital gain means the excess of (1) the sum of the gains from sales or exchanges

[16] Regulations Section 1.165-3(b).
[17] *United States v. Stewart,* 311 U.S. 60 (1940).
[18] I.R.C. Section 1242.
[19] I.R.C. Section 1221.

of capital assets, plus taxable income (computed without regard to personal exemptions) of the taxpayer or $1,000, whichever is smaller, over (2) the losses from these sales or exchanges.

Thus, in the taxable year, a corporation may only use a capital loss as an offset to capital gain. But other taxpayers may set the loss against other income (computed without the personal exemption) to the extent of $1,000. If the other income is less than $1,000, the deduction, of course, is similarly restricted.

Measuring the Holding Period. The holding period must be determined with reference to calendar months and fractions rather than with reference to days.[20] Thus, a holding period was deemed to be not more than six months, when 184 days were involved.[21]

In determining the holding period for capital assets, the date the property is acquired is excluded, and the date the property is disposed of is included.[22]

The following tabulation indicates the date that the holding period starts for various types of transaction:

Type of Item	*Date Holding Period Starts*
Bequests.	Decedent's death. *McFeeley v. Commissioner*, 296 U.S. 102 (1936).
Commodity acquired in satisfaction of a commodity futures contract.	Acquisition of the contract if it was a capital asset. I.R.C. Section 1223(8).
Gift after 1920.	If gain, donor's acquisition; if loss, date of donor's acquisition or of gift, dependent upon when value was lower. I.R.C. Section 1223(2).
Involuntary conversion.	Acquisition of original asset. I.R.C. Section 1223(1)(A).
Listed securities.	Day after purchase. G.C.M. 21503, 1939–2 CB 205.
New residence replacing old.	Acquisition of old residence. I.R.C. Section 1223(7).
New York Stock Exchange seat.	Date of approval by governing committee. *Herman Krech*, B.T.A. Memo., July 26, 1933.

[20] I.T. 3985, 1941–2 CB 51.
[21] *Weir v. Commissioner*, 173 F.2d 222 (3d Cir., 1949).
[22] Revenue Ruling 54–607, 1954–2 CB 177.

Type of Item	*Date Holding Period Starts*
Parts of building.	Completion of each part. *Paul v. Commissioner*, 206 F.2d 963 (3d Cir., 1953).
Patent.	Date invention was reduced to actual practice. G.C.M. 21507, 1939–2 CB 189.
Property distributed by partnership.	Date acquired by partnership. I.R.C. Section 735(b).
Real property.	Day after title passes or delivery is made. Revenue Ruling 55–607, 1954–2 CB 177.
Securities acquired after a wash sale.	Date of acquisition of original holding. I.R.C. Section 1223(4).
Stock of controlled corporation received from distributor.	Date of acquisition by distributor. Regulations Section 1.1223–1.
Stock or securities obtained by exercising rights.	Date rights were exercised. I.R.C. Section 1223(6).
Stock or securities received in tax-free distribution.	Date of original holding acquisition. I.R.C. Section 1223(3).
Substituted basis property.	Date transferor acquired same. I.R.C. Section 1223(2).
Tax-free rights.	Date of original stock. I.R.C. Section 1223(5).
Tax-free reorganization.	Date of original holding acquisition. I.R.C. Section 1223(1).

Specially Treated Capital Transactions

Bonds and Other Evidences of Indebtedness. Any amount received by the holder upon the retirement of an obligation will be considered as an amount received in exchange for this obligation. That is, capital gain or loss results. This refers to any bond, debenture, note, or certificate or other indebtedness (1) which is a capital asset in the hands of the taxpayer and (2) which is issued by any government or political subdivision. But as to bonds or other evidences of indebtedness issued before 1955, this rule applies only to those issued with interest coupons or in registered form, or to those in such form on March 1, 1954.[23] Assigned depositor claims against an insolvent bank are not regarded as certificates of indebtedness for this purpose.[24]

[23] I.R.C. Section 1232.
[24] *Cooper v. Commissioner*, 209 F.2d 154 (4th Cir., 1954).

Sometimes bonds or other evidences of indebtedness are issued without interest coupons and not in registered form, in the manner of the United States Treasury Series E bonds. Interest as such is not payable; but in lieu of interest, the bonds at maturity are redeemed at a price in excess of issue price. In *Commissioner v. Caulkins,* 144 F.2d 482 (6th Cir., 1944), the increment was treated as capital, on the grounds that where the bonds did not provide for interest the Internal Revenue Service could not regard any part of the increment as the equivalent of interest. The law has been modified, and it is now provided that gain realized upon the sale or exchange of obligations issued at a discount after 1954, where the taxpayer had held them for more than six months, will be considered ordinary income to the extent of the "original issue discount" recovered, the balance of the gain being regarded as long-term capital gain. "Original issue discount" means the difference between the issue price and the stated redemption price at maturity, the latter price being determined without regard to optional call dates. If the original issue discount is less than one-fourth of 1% of the stated redemption price at maturity, multiplied by the number of full years from the date of original issue to maturity, then the discount will be considered to be zero. For example, a 10-year bond with a stated redemption price at maturity of $100 issued at $98 would be regarded as having an original issue discount of zero. Thus, any gain realized by the holder would be a long-term capital gain, if the bond were a capital asset in his hands and had been held for more than six months. But if the bond were issued at $97.50 or less, the original issue discount would not be considered zero.[25]

The amount of the original issue discount considered to be recovered by the holder is computed by multiplying the original issue discount by a fraction, the numerator of which is the number of full months the obligation was held by the holder and the denominator of which is the number of full months from the date of original issue to the date specified as the redemption date at maturity. (The number of months the obligation was held by the holder includes the holding period of any other person from whom the holder has a continuation of basis. See Chapter 6.)

Illustration. An individual purchases a 10-year, 3% coupon bond for $900 on original issue on February 1, 1956, and sells it on February 20, 1961, for $940. The redemption price is $1,000. The bond has been held by the taxpayer for 60 full months, fractional periods not being taken into account. The number of completed months from date of issue to date of maturity is 120 (10 years). The fraction 60/120 multiplied by the discount of $100 is equal to $50 which repre-

[25] Regulations Section 1.1232–3(b).

sents the proportionate part of the original issue discount attributable to the period of ownership by the taxpayer. Accordingly, any part of the gain up to $50 will be treated as ordinary income. Therefore, in this illustration the entire gain of $40 is treated as ordinary income. If the selling price of the bond is $970, $50 of the gain of $70 is treated as ordinary income and the balance of $20 is treated as long-term capital gain. If the selling price of the bond is $800, the individual has a long-term capital loss of $100.

This rule does not apply to obligations where the interest is not included in gross income as a governmental obligation. Nor does it apply to any holder who purchased an obligation at a premium.

Even though the United States Treasury Series E bonds are issued on a discount basis, the above rule does not apply. Under the terms of the law under which these bonds were issued, the increment always is regarded as ordinary income.

Bonds that are in default in some respect, such as the payment of interest, frequently are dealt in "flat"; that is, the price paid does not include accrued interest. Any payments received by the bondholder as interest for a period prior to his acquisition of the bond are treated as a recovery of part of his cost, rather than as ordinary income. If he recovers more than his cost but less than the principal amount of the bonds, he has capital gain.[26] But where "there is a reasonable expectancy that their principal will ultimately be collected," amounts paid as interest are treated as ordinary income.[27] Interest covering a period subsequent to the purchase date of a flat bond represents ordinary income.

Short Sales. A short sale is one where a person sells property that he does not own, with the expectation that he will be able to purchase property to fulfill his contract at a later date, by which time, he believes, prices will be lower. According to an old jingle,

> "He who sells what isn't his'n,
> Must buy it back or go to prison."

For income tax purposes, a short sale is not deemed to be consummated until delivery of property to close the short sale. Whether the recognized gain or loss from a short sale is capital gain or loss, or ordinary gain or loss, depends upon whether the property delivered to close the short sale constitutes a capital asset in the hands of the taxpayer.[28]

Illustration. If a dealer in securities makes a short sale of stock in a certain corporation, ordinary gain or loss results on closing of the short sale if the stock

[26] *Hamilton C. Rickaby Estate,* 27 T.C. 886 (1957).
[27] Revenue Ruling 55–433, 1955–2 CB 515.
[28] I.R.C. Section 1233.

used to close this short sale was shares which he held primarily for sale to customers in the ordinary course of his trade or business. If the stock used to close the short sale was a capital asset in his hands (for example, something that he had purchased as an investment rather than for resale in the ordinary course of his business), or if he were not a dealer, a capital gain or loss would result.

Hedging operations do not produce capital gain if they are carried on in the regular conduct of the business.[29] This includes transactions in commodity futures entered into by flour millers, producers of cloth, operators of grain elevators, etc. Gain or loss from a sale of commodity futures which does not qualify as a hedging operation will be considered to be capital gain or loss, if the commodity future used to close the short sale constitutes a capital asset in the taxpayer's hands.[30]

Special rules are provided where capital gain or loss results from a short sale and, at the time of this sale or before the date of closing the short sale, the taxpayer holds property substantially identical to that sold short. For this purpose, "property" includes only stocks and bonds (including those dealt with on a "when issued" basis) and commodity futures which are capital assets in the taxpayer's hands.

Rule (*1*). Any gain upon the closing of a short sale of the type described above will be considered as a short-term capital gain, regardless of the actual holding time of the property used to close the short sale.

Rule (*2*). The holding period of the substantially identical property will be considered to begin on the earlier of (a) the date of the closing of the short sale or (b) the date of a sale, gift, or other disposition of the property.

Rule (*3*). Any loss upon the closing of the short sale will be considered as a long-term capital loss, despite the actual holding period of property used to close the short sale.

For the purpose of Rule (3), the acquisition of an option to sell property at a fixed price is not considered a short sale, and the exercise or failure to exercise such option is not considered as the closing of a short sale. But, for the purposes of Rules (1) and (2), the acquisition of an option to sell property at a fixed price will be considered a short sale, and the exercise or failure to exercise the option will be considered as a closing of the short sale, with this election as to options acquired on or after August 17, 1954: short sale treatment will not be involved provided that either the option and property identified as intended to be used in its exercise are acquired

[29] *Corn Products Refining Co. v. Commissioner*, 350 U.S. 46 (1955).
[30] Regulations Section 1.1233–1(4)(b).

on the same date. This exception does not apply, if the option is exercised, unless it is exercised by the sale of the property so identified. In the case of any option not exercised which falls within this exception, the cost of the option will be added to the basis of the property with which the option is identified.[31]

Illustration. An individual buys 100 shares of a certain stock at $10 per share on February 1, sells short 100 shares of the same company's stock at $16 per share on July 1 next, and closes the short sale on August 2 next by delivering the 100 shares of stock purchased on February 1 to the lender of the stock used to effect the short sale. Inasmuch as 100 shares of the stock had been held by the individual on the date of the short sale for not more than six months, the gain of $600 realized upon the closing of the short sale is, under Rule (1), a short-term capital gain.

Illustration. An individual buys 100 shares of a certain stock at $10 per share on February 1, sells short 100 shares of the same company's stock at $16 per share on July 1 next, closes the short sale on August 1 next with 100 shares of stock purchased on that date at $18 per share, and on August 2 sells at $18 per share the 100 shares purchased on February 1. The $200 loss sustained upon the closing of the short sale is a short-term capital loss not covered by the general rule. But by the application of Rule (2), the holding period of the 100 shares purchased on February 1 and sold on August 2 is considered to begin on August 1, the date of the closing of the short sale. The $800 gain realized upon the sale of this stock is, therefore, a short-term capital gain.

Illustration. An individual buys 100 shares of a certain stock at $10 per share on February 1, sells short 100 shares of the same company's stock at $16 per share on September 1 next, sells on October 1 next at $18 per share the 100 shares of stock purchased on February 1, and closes the short sale on October 1 with 100 shares of stock purchased on that date at $18 per share. The $800 gain realized upon the sale of the 100 shares purchased on February 1 is a long-term capital gain not covered by the general rule. Inasmuch as he had held 100 shares on the date of the short sale for more than six months, the $200 loss sustained upon the closing of the short sale is, by the application of Rule (3), a long-term capital loss. If, instead of purchasing the stock on October 1, the individual closed the short sale with the stock purchased on February 1, the $600 gain realized on the closing of the short sale would be a long-term capital gain not covered by the special rule.

Illustration. An individual sells short 100 shares of stock of a certain company at $16 per share on February 1. He buys 250 shares of stock of the same corporation on March 1 next at $10 per share and holds the latter stock until September 2 (more than six months), at which time, 100 shares of the 250 are delivered to close the short sale made on February 1. Inasmuch as substantially identical property was acquired by the individual after the short sale and before it was closed, the $600 gain realized on the closing of the short sale is, by the application of Rule (1), a short-term capital gain. The holding period of the remaining 150 shares of stock is not affected by the general rule inasmuch as this amount of the substantially identical property exceeds the quantity of the property sold short.

[31] Regulations Section 1.1233–1(c)(3).

Where listed bonds were convertible into common stock of the issuing corporation and the bond prices fluctuated in direct relation to the market price of the stock, sellers of stock could purchase bonds to obtain stock for delivery. "These transactions are known as arbitrage operations." Sales of the stock under these circumstances constituted short sales.[32]

"Substantially identical property" has no general definition. Ordinarily, stocks or bonds of one corporation are not considered substantially identical to stocks or bonds of another corporation. In the case of a corporate reorganization (see Chapter 17), the stocks and bonds of a predecessor and successor corporation may be regarded as substantially identical. In general, bonds or preferred stock of a corporation are not considered substantially identical to the common stock of the same corporation; but under appropriate circumstances, as where one stock is convertible into another, the character of substantially identical may be present.

As to commodity futures, one requiring delivery in a specified month will not be considered as substantially identical to a future calling for delivery in another month. Futures in different commodities which are not generally through custom of the trade used as hedges for each other (such as corn and wheat, for example) are not considered substantially identical property.

Where a taxpayer enters into two commodity futures transactions on the same day, one requiring delivery by him in one market, and the other requiring delivery to him of the same (or substantially identical) commodity in the same calendar month in a different market, and the taxpayer subsequently closes both of these transactions on the same day, the general rule will have no application to so much of the commodity involved in either transaction as does not exceed in quantity the commodity involved in the other.[33]

In the case of a short sale of property by an individual, the short sales provisions are deemed to mean by the term "taxpayer" the broader term "taxpayer or his spouse."[34] Thus, if the spouse of a taxpayer holds or acquires property substantially identical to that sold short by the taxpayer, the tax treatment will be the same as if the taxpayer individually held or acquired the substantially identical property.

Options To Buy or To Sell. In determining whether or not a capital transaction is involved, the character of the property to

[32] Revenue Ruling 151, 1953–2 CB 173.
[33] I.R.C. Section 1233(e)(3).
[34] I.R.C. Section 1233(e)(2)(C).

which the option relates is controlling.[35] Thus, if the property covered by an option would be capital in the taxpayer's hands, gain or loss attributable to the sale, exchange of, or loss on the failure to exercise the privilege will be given capital treatment. The period for which the taxpayer has held the option determines whether the capital gain is long-term or short-term.[36]

If the holder of an option to buy or to sell property incurs a loss on failure to exercise the option, the option is deemed to have been sold or exchanged upon the date that it expired. Thus, if the taxpayer never acquires the property subject to the option, the nature of his gain or loss is determined by whether the property would have been a capital asset if he had acquired it.

Illustration. A dealer in industrial property acquires an option to buy an industrial tract but fails to exercise his privilege. The loss would be an ordinary one, inasmuch as he normally holds such property for sale to customers in the ordinary course of his trade or business. But, if he is considering the purchase of a new home for himself and he acquires an option to buy a house, which option he sells at a gain, he would have capital gain.

This section does not apply to a loss on the failure to exercise an option to sell property at a fixed price, which is acquired on the same day on which the property identified as intended to be used in exercising the option is acquired. The loss is not recognized, but the cost of the option is added to the basis of the property with which it is identified.[37]

Gain or loss realized by a dealer in options from the sale or exchange of an option is considered ordinary income.

Gain resulting from the sale or exchange of an option is not governed by Section 1234 in these circumstances:

(1) Where the gain is in the nature of compensation; *e.g.*, employee stock options. See Chapter 11.

(2) Where the option is treated as Section 306 stock; *e.g.*, a preferred stock dividend to holders of common stock. See Chapter 17.

(3) Where the gain is in effect a distribution of corporate earnings and profits taxable as a dividend. See Chapter 8.

Puts and Calls. Detailed rules as to puts and calls may be found in Revenue Ruling 58–234, I.R.B. 1958–20, 20. The holder of a put may require the seller thereof to buy a certain quantity of stock at a named price within a stipulated period; the holder of a call may

[35] I.R.C. Section 1234.
[36] Regulations Section 1.1234–1(a).
[37] Regulations Section 1.1234–1(c).

require the seller thereof to deliver to him the covenanted items at named prices within the time limit.

Patents. A transfer (other than by gift, inheritance, or devise) of property consisting of all substantial rights evidenced by a patent, or of an undivided interest in all rights to a patent, by a holder to a person other than a related person is treated as a long-term capital transaction. It is immaterial whether the payments for the patent are (1) payable periodically over a period ending with the transferee's use of the patent or (2) contingent on the productivity, use, or disposition of the property transferred.[38]

To be treated as a transfer of a patent within the scope of this section, there must be a conveyance of exclusive rights to make, use, or vend the patented item. A conveyance of anything less would not be such an assignment but merely a license.[39] Thus there must be monopoly rights. The statute uses the term "all substantial rights," which means all rights that are of value at the time the rights to the patent (or an undivided interest therein) are transferred. A transfer limited in duration by the terms of the instrument to a period less than the remaining life of the patent is not a transfer of all substantial rights to a patent.[40]

Rights which are not considered substantial may be retained by the holder. Examples are: retention by the transferor of legal title for the purpose of securing performance or payment by the transferee in a transaction involving transfer of an exclusive license for the life of the patent, or the retention by the transferor of rights in the property which are not inconsistent with the passage of ownership, such as the retention of a vendor's lien or a provision for forfeiture on account of nonperformance.

The term "patent" means a patent granted under the provisions of Title 35 of the United States Code, or any foreign patent granting rights generally similar to those under a United States patent. It is not necessary that the patent or patent application be in existence if the requirements of this section are otherwise met.

The term "holder" means an individual whose efforts created the patent property, or who acquired his interest in the patent property in exchange for consideration in money or the equivalent actually paid to the creator prior to the time when the invention actually is reduced to practice. Individuals not eligible to qualify as the "first and original" inventor are not covered; for example,

[38] I.R.C. Section 1235.
[39] *Vincent A. Marco,* 25 T.C. 544 (1955).
[40] Regulations Section 1.1235-2(b).

the inventor's employer may not here qualify, even though he may be the equitable owner of the patent by reason of an employment relationship with the inventor. Nor is coverage afforded to any individual who is related to the creator as ancestor, spouse, lineal descendant, or other relationships outlined in I.R.C. Section 267 (except that brothers and sisters may qualify here). Although a partnership cannot be a holder, each member of a partnership who is an individual may qualify as a holder as to his share of a patent owned by the partnership.

The section applies to all qualifying individuals, whether amateur or professional, regardless of how often they may have sold their patents. The section is not applicable to any other purchasers or assignees.

The term "actual reduction to practice" means that the invention has been tested and operated under operating conditions.

If the other conditions are met, long-term capital gain treatment is afforded to the holder of the patent for all amounts received or accrued for any taxable year beginning after 1953 and ending after August 16, 1954, even if the transfer occurred in a taxable year prior to the effective date of the present law.

Dealers in Securities. *Gain* realized by a dealer in securities from the sale or exchange of a security (as defined below) will not be treated as capital unless (1) within 30 days of the time of its acquisition the security is identified in his records as one held for investment. If the security had been acquired before October 20, 1951, the identification must have been made before November 20, 1951. (2) The security is not held by the dealer primarily for sale to customers in the ordinary course of his trade or business at any time after the identification has been made. Unless *both* of these requirements are met, ordinary income will result.[41]

Loss sustained by a dealer from the sale or exchange of a security will not be treated as ordinary if at any time after November 19, 1951, the security has been clearly identified in the dealer's records as a security held for investment. Once a security has been identified after November 19, 1951, as being held by a dealer for investment, it retains that character for purposes of determining loss on its ultimate disposition, even though at the time of its disposition the dealer holds it primarily for sale to his customers in the ordinary course of his business. But this does not refer to a bank's losses on securities, which is governed by I.R.C. Section 582(c). See Chapter 16.

[41] I.R.C. Section 1236.

For purposes of this section, the term "security" means any share of stock in any corporation, any certificate of stock or interest in any corporation, any bond, note, debenture, or other evidence of indebtedness, or any evidence of any interest in, or right to subscribe to or to purchase any of the foregoing.[42] "Dealer in securities" is defined as "a merchant of securities, whether an individual, partnership, or corporation, with an established place of business, regularly engaged in the purchase of securities and their resale to customers . . ."[43]

Real Estate Subdivided for Sale. According to the standard rule, if an individual is not a dealer in real estate, he will have capital gain to report on the sale at a profit of realty that he held for investment. But, if he subdivides the property and makes sales piecemeal, there will be ordinary income to report. Section 1237, however, permits an individual who is not otherwise a real estate dealer to dispose of a tract of real estate held for investment purposes by subdividing it, without necessarily being treated as a real estate dealer with respect to all of his long-term gain.

If the necessary conditions are met and there is no other substantial evidence that a taxpayer holds real estate primarily for sale to customers in the ordinary course of his business, he will not be considered a real estate dealer holding it primarily for sale merely because he has (1) subdivided the tract into lots (or parcels) and (2) engaged in advertising, promotion, selling activities, or the use of sales agents in connection with the sale of lots in this subdivision. If the only evidence of the taxpayer's purpose in holding real estate consisted of not more than one of the following in the year in question, that fact would not be considered substantial other evidence; *e.g.*, holding a real estate dealer's license, selling other real property which was clearly investment property, acting as a salesman for a real estate dealer (but without any financial interest in the business), or mere ownership of other vacant real property without engaging in any selling activity whatsoever with respect to it.[44]

Before Section 1237 applies, the taxpayer must meet three basic conditions:

(1) He cannot have held any part of the tract at any time previously for sale in the ordinary course of the business, nor in the year of sale held any other real estate for sale to customers.

[42] Regulations Section 1.1238-1(c).
[43] Regulations Section 1.471-5.
[44] Regulations Section 1.1237-1(a).

(2) He cannot make substantial improvements on the tract which increases the value of the lot sold substantially. The improvement will be deemed to have been made by the taxpayer if, during the time he held this property, the improvements were made by his brothers and sisters, spouse, ancestors, and lineal descendants; or by a corporation in which, directly or indirectly, he held more than 50% of the stock; or by a partnership of which he was a member at the time the improvements were made; or by a lessee, if the improvement takes the place of rent; or by a Federal or local government, if the improvement results in an increase in the taxpayer's basis for the property. If he erects a shopping center on a part of a remote tract of unimproved real property and then subdivides and sells the remaining lots, the improvement on the shopping center part of the tract has been clearly substantial, and the section will not apply. Putting in all public utilities in the tract would be a substantial improvement. But a substantial improvement of a portion of the tract may be made which does not substantially increase the value of the remainder of the lots in the tract, although it may enhance their salability, such as the erection by the taxpayer of his personal residence on one of the lots. Also, improvements which are not substantial in and of themselves, although resulting in a substantial increase in the value of the lots of the tract, as where the taxpayer builds an inexpensive dirt access road across the tract. The taxpayer may make certain improvements where they are necessary to make the property marketable if he elects neither to add their cost to the basis of the property (or of any other property), nor to deduct the cost as an expense, and he has held the property for at least ten years.

(3) He must have owned the property at least five years, unless he inherited it.

If the taxpayer has not made more than five sales of lots from a single tract of real property, through the end of the taxable year, the entire proceeds will be treated as capital. All sales made during or after the year in which the sixth lot from a single tract is sold come under a special 5% rule. Gain on these sales will be reported as ordinary income up to, but not exceeding, an amount equal to 5% of the selling price. The remainder will be used in determining the amount realized on the sale of a capital asset. The rule for allocating the expenditures of sale is that expenditures may be taken as deductions from gross income in determining taxable income only to the extent that the gain was reported as ordinary income. The remainder of the selling expenditures will be used in determining the amount realized on the sale of a capital asset.

Illustration. An individual meets all the conditions of Section 1237 in subdividing and selling a single tract. In 1961 he sells four lots to four purchasers. In the same year, he sells three adjacent lots to one buyer. Since the seller has sold only five lots or parcels from the tract, any gain realized on the sale will be capital gain.

Illustration. If the taxpayer has sold the sixth lot or parcel from the same tract within the taxable year, then the amount, if any, by which 5% of the selling price of each lot exceeds the expenses incurred in connection with its sale or exchange will, to the extent that it represents gain, be ordinary income. Any part of the gain not treated as ordinary income will be treated as capital gain. Assume the selling price of the sixth lot of a tract is $10,000, the basis of the lot in the hands of the seller is $5,000, and the expenses of sale are $300. The amount of gain realized by the taxpayer is $4,700, of which the amount of ordinary income attributable to the sale is $200, computed as follows:

Selling price		$10,000
Basis		5,000
Excess over basis		$ 5,000
5% of selling price	$500	
Expenses of sale	300	
Amount of gain realized treated as ordinary income		200
Excess over basis		5,000
5% of selling price	$500	
Excess of expenses over 5% of selling price	0	500
Amount of gain realized from sale of property not held for sale in ordinary course of business		$ 4,500

In the case of an exchange, the term "selling price" means the fair market value of property received plus any money received in exchange for the lot.

The term "tract" for this purpose means either (1) a single piece of real property or (2) two or more pieces of real property if they were contiguous at any time while held by the taxpayer, or would have been contiguous but for the interposition of a road, street, railroad, stream, or similar property. Properties are contiguous if their boundaries meet at one or more points.

If the taxpayer sells or exchanges no lots from the tract for a period of five years after the sale or exchange of at least one lot in the tract, then the remainder of the tract will be deemed a new tract for the purpose of counting the number of lots sold from the same tract. The pieces in the new tract need not be contiguous. The 5-year period is measured between the dates of the sales or exchanges.

The rule is not applicable to dealers in real estate or to corporations, although under certain circumstances a corporation making such sales in a taxable year beginning after 1954 may qualify. Such a corporation may qualify if (1) the property in question was acquired through the foreclosure of a lien, or (2) the lien foreclosed secured the payment of an indebtedness to a creditor who has transferred the foreclosure bid to the corporation in exchange for all of the stock and other consideration, or (3) no shareholder holds real property for sale to customers in the ordinary course of the trade or business or holds a controlling interest in another corporation which actually so holds real estate.[45] Sale of subdivided land may not be claimed as a capital loss.[46]

Election to make use of Section 1237 is made on a statement that is filed with the income tax return for the year of sale. See details in Chapter 23 under the heading "Burden of Proof."

Sale of Emergency Facility. To some extent, capital gain treatment is available in the case of disposition of an asset subject to special amortization under Section 168.[47] This subject is treated in Chapter 10.

Taxability to Employee of Termination Payments. Under certain circumstances, payments of lump-sum amounts to retiring employees under a qualified benefit plan are treated as long-term capital gains.[48] See Chapter 11.

Cancellation of Lease or Distributor's Agreement. Payments received by a lessee for the cancellation of a lease or by a distributor for cancellation of a distributor's agreement are treated as received in exchange therefor.[49] Therefore, if the lease or the distributor agreement is a capital asset in the hands of the lessee or distributor, capital treatment will be afforded.

Sale of a lease by the lessee has been treated as capital gain.[50] Such also was a finding where a lessee released to the lessor a restrictive covenant in the lease.[51]

For this purpose, "cancellation" means a termination of all the contractual rights of a lessee or distributor with respect to particular premises or a particular distributorship, other than by the expiration of the lease or agreement in accordance with its terms. A payment made in good faith for a partial cancellation will be treated as having been received in cancellation if it relates to a severable economic unit, such as a portion of the premises covered by a lease, or a distributorship in one of several areas or of one of

[45] Regulations Section 1.1237–1(c)(2)(iv).
[46] Regulations Section 1.1237–1(a)(4).
[47] I.R.C. Section 1238.
[48] I.R.C. Section 1240.
[49] I.R.C. Section 1241.
[50] *Commissioner v. Golonsky et al.,* 200 F.2d 72 (3d Cir., 1952).
[51] *Commisssioner v. Ray,* 210 F.2d 390 (5th Cir., 1954).

several products. Payments made for other modifications of leases or distributorship agreements, however, are not recognized as amounts received for cancellation under Section 1241.[52]

But what a lessor received from a lessee for the unexpired term of a lease was not capital. It was ordinary income, being "clearly a substitute for rental payments." [53]

Other Capital Transactions

Good will is a capital asset.[54] So are trade names.[55] A franchise may be regarded as a capital asset.[56] But if the franchise is of short duration, it may be deemed to be depreciable property used in the trade or business. See discussion of Section 1231 in this chapter.

"While contracts are property, the decisions are to the effect that not all property rights constitute capital assets. Whether or not they are depends, at least in part, upon the nature of the income that would normally result from the fulfillment of the terms of the contract. . . . [Here] the disputed amount was essentially a substitute for sales commissions . . . [which] must be regarded as ordinary income." [57]

Customarily, payment for a covenant not to compete is regarded as ordinary income. "Where a covenant not to compete constitutes a nonseverable element of a transaction in which the owner of a going concern sells the property and transfers the good will of the business, the covenant is to be treated as a contributory element of the assets transferred and the entire revenue received is subject to tax on the basis of a capital gain. . . . But if a covenant not to compete can be segregated in order to be assured that a separate item has actually been dealt with, then so much as is received for the covenant is ordinary income rather than income from the sale of a capital asset." [58]

An unprofitable investment in a cooperative apartment venture is a capital loss. The investment was not in a lease but in stock.[59]

A nonbusiness bad debt is treated as a capital loss.[60] See Chapter 13.

[52] Regulations Section 1.1241–1(b).

[53] *Hort v. Commissioner,* 313 U.S. 28 (1941).

[54] *Ensley Bank & Trust Co. v. United States,* 154 F.2d 968 (5th Cir., 1946).

[55] *Commissioner v. Rainier Brewing Co.,* 165 F.2d 217 (9th Cir., 1948).

[56] *Constantine H. Kalvaris,* T.C. Memo., Docket #4209, entered January 16, 1946.

[57] *Joseph Roscoe,* T.C. Memo., Docket ##36905–8, entered May 25, 1953, *aff'd,* 215 F.2d 478 (5th Cir., 1954).

[58] *Hamlin Trust et al. v. Commissioner,* 209 F.2d 761 (10th Cir., 1954).

[59] *Junius B. Peake et al.,* T.C. Memo., Docket #27637, entered June 15, 1951.

[60] I.R.C. Section 166(d)(1)(B).

Gain or loss on the sale of stock received under a restricted stock option may receive capital treatment, in whole or in part.[61] See Chapter 11.

Certain distributions from regulated investment companies are given capital gains treatment.[62] See Chapter 16.

With certain exceptions, amounts received by shareholders upon the liquidation of a corporation are treated as capital gains or losses.[63] This subject and the various exceptions are discussed in Chapter 17.

Where stockholders of a dissolved corporation were obliged as transferees to pay a subsequently imposed corporate tax deficiency, such payments represented capital loss to these stockholders.[64]

Property Used in the Trade or Business

Some assets are, under appropriate circumstances, given capital gains treatment, even though they are not capital assets.[65] These are (1) depreciable business property and business real estate held for more than six months (other than stock in trade and certain copyrights and artistic property); (2) timber and coal, to the extent that I.R.C. Section 631 is applicable; and (3) certain livestock and unharvested crops.

Section 1231 does not apply to capital assets, except where they have been involuntarily converted.

The advantage of Section 1231 to the taxpayer is considerable. If assets of this type are held for more than six months and are sold at a gain, long-term capital gains treatment will be afforded, with the resultant limitation of tax. But where Section 1231 assets are sold at a loss, the loss is fully deductible. The result, however, is obtained each year on a *net* basis. The taxpayer must aggregate his recognized gains and losses from (1) the sale, exchange, or involuntary conversion of Section 1231 assets and (2) the involuntary conversion (but not a sale or exchange) of long-term capital assets. Thus, in a single year, it is not possible to take the advantage of long-term capital gain on one Section 1231 asset and the advantage of a fully deductible ordinary loss on another such asset. The section does not apply to (1) inventory or items held primarily for sale to customers in the ordinary course of business; (2) a copyright,

[61] I.R.C. Section 421.
[62] I.R.C. Section 854(a).
[63] I.R.C. Sections 301 *et seq.*
[64] *Arrowsmith v. Commissioner,* 344 U.S. 6 (1952).
[65] I.R.C. Section 1231.

a literary, musical, or artistic composition, or similar property in the hands of the creator, or one who has his basis (*e.g.*, one who received the asset as a gift); (3) livestock held for draft, breeding, or dairy purposes, except to the extent mentioned below under "Cattle," or (4) unharvested crops if the taxpayer retains any right or option to reacquire the land on which the crop is, directly or indirectly, other than a right customarily incident to a mortgage or other security transaction.

Section 1231 is inapplicable in the case of losses where the taxpayer is not compensated for the loss by insurance, if the loss arises from fire, storm, shipwreck, or other casualty, or from theft. This treatment is to apply, however, only in the case of property used in the trade or business and in the case of capital assets held for more than six months and held for the production of income.

All gains and losses to which Section 1231 applies must be taken into account in determining to what extent the gains exceed the losses. But the capital loss limitations of Section 1211 do not apply. With that exception, gains are included only to the extent that they are taken into account in computing gross income, and losses are included only to the extent that they are taken into account in computing taxable income. Here are examples of gains and losses not included in the computation under Section 1231: (1) losses of a personal nature, such as from the sale of personal jewelry; (2) losses which are not permitted under some specific section of the Code, such as transactions between related taxpayers (see Chapter 27); (3) gains and losses that are not taxable because they are deemed to be tax-free exchanges (see Chapter 17).

Illustration. An individual makes his income tax return on the calendar year basis. His recognized gains and losses for 1961 of the kind described in Section 1231 are as follows:

	Gains	Losses
Gain on sale of machinery, used in the business and subject to an allowance for depreciation, held for more than six months. .	$ 4,000	
Gain reported in 1961 on installment sale in 1960 of factory premises used in the business (including building and land, each held for more than six months)	6,000	
Gain reported in 1961 on installment sale in 1961 of land held for more than six months, used in the business as a storage lot for trucks	2,000	
Gain on proceeds from requisition by Government of boat, held for more than six months, used in the business and subject to a depreciation allowance	500	
Loss upon the destruction by fire of warehouse, held for more than six months and used in the business (excess of adjusted basis of warehouse over compensation by insurance, etc.)		$3,000

	Gains	Losses
Loss upon theft of unregistered bearer bonds, held for more than six months		$5,000
Loss in storm of pleasure yacht, purchased in 1954 for $1,800 and having a fair market value of $1,000 at the time of the storm		1,000
Total gains	$12,500	
Total losses		$9,000
Excess of gains over losses	$ 3,500	

Inasmuch as the aggregate of the recognized gains ($12,500) exceeds the aggregate of the recognized losses ($9,000), the gains and losses are treated under Section 1231 as gains and losses from the sale or exchange of capital assets held for more than six months.

Insofar as a corporation is concerned, all assets may be assumed to be used in the trade or business, a prerequisite for the use of Section 1231. In the case of other taxpayers, such usage is the subject of proof by the taxpayer, as is the case with almost any other position maintained by the taxpayer. A taxpayer can be engaged in more than one business.[66]

"'Used in the trade or business' means 'devoted to the trade or business,' and includes all such property, whether actually in use during the taxable year or not."[67] This "includes property purchased with a view to its future use in the business even though this purpose is later thwarted by circumstances beyond the taxpayer's control."[68] "[P]roperty once used in the business remains in such use until it is shown to have been withdrawn from business purposes."[69] If property would have been used in the trade or business had business conditions justified such employment, it is "used in the trade or business."[70] Land left after a rented house was destroyed by hurricane does not lose its character as property used in business (renting) where it was promptly sold to minimize the loss.[71]

Timber. Certain taxpayers have an election to treat the difference between (1) the actual cost or other basis of certain timber cut during the taxable year and (2) its fair market value as standing timber on the first day of that year as gain or loss from a sale or exchange of a Section 1231 asset.[72] The election must be made by the taxpayer in his income tax return for the taxable year in which the election is applicable; the election cannot be made on an amended return.

[66] *Oliver v. Commissioner,* 138 F.2d 910 (4th Cir., 1943).
[67] *Carter-Colton Cigar Co.,* 9 T.C. 219 (1947).
[68] *Alamo Broadcasting Co., Inc.,* 15 T.C. 534 (1950).
[69] *Kittredge v. Commissioner,* 88 F.2d 632 (2d Cir., 1937).
[70] *Yellow Cab Co. of Pittsburgh v. Driscoll,* 24 F. Supp. 993 (D.C., Pa., 1938).
[71] *Solomon Wright, Jr.,* 9 T.C. 173 (1947).
[72] I.R.C. Section 631.

If the cutting of timber is considered as a sale or exchange, gain or loss is recognized to the taxpayer in an amount equal to the difference between the adjusted basis for depletion in the hands of the taxpayer of the timber which has been cut during the taxable year and the fair market value of that timber as of the first day of the taxable year in which the timber is cut. The fair market value as of the beginning of the taxable year will be considered to be the cost of that timber, in lieu of the actual cost or other basis.[73]

For any taxable year for which the cutting of timber is considered to be a sale or exchange, the timber so cut will be considered as property used in the trade or business for the purpose of Section 1231, regardless of whether it would be of the type that otherwise would be included in inventory.

In case the products of the timber are sold after cutting, either in the form of logs or lumber or in the form of manufactured products, the income from these actual sales will be considered as ordinary income. When the election is in effect, the cost of standing timber cut during the taxable year is determined as if the taxpayer had purchased the timber on the first day of the taxable year. Thus, in determining the cost of the products so sold, the cost of the timber will be the fair market value on the first day of the taxable year in which the standing timber was cut, in lieu of the actual cost or other basis of the timber. This is also the rule in case the products of the timber cut during one taxable year for which an election has been made are sold during a subsequent taxable year, whether or not the election is applicable to the later years.

If an owner disposes of timber held for more than six months, under any type of contract whereby he retains an economic interest in the timber, the disposal will be treated as a sale of the timber. The difference between the amounts realized from disposal of timber in any year and the adjusted basis for depletion will be considered to be a gain or loss on the sale of timber in that year. The date of disposal of timber will be deemed to be the date when it is cut. But if the payment is made to the owner under the contract for timber before it is cut, the owner may elect to treat the date of payment as the date of disposal of the timber.

Amounts received or accrued prior to cutting (such as advance royalty payments or minimum royalty payments) are treated as realized from the sale of timber if the contract of disposal provides that these amounts are to be applied as payment for timber subsequently cut. It is immaterial whether an election has been made to treat the date of payment as the date of disposal. But if the right

[73] Regulations Section 1.631-1(d)(4).

to cut timber under the contract expires, terminates, or is abandoned before the timber which has been paid for is cut, the taxpayer must treat payments attributable to the uncut timber as ordinary income.

The provisions of this section apply only to an owner of timber. This means any person who owns an interest in timber, including a sublessor and a holder of a contract to cut timber. The owner of timber must have a right to cut timber for sale on his own account or for use in his trade or business in order to own an interest in timber for this purpose.[74]

Coal. Rather similar to the tax treatment of timber royalties are coal royalties. An election is available to an owner who disposes of coal (including lignite) held for more than six months under any type of contract whereby he retains an economic interest in the coal. The difference between (1) the amount realized from the disposal of coal in any taxable year and (2) the adjusted depletion basis plus the deductions disallowed under I.R.C. Section 272 will be the gain or loss upon the sale of the coal.[75] Section 272 provides that where the disposal of coal is covered by Section 531, no deduction will be allowed for expenditures attributable to the making and administration of the disposal contract, except that if in any taxable year these expenditures plus the adjusted depletion basis of the coal disposed of exceed the amount realized under the contract, the unavailed of excess will be deductible.

In the case of a disposal of the coal, it will be treated as a Section 1231 asset. The date of disposal will be the date the coal is mined. If the coal has been held for more than six months on the date it is mined, it is immaterial that it has been held for not more than six months on the date of the contract. Percentage depletion (see Chapter 10) will not be allowed where the coal is treated as a Section 1231 asset.[76]

A lessee who is also a sublessor may dispose of coal as an "owner." An "owner" means any person who owns an economic interest in coal in place, including a sublessor. A person who merely acquires an economic interest and has not disposed of coal under a contract retaining an economic interest does not qualify.

Payments received in advance of mining are handled in a manner similar to timber, above.

Certain Livestock and Unharvested Crops. Section 1231 applies to the sale, exchange, or involuntary conversion of livestock, regard-

[74] Regulations Section 1.631-2(c)(3).
[75] I.R.C. Section 631(c).
[76] Regulations Section 1.631-3(b)(1).

less of age, held by the taxpayer for draft, breeding, or dairy purposes, if held by him for twelve months or more from the date of acquisition. For this purpose, "livestock" includes cattle, hogs, horses, mules, donkeys, sheep, goats, fur-bearing animals, and other mammals. It does not include poultry, chickens, turkeys, pigeons, geese, other birds, fish, frogs, reptiles, etc.[77] Whether or not the livestock is held by the taxpayer for draft, breeding, or dairy purposes depends upon all of the facts and circumstances in each case.

Section 1231 does not apply to a sale, exchange, or involuntary conversion of an unharvested crop if the taxpayer retains any right to reacquire the land on which the crop is, directly or indirectly (other than a right customarily incident to a mortage or other security transaction). The length of time for which the crop (as distinguished from the land) is held is immaterial. A leasehold or estate for years is not "land" for the purpose of Section 1231.[78]

Conversion of Ordinary Income into Capital Gain

Certain methods of converting what would be ordinary income into what is treated as capital gain are specifically authorized by the Code, such as the election for timber under I.R.C. Section 631. Other techniques are clouded with uncertainty. Still others are not permitted.

Where a taxpayer sells stock before it goes on an ex-dividend basis, what would be taxed as ordinary income (the dividend) is converted to a capital basis. A life beneficiary would have received ordinary income from an estate; but by selling his life estate to the remainderman, he received capital treatment.[79] Proceeds of a life insurance or endowment policy upon surrender or maturity produce ordinary income to the extent of the excess of proceeds over cost; but capital gain results where the policy is sold before maturity or surrender.[80]

Where personal assets are allegedly converted to business use, so that the assets would qualify for Section 1231 treatment, the question is whether the conversion actually has taken place.[81] But the difficulty of establishing that a personal residence, once utilized, is now converted to business use is not present where property that

[77] Regulations Section 1.1231–1(a).

[78] Regulations Section 1.1231–1(f).

[79] *Bell v. Commissioner,* 137 F.2d 454 (8th Cir., 1943).

[80] *Jules J. Reingold,* B.T.A. Memo., Docket #100878, entered June 20, 1941.

[81] *Leland Hazard,* 7 T.C. 372 (1946); *Rumsey v. Commissioner,* 82 F.2d 158 (2d Cir., 1936); *George W. Carnick,* 9 T.C. 756 (1947).

has been inherited is immediately placed upon the market.[82] Intent to discontinue business does not change the nature of the assets.[83] It is essential to keep good records to establish the use to which assets have been put. Capital gain did not result where there was no proof that certain cars of an automobile distributor were used as demonstrators.[84] But the assets were deemed capital under similar facts, where the records were more carefully kept.[85] In the last-named case, ten categories of use of the cars (other than as inventory) were shown.

An anticipatory assignment of what would be ordinary income does not beget capital gain treatment.[86]

Disallowance of Capital Gains or Losses

Capital gains or losses may be disallowed in the following situations:

(1) Any gain from the sale or exchange of depreciable property between a husband and a wife, or between an individual and a corporation controlled by him to the extent of at least 80%, will be treated as ordinary income.[87]

(2) Any loss on transactions between certain related persons will be disallowed.[88] See Chapter 27.

(3) Transactions between parties under common control may be reallocated by the Secretary of the Treasury.[89] See Chapter 27.

(4) Where a corporation has the status of "collapsible," certain gains by the taxpayer that otherwise would be capital may be treated as ordinary income.[90] See Chapter 17.

(5) Although a sale of a partnership is generally treated as capital, ordinary income may be spelled out of transactions in unrealized receivables and inventories.[91] See Chapter 19.

(6) Corporate distributions, although allegedly not of earnings, may be treated as ordinary income rather than capital under a number of the reorganization sections of the Internal Revenue Code. See Chapter 17.

[82] *Anna C. Newberry et al.*, T.C. Memo., Docket ##3901 and 3926, entered February 27, 1945.
[83] *Grace Bros., Inc. v. Commissioner,* 173 F.2d 170 (9th Cir., 1949).
[84] *W. R. Stephens Co. v. Commissioner,* 199 F.2d 665 (8th Cir., 1952).
[85] *Latimer-Looney Chevrolet, Inc.,* 19 T.C. 120 (1952).
[86] *Commissioner v. Hawn,* 231 F.2d 340 (5th Cir., 1956).
[87] I.R.C. Section 1239.
[88] I.R.C. Section 267.
[89] I.R.C. Section 482.
[90] I.R.C. Section 341.
[91] I.R.C. Section 751.

(7) Where an acquisition was made to evade or to avoid income tax, the Secretary may disallow any deduction, credit, or allowance, if the principal purpose was evasion or avoidance.[92] See Chapter 17.

(8) The utilization of a corporation's unused capital loss carryover by a successor is greatly limited.[93] See Chapter 14.

Supplementary Material

A. Suggested Reading.

Raymond A. Hoffman, "Accounting Treatment Counts in Determining Net Taxable Income," *TAXES—The Tax Magazine,* December, 1957, Vol. XXXV, #12, p. 918.

Dan Throop Smith and J. Keith Butters, *Taxable and Business Income* (New York: National Bureau of Economic Research, 1949).

C. F. Riemer, *Differences in Net Income for Accounting and Federal Income Taxes* (Chicago: Commerce Clearing House, Inc., 1949).

Stanley S. Surrey, "Definitional Problems in Capital Gains Taxation," *Harvard Law Review,* April, 1956, Vol. LXIX, #5, p. 995.

Peter Miller, "Capital Gains Taxation of the Fruits of Personal Effort . . . ," *Yale Law Journal,* November, 1954, Vol. LXIV, #1, p. 1.

Lawrence H. Seltzer, *The Nature and Tax Treatment of Capital Gains and Losses* (Princeton: Princeton University Press, 1951).

Harry M. Halstead, "Sales of Land with Growing Crops—Tax Treatment," *TAXES—The Tax Magazine,* January, 1953, Vol. XXXI, #1, p. 55.

Charles S. Lowrimore, "Tax Savings and Capital Increase in Livestock Raising," *TAXES—The Tax Magazine,* January, 1953, Vol. XXXI, #1, p. 64.

B. Leading Cases.

Capital gains are income. *Merchants Loan & Trust Co. v. Smietanka,* 255 U.S. 509 (1921).

Power of the Government to tax capital gains. *Willcutts v. Bunn,* 282 U.S. 216 (1931).

Capital gain must be realized. *MacLaughlin v. Alliance Insurance Company of Philadelphia,* 286 U.S. 244 (1932).

C. Questions.

1. How can an asset be capital in the hands of one person and noncapital in the hands of another?
2. How is it possible to convert ordinary income into capital gain?
3. Is capital gains treatment limited to capital assets?
4. How may the sale of an asset be removed from the capital gains provisions of the Code?
5. Is it always desirable to have a disposition of assets be treated as capital rather than ordinary?
6. An asset held for precisely six months was sold at a gain. Is this long-term or short-term?

[92] I.R.C. Section 269.
[93] I.R.C. Section 381.

7. Is the 25% capital gains limitation available where an individual's only transaction for the year was a short-term capital gain?
8. Are all taxpayers with net capital losses entitled to a deduction from other income of the amount of the loss up to $1,000 a year?
9. Is the 25% capital gains limitation available to all taxpayers? Is it mathematically advantageous in every situation?
10. Is gain from the disposition of a United States Treasury Series E bond capital or ordinary?
11. What are the tax aspects of a bond that is sold "flat"?
12. How is the holding period determined in the case of a short sale?
13. Is gain from the sale of an option capital or ordinary?
14. May a dealer in securities receive capital treatment on a securities transaction?
15. A sum of money is paid to effect the cancellation of a lease. Is this capital gain or ordinary income when the payment is made by (a) the lessor or (b) the lessee?
16. A businessman is paid a sum in return for a covenant not to compete with the payor. Is this capital gain or ordinary income to him?
17. Discuss the tax aspects of disposition of Section 1231 assets.
18. How may a noncapital asset be converted into a capital asset?
19. Are there any restrictions upon transactions that might deprive a transaction of capital treatment?
20. Will disposition of capital assets always be given capital treatment? Does the taxpayer have any election?
21. Is appreciation in value of a capital asset the equivalent of capital gain?
22. Is capital treatment available upon the disposition of a personal asset?
23. An eminent tax attorney, Harry J. Rudick, has written: "If it were not for the limited capital gains rate, the special allowances to the investor in oil, and other preferments for property owners, it is probable that the number of millionaires in this country would have remained static since 1932." Discuss this point of view.

6

RECOGNITION OF GAIN OR LOSS

Realization

Before there can be gain or loss for tax purposes, there must be a *realization* of income. "[A] mere growth or increment in the value of an asset, which is not sold or otherwise disposed of by the owner, is not income."[1] "Generally speaking, appreciation in the value of property, or, to state it differently, unrealized profit thereon, is not taxable. The gain or profit must be realized."[2]

"From the beginning the revenue laws have been interpreted as defining 'realization' of income as the taxable event rather than the acquisition of the right to receive it. And 'realization' is not deemed to occur until the income is paid. But decisions and regulations have consistently recognized that receipt in cash or property is not the only characteristic of realization of income. . . . Where the taxpayer does not receive payment of income in money or property realization may occur when the last step is taken by which he obtains the fruition of the economic gain which has already accrued to him."[3] "Gain may occur as a result of exchange of property, payment of taxpayer's indebtedness, or other profit realized from the completion of a transaction."[4]

Actual Realization. Realization takes place when income *actually* is realized, or when income is *assumed* to be realized. Actual realization includes sales, exchanges that are not tax-free (see Chapter 17), the maturing of an obligation. The relinquishment of a restrictive covenant in a contract was deemed to be a sale or exchange.[5] The cancellation of a lease was treated as a realization of income.[6] An involuntary conversion of an asset is realization unless the special rule as to replacements of statutory involuntary conver-

[1] *United States v. Carter et al.*, 19 F.2d 121 (5th Cir., 1927).
[2] *H. Elkan & Co.*, 2 T.C. 597 (1943).
[3] *Helvering v. Horst*, 311 U.S. 112 (1940).
[4] *Helvering v. Bruun*, 309 U.S. 461 (1940).
[5] *Commissioner v. Ray*, 210 F.2d 390 (5th Cir., 1954).
[6] *Commissioner v. Golonsky et al.*, 200 F.2d 72 (3d Cir., 1952).

sions applies.[7] Payment of a debt with property is a sale.[8] The equivalent of a sale took place when an executor gave a beneficiary certain property in satisfaction of a legacy.[9] A tax sale of property is still a sale.[10]

Pledge of property as collateral for a loan is not a sale.[11] But if the creditor sells the property in payment of the loan, there is a sale, even if it is involuntary.[12]

"There must always first be a transaction in respect to property which so ends or changes the taxpayer's interest in it that resulting gain is 'realized.'"[13] "A transaction whereby nothing of exchangeable value comes to or is received by a taxpayer does not give rise to or create taxable income."[14]

Assumed Realization. Income is assumed, or is imputed to a taxpayer, under certain circumstances. A corporation is assumed to have realized income when it makes distributions of certain property to its shareholders: Lifo inventories (see Chapter 7 for explanation of "Lifo"), liabilities in excess of basis, or any assets where collectibility by the shareholder actually involves an anticipatory assignment of income by the corporation. See Chapter 8, "Dividends."

Income is assumed to be the taxpayer's when the payee was only a nominee of his. "[T]he rule that income is not taxable until realized has never been taken to mean that the taxpayer, even on the cash receipts basis, who has fully enjoyed the benefit of the economic gain represented by his right to receive income, can escape taxation because he has not himself received payment of it from his obligor."[15] Thus, where a parent enters a prize contest which provides that any award is payable to his child, the parent will be deemed to have realized the income.[16]

An unexplained increase in a taxpayer's net worth may be assumed to represent the realization of income.[17] See Chapter 3.

If a security which is a capital asset in the taxpayer's hands becomes worthless, the resultant loss will be treated as a loss from the

[7] I.R.C. Section 1231.
[8] *Kenan v. Commissioner,* 114 F.2d 217 (2d Cir., 1940).
[9] *Suisman & Blumenthal, Inc. v. Eaton,* 83 F.2d 1019 (2d Cir., 1936).
[10] *Helvering v. Nebraska Bridge Supply & Lumber Co.,* 312 U.S. 666 (1941).
[11] *W. P. Sewell et al.,* T.C. Memo., Docket ##112298–9 and 112339, entered February 7, 1944.
[12] *Helvering v. Hammel,* 311 U.S. 504 (1941).
[13] *Gutbro Holding Co. v. Commissioner,* 138 F.2d 16 (2d Cir., 1943).
[14] *Dallas Transfer and Terminal Warehouse Co. v. Commissioner,* 70 F.2d 95 (5th Cir., 1934).
[15] *Helvering v. Horst,* 311 U.S. 112 (1940).
[16] Revenue Ruling 58–127, I.R.B. 1958–13, 11.
[17] *Friedberg v. United States,* 348 U.S. 142 (1954).

sale or exchange of a capital asset on the last day of the taxable year.[18] (The loss will not be capital where certain securities in affiliated corporations are involved.[19] See Chapter 27.)

The parties in interest may not determine between themselves whether there has been a realization of income. "The recital in the contract that 'any surplus remaining over and above the expenses of handling this slag during the summer months will not be considered as profit' is immaterial so far as the present question is here. It was not within the power of the parties to render the income nontaxable." [20]

Basis

Originally, the Internal Revenue Service sought to tax *all* proceeds of the disposition of assets. Such efforts were not successful. "We must reject . . . the broad contention submitted in behalf of the government that all receipts—everything that comes in—are income within the proper definition of the term 'gross income,' and that the entire proceeds of a conversion . . . should be treated as gross income." [21] Income is only what the taxpayer receives in excess of the value of his original investment. "In order to determine whether there has been gain or loss, and the amount of the gain, if any, we must withdraw from the gross proceeds an amount sufficient to restore the capital value that existed at the commencement of the period under consideration." [22]

These two cases mark the start of the present theory of basis; that is, that gain or loss is the difference between the proceeds of a disposition and a *basic* amount, which amount may be the cost of the asset disposed of or some other determinant of value.

Importance of Basis. Basis has several important functions, the most important being: (1) The establishment of a figure used to determine gain or loss upon disposition. Realization minus basis equals the taxable gain or loss. (2) The creation of a figure to which appropriate percentages may be applied for write-offs for depreciation, depletion, amortization, and obsolescence. (3) The setting up of a *tax cost* for a variety of purposes.

Types of Basis. Basis, like Gaul, may be divided into three parts, or types: (1) unadjusted basis, (2) adjusted basis, and (3) substituted basis.

[18] I.R.C. Section 165(g)(1).
[19] I.R.C. Section 165(g)(3).
[20] *Standard Slag Co. v. Commissioner*, 63 F.2d 820 (App. D.C., 1933).
[21] *Southern Pacific Co. v. Lowe*, 247 U.S. 330 (1918).
[22] *Doyle v. Mitchell Brothers Co.*, 247 U.S. 179 (1918).

(1) Unadjusted basis refers to the bare cost.

(2) Adjusted basis is the cost or other basis as set by the Code, adjusted to the extent provided by other sections of the Code.[23] The principal adjustments are:

(A) Expenditures, receipts, losses, or other items, properly chargeable to capital account. But no adjustment is made for carrying charges or circulation expenses for which the taxpayer has taken deductions in determining taxable income for any taxable year or prior taxable years.

Illustration. A taxpayer pays $50,000 for a warehouse. A new type of roof (not a repair) is installed at a cost of $10,000. The adjusted basis of the warehouse is $60,000.

(B) Exhaustion, wear and tear, obsolescence, amortization, and depletion. See Chapter 10.

(C) In the case of stock (to the extent not provided for in the above references) for the amount of distributions previously made which either were tax-free or were applicable in reduction of basis. This does not refer to personal service corporations.

Illustration. A corporation effects a bona fide contraction of its business, and there is a partial liquidation of stock. Amounts received by the shareholders reduce the basis of the stock.

(D) In the case of any bond the interest on which is wholly tax-exempt, to the extent of the amortizable bond premium disallowable as a premium; and in the case of any other bond, to the extent of the deductions allowable as amortizable bond premium.

(E) In the case of any short-term municipal bond, to the extent of the amortizable bond premium.

(F) In the case of a residence the acquisition of which resulted in the nonrecognition of any part of the gain realized on the disposition of another residence, to the extent provided in Section 1034.

(G) In the case of property pledged to the Commodity Credit Corporation, to the extent of the amount received as a loan from that organization and treated by the taxpayer as income for the year in which received pursuant to Section 77, and to the extent of any deficiency on such loan with respect to which the taxpayer has been relieved from liability.

(H) For amounts allowed as deductions as deferred expenses under Section 616(b) (relating to certain expenditures in the development of mines) and resulting in a reduction of the tax-

[23] I.R.C. Section 1011.

payer's taxes, but not less than the amounts allowable for the taxable year and prior years.

(I) For amounts allowed as deductions as deferred expenses under Section 515(b) (relating to exploration costs) and resulting in a reduction of the taxpayer's taxes but not less than the amounts allowable for the taxable year and prior years.

(J) For deductions to the extent disallowed under Section 268 (relating to sale of land with unharvested crops).

(K) To the extent provided in Section 28(h) of the Internal Revenue Code of 1939 in the case of amounts specified in a shareholder's consent made under Section 28 of that Code.

(L) To the extent provided in Section 551(f) in the case of the stock of United States shareholders in a foreign personal holding company.

(M) For amounts allowed as deductions as deferred expenses under Section 174(b)(1) (relating to research and experimental expenditures) and resulting in a reduction of the taxpayer's taxes, but not less than the amounts allowable for the taxable year and prior years.

(N) For deduction to the extent disallowed under Section 272 (relating to the disposal of coal).

(O) For amounts allowed as deductions for expenditures treated as deferred expenses under Section 177 (relating to trademark and trade name expenditures), and resulting in a reduction of the taxpayer's taxes, but not less than the amounts allowable for the taxable year and prior years.[24]

(P) For amounts excluded from gross income under Section 108(a) on account of a discharge of indebtedness during the taxable year. Where a discharge of indebtedness otherwise would result in taxable income, adjustment may be elected in the following order (but in the case of an individual, Items (i) to (iv), inclusive, apply only to property used in any trade or business):

(i) In the case of indebtedness incurred to purchase specific property (other than inventory or receivables), the cost or other basis of the property will be decreased by the amount excluded from gross income.

(ii) In the case of specific property (other than inventories and receivables) against which, at the time of the discharge of the indebtedness, there is a lien (other than one securing indebtedness incurred to purchase that property) the cost or other basis of the property will be decreased by the amount excluded from gross income.

[24] I.R.C. Section 1016.

(iii) Any part of the exclusion from gross income not absorbed by (i) and (ii) will next be applied to reduce the cost or other basis of the debtor's property (other than inventories and receivables) as follows: The cost or other basis of each unit of property will be decreased in an amount equal to the proportion of the excess as the adjusted basis (without reference to this section) of each unit of property bears to the sum of adjusted bases (without reference to this section) of all the property of the debtor other than inventory and receivables.

(iv) Any excess of the total amount excluded from gross income over the sum of the above three adjustments will next be applied to reduce the cost or other basis of inventory and receivables as follows: The cost or other basis of inventory or receivables will be decreased in an amount equal to such proportion of the excess as the adjusted basis of the inventory and receivables bears to the sum of the adjusted bases of the inventory and receivables.

(v) In the case of an individual, any excess of the total amount excluded from gross income over the sum of the above four adjustments will next be applied to reduce the cost or other basis of his property held for the production of income as follows: The cost or other basis of each unit of this property will be decreased in an amount equal to such proportion of the excess as the adjusted basis (without reference to this section) of each unit of property bears to the sum of the adjusted bases (without reference to this section) of all of such property of the debtor.

(vi) In the case of an individual, any excess of the total amount excluded from gross income over the sum of the above five adjustments will next be applied to reduce the cost or other basis of his property held for the production of income as follows: The cost or other basis of each unit of the property will be decreased in an amount equal to such proportion of the excess as the adjusted basis (without reference to this section) of each unit of property bears to the sum of the adjusted bases (without reference to this section) of all of such property of the debtor.[25]

(vii) The taxpayer may make application to the Internal Revenue Service for other reduction in basis.[26]

(Q) Ordinarily, the Federal Bankruptcy Act provides for the reduction of basis where indebtedness is canceled. But this reduc-

[25] Regulations Section 1.1017–1(a).
[26] Regulations Section 1.1017–2(a).

tion is not required if the indebtedness was canceled by adjustment of the capital or debt structure of an insolvent corporation where the final judgment was entered before September 22, 1938.[27]

(R) No reduction is required for the cancellation of indebtedness in an insolvency reorganization under Section 371.[28] See Chapter 17.

(S) Basis is not to be reduced in certain railroad reorganizations.[29]

(3) Substituted basis is a basis determined by reference to the basis in the hands of a transferor, donor, or grantor, or by reference to other property held at any time by the person for whom the basis is to be determined.[30] Where the basis of property in the hands of the taxpayer is a substituted basis, any required adjustments will be made after first making adjustments of a similar nature for the period during which the property was held by the transferor, donor, or grantor, or during which the other property was held by the person for whom the basis is to be determined.[31]

Illustration. Senior in 1942 purchased the X Building and subsequently gave it to Junior. Junior exchanged the X Building for the Y Building in a tax-free exchange (see Chapter 17), and then gave the Y Building to his wife. The wife, in determining the gain from the sale or disposition of the Y Building in 1961, is required to reduce the basis of the building by deductions for depreciation which were successively allowed (but not less than the amount allowable) to Senior and Junior upon the X Building and to Junior upon the Y Building, in addition to the deductions for depreciation allowed (but not less than the amount allowable) to herself during her ownership of the Y Building.

General Rule. In general, the basis of the property is the cost thereof.[32] The cost is the amount paid for this asset in cash or other property. But there are certain exceptions to this general rule.

(1) *Property included in inventory.* The basis of property required to be included in inventory is the value at which it had been included in the preceding inventory.[33]

(2) *Property acquired from a decedent.* The basis of property acquired from a decedent is the fair market value of this property at the date of the decedent's death, or, if the decedent's executor so elects, at the value one year later.[34] (But if the executor disposes of the asset between the date of death and one year later, then,

[27] I.R.C. Section 1018.
[28] I.R.C. Section 372(a).
[29] I.R.C. Section 373(b).
[30] I.R.C. Section 1016(b).
[31] Regulations Section 1.1016–10(a).
[32] I.R.C. Section 1012.
[33] I.R.C. Section 1013.
[34] I.R.C. Section 1014.

should the election as to later valuation date have been made, the value will be as of the date of disposition.)[35] "Property acquired from a decedent" includes all assets that must be listed as part of the gross estate for estate tax purposes; for example, property which presumably had been given away by the donor before his death, but which must be listed with the estate assets before the decedent had retained incidents of ownership not permitted by the Code, such as the right to revoke a gift. (But if the donee has disposed of this property within one year after the date of the decedent's death, the basis is value as of this date of disposition.)[36] If no estate tax return is required to be filed, the alternate valuation date may not be used.[37]

(3) *Property acquired by gifts and transfers in trust.*

(A) *After December 31, 1920.* The basis of the property for purpose of determining *gain* is the same as it would be in the hands of the donor or the last preceding owner by whom it was not acquired by gift. In the case of gifts made on or after September 2, 1958, the basis is increased by any gift tax paid by either donor or donee. For the purpose of determining *loss,* the basis is the lower of (i) donor's basis or (ii) fair market value at the time of gift. Because of these two distinct rules, it is possible that there may be neither gain nor loss on the disposition of an asset received by gift: applying the rule for determining gain, there is no gain; applying the rule for determining loss, there is no loss.

Illustration. Senior buys property for $5,000. It is worth $4,000 when he gives the property to Junior. If Junior sells the property for

Realization	Basis	Gain or (Loss)
$6,000	$5,000	$1,000
3,000	4,500	(1,000)
4,500	5,000 for determining gain	0
	4,000 for determining loss	0

It is immaterial whether the gift was by a transfer of trust or otherwise.

(B) *Before January 1, 1921.* In the case of property acquired by gift or transfer in trust before January 1, 1921, the basis of the property is the fair market value at the time of the gift or at the time of the transfer in trust.[38]

(4) *Property acquired before March 1, 1913.* The basis for determining gain is the greater of cost or fair market value as of March

[35] I.R.C. Section 2032.
[36] Regulations Section 1.1014–3(e)(2).
[37] Regulations Section 1.1014–3.
[38] I.R.C. Section 1015.

1, 1913. The basis for determining loss is cost. Where cost is used, depreciation adjustments to March 1, 1913, must be made.

(5) *Property held for productive use or investment.* If there has been a tax-free exchange of property held for productive use or investment in trade or business or for investment for property of a like kind, a basis adjustment may be necessary.[39] This will be discussed under the heading of "Tax-free Exchanges" in Chapter 17.

(6) *Corporate reorganizations.* Basis adjustments are required in various types of corporate reorganizations, and a detailed discussion will be provided in Chapter 17 under these headings:

Subject	*I.R.C. Section*
Assumption of liabilities.	357
Bankruptcy.	371
Boot.	358
Complete liquidation of subsidiary.	334
Contributed property.	362
Distribution of property.	301
In general.	301
One-year liquidation.	337
Qualified electing shareholder	333
Redemptions.	302, 306, 331
Transfer to controlled corporation.	351

(7) *Transfers involving partnerships.* The basis adjustments when assets are transferred to or from partnerships, or when there is a revaluation of partnership assets, will be discussed in Chapter 19.

(8) *Stock rights.* The allocation of basis when stock rights are involved is considered in Chapter 8.

(9) *Wash sales.* Basis adjustments in the case of losses from wash sales on stock and securities will be considered in Chapter 7.

Involuntary Conversions

The principle of involuntary conversion was written into the tax law by experiences of World War I. Property owners sometimes lost their assets because of governmental commandeering or enemy action. The new assets acquired to make up for this loss, for obvious mathematical reasons, generally had a basis different from that of the assets lost. If gain had to be recognized when assets were involuntarily disposed of, high wartime taxes might have erased virtually all of the profit. The tax law is based upon the general

[39] I.R.C. Section 1031(d).

premise that persons enter into a transaction because they want to; that purchase price and other terms are subject to untrammeled exercise of bargaining power; that a person cannot be compelled to dispose of an asset and pay the resultant gains tax if he is more disposed not to do so. The principle of involuntary conversion replacements was devised to reflect this situation.

An involuntary conversion refers to (1) the destruction of property in whole or in part; (2) theft; and (3) the seizure of property, or its requisition or condemnation, or the threat or imminence of requisition or condemnation of property.[40] Other types of involuntary conversion, although similar in effect to the three forms mentioned in the statute, are not afforded the same tax treatment. "An involuntary conversion under the statute may only result from the three specified causes." [41]

The conversion must be the aftermath of one of the causes set forth in the Code. Thus where a taxpayer finally gave in to moral suasion advanced by a chamber of commerce and sold his property, it was held that an involuntary conversion did not take place.[42] Nor is involuntary conversion involved where there is a foreclosure of property.[43] Where a taxpayer sold his property to a railroad under a threat that the right of eminent domain would be invoked if he did not do so, it was held that statutory involuntary conversion had resulted.[44]

But the calling of a bond by the obligor is not an involuntary conversion, for the purchaser had acquired the bond subject to this condition.[45]

Investment in property similar in character and devoted to a similar use does not occur if (1) the proceeds of unimproved real estate (taken upon condemnation proceedings) are invested in improved real estate, or (2) the proceeds of conversion of real property are applied in reduction of indebtedness previously incurred in the purchase of a leasehold, or (3) the owner of a requisitioned tug uses the proceeds to buy barges.

A loss resulting from an involuntary conversion is recognized. But a gain is not recognized where property is converted into other property similar in service or use to the converted property, regardless of when the disposition of the converted property occurred and regardless of whether or not the taxpayer elects to have the gain not

[40] I.R.C. Section 1033.
[41] *Davis Co.,* 6 B.T.A. 281 (1927).
[42] *Davis Co.,* 6 B.T.A. 281 (1927).
[43] *Cooperative Publishing Co. v. Commissioner,* 115 F.2d 1017 (9th Cir., 1940).
[44] *Davis Regulator Co.,* 36 B.T.A. 437 (1937).
[45] I.T. 1354, I-1 CB 190.

recognized. In other types of involuntary conversion cases, the proceeds arising from the disposition of the converted property must be reinvested in similar property in order to avoid recognition of any gain realized.

To the extent that proceeds of an involuntary conversion are not reinvested in other property similar in service or use to the converted property, gain will be recognized.

Illustration. A taxpayer's ship, which has an adjusted basis of $100,000, is destroyed in 1960, and the owner receives in 1961 insurance in the amount of $200,000. If he invests $150,000 in a new ship, taxable gain to the extent of $50,000 would be recognized. The basis of the new ship is $100,000; that is, the adjusted basis of the old ship ($100,000) minus the money received by the taxpayer which was not expended in the acquisition of the new ship ($50,000) plus the amount of gain recognized upon the conversion ($50,000). If any amount in excess of the proceeds of the conversion is expended in the acquisition of the new property, this amount may be added to the basis.

Illustration. A taxpayer realizes $22,000 from the involuntary conversion of his barn in 1961. The adjusted basis of the barn to him was $10,000, and he spent in the same year $20,000 for a new barn, which resulted in the nonrecognition of $10,000 of the $12,000 gain on the conversion. The basis of the new barn to the taxpayer would be $10,000: the cost of the new barn ($20,000) less the amount of the gain not recognized on the conversion ($10,000). The basis of the new barn would not be a substituted basis in the hands of the taxpayer. If the replacement of the converted barn had been made by the purchase of two smaller barns which, together, were similar or related in service or use to the converted barn and which cost $8,000 and $12,000, respectively, then the basis of the two barns would be $4,000 and $6,000, respectively, the total basis of the purchased property ($10,000) allocated in proportion to their respective costs. $\frac{\$8,000}{\$20,000}$ of $10,000 ($4,000) plus $\frac{\$12,000}{\$20,000}$ of $10,000 ($6,000) equals $10,000.

Property or stock purchased before the disposition of the converted property will be considered to have been purchased for the purpose of replacing the converted property only if this property or stock is held by the taxpayer on the date of the disposition of the converted property.

The replacement of an involuntary conversion must take place not later than the last day of the taxable year following the year in which any part of the gain upon the conversion is realized. But if it is believed that a replacement cannot be purchased within that time, the taxpayer may file Form 1114, "Application To Establish a Replacement Fund." The Internal Revenue Service may grant a longer period of time for the replacement, the length of time depending upon the scarceness of the asset and the difficulty of finding a proper replacement. Assets must be purchased, or control of a corporation owning such property. Acquisition of an interest in a partnership owning such property does not qualify.

The taxpayer will not be deemed to have purchased replacement property or stock, unless the adjusted basis would be cost.[46] Thus a gift of replaced property would not qualify.

If, after having made an election, the taxpayer does not replace the converted property within the required time, or the replacement is made at a lower cost than was anticipated at the time of the election, or a decision is made not to replace, an amended tax return should be filed for the year or years originally covered by the election.[47]

Involuntary conversions are not treated as sales or exchanges for tax purposes.[48]

The proceeds of a use and occupancy insurance contract, which by its terms insured against actual loss sustained of net profits in the business, are not proceeds of an involuntary conversion but are income in the same manner that the profits for which they are substituted would have been.

Special rules apply where the disposition of the converted property occurred before January 1, 1951.[49]

Sale or Exchange of Residence

Involuntary Conversion. The regular rules as to an involuntary conversion apply where the property used by an individual as his principal residence is converted by destruction, theft, or seizure, which occurs after 1953.[50]

Regular Rule. Nonrecognition of gain is possible in certain cases where a taxpayer sells one residence after 1953 and buys, or builds, and uses as his principal residence another residence within specified time limits, before or after the sale. If the taxpayer invests in a new residence an amount at least as large as the adjusted sales price of his old residence, no gain is recognized on the sale of the old residence. But if the new residence costs the taxpayer less than the adjusted sales price of the old residence, gain is recognized to the extent of the difference. If there is no investment in a new residence, the special rule does not apply, and all of the gain will be recognized.[51]

[46] I.R.C. Section 1033(a)(3)(A)(ii).
[47] Regulations Section 1.1033(a)–2(c)(2).
[48] Revenue Ruling 56–372, 1956–2 CB 187.
[49] I.R.C. Section 1033(a)(2).
[50] Regulations Section 1.1033(b)–1.
[51] I.R.C. Section 1034.

If, as a result of the application of Section 1034, any or all of the gain realized on the sale of an old residence is not recognized, a corresponding reduction must be made in the basis of the new residence.

The provisions of this section are mandatory; an election cannot be made as to when or whether gain will be recognized. Only gains are involved; losses are recognized or not recognized without regard to the provisions of Section 1034.[52]

Definitions. Several of the terms used in this section have specialized meanings:

Old residence. The property used by the taxpayer as his principal residence which is the subject of a sale by him after 1953. This may be a building, trailer, boat, or stock in a cooperative apartment corporation.

New residence. Property used by the taxpayer as his principal residence, which is the subject of a purchase by him.

Adjusted sales price. The amount realized as reduced by the fixing-up expenses.

Amount realized. The consideration (money, fair market value of property received, assumption of a liability) less offsets against the consideration, such as commissions, advertising expense in connection with the sale, and other legal services in connection with the sale.

Gain realized. The excess (if any) of the amount realized over the adjusted basis of the old residence.

Fixing-up expenses. The aggregate of the expenses for work performed on the old residence in order to assist in its sale, provided that these expenses (1) are incurred for work performed during the 90-day period ending on the day on which the contract to sell the old residence is entered into and (2) are paid on or before the 30th day after the date of the sale of the old residence; and (3) are neither allowable as deductions in computing taxable income nor taken into account in computing the amount realized from the sale of the old residence. Fixing-up expenses do not include expenditures which are properly chargeable to capital account and which would, therefore, constitute adjustments to the basis of the old residence.

Cost of purchasing the new residence. The total of all amounts which are attributable to the acquisition, construction, reconstruction, and improvements constituting capital expenditures, made during the period ending one year before the date of sale of the old residence and ending either (1) one year after that date in the case

[52] Regulations Section 1.1034–1(a).

of a new residence purchased but not constructed by the taxpayer, or (2) 18 months after that date in the case of a new residence the construction of which was commenced by the taxpayer before the expiration of one year after that date.

Sale of residence. A sale or an exchange of a residence for other property which occurs after 1953.

Purchase of a new residence. A purchase or an acquisition of a residence on the exchange of property or the partial or total construction or reconstruction of a residence by the taxpayer. But the mere improvement of a residence, not amounting to reconstruction, does not constitute a purchase of a residence for this purpose.

Application. Gain realized from the sale after 1953 of an old residence will be recognized only to the extent that the taxpayer's adjusted sales price of the old residence exceeds his cost of purchasing the new residence, provided that he either (1) within a period beginning one year before the date of the sale and ending one year after that date purchases property and uses it as his principal residence, or (2) within a period beginning one year before the date of the sale and ending 18 months after that date uses as his principal residence a new residence the construction of which was commenced by him at any time before the expiration of one year after the date of the sale of the old residence. This rule applies to a new residence purchased by the taxpayer before the date of sale of the old residence, provided the new residence is still owned by him on that date.

In applying this rule, the taxpayer should first subtract the commissions and other selling expenses from the selling price of his old residence, to determine the amount realized. A comparison of the amount realized with the cost or other basis of the old residence will then indicate whether there is any gain realized on the sale. Unless the amount realized is greater than the cost or other basis, no gain is realized, and Section 1034 does not apply. If the amount realized exceeds the cost or other basis, the amount of this excess constitutes the gain realized. The amount realized should then be reduced by the fixing-up expenses (if any) to determine the adjusted sales price. A comparison of the adjusted sales price of the old residence with the cost of purchasing the new residence will indicate how much (if any) of the realized gain is to be recognized. If the cost of purchasing the new residence is the same as, or greater than, the adjusted sales price of the old residence, then none of the realized gain is to be recognized. On the other hand, if the cost of purchasing the new residence is smaller than the adjusted sales price of the old residence, the gain realized is to be recognized to the extent of the difference.

Illustration. A taxpayer decides to sell his residence, which has a basis of $17,500. To make it more attractive to buyers, he paints the outside, at a cost of $300, in April. He pays for the painting when the work is finished. In May, he sells the house for $20,000. Brokers' commissions and other selling expenses are $1,000. In October, he buys a new residence for $18,000.

Selling price	$20,000	
Less: Commissions and other selling expenses	1,000	
Amount realized	$19,000	
Less: Basis	17,500	
Gain realized		$1,500
Amount realized	$19,000	
Less: Fixing-up expenses	300	
Adjusted sales price	18,700	
Cost of purchasing new residence	18,000	
Gain recognized		$ 700
Gain realized but not recognized		800
Adjusted basis of new residence	$17,200	

Illustration. If the facts are the same as in the preceding illustration, except that the selling price of the old residence is $18,500, the computation would be:

Selling price	$18,500
Less: Commissions and other selling expenses	1,000
Amount realized	$17,500
Less: Basis	17,500
Gain realized	$ 0

NOTE: Inasmuch as no gain is realized, Section 1034 is inapplicable; it is, therefore, unnecessary to compute the adjusted sales price of the old residence and compare it with the cost of purchasing the new residence. No adjustment to the basis of the new residence is to be made.

Illustration. The facts are the same as in the first illustration, except that the cost of purchasing the new residence is $17,000.

Selling price	$20,000
Less: Commissions and other selling expenses	1,000
Amount realized	$19,000
Less: Basis	17,500
Gain realized	$ 1,500
Amount realized	$19,000
Less: Fixing-up expenses	300
Adjusted sales price	$18,700
Cost of purchasing the new residence	17,000
Gain recognized	$ 1,500

NOTE: Inasmuch as the adjusted sales price of the old residence exceeds the cost of purchasing the new residence by $1,700, which is more than the gain realized, all of the gain realized is recognized. No adjustment to the basis of the new residence is to be made.

Gain realized but not recognized	$ 0

Principal Residence. Whether or not property is used by the taxpayer as his residence, and whether (if he has more than one residence) it is his *principal* residence, depends upon all of the facts and circumstances, including the good faith of the taxpayer. The mere fact that property is, or has been, rented is not determinative that this property is not used by him as his principal residence. Property used by him as his principal residence does not include personal property (such as a piece of furniture, a radio, etc.) which, in accordance with the applicable local law, is not a fixture.

Where part of a property is used by a taxpayer as his principal residence and part is used for other purposes, an allocation must be made to determine the application of Section 1034.

If the taxpayer and his spouse file a consent form used for this purpose, then the "taxpayer's adjusted sales price of the old residence" means the taxpayer's and his spouse's adjusted sales price of the old residence. Similarly, the cost of purchasing a new residence means the cost to the taxpayer and/or his spouse.

Several Residences. If a residence is purchased by the taxpayer prior to the date of the sale of the old residence, the purchased residence will in no event be treated as a new residence if this purchased residence is sold or otherwise disposed of by him prior to the date of the sale of the old residence. If, during the period within which the purchase and use of the new residence must be made in order to have nonrecognition of gain on the sale of the old residence, he purchases more than one property which is used by him as his principal residence during the one year (or 18 months in the case of the construction of the new residence) succeeding the date of the sale of the old residence, only the *last* of these properties will be considered a new residence.

Illustration. An individual sells his old residence on January 15 and purchases another residence on February 15. On March 15, he sells the residence which he bought on February 15 and purchases another residence on April 15. The gain on the sale of the old residence on January 15 will not be recognized except to the extent to which his adjusted sales price of the old residence exceeds the cost of purchasing the residence which he purchased on April 15. Gain on the sale of the residence which was bought on February 15 and sold on March 15 will be recognized.

Basis of New Residence. Where the purchase of a new residence results in the nonrecognition of any part of the gain realized upon the sale of an old residence, then, in determining the adjusted basis of the new residence as of any time following the sale of the old residence, the adjustments to basis will include a reduction by an amount equal to the amount of the gain which was not recognized upon the sale of the old residence. Such a reduction is not to be made for the purpose of determining the adjusted basis of the new residence as of any time preceding the sale of the old residence.

Armed Forces. The time limitations of Section 1034 are liberalized for members of the armed forces. See Chapter 15.

Statute of Limitations. Where a taxpayer sells property used as his principal residence at a gain, the period allowed to the Internal Revenue Service for the assessment of a tax deficiency attributable to any part of this gain will not expire until three years after the appropriate District Director of Internal Revenue receives written notice from the taxpayer of (1) his cost of purchasing the new residence, (2) his intention not to purchase a new residence within the period where nonrecognition of gain is possible, or (3) his failure to make the purchase within the period allowed.

Elections To Capitalize

In certain instances, the Code gives taxpayers the election to *deduct* a payment as an expenditure or to *capitalize* the expenditure. When the latter choice is made, there is an adjustment to basis.

Carrying Charges. The following items may be capitalized at the election of the taxpayer:

(1) In the case of unimproved and unproductive real property, annual taxes, interest on a mortgage, and other carrying charges.

(2) In the case of real property whether improved or unimproved and whether productive or nonproductive, expenditures (otherwise deductible) paid or incurred in the development thereof or in the construction of an improvement thereon, up to the time the development or construction work has been completed. This includes interest on a loan to furnish funds for this purpose, payroll taxes and taxes on the purchase or use of materials for the project, and other necessary expenditures paid or incurred up to the time the development or construction work has been completed.

(3) In the case of personal property, payroll taxes of an employer in connection with the obtaining and installing of fixed assets; interest on a loan to finance acquisition, transportation, and installation of these assets; taxes on the purchase or use of materials for the project.

(4) Any other taxes and carrying charges with respect to property, otherwise deductible, which in the opinion of the Commissioner are, under sound accounting principles, chargeable to capital account.[53]

[53] I.R.C. Section 266; Regulations 118, Section 39.24(a)–8.

If a taxpayer elects to capitalize an item, the election is exercised by filing with the original tax return a statement indicating what is to be capitalized.

Circulation Expenses. All expenditures to establish, to maintain, or to increase the circulation of a newspaper, magazine, or other periodical may be expensed or capitalized.[54] But deduction is only allowed to the publisher making the circulation expenditures. Deduction is not allowed for expenditures for the purchase of land or depreciable property and for the acquisition of circulation through the purchase of any part of the business of another publisher.[55]

Research Expenditures. Research or experimental expenditures paid or incurred by the taxpayer in connection with his trade or business may be (1) treated as expenses not chargeable to capital account and deducted in the year in which they are paid or incurred or (2) deferred and amortized.[56] These expenditures may relate either to a general research program or to a particular project. See Chapter 9.

Conversion to Business Use

Depreciation may not be taken upon property not used in the taxpayer's trade or business, nor is loss recognized upon disposition. But such property may be converted to business use. Then (if the fact of conversion may be proved), the deductions may be allowed.

The question of whether conversion to business use has occurred is one of fact, and the controlling factor is the intent of the taxpayer.[57] The mere listing of a house for sale at a price that would return a nice profit is not enough to lose the characteristic of a personal house.[58] Paying off of the liens on a house is not proof that the property was not to be retained as a home.[59]

Where residential property is appropriated to rental purposes, loss upon sale may not exceed the lower of (1) the fair market value of the property at the time it was converted to business use (with proper adjustment for depreciation) or (2) the adjusted basis of the property at the time it was converted to business use (with proper adjustment for depreciation) over the amount realized from the sale. Similarly, the basis for computing depreciation will

[54] I.R.C. Section 173.
[55] Regulations Section 1.173–1(a).
[56] I.R.C. Section 174.
[57] *Dupuy G. Warrick,* 44 B.T.A. 1068 (1942).
[58] *Warren Leslie, Sr.,* 6 T.C. 488 (1946).
[59] *Seletos v. Commissioner,* 254 F.2d 794 (8th Cir., 1958).

be the fair market value of the property at the time it was converted to business use, or the adjusted basis on that date, whichever is the lesser.

Illustration. Residential property was purchased by a taxpayer in 1946 for use as his personal residence at a cost of $25,000, of which $15,000 was allocable to the building. He used the property as a home until January 1, 1955. From that date to January 1, 1961, when the property was sold, it was rented by the taxpayer. The fair market value of the property at the time it was rented on January 1, 1955, was $22,000, of which $12,000 was allocable to the building. The building had an estimated life of twenty years on January 1, 1955. The property was sold on January 1, 1961, for $16,000. The loss from the sale allowable as a deduction (without regard to the capital loss limitation) is $2,400, computed as follows:

Cost of property in 1946	$25,000
Less: Depreciation allowed (not less than the amount allowable) on the building (depreciation for six years at 5% on the straight line method based on $12,000, the value of the building when converted to business use)	3,600
	$21,400
Amount realized	16,000
Loss	$ 5,400
Value of building at time it was rented on January 1, 1955	$22,000
Less: Depreciation allowed or allowable	3,600
	$18,400
Amount realized	16,000
Portion of $5,400 loss which is deductible (except as limited by capital loss limitation)	$ 2,400

Apportionment of Basis

Sometimes there is a single cost or other basis figure for an asset, which subsequently is disposed of piecemeal. Then an allocation of basis is required. "When it is remembered that income is stated in annual periods, it would be a distortion to construe the Revenue Act as permitting a taxpayer to sell part of a large block of stock in the year of the sale and report, without cost, the gain from the remaining shares as sold in small blocks each year. Fairness to both the taxpayer and the Government requires an allocation of the cost on a share basis, and the cost deducted from each share as sold for the purpose of determining gain or loss." [60]

Where it is impossible to allocate the basis between two or more assets, no loss is permitted until there is disposition of the last property.[61] But gain would result, regardless of how many items still remained, as soon as the basis had been recovered.

[60] *Leake v. Commissioner,* 140 F.2d 451 (6th Cir., 1944).
[61] *Spreckels-Rosekrans Investment Co. v. Lewis,* 146 F.2d 982 (9th Cir., 1945).

If consideration is paid for a mixed group of assets and it is possible to establish a cost basis for each asset, the total consideration may be allocated to each asset in accordance to its relative value to the whole at the time of acquisition.[62]

The advantage of establishing separate basis for each asset acquired in a bulk acquisition is shown in Chapter 28.

United States Savings Bonds

The gain on United States savings bonds is taxed according to the terms of the bonds themselves.

Series E Bonds. These bonds are issued on a discount basis of 75% of their maturity value. No interest as such is paid on the bonds, but they increase in redemption value at the end of each half-year period from the issue date; a table of these increments is engraved on the reverse of each bond. The entire increment is treated as interest; thus, no capital gains treatment is possible. The interest is fully subject to Federal income tax.[63]

A taxpayer (1) may report each year's increment as income for that year. Or (2) he may wait until the bond matures and report the entire increment in that year. If he elects under alternative (1), the same treatment must be afforded to all bonds of this type that he owns at the beginning of the year covered by his election, and all similar bonds subsequently acquired will be covered by the election, unless the Secretary of the Treasury permits a change in election to be made.[64]

If a taxpayer (other than a corporation) holds a Series E bond at the date of maturity, and he elects to hold the bond for an additional 10-year period, the increase in redemption value not previously includible in gross income in excess of the cost of the bond is includible in gross income in the taxable year in which the obligation is finally redeemed or in the taxable year of final maturity, whichever is earlier.[65]

Establishment of Basis

If a person has several assets that are indistinguishable (*e.g.,* shares of stock in the same corporation), the first-in, first-out rule will be applied.[66] That is, the basis of what is sold will be the basis

[62] *L. M. Graves,* T.C. Memo., Docket #28049, entered May 14, 1952.
[63] Treasury Department Circular No. 653, Fourth Revision, April 22, 1957.
[64] I.R.C. Section 454(a).
[65] Regulations Section 1.454–1.
[66] *Towne v. McElligott,* 274 Fed. 960 (D.C., N.Y., 1921).

of the asset first acquired. This result may be avoided by earmarking the asset that is to be sold: physical segregation, serial number, etc.

If the taxpayer cannot establish the basis of an asset, it is zero.

After an income tax examination, the Secretary of the Treasury may enter into a closing agreement with the taxpayer, finalizing various aspects of the case.[67] See Chapter 26. Form 906 may be used, for example, to establish the basis of an asset.

Supplementary Material

A. Suggested Reading.

John M. Stoy, "Accounting Theory and Taxable Income," *TAXES—The Tax Magazine,* May, 1950, Vol. XXVIII, #5, p. 442.

Benjamin Harrow, "*Helvering v. Horst.* Some Notes on Recent Applications of the Doctrine," *Proceedings of the New York University Sixth Annual Institute on Federal Taxation* (Albany: Matthew Bender & Co., Inc., 1948), p. 1127.

B. Leading Cases.

Realization. *Helvering v. Horst,* 311 U.S. 112 (1940).
Forms of gain. *Helvering v. Bruun,* 309 U.S. 461 (1940).
Net worth. *Friedberg v. United States,* 348 U.S. 142 (1954).
Recovery of basis. *Southern Pacific Co. v. Lowe,* 247 U.S. 330 (1918).

C. Questions.

1. Why is it necessary to have a realization of income before tax can be imposed?
2. An individual owned a home in which he lived. When he entered the United States Navy for a 3-year hitch, he listed the house for sale with a broker. Actually no sale was effected, and after his tour of duty, the individual moved back into the house. Was he entitled to a depreciation deduction for the house during the period that it was listed for sale? Would your answer be different if he had listed the house for rental at (a) $2,000, the going rate according to the broker, or (b) $1,000,000?
3. A man gave identical pieces of property to his children, Sibyl and John. The properties each had cost him $5,000 in 1953 and were worth $6,000 at the time of the gift. Sibyl sold her property for $7,000; John sold his for $4,000. What was the gain or loss to each person?
4. A calendar year basis taxpayer owned a pier that was seized by the Government on April 21, 1961. By what date must the property be replaced to take advantage of the provisions of a statutory involuntary conversion? Would your answer be different if he had filed an application to establish a replacement fund?
5. In return for merchandise, Mr. Edwards received stock in a corporation. He is unable to obtain any information about the corporation,

[67] I.R.C. Section 7121.

its assets, or its earnings, nor can he find a quotation for the stock. How does he determine gain or loss on the disposition of the merchandise?

6. A father provided by will that his son would get a certain property that had cost $10,000. At the date of the father's death, the property had a fair market value of $13,000. One year thereafter, the property had a fair market value of $12,000. Because of the smallness of the estate, no estate tax return was filed. What is the basis of the property in the son's hands?
7. An individual purchased a home for $17,500. He sold it for $20,000 and immediately purchased another home that served as his principal residence. What was his recognized gain or loss if the second home cost him (a) $21,000 or (b) $19,000?
8. A taxpayer paid $10,000 for a quantity of scrap metal. He assembled the metal into ten equal piles, which he sold for $1,800 each. Five lots were sold in the first year; two in the second; three in the third. What was his recognized gain or loss in each year?
9. Senior gave some property to his son, Junior, as a gift. The property was a building that had cost Senior $10,000 some years ago, but which had been subject to a depreciation deduction as a business asset in the amount of $2,000 since acquisition. At the time of the gift the property had a fair market value of $11,000. What was the (a) unadjusted basis, (b) adjusted basis, and (c) substituted basis of the property?
10. Mr. Soandso, an officer of the S and S Corporation, was permitted to buy stock in that company on very favorable terms, provided he agreed to sell the stock back to the corporation at cost if he should be discharged for cause. He was. Reluctantly he sold the stock back to the company, despite the greatly enhanced value of the stock. Was this very involuntary act an involuntary conversion?
11. An individual who worked in New York City had an apartment in New York and a house in Westport, Connecticut. By factual evidence it could be established that he spent the same amount of time in each house during the taxable year. On December 31 he sold his Westport home, and a few weeks later he purchased another home in Allentown, Pennsylvania. Is he entitled to the preferential tax treatment afforded to the sale and purchase of a principal residence?
12. Charles Martel bequeathed his niece certain property, which had cost him $12,000. On the date of his death, the property had a fair market value of $14,000, which value had risen to $17,000 one year later. Ten months after his death, the niece sold the property for $13,000. What was her recognized gain or loss?
13. A holding company owned some hotel corporation stocks. The United States Department of Justice ordered the disposition of certain stocks (which allegedly were held in restraint of trade), as they represented all of the hotels in a certain city. Was the sale an involuntary conversion?
14. A county sheriff sold at auction the property of an individual who had not paid his property taxes for several years. The individual was given a check for the sales proceeds, less back property taxes. Would recognized gain or loss result? If so, what is the measure of his gain or loss?

15. An individual owned an automobile that was used for both business and pleasure. It originally had cost $3,600, and depreciation had been claimed and allowed on it in the amount of $1,350 in prior years. He traded it in for a new car which was priced at $4,000, and was given a trade-in allowance of $1,200. Based on mileage, the automobile was driven two-thirds for business use and one-third for personal use. What was the depreciable portion of the basis of the new car?
16. An octogenarian used in his business a building which he had purchased some years ago for $35,000. He had made certain permanent improvements at a cost of $10,000, and depreciation had been allowed in the amount of $5,000. The building was sold for $50,000 cash, plus other property having a fair market value of $10,000. The buyer assumed the current real estate taxes of $1,500 and the mortgage of $8,500. The selling expenses were $2,000. What was the gain or loss on the sale?
17. In 1958 an individual purchased for $80,000 real property to be used as a factory. In addition to the purchase price he paid commissions of $2,000 and title search and legal fees of $600. The total cost of $82,600 was allocated $10,325 to the land and $72,275 to the building. He immediately spent $20,000 in remodeling the building. He was allowed depreciation of $9,600 for each year 1958, 1959, 1960, and 1961. In 1961 he suffered a casualty loss to the building of $5,000 as a result of a flood not covered by insurance, and the loss was claimed as a deduction. What was the adjusted basis of the property as of January 1, 1962?
18. A taxpayer had property that cost $50,000 in 1959. Its adjusted basis (cost less depreciation) was $42,000 in 1961, when it was destroyed by boll weevils. The insurance company paid him $60,000 on his claim. What was the recognized gain or loss if he purchased a replacement property for (a) $55,000 or (b) $62,000?

7

SALES; COST OF SALES; INVENTORIES

Sales

When Is a Sale? The basic principle is that a *closing* is an essential prerequisite to taxation of gain from a sales transaction.

On the cash basis, a taxable sale takes place when there is receipt of cash or the equivalent, actually or constructively.

On the accrual basis, a sale is not reported until there is unconditional liability on the part of the vendee for the purchase price.[1] Thus, where the vendor retains title and right of possession until a transaction is closed, there is no unconditional liability on the part of the vendee for the purchase price until all the formalities have been met, and the vendor may not report income until that time. If a condition is imposed, the sale may not be final in the year of origin.[2] When the buyer gets substantially all the rights, there has been a sale.[3] A court-ordered sale may only confirm the date of an earlier sale, as where the seller reneged.[4] Where the terms of a sale are complete, the fact of nondelivery of the subject matter of the sale does not prevent the sale from taking effect if it were the intention of the parties that it was to take effect as of a certain date.[5]

Even where the entire consideration is paid, if the sale is made conditional upon the purchaser's acceptance of the property, the salc will not be deemed closed and the gain from the sale realized until the property is accepted.[6] But where the consideration is paid and the buyer immediately receives the "economic consequences of ownership," it is immaterial that he does not also immediately receive the property which he has purchased; the sale will be considered as occurring and closed at the time the consideration is paid.[7]

[1] *Lucas v. North Texas Lumber Co.,* 281 U.S. 11 (1930).
[2] *John J. Hessian Estate,* T.C. Memo., Docket #110139, entered April 29, 1943.
[3] *Brunton v. Commissioner,* 42 F.2d 81 (9th Cir., 1930).
[4] *Commissioner v. North Jersey Title Insurance Co.,* 79 F.2d 392 (3d Cir., 1935).
[5] *Stanton et al. v. Commissioner,* 98 F.2d 739 (2d Cir., 1938).
[6] *Web Press Co., Ltd.,* 3 B.T.A. 247 (1927).
[7] *Commissioner v. Sporl & Co., Inc.,* 118 F.2d 283 (5th Cir., 1941).

Disposition Is Necessary. In order to effect a sale for tax purposes, there must be an actual disposition of property. Transfer of property for cash is the cleanest example of a disposition. Reimbursement for property may not involve the necessary element of a taxable disposition. Demolition of property and subsequent compensation for its loss by an insurance company is not a sale or exchange.[8] An amount received from an insurance company as compensation for the loss of property destroyed by fire is not a sale or exchange.[9] Involuntary conversions in general are not sales.[10] Withdrawal from common trust funds is treated as a sale or exchange.[11]

Death is not a disposition; that is, gain or loss does not result when property passes from the decedent to the executor.[12] But the executor may derive taxable gain on the transfer of property in settlement of a beneficiary's claim.[13]

Nature of the Consideration. A purchase and sale transaction customarily is for money. "[T]he distinction between a 'purchase' and an 'exchange' is largely verbal. There would certainly be nothing outrageous in speaking of 'exchange' of money for goods; that is what in effect actually happens in connection with every so-called 'purchase.' Nevertheless, we ordinarily use the word 'exchange' to describe a transaction where one piece of property, usually something other than money or its equivalent, is given in return for another such piece of property." [14]

The amount realized from a sale or other disposition of property is the sum of any money received plus the fair market value of any other property received. The fair market value of property is a question of fact, but only in rare and extraordinary cases will property be considered to have no fair market value.[15]

Only cash or its equivalent constitutes income.[16] Nonnegotiable promissory notes may not be the equivalent of cash.[17] Although what is received need not be cash, there is no amount realized upon a taxable disposition unless what is received is the equivalent of cash.[18]

[8] *Helvering v. Hammel et al.,* 311 U.S. 504 (1941); *Fairbanks v. United States,* 306 U.S. 436 (1939).

[9] *Helvering v. William Flaccus Oak Leather Co.,* 313 U.S. 247 (1941).

[10] Revenue Ruling 56–372, 1956–2 CB 187.

[11] I.R.C. Section 584(e).

[12] O.D. 731, 3 CB 210.

[13] *Herbert v. Commissioner,* 139 F.2d 756 (3d Cir., 1944).

[14] *Hadley Falls Trust Co. v. United States,* 110 F.2d 887 (1st Cir., 1940).

[15] Regulations Section 1.1001–1.

[16] *John B. Atkins,* 9 B.T.A. 140 (1927).

[17] *Dudley T. Humphrey,* 32 B.T.A. 280 (1936).

[18] *Nina J. Ennis,* 17 T.C. 465 (1951).

Receipt of a consideration of unascertainable value, such as a contingent contractual right, does not result in a closed transaction, but rather in a transaction which remains open as long as payments are made under the contract. The time for reporting the gain on such a sale is deferred until after the taxpayer has recouped his cost basis.[19]

Special Types of Sale. Certain forms of sale are not treated in the ordinary manner. The principal examples are:

(1) *Installment sales.* If the proper conditions are met, the sales proceeds are spread over the years of collection. See Chapter 28.

(2) *Sales and lease-backs.* Where property is sold to an investor, who immediately leases it back to the original owner, the Internal Revenue Service may take the position that a sale actually did not take place, for the original owner is, for practical purposes, right where he started. See Chapter 28.

(3) *Long-term contracts.* Certain types of sales actually involve the construction of an asset over a period of several years. Where the conditions of the Code are met, sales proceeds may be spread. See Chapter 28.

(4) *Related parties.* Where a sale is made to a related party, or to a party under common control, the Internal Revenue Service may not be bound by the terms of the agreement. See Chapter 27.

(5) *Bargain sales.* Where an employer makes sales to an employee at a bargain, compensation generally is found to the extent that the employee gained an economic benefit from being an employee. See Chapter 11. If a corporation makes a bargain sale to a stockholder, the latter may be found to have received a dividend to the extent of the advantage that he received merely because he was a shareholder. See Chapter 8.

(6) *Lease with option to purchase.* Where the purported lessee is permitted to purchase the property, past rent payments thereby being credited against the purchase price, the entire transaction may be regarded by the Internal Revenue Service as a sale and not a lease. See Chapter 28.

(7) *Inventions.* Sales by inventors may, under proper circumstances, be treated on a capital basis. See Chapter 5.

(8) *Collapsible corporations.* Sales of assets involving a corporation that was availed of primarily for liquidation or for disposition purposes may be taxed by the Internal Revenue Service as ordinary income. See Chapter 17.

(9) *Personal residence.* The sale of a personal residence sometimes does not result in taxable gain. See Chapter 5.

[19] *Burnet v. Logan,* 283 U.S. 404 (1931).

(10) *Sales in escrow.* Such transactions present a special problem because it is recognized that such sales afford a taxpayer who wishes to report them in taxable periods other than those in which the sale really occurred an opportunity to do so. Where the evidence shows that the escrow arrangement was not motivated solely by tax reasons, orthodox rules will be applied.[20]

(11) *"Who makes the sale?"* Where a corporation owns assets which subsequently are sold by the shareholders, the question arises as to who should be taxed, the corporation or the shareholders. Ascertainment of the seller for tax purposes is discussed in Chapter 17.

(12) *Exchanges.* Inasmuch as a sale may be a transfer of property for property, cash not being required, an exchange may be a taxable disposition, the equivalent of a sale. But under certain circumstances, the asset surrendered and the one received back are deemed to be the same asset for tax purposes. In such an event, there is a tax-free exchange rather than a taxable disposition. See Chapter 17.

(13) *Wash sales.* A taxpayer cannot deduct any loss from the sale or other disposition of stock or securities if, within a period beginning 30 days before the date of the disposition and ending 30 days after that date, he has acquired (by purchase or by an exchange upon which the entire amount of gain or loss was recognized), or has entered into a contract or option so to acquire, substantially identical stock or securities.[21] But this prohibition does not apply (1) in the case of a taxpayer (not a corporation) if the sale or other disposition of securities is made in connection with the taxpayer's trade or business or (2) in the case of a corporation, a dealer in stock or securities, if the sale or other disposition is made in the ordinary course of its business as a dealer.

Where more than one loss is claimed within the taxable year from the disposition of stock or securities, the wash sales provisions will be applied to the losses in the order in which the dispositions occurred; and if the order of disposition of stock or securities disposed of at a loss on the same day cannot be determined, the stock or securities will be considered to have been disposed of in the order in which they were originally acquired.

Where the amount of stock or securities acquired within the 61-day period (that is, 30 days before and 30 days after the disposition) is less than the amount of stock or securities disposed of, then the

[20] *K. E. Merren,* 18 B.T.A. 156 (1930); *Bedell v. Commissioner,* 30 F.2d 622 (2d Cir., 1929).

[21] I.R.C. Section 1091.

particular shares or securities whose loss on disposition is not deductible will be ascertained by matching in accordance with the order of acquisition. A comparable rule is applied where the amount of stock or securities acquired within the 61-day period is not less than the amount of stock or securities disposed of.

Illustration. An individual using the calendar year basis purchased, on December 1, 100 shares of common stock of a certain corporation for $10,000. On the following December 15 he purchased an additional 100 shares of the same corporation's stock for $9,000. On January 3 following, he sold the 100 shares purchased on December 1 for $9,000. No loss from the sale is allowable as a deduction.

Illustration. An individual using the calendar year basis on September 21 purchased 100 shares of the common stock of a certain corporation for $5,000. On December 21 of the same year, he purchased 50 shares of substantially identical stock for $2,750, and on December 27 he purchased 25 additional shares for $1,125. On January 3 next, he sold for $4,000 the 100 shares purchased on September 21. There is an indicated loss of $1,000 on the sale of the 100 shares. But since, within the 61-day period, he purchased 75 shares of substantially identical stock, the loss on the sale of 75 of the shares ($3,750 minus $3,000, or $750) is not allowable as a deduction. The loss on the sale of the remaining 25 shares ($1,250 minus $1,000, or $250) is deductible. The basis of the 50 shares purchased December 21, the acquisition of which resulted in the nondeductibility of the loss ($500) sustained on 50 of the 100 shares sold on January 3, is $2,500 (the cost of 50 of the shares sold on January 3) plus $750, the difference between the purchase price ($2,750) of the 50 shares acquired on December 21 and the selling price ($2,000) of 50 of the shares sold on January 3, or $3,250. Similarly, the basis of the 25 shares purchased on December 27, the acquisition of which resulted in the nondeductibility of the loss ($250) sustained on 25 of the shares sold on January 3, is $1,250 plus $125, or $1,375.

Illustration. An individual using the calendar year basis on September 15 purchased 100 shares of the common stock of a certain corporation for $5,000. He sold these shares on the following February 1 for $4,000. On each of the four days from February 15 to 18, inclusive, he purchased 50 shares of substantially identical stock for $2,000. There is an indicated loss of $1,000 from the sale of the 100 shares on February 1, but, since within the 60-day period he purchased not less than 100 shares of substantially identical stock, the loss is not deductible. The particular shares of stock the purchase of which resulted in the nondeductibility of the loss are the first 100 shares purchased within the period, that is, the 50 shares purchased on February 15 and the 50 shares purchased on February 16. In determining the period for which the 50 shares purchased on February 15 and the 50 shares purchased on February 16 were held, there is to be included the period for which the 100 shares purchased on September 15 and sold on the following February 1 were held.

In the case of stock or securities where nondeductibility resulted from the sale or other disposition of substantially identical stock or securities, the basis will be that of the stock or securities disposed of, increased or decreased (as the case may be) by the difference (if any) between the price at which the property was acquired and the price at which the substantially identical items were disposed of.

Illustration. An individual purchased a share of common stock of a certain corporation for $100, which he sold for $80 twenty years later. Two weeks after the sale, he purchased a share of common stock of the same corporation for $90. No loss from the sale is recognized. The basis of the new share is $110; that is, the basis of the old share ($100) increased by $10, the excess of the price at which the new share was acquired ($90) over the price at which the old share was sold ($80).

Illustration. An individual purchased a share of the common stock of a certain corporation for $100; twenty years later he sold it for $80. Two weeks after the sale he purchased a share of stock of the same corporation for $70. No loss from the sale is recognized. The basis of the new share is $90; that is, the basis of the old share ($100), decreased by $10, the excess of the price at which the old share was sold ($80) over the price at which the new share was acquired ($70).

It should be noted that the wash sales provisions:

(1) Do not apply to gains. Only losses are disallowed.

(2) Do not apply to any assets other than stock or securities.

(3) Apply whether the disposition was voluntary or involuntary.

(4) Apply even if more than one calendar or taxable year is involved.

Illustration. An individual using the calendar year basis sells 100 shares of common stock of a particular corporation on December 21. He purchases 100 shares of the same stock on the following January 3. Two taxable years are affected, but the wash sales provisions nonetheless apply.

First-In, First-Out Rule. Where a taxpayer has several lots of property of identical type, he is deemed to have sold the assets in the order of acquisition.[22] In making a sale, the taxpayer has the burden of proof of establishing a deviation from this rule. This may be done by supplying the specific stock certificates or other assets that are to be sold, giving detailed instructions ("Sell the property that I acquired on June 10, 1960"), or supplying certificate numbers or other identifying characteristics.[23]

Cost of Sales

The figure of sales, less sales returns, is not gross income for tax purposes. "In a manufacturing, merchandising, or mining business, 'gross income' means the total sales, less the cost of goods sold, plus any income from investments and from incidental or outside operations or sources." [24]

[22] *Skinner v. Eaton,* 45 F.2d 568 (2d Cir., 1930).

[23] *Herbert H. Franklin,* 37 B.T.A. 471 (1938).

[24] Regulations Section 1.63–3(a).

Gross profit from sales is net sales less cost of sales. Cost of sales is obtained as follows:

Opening inventory at the same figure as the previous year's closing inventory.

Plus merchandise purchased (less any items withdrawn from business for personal use).

Plus cost of labor. This may include an allocation of executive or administrative salaries, but no compensation of a sales nature.

Plus materials and supplies. The cost of transportation in acquiring the materials ("freight in") is included here, but not the cost of getting material to customers ("freight out"). Trade discounts are deducted. When he starts business, the taxpayer elects whether to deduct cash discounts on purchases from the cost of materials purchased or whether to show such discounts as other income; thereafter this election must be adhered to consistently.

Plus other costs.

Minus closing inventory.

Depreciation and cost depletion (see Chapter 10) may be included in cost of sales if this practice is uniformly followed.[25]

For one specific purpose, gross income from a manufacturing or merchandising operation does not mean sales less cost of sales. The ordinary 3-year statute of limitations for tax return purposes (see Chapter 26) is extended to six years if gross income is understated by 25% or more. For this one purpose, gross income is not determined after the deduction of cost of sales.[26]

Inventory

In most manufacturing and merchandising operations, the most important element in cost of sales is inventory. "The inventory is not taxed. It is used to compute the cost of goods actually sold." [27]

In all cases in which the production, purchase, or sale of merchandise of any kind is an income-producing factor, merchandise on hand (including finished goods, work in process, raw materials, and supplies) at the beginning and end of the year must be taken into account.[28] In other words, the taxpayer must be on the accrual basis. If the taxpayer has inventories but does not use the accrual method, he may anticipate that the Internal Revenue Service, upon audit, will require the change to be made. Actually, this change may only be directed if the Secretary of the Treasury makes a find-

[25] Revenue Ruling 141, 1953-2 CB 101.

[26] I.R.C. Section 6501(e).

[27] *Boynton v. Pedrick,* D.C., N.Y., 1954, *aff'd on another issue,* 228 F.2d 745 (2d Cir., 1956).

[28] Regulations Section 1.446-1(a)(4)(i).

ing that the taxpayer's inventory method does not clearly reflect income.[29] But such a finding is easily made.

Failure To Keep Inventories. If inventories are not taken into account in the computation of taxable income, or if the tax return gives no information as to inventories, delinquency and negligence penalties may attach.[30] A negligence penalty may be imposed for failure to preserve inventory records and supporting data for the period during which the tax return is open for audit.[31] There is no specific requirement as to *how* inventory records are maintained. They do not have to be an integral part of the books of account; they may be separately kept on loose sheets of paper.[32]

A formula to arrive at gross profit without the use of inventories is not likely to prevail. The Secretary of the Treasury probably has more extensive data than the taxpayer as to industry experience.[33]

A taxpayer may not use an estimated inventory to his advantage when his actual figure is available at the time the return is filed.[34]

If book or perpetual inventories are kept, they should be verified and adjusted by physical count at reasonable periods.[35]

Inventories To Be Carried. The inventory should include all finished or partly finished goods and, in the case of raw materials and supplies, only those which have been acquired for sale or which will physically become a part of merchandise intended for sale. This includes containers (such as kegs, bottles, and cases), whether returnable or not, if title thereto will pass to the purchaser of the product to be sold therein. Merchandise should be included in inventory only if title to the merchandise is vested in the taxpayer. Accordingly, the seller should include in his inventory goods under contract for sale but not yet segregated and applied to the contract, as well as goods out upon consignment, but should exclude from inventory goods sold (including containers), title to which has passed to the purchaser. A purchaser should include in inventory merchandise purchased (including containers), title to which has passed to him, although this merchandise is in transit or for other reasons has not been reduced to physical possession. But he should

[29] *Glenn v. Kentucky Color and Chemical Co., Inc.,* 186 F.2d 975 (6th Cir., 1951).
[30] *Carmichael Tile Co.,* T.C. Memo., Docket #22858, entered April 21, 1950.
[31] *Bechelli v. Hofferbert,* 111 F. Supp. 631 (D.C., Md., 1953).
[32] *Commissioner v. Dwyer,* 203 F.2d 522 (2d Cir., 1953).
[33] *Lee J. Omelian et al.,* T.C. Memo., Docket ##32675–6, entered March 23, 1953.
[34] *American Pitch Pine Export Co. v. Commissioner,* 188 F.2d 721 (5th Cir., 1951).
[35] *College Point Boat Corp.,* 1 B.T.A. 534 (1924).

not include goods ordered for future delivery, where the transfer of title has not been effected as yet.

Manufacturers and processors may combine in one category raw materials and the raw material content of goods in process and finished goods. Combination of similar but not identical raw materials in single groups is permitted.[36]

If a taxpayer carries incidental materials or supplies on hand for which no record of consumption is kept or of which physical inventories at the beginning and end of the year are not taken, he may include in his expenses and deduct from gross income the total cost of these supplies and materials that were purchased during the taxable year, provided the taxable income is clearly reflected by this method.[37] No inventorying is then required.

Valuation of Inventories

Inventory must conform to two tests: (1) it must conform as nearly as possible to the best accounting practice in the trade or business and (2) it must clearly reflect the income.[38] It follows, therefore, that inventory rules cannot be uniform but must give effect to trade customs that come within the scope of the best accounting practice in the particular trade or business. In order clearly to reflect income, the inventory practice of a taxpayer should be consistent from year to year, and greater weight is to be given to consistency than to any particular method of inventorying or basis of valuation, so long as the method or basis used is substantially in accord with the Code.

The bases of valuation most commonly used by business concerns are (1) cost and (2) cost or market, whichever is lower. Other methods are market, the retail method, and Lifo. A special technique is available for defective or substandard goods. The following methods are not acceptable:

(1) Deducting from the inventory a reserve for price changes, or an estimated depreciation in the value thereof.

(2) Taking work in process, or other parts of the inventory, at a nominal price or at less than its proper value.

(3) Omitting portions of the stock on hand.

(4) Using a constant price or nominal value for a so-called normal quantity of materials or goods in stock.

(5) Including stock in transit, shipped either to or from the taxpayer, the title to which is not vested in the taxpayer.

[36] T.D. 5407, 1944 CB 83.
[37] Regulations Section 1.162–3.
[38] I.R.C. Section 471.

Cost. Cost means, in the case of merchandise on hand at the beginning of the taxable year, the inventory price. Where merchandise was purchased since the beginning of the taxable year, cost is the invoice price less trade or other discounts (except cash discounts approximating a fair interest rate, which may consistently be deducted or not at the taxpayer's option); "freight-in" should be included. Where merchandise was produced by the taxpayer since the beginning of the taxable year, cost means (1) the cost of raw materials and supplies entering into or consumed in connection with the product, (2) expenditures for direct labor, (3) indirect expenses incident to and necessary for the production of the particular article, including in such indirect expenses a reasonable proportion of management expenses, but not including any cost of selling or return on capital whether by way of interest or profit.

In any industry where the usual rules for computation of cost of production are inapplicable, costs may be approximated upon a basis that is reasonable and is in conformity to established practice in the particular trade or industry. This includes farmers and raisers of livestock; miners and manufacturers who by a single process or uniform series of processes derive a product of two or more kinds, sizes, or grades, the unit cost of which is substantially alike; and retail merchants.

Cost or Market, Whichever Is Lower. Market means the current bid price prevailing at the date of the inventory for the particular merchandise in the volume in which usually purchased by the taxpayer. It is applicable in the cases of (1) goods purchased and on hand, and (2) basic elements of cost (materials, labor, and burden) in goods in process of manufacture and in finished goods on hand. This does not include goods on hand or in process of manufacture for delivery upon firm sales contracts (that is, those not legally subject to cancellation by either party) at fixed prices entered into before the date of the inventory, under which the taxpayer is protected against actual loss. Such goods must be inventoried at cost.

If no market exists, or if quotations are nominal, because of inactive market conditions, the taxpayer must use such evidence of a fair market price at the date or dates nearest the inventory as may be available, such as specific purchases or sales by the taxpayer or others in reasonable volume that were made in good faith, or compensation paid for cancellation of contracts for purchase commitments.

Where the inventory is valued upon the basis of cost or market, whichever is lower, the market value of each article on hand at the inventory date will be compared with the cost of the article, and the lower of these values will be taken as the inventory value of the article.

Illustration. If at the end of a taxable year the following items were on hand, the value of the closing inventory would be $600.

Items	Cost	Market	Whichever Is Lower
Stock #1	$300	$500	$300
Stock #2	200	100	100
Stock #3	450	200	200
Totals	$950	$800	$600

Expert testimony has been accepted as evidence of market.[39]

Market. Market may be used as the basis of inventory valuation in the case of certain dealers in securities in commodities listed on an exchange, and farmers.

A dealer in securities who in his books of account regularly inventories unsold securities on hand at cost, at the lower of cost or market, or at market may make his return upon the basis upon which his accounts are kept, provided that a description of the method employed accompanies the tax return. Additional requirements are that all the securities be inventoried by the same method and that the method be consistently followed in subsequent years. For this purpose, a dealer in securities is a merchant of securities, whether an individual, partnership, or corporation, with an established place of business, regularly engaged in the purchase of securities and their resale to customers. If this business is simply a branch of the activities carried on by this person, the securities inventories under this rule may include only those held for purposes of resale and not for investment.

Dealers in cotton, grain, and other commodities dealt in on organized exchanges may use the market method.[40]

For the market method of inventory as applied to farmers, see Chapter 15.

Retail Method. Retail merchants who employ what is known as the retail method of pricing inventories may make their tax returns upon that basis, provided that the use of this method is indicated upon the return, that accurate records are kept, and that this method is consistently followed.

This method involves taking from the price tags of the merchandise in stock on the day of the closing inventory a total *for each department,* which, of course, represents the retail price on that day

[39] *Bloom Brothers, Inc.,* 10 B.T.A. 710 (1927).
[40] I.T. 3123, 1937-2 CB 114.

of the goods then on hand. From this there is deducted the department's average mark-on for the year, and the resulting figure, representing a theoretical conversion back to the cost of the goods on the shelves, is the closing inventory of the department in question.

The mark-on or difference between the cost to the store and its selling price is obtained by recourse to the original invoices. During the year, as goods are received, the invoices are extended by a notation of the retail price at which such goods are to be sold. These invoices form the records from which the mark-up for the year is computed by comparing the total of the costs they show with the total retail prices extended on them.

The dollar amount of the inventory so determined is then used like any other in computing the cost of goods sold, gross merchandising profit, and ultimate net income of the store. The immediately apparent consequences of the retail method are that the goods in a single department are treated for inventory purposes as being entirely fungible, even though in fact they may, and generally do, differ considerably as to type, quality, and price.

"The underlying principle of the retail inventory method is the determination of inventory value by applying the complement of the percentage of mark-up to the retail value of the inventory." [41]

Mark-downs are permitted if the merchandise actually was offered for sale at these prices.

Illustration. On the last day of the taxable year, the records disclose the following:

Item	Cost	Retail Value
Opening inventory	$52,000	$60,000
Purchases during year	53,000	78,500
Sales		98,000
Mark-ups		2,000
Mark-downs		500

Using the retail method, closing inventory is determined as follows:

Item		Cost	Retail Value
Opening inventory		$ 52,000	$ 60,000
Add: Purchases during year		53,000	
Mark-ups	$2,000		
Mark-downs	500		1,500
Totals (Mark-up percentage, 25%)		105,000	$140,000
Less: Sales			98,000
Closing inventory at retail			$ 42,000
Less: Mark-up percentage (25%)			10,500
Closing inventory at cost			$ 31,500

In this illustration, the mark-up is equal to the difference ($35,000) between the cost ($105,000) and the retail value ($140,000), which includes inventory at sales

[41] *Desmonds, Inc.*, 15 B.T.A. 738 (1928).

prices and purchases at sales prices. The total mark-up, divided by the total retail value, gives the percentage (25%) of purchase mark-up.

The retail method may be used in conjunction with the last-in, first-out method (see below), as well as in conjunction with the first-in, first-out and specific identification methods.

Valuation *at retail* is not a recognized method of inventory valuation.[42]

Lifo. Lifo is an anagram, formed from the words *last-in, first-out* inventories. It is thus an exception to the general rule that where like assets may be mingled, the one first acquired is deemed to be the one first sold in the absence of evidence to the contrary (the "Fifo" rule).

The theory of Lifo is that a stipulated amount of inventory must be carried in order to conduct the business. This inventory is more in the nature of a fixed asset than a current asset. As long as the inventory is maintained intact (that is, as long as the stipulated number of units is on hand), any fluctuations in the value of this fixed or basic inventory are unrealized profit or unsustained loss that should not be reflected in taxable income. While this basic inventory is maintained, any additional purchases are matched with sales. Thus purchases and sales are considered to be made at approximately the same time. Thus, gross profit on sales will tend to be steady. Lifo, in effect, levels years of rising and falling prices. It reduces gains in a rising or high market and eliminates from taxable income the profits realized in this market to the extent that these profits are reinvested in a more expensive inventory. Advocates of this system claim that they wish to derive gain or loss from normal manufacturing or selling operations, rather than from market fluctuations. Opponents of the system maintain that it is customary to calculate gain or loss by the difference between cost and realization, and that cost should not be the football of circumstances beyond the control of the management. Furthermore, the Lifo method requires considerable additional paperwork.

On a rising market, profits are kept down by the use of higher costs. On a falling market, low costs may produce taxable income where otherwise a deficit would result. The method has the greatest appeal to taxpayers whose inventory value is large compared with other factors, where inventory values are subject to wide fluctuations, and where inventory turnover is relatively slow (that is, cost otherwise is not reflective of the conditions prevailing when the inventories are sold).

[42] Revenue Ruling 55–285, 1955–1 CB 69.

The Lifo method cannot be imposed upon a taxpayer by the Secretary of the Treasury. It is entirely optional. The method is not dependent upon the character of the business in which the taxpayer is engaged, or upon the identity or want of identity through commingling of any of the goods on hand, and may be adopted by the taxpayer as of the close of any taxable year.[43]

Under Lifo, the taxpayer is permitted to treat those goods remaining on hand at the close of the taxable year as being (1) those included in the opening inventory of the taxable year, in the order of acquisition and to the extent thereof, and (2) those acquired during the taxable year.

If the Lifo inventory method is used by a taxpayer who regularly and consistently (in a manner similar to hedging on a futures market) matches purchases with sales, then firm purchases and sales contracts entered into at fixed prices on or before the date of the inventory may be included in purchases or sales, as the case may be, for the purpose of determining the cost of goods sold and the resulting profit, if this is consistently done.

A manufacturer or processor who has adopted the Lifo method for a class of goods may elect to have this method apply to the raw materials only (including those in goods in process and in finished goods) expressed in terms of appropriate units. If this method is adopted, the adjustments are confined to costs of the raw material in the inventory and the cost of the raw material in goods in process and in finished goods produced by him and reflected in the inventory.

Illustration. Opening inventory had 10 units of raw material, 10 units of goods in process, and 10 units of finished goods. Raw material cost was 6 cents a unit, the processing cost 2 cents a unit, and overhead cost 1 cent a unit. It is assumed that the entire amount of goods in process was 50% processed.

	Opening Inventory		
	Raw Material	Goods in Process	Finished Goods
Raw material	$0.60	$0.60	$0.60
Processing cost		.10	.20
Overhead		.05	.10
Total	$0.60	$0.75	$0.90

In the closing inventory there are 20 units of raw material, 6 units of goods in process, and 8 units of finished goods. Costs were: Raw material 10 cents, processing 4 cents, and overhead 1 cent.

[43] I.R.C. Section 472.

	Closing Inventory		
	Raw Material	Goods in Process	Finished Goods
Raw material	$2.00	$0.60	$0.80
Processing cost		.12	.32
Overhead		.03	.08
Total	$2.00	$0.75	$1.20

There were 30 units of raw material in the opening inventory and 34 units in the closing inventory. The adjustments to the closing inventory would be as follows:

	Closing Inventory as Adjusted		
	Raw Material	Goods in Process	Finished Goods
Raw material:			
20 at 6 cents	$1.20		
6 at 6 cents		$0.36	
4 at 6 cents			$.024
4 at 10 cents			.40
Processing costs		.12	.32
Overhead		.03	.08
Total	$1.20	$0.51	$1.04

The only adjustment to the closing inventory is the cost of the raw material; the processing costs and overhead cost are not changed.

Illustration. Assume that the opening inventory had 5 units of raw material, 10 units of goods in process, and 20 units of finished goods, with the same prices as in the previous illustration. Assume further that the closing inventory had 20 units of raw material, 20 units of goods in process, and 10 units of finished goods, with raw material costs as in the closing inventory in the preceding illustration. The adjusted closing inventory would be as follows insofar as the raw material is concerned:

Raw material, 20 at 6 cents	$1.20
Goods in process:	
15 at 6 cents	.90
5 at 10 cents	.50
Finished goods:	
None at 6 cents	0
10 at 10 cents	1.00

The 20 units of raw material in the raw state plus 15 units of raw material in goods in process make up the 35 units of raw material that were contained in the opening inventory.

For this purpose, raw material in the opening inventory must be compared with similar raw material in the closing inventory. There may be several types of raw materials, depending upon the character, quality, or price, and each type of raw material in the opening inventory must be compared with a similar type in the closing inventory. For example, in the cotton textile industry, there may be different raw materials depending upon market differences in length of staple, in color, or in grade of the cotton. But where different staple lengths or grades of cotton are being used at different times in the same mill to produce the same class of goods, these differences would not necessarily require the classification into different raw materials. Where the finished product contains two or more different raw materials as in the case of cotton and rayon mixtures, each raw material is treated separately and adjustments made accordingly.

Upon written notice addressed to the Commissioner of Internal Revenue, Attention T:R, Washington 25, D.C., a taxpayer who previously adopted the Lifo method may limit the election to the raw material. The election may also be limited to that phase in the manufacturing process where a product is produced that is recognized generally as a salable product as, for example, in the textile industry, where one phase of the process is the production of yarn. The election may be limited to that portion of the process when yarn is produced. The election may also apply to any one raw material, when two or more raw materials enter into the composition of the finished product; for example, in the case of cotton and rayon yarn, the taxpayer may elect to inventory the cotton only.

If a taxpayer using the retail method of pricing inventories elects to use in connection therewith the Lifo method, the apparent cost of the closing inventory must be adjusted to the extent of price changes therein taking place after the close of the preceding taxable year. The amount of any apparent inventory increase or decrease to be eliminated in this adjustment will be determined by reference to acceptable price indices, such as those prepared by the United States Bureau of Labor Statistics. If a taxpayer uses consistently the so-called dollar-value method of pricing inventories, or any other method of computation that the Commissioner accepts as reasonably acceptable, the opening and closing inventories will be determined "by the use of the appropriate adaptation." [44]

The adoption and use of the Lifo method is subject to the following requirements:

(1) The taxpayer must file an application on Form 970, indicating the goods to which it is to be applied.

(2) The inventory must be taken at cost regardless of market value.

(3) Goods of the specified type in the opening inventory of the taxable year for which the method is first used will be considered as having been acquired at the same time and at a unit cost equal to the actual cost of the aggregate divided by the number of units on hand. The actual cost of the aggregate will be determined in

[44] Regulations Section 1.472–1(l).

accordance with the inventory method employed by the taxpayer under the regulations applicable to the prior taxable year with the exception that restoration will be made of any write-down to market values resulting from the pricing of former inventories.

(4) Goods of the specified type on hand as of the close of the taxable year in excess of what were on hand as of the beginning of the year will be included in the closing inventory, regardless of identification with specific invoices and regardless of specific cost accounting records at costs determined under (A) or (B), below, dependent upon the character of the transactions in which the taxpayer is engaged.

(A) In the case of a taxpayer engaged in the purchase and sale of merchandise (such as a retail grocer or druggist) or engaged in the initial production of merchandise and its sale without processing (such as a miner selling his ore output without smelting or refining), his costs will be determined:

(i) By reference to the actual cost of the goods most recently purchased or produced;

(ii) By reference to the actual cost of the goods purchased or produced during the taxable year in order of acquisition;

(iii) By application of an average unit cost equal to the aggregate cost of all of the goods purchased or produced throughout the taxable year divided by the total number of units so purchased or produced, the goods reflected in the inventory increase being considered for this purpose as having been acquired all at the same time; or

(iv) Pursuant to any other proper method which, in the opinion of the Commissioner, clearly reflects income.

Whichever of these methods of valuing the inventory increase is adopted must be followed consistently as long as the Lifo method is used by the taxpayer.

Illustration. A taxpayer adopts the Lifo inventory method for the taxable year 1960 with an opening inventory of 10 units at 10 cents per unit. In 1960, he makes purchases of 10 units as follows:

January	1 at	$0.11, or	$0.11
April	2 at	.12, or	.24
July	3 at	.13, or	.39
October	4 at	.14, or	.56
	10		$1.30

The 1960 closing inventory is 15 units. This closing inventory, depending upon the method of valuing inventory increases which is employed by the taxpayer, will be computed as shown on the following page.

(i) Most recent purchases—

	10 at $0.10	$1.00
	4 at .14 (October)	.56
	1 at .13 (July)	.13
Totals	15	$1.69

or

(ii) In order of acquisition—

	10 at $0.10	$1.00
	1 at .11 (January)	.11
	2 at .12 (April)	.24
	2 at .13 (July)	.26
Totals	15	$1.61

or

(iii) At an annual average—

	10 at $0.10	$1.00
	5 at .13 (130/10)	.65
Totals	15	$1.65

Illustration. Suppose that the taxpayer's closing inventory for 1961, the year following that involved in the preceding illustration, reflects an inventory decrease for the year, and not an increase; suppose that there is, accordingly, a 1961 closing inventory of 13 units. Inasmuch as the decreased closing inventory will be determined wholly by reference to the 15 units reflected in the opening inventory for the year, and will be taken "in the order of acquisition" and inasmuch as the character of the taxpayer's opening inventory for 1961 will be dependent upon its method of valuing its 5-unit inventory increase for 1961, the closing inventory for 1961 will be computed as follows:

(i) In case the increase for 1960 was taken by reference to the most recent purchases—

	10 at $0.10 (from 1959)	$1.00
	1 at .13 (July, 1960)	.13
	2 at .14 (October, 1960)	.28
Totals	13	$1.41

or

(ii) In case the increase for 1960 was taken in the order of acquisition—

	10 at $0.10 (from 1959)	$1.00
	1 at .11 (January, 1960)	.11
	2 at .12 (April, 1960)	.24
Totals	13	$1.35

or

(iii) In case the increase for 1960 was taken on the basis of an average—

	10 at $0.10 (from 1959)	$1.00
	3 at .13 (from 1960)	.39
Totals	13	$1.39

(B) In the case of a taxpayer engaged in manufacturing, fabricating, processing, or otherwise producing merchandise, costs will be determined:

(i) In the case of raw materials purchased or initially produced by the taxpayer, in the manner elected by the taxpayer under (A), above, to the same extent as if he were engaged in purchase and sales transactions; and

(ii) In the case of goods in process, regardless of the stage to which the manufacture, fabricating, or processing may have advanced, and in the case of finished goods, pursuant to any proper method which, in the opinion of the Commissioner, clearly reflects income.

To the satisfaction of the Commissioner, the taxpayer must establish that he, in ascertaining the income, profit, or loss for the taxable year for which the Lifo method is first used or for any subsequent year, the Lifo method is used for statement, credit, and shareholder purposes. "The taxpayer's use of market value in lieu of cost or his issuance of reports or credit statements covering a period of operations less than the whole of the taxable year is not considered at variance with this requirement."[45]

For the year in which Lifo first is used, the previous year's closing inventory must be calculated at cost.

To adopt the Lifo method, the taxpayer must file his election on Form 970 with his income tax return for the first year to be covered. All necessary facts and figures must be supplied to show the basis of the computation. "In the case of a manufacturer, this analysis shall show in detail the manner in which costs are computed with respect to raw materials, goods in process, and finished goods, segregating the products (whether in process or finished goods) into natural groups on the basis of either (1) similarity in factory processes through which they pass, or (2) similarity of raw materials used, or (3) similarity in style, shape, or use of finished products. Each group of products shall be clearly described."[46]

The Commissioner decides whether approval of the method will be granted. Where the taxpayer is engaged in more than one trade or business, the Commissioner may require that if Lifo is used in one trade or business, it must be used in the others.

A taxpayer may not change to the Lifo method unless, at the time he files his application for adoption of the system, he agrees to those adjustments incident to the change as may be deemed necessary by the Internal Revenue Service properly to reflect taxable income.

Once adopted, the method must be used, unless (1) the Commissioner approves a change to a different method or (2) the Com-

[45] Regulations Section 1.472–2(e).

[46] Regulations Section 1.472–3(a).

missioner determines that the taxpayer has used a different method for other report purposes.

An election to use Lifo is irrevocable, unless the Commissioner consents to a change, or orders it.

If a change from the Lifo method is made, the inventory for the year of the change and for each succeeding year will be taken (1) in conformity with the method used by the taxpayer for inventories other than those on the Lifo basis; or (2) if Lifo is used on all inventories, then under the method used prior to the adoption of Lifo; or (3) if all inventories were under the Lifo method and no inventories ever had been carried under any other method, then under any system that the taxpayer adopts and the Commissioner approves; or (4) in conformity with any method to which the taxpayer changes, with the Commissioner's approval.

Defective or Substandard Goods. Defective or substandard goods may be valued at estimated sales price less estimated cost of disposition. Used motorcar inventories, for example, could be valued by adding to the trade-in allowance the cost of reconditioning, less the cost of selling.[47]

This treatment is available for any goods in inventory which are unsalable at normal prices or unsalable in the normal way because of damage, imperfections, shop wear, changes of style, odd or broken lots, or other similar causes, including secondhand goods taken as trade-ins. The method may be used regardless of whether the regular inventory basis is cost or the lower of cost or market.

Write-downs and Write-offs

If an inventory is carried at market, or at the lower of cost or market, a write-down is possible whenever the arithmetic of the situation justifies this action. As mentioned in the second preceding paragraph, write-downs may be possible for defective or substandard goods. But inventories may not be written down on an over-all percentage basis, as, for example, in the case of merchandise allegedly shopworn.[48] Nor could inventory be written down upon the basis of an evaluation of an employee that stock items could all be categorized as "good," "fair," or "poor."[49]

Loss resulting from inventory shortage is deductible from gross income.[50]

[47] *Pierce-Arrow Motor Co. v. United States,* 11 F. Supp. 161 (Ct. Cl., 1935).
[48] *Gem Jewelry Co., Inc.,* T.C. Memo., Docket #8921, entered January 13, 1947.
[49] *John L. Asche, Inc. v. Commissioner,* 214 F.2d 13 (5th Cir., 1954).
[50] *Lang Broom Co.,* 9 B.T.A. 39 (1927).

General

If the Internal Revenue Service makes an adjustment to a taxpayer's closing inventory, a corresponding adjustment must be made in opening inventory.[51]

Where stock is acquired in order to get inventories, any loss on the sale of the stock may be considered to be part of the cost of the inventories.[52]

Under certain circumstances, a corporation derives taxable income from the distribution to shareholders of inventories that were valued under the Lifo method.[53] Corporate earnings and profits may be increased as the result of an inventory distribution.[54] Both of these subjects will be discussed in Chapter 17.

Inventory treatment afforded to a successor corporation after a tax-free reorganization depends upon the nature of the reorganization.[55] See Chapter 14.

A request to change an inventory method from cost to the lower of cost or market "should be carefully scrutinized and the request refused if it appears that the principal reason therefor is to reduce the tax payable . . ." [56]

Supplementary Material

A. Suggested Reading.

John C. Bruton, "'Closings' in Sales Transactions," *TAXES—The Tax Magazine,* February, 1954, Vol. XXXII, #2, p. 110.

Robert S. Holzman, "How To Buy and Sell Real Estate, Business Property, and Business Assets," *Proceedings of the New York University Sixth Annual Institute on Federal Taxation* (Albany: Matthew Bender & Co., Inc., 1948), p. 395.

T. Hartley Pollock, "General Outline of Tax Considerations in Sales Decisions," *The Encyclopedia of Tax Practices* (Englewood Cliffs, N.J.: Prentice-Hall, Inc., 1956), p. 919.

William A. Schan, "Tax Effects of Different Methods of Reporting Sales: Accrual, Instalment, Deferred," *Proceedings of the New York University Seventeenth Annual Institute on Federal Taxation* (Albany: Matthew Bender & Co., Inc., 1959), p. 241.

David Schaff, "When Is a Lease a Sale for Tax Purposes?" *The Controller,* February, 1959, Vol. XXVII, #2, p. 70.

[51] *Eureka Fire Brick Works,* T.C. Memo., Docket #7641, entered December 26, 1946.

[52] *Western Wine and Liquor Co.,* 18 T.C. 1090 (1952).

[53] I.R.C. Section 311(b).

[54] I.R.C. Section 312(b).

[55] I.R.C. Section 381(c)(5).

[56] A.R.M. 38, 2 C.B. 54.

J. Keith Butters and Powell Niland, *Effects of Taxation—Inventory Accounting and Policies* (Boston: Harvard University, Graduate School of Business Administration, Division of Research, 1949).

Raymond A. Hoffman, "Current Developments in the Use of LIFO," *Proceedings of the New York University Sixteenth Annual Institute on Federal Taxation* (Albany: Matthew Bender & Co., Inc., 1958), p. 599.

B. Leading Cases.

When is a sale? *Lucas v. North Texas Lumber Co.*, 281 U.S. 11 (1930).

Delayed closing. *United States Industrial Alcohol Company (West Virginia) v. Helvering*, 137 F.2d 511 (2d Cir., 1943).

Unconditional liability. *Fordyce v. Helvering*, 76 F.2d 431 (App. D.C., 1935).

C. Questions.

1. An individual purchased property for $10,000. It was worth $12,000 upon his death two years later. What taxable gain or loss was recognized upon the executor's taking possession of the decedent's property?
2. A manufacturer sent a dealer certain goods on consignment. Should they be included in the dealer's inventory if physically on his premises?
3. A dealer had certain merchandise that was destroyed by fire twenty days before the end of the taxable year. If settlement had not been made as yet with the insurance company, are the destroyed items still to be listed in the closing inventory?
4. In order to get a favorable location at a world's fair, a concessionaire was obliged to purchase a certain amount of the fair's bonds. Could he consider this as part of his cost of making sales at the fair?
5. It is stated in the text that the Lifo method of inventory requires considerable additional paperwork. Why is this?
6. By reason of highly confidential reports of a revolution that was brewing, an exporter believed that merchandise in that country would have to be disposed of at prices below market, which was the inventory basis used. Is an inventory write-down permitted under the circumstances?
7. Are import duties to be included in an importer's inventory of his foreign merchandise stock in this country?
8. A manufacturer of chrome widgets used the lower of cost or market method. As of a particular date, cost was $1.25 each, while the regular market price was $1.31. A bank, however, sold a lot of similar widgets that had been collateral for an unpaid loan, and $1.17 was the price realized at public auction. How should the manufacturer value his inventory?
9. An individual owned three lots of 100 shares each of a company that he had purchased at various times at these prices, in order of time of acquisition: $1,000, $2,000, $3,000. He sold 100 shares for $2,500. (a) What was his recognized gain or loss? (b) Would the answer be different if he had given his broker, along with the sale order, the stock certificate that had cost $2,000?
10. A retail dealer had purchased inventory too heavily, but he was not allowed to return any stock to his manufacturers. He decided to write down his excessive inventory to estimated sales price at bargain

figures (below his cost) less estimated cost of disposition. Is this permitted for tax purposes?

11. Alpha sold property that had cost him $8,000 to Beta for $12,000. It was agreed that no cash would pass but that Beta would promise to give Alpha a $1,000 cash discount on every truck that Alpha bought from Beta in the next ten years. There would be no price adjustment regardless of how many trucks were bought in that period. What was Alpha's gain or loss?
12. May a taxpayer use the Lifo method for part of his inventory and the lower of cost or market for the remainder?
13. If a taxpayer owns inventories but reports on the cash basis, what consequences, other than specific penalties, may result?
14. An individual on the calendar year basis sold stock on December 17 for a loss of $1,000. He purchased substantially the same stock on the following January 12 for $12,000. (a) Will the loss be recognized in either year? (b) What is the basis of the stock he purchased on January 12?
15. A manufacturer of cowboy supplies followed the practice of carrying inventories of raw materials and inventories of finished products. Goods in process were not inventoried, as the manufacturing process was long and complicated, and physical count of goods in process would be difficult to take. Is this acceptable to the Internal Revenue Service?
16. Must the entire inventory of a taxpayer be carried on the same basis?
17. A dealer on the accrual basis made sales to a buyer whose credit status was questionable. Must the sales be reflected in income in view of the uncertainty that there ever will be a realization?
18. A taxpayer adopted the Lifo method for the taxable year with an opening inventory of 10 units at 10¢ per unit. Purchases of an additional 10 units were made as follows:

January	1 at 11¢,	or 11¢
April	2 at 12¢,	or 24¢
July	3 at 13¢,	or 39¢
October	4 at 14¢,	or 56¢
Totals	10	$1.30

The closing inventory was 15 units. How is the closing inventory valued under the following alternatives: (a) most recent purchases, (b) in order of acquisition, (c) at an annual average?

8

DIVIDENDS

A dividend is a distribution to shareholders of corporate earnings that have been earned since the effective date of the present Federal income tax system, February 28, 1913. In general, the distribution must be of the actual earnings of the payor. But under appropriate circumstances, earnings may be *implied* for this purpose. The earnings need not even be those of the payor, under certain reorganization conditions. All distributions are not dividends. There is, however, a strong presumption that what a shareholder receives from a corporation *is* a dividend, unless he can prove to the contrary.

A dividend for income tax purposes is any distribution of cash or other property made by a domestic or foreign corporation to its shareholders out of either (1) earnings and profits accumulated since February 28, 1913 or (2) earnings and profits of the taxable year computed without regard to the amount of earnings and profits (whether of that year or accumulated since February 28, 1913) at the time the distribution was made.[1] If a corporation has earnings in excess of cash distributions in a taxable year, the distributions may be dividends, even though, because of an opening deficit, there would be a deficit at the close of the year regardless of whether or not distributions were made in the taxable year.[2]

If a shareholder is not a corporation, the amount of any distribution will be the amount of money received plus the fair market value of the other property received. If the shareholder is a corporation, the amount of any distribution is the amount of the money received plus the lesser of (1) the fair market value of the other property received or (2) the adjusted basis (in the hands of the distributing corporation immediately before the distribution) of the other property received. The latter amount is increased by the amount of gain to the distributing corporation under either of two conditions:

(1) If a corporation inventorying goods under the Lifo method (see Chapter 7) distributes inventories, there will be gain to the

[1] I.R.C. Section 316.
[2] *Stanley M. Waldheim et al.*, 25 T.C. 839 (1956).

extent that (A), the inventory valuation other than under Lifo, exceeds (B), the valuation under the Lifo method. If a corporation uses the retail method, that valuation will be used for (A); otherwise, the lower of cost or market method will be used.

(2) If a corporation distributes to its shareholders property which is subject to a liability, or the shareholders assume a corporate liability in connection with the distribution, gain will be recognized to the distributing corporation in an amount equal to the excess of the liability over the adjusted basis as if the property had been sold at the time of the distribution.[3]

Illustration. If property which is a capital asset having an adjusted basis to the distributing corporation of $100 and a fair market value of $1,000 (but subject to a liability of $900) is distributed to a shareholder, the distribution is taxable to the corporation (as long- or short-term capital gain, as the case may be) to the extent of the excess of the liability ($900) over the adjusted basis ($100) or $800. If the property subject to a liability were not a capital asset in the hands of the distributing corporation, the gain would be taxable as ordinary income.

Except for these two circumstances, a corporation does not derive gain from the distribution to its shareholders of inventory.

Where a corporation distributes property to its shareholders on or after June 22, 1954, the amount of the distribution which is a dividend to them may not exceed the earnings and profits of the distributing corporation.[4]

Illustration. Two individuals each own one-half of the stock of a certain corporation which has earnings and profits of $10,000. The corporation distributes the property having a basis of $6,000 and a fair market value of $16,000 to its shareholders, each shareholder receiving property with a basis of $3,000 and with a fair market value of $8,000. The amount taxable to each shareholder as a dividend is $5,000.

That portion of a distribution which is a dividend is to be included in the recipient's gross income; that is, a distribution of corporate earnings since February 28, 1913. That portion of the distribution which is not a dividend will first be applied against the adjusted basis of the stock as a reduction. To the extent that the portion of the distribution which is not a dividend exceeds the adjusted basis of the stock, this portion will be treated as gain from the sale or exchange of property. That portion of the distribution which exceeds the adjusted basis of the stock but which is out of increase in value accrued before March 1, 1913, will be exempt from tax.[5]

[3] I.R.C. Section 311(b), (c).
[4] Regulations Section 1.316–1(a)(2).
[5] I.R.C. Section 301(c).

Every corporate distribution is deemed to be made out of earnings and profits to the extent thereof and from the most recently accumulated earnings and profits. In determining the source of a distribution, consideration should be given first to the earnings and profits of the taxable year; second, to the earnings and profits accumulated since February 28, 1913, only in the case where, and to the extent that, the distributions made during the taxable year are not regarded as out of the earnings and profits of that year; third, to the earnings and profits accumulated before March 1, 1913, only after all the earnings and profits of the taxable year have been distributed; and fourth, to sources other than earnings and profits only after the earnings and profits have been distributed.[6]

If the earnings and profits of the taxable year (computed as of the close of the year without diminution by reason of any distributions made during the year and without regard to the amount of the earnings and profits at the time of the distribution) are sufficient in amount to cover all the distributions made during that year, then each distribution is a taxable dividend. If the distributions made during the taxable year consist only of money and exceed the earnings and profits of that year, then that proportion of each distribution which the total of the earnings and profits of the year bears to the total distributions made during the year will be regarded as out of the earnings and profits of that year. The portion of each distribution which is not regarded as out of earnings and profits of the taxable year will be considered as a taxable dividend to the extent of the earnings and profits accumulated since February 28, 1913, and available on the date of the distribution. In any case in which it is necessary to determine the amount of earnings and profits accumulated since February 28, 1913, and the actual earnings and profits to the date of a distribution within any taxable year (whether beginning before January 1, 1936, or, in the case of an operating deficit, on or after that date) cannot be shown, the earnings and profits for the year (or accounting period, if less than a year) in which the distribution was made will be prorated to the date of the distribution, not counting the date on which the distribution was made.

Illustration. At the beginning of a taxable year, a corporation had $12,000 in earnings and profits accumulated since February 28, 1913. Its earnings and profits for that year amounted to $30,000. During the year it made quarterly cash distributions of $15,000 each. Of each of the four distributions made, $7,500 (that portion of $15,000 which the amount of $30,000, the total earnings and profits of the taxable year, bears to $60,000, the total distributions made during

[6] Regulations Section 1.316–2(a).

the year) was paid out of the earnings and profits of the taxable year; and of the first and second distributions, $7,500 and $4,500, respectively, were paid out of the earnings and profits accumulated after February 28, 1913, and before the taxable year, as follows:

DISTRIBUTIONS DURING TAXABLE YEAR

Date	Amount	Portion Out of Earnings and Profits of Taxable Year	Portion Out of Earnings Accumulated Since Feb. 28, 1913, and Before the Taxable Year	Taxable Amount of Each Distribution
March 10	$15,000	$7,500	$7,500	$15,000
June 10	15,000	7,500	4,500	12,000
September 10	15,000	7,500		7,500
December 10	15,000	7,500		7,500
Total amount taxable as dividends......................				$42,000

Earnings of Another. Where a corporation acquires the earnings and profits of another corporation in a tax-free reorganization, the earnings of the acquired company retain their character as *earnings* and hence any distribution from them is a taxable dividend.[7] It is immaterial what the earnings are called or to what account they have been reclassified. It does not matter who received the dividends; they are includible in gross income.[8] But even where there is a tax-free reorganization, if new capital and new stockholders are introduced, the prereorganization earnings of the predecessor will not be taken into account in appraising the nature of the successor's subsequent distributions.[9]

The rule does not apply as to deficits. Losses of acquired corporations may not be used to reduce the earnings and profits of a successor corporation in reorganization in ascertaining the amount of earnings available for distribution as taxable dividends.[10]

A parent corporation could not reduce its accumulated earnings available for distribution by losses of a subsidiary, despite an oral agreement between the officers of the corporations that provided for the transfer of the subsidiary's profits and losses to the parent during a period of expansion. Although the parent actually paid the subsidiary's losses, "this operated to increase its capital investment, and it may not be charged against its profits or earnings." [11]

What Are Dividends? A dividend is a distribution to a shareholder in his capacity as such. Thus a distribution of property to a shareholder who is a creditor of the corporation in satisfaction of

[7] *Commissioner v. Sansome,* 60 F.2d 951 (2d Cir., 1932).
[8] *Putnam v. United States,* 149 F.2d 721 (1st Cir., 1945).
[9] *Campbell v. United States,* 144 F.2d 177 (3d Cir., 1944).
[10] *Commissioner v. Phipps,* 336 U.S. 410 (1949).
[11] *Freedman et al. v. United States,* 157 F. Supp. 613 (D.C., Okla., 1958).

his claim against the corporation would not be covered. So-called dividends paid by insurance companies to their policyholders are only an adjustment of the cost.[12] A municipality may issue what is called corporate stock; but payments for the use of the investor's money are not dividends in the tax sense; they are interest. Some banks or savings and loan associations call their payments to depositors dividends, but actually interest is involved.

Distributions from organizations which are taxed as corporations are treated as corporate dividends.[13]

What Are Earnings and Profits? "It is clear that the Congress intended the income tax laws 'to tax earnings and profits less expenses and losses.' *Higgins v. Smith,* 308 U.S. 473, 477 (1940), carrying out a broad basic policy of taxing 'net, not . . . gross, income . . .' *McDonald v. Commissioner,* 323 U.S. 57, 66–67." [14]

In determining the amount of earnings and profits, due consideration must be given to the facts; and while mere bookkeeping entries increasing or decreasing surplus will not be conclusive, the amount of the earnings and profits in any case will be dependent upon the method of accounting properly employed in computing taxable income. Among the items entering into the computation are all income exempted by statute.[15] A reduction is permitted for any fraud penalties payable, even though these are not deductible in arriving at taxable income.[16]

The computation of earnings and profits for a taxable year begins with taxable income. This is reduced by such items as the following: Federal income taxes paid or accrued, premiums on life insurance carried on officer or employee, charitable contributions in excess of those permitted by statute, and special assessments that are not deductible. The computation next is increased by such items as these: the corporate dividends received deduction, net operating losses from other taxable years, tax-exempt interest, life insurance proceeds paid upon the death of the insured, the excess of percentage depletion over cost depletion, and corporate indebtedness to a shareholder where collection is barred by the statute of limitations.

Earnings and profits must be adjusted in the case of dividend payments. If the distribution is in cash, the earnings are decreased by the amount of this cash; and if it is an obligation of the distributing corporation, the earnings are decreased by the principal amount

[12] Regulations Section 1.316–1(a)(1).
[13] G.C.M. 12605, XIII–1 C.B. 166.
[14] *Tank Truck Rentals, Inc., v. Commissioner,* 356 U.S. 30 (1958).
[15] Regulations Section 1.312–6(a).
[16] *Esther M. Stein Estate,* 25 T.C. 940 (1956).

of the obligation. If the distribution is in property, the amount of the decrease is by the adjusted basis of this property. This rule is applicable whether the property has appreciated or depreciated in value.

Illustration. If property with a value of $100 is distributed but there are only $75 of earnings and profits from which the distribution can be made, the taxable amount will be only $75. If the property, however, only cost the corporate distributor $50, its earnings and profits will be reduced only by $50, and $25 will remain in its earnings and profits account.

An upward adjustment of earnings and profits is required where appreciated inventory assets are distributed. If inventory assets (that is, inventories and unrealized receivables from sales of other than inventory assets) are distributed, and if the fair market value exceeds the basis, then the corporate earnings are to be increased by the amount of this excess and are to be decreased by the lesser of the fair market value or the earnings and profits (so increased). But the required adjustments may not serve to create a deficit in earnings and profits.[17]

Illustration. A corporation distributes to its sole stockholder property with a value of $10,000 and a basis of $5,000. It has $12,500 in earnings and profits. The reduction in earnings and profits by reason of this distribution is $5,000. This is the reduction even though the amount of $10,000 is includible in the income of the shareholder (other than a corporation) as a dividend.

Illustration. The facts are the same as in the preceding illustration, except that the property has a basis of $15,000 and the earnings and profits of the corporation are $20,000. The reduction in earnings and profits is $15,000. This is the reduction even though only the amount of $10,000 is includible in the income of the shareholder as a dividend.

Another adjustment to the earnings and profits must be made if property distributed is subject to a liability, where the distributee assumes a liability in connection with the distribution and where gain is recognized to the distributing corporation under I.R.C. Section 311(b) or (c); that is, there has been a distribution of Lifo inventory or of property subject to indebtedness in excess of its basis. See page 8·2.

Illustration. A corporation distributed to an individual, its sole shareholder, as a dividend in kind a vacant lot which is not an inventory asset. On the date of the distribution, the lot had a fair market value of $5,000 and was subject to a mortgage of $2,000. The adjusted basis of the lot was $3,100. The amount of the earnings and profits was $10,000. The amount of the dividend received by the stockholder is $3,000 ($5,000, the fair market value, less $2,000, the amount of the mortgage), and the reduction in the earnings and profits of the paying corporation is $1,100 ($3,100, the basis, less $2,000, the amount of the mortgage).

[17] I.R.C. Section 312(b).

Illustration. The facts are the same as in the preceding illustration, with the exception that the amount of the mortgage to which the property was subject was $4,000. The amount of the dividend received by the shareholder is $1,000, and there is no reduction in the earnings and profits of the corporation (disregarding any reduction that may result from an increase in tax to the paying corporation because of gain resulting from the distribution). There is a gain of $900 recognized to the corporation, the difference between the basis of the property ($3,100) and the amount of the mortgage ($4,000) and an increase in earnings and profits of $900.

Illustration. A corporation, having accumulated earnings and profits of $100,000, distributed in kind to its shareholders (not in liquidation) inventory assets which had a basis on the Lifo method of $46,000 and on the basis of cost or market of $50,000. The inventory had a fair market value of $55,000 and was subject to a liability of $35,000. This distribution results in a net decrease of earnings and profits of the paying corporation of $11,000 (without regard to any tax on the corporation), computed as follows:

Regular basis of inventory	$50,000	
Less: Lifo basis of inventory	46,000	
Gain recognized—addition to earnings and profits		$ 4,000
Adjustment to earnings and profits required:		
Fair market value of inventory	$55,000	
Less: Lifo basis plus adjustment	50,000	5,000
Total increase in earnings and profits		$ 9,000
Decrease in earnings and profits		20,000
Net decrease in earnings and profits		$11,000

The distribution of stock or securities by a corporation will not be considered a distribution of earnings and profits. This is true if no gain to the distributee was recognized. Thus, a distribution of stock in lieu of currently owing dividends on preferred stock would be considered a distribution of earnings, inasmuch as gain is recognized to the distributee in such a case. The distribution of a nontaxable stock dividend will not affect the earnings and profits of the corporation for the purpose of future distributions. This includes rights.[18]

In the case of a partial liquidation or a redemption, corporate earnings will not be decreased by the portion of the distribution properly chargeable to capital account.

In the case of a corporation in which depreciation or depletion is a factor in the determination of income, the only depreciation or depletion deductions to be considered in the computation of the total earnings and profits are those based on cost or other basis without regard to the March 1, 1913, value.

Earnings and profits will be adjusted by the sale or other disposition of property only to the extent that gain or loss is recognized

[18] I.R.C. Section 312(d).

in computing taxable income. Thus, in the case of tax-free distributions, no adjustment may be required.

Where there is a corporate separation under Section 355 (see Chapter 17), earnings and profits of the original corporation have to be allocated between the companies. But in no case may the earnings and profits of a corporation exceed its total net worth.

Where a corporation makes a distribution of the proceeds of a loan insured by the United States, the earnings and profits will be increased by the excess of the Government loans outstanding over the adjusted basis of the property, without regard to any adjustments to basis, such as depreciation.

The reduction in earnings and profits by the amount of dividends paid to shareholders may include a dividend paid after the close of a taxable year, provided the payment is on or before the fifteenth day of the third month following the close of that year. Such a dividend, of course, may not be utilized again in a computation for the year in which payment actually is made.[19]

Requirements of a Dividend. A dividend payment may be spelled from the facts. Formal declaration is not necessary.[20] The parties may not have intended that there be a dividend.[21] The question is: *Was* there a dividend in fact?

Any informal withdrawal of cash or other property from a corporation by its shareholders may be treated as a dividend. Thus, shareholder loans may be treated as dividends if it does not appear that there was any intention to repay the loans.[22] To the extent that a salary to a shareholder is excessive, it may be a dividend.[23] Bargain sales to shareholders, to the extent of the preference, may be dividends.[24] Purchase of property by a corporation from its shareholders may be a dividend to the extent that the price was too high.[25] Where a corporation pays insurance premiums for shareholders, a dividend may be found.[26] The cancellation of a stockholder debt may be regarded as a dividend.[27]

Even more dangerous, because of the abstruse philosophical concepts that sometimes are involved, is a distribution that is deemed

[19] I.R.C. Section 563.

[20] *Helvering v. Gordon,* 87 F.2d 663 (8th Cir., 1937).

[21] *J. W. Allen & Co.,* 3 B.T.A. 1135 (1926).

[22] *Commissioner v. Cohen,* 121 F.2d 348 (5th Cir., 1941).

[23] *University Chevrolet Co., Inc. v. Commissioner,* 199 F.2d 629 (5th Cir., 1952).

[24] *Palmer v. Commissioner,* 302 U.S. 63 (1937).

[25] *H. K. L. Castle,* 9 B.T.A. 931 (1927).

[26] *Earl Everett Jameson,* B.T.A. Memo., Docket #106788, entered January 22, 1942.

[27] *Ida L. Dowling,* 13 B.T.A. 787 (1928).

to be essentially equivalent to the distribution of a taxable dividend. To be *essentially equivalent,* there is no requirement of intention. "Neither artifice, subterfuge, nor bad faith need be present to bring the transaction within the meaning of the statute here involved, for as we read the law a taxpayer may well act with the utmost good purpose and without even intent and yet his transactions may in effect be the equivalent of the distribution of a taxable dividend." [28]

Even if state law, or a company by-law, provides that there can be no dividend payment unless a dividend is affirmatively voted upon by a majority of the directors at a meeting especially called for the purpose, the Internal Revenue Service may tax a payment as a dividend. In the face of technicalities, the Service merely states that the transaction may not be a dividend, but it is being taxed as the equivalent of one. "The net effect of the redemption was clearly to distribute to taxpayer the corporate earnings just as if a cash dividend had been declared." [29] In its simplest essence, any economic benefit that a person gets because he is a stockholder may be treated as a dividend.

What the parties call the transaction is not decisive. It is immaterial that a distribution is deemed by the payor corporation to be partially a current dividend and partially a payment on account of accumulated dividends.[30]

If the nature of a corporate payment cannot be proved, it will be treated as a dividend.[31]

A distribution of property of a type not used in the taxpayer's trade or business may be taxed as a dividend if "the availability of the property for distribution does not result from the termination of a trade or business by the corporation." [32] No dividend was found where a corporation purchased cars for use of its officers, as the corporation retained title.[33]

Even if a distribution by a corporation is of income that was entirely tax-exempt to the corporation, the dividend will be includible in the stockholder's gross income. The character of income is lost in the hands of a subsequent recipient via the dividend route.[34]

[28] *McGuire v. Commissioner,* 84 F.2d 431 (7th Cir., 1936).
[29] *Commissioner v. Roberts,* 203 F.2d 304 (4th Cir., 1953).
[30] Revenue Ruling 56–211, 1956–1 CB 155.
[31] *Wade E. Moore,* 7 T.C. 1250 (1946), *appeal dismissed on stipulation sub nomine Forcum-James v. Commissioner,* 176 F.2d 311 (6th Cir., 1949).
[32] Revenue Ruling 56–512, 1956–2 CB 173.
[33] *Joseph Morgenstern et al.,* T.C. Memo. 1955–86, filed April 14, 1955.
[34] I.T. 2222, III–2 CB 12.

Purpose of the Distribution. If a sound business purpose for a payment by a corporation to the chief stockholder is lacking, the payment may be regarded as a dividend.[35] Where a subsidiary corporation declared a dividend in property so that the parent corporation could sell these assets, "It was not a distribution for the purposes of the Parent's business, but only in order to escape a tax and such a 'distribution' is not among those contemplated in the section." [36] Inasmuch as the subsidiary was found not to have paid out the property as a dividend, profit on a subsequent sale of this property to an outsider was taxed to the subsidiary.

Distributions That Are Not Taxable. If a corporation does not have earnings accumulated since February 28, 1913, either actual or imputed, there is no dividend.

Even if a corporation has accumulated earnings, a dividend will not be found if a distribution actually is in redemption of some or all of the stock.[37]

A redemption of shares where there is no liquidation will not be regarded as a dividend if any of the following four conditions obtain:

(1) The redemption is not essentially equivalent to a dividend. Stated affirmatively, a redemption may be treated as a dividend if it is equivalent to a dividend. If a corporation declares a stock dividend that is tax-free to the shareholders, and shortly thereafter the corporation redeems the stock without a business reason, the redemption will be regarded as a dividend.

(2) There has been a substantially disproportionate redemption of stock. A distribution will be substantially disproportionate with respect to a shareholder only if the ratio which the voting stock owned by the shareholder after the redemption bears to all the voting stock of the corporation at that time is less than 80% of the ratio which the voting stock he owned immediately before the redemption bears to all the voting stock of the corporation at that time. In addition, in order that a distribution may qualify as "substantially disproportionate," it is necessary that the shareholder's ownership of voting or nonvoting common stock (that is, his participating interest) in the corporation also be reduced by the percentage required with respect to voting stock.

(3) The distribution must be in complete redemption of all of the stock of a corporation owned by a shareholder.

(4) The redemption is of stock issued by a railroad corporation,

[35] *W. H. Armston Co., Inc. et al. v. Commissioner,* 188 F.2d 531 (5th Cir., 1951).

[36] *Commissioner v. Transport Trading & Terminal Corp.,* 176 F.2d 570 (2d Cir., 1949).

[37] I.R.C. Section 331(a).

as defined in Section 77(m) of the Bankruptcy Act, pursuant to a plan of reorganization under Section 77 of the Bankruptcy Act.[38]

A redemption of stock to pay death taxes will not be treated as a dividend under appropriate conditions. The amount involved must be distributed within ninety days after the assessment period of the Federal estate tax, which, in general, means within three years and ninety days after the estate tax return is to be filed. The rule applies in the case of a taxpayer whose stock interest in the corporation comprised more than 35% of his gross estate or 50% of the net estate. If the decedent did not hold enough stock in one corporation to meet either of these tests, there may be added his holdings in two or more corporations if more than 75% in value of the outstanding stock of each such corporation was owned by him. The distribution will not be regarded as a dividend to the extent utilized to pay death taxes and funeral and administration expenses.[39] See Chapter 17.

Redemption Through a Related Corporation. Where one or more persons who are in control of each of two corporations sell the stock of one of the corporations to another of these corporations, the proceeds of this sale will be considered to be an amount distributed in redemption of the stock of the corporation which purchased the stock. The stock thus acquired will be treated as a contribution to the capital of the acquiring corporation made by the shareholder, and accordingly will take as its basis the basis in the hands of the shareholder. Constructive rules of stock ownership will apply.[40] See Chapter 17.

Section 306 Stock. A type of distribution which may be taxed somewhat in the nature of a dividend relates to what is known as Section 306 stock. This is any stock (other than common shares issued with respect to common stock) distributed to the shareholder on a tax-free basis. Most commonly, it is a dividend on common stock, payable in the form of preferred stock. The receipt of Section 306 stock is not taxable. But when the Section 306 stock is sold, the amount realized is treated as ordinary income to the extent of the stock's ratable share of earnings and profits of the distributing corporation at the time of its *distribution*.[41]

Illustration. On December 15, A and B owned equally all of the stock of Corporation X, which files its income tax return on a calendar year basis. On that date, Corporation X distributed, pro rata, 100 shares of preferred stock as a

[38] I.R.C. Section 302(b).
[39] I.R.C. Section 303.
[40] I.R.C. Section 304.
[41] I.R.C. Section 306.

dividend on its outstanding common stock. The preferred stock had a fair market value at that time of $10,000. On December 31, the earnings and profits of Corporation X were $20,000. The 50 shares of preferred stock so distributed to A had an allocated basis to him of $10 per share or a total of $500 for the 50 shares. The shares had a fair market value of $5,000 when issued. A sold the 50 shares on the following July 1 for $6,000. Of this amount, $5,000 will be treated as ordinary income; $500 ($6,000 minus $5,500) will be treated as gain from the sale of a capital or noncapital asset as the case may be.

If Section 306 stock is redeemed, the amount realized will be treated as a distribution. Thus if the Section 306 stock were distributed at a time when there was an amount of corporate earnings attributable to it equal to its full fair market value at that time, but if there were no corporate earnings (accumulated or current) at the time of redemption, the amount realized on redemption of the stock would be treated as a return of capital. No loss would be allowed in that case.

If stock is acquired through the exercise of stock rights, this stock will be treated as Section 306 stock to the extent that the rights themselves had the character of Section 306 stock at the time of distribution.

Where Section 306 stock is disposed of by a nonresident alien or foreign corporation, it will be treated as if the amount of the proceeds had been received from the corporation as a dividend at the time of the distribution of the Section 306 stock.

The rules of Section 306 do not apply in the following circumstances:

(1) If a shareholder sells his entire stock interest in the corporation to a person other than one covered by the rules of constructive ownership of stock.

(2) If the Section 306 stock is redeemed pursuant to a partial or complete liquidation.

(3) If gain or loss to the shareholder is not recognized with respect to the disposition of the Section 306 stock; *e.g.*, a tax-free exchange under Section 1033. See Chapter 17.

(4) If it is established to the satisfaction of the Secretary of the Treasury that the transaction was not in pursuance of a plan having as one of its principal purposes the avoidance of Federal income tax.

Stock Dividends. A stock dividend refers to a distribution to a shareholder of stock of the distributing corporation, or rights to acquire such stock. Except where the distribution is "in lieu of money," a stock dividend will not be included in the gross income of the recipient. A distribution is in lieu of money under either of two circumstances:

(1) If the distribution is made in discharge of preference dividends on stock of the corporation for the taxable year of the distribution or for the preceding taxable year.

(2) If the distribution of stock or rights is, at the election of any of the shareholders, payable either in such stock or rights, or in property (such as cash). The amount of this distribution will be measured by reference to the property subject to the election.[42]

If stock or rights are acquired as a tax-free distribution, the basis of such stock or rights will be the same as that of the original stock, allocated between the original stock and the new stock or rights in proportion to their respective fair market values at the time of the distribution.[43]

Illustration. A taxpayer purchased 100 shares of common stock at $100 per share in 1954. In 1961, by reason of the ownership of this stock, he acquired 100 rights entitling him to subscribe to 100 additional shares of such stock at $90 per share. Immediately after the issuance of the rights, each of the shares of stock in respect of which the rights were acquired had a fair market value (ex-rights) of $110, and the rights had a fair market value of $19 each. The basis of the rights and the common stock for the purpose of determining the basis for gain or loss on a subsequent sale or exercise of the rights or a sale of the old stock is computed as follows:

100 (shares) × $100 = $10,000, cost of old stock (stock in respect of which the rights were acquired).
100 (shares) × $110 = $11,000, market value of old stock.
100 (rights) × $19 = $1,900, market value of rights.
$\frac{11,000}{12,900}$ of $10,000 = $8,527.13, cost of old stock apportioned to such stock.
$\frac{1,900}{12,900}$ of $10,000 = $1,472.87, cost of old stock apportioned to rights.

If the rights are sold, the basis for determining gain or loss will be $14.7287 per right. If the rights are exercised, the basis of the new stock acquired will be the subscription price paid therefor ($90) plus the basis of the rights exercised ($14.7287 each) or $104.7287 per share. The remaining basis of the old stock for the purpose of determining gain or loss on a subsequent sale will be $85.2713 per share.

There is a special rule for the treatment of certain stock rights, which have a minimal value in relationship to the stock with respect to which these stock rights were distributed. A simple rule was intended which will eliminate, unless the recipient elects otherwise, the problems of allocation as shown in the above illustration.[44]

Under this special rule, if rights are acquired and the fair market value of these rights is less than 15% of the fair market value of the

[42] I.R.C. Section 305.
[43] I.R.C. Section 307.
[44] I.R.C. Section 307(b).

stock with respect to which these rights were distributed, then the basis of the rights will be zero, unless the taxpayer elects to determine the basis under the allocation method shown in the above illustration. The election is to be made in the return for the taxable year in which the rights were received. The election when made is irrevocable.

Timing of Dividends. Where stock is sold, and a dividend is both declared and paid after the sale, this dividend is not included in the seller's gross income. When stock is sold after the declaration of a dividend and after the date on which the seller becomes entitled to the dividend, the dividend ordinarily is income to the seller. But when stock is sold between the time of declaration and the time of payment of the dividend, this dividend is not included in the seller's gross income.[45]

Dividends are gross income to the shareholders in the year in which they are made available without substantial limitation. If a dividend is declared payable on the last day of the taxable year and the corporate payor intended to and did follow its practice of paying the dividends by checks mailed so that the shareholders would not receive them until the first days of the following year, the dividends would not be considered to have been unqualifiedly made subject to the demand of the shareholders prior to the second year. The Internal Revenue Service could not take the position that checks would have been available to any shareholder who actually went to the payor's office on the last day of the taxable year, for, in the case of large corporations at least, it is standard practice to mail the checks. "Confusion would result if the stockholders of any large corporation descended in a body on the treasurer's office and demanded forthwith payment of their dividends." [46]

Where a dividend is paid in one year but is rescinded in a subsequent year, the income of the earlier year is not subject to reduction. The claim of right under which the shareholder received the dividend made it taxable in the year of receipt.[47]

Patronage Dividends. Patronage dividends from purchases of merchandise or other property for personal use are not included in gross income. If these dividends result from purchases of capital assets or depreciable property used in the trade or business, the cost of the items purchased is reduced. But patronage dividends from the purchase of expendable assets used in the business as well

[45] Regulations Section 1.61–9(c).
[46] *Commissioner v. Fox,* 218 F.2d 347 (3d Cir., 1954).
[47] *St. Regis Paper Co. v. Commissioner,* 157 F.2d 884 (2d Cir., 1946).

as merchandise purchased for resale may be reported as gross income or as a reduction of the cost of these items.[48]

Regulated Investment Companies. The specialized treatment of dividends from regulated investment companies will be dealt with in Chapter 16.

Consent Dividends. If a corporation desires to retain its cash (*e.g.*, for expansion purposes) but the retention of earnings would subject the company to a penalty such as the personal holding company tax (see Chapter 16), the shareholders may *consent* to be taxed on their respective proportions of the amount that the corporation would claim as a dividends paid credit. Actually, the corporation does not pay out the funds. But each consenting shareholder would include in gross income his respective share of the consent dividend.[49]

Dividends Exclusion

An individual may exclude from gross income the first $50 of dividends from domestic corporations. In the case of a joint return of husband and wife, each spouse is entitled to the exclusion (in an amount not in excess of $50) with respect to the dividends received.[50]

Illustration. If a husband receives $200 of dividends in the taxable year and his wife $100, the amount to be included in gross income is $200 ($150 of the husband's dividends and $50 of the wife's). If the wife receives only $30 of dividends, the entire $30 is excludable; and there is included in gross income in the joint return only $150, consisting of the dividends received by the husband ($200 less his $50 exclusion).

Where two or more persons hold stock as tenants in common, as joint tenants, or as tenants by the entirety, the dividends received with respect to this stock will be considered as being received by each tenant to the extent that he is entitled under local law to a share of the dividends. Where dividends constitute community property under local law, each spouse will be considered as receiving one-half of the dividends.[51]

If a husband owned all of the dividend-paying stocks, he would have to make a bona fide gift to his wife of stocks paying at least $50 a year in dividends to get the maximum exclusion possible on a joint return.

[48] Regulations Section 1.61–5.
[49] I.R.C. Section 565.
[50] I.R.C. Section 116.
[51] Regulations Section 1.116–1.

The $50 exclusion is not allowed in the case of distributions from an insurance company, a China Trade Act Corporation, a corporation dealing with possessions of the United States (and taxed as such), and tax-exempt organizations. Nonresident alien individuals are not entitled to the exclusion.[52]

Dividends Received Credit

An individual is entitled to a credit against his Federal income tax equal to 4% of the dividends received from domestic corporations, provided these amounts are included in gross income. Thus, the $50 exclusion is not subject to this credit. The credit is against the tax itself; that is, it may not be set against penalties or interest.[53]

If a joint return is filed, the credit is determined on the basis of the dividends received by both spouses after taking into account the dividend exclusion. The credit is allowable on account of the dividends received by each spouse without regard to whether the spouse would be liable for the tax had not the joint return been filed. It makes no difference whether the tax, the credit, or the taxable income is attributable to one or the other spouse.

Illustration. H and W, husband and wife, make a joint return for the taxable year. The total dividends received are $400 payable to H. Subject to a limitation to be detailed below, the credit amounts to $14 (4% of $350, the dividends included in gross income after the exclusion). If W also received a dividend of $30, the computation of the tax credit would not be affected, as this additional dividend is less than the maximum amount allowable as an exclusion.

Illustration. H and W make a joint return for the taxable year. Each received a $400 dividend. Since H and W may each exclude $50 of the dividends received, $700 of dividend income is included in gross income. Subject to a limitation mentioned below, the credit against the joint return tax amounts to $28 (4% of $700).

Where two or more persons hold stock as tenants in common, as joint tenants, or as tenants by the entirety, the dividends received with respect to such stock will be considered as being received by each tenant to the extent that he is entitled under local law to a share of these dividends. Where dividends constitute community property under local law, each spouse will be considered as receiving one-half of the dividends.[54]

The credit may not exceed the lesser of either—

(1) The amount of the tax for the taxable year reduced by the foreign tax credit (see Chapter 22) or

[52] Regulations Section 1.34–4(a).
[53] I.R.C. Section 34.
[54] Regulations Section 1.34–1(d).

(2) 4% of the taxable income for that taxable year.

In the case of a taxpayer with adjusted gross income who uses the optional tax table or who uses the standard deduction (see Chapter 24), the taxable income for the taxable year is the adjusted gross income reduced by the standard deduction and the deductions for personal exemptions (see Chapter 24). Where the alternative tax on capital gains is imposed, the taxable income is the taxable income reduced by 50% of the excess of net long-term capital gain over net short-term capital loss.

Illustration.

Computation of tax liability without regard to the dividend received credit:	
(1) Gross income	$7,500
(2) Deductions	2,900
(3) Taxable income	4,600
(4) Income tax liability	996
(5) Foreign tax credit	816
(6) Income tax liability − foreign tax credit	180
Computation of limitation:	
(7) Dividends for which credit is allowable	$2,500
(8) Dividends received credit ($2,500 × 4%)	100
(9) Dividends received credit as limited (Item (6) or Item (8), whichever is lesser)	100
OR	
(10) Taxable income	$4,600
(11) Dividends received credit ($4,600 × 4%)	184
Dividends received credit allowable:	
Item (6), Item (8), or Item (11), whichever is lesser	$ 100

The dividends to which the credits apply are the ones mentioned above as subject to the dividend exclusion. Taxpayers not entitled to the credit are those listed above as not entitled to the exclusion.

Dividends Received Deduction

A corporation is entitled to a deduction from gross income for taxable dividends received from a domestic corporation. The deduction is an amount equal to 85% of such dividends.[55]

Instead of 85%, the figure is 100% in the case of dividends received by small investment companies, as defined, from taxable domestic corporations.[56] See Chapter 16.

This deduction is determined without regard to dividends received on the preferred stock of a public utility, with respect to which a deduction is allowed by Section 247 (relating to dividends paid on certain preferred stock of public utilities). But if a deduc-

[55] I.R.C. Section 243.
[56] I.R.C. Section 1242.

tion for dividends paid is not allowable to a domestic public utility corporation, dividends from such a company are includible in the dividends received deduction.

For the purpose of this deduction, the following items are not considered as dividends: dividends paid by mutual savings banks, cooperative banks, and domestic building and loan associations.[57] Dividends received from a regulated investment company are not considered as dividends to the extent that they are capital gain dividends (see Chapter 16).[58]

Dividends Received on Certain Preferred Stock. A corporation may include in the base for the dividends received deduction those dividends received on certain preferred stock of a taxable public utility corporation. The deduction is allowable only for dividends received on the preferred stock of a public utility with respect to which the deduction for dividends paid on certain preferred stock of public utilities is allowable to the distributing corporation.[59]

The deduction is equal to 85% of the dividends received out of (1) its earnings and profits of the taxable year and (2) that part of its earnings and profits accumulated after February 28, 1913, that have accumulated after the beginning of the uninterrupted period. But in both (1) and (2), the amount cannot exceed the ratio of dividends received from these earnings and profits that the gross income of the foreign corporation for the period from sources within the United States bears to its gross income from all sources for that same period.

Illustration. Corporation A, which files its income tax returns on the calendar year basis, received in the taxable year $100,000 as dividends on the preferred stock of Corporation B, a taxable public utility corporation. Corporation B is entitled to a deduction for dividends that it pays. The corporation normal and surtax rates for the taxable year are 30% and 22%, respectively. The deduction allowable to Corporation A for the taxable year with respect to these dividends is $62,115.38, computed as follows:

Dividends received on preferred stock of Corporation B........	$100,000.00
Less: $\frac{14}{52} \times \$100{,}000$	26,923.08
Amount subject to 85% deduction............................	$ 73,067.92

If the normal and surtax rates were, respectively, 25% and 22%, the denominator in the fraction would be 47.

Foreign Corporation Dividends. A corporation is allowed a deduction for dividends received from a foreign corporation (other

[57] Regulations Section 1.243-2.
[58] I.R.C. Section 854(a).
[59] I.R.C. Section 244.

than a foreign personal holding company) if (1) for an uninterrupted period of not less than 36 months ending with the close of the foreign corporation's taxable year in which the dividends are paid the foreign corporation has been engaged in trade or business within the United States and (2) has derived 50% or more of its gross income from sources within the United States.[60] If the foreign corporation has been in existence less than 36 months as of the close of the taxable year in which the dividends are paid, then the necessary period of activity in the United States is the entire period of existence as of the close of the taxable year. An uninterrupted period which satisfies the twofold requirement with respect to business activity and gross income may start at a date later than the date on which the foreign corporation first commenced an uninterrupted period of engaging in trade or business within the United States, but the applicable uninterrupted period is in any event the longest uninterrupted period which satisfies this twofold requirement.[61]

Illustration. Corporation A (a foreign corporation filing its income tax returns on a calendar year basis) whose stock is 100% owned by Corporation B (a domestic corporation filing its income tax returns on a calendar year basis) for the first time engaged in trade or business within the United States on January 1, 1950, and qualifies for the entire period beginning on that date and ending on December 31, 1961. Corporation A had accumulated earnings and profits of $50,000 immediately prior to January 1, 1950, and had earnings and profits of $10,000 for each taxable year during the uninterrupted period from January 1, 1950, through December 31, 1961. It derived for the period from January 1, 1950, through December 31, 1960, 90% of its gross income from sources within the United States and in 1961 derived 95% of its gross income from sources within the United States. During the calendar years 1950, 1951, 1952, 1953, and 1954 Corporation A distributed in each year $15,000; during the calendar years 1955, 1956, 1957, 1958, 1959, and 1960 it distributed in each year $5,000; and during the year 1961, $50,000.

An analysis of the accumulated earnings and profits under the above statement of facts discloses that at December 31, 1960, the accumulation amounted to $55,000, of which $25,000 was accumulated prior to the uninterrupted period and $30,000 was accumulated during the uninterrupted period. For 1961 a deduction of $31,025 ($8,075 on 1961 earnings of the foreign corporation, plus $22,950 from the $30,000 accumulation at December 31, 1960) for dividends received from a foreign corporation is allowable to Corporation B with respect to the $50,000 received from Corporation A, computed as follows:

(1) $8,075, which is $8,500 (85% of the $10,000 of earnings and profits of the taxable year) multiplied by 95% (the portion of the gross income of Corporation A derived during the taxable year 1961 from sources within the United States) plus

[60] I.R.C. Section 245.
[61] Regulations Section 1.245-1(a).

(2) $22,950, which is $25,500 (85% of $30,000, the part of the earnings and profits accumulated after the beginning of the uninterrupted period) multiplied by 90% (the portion of the gross income of Corporation A derived from sources within the United States during that portion of the uninterrupted period ending at the beginning of the taxable year 1961.

Limitation on Aggregate Amount of Deductions. Except in the case of a net operating loss, there is a limitation of 85% of the taxable income of the corporation to the sum of these deductions: dividends received by corporations under Section 243, dividends received on certain preferred stock under Section 244, and dividends received from certain foreign corporations under Section 245. The taxable income of the corporation for this purpose is computed without regard to the net operating loss deduction (see Chapter 14), the deduction for dividends paid on certain preferred stock of public utilities, and the three deductions mentioned in the preceding sentence.[62]

If the shareholder corporation has a net operating loss for a taxable year, the limitation of the previous paragraph is not applicable. In that event, the three types of deduction mentioned in the first sentence of the preceding paragraph will be allowable for all tax purposes to the shareholder corporation for that taxable year without regard to the limitation.

Denial of Deduction. The dividends received deduction is denied on stock that is sold within fifteen days after its acquisition. The deduction also is denied to the extent that the taxpayer is under an obligation to make corresponding payments with respect to substantially identical stock or securities. If the stock is cumulative preferred stock where dividends are in arrears, the shares must be held for more than ninety days in order to receive the dividends received deduction where the corporate shareholder receives more than a year's dividends.[63]

Supplementary Material

A. Suggested Reading.

Victor R. Wolder and Stanley Wolder, "The Dividend," *TAXES—The Tax Magazine,* October, 1947, Vol. XXV, #10, p. 911.

L. William Seidman, "The Unexpected, Untimely and Uninvited Dividend," *TAXES—The Tax Magazine,* March, 1958, Vol. XXXVI, #3, p. 166.

Daniel M. Holland, *Income-Tax Burden on Stockholders* (Princeton: Princeton University Press, 1958).

[62] I.R.C. Section 246.
[63] I.R.C. Section 246(a).

Charles R. Cutler, "Dividend Arrearages," *TAXES—The Tax Magazine,* April, 1959, Vol. XXXVII, #4, p. 309.

Martin Lore, *Thin Capitalization* (New York: The Ronald Press Co., 1958).

William J. Schwanbeck, "The Accountant's Problem in Working with 'Earnings and Profits' for Tax Purposes," *The Journal of Taxation,* January, 1959, Vol. X, #1, p. 22.

Herman T. Rehling, "The Law of Income Taxation and Corporate Distributions," *Notre Dame Lawyer,* March, 1956, Vol. XXXI, #2, p. 147.

B. Leading Cases.

Essentially equivalent to a dividend. *McGuire v. Commissioner,* 84 F.2d 431 (7th Cir., 1936).

Effect of a distribution of a dividend. *Commissioner v. Edward T. Bedford Estate,* 325 U.S. 283 (1945).

Dividend or interest. *John Kelley Company v. Commissioner; Talbot Mills v. Commissioner,* 326 U.S. 521 (1946).

Surplus of predecessor corporation in a reorganization. *Commissioner v. Sansome,* 60 F.2d 951 (2d Cir., 1932).

C. Questions.

1. Discuss the taxability of stock dividends.
2. In order to be taxable, must a dividend be paid on a pro rata basis?
3. An individual stockholder of the Borgia Wine Company purchased property from that corporation for $20. The fair market value of this property was $100, and its basis in the hands of the corporation was $25. The amount of the distribution is how much? What would your answer be if the stockholder were a corporation?
4. A corporation's only income in the taxable year was interest on City of Des Moines bonds. A distribution of this same amount is immediately made to the shareholders. Is it taxable?
5. How may it be established that a distribution is from earnings accumulated prior to March 1, 1913? What is the tax significance?
6. The Secondhand Paint Corporation had an accumulated deficit of $80,000 on December 31, 1961, the close of its taxable year. In 1962 there were earnings for the year of $10,000. The shareholders received a distribution of $20,000. Is any of this taxable as ordinary income? If any portion is not ordinary income, how is it treated for tax purposes?
7. Can a redemption of stock be treated as a taxable dividend? Explain.
8. An individual owned stock, dividends on which were $500 in the taxable year. What is the dividend exclusion on a joint return that he files with his wife? Is there any legitimate way that he may increase the exclusion?
9. The Anonymous Corporation is on the calendar year basis. In 1960, earnings were $50,000, but no distribution was made until the day after the accountant's report was received on March 1, 1961. May the corporation treat this as a dividend paid in 1960? May the corporation regard this as a dividend paid in 1961?
10. In the preceding question, is it a matter of concern to the corporation as to which year the dividend was deemed to be paid?
11. If a corporation without accumulated earnings makes a distribution to

its shareholders, can they be taxed upon dividends? If so, how is the amount of the taxable distribution computed?

12. A certain individual owns all of the stock and all of the bonds of a corporation. The corporation sends him a check, allegedly for interest. May the Internal Revenue Service label this as a dividend?
13. The Internal Revenue Service argued that a dividend took place in the taxable year; but the shareholders argued that under the laws of the state of incorporation, a dividend could not have been paid, as affirmative action on the part of the directors was required, and no meeting ever had been held. Is this argument valid?
14. If a corporation has only common stock outstanding, what are the tax consequences should a dividend be issued in the form of preferred stock?
15. Is the dividends received deduction of a corporation limited to dividends from domestic corporations?
16. A corporation owns securities that cost $50,000. Subsequently, when they are worth $75,000, the securities are given to the shareholders as a distribution. What is the income tax effect upon (a) the distributing corporation, (b) shareholders that are not corporations, and (c) shareholders that are corporations?
17. An individual receives dividends from domestic corporations in the amount of $600 in the taxable year. He also receives $80 in dividends on a deposit in a commercial bank and $100 in patronage dividends from an agricultural marketing cooperative association. What is his dividends received credit?
18. Amy purchased 100 shares of common stock of a certain corporation for $1,000. In the taxable year, she received a stock dividend of 10% payable in common stock of the same company. At the time of the dividend, the stock had a fair market value of $14 a share. What is the basis of each share of stock?
19. A corporation has a loss from operations of $20,000 in the taxable year. It also received $100,000 in dividends from domestic corporations. The corporation's taxable income is $80,000 before the deduction for dividends received is considered. After deducting 85% of dividends received ($85,000), the result is a net operating loss of $5,000. Will the deduction for dividends received be limited to 85% of taxable income?
20. In the preceding question, assume that taxable income is $90,000 before the deduction for dividends received is considered. What deduction will be recognized for dividends received?
21. An individual has gross income of $7,500, deductions of $2,900, and taxable income of $4,600. His income tax liability was $996, against which he applied a foreign tax credit of $816, leaving a net tax liability of $180. Assuming that he received $2,500 in dividends from domestic corporations, what is the dividends received credit that is allowable?

9

DEDUCTIONS

Items of income and of expense (or deduction or credit) are not treated in the same manner for tax purposes. Insofar as the taxpayer is concerned, all income is taxable, unless he can show authority why it should not be. But nothing is deductible, unless he can show authority for the deduction. "The income taxed is described in sweeping terms and should be broadly construed in accordance with an obvious purpose to tax income comprehensively. The exemptions, on the other hand, are specifically stated and should be construed with restraint in the light of the same policy."[1]

"We examine the argument in the light of the now familiar rule that an income tax deduction is a matter of legislative grace and that the burden of clearly showing the right to the claimed deduction is on the taxpayer."[2] "Deductions are a matter of grace and Congress can, of course, disallow them as it chooses."[3] A taxpayer seeking a deduction must show that he comes within the terms of the statute relied upon.[4] An exemption statute is to be construed against the taxpayer.[5]

Types of Deduction. A deduction may be lost for tax purposes for one of three main reasons: (1) The deduction is personal. But as will be seen below, certain types of deduction are allowed whether of a personal or business nature. (2) The deduction must be capitalized; that is, the expenditure is not allowed in full at the time of the outlay, but the total may be taken in the form of deductions over a period of years. For example, a truck is purchased for business purposes at a cost of $5,000. Assuming that the truck has a useful life of five years and that there will be no salvage value at the end of that time, a deduction of $1,000 per year may be taken for five years under the straight line method (see Chapter 10).

[1] *Commissioner v. Jacobson,* 336 U.S. 28 (1949).
[2] *Interstate Transit Lines v. Commissioner,* 319 U.S. 590 (1943).
[3] *Commissioner v. Sullivan et al.,* 356 U.S. 27 (1958).
[4] *New Colonial Ice Co. v. Helvering,* 292 U.S. 435 (1934).
[5] *Pierce v. Commissioner,* 146 F.2d 388 (2d Cir., 1945).

(3) The deduction is disallowed because it is expressly or impliedly forbidden by the Internal Revenue Code or some other law.

A business deduction may be lost because it is of a capital nature or because it is forbidden by some statute.

Any deduction may be lost because it is not ordinary, necessary, or reasonable in amount.

Personal Expenses

The following items are deductible regardless of whether the expenditure was incurred for business reasons or otherwise:

(1) *Interest,* unless the money was borrowed for the purpose of buying or carrying tax-exempt securities.[6] Or unless the indebtedness was incurred to purchase single-premium life insurance, endowment, or annuity contracts.[7] See Chapter 12. Interest may even be deducted where not charged to the debtor under installment purchases. Whenever there is a contract for the purchase of personal property providing for the payment of part or all of the purchase price in installments, and there is a separately stated carrying charge (including a finance charge, service charge, or the like) but the actual interest charge cannot be ascertained, a portion of the payments made during the taxable year under the contract will be treated as interest. The portion of any such payments to be treated as interest is equal to 6% of the average unpaid balance under the contract during the taxable year. For purposes of this computation, the average unpaid balance is the sum of the unpaid balance outstanding on the first day of each month beginning during the taxable year, divided by twelve.

Illustration. On January 20, a taxpayer purchased a television set for $400, including a stated carrying charge of $25. The down payment was $50, and the balance was paid in fourteen monthly installments of $25 each, on the twentieth day of each month commencing with February. Assuming that he is on a cash method, that he uses the calendar year, and that no other installment purchases were made, the amount to be treated as interest in the taxable year is $12.38, computed as follows:

First Day of	Unpaid Balance Outstanding
January	$ 0
February	350
March	325
April	300
May	275
June	250
July	225

[6] I.R.C. Section 265.

[7] I.R.C. Section 264(a)(2).

First Day of	Unpaid Balance Outstanding
August	200
September	175
October	150
November	125
December	100
	$2,475

Sum of the unpaid balances, $2,475, divided by twelve, is $206.25, and 6% of this is $12.38.

An interest deduction will be denied when the transaction appears to have been entered upon primarily for the purpose of getting an interest deduction. Prepaid interest payments were disallowed where there was no business purpose to buy bonds.[8] Deduction was not allowed where Treasury bonds were purchased with borrowed funds only to get a tax deduction.[9] A fully paid-up annuity contract was purchased by utilizing funds borrowed from a bank, the contract being pledged as collateral for the bank's loan; interest could not be deducted.[10] Alleged borrowing to make investments in Treasury bonds did not create deductible interest where there was no real intent to buy the bonds and the borrower ended up without them.[11]

(2) *Taxes.* But these are deductible only by the person upon whom the tax is specifically imposed, regardless of who actually pays the tax.[12] Furthermore, certain taxes are not deductible by any person for income tax purposes: Federal income taxes; Federal import duties, excises, and stamp taxes (unless the expense relates to the taxpayer's trade or business, or is an expense for the production of income); estate, inheritance, legacy, succession, and gift taxes; income, war profits, and excess profits taxes imposed by the authority of any foreign country or posession of the United States, if the taxpayer elects to take the foreign tax credit (see Chapter 22); taxes on real property, to the extent that these taxes are treated as imposed on another taxpayer; taxes assessed against local benefits of a kind tending to increase the value of the property assessed. As to the last-named classification, there is loss of deduction of (A) so much of these taxes as is properly allocable to maintenance or interest charges or (B) taxes levied by a special taxing district if (i) the district covers the whole of at least one county, (ii) at least 1,000 persons are subject to the taxes levied by the

[8] *Leslie Julian et ux.*, 31 T.C., #99 (1959).
[9] *Egbert J. Miles et ux.*, 31 T.C., #100 (1959).
[10] *W. Stuart Emmons*, 31 T.C. 4 (1958).
[11] *George G. Lynch et al.*, 31 T.C., #98 (1959).
[12] Regulations Section 1.164–1.

district, and (iii) the district levies its assessments annually at a uniform rate on the same assessed value of real property, including improvements, as is used for purposes of the real property tax generally.[13] Any amount representing a state or local sales tax paid by a consumer of services or tangible personal property is deductible by him as a tax, provided it is separately stated and not paid in connection with his trade or business. The fact that, under the law imposing it, the incidence of the state or local sales tax does not fall on the consumer is immaterial.[14]

(3) *Contributions.* These will be discussed in greater detail later in this chapter.

(4) *Casualty losses.* See Chapter 13.

Personal expenses of the following types are not allowed as deductions:

(1) Premiums paid for life insurance by the insured.

(2) The cost of insuring a dwelling owned and occupied by the taxpayer as a personal residence.

(3) Expenses of maintaining a household (rent, utilities, domestic service, etc.). If part of the house is used for business purposes, an allocation of expenses is permitted.

(4) Losses sustained by the taxpayer upon the sale or other disposition of property held for personal, living, and family purposes.

(5) Expenses incurred in traveling away from home and any other transportation expenses, other than for business or nonbusiness purposes.

(6) Amounts paid as damages for breach of promise to marry, including costs (attorneys', etc.).

(7) The cost of equipment of a member of the armed forces is deductible only to the extent that it exceeds nontaxable allowances received for this equipment, and to the extent that this equipment is especially required by his profession and does not merely take the place of articles required in civilian life.

Certain personal expenses, however, are deductible:

(1) Interest, taxes, contributions, and casualty losses, as mentioned above.

(2) Alimony of certain types. See Chapter 15.

(3) Medical, dental, and similar expenses, within limitations. See Chapter 15.

(4) Expenses for care of certain dependents. See Chapter 24.

[13] I.R.C. Section 164(b).

[14] Regulations Section 1.164-5(a).

Ordinary and Necessary

To be deductible, business and nonbusiness expenses must be both ordinary and necessary.

The fact that it is *necessary* to make an expenditure in order to get business, or to maintain one's resources, does not mean that there is a permissible tax deduction. For example, it might be necessary to bribe a purchasing agent in order to obtain a contract from a hypothetical governmental agency. The expense is not ordinary; in the ordinary sense of things, one does not have to bribe another in order to get a contract. "Now, what is ordinary, though there must always be a strain of constancy within it, is none the less a variable affected by time and place and circumstance. Ordinary in this context does not mean that the payment must be habitual or normal in the sense that the same taxpayer will have to make them often. . . . The situation is unique in the life of the individual affected, but not in the life of the group, the community, of which he is a part." [15]

If transactions reflect a nationwide practice, they are *ordinary* in the generally accepted meaning of that word.[16] "[T]he expense is 'ordinary,' if it is of a kind similar to what arises in other similar situations." [17]

Where a business dispute ends up in a murder, legal expenses connected with one's defense are not deductible. "It cannot be said that settlement of a dispute or defense of honor in this matter was ordinary to the business or to business in general." [18]

Legal fees are deductible as ordinary and necessary if incurred in the defense of a business which allegedly had violated the law, even where the violation was sustained.[19] Here the deduction did not frustrate the law, which was aimed only at preventing the illegal use of the mails. Likewise, kickbacks by a manufacturer of optical goods to physicians were allowed as a deduction, for the allowance did not frustrate sharply defined national or state policies prescribing particular types of conduct.[20] Nothing in the tax law prohibits the deduction of ordinary and necessary expenses on the ground that they violate or frustrate public policy. Thus a bookie could deduct rent and wages. "The amounts paid as wages to employees

[15] *Welch v. Helvering,* 290 U.S. 111 (1933).
[16] *Deputy v. du Pont,* 308 U.S. 488 (1940).
[17] *Amtorg Trading Corp. v. Commissioner,* 65 F.2d 583 (2d Cir., 1933).
[18] *B. W. Sturdivant,* 15 T.C. 880 (1950).
[19] *Commissioner v. Heininger,* 320 U.S. 467 (1943).
[20] *Lilly et al. v. Commissioner,* 343 U.S. 90 (1952).

and to the landlord as rent are 'ordinary and necessary expenses' in the accepted meaning of the words." [21]

But payments in connection with an illegal business are not deductible, as where fines and court costs were paid by a partnership that took bets on the ponies, contrary to municipal law.[22] The owner of a fleet of trucks could not deduct fines for violation of state overweight laws. "Deduction of fines and penalties uniformly has been held to frustrate state policy in severe and direct fashion by reducing the 'sting' of the penalty prescribed by the state legislature." [23] The payment of fines was not "necessary" in the operation of a trucker's business.[24]

Amounts paid to "hoods" for protection are not deductible, for "while legitimate expenses incurred in an illegitimate business are deductible, amounts paid for protection are not legitimate business expenses." [25]

Amounts paid in compromise of a state antitrust suit are not deductible, for "to permit the violator to gain a tax advantage through deducting the amount of the penalty as a business expense, and thus to mitigate the degree of his punishment, would frustrate the purpose and effectiveness of that public policy." [26]

The Internal Revenue Service may disallow deductions that are contrary to state law; for example, gratuities that are specifically forbidden.[27]

Reasonable

Although the statute only spells out a requirement of reasonableness in the case of compensation, "the element of reasonableness is inherent in the phrase 'ordinary and necessary.' " [28] "[R]entals or other payments for the use of property which are excessive in amount, taking into consideration all the facts of the particular case, do not constitute ordinary and necessary business expenses. . . ." [29]

According to a release of the Internal Revenue Service, "To be deductible, such items must be both ordinary and necessary, and

[21] *Commissioner v. Sullivan et al.*, 356 U.S. 27 (1958).
[22] *Harry Wiedetz et al.*, 2 T.C. 1262 (1943).
[23] *Tank Truck Rentals, Inc. v. Commissioner*, 356 U.S. 30 (1958).
[24] *Hoover Motor Express Co., Inc. v. United States*, 356 U.S. 38 (1958).
[25] *Max Cohen et al. v. Commissioner*, 176 F.2d 394 (10th Cir., 1949).
[26] *Commissioner v. Longhorn Portland Cement Co.*, 148 F.2d 276 (5th Cir., 1945).
[27] *Fred D. Newman*, T.C. Memo., Docket #28955, entered August 29, 1952.
[28] *Commissioner v. Lincoln Electric Co.*, 176 F.2d 815 (6th Cir., 1949).
[29] *Limericks, Inc. v. Commissioner*, 165 F.2d 483 (5th Cir., 1948).

must be reasonable in amount in the light of existing circumstances in each case." [30]

Business Expenses

Business expenses deductible from gross income include the ordinary and necessary expenses directly connected with or pertaining to the taxpayer's trade or business, except items which are used as the basis for a deduction or credit under some provision of the Code other than Section 162. Among the items included in business expenses are management expenses, commissions, labor, supplies, incidental repairs, operating expenses of automobiles used in the trade or business, advertising and other selling expenses, insurance premiums against business loss or casualty, and rental for the use of business property. No such item may be included in business expenses, however, to the extent that it is used by the taxpayer in computing the cost of property included in inventory or used in determining the gain or loss basis of its plant, equipment, or other property.[31]

Business Expenses of Employees. An employee need not report on his tax return (either itemized or in totaled amount) expenses for travel, transportation, entertainment, and similar purposes incurred by him solely for the benefit of his employer *for which he accounts to his employer* and which are charged directly or indirectly to the employer, or for which the employee is paid through advances, reimbursements, or otherwise. The employee must state in the return that the amounts charged to the employer (directly or indirectly) or received from the employer as advances or reimbursements did not exceed the ordinary and necessary business expenses paid or incurred by the employee. In case the total did exceed these expenses, the employee must state on the return that the excess has been included in income.

An employee must submit the following information on his tax return in connection with expenses for travel, etc., incurred by him *for which he does not account to his employer* and which are paid or incurred by the employee under a reimbursement or other expense allowance arrangement with his employer or are otherwise charged directly or indirectly to his employer (or if not so paid, incurred, or charged are claimed as deductions on the employee's return): (1) the total of any such charges paid or borne by the

[30] S-2979, February 26, 1952.
[31] Regulations Section 1.162-1(a).

employer and of any other amounts received from the employer for payment of expenses whether by means of advances, reimbursements, or otherwise; and (2) a statement showing the nature of his occupation; the number of days away from home on business; and the amount of these expenses that constitute ordinary and necessary expenses (including those charged directly or indirectly to the employer), broken down into such broad categories as transportation, meals and lodgings, entertainment expense, and other business expenses.

To "account to his employer" means the submission of an expense account or other written statement. A reasonable *per diem* allowance may be approved as being the equivalent of an accounting.

Nonbusiness Expenses

Nonbusiness expenses are treated in the same manner as those incurred in carrying on a trade or business. Despite the label, nonbusiness expenses do not mean personal expenses; they are ordinary and necessary expenses paid or incurred during the taxable year (1) for the production or collection of income; (2) for the management, conservation, or maintenance of property held for the production of income; or (3) in connection with the determination, collection, or refund of any tax.[32] The term "income" for this purpose means not merely income of the taxable year but also income which the taxpayer has realized in a prior taxable year or may realize in subsequent taxable years, and is not confined to recurring income but applies as well to gains from the disposition of property.

Expenses of carrying on transactions primarily as a sport, hobby, or recreation are not allowable as nontrade or nonbusiness expenses.

Among expenditures not allowable under this heading are commuters' expenses; most expenses of taking special courses or training; expenses for improving personal appearance; the cost of rental of a safe-deposit box for storing jewelry and other personal effects; expenses such as those paid or incurred in seeking employment or in placing one's self in a position to begin rendering personal services for compensation; campaign expenditures of a candidate for public office; bar examination fees and other expenses paid or incurred by professional men for securing the right to practice.[33]

Ordinary and necessary expenses paid or incurred in connection with the management, conservation, or maintenance of property held as a residence by the taxpayer are not deductible.

[32] I.R.C. Section 212.
[33] Regulations Section 1.212–1(f).

Capital expenditures are not allowable as nontrade or nonbusiness expenses.

Nontrade or nonbusiness expenses are deductible "upon the basis of their immediate purposes rather than upon the basis of the remote contributions they might make to the conservation of a taxpayer's income-producing assets. . . ."[34]

Capital Expenditures

Deduction is not permitted for expenditures which add to the value of property. This includes such items as the following:

(1) The cost of acquisition, construction, or erection of buildings, machinery, equipment, furniture, fixtures, and similar property having a useful life substantially beyond the taxable year.

(2) Amounts expended for securing a copyright and plates, which remain the property of the person making the payments.

(3) The cost of defending or perfecting title to property.

(4) Commissions paid in purchasing securities. Commissions paid in selling securities are an offset against the selling price, except that in the case of dealers in securities, the commissions may be treated as ordinary and necessary expense.

(5) Amounts assessed and paid under an agreement between the bondholders or shareholders of a corporation to be used in a reorganization of the corporation or voluntary contributions by shareholders to the capital of the corporation for any corporate purpose. These amounts are capital investments and are not deductible.

(6) A holding company which guarantees dividends at a specified rate on the stock of a subsidiary corporation for the purpose of securing new capital for the subsidiary and increasing the value of its stockholdings in the subsidiary may not deduct amounts paid in carrying out this guaranty in computing its taxable income. These payments are capital expenditures to be added to the cost of its stock in the subsidiary.

(7) The cost of good will in connection with the acquisition of the assets of a going concern is a capital expenditure.

Special rules apply to the following types of expenditure:

(1) Development of mines or deposits.

(2) Research and experimental expenditures. This subject will be developed in the present chapter.

(3) Soil and water conservation expenditures.

(4) Expenditures for advertising and good will. If a corporation for the purpose of computing its excess profits credit under the

[34] *Lykes v. United States,* 343 U.S. 118 (1952).

1939 Code made an election to take the benefits of Section 733 or 451 of that Code, no deduction is presently allowable for expenditures for advertising or the promotion of good will which otherwise might be regarded as capital investments.

(5) Intangible drilling and development costs in the case of oil and gas wells.

Repairs. "The cost of incidental repairs which neither materially add to the value of the property nor appreciably prolong its life, but keep it in an ordinarily efficient operating condition, may be deducted as an expense, provided the cost of acquisition or production or the gain or loss basis to the taxpayer's plant, equipment, or other property, as the case may be, is not increased by the amount of such expenditures. Repairs in the nature of replacements, to the extent that they arrest deterioration and appreciably prolong the life of the property, shall either be capitalized and depreciated in accordance with Section 167 or charged against the depreciation reserve if such an account is kept." [35]

Even when there was no income tax, the Supreme Court had said: "Theoretically, the expenses chargeable to earnings include the general expenses of keeping up the organization of the company, and all expenses incurred in operating the works and keeping them in good condition and repair; whilst expenses chargeable to capital include those which are incurred in the original construction of the works, and in the subsequent enlargement and improvement thereof." [36]

With remarkable consistency, the courts have decided cases by their conformity or nonconformity to this definition: "To repair is to restore to a sound state or to mend, while a replacement connotes a substitution. A repair is an expenditure for the purpose of keeping the property in an ordinarily efficient operating condition. It does not add to the value of the property, nor does it appreciably prolong its life. It merely keeps the property in an operating condition over its probable useful life for the uses for which it was acquired. Expenditures for that purpose are distinguishable from those for replacements, alterations, improvements, or additions which prolong the life of the property, increase its value, or make it adaptable to a different use. The one is a maintenance charge, while the others are additions to capital investment which should not be applied against current earnings." [37]

[35] Regulations Section 1.162–4.
[36] *Union Pacific Rail Road Company v. United States,* 99 U.S. 401 (1879).
[37] *Illinois Merchants' Trust Co.,* 4 B.T.A. 103 (1926).

This classic definition is not confined to repairs as such. "The term 'replacement' in its loose sense is not excluded from this definition of 'repairs.' For example, it could hardly be said that the replacement of a burnt-out electric bulb in an elevator shaft is not an ordinary repair." [38]

Maintenance of the *status quo* is the objective of a deductible repair. If the expenditure is confined to this purpose and is not for additions, improvements, or betterments, the expenditure will be allowed.[39]

It is convenient to think of replacements as a type of repair. Thus, if an accident occurs, the taxpayer is under no compulsion to use his asset in damaged condition, even though it is still usable; he may restore the impaired property to its normal condition. But this restoration, to be recognized, may not prolong the normal life of the property nor increase its value; the *status quo ante* is that prevailing just before the accident or other actuating force that necessitated the repair.[40]

The wear and tear to be replaced need not be the result of an identifiable event, as in the case of a casualty loss (see Chapter 13). The ravages of deterioration may be similarly subject to deductible repairs, if the expenditures were "solely to mend deteriorated portions of the old [property] in order to restore it to a sound condition," a proviso being that these repairs may not "appreciably prolong the original useful life of the property." [41]

The replacement must be comparable to the original asset, similar materials being used. But the replacement need not even be a reasonable facsimile of the original, if it is of equal efficiency and cost, as in the case of a different type of elevator.[42] Where the replacement is with the same type of asset but in an improved version, capitalization will be required.[43] Technological improvements as such are not repairs; *e.g.,* the addition of automatic attachments to looms.[44]

Inasmuch as determination of the tax treatment of a repair often is of a borderline character, the purpose of the work should be kept clearly in mind. Deduction was allowed where "The purpose of the expenditure was to enable petitioner to continue the plant in opera-

[38] *Mellie Esperson,* B.T.A. Memo., Docket #98737, entered February 5, 1941.

[39] *Zimmern v. Commissioner,* 28 F.2d 769 (2d Cir., 1928).

[40] *Claremont Waste Manufacturing Co.,* T.C. Memo., Docket #3361, entered March 12, 1945.

[41] *Farmers Creamery Co.,* 14 T.C. 879 (1950).

[42] *Mellie Esperson,* B.T.A. Memo., Docket #98737, entered February 5, 1941.

[43] *Robert M. Craig,* T.C. Memo., Docket #13843, entered July 29, 1948.

[44] *Banana Manufacturing Co.,* 1 B.T.A. 1037 (1925).

tion not on any new or better scale but on the same scale and, so far as possible, as efficiently as it had operated before." [45]

If the property is made more adaptable to use by the putative repair, the cost must be capitalized.[46]

The reason for the repair is immaterial, provided the repair is necessary. Thus, a replacement occasioned by the taxpayer's negligence was deductible.[47]

Where repairs are made to an asset immediately after its acquisition, the Internal Revenue Service may not claim that such work *ipso facto* is capital.[48] Nor is capitalization implied by the fact that the bill was very expensive, amounting in one case to 35% of the cost of the asset.[49]

Advertising

To be deductible, an advertising expense must be ordinary, necessary, and reasonably related to the nature of the business.[50] "The cost of a big game hunt in Africa does not sound like an ordinary and necessary expense of a dairy business in Erie, Pennsylvania, but the evidence in this case shows clearly that it was and was so intended." [51] The resultant newspaper publicity was deemed to be a means of advertising a restaurant chain.[52] But a jeweler could not deduct as advertising the cost of entering a horse in a show, as there was no demonstrated relationship between the expenditure and an anticipated business benefit.[53]

Advertisements do not have to praise a product directly.[54]

Lobbying

It is an old-fashioned custom in democracies that the legislature may be petitioned to redress wrongs; and that sometimes takes time and money. "Congress shall make no law . . . abridging . . . the rights of the people . . . to petition the Government for a redress of grievances." [55] But lobbying expenses are not deductible as ordinary

[45] *Commissioner v. American Bemberg Corp.*, 177 F.2d 200 (6th Cir., 1949).
[46] *The P. Dougherty Co. v. Commissioner,* 159 F.2d 265 (4th Cir., 1946).
[47] *Brier Hill Collieries,* 12 B.T.A. 500 (1928).
[48] *Osage Steamship Co., Ltd.*, 3 B.T.A. 141 (1925).
[49] *Buckland v. United States,* 66 F. Supp. 681 (D.C., Conn., 1946).
[50] I.T. 3564, 1942-2 CB 87.
[51] *Sanitary Farms Dairy, Inc.*, 25 T.C. 463 (1955).
[52] *Rodgers Dairy Co.*, 14 T.C. 66 (1950).
[53] *James Schulz,* 16 T.C. 401 (1951).
[54] *Denise Coal Co. et al.*, 29 T.C. 528 (1957).
[55] Constitution of the United States, Article I.

and necessary.[56] Expenditures made for the exploitation of propaganda or the promotion or defeat of legislation are not deductible as business expenses.[57]

Entertaining of public officials also may be disallowed on the ground of undue efforts to influence a governmental agency.[58]

Research and Experimental Expenditures

There are two methods for treating research or experimental expenditures paid or incurred by the taxpayer in connection with his trade or business. These expenditures may be (1) deducted as expenses in the year in which they are paid or incurred or (2) deferred and amortized.[59] If the taxpayer does not elect to use either of these methods, the expenditures must be charged to capital account.

The term "research or experimental expenditures" means expenditures incurred in connection with the taxpayer's trade or business which represent research and development costs in the experimental or laboratory sense. The term includes generally all such costs incident to the development of an experimental or pilot model, a plant process, a product, a formula, an invention, or similar property, and the improvement of an already existing property of the type mentioned. The term does not include expenditures such as those for the ordinary testing or inspection of materials or products for quality control or those for efficiency surveys, management studies, consumer surveys, advertising, or promotions. The term, however, includes the costs of obtaining a patent, such as attorneys' fees expended in making and perfecting a patent application. On the other hand, the term does not include the costs of acquiring another's patent, model, production, or process, nor does it include expenditures paid or incurred for research in connection with literary, historical, or similar projects.[60]

These provisions apply not only to costs paid or incurred by the taxpayer for research or experimentation undertaken directly by him, but also to expenditures paid or incurred for research or experimentation carried on in his behalf by another person or organization; but any such expenditures carried on in the taxpayer's behalf by another person are not covered to the extent that they represent

[56] *Textile Mills Securities Corp. v. Commissioner,* 314 U.S. 326 (1941).
[57] *Roberts Dairy Co.,* T.C. Memo., Docket #20442, entered October 31, 1950.
[58] *Raymond F. Flangan,* 47 B.T.A. 782 (1942).
[59] I.R.C. Section 174.
[60] Regulations Section 1.174-2(a).

expenditures for the acquisition or improvement of land or depreciable property. Expenditures by the taxpayer for the acquisition or improvement of land, or of depreciable or depletable property, are not covered by the research elections, irrespective of the fact that the property or improvements may be used by him in connection with research or experimentation. But depreciation or depletion allowances are considered as research or experimental expenditures to the extent that the property is used in connection with research or experimentation.

If expenditures for research or experimentation are incurred in connection with the construction or manufacture of depreciable property by another, they are deductible only if made upon the taxpayer's order and at his risk.

Expenditures for research or experimentation which result, as an end product of the research or experimentation, in depreciable property to be used in the taxpayer's trade or business may be allowable as a current deduction; these expenditures cannot be amortized. These deductions are limited to amounts expended for research or experimentation, and do not include the costs of the component materials of the depreciable property, the costs of labor or other elements involved in its construction and installation, or costs attributable to the acquisition of the property.

Illustration. A taxpayer undertakes to develop a new machine for use in his business. He expends $30,000 on the project of which $10,000 represents the actual costs of material, labor, etc., to construct the machine and $20,000 represents research costs which are not attributable to the machine itself. The taxpayer would be permitted to deduct the $20,000 as expenses, but the $10,000 must be charged to the asset account (the machine).

These rules are not applicable to any expenditures paid or incurred for the purpose of ascertaining the existence, location, extent, or quality of any deposit of ore, oil, gas, or other mineral.

Adoption and Change of Method. Research or experimental expenses may be deducted currently, if the taxpayer adopts this method. If adopted, the method will apply to all research and experimental expenditures paid or incurred in the year of adoption and all subsequent taxable years, unless the Commissioner gives permission to use a different method. The Commissioner's permission is not required to adopt the method, if this is done for the first taxable year in which such expenditures are paid or incurred. But with the Commissioner's permission, the method may be adopted at any time. An application for permission to change to a different method of treating research or experimental expenditures must be in writing, addressed to the Commissioner of Internal Revenue, Attention: T:R, Washington 25, D.C.

Treatment as Deferred Expenses. If the taxpayer has not elected to take research or experimental expenditures as expenses, he may elect to treat them as deferred expenses. This election applies only to those expenditures which are chargeable to capital account but which are not chargeable to property subject to depreciation or depletion. Thus, the election applies only if the property resulting from the research or experimentation has no determinable useful life; otherwise, the capitalized expenditures must be amortized or depreciated over the determinable useful life.

Expenditures which are treated as deferred expenses are allowable as a deduction ratably over a period of not less than sixty consecutive months beginning with the month in which the taxpayer first realizes benefits from the expenditures. The length of the period is to be selected by the taxpayer at the time he makes the election to defer the expenditures. If he has two or more separate projects, he may select a different amortization period for each project.

If expenditures which the taxpayer has elected to defer and deduct ratably over a period of time result in the development of depreciable property, deductions for the unrecovered expenditures, beginning with the time the asset becomes depreciable in character, will be determined under customary depreciation rules (see Chapter 10).

The election will be applicable to all research and experimental expenditures paid or incurred by the taxpayer or, if so limited by the taxpayer's election, to all such expenditures with respect to the particular project.

Education

In general, the cost of acquiring an education is not deductible. "Reputation and learning are akin to capital assets. . . . For many, they are the only tools with which to hew a pathway to success. The money spent in acquiring them is well and wisely spent. It is not an ordinary expense of the operation of a business." [61] But this basically harsh rule has been subjected to many exceptions.

Expenditures made by a taxpayer for his education are deductible if they are for education (including research activities) undertaken primarily for the purpose of (1) maintaining or improving skills required by the taxpayer in his employment or other trade or busi-

[61] *Welch v. Helvering,* 290 U.S. 111 (1933).

ness or (2) meeting the express requirements of a taxpayer's employer, or the requirements of applicable law or regulations, imposed as a condition to the retention by the taxpayer of his salary, status, or employment.[62]

If it is customary for other established members of the taxpayer's trade or business to undertake such education, the taxpayer ordinarily will be considered to have undertaken this education for permissible purposes. Education expenditures are deductible only to the extent that they are required by the taxpayer's employer, or by applicable law or regulations, as a condition to retaining one's salary, status, or employment. The requirement must be primarily for a bona fide business purpose of the taxpayer's employment and not primarily for the taxpayer's ends. This is something that the taxpayer may have to prove.

Education expenses are not deductible if they are undertaken primarily for the purpose of obtaining a new position or substantial advancement in position, or primarily for the purpose of fulfilling the general educational aspirations or other personal purposes of the taxpayer. If education is required in order to meet the minimum requirements for qualification or establishment in his intended trade or business, or specialty therein, the expense is personal in nature and hence nondeductible.

In general, a taxpayer's expenditures for travel (including travel while on sabbatical leave) as a form of education will be considered as primarily personal in nature and therefore not deductible.

If a taxpayer travels away from home primarily to obtain education which is a deductible item, his expenditures for travel, meals, and lodging while away from home are deductible.[63] But if, as an incident to the trip, he engages in some personal activity, such as sightseeing or social visiting, a portion of the expenditure will be regarded as nondeductible. Expenses in the nature of commuters' fares are not deductible.

Illustration. A is employed by an accounting firm. In order to become a certified public accountant, he takes courses in accounting. Inasmuch as the education was undertaken prior to the time he became qualified in his chosen profession as a certified public accountant, his expenditures for these courses and expenses for any transportation, meals, and lodging while away from home are not deductible.

Illustration. B, a general practitioner of medicine, takes a course of study in order to become a specialist in pediatrics. C, a general practitioner, takes a 2-week course reviewing developments in several specialized fields, including

[62] Regulations Section 1.162–5.

[63] Regulations Section 1.162–5(d).

pediatrics, for the purpose of carrying on his general practice. B's expenses are not deductible because the course of study qualified him for a specialty within his trade or business. C's expenses for his education and any transportation, meals, and lodging while away from home are deductible because they were undertaken primarily to improve skills required by him in his trade or business.

Illustration. D is required by his employer (or by state law) either to read a list of books or to take certain courses giving six hours of academic credit every two years in order to retain his position as a teacher. D fulfills the requirement by taking the courses and thereby receives an automatic increase in salary in his present position. Also, as the result of taking the prescribed courses, at the end of ten years he receives a master's degree and becomes automatically eligible for an additional salary increase. Inasmuch as his purpose in taking the courses was primarily to fulfill the educational requirement of his employer, his expenses for such education and transportation, etc., are deductible.

Illustration. The facts are the same as in the preceding illustration except that, solely because of a shortage of qualified teachers, D's employer does not enforce the prescribed educational requirements in that other teachers who do not fulfill those requirements are retained in their positions. D's expenses are nevertheless deductible.

Illustration. E, a high school teacher of physics, in order to improve skills required by him and thus improve his effectiveness as a teacher, takes summer school courses in nuclear physics and educational methods. E's expenses for these courses are deductible.

Illustration. F takes summer school courses in order to improve skills required by him in his employment as a teacher. As a result of taking these courses, he receives an in-grade increase in salary in his present position pursuant to a salary schedule established by the school system for which he works. His expenditures for these courses are deductible.

Illustration. G, a graduate student at a university, plans to become a university professor. In order to qualify as a regular faculty member, he must obtain a graduate degree. While taking the required graduate courses, he is engaged in teaching at the university. His expenses are not deductible inasmuch as he has not completed the education required to become qualified as a regular faculty member at the time he takes these courses.

Illustration. H, a self-employed tax consultant, decides to take a 1-week course in taxation, which is offered in City X, 500 miles away from his home. His primary purpose in going to X is to take the course, but he also takes a side trip to City Y (50 miles from X) for one day, takes a sightseeing trip while in X, and entertains some personal friends. His transportation expenses to City X and return to his home are deductible, but not his transportation to City Y. His expenses for meals and lodging while away from home will be allocated between his educational pursuits and his personal activities. Those expenses which are entirely personal, such as sightseeing and entertaining friends, are not deductible to any extent.

Illustration. The facts are the same as in the preceding example, except that H's primary purpose in going to City X is to take a vacation. This purpose is indicated by several factors, one of which is the fact that he spends only one week attending the tax course and devotes five weeks entirely to personal activities. None of his transportation expenses is deductible and his expenses for meals and lodging while away from home are not deductible to the extent attributable to personal activities. His expenses for meals and lodging allocable to the week attending the tax course are, however, deductible.

Expenses of attending summer school were deductible where the position could not be *retained* unless courses were taken.[64] Educational expense is not deductible if the purpose is to *obtain,* rather than merely to retain, a teaching position, or if the purpose is to qualify for permanent status or a higher position.[65] But graduate study to get a doctorate in order to qualify a tutor for a permanent position was deductible, where he had a temporary status and might be reappointed.[66] Expenses of getting a doctorate were not deductible where a professor obtained a position that required him to get this degree. He was not maintaining a position, for he was not established in it "until the basic requirement of holding a doctorate degree was met." [67]

Expenses of a trip to Europe to study marketing *in preparation for* starting one's own business were not deductible.[68]

Expenses in connection with a doctoral dissertation were denied a college professor, who was not required to take advanced academic credits.[69] A professor could not deduct the cost of a foreign trip for study on research, allegedly to fit him better for the duties he was engaged to perform, for there was no requirement that he do so.[70]

The nature of the subject studied may have some bearing on the tax treatment. It was said of a course in taxation, "Even if in its cultural aspect knowledge should for tax purposes be considered in the nature of a capital asset . . . the rather evanescent character of that for which the petitioner spent his money deprives it of the sort of permanency such a concept embraces." [71]

A schoolteacher's cost of daily travel to school in a nearby town plus the cost of her midday meal were nondeductible personal expenses.[72]

[64] *Hill v. Commissioner,* 181 F.2d 906 (2d Cir., 1950).
[65] I.T. 4044, 1951–1 CB 16.
[66] *Marlor v. Commissioner,* 251 F.2d 615 (2d Cir., 1958).
[67] *Robert M. Kamins et ux.,* 25 T.C. 1238 (1956).
[68] *Harold V. Bell, Jr. et ux.,* T.C. Memo. 1958–33, filed February 28, 1958.
[69] *Richard Henry Lamphin,* T.C. Memo., Docket #26814, entered June 9, 1952.
[70] *Manoel Cardozo,* 17 T.C. 3 (1951).
[71] *Coughlin v. Commissioner,* 203 F.2d 307 (2d Cir., 1953).
[72] *E. M. and Rose Ann Taylor,* T.C. Memo., Docket #27540, entered June 24, 1952.

Professional Expenses

A professional man may deduct the cost of supplies used by him in the practice of his profession, expenses paid or accrued in the operation and repair of an automobile used in making professional calls, dues to professional societies and subscriptions to professional journals, office rent, office utilities, and the hire of office assistants. Expenditures for books, furniture, and instruments and equipment with a short useful life may be deducted rather than being subjected to depreciation.[73]

The cost of attending a professional seminar is deductible.[74] So is the cost of attending a professional convention.[75]

Contributions

Charitable contributions (to be defined below) are deductible *in the year actually paid,* regardless of the accounting method used by the taxpayer. Under certain circumstances, an accrual-basis corporation may deduct a contribution either in the year of pledge or the year of payment; see Chapter 16. The amount of the contribution allowable is subject to over-all limitations that will be developed below.[76]

The term "charitable contribution" means a contribution or gift to or for the use of:

(1) A state, territory, possession of the United States, or political subdivision of one of these, or the United States or the District of Columbia, but only if the contribution is made for exclusively public purposes.

(2) A corporation, trust, or community chest, fund, or foundation—

(A) Created or organized in the United States or one of its possessions, or under the law of the United States, possession, state, territory, or the District of Columbia;

(B) Organized and operated exclusively for religious, charitable, scientific, literary, or educational purposes, or for the prevention of cruelty to children or animals;

(C) No part of the net earnings of which inures to the benefit of any private shareholder or individual; and

[73] Regulations Section 1.162–6.
[74] *Musser v. United States,* D.C., Calif., 1957.
[75] *Robert C. Coffey,* 21 B.T.A. 1242 (1930).
[76] I.R.C. Section 170.

(D) No substantial part of the activities of which is carrying on propaganda, or otherwise attempting to influence legislation.

A contribution or gift by a corporation to a trust, chest, fund, or foundation may be deductible only if it is to be used within the United States or any of its possessions exclusively for the purposes mentioned in (B), above.

(3) A post or organization of war veterans, or an auxiliary unit or society of, or trust or foundation for, any such post or organization—

(A) Organized in the United States or any of its possessions, and

(B) No part of the net earnings of which inures to the benefit of any private shareholder or individual.

(4) In the case of a contribution or gift by an individual, a domestic fraternal society, order, or association, operating under the lodge system, but only if the contribution or gift is to be used exclusively for religious, charitable, scientific, literary, or educational purposes, or for the prevention of cruelty to children or animals.

(5) A cemetery association owned and operated exclusively for the benefit of its members, or any corporation chartered solely for burial purposes as a cemetery corporation and not permitted by its charter to engage in any business not necessarily incident to that purpose, if this company is not operated for profit and no part of the net earnings inures to the benefit of any private shareholder or individual.

A schedule of organizations, contributions to which (within the applicable limits) are deductible for tax purposes may be purchased from the Superintendent of Documents in Washington.[77]

An "educational organization" for this purpose is one the primary function of which is the presentation of formal instruction and which normally maintains a regular faculty and curriculum and normally has a regularly enrolled body of students in attendance at the place where its educational activities are regularly carried on. This includes primary, secondary, preparatory or high schools, and colleges and universities. It includes Federal, state, and other publicly supported schools which otherwise come within the definition. It does not include organizations engaged in both educational and noneducational activities, unless the latter are merely incidental to and growing out of the educational activities. A recognized university which incidentally operates a museum or sponsors concerts is an educational organization. But the operation of a school

[77] *Cumulative List, Organizations Described in Section 170(c) of Internal Revenue Code of 1954.*

by a museum does not qualify the museum as an educational organization.

The term "hospital" means an organization the principal purposes or functions of which are providing hospital or medical care. It does not include medical education or research organizations. It does not include convalescent homes, homes for children or the aged, or institutions the principal purposes of which are to train handicapped individuals to pursue some vocation.

Limitations on Individuals. The deduction allowed to an individual is limited to 20% of his adjusted gross income (computed without regard to any net operating loss carryback to the taxable year). See Chapter 14. If a husband and a wife make a joint return, the deduction for contributions is the aggregate of the contributions made by both spouses, and the limitation is on the aggregated gross incomes. In addition to this 20% figure, an individual may deduct contributions made during the taxable year *to* (but not merely *for the use of*) a church or convention of churches, an educational organization, or a hospital to the extent that these contributions in the aggregate do not exceed 10% of his adjusted gross income (without loss carryback).

Illustration. An individual reports his income on the calendar year basis, and for the taxable year he has an adjusted gross income of $10,000. During the year, he made the following charitable contributions:

		Deductible Contributions
(1) Contributions qualifying for the additional 10% deduction	$2,400	
(2) Other charitable contributions	700	
(3) Total contributions paid	$3,100	
(4) Contributions qualifying for the additional 10% deduction	$2,400	
(5) Special limitation: 10% of adjusted gross income	1,000	
(6) Deductible amount: Line 4 or line 5, whichever is the lesser		$1,000
(7) Excess of line 4 over line 5	$1,400	
(8) Add: Other charitable contributions	700	
(9) Contributions subject to the 20% limitation	$2,100	
(10) Limitation of 20% of adjusted gross income	2,000	
(11) Deductible amount: Line 9 or line 10, whichever is the lesser		$2,000
(12) Contributions not deductible	$ 100	
(13) Total deduction for contributions		$3,000

No deduction is allowable for contribution of services. Nor does a donation of blood qualify as a charitable deduction.[78]

[78] Revenue Ruling 162, 1953–2 CB 127.

A taxpayer who gives his services gratuitously to an association, contributions to which are tax-deductible, and who incurs unreimbursed travel expenses (including meals and lodgings) while away from home in connection with the affairs of the association, and at its direction, may deduct such amounts.[79] Out-of-pocket expenses incurred by an individual for transportation to and from a local hospital or church for the purpose of rendering volunteer services to the Red Cross or church are contributions. But meals are not deductible unless the taxpayer is away from home overnight.[80]

Actual unreimbursed expenses incurred by a lay member of a church to attend as a delegate a church convention are contributions. Such also is the case with an American Legion member attending a convention as a delegate.[81]

A contribution by an individual to an organization of the type described is deductible even though some portion of the funds of the organization may be used in foreign countries for charitable and educational purposes.

Unlimited Deduction for Individuals. The above percentage limitations do not apply if in the taxable year and each of eight of the ten preceding taxable years the sum of an individual's charitable contributions paid during the year, plus his payments during the year on account of Federal income taxes, is more than 90% of his taxable income for the year.[82] For the purpose of the preceding sentence, taxable income is determined without regard to the deduction for charitable contributions, for personal exemptions, or for a net operating loss carryback.

For the purpose of the previous paragraph, in lieu of the amount of income tax paid during any year, there may be substituted the amount of tax paid *for* that year.

Limitation on Corporations. The deduction by a corporation in any taxable year for charitable contributions is limited to 5% of its taxable income for the year, computed without regard to:

(1) The deduction for charitable contributions,

(2) The special deductions for corporations allowed under Sections 241 through 247 (see Chapter 16),

(3) Any net operating loss carryback to the taxable year, and

(4) The special deduction for Western Hemisphere Trade Corporations under Section 922 (see Chapter 2).

[79] Revenue Ruling 55–4, 1955–1 CB 291.
[80] Revenue Ruling 56–508, 1956–2 CB 126.
[81] Revenue Ruling 58–230, I.R.B. 1958–21, 18.
[82] I.R.C. Section 170(b)(1)(C).

A contribution by a corporation to a trust, chest, fund, or foundation organized and operated exclusively for one of the authorized purposes previously mentioned is deductible only if the contribution is to be used in the United States or its possessions for these purposes.

Any contributions made by a corporation in excess of the 5% limitation are deductible in each of the two succeeding taxable years in order of time, but only to the extent of the lesser of the following amounts: (1) the excess of the maximum amount deductible for the succeeding year under the 5% limitation over the contributions made in that year and (2) in the case of the first succeeding taxable year, the amount of the excess contributions; and in the case of the second succeeding taxable year, the portion of the excess contributions not deductible in the first succeeding taxable year.

Illustration. A corporation which reports its income on the calendar year basis makes a charitable contribution of $10,000 in June, 1960, anticipating taxable income for 1960 of $200,000. Its actual taxable income (without regard to charitable deductions) for 1960 is only $50,000 and the charitable deduction for that year is limited to 5% of that figure, or $2,500. The excess charitable contribution not deductible in 1960 ($7,500) represents a carryover potentially available as a deduction in the two succeeding taxable years. The corporation has taxable income (without regard to charitable contributions) of $150,000 in 1961 and makes a charitable contribution of $2,500 in that year. For 1961, the corporation may deduct as a charitable contribution the amount of $7,500 (5% of $150,000). This amount consists first of the $2,500 contribution made in 1961, and $5,000 of the $7,500 carried over from 1960. The remaining $2,500 carried over from 1960 and not allowable as a deduction in 1961 because of the 5% limitation may be carried over to 1962. The corporation has taxable income (without regard to charitable contributions) of $100,000 in 1962 and makes a charitable contribution of $3,000. For 1962, the corporation may deduct the amount of $5,000 (5% of $100,000). This amount consists first of the $3,000 contributed in 1962, and $2,000 of the $2,500 carried over from 1960 to 1962. The remaining $500 of the carryover from 1960 is not allowable as a deduction in any year because of the 2-year limitation.

There is a special rule for corporations having net operating loss carryovers. The excess of total contributions over allowable contributions must be reduced to the extent that this excess reduces taxable income and increases a net operating loss carryover to a succeeding taxable year.

Travel and Entertainment Expenses

"There shall be allowed as a deduction all the ordinary and necessary expenses paid or incurred during the taxable year in carrying on any trade or business, including . . . traveling expenses (including the entire amount expended for meals and lodging) while away from home in the pursuit of a trade or business . . ." [83]

Traveling expenses also include expenses for sample rooms, telephone and telegraph, public stenographers.[84] Likewise covered are tips, luggage, taxicabs, and sundry transportation.[85] Where a taxpayer's wife accompanies him on a business trip, expenses attributable to her travel are not deductible unless it can be adequately shown that her presence on the trip has a bona fide business purpose. Her performance of some incidental service does not cause her expenses to qualify as deductible business expenses.[86]

"We have been taking a close look at expense deductions claimed involving such items as club dues, entertainment, travel, maintenance of automobiles, yachts, and airplanes, maintenance of company-supported residences, and so forth.

"One area which requires close attention involves the use of alleged branch offices established in resort cities for the sole purpose of sending business executives to such cities for vacations. Other instances involve deductions for the expenses of purported business trips by executives vacationing at resort hotels, expenses of hunting trips, expenses of attendance at sporting events in distant cities, and for other nonbusiness purposes, under the guise of necessary business trips.

"We obviously have no desire to tell taxpayers how to spend their money, but we cannot permit expenditures to be deducted for tax purposes without proper justification." [87]

"[T]he travel expense must have a direct connection with the carrying on of the trade or business of the taxpayer or his employer. It must be necessary or appropriate to the development and pursuit of the business or trade." [88] Traveling expenses in pursuit of business can arise only when the business forces the taxpayer to travel and to live temporarily at some place other than his post of duty, thereby advancing the interests of the business. "The exigencies of business rather than the personal conveniences and necessities of the traveler must be the motivating factors." [89]

Where one maintains a second residence for business convenience, it is nonetheless regarded as a personal matter.[90] Personal reasons

[83] I.R.C. Section 162(a)(2).
[84] Regulations Section 1.162–2(a).
[85] I.T. 3728, 1945 CB 78.
[86] Revenue Ruling 56–168, 1956–1 CB 93.
[87] IR-Circular No. 57–85, June 20, 1957.
[88] *United States v. Woodall et al.,* 255 F.2d 370 (10th Cir., 1958).
[89] *Commissioner v. Flowers,* 326 U.S. 465 (1946).
[90] *Wilbur H. Clayton,* T.C. Memo., Docket #13650, entered June 4, 1958.

for maintaining a home distant from the place of work are immaterial.[91]

The Internal Revenue Service has announced that the deduction is permitted for "reasonable and necessary expenses of traveling away from home overnight in pursuit of your business or employment." [92] But it has been ruled that there is no requirement of "overnight." [93]

Some persons may not deduct any expenses while away from home, as they have no homes; *e.g.*, a circus performer, whose home was adjudged to be wherever the circus was at a particular time.[94]

Commuters' fares are not deductible.[95] Nor are expenses incurred to obtain employment.[96] Expenses of a trip to Washington in connection with an additional tax assessed on the taxpayer's trade or business are deductible.[97]

The cost of a European trip of a physician and his wife (who helped him in his sanitarium) was largely disallowed as personal. Most of the prominent sightseeing places in Great Britain and the Continent were visited on the trip, which lasted 85 days, of which 56 were spent in travel; and a travel agent had worked out the itinerary. No preliminary arrangements had been made to visit hospitals and the like, and the visits may have been the result of natural curiosity that any professional man would have felt. The court allowed but $200 of the $7,881 claimed.[98] The case illustrates the problem of proof when personal pleasure is involved in a business trip. Taxpayers are permitted to use Form 2106, a work sheet calling for a detailed analysis of expenditures.

The entertainment expense deduction for taking a client to lunch includes only that portion of the check representing the client. What the host spent on his own meal, it was assumed, was personal; he would have had to eat lunch even if he had been alone.[99]

Uniforms

As to a business expense deduction for the cost and maintenance of uniforms, there is no uniform rule. In general, the cost is de-

[91] *Beatrice H. Albert,* 13 T.C. 129 (1949).

[92] *Your Federal Income Tax* (Washington, D.C.: Government Printing Office, 1958), p. 34.

[93] *Kenneth Waters,* 12 T.C. 414 (1949).

[94] *Nat Lewis et al.,* T.C. Memo. 1954-233, filed December 27, 1954.

[95] Regulations Section 1.162-2(e).

[96] *United States v. Woodall et al.,* 255 F.2d 370 (10th Cir., 1958).

[97] O.D. 849, 4 CB 123.

[98] *Ralph E. Duncan et al.,* 30 T.C. 386 (1958).

[99] *Richard A. Sutter,* 21 T.C. 170 (1953).

ductible where (1) the uniforms are of a type specifically required as a condition of employment and (2) are not adaptable to general or continued usage to the extent that they take the place of ordinary clothing.[100] Thus, a fireman's leather helmet would seem to represent a deduction; for although he could use it as a hat for street and social use, thereby saving the cost of a more conventional hat, he would not be likely to do so. "In any case . . . where a uniform 'does not merely take the place of articles required in civilian life,' deduction of amounts expended in the purchase and maintenance of such a uniform would not be precluded . . ." Thus, the uniform of an army reservist "does not merely take the place of articles required in civilian life." [101]

An advertising agent could not deduct one-fifth of the cost of a mink coat he had purchased for his wife, allegedly on the ground that it was a business expense, as an aura of prosperity would aid his business. The court denied that "the purchase of a mink coat for his wife is an 'ordinary' expense of the business engaged in by a public relations or advertising agent." [102]

Amortizable Bond Premium

Bond premium is the excess of (1) the bond's cost or other basis in the hands of the bondholder over (2) the amount payable at maturity (or, in the case of a callable bond, the earlier call date). Where a premium was paid, the bondholder will get back less than he paid for the bonds. Amortization of premium is a process by which this loss may be taken ratably over the remaining life of the bonds.[103]

Amortization of bond premium is *required* in the case of—

(1) Fully tax-exempt bonds (the interest on which is excludable from gross income), whether the owner is a corporation, individual, or other taxpayer.

(2) Partially tax-exempt bonds owned by a corporation.

Amortization is *optional,* at the election of the taxpayer, in the case of—

(3) Fully taxable bonds, regardless of the nature of the owner.

(4) Partially tax-exempt bonds owned by taxpayers other than corporations.

[100] Mimeograph 6463, 1950–1 CB 29.

[101] Revenue Ruling 55–109, 1955–1 CB 261.

[102] *Paul E. Jackson et al.,* T.C. Memo. 1954–235, filed December 27, 1954.

[103] I.R.C. Section 171.

Operation. In the case of (1), the amortizable bond premium is simply an adjustment to the adjusted basis of the bond. If the premium is $1, the adjusted basis of the bond is reduced by $1.

In the case of (2), the amortizable bond premium is applied both as an adjustment to adjusted basis and as a deduction in computing taxable income.

In the case of (3), the amortizable bond premium for the taxable year is used for the following purposes:

(A) As an adjustment to the basis of the bond.

(B) As a deduction in computing taxable income.

(C) As a credit or deduction for partially tax-exempt interest.

Illustration. An individual has elected to amortize the premium on a partially tax-exempt bond. The interest on the bond is $30 for the year. The bond has an adjusted basis of $1,036. The amortizable bond premium is $6 for the year. In such case, the $30 must be included in gross income, the $6 will be allowed as an amortization deduction, the adjusted basis will be reduced by $6 to $1,030, and a credit of $0.72 (3% of $24 ($30 minus $6)) will be allowed against the tax for the year. If the taxpayer was a corporation, it would be required to amortize and deduct the bond premium. The $30 would be included in gross income. The $6 would be allowed as an amortization deduction. The adjusted basis would be reduced by $6 to $1,030, and an adjustment of $7.20, which is 30% of $24, would be allowed against the tax for the year.

If a wholly taxable bond, regardless of the date of issue, is acquired after 1957, the amount of the bond premium is to be determined with reference to (1) the amount payable on maturity or (2) if the bond premium determined with reference to the amount payable on earlier call date results in a smaller amortizable bond premium attributable to the period of the earlier call date, with reference to the latter date.

Illustration. On January 1, 1958, the taxpayer (who was on a calendar year basis) paid $1,200 for a $1,000 wholly taxable bond which matures on December 31, 1977. The bond is callable on January 1, 1963, at $1,165. The premium computed with reference to the maturity date of the bond is $200. The premium computed with reference to earlier call date is $35. Although the premium amortized ratably to maturity would yield a deduction of $10 for each year ($200 divided by 20 years), under the amendment the deduction for each taxable year for the period before January 1, 1963, will be $7 ($35 divided by 5 years). If the bond is not called, the deduction for each taxable year in the period from 1963 through 1977 will be $11 ($165 divided by 15 years). If the earliest call date in this example had been January 1, 1961, instead of January 1, 1963, the premium amortized ratably to maturity would be used to obtain a deduction of $10 per year since this would be less than the premium amortized ratably to earlier call date of $11.67 ($35 divided by 3, the number of years to the earliest call date).

Election. The election to amortize bond premium is made by claiming the deduction on the return for the first taxable year where the application is desired. A statement of the computation should be attached to the return.

Supplementary Material

A. Suggested Reading.

William Carson and Herbert Weiner, *Ordinary and Necessary Expenses* (New York: The Ronald Press Co., 1959).

Michael Kaminsky, "Are All Deductions a Matter of Privilege?" *TAXES—The Tax Magazine,* February, 1959, Vol. XXXVII, #2, p. 137.

John E. Hamilton, "Non-Business Expenses," *American University Tax Institute Lectures* (Albany: Matthew Bender & Co., Inc., 1954), Vol. VI, p. 117.

James C. Wriggins and George Byron Gordon, *Repairs vs. Capital Expenditures* (New York: The Ronald Press Co., 1958).

Robert L. Merritt, "The Tax Incentives for Charitable Giving," *TAXES—The Tax Magazine,* September, 1958, Vol. XXXVI, #9, p. 646.

Richard F. Palmer, "Tax Saving Through Charitable Giving," *TAXES—The Tax Magazine,* January, 1958, Vol. XXXVI, #1, p. 40.

J. K. Lasser, *How Tax Laws Make Giving to Charity Easy* (New York: Funk & Wagnalls Co., 1948).

Clark E. Bowen, "How You Should Handle Advertising Costs," *TAXES—The Tax Magazine,* January, 1957, Vol. XXXV, #1, p. 11.

Clark E. Bowen, "Teachers and Taxes," *TAXES—The Tax Magazine,* January, 1954, Vol. XXXII, #1, p. 57.

B. Leading Cases.

Deductions are matters of grace. *Commissioner v. Sullivan et al.,* 356 U.S. 27 (1958).

Ordinary and necessary. *Welch v. Helvering,* 290 U.S. 111 (1933).

Kickbacks. *Libby et al. v. Commissioner,* 343 U.S. 90 (1952).

Reasonableness. *Commissioner v. Lincoln Electric Co.,* 176 F.2d 815 (6th Cir., 1949).

Repairs. *Illinois Merchants' Trust Co.,* 4 B.T.A. 103 (1926).

Lobbying. *Textile Mills Securities Corp. v. Commissioner,* 314 U.S. 326 (1941).

Away from home. *Commissioner v. Flowers,* 326 U.S. 465 (1946).

C. Questions.

1. Do you believe that the rule as to income and expenses should be the same; that is, that all income and all expenses should be taken into account, or that income and expenses should only be taken into account if specifically mentioned in the statute?
2. The distributor of Cougar Brand footwear rented a live cougar to advertise his products. A Revenue Agent questioned the deduction for cost of food, as the Internal Revenue Code makes no reference to victuals for cougars. Is the deduction allowable?
3. Distinguish between a repair that is deductible for tax purposes and one that is not.

4. A manufacturer spent $10,000 in endeavoring to produce a hair oil with fewer impurities than existing brands. The resultant product, it was believed, would be profitable for fifteen years. May the full cost be deducted in the one year of incurrence?
5. A salesman is away from home for a month on business. Is his laundry a deductible expense?
6. Why is no deduction allowed for interest on money borrowed to purchase municipal bonds?
7. A businessman deducted certain expenses to prevent possible flood damages. A Revenue Agent claimed that as the business had not experienced a flood in its 20-year history, such expenses were not *ordinary* and hence could not be deducted. Do you agree?
8. A road construction company paid bribes to the State Commissioner of Highways to get approval on work done. The laws of that state did not specifically prohibit bribes to state employees. Is the deduction valid for Federal tax purposes?
9. The driver of a milk truck, who received both salary and commissions, was permitted to wear any clothing he chose (within obvious limits), but he preferred to wear white garb that seemed appropriate to what he regarded as his professional status. This clothing required more frequent laundering than conventional dark clothes. Is the additional cost a tax deduction?
10. A Texan paid $1,200 on January 1, 1961, for a City of Fort Worth bond of $1,000 principal amount, with a 20-year maturity, of which ten years were yet to run. He amortized the premium. What is his annual deduction? What would the deduction be if the obligor had the right to call the bond at any time on or after January 1, 1966?
11. A certain excise tax is imposed upon manufacturers of automobiles. If a manufacturer passes the tax along so that the ultimate purchaser of a car really pays the tax, is this purchaser entitled to the tax deduction? Would your answer be different if the car were purchased for business purposes rather than for pleasure?
12. A manufacturer spent money on the development of two technical processes. May he elect to expense the cost of one and to capitalize the other?
13. An individual wishes to sit for a state certified public accountant's examination, but he finds the examination is open only to persons with college degrees. May he deduct the cost of a 4-year liberal arts program that will lead to such a degree?
14. An attorney lived in the suburbs of a city. He was severely injured in an accident, and after he left the hospital he could only get to his office if he used a taxi. Are the taxi bills deductible, on the ground that without the cabs he could earn no taxable income?
15. In 1961, a taxpayer paid $1,500 to a broker to locate a certain type of merchandise that was purchased. This fee was added to the cost of the inventory; but no sales were made in that year. May the fee be claimed as a business expense for 1961?
16. A retired person, who was no longer engaged in any business, used the proceeds of an inheritance to buy some lots for rental purposes in another city. Is he entitled to a tax deduction for his traveling expenses when he went to see a broker about getting tenants for his land?

17. The doors of a commercial garage were damaged to an extent that required replacement, and the proprietor purchased gates that were larger than previously used so that trucks could be stored as well as passenger cars. Is this a deductible repair, assuming that the new doors were made of the same type and quality of wood as the old ones?
18. A retailer purchased advertising space to urge that the state legislature be deluged with letters from persons who wanted to have a state fair trade law repealed. Is the advertising cost deductible?
19. To what extent may an individual take a deduction for rental of a safe-deposit box in a bank?
20. A creditor took out life insurance, payable to his own order, on the life of a purchaser of merchandise, to insure payment should the customer die before the bill was settled. May the creditor deduct the cost of the insurance premium?
21. A traveling salesman received commissions on sales that he effected and also $250 per month as expense money. He did not have to submit an expense account. In the taxable year, he received $3,000 in expense money; his actual expenses were $2,500. Are there any tax consequences to him? Would your answer be different if he actually spent $3,300?
22. To what extent may a person who travels for business reasons deduct the travel expenses of his wife who accompanies him?
23. A corporation had $100,000 income in 1961 and $150,000 in 1962. A $10,000 charitable contribution was made in 1961. What is the maximum allowable deduction for 1962? If a $15,000 contribution were made in 1962, how much of a carryover into 1963 is allowed? Is any unused portion of the 1962 contribution carried back to 1960?

10

DEPRECIATION; AMORTIZATION; OBSOLESCENCE

Depreciation

Depreciation has been variously defined by economists, engineers, accountants, and others. But for tax purposes, the United States Supreme Court has said the final word: "The depreciation charge permitted as a deduction from the gross income in determining the taxable income of a business for any year represents the reduction, during the year, of the capital assets through wear and tear of the plant used. The amount of the allowance for depreciation is the sum which should be set aside for the taxable year, in order that, at the end of the useful life of the plant in the business, the aggregate of the sums set aside will (with the salvage value) suffice to provide an amount equal to the original cost. The theory underlying this allowance for depreciation is that by using up the plant a gradual sale is made of it. The depreciation charged is the measure of the cost of the part which has been sold. When the plant is disposed of after years of use, the thing then sold is not the whole thing originally acquired. The amount of the depreciation must be deducted from the original cost of the whole in order to determine the cost of that disposed of in the final sale of the properties." [1]

"Or as a layman might put it, the machine in its lifetime must pay for itself before it can be said to pay anything to its owner." [2]

There is allowed to the taxpayer each year a reasonable allowance for the exhaustion and wear and tear (including a reasonable allowance for obsolescence) of (1) property used in the trade or business or (2) property held for the production of income.[3] This *reasonable amount* is that amount which should be set aside for the taxable year in accordance with a reasonably consistent plan (not necessarily at a uniform rate), so that the aggregate of the amounts set

[1] *United States v. Ludey,* 274 U.S. 295 (1927).
[2] *Detroit Edison Co. v. Commissioner,* 319 U.S. 98 (1943).
[3] I.R.C. Section 167.

aside, plus the salvage value, will, at the end of the estimated useful life of the depreciable property, equal the cost or other basis of the property. An asset may not be depreciated below a reasonable salvage value under any method of computing depreciation. The amount may not reflect amounts representing a mere reduction in market value.[4]

Basis. The basis on which depreciation is allowed is the adjusted basis for the purpose of determining gain on the sale or other disposition of the property; that is, *plus* adjustments are made for capital additions (such as improvements that are more than replacement repairs) and *minus* adjustments are made for annual depreciation write-offs, damage to the property, and partial dispositions.[5] Except in the case of declining balance depreciation (see below), the adjusted basis must be reduced by the amount of estimated salvage value at the end of the asset's useful life. Salvage, when reduced by the cost of removal, is known as net salvage. The time at which an asset is retired from service may vary according to the policy of the taxpayer. If the taxpayer's policy is to dispose of assets which are still in good operating condition, the salvage value may represent a relatively large proportion of the original basis of the asset. But if he customarily uses an asset until its inherent useful life has been exhausted substantially, salvage value may represent no more than junk value. Occasionally it is zero.

What Is Depreciable? The depreciation deduction is allowed only on business property, or on property held for the production of income. Land is not subject to the allowance. A railroad company was denied depreciation on its roadbed and grading because it could not be shown what the ratable amount was that had to be set aside "to recover during the remaining useful life of the property the unrecovered cost or other basis." [6]

Property used for personal purposes is not subject to the depreciation allowance. But if personal property (such as the residence in which the taxpayer had lived) is converted to business use or is held for the production of income, depreciation may be taken from that time. Depreciation henceforth will be taken on the fair market value on the date of this conversion or on the adjusted basis of the property at that time, whichever is *lower*.[7] Unless a person actually rents out a residence in which formerly he had lived, or unless he

[4] Regulations Section 1.167(a)–1(a).
[5] I.R.C. Section 1011.
[6] *The Texas and Pacific Railway Co.*, T.C. Memo., Docket #105730, entered March 25, 1943.
[7] Regulations Section 1.167(f)–1.

physically converts it into such a form that it no longer may be used as a residence, he is unlikely to establish that the property actually has been converted to business use. The mere listing of the property for rental is not likely to suffice.

The depreciation allowance applies only to that part of the property which is subject to wear and tear, to decay or decline from natural causes, to exhaustion, and to obsolescence. It does not apply to inventories or stock in trade. It does not apply to natural resources which are subject to a depletion allowance (to be discussed later in this chapter).

If an intangible asset is known from experience or other factors to be of use in the business or in the production of income for only a limited period, the length of which can be estimated with reasonable accuracy, this intangible asset may be the subject of a depreciation allowance; *e.g.*, patents and copyrights. But where the useful life is not limited, there is no depreciation allowance. No allowance will be permitted merely because, in the unsupported opinion of the taxpayer, the intangible has a limited useful life.[8] Good will is not depreciable.

No deduction is allowed for exhaustion of trademarks, trade names, or trade brands, which are regarded as a phase of good will.[9]

A taxpayer is entitled to take depreciation on property in which he has made an investment.[10] If property (other than money) is acquired by a corporation as a contribution to capital, and is not contributed by a shareholder as such, the basis of the property to the corporation will be zero, which means that there can be no depreciation allowance. If money is received by a corporation as a contribution to capital (and is not contributed by a shareholder as such), then the basis of any property acquired with this money during the 12-month period beginning on the day the contribution is received will be reduced by the amount of this contribution.[11]

Illustration. In order to induce a corporation to locate its plant in the community, a chamber of commerce offers $25,000, which is paid in cash on February 15. On the following October 1, the corporation spends $100,000 in purchasing machinery to install on rented premises. Depreciation may be taken on $75,000, which is the corporation's actual investment.

Who May Take Depreciation? Depreciation may be taken by a person with economic ownership of property.

[8] Regulations Section 1.167(a)–3.
[9] *Norwich Pharmacal Co.*, 30 B.T.A. 326 (1934).
[10] *Detroit Edison Co. v. Commissioner*, 319 U.S. 98 (1943).
[11] I.R.C. Section 362(c).

In the case of property held by one person for life with the remainder to another person, the deduction will be taken by the life tenant as though he were the absolute owner of the property. In the case of property held in trust, the deduction will be apportioned between the income beneficiaries and the trustee in accordance with the pertinent provisions of the trust instrument; if there are no such provisions, then on the basis on the trust income allocable to each. In the case of an estate, the depreciation deduction is apportioned between the estate and the heirs, legatees, and devisees on the basis of the income of the estate allocable to each.[12]

In the case of improvements on leased property, depreciation or amortization must be over the shorter of (1) the life of the asset or (2) the term of the lease, *including optional renewal periods.* But depreciation may be taken for the term of the lease *without renewal periods* (1) if the unexpired lease period (determined without regard to any unexercised option to renew) is 60% or more of the useful life of the improvement or (2) in respect of any cost of acquiring the lease if 75% or more of the cost is attributable to the unexpired lease period. But if the option to renew has been exercised or there is a reasonable certainty that it will be, the renewal period will be taken into account despite the tests. Where lessor and lessee are related parties (see Chapter 27), depreciation must be taken over the useful life of the improvement.

A lessee making improvements that would revert to the lessor could not take depreciation.[13] Where the lessor of land contributed funds to the lessee, who erected a building there, the lessee could take depreciation; he "paid" for the advance via rent.[14]

Where a taxpayer erects leasehold improvements on rented premises, depreciation may be taken on the shorter of (1) life of the assets or (2) length of the lease. If the lease is the subject of renewal clauses, depreciation may be taken on the basis of time until the expiration of the original lease. The benefits of this treatment are not lost merely because lessor and lessee are related parties, if the terms are fair.[15]

A lessee may not amortize the cost of capital improvements where the lease is for an indefinite period of time, and there is no way to determine the proper period for amortization purposes.[16]

Depreciation must be taken over the life of property, where the assets were located on premises leased for five years, at the expira-

[12] I.R.C. Section 167(g).
[13] *Reinsinger v. Commissioner*, 144 F.2d 475 (2d Cir., 1944).
[14] *Commissioner v. Revere Land Co.*, 169 F.2d 469 (3d Cir., 1948).
[15] *Fort Wharf Ice Co.*, 23 T.C. 202 (1954).
[16] *B. Kirk Rankin*, 17 B.T.A. 1301 (1930).

tion of which the taxpayer remained in possession as a tenant at will. The landlord had a policy of renewal as long as the property was productive.[17]

Useful Life. The first step in figuring depreciation is to determine the useful life of each asset. This life generally is calculated according to the number of years that the asset is supposed to last, or to render useful service, but occasionally life is determined according to the number of units the asset is supposed to furnish. The useful life of an asset depends upon such things as the amount of use; age when acquired; policy as to repairs, upkeep, and replacements; climate and other conditions.

The estimated useful life of an asset is not necessarily the useful life inherent in the asset but is the period over which the asset may reasonably be expected to be useful to the taxpayer. The estimated useful life may be subject to modification by reason of conditions known to exist at the end of the taxable year and may be redetermined, when necessary, regardless of the method of computing depreciation. But a redetermination of the remaining useful life will be made only when the change is significant, and there is a clear and convincing basis for the redetermination.

A taxpayer may estimate the remaining useful life of an asset by any method, including the following: opinion of the manufacturer or vendor; the taxpayer's own experience; the findings of an examiner, appraiser, engineer, or other expert; Bulletin "F" of the United States Treasury Department. Bulletin "F" was prepared as a guide to taxpayers and should not be regarded as definitive. It is a table of useful lives of depreciable property according to industries.

When group, classified, or composite accounts are used with average useful lives, and a normal retirement occurs, the full cost or other basis of the asset retired (unadjusted for depreciation or salvage) will be removed from the asset account and will be charged to the depreciation reserve. Amounts representing salvage ordinarily are credited to the depreciation reserve. Where an asset is disposed of for reasons other than normal retirement (*e.g.*, casualty), the full cost or other basis of the asset will be removed from the asset account, and the depreciation reserve will be charged with the depreciation applicable to the retired asset.

Accounting for Depreciable Property. Depreciable property may be accounted for by treating each individual item as an account, or by combining two or more assets in a single account. Assets may

[17] *Kerr-Cochran, Inc.*, 30 T.C. 69 (1958).

be grouped in an account in a variety of ways. For example, assets similar in kind with approximately the same useful lives may be grouped together. The resultant account is commonly known as a group account. Another appropriate grouping might consist of assets segregated according to the use without regard to useful life, for example, machinery and equipment, furniture and fixtures, or transportation equipment. The resultant account is commonly known as a classified account. A broader grouping, where assets are included in the same account regardless of their character or useful lives, is commonly known as a composite account. For example, all the assets used in a business may be included in a single account. Group, classified, or composite accounts may be further broken down on the basis of location, dates of acquisition, cost, character, use, etc.

Bulletin "F" presents a variety of composite rates in addition to the tables of average useful life in years.

The figures in Bulletin "F" are for new properties only and not for used assets.

A taxpayer may establish as many accounts for depreciable property as he desires. Depreciation allowances will be computed separately for each account. The Internal Revenue Service prefers that the depreciation be recorded in a depreciation reserve account. Where depreciation reserves are maintained, a separate reserve account must be maintained for each asset account. There must be shown (in the regular books or in a subsidiary record) for each account the basis of the property (including adjustments, such as obsolescence, capitalized taxes, etc.). In the event that reserves for book purposes do not correspond with reserves maintained for tax purposes, permanent auxiliary records must be maintained with the regular books of account reconciling the differences in depreciation for tax and book purposes. Depreciation schedules filed with the tax returns must show the accumulated reserves computed in accordance with the allowances for income tax purposes.

Taxpayers claiming the depreciation deduction must maintain full and complete information regarding (1) the cost or other basis, (2) the age, condition, and remaining useful life of the assets, (3) the portion of the cost or other basis which has been recovered through depreciation allowances for prior taxable years, and (4) such other information as may be required to establish the correctness of the deduction claimed, or to determine the amount of the deduction properly allowable.[18] The Revenue Agent should verify the correctness of any summarized schedules filed from the tax-

[18] T.D. 4422, XIII-1 CB 58.

payer's records; but the inclusion in the schedule of a voluminous mass of detail is not ordinarily necessary.[19]

In classified or composite accounts, the average useful life and rate are to be redetermined whenever additions, retirements, or replacements substantially alter the relative proportion of types of assets in the accounts.[20]

Methods of Computing Depreciation

Any reasonable and consistently applied method of computing depreciation may be used. But regardless of the method used, the deduction may not exceed the amount necessary to recover the unrecovered cost or other basis, less salvage value, during the remaining useful life of the property.

Straight Line Method. Under the straight line method, the cost or other basis of the property less its estimated salvage value is deductible in equal annual amounts over the period of the estimated useful life of the property. The allowance for the taxable year is determined by dividing the adjusted basis of the property at the beginning of the taxable year, less salvage value, by the remaining useful life of the property at that time. As a rule, the amount so determined is expressed as a percentage or fraction. If the taxpayer has not adopted a different acceptable method of depreciation, he must use the straight line method.

Illustration.

Year	Item	Cost or Other Basis Less Salvage	Useful Life	Depreciation Allowable 1960	1961	1962
1960	Asset A	$ 1,600	4	$200*	$400	$400
	Asset B	12,000	40	150*	300	300

* In this example it is assumed that the assets were placed in service on July 1, 1960.

In group, classified, or composite accounting, a number of assets with the same or different useful lives may be combined into one account, and a single rate of depreciation (that is, the group, classified, or composite rate) used for the entire account. In the case of group accounts (that is, accounts containing assets which are similar in kind and which have approximately the same estimated useful lives), the group rate is determined from the average of the useful lives of the assets. In the case of classified or composite accounts,

[19] Mimeograph 4170, XV-2 CB 148.
[20] Regulations Section 1.167(a)-7.

the classified or composite rate is generally computed by determining the amount of one year's depreciation for each item or each group of similar items, and by dividing the total depreciation thus obtained by the total cost or other basis of the assets. The average rate so obtained is to be used as long as subsequent additions, retirements, or replacements do not substantially alter the relative proportions of different types of asset in the account.

Illustration.

Cost or Other Basis	Estimated Useful Life	Annual Depreciation
$10,000	5 years	$2,000
10,000	15 years	667
$20,000		$2,667

Average rate is 13.33% ($2,667 divided by $20,000) unadjusted for salvage. Assuming the estimated salvage value is 10% of the cost or other basis, the rate adjusted for salvage will be 13.33% minus 10% of 13.33% (13.33% minus 1.33%), or 12%.

"The straight-line method of depreciation is essentially an accounting concept which to a considerable extent is a matter of hypothesis and computation. . . . It is generally . . . based on a conjecture not shown to have any connection with actuality that depreciation will be at a constant rate throughout an estimated life."[21] The method has the advantages of consistency, simplicity, and relative freedom from manipulation. But a strong disadvantage is that the straight line method is harshly inflexible. The actual use or particular operating conditions of a machine will have an effect upon useful life and annual wear and tear, but the straight line method blithefully assumes that wear and tear is constant. In actual fact, an asset will wear out more rapidly under such circumstances as: more overtime than had been anticipated when rates were set, 3-shift operation so that the machine has inadequate time for "cooling off" or for proper maintenance, lack of proper replacement parts or lubrication, absence of trained operators or maintenance men, processing of materials of heavier or harder type than standard. It was held that more rapid depreciation could not be taken when assets were subjected to overtime use and unskilled labor. "It is not necessarily true that machinery will deteriorate in a direct ratio to its use."[22] That decision is far more typical than one finding that shorter life could be claimed where tractors and trailers were operated in mountainous country, with two-man operations on a 20-

[21] *United States Industrial Alcohol Co.*, 42 B.T.A. 1323 (1940), *aff'd*, 137 F.2d 511 (2d Cir., 1943).

[22] *Donald V. Smith et al.*, T.C. Memo., Docket #5839, entered May 21, 1947.

hour day.[23] Furthermore, assets lose a greater part of their value in the market place in the earlier years, a fact which is not taken into account in the straight line method. The weakness of the straight line method by reason of its failure to correlate usage and depreciation deduction is taken into account by the unit of production method (to be discussed later in this chapter). The weakness of the straight line method's failure to reflect the serious value-declines in the market place during the first few years is taken into account by the declining balance and sum of the years-digits methods.

Declining Balance Method. Under the declining balance method, a uniform rate is applied each year to the unrecovered cost or other basis of the property. (The unrecovered basis for this purpose means basis adjusted for depreciation previously allowed or allowable, and for all other adjustments properly taken into account in computing depreciation: capitalized taxes, "repairs" that were more than replacements, casualty losses, etc.) The depreciation rate to be used is the taxpayer's choice, but this rate may not be more than twice the appropriate straight line rate computed without adjustment for salvage; and in actual practice, the declining balance rate invariably seems to be exactly double the straight line rate. Unlike the straight line method, salvage is not taken into account in determining the annual depreciation allowance under this method; but an asset or account may not be depreciated below a reasonable salvage value.

Illustration. A new asset having an estimated useful life of 20 years was purchased on January 1, 1960 for $1,000. The normal straight line rate (without adjustment for salvage) is 5%, and the declining balance rate at twice the normal straight line rate is 10%. The annual depreciation allowances for 1960, 1961, and 1962 are as follows:

Year	Basis	Declining Balance Rate	Depreciation Allowance
1960	$1,000	10%	$100
1961	900	10%	90
1962	810	10%	81

Sum of the Years-Digits Method. Under the sum of the years-digits method, annual allowance for depreciation is computed by applying changing fractions to the cost or other basis of the property reduced by estimated salvage. The numerator of the fraction changes each year to a number which corresponds to the remaining useful life of the asset (including the year for which the allowance is being computed), and the denominator (which remains constant)

[23] *Pilot Freight Carriers, Inc.,* T.C. Memo., 1956–195, filed August 27, 1956.

is the sum of all the years' digits corresponding to the estimated useful life of the asset.

Illustration. A new asset having an estimated useful life of five years was acquired on January 1, 1960, for $1,750. The estimated salvage is $250. For a taxpayer filing his returns on a calendar year basis, the annual depreciation allowances are as follows:

Year	Cost or Other Basis Less Salvage	Fraction *	Allowable Depreciation	Depreciation Reserve
1960	$1,500	5/15	$500	$ 500
1961	1,500	4/15	400	900
1962	1,500	3/15	300	1,200
1963	1,500	2/15	200	1,400
1964	1,500	1/15	100	1,500
Unrecovered value (salvage)				$ 250

* The denominator of the fraction is the sum of the digits representing the years of useful life, that is, 5, 4, 3, 2, and 1, or 15. The same figure may be obtained by using the mathematical formula for a progression:

$$s = \frac{n}{2}(a + l)$$

The *sum, s,* equals the ***number*** of years, 5, divided by 2, times the total of the first year, *a,* and the last year, *l.*

$$s = \frac{5}{2}(1 + 5)$$
$$= \frac{5}{2}(6)$$
$$= 15$$

Illustration. Assume in connection with an asset acquired in 1960 that three-quarters of a year's depreciation is allowable in that year. A reasonable method of allocating depreciation is:

	Deprecia-tion for 12 Months	Allowable Depreciation 1960	1961	1962
1st year	$500	$375(¾)	$125(¼)	
2d year	400		300(¾)	$100(¼)
3d year	300			225(¾)
		$375	$425	$325

Where in the case of a single asset, a change is justified in the useful life, subsequent computations will be made as though the remaining useful life at the beginning of the taxable year of change were the useful life of a new asset acquired at that time and with a basis equal to the unrecovered cost or other basis of the asset at that time.

Illustration. A new asset with an estimated useful life of ten years is purchased in 1960. At the time of making out his return for 1965, the taxpayer finds that the asset has a remaining useful life of seven years from January 1, 1965. Depreciation for 1965 should then be computed as though 1965 were the first year of the life of an asset estimated to have a useful life of seven years, and the allowance for 1965 would be 7/28 of the unrecovered cost or other basis of the asset after adjustment for salvage.

Under the sum of the years-digits method, annual allowances for depreciation may also be computed by applying changing fractions to the unrecovered cost or other basis of the asset reduced by estimated salvage. The numerator of the fraction changes each year to a number which corresponds to the remaining useful life of the asset (including the year for which the allowance is being computed), and the denominator changes each year to a number which represents the sum of the digits corresponding to the years of estimated remaining useful life of the asset.

Illustration. A new asset with an estimated useful life of ten years is purchased on January 1, 1960, for $6,000. The salvage value is computed at $500. Using the decimal equivalents of the fractions, the depreciation allowance for 1960 is $1,000 ($5,500 times 0.1818). For 1961, the unrecovered balance is $4,500, and the remaining life is nine years. The depreciation allowance for 1961 would then be $900 ($4,500 times 0.2000). Decimal equivalents for use in connection with the sum of the years-digits method, based on the remaining life, are published by the Internal Revenue Service.[24] These decimal equivalents were derived from the following formula:

$$D = \frac{2R}{(W + 2F)(W + 1)}$$

where $D =$ Decimal equivalent
$R =$ Remaining life
$W =$ Whole number of years in remaining life
$F =$ Fractional part of year in remaining life

The sum of the years-digits method may be applied to group, classified, or composite accounts.

A variant on the sum of the years-digits method is the *remaining life plan.* Under this plan, the denominator of the fraction changes each year to a number equal to the total of the digits representing the estimated remaining useful life of the property. The numerator of the fraction changes each year to a number which represents the years of useful life remaining at the beginning of the year for which the computation is made.

Illustration. New property with an estimated useful life of five years is purchased for $6,500 and placed in service January 1, 1960. Assuming a salvage value of $500, the depreciation allowance for 1960 is $2,000, that is, 5/15 of $6,000. For 1961, the unrecovered balance is $4,000, and the remaining life is four years. The sum of the digits 4, 3, 2, and 1 is 10, and the depreciation allowance for 1961 would be $1,600, that is, 4/10 of $4,000 ($6,000 less $2,000). For 1962, 1963, and 1964, the depreciation allowances, respectively, would be $1,200

[24] Regulations Section 1.167(b)–3(a)(2)(ii).

(3/6 of $2,400, or $4,000 less $1,600), $800 (2/3 of $1,200, or $2,400 less $1,200), and $400 (1/1 of $400, the unrecovered cost in the last year of useful life). Taxpayers who wish to use the sum of the years-digits method in accordance with a sum of the years-digits plan other than the remaining life plan must get the consent of the Commissioner of Internal Revenue.

Comparative Write-offs Under Three Methods. Assume that a new asset with an estimated life of five years is bought on January 2, 1960, for $11,000. Its salvage value is estimated to be $1,000 at the end of its useful life.

Straight line method.

Year	Cost Less Salvage	Rate	Deduction	Reserve December 31
1960	$10,000	20%	$2,000	$ 2,000
1961	10,000	20%	2,000	4,000
1962	10,000	20%	2,000	6,000
1963	10,000	20%	2,000	8,000
1964	10,000	20%	2,000	10,000

Declining balance method.

Year	Unrecovered Cost January 1	Rate	Deduction	Reserve December 31
1960	$11,000	40%	$4,400	$ 4,400
1961	6,600	40%	2,640	7,040
1962	3,960	40%	1,584	8,624
1963	2,376	40%	950	9,574
1964	1,426	40%	426	10,000

Only $426 is allowable in 1964, since the asset must not be depreciated below the $1,000 estimated salvage value.

Sum of the years-digits method—general rule, used for single asset accounts only.

Year	Cost Less Salvage	Fraction	Deduction	Reserve December 31
1960	$10,000	5/15	$3,333	$ 3,333
1961	10,000	4/15	2,667	6,000
1962	10,000	3/15	2,000	8,000
1963	10,000	2/15	1,333	9,333
1964	10,000	1/15	667	10,000

Sum of the years-digits, remaining life plan.

Year	Cost Less Salvage	Unrecovered Cost Less Salvage January 1	Fraction	Depreciation Allowance	Reserve December 31
1960	$10,000	$10,000	5/15	$3,333	$ 3,333
1961	10,000	6,667	4/10	2,667	6,000
1962	10,000	4,000	3/6	2,000	8,000
1963	10,000	2,000	2/3	1,333	9,333
1964	10,000	667	1/1	667	10,000

Other Methods. A taxpayer may use any consistent method of computing depreciation, provided the allowances do not result in accumulated allowances at the end of any taxable year greater than the total of the accumulated allowances which would have resulted from the use of the declining balance method. This limitation applies only during the first two-thirds of the useful life of the property.

Illustration. An asset costing $1,000, having a useful life of six years may be depreciated under the declining balance method at a rate of 33⅓%. During the first four years or two-thirds of its useful life, maximum depreciation allowances under the declining balance method would be as follows:

	Current Depreciation	Accumulated Depreciation	Balance
Cost of asset			$1,000
1st year	$333	$333	667
2d year	222	555	445
3d year	148	703	297
4th year	99	802	198

An annual allowance computed by any other method could not exceed $333 for the first year, and at the end of the second year the total allowances for the two years could not exceed $555. Likewise, the total allowances for the three years could not exceed $703 and for the four years could not exceed $802. This limitation would not apply to the fifth and sixth years.

The *unit of production method* of depreciation may be used where the useful life of an asset reasonably may be determined by reference to actual usage; that is, the obsolescence factor is not important, and the asset does not deteriorate markedly from mere passage of time.[25] Here the cost of the asset, less estimated salvage, is divided by the number of units that are expected to be produced, processed, etc., by the asset. The net cost per unit of production is then determined. This cost is multiplied by the actual usage of the asset, and the asset thus is written off in strict conformity to usage. But where an asset is used for several functions, or where it works on different substances (as nickel and copper), the method would not be practical. A variation is the *unit of mileage.* The cost of a truck, less estimated salvage, would be divided by the number of miles the vehicle would be expected to travel. Every mile that the truck was used, the unit would be multiplied accordingly.

The *operating day method* is confined to assets where the major factor in depreciation is wear and tear arising from use; for example, rotary oil drilling rigs. The life of a particular piece of equipment is estimated in terms of the total number of days it can be operated, and the depreciable basis is prorated on the actual number of days used. Salvage is taken into account.[26]

[25] *Hillyer, Deutsch, Edwards, Inc.*, 21 B.T.A. 452 (1930).
[26] Revenue Ruling 56–652, 1956–2 CB 125.

Under the *retirement method,* there are no annual depreciation charges as such, and hence no annual adjustments are made in the book values of the various assets. Only upon the ultimate retirement or replacement with betterments of any particular item of property or equipment is any change made in the investment account; and on that occasion, the full initial book value of the asset is taken out of the capital account. This sum, diminished by the net salvage proceeds, is then charged to current expense. Meanwhile, any repairs or minor replacements made during the life of the property are charged directly to current expense and are never reflected in the capital account.[27]

The *annual inventory method* involves depreciation write-offs on the basis of determinations "by officials of the company who had been connected with the management for many years and who possessed accurate and technical knowledge of the plant, its assets, and equipment. They were familiar with the actual use and operation of the plant, knew the age, cost, and probable useful life of its various items of equipment, and the current cost of repairs and replacements." [28] There is little precedent for this in tax matters.

Limitations on Choice of Method. A taxpayer may not use the so-called "rapid depreciation" methods at will. The declining balance method and the sum of the years-digits method may be used only in the case of (1) tangible property having a useful life of three years or more where (2) the original use of the property commences with the taxpayer and commences after 1953. The term "original use" means the first use to which the property is put, whether or not this use corresponds to the use of this property by the taxpayer. For example, a reconditioned or rebuilt machine will not qualify. Use of this method is not available to a corporation, where the property had been acquired new by an individual, who subsequently transferred the asset to this corporation in a nontaxable transaction for stock.[29]

Change in Depreciation Method. Subject to these limitations on the use of the so-called rapid depreciation methods, a taxpayer may use any method of depreciation that properly reflects taxable income. A method of computing depreciation is an accounting method.[30] Therefore, no change in method may be made without

[27] *Boston & Maine Railroad v. Commissioner,* 206 F.2d 617 (1st Cir., 1953).

[28] *The Cumberland Glass Manufacturing Co. v. United States,* 44 F.2d 455 (Ct. Cl., 1930).

[29] Revenue Ruling 56-265, 1956-1 CB 156.

[30] I.T. 3813, 1946-2 CB 42.

the consent of the Commissioner of Internal Revenue, with one exception to be mentioned in the following paragraph. A change in method of computing depreciation will be permitted only with respect to all the assets contained in a particular account.

A change from the declining balance method to the straight line method may be made without consent, unless there is in existence a depreciation agreement between the taxpayer and the Commissioner (see below) which provides that no such change will be made. When the change is made, the unrecovered cost or other basis (less a reasonable estimate for salvage) will be recovered through annual allowances over the estimated remaining useful life determined under the circumstances existing at that time. As to any account, this change will be permitted only if applied to all the assets in the account. The taxpayer must furnish a statement showing the date of acquisition of the property covered by the change, cost or other basis, amounts recovered through depreciation and other allowances, the estimated salvage value, the character of the property, and the remaining useful life of the property. This statement must be attached to the tax return for the year in which the change is being made. The change must be adhered to for the entire taxable year of the change and all subsequent years, unless the Commissioner consents to some other treatment.[31]

When Is Depreciation Taken? A taxpayer should deduct the proper depreciation allowance each year and may not increase his depreciation allowance in later years by reason of his failure to deduct any depreciation allowance or of his action in deducting an allowance plainly inadequate under the known facts in prior years.[32] "Wear and tear do not wait on net income. Nor can depreciation be accumulated and held for use in that year in which it will bring the taxpayer the most tax benefit. Congress has elected to make the year the unit of taxation." [33]

The period for depreciation of an asset begins when the asset is placed in service and ends when the asset is retired from service. A proportionate part of one year's depreciation is allowable for that part of the first and last year during which the asset was in service. But in the case of a multiple asset account, the amount of depreciation may be determined by using what is commonly described as an "averaging convention," that is, by using an assumed timing of additions and retirements. For example, it may be assumed that all additions and retirements to the asset account occur uniformly

[31] Regulations Section 1.167(e)–1.
[32] Regulations Section 1.167(a)–10(a).
[33] *Virginian Hotel Corp. of Lynchburg v. Helvering,* 319 U.S. 523 (1943).

throughout the taxable year, in which case depreciation is computed on the average of the beginning and ending balances of the asset account for the taxable year. One permissible averaging convention assumes that all additions and retirements during the first half of a given year were made on the first day of that year and that all additions and retirements during the second half of the year were made on the first day of the following year.

The taxpayer "must claim the deduction in his tax return for the year when the depreciation occurs, and may not take it in a later year."[34] The general rule is that the cost or other basis of property must be decreased for depreciation in the greater of the amount *allowed* or *allowable*.[35] *Allowed* means the extent resulting in a reduction of the taxpayer's income taxes. *Allowable* means the amount that should have been deducted. The determination of the amount allowable must be made on the basis of facts reasonably known to exist at the end of the taxable year. If in prior years the taxpayer has consistently taken proper deductions for depreciation under one method, the amount allowable for any prior years may not be increased even though a greater amount would have been allowable under another proper method.

Illustration. An asset was purchased on January 1, 1956, at a cost of $10,000. The useful life of the asset is ten years, and it has no salvage value. Depreciation was deducted and allowed for 1956 to 1960 as follows:

1956	$ 500
1957	0
1958	1,000
1959	1,000
1960	1,000
Total amount allowed	$3,500

The correct reserve as of December 31, 1960, is computed as follows:

December 31:	
1956 ($10,000 ÷ 10)	$1,000
1957 ($9,000 ÷ 9)	1,000
1958 ($8,000 ÷ 8)	1,000
1959 ($7,000 ÷ 7)	1,000
1960 ($6,000 ÷ 6)	1,000
Reserve, December 31, 1960	$5,000

Depreciation for 1961 is computed as follows:

Cost	$10,000
Reserve as of December 31, 1960	5,000
Unrecovered cost	$ 5,000
Depreciation allowable for 1961 ($5,000 ÷ 5)	1,000

34 *Kittredge v. Commissioner*, 88 F.2d 532 (2d Cir., 1937).

35 I.R.C. Section 1016(a)(2).

If the taxpayer has not taken a depreciation deduction either in the taxable year or for any prior taxable year, adjustments to basis of the property for depreciation allowable must be determined by using the straight line method.

If the taxpayer has taken a depreciation deduction properly under one method for one or more years but has omitted the deduction in other years, the adjustment to basis will be made under the method which was used by the taxpayer.

For the reduction in basis, it may be necessary to determine the extent to which the amount allowed as depreciation deduction resulted in a reduction for any taxable year of the taxpayer's income taxes (which does not mean for this purpose the self-employment tax under Social Security Act legislation). This amount is referred to as the "tax benefit amount allowed," and the mechanism is referred to as the *tax benefit* rule. In order to determine whether the tax benefit amount allowed exceeded the amount allowable, a determination must be made of that portion of the excess of the amount allowed over the amount allowable which, if disallowed, would not have resulted in an increase in any such tax previously determined. If the entire excess of the amount allowed over the amount allowable could be disallowed without any increase in tax, the tax benefit amount allowed may not be considered to have exceeded the amount allowable. In such a case, the reduction in basis would be the amount properly allowable as a deduction. If only part of this excess could be disallowed without any increase in tax, the tax benefit amount allowed will be considered to exceed the amount allowable to the extent of the remainder of this excess. In this case, the reduction in basis would be the amount of the tax benefit amount allowed.

The only adjustments made in determining whether there would be an increase in tax are those resulting from the disallowance of the amount allowed. The taxable years for which the determination is made will be the taxable year for which the deduction was allowed and any other taxable year which would be affected by the disallowance of the deduction. Examples of other taxable years are years to which there was a carryover or carryback of a net operating loss from the taxable year for which the deduction was allowed (see Chapter 14) and taxable years for which a computation was made because of recoveries (bad debts, prior taxes, and delinquency amounts) or comparable adjustments.

A taxpayer who seeks to limit the adjustment to basis to the tax benefit amount allowed for any period, in lieu of the amount allowed, must establish the tax benefit amount allowed.

Agreement as to Useful Life and Rates of Depreciation. A taxpayer may enter into an agreement with respect to the estimated useful life, method and rate of depreciation, and treatment for salvage of any property which is subject to the depreciation allowance. An application for this agreement must be made in quadruplicate on Form 2271 with the District Director of Internal Revenue where the tax return is to be filed. The agreement will set forth its effective date, the estimated remaining useful life, the estimated salvage value, and rate and method of depreciation of the property and the facts and circumstances taken into consideration in adoption of the agreement. The agreement is only prospective; rates, etc., prior to the effective date are not covered. The agreement is binding on both parties until the party who wishes to change it can prove the existence of facts and circumstances not previously taken into account.[36]

Even in the absence of such an agreement, it is the announced policy of the Internal Revenue Service not to disturb depreciation deductions except where there is a clear and convincing basis for the change.[37]

In the absence of an agreement, the taxpayer has the burden of proof in upsetting the Internal Revenue Service's determination of depreciation.[38]

Additional First-Year Depreciation. For taxable years ending after June 30, 1958, a taxpayer may elect to deduct 20% of the cost of qualifying property (determined without regard to salvage value) in addition to regular depreciation. This deduction is allowed only in the first taxable year for which a depreciation deduction is allowable on the property. Trusts do not qualify for the deduction.

The cost of property on which the additional allowance is possible is limited to $10,000 on a separate return and $20,000 on a joint return. The taxpayer may select the items upon which the deduction will be claimed.

Qualifying property is tangible personal property purchased after 1957, having a useful life of at least six years (determined at the date of acquisition). It must be purchased for use in business or for the production of income. It may be new or used property. Property does not qualify if acquired by gift or inheritance. It must be purchased.

Depreciation is allowed for the full year even though the property is acquired during the year.

[36] I.R.C. Section 167(d).
[37] Revenue Rulings 90 and 91, 1953–1 CB 43, 44.
[38] *Park Hosiery Mills v. Commissioner,* 183 F.2d 583 (6th Cir., 1950).

Illustration. A calendar year taxpayer purchased on July 1, 1960, a used piece of business equipment for $13,500. It had an estimated useful life of ten years and a salvage value of $500. The depreciation deduction on a separate return would be:

20% of $10,000 ($13,500 limited to $10,000)	$2,000
10% of $11,000 ($13,500 − $2,000 − $500 salvage) × ½ year	550
Depreciation for 1960 on separate return	$2,550

Amortization

A special type of depreciation is the amortization of emergency facilities. A person (including an estate, trust, or partnership) may elect to write off the cost or other basis of an emergency facility over a period of sixty months, instead of the actual useful life of the asset. The taxpayer may elect to begin the 60-month amortization with (1) the month following the month in which the facility was completed or acquired or (2) the taxable year succeeding that in which the facility was completed or acquired.[39]

The amortization deduction is an amount equal to the adjusted basis of the facility at the end of each month divided by the number of months (including the particular month for which the deduction is computed) remaining in the 60-month period. The amortization deduction is in lieu of a depreciation deduction.

Illustration. On July 1, a corporation which makes its income tax returns on the calendar year basis begins the construction of an emergency facility, which is completed on September 30 at a cost of $240,000. The certificate covers the entire construction. The corporation elects to take amortization deductions with respect to the facility and to begin the 60-month amortization period with October, the month following its completion. The adjusted basis of the facility at the end of October is $240,000. The allowable amortization deduction with respect to this facility for the taxable year is $12,000, computed as follows:

Monthly amortization deductions:	
October: $240,000 ÷ 60	$ 4,000
November: $236,000 ($240,000 − $4,000) ÷ 59	4,000
December: $232,000 ($236,000 − $4,000) ÷ 58	4,000
Total amortization deduction for taxable year	$12,000

An election to take amortization is made by filing a statement to that effect for the taxable year in which the first deduction is claimed. The amortization deduction may be discontinued by filing a written notice with the District Director of Internal Revenue where the taxpayer's returns are filed. Upon the discontinuance of the amortization deduction, depreciation is taken on the adjusted basis of the property as of the beginning of the month of the change.

[39] I.R.C. Section 168.

"Emergency facility" means any facility, land, building, machinery, or equipment, or any part thereof, the acquisition of which occurred after 1949, or the construction, reconstruction, erection, or installation of which was completed after that date, and with respect to which a *certificate of necessity* was issued by the certifying authority.[40] At the present time the certifying authority is the Office of Defense Mobilization. "Emergency facility" includes improvements of land, such as the construction of roads, bridges, and airstrips, and the dredging of channels. It may include machinery for producing war goods or vehicles intended for civilian transportation.

Certain payments may be made by the United States to a taxpayer as compensation for the unamortized cost of an emergency facility; for example, if the Government cancels a procurement contract. If any such payment is properly includible in gross income, a taxpayer which is recovering the adjusted basis of an emergency facility through amortization rather than depreciation may elect to take an amount equal to this payment as an amortization deduction with respect to this facility for the month in which this payment is includible. This amortization deduction will be in lieu of the regular amortization deduction for that month, but it may not exceed the adjusted basis of the facility as of the end of the month (computed without regard to any amortization deduction for that month). The election is made in the return for the taxable year in which the payment is includible in gross income.

Amortization over a 60-month period also is permitted in the case of certain grain-storage facilities. The election is available to the original owner of a grain-storage facility and to any subsequent owner.[41]

"Grain-storage facility" means any corn crib, grain bin, or grain elevator, or any similar structure suitable for the storage of grain; but only if the taxpayer at the time of his election to take the amortization deduction intends that the facility be used for the storage of grain produced by him. It also includes any public grain warehouse or elevator permanently equipped for receiving, elevating, conditioning, and loading out grain. In either instance, the construction, reconstruction, or erection of the facility must have been completed after 1952 and on or before December 31, 1956.

Termination of the election, and the subsequent depreciation treatment, are similar to what has been mentioned above for emergency facilities.

[40] Regulations Section 1.168–4(b).

[41] I.R.C. Section 169.

Obsolescence

The depreciation allowance includes an allowance for *normal* obsolescence which should be taken into account to the extent that the expected useful life of property will be shortened by reason thereof. Obsolescence may render an asset economically useless to the taxpayer regardless of its physical condition.[42]

"Obsolescence may arise as the result of laws regulating or forbidding the particular use of the property as well as from changes in the art, the shifting of business centers, loss of trade, inadequacy or other causes."[43] It may arise from "things which, apart from physical deterioration, operate to cause plant elements or the plant as a whole to suffer diminution in value."[44]

In any case in which the taxpayer shows that the estimated useful life previously used should be shortened by reason of obsolescence greater than had been assumed in computing this estimated useful life, a change to a new and shorter estimated useful life computed in accordance with this showing will be permitted. But no such change will be permitted merely because in the unsupported opinion of the taxpayer the property may become obsolete.

Abnormal obsolescence is the term sometimes used to distinguish the obsolescence deduction as such from the element already included in depreciation as *normal* obsolescence.

Land is not the subject of an obsolescence deduction.[45]

No obsolescence was allowed on intangible property where the obsolescence resulted from the asset's losing its value because of an act of Congress; specifically, the National Prohibition Act.[46] But obsolescence of tangible property was allowed under the same circumstances.[47]

Depletion

"In essence, the deduction for depletion does not differ from the deduction for depreciation."[48]

"Oil and gas reserves, like other minerals in place, are recognized as wasting assets. The production of oil and gas, like the mining of

[42] Regulations Section 1.167(a)–9.
[43] *Burnet v. Niagara Falls Brewing Co.*, 282 U.S. 648 (1931).
[44] *United States Cartridge Co. v. United States*, 284 U.S. 511 (1932).
[45] L.O. 862, 1 CB 127.
[46] *Clarke v. Haberle Crystal Springs & Brewing Co.*, 280 U.S. 384 (1930).
[47] *Gambrinus Brewing Co. v. Anderson*, 282 U.S. 538 (1931).
[48] *United States v. Ludey*, 274 U.S. 295 (1927).

ore, is treated as an income-producing operation, not as a conversion of capital investment as upon a sale, and is said to resemble a manufacturing business carried on by the use of the soil. . . . The depletion effected by production is likened to the depreciation of machinery or the using up of raw materials in manufacturing."[49]

As to mines, oil and gas wells, other natural deposits, and timber, a reasonable allowance for depletion is permitted.[50] In the case of standing timber, the depletion allowance is computed solely upon the adjusted basis of the property. In the case of other exhaustible natural resources, the depletion allowance is computed upon either (1) the adjusted depletion basis of the property or (2) a percentage of gross income from the property. In no case will depletion based upon discovery value be allowed. These two methods are known, respectively, as *cost depletion* and *percentage depletion.*

Who May Take Depletion? Annual depletion deductions are allowed only to the owner of an economic interest in mineral deposits or standing timber. An economic interest is possessed in every case in which the taxpayer has acquired (by investment or otherwise) a capital interest in mineral in place or standing timber and secures, by any form of legal relationship, income derived from the severance or sale of the mineral or timber, to which he must look for a return of his capital. The holder of a royalty interest is deemed to have an economic interest in oil in place which is depleted by severance.[51] Cash bonus payments, when included in a royalty lease, are regarded as advance royalties and are given the same tax consequences.[52] A share in the net profits derived from development and operation, on the contrary, does not entitle the holder of this interest to a depletion allowance even though continued production is essential to the realization of profits.[53] Similarly, the holder of a favorable contract to purchase wet gas at the mouth of the well is denied a depletion allowance on the difference between the contract price and the fair market value. Such an interest has been characterized as a "mere economic advantage derived from production, through a contractual relation to the owner."[54]

The lessor's right to a depletion allowance does not depend upon his retention of ownership or any other particular form of legal interest in the content of the land. It is enough, if by virtue of

[49] *Anderson et al. v. Helvering,* 310 U.S. 404 (1940).
[50] I.R.C. Section 611.
[51] *Palmer v. Bender,* 287 U.S. 551 (1933).
[52] *Burnet v. Harmel,* 287 U.S. 103 (1932).
[53] *Helvering v. O'Donnell,* 303 U.S. 370 (1938).
[54] *Helvering v. Bankline Oil Co.,* 303 U.S. 362 (1938).

the leasing transaction, he has retained a right to share in the minerals produced. If so, he has retained an economic interest in the minerals in place, which is depleted by production.[55]

No depletion deduction will be allowed the owner with respect to any timber or oil that he has disposed of under any form of contract by virtue of which he retains an economic interest in the timber or coal.

Depletion deductions with respect to an economic interest of a corporation are allowed to the corporation and not to its shareholders.

In the case of a lease, the depletion deduction is equitably apportioned between lessor and lessee. In the case of a lease or other contract providing for the sharing of economic interests in a mineral deposit or standing timber, the deduction is computed by reference to the respective adjusted bases of each interested party.

In the case of property held by one person for life with remainder to another person, the depletion deduction is computed as if the life tenant were the absolute owner of the property so that he will be entitled to the deduction during his life, after which the remainderman will be entitled to it.

If property is held in trust, the allowable depletion deduction is apportioned between the income beneficiaries and the trustee on the basis of the trust income allocable to each, unless the governing instrument (or local law) requires or permits the trustee to maintain a reserve for depletion. In the latter case, the deduction is first allocated to the trustee to the extent that income is set aside for a reserve, and any part of the deduction in excess of the income thus set aside will be apportioned on the basis of the trust income allocable to each.

In the case of property held by an estate, the depletion deduction is apportioned between the estate and the beneficiaries on the basis of income of the estate which is allocable to each.

Cost Depletion. In general, cost depletion is computed by dividing the total number of recoverable units (tons, barrels, etc., determined in accordance with prevailing industry methods) in the deposit into the adjusted basis applicable to the mineral property, and multiplying the resulting rate per unit by (1) the number of units for which payment is received during the taxable year if the cash receipts method is used or (2) the number of units sold if the accrual method is used. No further deduction for cost depletion will be allowed when the sum of the credits for depletion equals the cost

[55] *Bankers Pocahontas Coal Co. v. Burnet*, 287 U.S. 308 (1932).

or other basis of the property, plus allowable capital additions. But depletion deductions may be allowable thereafter computed upon a percentage of gross income from the property. In no event may percentage depletion in excess of cost or other basis of the property be credited to the improvements account or the depreciation reserve account.

The number of units in place in any natural deposit is primarily an engineering problem, and the burden of proof as to the number of units recoverable therefrom is upon the taxpayer.

Percentage Depletion. Percentage depletion is determined by applying a certain percentage (see table below) to the *gross income from the property*. The deduction may not exceed 50% of the taxpayer's *taxable income from the property* (computed without allowance for depletion). In no case will the depletion deduction on this basis be less than the deduction on a cost basis. Timber is not subject to this treatment.

"The term 'gross income from the property' means gross income from the oil and gas . . . and the term should be taken in its natural sense. . . . We do not think that we are at liberty to construct a theoretical gross income by recourse to the expenses of production operations." [56]

In the case of oil and gas wells, "gross income from the property" means the amount for which the taxpayer sells the oil or gas in the immediate vicinity of the well; if the oil or gas is not sold on the premises but is manufactured or converted into a refined product prior to sale, or is transferred from the premises prior to sale, the "gross income from the property" will be assumed to be equivalent to the representative market or field price of the oil or gas before conversion or transportation. The quoted phrase means, in the case of a property other than an oil or gas property, gross income from mining.

The term "taxable income from the property" (computed without allowance for depletion) means "gross income from the property" as defined in the previous paragraph, less allowable deductions (excluding any deduction for depletion) which are attributable to the mineral property with respect to which depletion is claimed. These deductions include administrative and financial overhead, operating expenses, selling expenses, depreciation, taxes, losses sustained, etc.

Depletion allowances may be computed as follows:

(1) *Without regard to situs of deposits.* The following rates are

[56] *Helvering v. Mountain Producers Corp.*, 303 U.S. 376 (1938).

applicable to the minerals listed below regardless of the situs of the deposits from which the minerals are produced:

(A) 27½%—

gas wells	oil wells

(B) 23%—

sulphur	uranium

(C) 15%—

ball clay	sagger clay
bentonite	rock asphalt
china clay	vermiculite
metal mines *	

(D) 10%—

asbestos *	perlite
brucite	sodium chloride
coal	wollastonite
lignite	

(E) 5%—

brick and tile clay	sand
gravel	scoria
mollusk shells (including clam shells and oyster shells)	shale
peat	stone (except dimension or ornamental stone)
pumice	

if from brine wells—

bromine	magnesium chloride
calcium chloride	

(2) *Production from United States deposits.* A rate of 23% is applicable to the minerals listed below if produced from deposits within the United States:

anorthosite †	ilmenite
asbestos	kyanite
bauxite	mica
beryl	olivine
celestite	quartz crystals (radio grade)
chromite	rutile
corundum	block steatite talc
fluorspar	zircon
graphite	

* Not applicable if the rate prescribed in (2) is applicable.

† This rate does not apply except for the production of alumina and aluminum compounds.

and ores of the following metals—‡

- antimony
- bismuth
- cadmium
- cobalt
- columbium
- lead
- lithium
- manganese
- mercury
- nickel
- platinum
- platinum group metals
- tantalum
- thorium
- tin
- titanium
- tungsten
- vanadium
- zinc

(3) *Other minerals.* A rate of 15% is applicable to the minerals listed below regardless of the situs of the deposits from which the minerals are produced, provided the minerals are not used or sold for use by the mine owner or operator as rip rap, ballast, road material, rubble, concrete aggregates, or for similar purposes. If, however, the minerals listed below are sold or used for the purposes just described, a rate of 5% is applicable to any of these minerals unless sold on bid in direct competition with a bona fide bid to sell any of the minerals listed in subdivision (C) of subparagraph (1), in which case the rate is 15%. In addition, the provisions of this paragraph are not applicable with respect to any of the minerals listed below if the rate prescribed in subparagraph (2) above is applicable:

- aplite
- barite
- bauxite *
- beryl *
- borax
- calcium carbonates
- clay, refractory and fire
- diatomaceous earth
- dolomite
- feldspar
- flake graphite *
- fluorspar *
- fullers earth
- garnet
- gilsonite
- granite
- lepidolite *
- limestone
- magnesite
- magnesium carbonates
- marble
- mica *
- phosphate rock
- potash
- quartzite
- slate
- soapstone
- spodumene *
- stone (dimension or ornamental) ††
- talc (including pyrophyllite) *
- thenardite
- tripoli
- trona
- all other minerals

‡ Applicable only to the extent that such metals are produced.
* Not applicable if the rate prescribed in (2) is applicable.
†† The 15% rate is applicable only to stone used or sold for use by the mine owner or operator as dimension stone or ornamental stone.

Illustration. A taxpayer owns oil property which was purchased in 1960 for $10,000. The accrual basis of accounting is used. In 1960, $50,000 was expended for intangible drilling and development costs, and an election to capitalize this amount had been made. It is estimated that the recoverable oil reserves are 1,500,000 barrels. Production of 50,000 barrels of oil takes place, and these are sold in 1961 for $2.25 per barrel. The purchaser deducts transportation charges of 20¢ and severance taxes of 10¢ per barrel. The taxpayer's operating and overhead expenses applicable are $20,000.

Sales of 50,000 barrels of oil at $2.25	$112,500.00
Less: Transportation (50,000 × 20¢)	10,000.00
Gross income from property	$102,500.00
Rate of depletion	27½%
Percentage depletion deduction	$ 28,187.50

While this deduction is equivalent to 27½% of gross depletable income from each unit (barrel) of property, the allowance is limited to 50% of the taxable income from this property, computed without an allowance for depletion, as follows:

Sales		$112,500.00
Less: Transportation		10,000.00
Gross income from property		102,500.00
Less: Severance taxes	$ 5,000.00	
Expenses	20,000.00	25,000.00
Taxable income from property		$ 77,500.00
Deduction limitation		50%
Maximum deduction		$ 38,750.00

Inasmuch as 50% of taxable income from this property is greater than 27½% of gross income, the above taxable income limitation does not decrease the percentage depletion allowance.

Under the cost method, the depletion under the above facts would be $2,000, that is, $60,000 cost, divided by 1,500,000 recoverable barrels, or 4¢, multiplied by 50,000 barrels sold, which equals $2,000. Inasmuch as the percentage depletion here is greater than cost depletion, the taxpayer would be entitled to a depletion deduction of $28,187.50.

Timber Depletion. Timber depletion is based on the cost of the timber and does not include any part of the cost of the land. Depletion takes place when standing timber is cut. Depletion must be computed by the cost method and not the percentage method.[57]

The deduction each year is the product of the timber units cut multiplied by the depletion unit. The depletion unit is the cost or other basis of the standing timber on hand divided by the total depletable units (thousand board feet, cords, etc.).

Illustration. A taxpayer purchases a timber tract for $20,000 in 1958; half of the cost was properly allocable to the timber under the facts. If the depletion unit was determined to be $10, based on an estimated one million board feet (1,000 thousand board feet) of standing timber, and the taxpayer felled 500,000

[57] I.R.C. Section 613 (a).

board feet of timber in 1960, his depletion deduction would be $5,000 for 1960 (500,000 at $10 per thousand).

Under certain circumstances, election may be made to treat the cutting of timber as a sale of a capital asset for its fair market value. See Chapter 5.

Statement as to Depletion. When a depletion allowance is claimed, a statement to that effect must accompany the income tax return. The following special forms must be attached to the tax return:

Coal	Form E
Mines and other natural deposits	Form M
Oil and gas	Form O
Timber	Form T

Supplementary Material

A. Suggested Reading.

George Terborgh, *Tax Depreciation Problem* (Washington, D.C.: Machine & Allied Products Institute, 1958).

Ned Fischer, "Methods of Depreciation: A Review," *TAXES—The Tax Magazine,* September, 1953, Vol. XXXI, #9, p. 681.

Willard J. Lassers, "Depreciation Under the 1954 Code," *TAXES—The Tax Magazine,* September, 1954, Vol. XXXII, #9, p. 695.

Lester M. Ponder, "Depreciation Under the New Code," *American Bar Association Journal,* August, 1955, Vol. XLI, #8, p. 726.

E. C. Brown, *Effects of Taxation—Depreciation Adjustments for Price Changes* (Boston: Harvard University, Graduate School of Business Administration, Division of Research, 1952).

F. J. Blaise, "What Every Tax Man Should Know About Percentage Depletion," *TAXES—The Tax Magazine,* June, 1958, Vol. XXXVI, #6, p. 395.

Clark W. Breeding and A. Gordon Burton, *Taxation of Oil and Gas Income* (New York: Prentice-Hall, Inc., 1954).

B. Leading Cases.

What is depreciation? *United States v. Ludey,* 274 U.S. 295 (1927).

On what is depreciation taken? *Detroit Edison Co. v. Commissioner,* 319 U.S. 98 (1943).

Time of deducting depreciation. *Virginian Hotel Corp. of Lynchburg v. Helvering,* 319 U.S. 523 (1943).

Obsolescence. *Burnet v. Niagara Falls Brewing Co.,* 282 U.S. 648 (1931).

Who may take depletion? *Palmer v. Bender,* 287 U.S. 551 (1933).

C. Questions.

1. Must estimated salvage value be taken into account when figuring depreciation?
2. A psychologist worked entirely with mentally disturbed children, who frequently gave his office furniture and equipment a pretty rough

time. May he deduct depreciation on these assets at a more rapid rate than customarily would be applied?

3. The operator of a fleet of taxicabs paid $3,000 per cab. Estimated useful life was four years, with salvage value of $500. But he preferred to replace his cabs every two years, when salvage value was $1,000. How much depreciation would he be allowed on a straight line basis?
4. An individual paid $20,000 for a house in 1951. In 1961, he rented the house to unrelated parties. On what figure will he take depreciation, assuming that he had paid $5,000 for a new roof in 1957?
5. A taxpayer acquires property subject to 5-year amortization to the extent of 50% of cost, which is $20,000. What amount of straight line depreciation may be taken annually, assuming no remaining salvage value and no utilization of the new asset rule? The asset has a 10-year life.
6. A company used the declining balance method on an asset with a 10-year life which had cost $10,000. After $2,000 had been claimed as depreciation, a switch was made to the straight line method. What annual depreciation will be taken henceforth, assuming salvage value of $800?
7. A manufacturer had machinery that would cost far more to replace than its original cost. Is he justified in taking depreciation in an amount that would provide the cost of new equipment at the end of the useful life of his present assets?
8. G leased property to D for 20 years, with a 10-year option allowing G to continue tenancy on the existing terms. G erected a leasehold improvement with a 30-year life for $10,000. What is the maximum allowable straight line depreciation per year?
9. On December 31, 1959, Mathewson & Bresnahan, a battery company, made plans to replace certain machinery with a new type used by certain competitors. On that date, the old machinery had an adjusted basis of $37,000 and a remaining useful life of ten years. It was anticipated that the new assets would be available on January 1, 1962, and that the purchase price of $100,000 would be reduced by $6,000 trade-in on the old assets. In what year or years is obsolescence allowed as a deduction, and in what amounts?
10. A partnership used the calendar year basis. On July 1, 1960, it purchased a used piece of equipment for $13,500. It had an estimated useful life of ten years and a salvage value of $500. What is the maximum depreciation on a straight line basis?
11. In the previous question, what would your answer be if the taxpayer were a married couple filing on a joint return basis?
12. A truck operator estimated that each vehicle would travel 100,000 miles. If trucks cost $6,000 each and had estimated salvage value of $600, what depreciation would be taken on the unit of production method in a year when the vehicle had traveled 12,000 miles? What depreciation would be taken in the following year, when, because of strikes, the trucks were not used at all?
13. A trust purchased a building and the land on which it stands for $30,000, $20,000 of which is allocated to the building. If the building has an estimated useful life of 33⅓ years and its salvage value is $5,000, what is the annual depreciation on the straight line method?

14. A taxpayer decides that depreciation for 1961 will be more useful to him in 1962 than in the proper year, 1961. If he fails to deduct for 1961, may he properly consider that there is still unclaimed depreciation to be recovered, for example, in 1962?
15. A building used for a railroad roundhouse for locomotives has a remaining physical life of 25 years. But revenues have been so poor that the railroad line is insolvent, and application has been made to the Interstate Commerce Commission for permission to discontinue operations in this locality. Over what period should depreciation be taken?
16. A municipality donated a factory costing $175,000, with an adjusted book value of $150,000 and a fair market value of $195,000, to a corporation that would agree to move into the community. If the factory has a 10-year remaining life, with no estimated salvage value, what annual depreciation would be taken on a straight line basis?
17. Giselle, a ballerina, purchased a full-length mirror for purposes of studying her technique. She was on a calendar year basis. The mirror was purchased on July 1 and had an estimated useful life of twenty years, at which time $100 of the $1,200 cost would represent salvage. What is the straight line depreciation in the year of purchase, assuming no election was made to accelerate first-year depreciation?
18. A business asset costing $20,000 in 1957, sold in 1961 for $19,000. Depreciation had been taken at $1,000 a year since 1957, the date of acquisition, except that for 1959, because of an honest error, no depreciation deduction had been claimed. What is the gain or loss on disposition?
19. On October 1, 1960, a calendar year corporation acquired an asset costing $50,000, for which a certificate of necessity was obtained. How much amortization is allowed in 1960? In 1961?
20. An asset having an estimated useful life of ten years is purchased on January 2 for $2,100. Its salvage value at the end of its useful life is estimated to be $100. Ignoring any special first-year depreciation election, construct a chart showing the annual depreciation for each of the ten years, with salvage value or unrecovered cost at the end of the tenth year, under the straight line, 200% declining balance, and sum of the years-digits methods.

11

COMPENSATION

As a general rule, compensation for personal services is ordinary income, taxable to the one performing the services in accordance with his accounting method; that is, the income is taxable (1) when paid to a cash-basis taxpayer or (2) when earned by an accrual-basis taxpayer.

The law is settled that the statutory definition of gross income "is broad enough to include in taxable income any economic or financial benefit conferred on the employee as compensation, whatever the form or mode by which it is effected." [1]

Payment for services is taxable to the person who rendered these services. "The statute could tax salaries to those who earned them and provide that the tax could not be escaped by anticipatory arrangements and contracts however skillfully devised to prevent the salary when paid from vesting even for a second in the man who earned it. That seems to us the import of the statute before us and we think that no distinction can be taken according to the motives leading to the arrangement by which the fruits are attributed to a different tree from that on which they grew." [2] Thus a person cannot escape tax upon compensation which is paid to a relative or other nominee. Even if the payment is made directly by the beneficiary of the services to a charitable organization, the one performing the services is taxed.[3]

Where an employee owns more than 50% of the stock of a corporation, directly or indirectly, the corporation only is entitled to the deduction if the amount is paid (actually or constructively) within two and a half months after the close of the taxable year.[4]

Compensation for services is taxable regardless of the form of payment; it need not be in cash. Where property is given for services, the valuation is fair market value at the time of distribution.[5]

[1] *Commissioner v. LoBue,* 351 U.S. 243 (1956).
[2] *Lucas v. Earl,* 281 U.S. 111 (1930).
[3] T.D. 5151, 1942-1 CB 34.
[4] I.R.C. Section 267(a)(2).
[5] I.T. 3795, 1946-1 CB 15.

Christmas gifts of nominal value given to employees as merchandise (turkeys, hams, and the like) are not taxable, even though the employer gets a tax deduction. But this exception does not extend to cash, gift certificates, or similar items readily convertible into cash, regardless of the amount involved.[6]

As a general rule, anything of value that flows from the employer to the employee is regarded as compensation for services; why else did the employer make the payment? Where an employee is sold property at bargain prices, there is compensation to the extent of the differential.[7]

"The payment for services, even though entirely voluntary, was, nevertheless, compensation within the statute."[8]

If an employee voluntarily repays amounts that he has received as compensation (where there had been no mistake), his income for the year of original receipt is not reduced; the transaction is regarded as a gift or contribution of income already received.[9] Even the discovery of accounting errors several years later will not form the basis for adjusting the earlier year.[10]

Reasonableness

A payor is allowed as a deduction "all the ordinary and necessary expenses paid or incurred during the taxable year in carrying on any trade or business, including (1) a reasonable allowance for salaries or other compensation for personal services actually rendered. . . ." To the extent that the compensation is unreasonable, the payor is denied a deduction; but the recipient is, nonetheless, taxed upon the payment.

In appraising the reasonableness of compensation, it is desirable to view each salary individually, although there is some authority for permitting the Internal Revenue Service to make a lump-sum disallowance from an unreasonable aggregate.[11]

Determination of the reasonableness of compensation includes an individual analysis of such factors as: the employee's qualifications; the nature, extent, and scope of his work; the size and complexities of the business; a comparison of salaries paid with the gross income and the taxable income; the prevailing general economic conditions; comparison of salaries with distributions to stockholders; the pre-

[6] Revenue Ruling 59–58, I.R.B. 1959–8.
[7] *Hudson Motor Car Co. v. United States*, 3 F. Supp. 834 (Ct. Cl., 1933).
[8] *Old Colony Trust Co. v. Commissioner*, 279 U.S. 716 (1929).
[9] *Leicht v. Commissioner*, 137 F.2d 433 (8th Cir., 1943).
[10] *Haberkorn v. United States*, 173 F.2d 587 (6th Cir., 1949).
[11] *Bone v. United States*, 46 F.2d 1010 (D.C., Ga., 1931).

vailing rates of compensation for comparable positions in comparable concerns; the salary policy of the taxpayer as to all employees; the amount of compensation paid to the particular employee in previous years.[12]

A special problem exists in the case of salaries paid to persons who also are stockholders in the corporation making the payments. This problem is particularly acute in the case of closely held corporations. Was the payment actually a dividend, a nondeductible item? Any modification of salaries to stockholder-officers, or bonuses to them, should be specifically authorized in the corporate minutes, with the payments being keyed to *individual* rather than *corporate* performance.[13] But except in the case of stockholders, the action of a board of directors of a corporation in voting salaries for any given period is entitled to the presumption that these salaries are reasonable and proper.[14]

Considerable latitude is ordinarily achieved by using the contingent compensation method; that is, compensation or sales commissions are based upon a percentage of profits or of receipts. Such a method may provide room for a deduction in excess of amounts that would be allowed ordinarily. The method is much more apt to be recognized if the arrangement is made before the services are performed, if the arrangement is in writing, and if it is made at arm's length for services only. In one case, commissions running to seven times prior maximum earnings of officer-salesmen were allowed.[15] But large participation in war profits was not allowed despite a standing profit-sharing arrangement.[16]

Long-term Compensation

A special rule exists to relieve a taxpayer from the amount of tax which otherwise results when an amount of income which has been earned over a period of years is received or accrued in one taxable year. Because of the graduated income tax rates, this so-called bunching of income in one year usually subjects it to a higher rate of tax than would be payable if it had been received or accrued over the several years during which it was earned.

If an individual or partnership (1) engages in an employment as defined below, and (2) the employment covers a period of 36 months

[12] *Mayson Manufacturing Co. v. Commissioner,* 178 F.2d 115 (6th Cir., 1949).

[13] *Builders Steel Co.,* T.C. Memo., Docket #17796, entered March 25, 1949.

[14] *Ox Fibre Brush Co. v. Blair,* 32 F.2d 42 (4th Cir., 1929).

[15] *Eagle Office Equipment Co., Inc.,* T.C. Memo., Docket #8739, entered November 13, 1946.

[16] *Locke Machine Co. v. Commissioner,* 168 F.2d 21 (6th Cir., 1948).

or more (from the beginning to the completion of this employment), and (3) the gross compensation from the employment received or accrued in the taxable year of the individual or partnership is not less than 80% of the total compensation from this employment, then the tax attributable to any part of the compensation which is included in gross income may not be greater than the aggregate of the taxes attributable to this part had it been included in gross income ratably over that part of the period of the employment which precedes the date of receipt or accrual.[17]

Illustration. An individual who makes his income tax return on a calendar year basis and uses the cash method of accounting begins an employment as defined below on February 17,1957, and completes it on July 1, 1960. His total compensation from this employment was $9,000, of which he received $1,000 on July 1, 1959, and $8,000 on the completion date. Inasmuch as the employment covered more than 36 months and the $8,000 received in 1960 was not less than 80% of his total compensation from this employment, he is entitled to the benefits of this special rule in computing the tax payable with respect to the $8,000 reflected in his 1960 return. The rule does not apply to the $1,000 received in 1959. Under the special rule, the tax attributable to the $8,000 included in his gross income for 1960 is not greater than the aggregate of the taxes attributable to that amount had it been received ratably over the calendar months included in the period from February 17, 1957, to July 1, 1960. But if he had received an additional $5,000 in 1961 from this employment, he would not be entitled to the benefits of this rule with respect to either the $8,000 or the $5,000, inasmuch as he would not have received in one taxable year at least 80% of the total compensation from this employment.

Illustration. If, in the previous illustration, the individual had commenced the employment on March 3, 1960, and completed it on August 22, 1963, and had been paid a total compensation of $10,000 for that employment on July 5, 1962, he would be entitled to the benefits of the special rule. But the tax attributable to the $10,000 included in his gross income for 1962 cannot be greater than the aggregate of the taxes attributable to that amount had it been received ratably over the calendar months included in the period from March 3, 1960, to July 5, 1962, the date on which the $10,000 was received.

Amended returns are not filed for the years in which amounts were ratably earned or accrued. Instead, a rider is attached to the tax return for the year of receipt or accrual, limiting the tax in that year to the amount resulting from the application of the special rule.

Illustration. On January 1, 1958, an unmarried attorney was retained in an antitrust suit. This employment continued until June 30, 1961, when the action was terminated and he received a fee of $84,000 as total compensation for his services. Inasmuch as all the requirements of the special rule are met with respect to the $84,000, the following tax results will occur, assuming that his taxable income was as follows: 1957, $20,600 (which reflects a net operating loss

[17] I.R.C. Section 1301(a).

carryback from 1958); 1958, net operating loss $2,000; 1959, $50,600; 1960, $32,000; 1961, $100,000 ($16,000 plus the $84,000 fee).

(1) Allocation of fee to period of employment:

1961 (6 months)	$12,000
1960 (12 months)	24,000
1959 (12 months)	24,000
1958 (12 months)	24,000

(2) Tax for 1961 computed by including the $84,000 fee in gross income: $67,320.

(3) Tax for 1961 computed without including the $84,000 fee in gross income: $5,200.

(4) Taxes attributable to the $84,000 fee allocated to the various taxable years:

		Prior to Allocation Under Special Rule of Section 1301	Under Section 1301
(A) Tax attributable to 1961:			
Taxable income ($16,000 + $12,000)			$28,000
Tax		$11,980	
Less		5,200	
Amount of tax attributable to 1961			6,780
(B) Tax attributable to 1960:			
Taxable income	$32,000		$56,000
Tax	14,460	$31,320	31,320
Less		14,460	
Amount of tax attributable to 1960			16,860
(C) Tax attributable to 1959:			
Taxable income	$50,000		$74,000
Tax	28,916	$47,936	47,936
Less		28,916	
Amount of tax attributable to 1959			19,020
(D) Tax attributable to 1958:			
Taxable income ($2,000 net operating loss)			$21,400
Amount of tax attributable to 1958			8,984
(E) Tax attributablc to 1957:			
Taxable income	$20,000		$22,000
Tax	7,396	8,536	8,536
Less		7,396	
Amount of tax attributable to 1957			1,140
(F) Aggregate of taxes resulting from allocation of compensation under Section 1301:			
1961			$ 6,780
1960			16,860
1959			19,020
1958			8,984
1957			1,140
			$52,784

(5) Tax for 1961 under Section 1301: $57,984. Inasmuch as the tax for 1961 computed without including the $84,000 fee in gross income ($5,200), plus the

aggregate of taxes attributable to the allocation of that fee over the period of employment ($52,784) equals $57,984, which is a lesser sum than $67,320 (the amount of tax for 1961 computed by including the entire fee in income for 1961), $57,984 is the amount for tax for 1961 under the provisions of Section 1301.

Definition of an Employment. For this purpose, "an employment" means an arrangement or series of arrangements for the performance of personal services by an individual or partnership to effect a particular result, regardless of the number of sources from which compensation for these services is obtained. There must be an understanding for the performance of services to accomplish a particular result. An arrangement to perform general services is not an employment for this purpose either as to any particular project on which services are performed or as to the general service since there is no understanding that the services are to accomplish a particular result.[18]

To qualify as an employment, the services must relate to a particular project, such as a particular law case, and must not consist of a set of unrelated services performed for the same person. Furthermore, the individual steps performed by a taxpayer in connection with his project do not each constitute an employment; the services rendered by him with respect to the entire project represent the employment.

Partners. An individual who is a member of a partnership receiving or accruing compensation from an employment eligible for the special rule will be entitled to the benefits of Section 1301 only if (1) he has been a member of the partnership continuously for a period of 36 months immediately preceding the receipt or accrual of this compensation by the partnership or (2) he has been a member of the partnership continuously for the period of the employment immediately preceding this receipt or accrual. It is immaterial whether the individual actually rendered services with respect to the employment to which the compensation is attributed.

Back Pay. A similar rule exists for income from back pay. If the amount of back pay, as defined below, received or accrued by an individual during the taxable year exceeds 15% of his gross income for the year, the part of the tax attributable to the inclusion of the back pay in gross income for the taxable year may not be greater than the aggregate of the increases in the taxes which would have resulted from the inclusion of the respective portions of this back pay in gross income for the taxable years to which these portions are respectively attributable.[19]

[18] Regulations Section 1.1301–2(b).
[19] I.R.C. Section 1303.

For this purpose, back pay means remuneration including wages, salaries, pensions, retirement pay, and other similar compensation, received or accrued during the taxable year and includible in gross income by an employee for services performed prior to the taxable year for his employer and which would have been paid prior to the taxable year but for the intervention of any one of the following events: (1) bankruptcy or receivership of the employer; (2) dispute as to the liability of the employer to pay this remuneration, which is determined after the commencement of court proceedings; (3) if the employer is a government or governmental agency, lack of funds appropriated to pay this remuneration; or (4) any other event determined to be similar in nature.

Where the Internal Revenue Service pays a reward for information leading to the detection and punishment of persons guilty of violating tax laws, informers' fees that are paid do not result from such a contractual arrangement as to constitute an "employment." The amount received by the employee does not qualify as back pay.[20]

Deferred Compensation Plans

In order to protect an employee from the consequences of high taxes (as well as for various nontax reasons), an employer sometimes adopts a deferred compensation arrangement. Under such an arrangement, compensation that would be taxed if paid currently is deferred until a later date, with the double tax objective of (1) paying the employee at a time when he is in a lower tax bracket (*e.g.*, after retirement) and (2) spreading a portion of the current year's income over a number of years to avoid bunching. There is no immediate taxation of deferred payments unless either one of two conditions exists: (1) there is constructive receipt by the employee of whatever amount the employer had agreed to provide or (2) the employer's agreement is deemed to be the equivalent of cash. If the employer's liability to make payment is contingent upon something, this contingency may never be met and, hence, the employee will get nothing. On the other hand, if the contingency is so certain to be met that the employee is certain to get his payments, he will be taxed immediately and the so-called deferred compensation plan will be meaningless.

Certain employee benefit plans make the deferred payment idea very attractive both to employers and to their employees. Interesting tax features are available in the case of pension, profit-sharing, stock bonus, and annuity plans, and compensation paid under a

[20] Revenue Ruling 58–326, I.R.B. 1958–26, 17.

deferred payment plan. The tax advantages are: (1) the *employer* gets a Government subsidy in the form of immediate tax deduction for contributions irrespective of the fact that the employee may have received nothing. (2) The *employee* (or his beneficiary) is shielded from taxation until he gets his benefit, at which time the tax generally is lower because the employee usually will have retired and so probably will be in a lower tax bracket. (3) The *trust* that administers many forms of employee benefit plan is tax-exempt as to the employer contributions and as to its income on all but certain specified investments.

The deduction enables otherwise unusable tax dollars to be used as part of the employer contribution; this encourages funding the benefit over many years. Furthermore, by funding the benefit costs the employer may feel that he is acquiring an economic "hold" over the employee by creating a fund that the employee would forfeit if he went to work elsewhere. The employer may be a corporation, a partnership, or even a sole proprietorship. But partners and sole proprietors do not qualify as employees; hence, the full advantages of a plan are for corporations.

Types of Plan. A *pension plan* for this purpose is a plan established and maintained by an employer primarily to provide systematically for the payment of definitely determinable benefits to his employees over a period of years, usually for life, after retirement. Retirement benefits generally are measured by, and based on, such factors as years of service and compensation received by the employees. The determination of the amount of retirement benefits and the contributions to provide these benefits are not dependent upon profits. It must be possible to determine the employer contribution actuarially on the basis of definitely determinable benefits. Benefits are not definitely determinable if funds arising from forfeitures on termination of service, or other reason, may be used to provide increased benefits instead of being used to reduce the amount of the employer's contribution.[21]

A *profit-sharing plan* for this purpose is a plan established and maintained by an employer to provide for the participating in his profits by his employees or their beneficiaries. The plan must provide for a definite predetermined formula for allocating the contributions made to the plan among the participants and for distributing the funds accumulated under the plan after a fixed number of years, the attainment of a stated age, or upon the prior occurrence of some event such as layoff, illness, disability, retirement, death, or

[21] Regulations Section 1.401-1(b).

severance of employment. A formula for allocating the contributions among the participants is definite if, for example, it provides for an allocation in proportion to the basic compensation of each participant. In a very few cases, the courts have held that a definite formula was not needed.[22] But a formulaless plan seems highly dangerous in view of the specific language of the regulations.

A *stock bonus plan* is a plan established and maintained by an employer to provide benefits similar to those of a profit-sharing plan, except that the contributions by the employer are not necessarily dependent upon profits, and the benefits are distributable in stock of the employer company. For the purpose of allocating and distributing the stock of the employer which is to be shared among his employees or their beneficiaries, such a plan is subject to the same requirements as a profit-sharing plan.

The Plan. The term "plan" implies a permanent, as distinguished from a temporary, program. The plan may not be a mere subterfuge for the distribution of profits to shareholders.

Coverage. The plan must benefit the employees in general, although it need not provide benefits for all of the employees. There must be no discrimination in favor of shareholders, officers, supervisors, or highly paid employees. An otherwise acceptable plan was recognized where there was but one employee.[23] There is no minimum requirement as to the number of participants in a plan except in relation to the total number of employees of a particular employer. If 70% or more of all employees are covered by the plan or if 80% or more of all *eligible* employees are covered (provided that at least 70% of all employees are eligible), the plan may properly be set up.

An employer may disregard completely the following categories of employees without invoking the antidiscrimination provisions:

(1) Employees who have not been employed for a sufficiently long period, to be set by the employer. This may not exceed five years.

(2) Employees whose customary employment is for not more than a stipulated figure, which may not exceed twenty hours in one week.

(3) Employees who work in a seasonal occupation, which is for not more than five months in any calendar year.

[22] *Lincoln Electric Co. Employees Profit-Sharing Trust v. Commissioner,* 190 F.2d 326 (6th Cir., 1951); *Commisisoner v. Produce Reporter Co.,* 207 F.2d 586 (7th Cir., 1953).

[23] Revenue Ruling 55–81, 1955–1 CB 392.

Illustration. An employer provides a plan at a time when he has 1,000 employees. The plan provides that all full-time employees who have been employed by him for a period of two years and have reached the age of thirty are eligible to participate. The plan also requires participating employees to contribute 3% of their monthly pay. At the time the plan is made effective, 100 of the 1,000 employees have not been employed for a period of two years. Fifty of the employees were seasonal employees whose customary employment did not exceed five months in any calendar year. Twenty-five of the employees were part-time employees whose customary employment did not exceed 20 hours in any one week. One hundred and fifty of the full-time employees who had been employed for two years or more had not yet reached age thirty. The requirements will be met if 540 employees are covered by the plan, as shown below:

Total employees with respect to whom the percentage requirements are applicable (1,000 − 175, that is, 100 + 50 + 25)	825
Employees not eligible to participate because of age requirements	150
Total employees eligible to participate	675
Percentage of employees on first line, above, eligible to participate	81+%
Minimum number of participating employees to qualify the plan (80% of 675)	540

If only 70%, or 578 of the 825 employees satisfied the age and service requirements, then 462 (80% of 578) participating employees would satisfy the percentage requirements.

A plan which excludes all employees whose entire remuneration constitutes wages under the Federal Insurance Contributions Act, or a plan under which the contributions or benefits based on that part of an employee's remuneration which is excluded from wages under that act differ from the contributions or benefits based on an employee's remuneration which is not so excluded, or a plan under which the contributions or benefits differ because of any retirement benefit created under Federal or state law, will not be deemed discriminatory because of this exclusion or difference, provided the total benefits resulting under the plan and under this law establish an integrated and correlated retirement system. An illustration of a properly integrated plan is provided in Regulations Section 1.401-3(e)(2).

An employee benefit plan need not meet the tests as to eligibility (the 70% rule, etc.) at all times. But the tests must be met on at least one day in each quarter of the taxable year.

Pension Plans. A pension plan may be of two general forms: (1) contributory and (2) noncontributory. Under a contributory plan, both employer and employee pay a portion of the cost of providing the ultimate benefits. An employer customarily will only pay an amount for which a tax deduction is possible. Inasmuch as the objective of a plan is to provide employees (or their beneficiaries) with as large an amount as possible, the plan may be made contributory. In practice, however, most plans are noncontributory, as employees in general are not anxious to pay anything toward a distant pension. Should an employer adopt a contributory plan, it is indeed conceivable that no one would be benefited; for 80% or more of the eligible employees might not elect to be covered.

Plans also may be characterized according to the method by which they are *funded;* that is, the method by which the cost of the ultimate benefits is met. A convenient method to describe plans is as *trusteed* or *nontrusteed.* The distinction involves the question of whether the employer's contribution is paid directly to a trust for the benefit of the employees, or whether the employer prefers to handle the details of investment of funds, ultimate payments to persons entitled to them, etc., without the intervention (and expense) of a trust. Inasmuch as the employer, in order to get tax deduction, must show that he has parted with the funds irrevocably, the problem of proof is readily met when a trust is employed, especially where independent trustees handle the funds.

Getting the Tax Deduction. In the case of a pension plan, the employer may pay into the fund as large an amount as he chooses; but the income tax deduction is limited according to either of two methods. (1) Deduction is allowed for as much as 5% of the compensation of covered employees. (2) Deduction is allowed for the actual cost of providing the ultimate benefits as determined according to any generally accepted actuarial principles. This is the *current service* credit. In addition, if an employer chooses, he may provide ultimate benefits based upon the length of service (or some part of it) of an employee prior to the time when the pension plan and its current service credits were adopted. The past service cost is the actuarially determined amount required at a particular time to meet all future benefits provided under the plan and not funded by future normal costs and employee contributions with respect to the employees covered by the plan at that time. An employer may deduct the past service cost, but not more than 10% of this cost may be taken as a tax deduction annually in the absence of special permission from the Secretary of the Treasury.

In the case of a deferred profit-sharing plan, the employer's deduction is limited to 15% of the compensation of persons covered by the plan. The plan should carefully define the profits that are to be shared: book income, book income with specified adjustments (such as elimination of capital gains and/or nonoperating profits), income as determined by an independent certified public accountant, taxable income per the Federal income tax return as filed or as audited, etc.

There may be a combined pension and profit-sharing plan; that is, a small pension might be provided, while profits per formula would be used to provide additional retirement benefits, such as through the purchase of annuities. In such a case, the tax deduction would be limited to 25% of the compensation of covered employees.

But no tax deduction is available unless the various requirements of the Internal Revenue Code as to scope of coverage, as well as absence of discrimination, are met.

The employer should send all details of his employee benefit plan to the Commissioner of Internal Revenue with a request for a ruling as to whether the plan qualifies under Section 401 of the Code.

Taxability of Distributions. Payments made under a qualified pension or profit-sharing plan are regarded as annuities, even if made from a trust fund. If the employee had no cost basis (*e.g.*, the plan was noncontributory), the full receipt is taxable income.[24] If the employee has a cost basis not in excess of the first three years of annuity payments, there is no tax liability on guaranteed payments until the cost basis is recovered; thereafter, everything is included in gross income.[25] In other cases, the regular annuity rules apply; see Chapter 12.

If the total distributions payable with respect to any employee are paid within one taxable year on account of the employee's death or other separation from service, the amount paid is entitled to long-term capital gains treatment.[26]

A participating employee, or his beneficiary, is taxed when he received a payment, or when part of the fund is made available to him. A distribution may be deemed to have been made to an employee or beneficiary, with full tax consequences, even if nothing actually is received.[27] If the employee has the right to demand cash or property, he will be taxed as though he actually had received it.[28] But there will be no constructive receipt if there are substantial restrictions on the right or if, before the right is exercisable, the employee irrevocably defers it.[29]

[24] I.R.C. Section 72(a).
[25] I.R.C. Section 72(d).
[26] I.R.C. Section 402(a)(2).
[27] Regulations Section 1.451–2.
[28] Revenue Ruling 54–265, 1954–2 CB 239.
[29] Revenue Ruling 55–423, 1955–1 CB 41.

Unqualified Pension Plan

For the benefit of executives or other favored employees, a corporation may deliberately adopt a pension plan that will not qualify under the Internal Revenue Code because it is frankly discriminatory. Reserves are not deductible for tax purposes. But when pensions actually are paid to the favored participants, the corporation will get a tax deduction, provided these amounts plus other compensation paid to each employee are not unreasonable.

During his period of employment, an employee may build up rights or an expectancy as to future income on which no tax is paid until after retirement, at which time the employee will be in a lower tax bracket.

Stock Options

If an employee is given property by his employer at bargain rates (that is, below market), the rule is that the employee has ordinary income (compensation) to the extent of the differential. The same rule applies where a corporate employer gives an employee the right to buy stock in the company; the value of the option to be taxed is the difference between the option price and the fair market value of the stock at the time the option is granted. In the case of the ordinary (unrestricted) stock option, regardless of *why* it was issued to an employee, he realizes ordinary income upon exercise. Compensation is received in an amount equal to the difference between the fair market value of the stock when the option was exercised and the purchase price.[30] As it is compensation, the employer gets a deduction at the time of exercise. Sometimes the employer, by using its obvious dominion, can *persuade* the employee to exercise the option at the time when a deduction will give the employer the greatest tax advantage.

A stock option is exercised when an unconditional promissory note is given, even if the buyer does not get the stock till the note is paid.[31]

Very favorable tax treatment may be obtained in the case of a *restricted stock option.* A restricted stock option is an option granted after February 26, 1945, to an individual, for any reason connected with his employment by a corporation, if granted by the employer corporation (or its parent or subsidiary corporation) to purchase

[30] *Commissioner v. LoBue,* 351 U.S. 243 (1956).
[31] *Commissioner v. LoBue,* 256 F.2d 735 (3d Cir., 1958).

stock of any of these corporations. At the time the option is granted, the option price must be at least 85% of the fair market value of the stock. This option may not be transferable by the individual except by death (*e.g.*, by will or by the laws of intestacy), and during his lifetime it may be exercisable only by him. At the time the option is granted, he may not own stock possessing more than 10% of the total combined voting power of all classes of stock either of the employer corporation or of its parent or subsidiary corporation, unless the option is at least 110% of the fair market value of the stock at the time the option is granted. In determining whether the taxpayer owns more than 10% of the combined voting power of a corporation, an optionee is considered to own proportionately the present interests of qualifying relatives in a trust holding shares of stock in the corporation by which he has been granted the option, but is considered not to own remainder or other remote interests of those relatives, whether vested or contingent.[32]

If the option was granted after June 21, 1954, the option by its terms may not be exercisable after ten years from the date on which it was granted.[33] Options that had been granted prior to that date are not disturbed.

Taxability. An employee realizes no income from the exercise of a restricted stock option if he does not dispose of the stock before a date which is (1) at least two years after the option date *and* (2) at least six months after he receives the stock. Disposition does not take place for this purpose if it is by reason of the employee's death.

If the employee holds the stock for the required period of time, he will realize income only when he sells the shares. But the amount and nature of the gain depend upon whether the option price was (1) from 85% to 95% of the value of the stock at the option date or (2) at least 95% of the market value at that time.

(1) *If the option price is within the 85%–95% bracket,* he must include in his gross income as compensation for the year of the disposition the amount (if any) by which the option price is exceeded by the lesser of (A) the fair market value of the share at the time the option was granted or (B) the fair market value of the share at the time of disposition or death. The amount of this compensation must be included in the individual's gross income for the taxable year in which the disposition occurs or for the taxable year closing with his death, according to the circumstances of the disposition.

[32] Revenue Ruling 58–325, I.R.B. 1958–26, 15.
[33] I.R.C. Section 421(d).

The basis of any stock disposed of is increased by any amount treated as compensation for this purpose.

Illustration. On June 1, 1960, a corporation grants to an employee a restricted stock option to purchase a share of the corporation's stock for $85. The fair market value of the stock on that date is $100 per share. On June 1, 1961, he exercises the option and on that date the corporation transfers to him the share of stock. On January 1, 1963, he sells the share for $150, its fair market value on that date. He makes his income tax return on the calendar year basis. The income tax consequences to employee and to employer are as follows: (A) Compensation in the amount of $15 is includible in the employee's gross income for 1963, the year of the disposition of the share. The $15 represents the difference between the option price ($85) and the fair market value of the share on the date that the option was granted ($100), inasmuch as this value is less than the fair market value of the share on the date of disposition ($150). For the purpose of computing his gain or loss on the disposition of the stock, the employee's cost basis of $85 is increased by $15, the amount includible in his gross income as compensation. Thus, his basis for the share is $100. Inasmuch as the share was sold for $150, he realizes a gain of $50, which is treated as long-term capital gain. (B) The corporation is entitled to no deduction *at any time* with respect to the share thus transferred to the employee.

Illustration. Assume, in the previous illustration, that the employee sells the share of stock on January 1, 1964, for $75, its fair market value on that date. Inasmuch as $75 is less than the option price ($85), no amount in respect of the sale is includible as compensation in his gross income for 1964. His basis for determining gain or loss on the sale is $85. Inasmuch as he sold the share for $75, he realized a loss of $10 on the sale, which loss is treated as a long-term capital loss.

(2) *If the option price is 95% or more of the market value* on the option date, all of the gain is long-term capital gain or all of the loss is long-term capital loss. There will be no ordinary income from disposition of the stock.

Variable Stock Options. A special rule exists in the case of a variable stock option. The option may qualify as restricted where the purchase price is fixed or where it is determinable under a formula in which the value of the stock is the only variable. Under such an arrangement, an option may qualify where the price is determined by reference to the value of the stock on any particular day during a period of six months which includes the time when the option is exercised. Or the reference may be to an average value of the stock over either the entire 6-month period or over any shorter period included in that period. This 6-month period may begin with, end with, or in any other manner span the day on which the option is exercised.

Illustration. A corporation grants an option to an employee, giving him the right to purchase, after one year, 100 shares of the employer's stock at 85% of market value. The market value at the time the option is granted is $100 per share. One year later the market value of the stock is $200, and the employee exercises the option, buying 100 shares at $170 per share for a total of $17,000. After holding the stock for two years he sells it for $250 per share, or $25,000. Inasmuch as the purchase price of the stock under the option would have been $85 per share had the option been exercised at the date of the grant, the option qualifies. His gain will be the lesser of (A) $250 (market value when sold) minus $170 (price paid for stock) or (B) $100 (market value at the time the option was granted) minus $85 (the price that would have been paid for the stock had it been exercised at the date the option was granted). Consequently, upon the sale of the stock the employee will be taxable upon $15 per share ($1,500) ordinary income and $65 per share ($6,500) capital gain. In determining the capital gain, the amount taxable as ordinary income ($15) is added to the purchase price of the stock ($170).

If a variable stock option was granted after September 30, 1958, it will not meet the definition of *variable* should the formula provide for determining the option price by reference to the fair market value of the stock at any time before the option is exercised, if this value is greater than the average fair market value of the stock during the calendar month in which the option is exercised.[34]

Stock Purchase Warrants

A restricted stock option may be an excellent mechanism to obtain capital gain treatment when corporate stock becomes more valuable. But an investment is required. Stock purchase warrants differ from options in that the warrants are rights to purchase stock which are freely transferable. Thus, warrants may be sold without the need of actually purchasing and reselling stock. Capital treatment may be obtained.

Stock Purchase Plans

A stock purchase plan is an arrangement under which a corporation will enable an employee to buy corporate stock. The stock is not offered at a bargain; the differential would be ordinary income as compensation. Instead, the employer may facilitate financing of the stock for an employee, or the employee may be able to borrow with the stock as collateral but without personal liability for the loan.

One mechanism provides that the employer will sell stock to an employee subject to serious restrictions; for example, it may be nonassignable, nonvoting, subject to resale to the corporation at a very nominal figure when the employee leaves the company, etc.

[34] I.R.C. Section 421(d).

The stock, with all of these restrictions, will have a very low fair market value, and that is what the employee will pay. At some future time, without previous arrangement or commitment, the employer may lift the restrictions. The stock will then have a greatly increased value; but the gratuitous lifting of the restrictions does not constitute taxable income.[35]

Payment of Personal Expenses

As a rule, if the employer pays personal expenses of an employee, the payment is treated as constructive receipt of compensation by the employee. But payment of expenses of an employee *because* they were incurred as an employee are not taxable, if they can be substantiated. Deductible by the employer were legal fees to defend an executive who had been accused of stealing funds, where the resultant publicity was deemed adverse to the employer's business.[36]

If an employer pays the income taxes of an employee, there is constructive receipt of compensation.[37] Where an employer absorbs employee taxes instead of withholding them from compensation, the employee is deemed to have received additional income to this extent.[38] An officer was taxed upon a percentage of corporate profits that were placed in a trust fund for him.[39] But an exception is made where the employer absorbs all of the Social Security taxes of the employee; this is not treated as constructive income.[40]

Death Benefits

Amounts up to $5,000 which are paid by an employer to the beneficiaries or to the estate of an employee, or former employee, by reason of the death of the employee, are excluded from the gross income of the recipient. This exclusion does not apply to amounts constituting income payable to the employee during his lifetime as compensation for services. Nor does it apply to amounts received as an annuity under a survivorship arrangement, where the employee was the primary annuitant and the annuity starting date occurred before the death of the employee.[41]

[35] *Robert Lehman,* 17 T.C. 652 (1952); *Harold H. Kuchman,* 18 T.C. 154 (1952).
[36] *Catholic News Publishing Co.,* 10 T.C. 73 (1947).
[37] *Old Colony Trust Co. et al. v. Commissioner,* 279 U.S. 716 (1929).
[38] I.T. 3154, 1938–1 CB 113.
[39] *J. H. McEwen,* 6 T.C. 1018 (1946).
[40] Regulations Section 31.3121(a)(6)–1.
[41] I.R.C. Section 101(b).

The total amount excludable with respect to any employee may not exceed $5,000, regardless of the number of employers or the number of beneficiaries.

Payments to Survivor

Where an employer gratuitously continues to pay the compensation of a deceased employee to the widow, the tax treatment to the recipient depends upon the intentions of the parties, particularly the employer. Thus, a nontaxable gift was found where payment was "made without any legal or moral obligation, in recognition of, but not in payment of, former services of the Decedent." [42]

Insurance

The tax aspects of certain insurance premiums paid by the employer for the employee are treated in Chapter 12; for example, group insurance, other insurance, and split-dollar insurance.

Supplementary Material

A. Suggested Reading.

Gordon D. Henderson, ed., *The Effect of Tax Policy on Executive and Worker Compensation* (Princeton: Tax Institute, Inc., 1958).

Raymond E. Graichen, "Reasonable Compensation," *Proceedings of the New York University Seventeenth Annual Institute on Federal Taxation* (Albany: Matthew Bender & Co., Inc., 1959), p. 117.

Kenneth W. Bergen, "Deferred Compensation," *Proceedings of the New York University Seventeenth Annual Institute on Federal Taxation* (Albany: Matthew Bender & Co., Inc., 1959), p. 879.

John R. Lindquist, "Fundamentals of Deferred Compensation," *Illinois Bar Journal,* June, 1955, Vol. XLIII, #10, p. 756.

Harvey Luppescu, "Deferred Compensation for Executives," *The Price Waterhouse Review,* September, 1958, Vol. III, #3, p. 45.

Andrew C. Bailey, "Compensation with the Fringe on Top," *Proceedings of the New York University Sixteenth Annual Institute on Federal Taxation* (Albany: Matthew Bender & Co., Inc., 1958), p. 75.

Challis A. Hall, Jr., *Effects of Taxation—Executive Compensation and Retirement Plans* (Boston: Harvard University, Graduate School of Business Administration, Division of Research, 1951).

Robert L. Lawthers, "Federal Income Taxation of an Employee and His Beneficiaries Under a Qualified Pension or Profit-Sharing Plan," *The Journal of the American Society of Chartered Life Underwriters,* Spring, 1958, Vol. XII, #2, p. 130.

Robert S. Holzman, *Guide to Pension and Profit Sharing Plans* (New York: Farnsworth Publishing Co., 1956).

[42] *Bank of Southwest National Association, Houston, v. United States,* — F. Supp. — (D.C., Texas, 1958).

B. Leading Cases.

What is compensation? *Commissioner v. LoBue,* 351 U.S. 243 (1956).
Payment for services. *Old Colony Trust Co. v. Commissioner,* 279 U.S. 716 (1929).
Time of deduction. *Lucas v. Ox Fibre Brush Co.,* 281 U.S. 115 (1930).
Who is to be taxed? *Lucas v. Earl,* 281 U.S. 111 (1930).

C. Questions.

1. To what extent does *intent* of the payor determine whether the payee has received taxable compensation?
2. If an employer is satisfied that compensation paid to an employee is reasonable under all of the circumstances, does the Internal Revenue Service have any right to interfere?
3. A corporation makes no deductions for Social Security taxes of its employees but makes payments to the Internal Revenue Service out of its own funds. Are these deemed to be income to the employees?
4. In accordance with established policy, an employer gives $1,000 to each newborn baby of an employee. Is this taxable to (a) the employee or (b) the baby? If so, does the employer get a deduction?
5. On January 1, 1961, an employee was sent to prison because of charges of embezzlement brought by his employer. Late in 1963, the true culprit confessed, and the employee was released. The employer rehired him at a very substantial increase in compensation on December 31, 1963 and immediately gave him a check for the equivalent of his old salary for the three years he was in prison. Discuss the tax aspects of this payment with reference to each of the years.
6. A corporation adopts an employee benefit plan, which covers all employees except those who belong to unions. Will the plan be disqualified because of discrimination?
7. On various occasions, a certain corporation has rented a box at the Yankee Stadium for the entire baseball season. When there are no customers to entertain, employees are given tickets to the games without charge. Is this taxable compensation to them?
8. The sole stockholder of a corporation is on the cash basis; the company is on the accrual basis. He receives a year-end bonus, which, however, is not paid to him until after the accountants render their report three months later. Will the corporation be entitled to the deduction in the year of accrual or the year of payment?
9. For the summer vacation, a young man is hired by a corporation of which his father is an executive. The father, a highly ethical person, does not want the corporation to be charged for services of questionable value, so he arranges that $100 a week of his own compensation will be paid by the corporation to his son rather than to him. Who will be taxed?
10. A corporation adopts a qualified pension plan for the benefit of its employees. What are the tax benefits to each of the parties concerned?
11. A corporation paid all of its sales personnel (including the sales manager) nominal salaries plus a commission of 10% of sales made by each man. In 1961, the sales manager (whose average commissions for the past five years had been $15,000) earned $82,500. Do you believe that the corporation would lose any part of its deduction as unreasonable compensation?

12. A corporation adopts a contributory pension plan. Of the 100 employees, 18 voted not to be covered. Of the remainder, 6 have not been with the company for a long enough time to meet the eligibility requirements and 9 are excluded as part-time workers. Is the plan eligible for qualification?
13. If the Internal Revenue Service disallows a portion of an employee's salary as unreasonable, will the employee be relieved of tax on that amount which the employer may not take as a deduction?
14. When an employee of S Company retires, he is entitled under his corporate employer's plan to a lump-sum pension of $25,000, which, at the employee's option, the employer will retain and pay interest on at the rate of 6½% per annum to the employee. What are the tax implications to the employee?
15. An employer assumes the personal tax liability of persons who have been with the firm for more than ten years. Does this assumption constitute taxable income to these employees?
16. An employee is covered by a qualified benefit plan. After 31 years of service, he dies, and the company promptly pays his widow his accrued benefits in a lump sum. Is this ordinary income to her?
17. A company estimates that the payroll of persons covered by its pension plan is $100,000 per year. An actuary computes an annual cost of $6,789.21 for the plan. What is the maximum allowable tax deduction if the plan is qualified?
18. An employee is granted an option to buy 200 shares of stock in his employer-corporation at $90 per share. The fair market value of the stock is $100 per share at the time, January 1, 1959. The option will lapse in ten years and may not be disposed of by him. He owns no stock in the corporation at the time. On July 1, 1961, he exercises the option and receives stock, which he sells on February 11, 1962, for $102 per share. What are the tax consequences to him on (a) January 1, 1959, (b) July 1, 1961, and (c) February 11, 1962?
19. In 1961, an employee is given the right to buy stock in his employer-corporation at $80 per share at any time within ten years. The stock is valued at $100 per share on this date. In 1962, he exercises the option, at which time the stock is valued at $110 per share. In 1963, he sells the stock for $120 per share. (a) What are the tax consequences to him in each of the years involved? (b) Does the employer get a tax deduction at any time?
20. A corporation permits a new employee to buy stock, currently valued at $85 per share; but he is not permitted to vote the stock, to dispose of it other than to the company at cost, nor to retain it if he leaves the company. As a result of these conditions, the stock is deemed to be worth $50 per share, the price he pays. Two years later, in 1961, without any prior understanding that this would happen, the restrictions are lifted. In 1963, he sells the stock for $93 per share. What are the tax consequences to him in each of the years named?
21. An individual is given a restricted stock option to buy 100 shares of stock at $200 per share in the corporation that owns the stock of the company for which he works. The fair market value of the parent's stock on that date is also $200 per share. Three years later he acquires the stock and, eleven months later, he sells the shares for $190 each. Discuss the tax aspects of the matter.

12

INSURANCE AND ANNUITIES

Life Insurance

Deductibility of Premiums. Premiums on an individual's policy of life insurance are not deductible for income tax purposes; this is a personal expense. Certain premiums on personal life insurance for *business purposes* are deductible. For example, a company could claim a deduction on premiums on a policy on the life of a debtor, as such a payment is "related to its business, to wit, the preservation and conservation of its funds." [1] Deductible are premiums that a business pays on insurance premiums on the lives of valued employees, where the enterprise will be the beneficiary if the policy matures by reason of the death of the insured. "What corporate purpose could be considered more essential than key man insurance?" [2]

An employer may deduct the premiums on group insurance contracts covering the lives of his employees.[3]

But premiums are not deductible as trade or business expenses if they are paid on a life insurance policy covering the life of any officer or employee of the corporation, or any person (including the taxpayer) who is financially interested in any trade or business carried on by the taxpayer.[4]

If a taxpayer takes out a policy for the purpose of protecting himself from loss in the event of the death of the insured, the taxpayer is considered a beneficiary (directly or indirectly) under the policy. But if he is not a beneficiary under the policy, the premiums paid will not be disallowed merely because the taxpayer may derive a benefit from the increased efficiency of the officer or employee insured.[5]

A taxpayer is not entitled to a deduction for interest paid or accrued to purchase or to carry a single premium life insurance,

[1] *General Smelting Co.,* 4 T.C. 313 (1944).
[2] *The Emeloid Co., Inc. v. Commissioner,* 189 F.2d 230 (3d Cir., 1951).
[3] L.O. 1014, 2 CB 88.
[4] I.R.C. Section 264(a).
[5] Regulations Section 1.264–1(b).

endowment, or annuity contract. For this purpose, a policy will be treated as a single-premium contract if (1) substantially all the premiums on the policy are paid within a period of four years from the purchase date of the contract or (2) an amount is deposited after March 1, 1954, with the insurance company for payment of a substantial number of future premiums on the contract.[6]

According to the regulations, if an expenditure by a cash basis taxpayer is for an asset "which extends substantially beyond the close of the taxable year," a proration of the expenditure must be made over the years in which the benefit is derived.[7] Court decisions are in conflict. It has been held that prepaid insurance premiums may not be deducted at the time of payment by a cash basis taxpayer.[8] But there is authority to the contrary.[9]

Taxability of Proceeds. The general rule is that receipts of the proceeds of a life insurance policy by reason of the death of the insured are not taxable income. This is true whether payment is made in a single sum or otherwise.[10] This exemption applies to corporate beneficiaries as well as individuals.[11] Death benefit payments having the characteristics of life insurance proceeds payable by reason of death under contracts, such as workmen's compensation insurance contracts, endowment contracts, or accident and health insurance contracts, are covered by this provision. It is immaterial whether payment is made to the estate of the insured or to a beneficiary, whether it is made directly or in trust.

But where there is a transfer of a life insurance contract (or any interest in it) by assignment or otherwise for a valuable consideration, the amount excluded from gross income may not exceed the cost; that is, the actual consideration plus premiums or other amounts subsequently paid by the transferee.

Illustration. A pays premiums of $500 for an insurance policy in the face amount of $1,000 upon the life of B, and subsequently transfers the policy to C for $600. C receives the proceeds of $1,000 upon the death of B. The amount which C can exclude from his gross income is limited to $600 plus any premiums paid by C subsequent to the transfer.

This limitation on the amount excludable from the transferee's gross income does not apply (except in certain special cases in-

[6] I.R.C. Section 264(b).

[7] Regulations Section 1.461–1.

[8] *Commissioner v. Boylston Market Association,* 131 F.2d 966 (1st Cir., 1942).

[9] *Waldheim Realty and Improvement Co. v. Commissioner,* 245 F.2d 823 (8th Cir., 1957).

[10] I.R.C. Section 101(a)(1).

[11] *United States v. Supplee-Biddle Hardware Co.,* 265 U.S. 189 (1924).

volving a series of transfers), where the basis of the policy or interest transferred is determinable, in whole or in part, by reference to the basis in the hands of the transferor. Nor does the limitation apply where the policy or interest is transferred to the insured, to a partner of the insured, to a partnership in which the insured is a partner, or to a corporation in which the insured is a shareholder or officer.

Illustration. The O Corporation purchases for a single premium of $500 an insurance policy in the face amount of $1,000 upon the life of one of its employees, naming the O Corporation as beneficiary. The O Corporation transfers the policy to the N Corporation in a tax-free reorganization (the policy having a basis for determining gain or loss in the hands of the N Corporation determined by reference to its basis in the hands of O Corporation). O Corporation receives the proceeds of $1,000 upon the death of the employee. The entire $1,000 is to be excluded from N Corporation's gross income.

Illustration. The facts are the same as in the preceding illustration, except that, prior to the death of the employee, O Corporation transfers the policy to F Corporation for $600. F Corporation receives the $1,000 proceeds upon the employee's death. The amount which F Corporation may exclude from its gross income is limited to $600 plus any premiums paid by F Corporation subsequent to the transfer of the policy to it.

Illustration. The facts are the same as in the preceding illustration, except that, prior to the death of the employee, F Corporation transfers the policy to L Corporation, in which the employee is a shareholder. L Corporation receives the proceeds of $1,000 upon the employee's death. The entire $1,000 is to be excluded from the gross income of L Corporation.

In the case of a gratuitous transfer of a life insurance policy or any interest in it, the general rule is that the amount of the proceeds which is excludable from the transferee's gross income is limited to the sum of (1) the amount which would have been excludable by the transferor if no such transfer had taken place and (2) any premiums and other amounts subsequently paid by the transferee. But where the gratuitous transfer is made by or to the insured, a partner of the insured, a partnership in which the insured is a partner, or a corporation in which the insured is a shareholder or an officer, the entire amount of the proceeds attributable to the policy or interest transferred will be excludable from the transferee's gross income.

In the case of a series of transfers, if the last transfer of a life insurance policy or an interest in it is for a valuable consideration, the general rule is that the final transferee may exclude from gross income only the sum of (1) the actual value of the consideration paid by him and (2) the premiums and other amounts subsequently paid by him. But if the final transfer is to the insured, to a partner of the insured, to a partnership in which the insured is a partner, or to a corporation in which the insured is a shareholder or officer, the final transferee may exclude the entire amount of the proceeds from gross income.

Illustration. H pays premiums of $500 for an insurance policy in the face amount of $1,000 upon his own life, and subsequently transfers the policy to his wife, W, for $600. W later transfers the policy without consideration to their son, S. S receives the proceeds of $1,000 upon the death of H. The amount which S may exclude from gross income is limited to $600 plus any premiums paid by W and S subsequent to the transfer of the policy to W.

To be excludable, amounts received under an insurance policy must be as a primary and direct result of it. A corporation took out an insurance policy upon the life of an officer, and a corporate resolution declared that any proceeds collected would be given to the stockholders. When he died, the insurance proceeds that the corporation received were not excludable from the shareholders' gross incomes.[12]

Taxability of Premiums to Stockholders. If a corporation pays premiums on a policy on the life of an employee or shareholder, as the corporation's own investment, no tax consequences to the insured arise.[13] But if the corporation pays the premiums on a policy owned by the insured and of which he designates the beneficiary, the amount paid in premiums constitutes taxable income to him.[14]

It is necessary to establish whether the corporation or the stockholder is really the beneficial owner of the policy. In one case, a corporation paid premiums on policies where the stockholders were the beneficiaries; but the corporate minutes provided that, in the event of the death of the insured, proceeds of the policy would go to the corporation to buy out the insured's stock. It was held that, under state law, the stockholders held any rights they had in the policies for the benefit of the corporation; and, hence, the premiums paid on the policies by the corporation were not income to the shareholders.[15]

Where insurance policies were used to fund a stock retirement agreement (that is, to buy up the shares of a stockholder upon his death so that these shares would be canceled), premiums paid by the corporation were not deemed to be constructive dividends to the stockholders. Even if they had the right to designate the beneficiaries, there was no dividend if the corporation remained the owner of the cash surrender values and of all other rights under the

[12] *Cummings et al. v. Commissioner*, 73 F.2d 477 (1st Cir., 1934).
[13] *Lewis v. O'Malley*, 140 F.2d 735 (8th Cir., 1944).
[14] *Commissioner v. Bonwit*, 87 F.2d 764 (2d Cir., 1937).
[15] *Prunier et al. v. Commissioner*, 248 F.2d 818 (1st Cir., 1957).

policies. Here the purpose of the insurance was to finance an agreement to retire the stock of each shareholder at a guaranteed minimum price at his death. There were no benefits to the shareholders at the time the premiums were paid.[16]

Group Life Insurance Premiums. Although premiums paid by a corporation on ordinary life insurance policies on the lives of employees will be treated as income to the employees if they are permitted to name the beneficiaries, this rule does not apply to group life insurance premiums.[17] But this exclusion provided in the case of group life insurance does not extend to group *permanent* life insurance, where substantial economic benefits usually include increasing values of paid-up continued insurance or other benefits to the employees. Thus, under permanent forms of insurance, employees are provided with something more than current term insurance which does not have paid-up or other substantial values.[18]

Employee Death Benefits. There is a $5,000 exclusion from gross income of amounts paid by or *on behalf of* an employer to the beneficiaries or estate of an employee by reason of the death of the employee.[19] This payment may be made by an insurance company under an insurance policy.

This exclusion does not refer to amounts to which the employee had a nonforfeitable right before death, nor to amounts paid a surviving annuitant if the employee received or was entitled to receive any annuity before his death.

Insurance Dividends. Insurance dividends are not income but serve to reduce the cost of the policy. But shareholders in stock insurance companies will treat distributions of profits in the same manner as any other corporate dividends.

Payment of Life Insurance Proceeds at a Date Later than Death. If the amounts payable as proceeds of life insurance cannot in any event exceed the amount payable at the time of the insured's death, these amounts are fully excludable from the gross income of the recipient (or recipients) without regard to the time of payment. But the interest element contained in life insurance proceeds which are payable (in installments, as an annuity, or otherwise) at a date later than death are taxed to the beneficiary, except that the surviving spouse of the insured is entitled to an annual exclusion with respect to this interest in the amount of $1,000.[20]

[16] *Sanders et al. v. Fox,* 253 F.2d 855 (10th Cir., 1958).
[17] G.C.M. 16069, XV–1 CB 84.
[18] Mimeograph 6477, 1950–1 CB 16.
[19] I.R.C. Section 101(b).
[20] I.R.C. Section 101(d).

For the purpose of this exclusion, "surviving spouse" means the spouse of the insured as of the date of death, including a spouse legally separated, but not under a decree of absolute divorce. To the extent that the total payments, under one or more agreements, made in excess of the amounts determined by proration do not exceed $1,000 in the taxable year of receipt, they will be excluded from the gross income of the surviving spouse (whether or not payment of any part of this amount is guaranteed by the insurer).

Illustration. A surviving spouse elects to receive all of the life insurance proceeds with respect to one insured, amounting to $150,000 in ten annual installments of $16,500 each, based on a certain guaranteed interest rate. The prorated amount is $15,000 ($150,000 divided by ten). As to the second payment, the insurer pays $17,850, which exceeds the guaranteed payment by $1,350 as the result of earnings of the insurer in excess of those required to pay the guaranteed installments. The surviving spouse may include $1,850 on gross income and exclude $16,000, determined in the following manner:

Fixed payment (including guaranteed interest)	$16,500
Excess interest	1,350
Total payment	$17,850
Prorated amount	15,000
Excess over prorated amount	$ 2,850
Annual excess over prorated amount excludable	1,000
Amount includible in gross income	$ 1,850

The proration is based upon what the statute refers to as an "amount held by an insurer with respect to any beneficiary." This means an amount equal to the present value to the beneficiary (as of the date of death of the insured) of an agreement by the insurer under a life insurance policy (whether as an option or otherwise) to pay the beneficiary an amount at a date or dates later than the death of the insured. The present value of this agreement is to be computed as if the agreement under the policy had been entered into on the date of death of the insured, except that this value will be determined by the use of the mortality tables and interest rate used by the insurer in calculating payments to be made to the beneficiary under the agreement. Where an insurance policy provides an option for the payment of a specific amount upon the death of the insured in full discharge of the contract, this lump sum is the amount held by the insurer with respect to all beneficiaries under the contract.

In the ordinary case, one of the options in a life insurance contract is an option to take a specific amount in a lump sum. This lump-sum amount will be, in such cases, the "amount held by an insurer" and need only be prorated over the period payments which are to be made by the insurer.

Illustration. If, at the insured's death, $1,000 would have been payable in a single installment, but ten equal annual payments are made in lieu of this method, the portion of the installment to be excluded from gross income is $100 ($1,000 divided by ten). Any amount actually received as an installment in excess of $100 is to be excluded from gross income, except to the extent that the annual interest exclusion of a qualified beneficiary may apply. If payments for life were provided for instead of ten equal payments, the $1,000 lump sum would be divided by the present life expectancy in years of the beneficiary concerned. Assuming the beneficiary to have an expectancy of twenty years and the lump-sum payment to be $1,000, $50 of each installment payment would be excluded from gross income and the balance included in gross income ($1,000 divided by 20), again subject to the applicable annual interest exclusion.

Special problems arise where the insurance contract does not provide for a particular amount payable immediately upon the death of the insured as an option. These are to be solved by finding the value (with respect to each beneficiary on a particular policy) of the agreement, as of the date of death of the insured, discounted on the basis of the interest rate and mortality tables used by the insurer in determining the payments.

Illustration. If the surviving spouse were to receive an annuity for a fixed period (or life) under one option and under the remaining option she were to receive a different sum or the same sum for a different time, and the daughter were to receive an annuity for a given period, the values to each would be determined after the wife's selection of an option, as of the date of death of the insured. If the wife selected an option under which she is to receive $5,000 per year for her life, with an expectancy of twenty years, and the daughter $5,000 per year for ten years, the discounted value to the wife might be $60,000, and that of the daughter $35,000. The wife would then exclude $3,000 of each installment from gross income ($60,000 divided by 20) and an additional $1,000 of each installment because of her special exclusion. She would then exclude a total of $4,000 of each installment from her gross income, but include $1,000 of each installment in her gross income. The daughter would exclude $3,500 of each installment from her gross income ($35,000 divided by 10). The daughter would include $1,500 of each installment in gross income.

Payments made by reason of the death of a beneficiary (or beneficiaries) under a contract providing that these payments will be made in the event that the beneficiary (or beneficiaries) dies before receiving a specified number of payments or a specified total amount will be excluded from the gross income of the recipient to the extent that these payments are made solely by reason of this guaranty.

The rules as to exclusion of life insurance proceeds from gross income do not apply to interest payments on any amount held by an insurer under an agreement to pay interest thereon.[21]

[21] I.R.C. Section 101(c).

Exchanges of Insurance Policies. No gain or loss is recognized on the exchange of:

(1) A contract of life insurance for another contract of life insurance or for an endowment or annuity contract;

(2) A contract of endowment insurance for another contract of endowment insurance providing for regular payments beginning at a date not later than the date payments would have begun under the contract exchanged, or an annuity contract; or

(3) An annuity contract for another annuity contract; but this exchange is not tax-free if the policies exchanged do not relate to the same insured.[22]

For the purpose of this section, the following definitions have been provided:

"(1) Endowment contract.—A contract of endowment insurance is a contract with a life insurance company as defined in section 801 which depends in part on the life expectancy of the insured, but which may be payable in full in a single payment during his life.

"(2) Annuity contract.—An annuity contract is a contract to which paragraph (1) applies but which may be payable during the life of the annuitant only in installments.

"(3) Life insurance contract.—A contract of life insurance is a contract to which paragraph (1) applies but which is not ordinarily payable in full during the life of the insured." [23]

The exchanges of an endowment contract for a life insurance contract is taxable, as is the exchange of an annuity for a life insurance or endowment policy. This prevents avoidance of the tax on the maturity of endowment or annuity contracts by conversion to life insurance or endowment contracts, the proceeds of which (payable upon the death of the insured) are excluded from gross income.

Sales of Endowment Policies. The maturing of an endowment policy results in ordinary income to the extent that realization exceeds cost. It is not certain whether the sale of an endowment policy shortly before maturity will convert ordinary income into capital gain.

Twelve days before an endowment insurance policy on his life matured, an individual sold the policy to his partners for an amount in excess of his cost. This excess was treated as capital gain, even though his principal reasons for making the transfer were personal, such as to get capital gains treatment, to have cash available for what seemed to be an opportune investment time, and to assist his

[22] I.R.C. Section 1035(a).
[23] I.R.C. Section 1035(b).

son-in-law in acquiring a house. This was held to be a real and bona fide sale, as the buyers were not "stooges" and the transaction was not "an agency arrangement masquerading as a sale." [24]

But on substantially identical facts, it was held that the sale of an annuity shortly before maturity resulted in ordinary income, as the "purchase" of future income did not turn ordinary income into capital.[25]

Insurance as Alimony. If an alimony settlement provides that a man will pay premiums on a life insurance policy on his life for the benefit of his divorced wife, these premiums are deductible by him and are includible in her gross income. But she must be the irrevocable beneficiary.[26]

The wife was not taxed on her ex-husband's premiums on policies that he had assigned to her as trustee for a trust for the benefit of herself and the children. Here she was not personally a beneficiary nor did she acquire an interest in the increased cash or loan values of the policy.[27]

Grantor's Insurance Premiums. The grantor of a trust is taxed upon trust income to the extent that this income is applied to the payment of premiums on policies of insurance on his life, except policies irrevocably payable for a charitable purpose as specified in Section 170(c) of the Internal Revenue Code.[28]

Split-Dollar Life Insurance. Split-dollar life insurance is an arrangement whereby both employer and employee pay portions of the premium on insurance on the life of the employee.

Illustration. An employer enters into an agreement with an employee under which the former purchases as sole owner and beneficiary a policy of ordinary insurance on the latter's life. The employee is given the right to assist in the payment of premiums, in return for partial control over the distribution of death benefits under this policy.

Under the agreement, the gross premiums paid, less the amount of any dividends, will be paid by the employer to the extent of the increase in cash surrender value for any taxable year, the balance being paid by the employee. Both employer and employee will have separate ownership rights during the employee's lifetime, with the employee having the privilege of designating the beneficiary under the policy for that part of the proceeds equal to the excess of the

[24] *Percy W. Phillips et al.,* 30 T.C. 866 (1958).
[25] *Arnfeld et al. v. United States,* 163 F. Supp. 865 (Ct. Cl., 1958).
[26] I.T. 4001, 1950-1 CB 27.
[27] *Seligmann v. Commissioner,* 207 F.2d 489 (7th Cir., 1953).
[28] Regulations Section 1.677(a)-1.

face amount payable over the cash surrender value. The employer will be the beneficiary under the policy to the extent of the cash surrender value, which may be available for general corporate purposes.

The agreement may provide that upon the termination of the employee's employment, the employer will, upon the employee's election, (1) sell its ownership interest in the life insurance contract to him for an amount equal to the larger of the gross premiums it has paid or the guaranteed cash values in its portion of the policy or (2) assign to the employee all of the employer's ownership interest except an amount equal to the guaranteed cash surrender value at the date of the assignment, provided, however, that if the employee defaults on any future premiums, the employer may reassert its rights to ownership. Or the plan may provide that the employer will sell its interest to the employee at any time during the period of employment, should the employee wish to reimburse the employer for the latter's cost as of that time.

In effect, this arrangement is the same as if the employer makes annual loans without interest of a sum of money equal to the annual increases in the cash surrender value of the policy on the employee's life.

The employee will realize no taxable income upon the payment of the portion of the premium by the employer. The employer gets no deduction for the payment. The portion of the proceeds taxable upon the employee's death to the employer and to the designated beneficiary of the employee will not be included in the gross income of the employer or of the employee's beneficiary.[29]

Split-dollar insurance may also be used to take care of a dependent's financial future. A father, for example, may advance funds to buy insurance for his son, in the manner just described.

Other Insurance

General. Allowance for most types of business insurance premiums is provided by general language in the Code, for deduction is allowed for "all the ordinary and necessary expenses paid or incurred during the taxable year in carrying on any trade or business." [30] "Among the items included in business expenses are . . . insurance premiums against fire, storm, theft, accident, or other similar losses in the case of a business. . . . No such item shall be included in business expenses, however, to the extent that it is used by the

[29] Revenue Ruling 55-713, 1955-2 CB 23.
[30] I.R.C. Section 162.

taxpayer in computing the cost of property included in its inventory or used in determining the gain or loss basis of its plant, equipment, or other property." [31]

Unlike certain types of life insurance, there are no types of business insurance specifically disallowed by the Code. There is authority for deducting the following types of insurance premiums, in addition to those cited in the regulations:

Flood, wind, hurricane, marine, crop.[32]
Use and occupancy.[33]
Fidelity bond.[34]
Credit insurance.[35]
Automobile liability.[36]
Business overhead expenses during prolonged periods of disability due to injury or sickness.[37]
Workmen's compensation.[38]

Any expense for the business seems to fall within this category of ordinary and necessary expenses, except for the life insurance premiums specifically excluded. Even life insurance premiums may be deductible under certain circumstances, as where a creditor takes out a policy on the life of a debtor.[39]

To be deductible under this heading, the expenditure must be for the purchase of insurance. "Insurance" has been authoritatively defined as follows: "A contract whereby, for an agreed premium, one party undertakes to compensate the other for loss on a specified subject by specified perils." [40]

Personal Insurance Not Deductible. Insurance premiums, to be deductible, must be for business purposes. Deduction also may be allowed as a nonbusiness expense, as where the taxpayer (who was not a dealer or trader in that commodity) held turpentine for the production of income.[41]

If an asset is used in part for business and in part for personal purposes, an allocation must be paid, and only that portion of the premium attributable to business use is deductible. Such was the

[31] Regulations Section 1.162–1(a).
[32] O.D. 215, 1 CB 104.
[33] O.D. 645, 3 CB 89.
[34] T.D. 2090, CB December 14, 1914.
[35] A.R.R. 723, I–1 CB 113.
[36] I.T. 3015, XV–2 CB 136.
[37] Revenue Ruling 55–264, 1955–1 CB 11.
[38] O.D. 964, 5 CB 118.
[39] O.D. 38, 1 CB 104.
[40] *Bouvier's Law Dictionary,* 1946 Edition, p. 564.
[41] *Higgins v. United States,* 75 F. Supp. 252 (Ct. Cl., 1948).

case with an automobile insurance policy.[42] Such was the ruling as to liability insurance.[43]

Losses are allowed only to the extent not compensated for by insurance or otherwise. Where a taxpayer had a right to be reimbursed for a loss, and he did not avail himself of this right, there was no allowable deduction, as he could have been compensated "by insurance or otherwise." [44]

Deduction of Loss. Loss must be claimed as a deduction in the year of incidence. But if the loss is covered by insurance, and the insurer neither admitted nor settled its liability until a subsequent year, any reimbursed loss is deductible in the year of settlement.[45]

Premium Deduction. The rule as to deduction of a lump-sum insurance premium has been discussed earlier.

As long as the insured is contractually bound to pay premiums to the insurer, it is immaterial that the actual net cost of the insurance is not known in a particular year. An accrual-basis corporation purchased catastrophe insurance, the cost of the premium being determined by the amount of the payroll. It was held that inasmuch as liability had accrued during the year, the basis for the deduction was set, although the amount of the liability had not been ascertained definitely.[46]

Policies, the final net cost of which is not known in the taxable year, are a familiar form of coverage. This so-called retrospective rating plan takes into account the loss experience in the current policy year of the individual insured. A standard rate is tentatively paid; but the actual premium for the taxable year will be determined by the taxpayer's own experience. If losses have been less than the underwriters expected, a refund of a portion of the premium is made as a reward to the policyholder. If losses prove excessive as compared to the initial expectation of the underwriters, an additional premium or penalty is charged.

To be deductible, an expenditure must meet the statutory requirements as to its being ordinary and necessary.[47] Thus, *any* amount of premiums may not constitute an allowable deduction for tax purposes. Such may be the case with certain premiums on factory fire insurance mutuals. Here members are required to pay premiums that are higher than expected costs and losses, and it is

[42] *Marvin T. Blackwell et al.,* T.C. Memo. 1956–184, filed August 9, 1956.
[43] I.T. 3015, XV–2 CB 136.
[44] *Charles D. Whitney,* 13 T.C. 897 (1949).
[45] *Charles F. Jeffrey et al.,* T.C. Memo., Docket #30918, entered May 20, 1953.
[46] *Roundup Coal Mining Co.,* 20 T.C. 388 (1953).
[47] *Limericks, Inc. v. Commissioner,* 165 F.2d 483 (5th Cir., 1948).

"believed" that premiums will be refunded to the extent that they have been excessive. Such refunds may be treated as being, in part, dividends. The original premium might be regarded as consisting of two elements—part protection (deductible) and part future dividends.

An amount accrued and paid in one year as insurance premiums, although refunded in a subsequent year on the cancellation or expiration of the contract, is a proper deduction for tax purposes in the year of accrual and payment.[48] Where a corporation in a taxable period receives refunds of insurance premiums paid and properly deducted in a previous year, they represent taxable income to the corporation when returned to it.[49] Refunds of premiums on policies of workmen's compensation insurance represent ordinary income and not dividends to an employer.[50]

Use and Occupancy Insurance. If a taxpayer carries use and occupancy insurance, he will be reimbursed for lost profits resulting from a suspension of the business for stated causes, such as fire. The more common type of policy calls for reimbursement of a stipulated percentage of profits for a base period, although the compensation may be a set amount per day of business interruption. Reimbursement by the insurer is regarded as merely a replacement of profits; thus, the reimbursement is included in gross income.[51] This is the case even where the insured devotes the entire proceeds to the purchase of new physical assets for the business.[52]

The proceeds of overhead insurance (reimbursement for overhead during a stated business interruption) are included in gross income, but the elements of overhead involved are deductible.[53]

Accident and Health Plans. An employee does not include in gross income any contributions by his employer to accident or health plans (through insurance or otherwise) for personal injuries or sickness of the employee.[54]

Self-Insurance. Reserves for losses or contingencies are not deductible. A reserve set up for self-insurance equal to the estimated premiums that otherwise would be paid to insurance companies is

[48] *Louis S. Cohn Co.*, 12 B.T.A. 1281 (1928).
[49] *Jamaica Water Supply Co.*, 42 B.T.A. 359 (1940).
[50] *Houston Chronicle Publishing Co.*, T.C. Memo., Docket #838, entered October 12, 1944.
[51] *Oppenheim's, Inc. v. Kavanagh*, 90 F. Supp. 107 (D.C., Mich., 1950).
[52] *Miller v. Hocking Glass Co.*, 80 F.2d 436 (6th Cir., 1935).
[53] Revenue Ruling 55–264, 1955–1 CB 11.
[54] I.R.C. Section 106.

not deductible.[55] A reserve is nondeductible even though insurance is unobtainable, and hence no other provision seems possible.[56]

Annuities

Payments for a Period or for Life. There are three general forms of payment for a period of time or for life.

(1) Where proceeds of a life insurance (paid other than by reason of the death of the insured), endowment, or annuity contract are received in a lump sum, the tax is computed as though the proceeds were received during a 3-year period in accordance with the principles of long-term compensation from an employment. See Chapter 11.

(2) Where proceeds of an endowment contract are received in installments, the method of taxation is the same as in the case of an annuity. See (3), below.

(3) In the case of amounts received as an annuity (other than certain employee annuities), the proportionate part of each payment which is to be considered a return of investment (and thus excludable from gross income) is to be determined by the ratio which the investment in the contract bears to the expected return under the contract. The investment in the contract is determinable from actuarial tables. Once determined for a particular contract, the excludable portion of the payment remains fixed despite the fact that the individual may die before or after his life expectancy.[57]

General Rules. For the purpose of determining the extent to which amounts received represent a reduction or return of premiums or other considerations paid, there is a distinction between (1) "amounts received as an annuity" and (2) "amounts not received as an annuity." In general, (1) refers to amounts which are payable at regular intervals over a period of more than one full year from the date on which they are deemed to begin, provided the total of the amounts so payable or the period for which they are to be paid can be determined as of that date. Any other amounts are considered as belonging to (2). In the case of (1), a proportionate part of each amount so received is considered to represent a return of premiums or other considerations paid. In the case of (2), no amount received as an annuity is includible in the gross income of a recipient until the aggregate of all amounts received and excluded from gross income under the income tax law (the present Code or

[55] *Spring Canyon Coal Co. v. Commissioner,* 43 F.2d 78 (10th Cir., 1930).
[56] *L. A. Thompson Scenic Railway Co.,* 2 B.T.A. 664 (1925).
[57] I.R.C. Section 72.

the 1939 edition) exceeds the consideration contributed (or deemed to have been contributed) by the employee. Thereafter, all amounts so received are includible in the gross income of the recipient.[58]

A recipient is considered to be an "annuitant" if he receives amounts under an annuity contract during the period that the annuity payments are to continue, whether for a term certain or during the continuing life or lives of the person or persons whose lives measure the duration of the annuity. But a recipient will be considered a "beneficiary" rather than an "annuitant" if the amounts he receives under a contract are received after the term of the annuity for a life or lives has expired and these amounts are paid by reason of the fact that the contract guarantees that payments of some minimum amount or for some minimum period will be made.

Amounts received are regarded as "amounts received as an annuity" only in the event that all of the following tests are met:

(1) They must be received on or after the "annuity starting date."

(2) They must be payable in periodic installments at regular intervals (whether annually, semiannually, quarterly, monthly, weekly, or otherwise) over a period of more than one full year from the annuity starting date; and

(3) The total of the amounts payable must be determinable at the annuity starting date either directly from the terms of the contract or indirectly by the use of either mortality tables or compound interest computations, or both, in conjunction with such terms and in accordance with sound actuarial theory. But if amounts are to be received for a definite or determinable time under a contract which provides—

(A) That the amount of the periodic payments may vary in accordance with investment experience (as in certain profit-sharing plans), cost of living indices, or similar fluctuating criteria, or

(B) For specified payments the value of which may vary for income tax purposes (such as in the case of any annuity payable in foreign currency),

each such payment received will be considered as an amount received as an annuity only to the extent that it does not exceed the amount computed by dividing the investment in the contract, as adjusted for any refund feature, by the number of periodic payments anticipated during the time that the periodic payments are to be made. If payments are to be made more frequently than annually, the amount so computed will be multiplied by the number

[58] Regulations Section 1.72–1(c).

of periodic payments to be made during the taxable year for the purpose of determining the total amount which may be considered received as an annuity during that year.[59]

Exclusion Ratio. To determine the proportionate part of the total amount received each year as an annuity which is excludable from the gross income of a recipient in the taxable year of receipt (other than amounts received under certain employee annuities), an exclusion ratio is to be determined for each contract. In general, this ratio is determined by dividing the investment in the contract by the expected return under this contract. Where a single consideration is given for a particular contract which provides for two or more annuity elements, an exclusion ratio will be determined for the contract as a whole by dividing the investment in this contract by the aggregate of the expected returns under all the annuity elements provided.

The exclusion ratio for the particular contract is then applied to the total amount received as an annuity during the taxable year by each recipient. Any excess of the total amount received as an annuity by the application of the exclusion ratio to the total amount will be included in the gross income of the recipient for the taxable year of receipt.

Illustration. A taxpayer purchased an annuity contract providing for payments of $100 per month for a consideration of $12,650. Assuming that the expected return under this contract is $16,000, the exclusion ratio to be used by him is $\frac{\$12,650}{\$16,000}$, or 79.1% (79.06 rounded to the nearest tenth). If twelve such monthly payments are received by him during his taxable year, the total amount he may exclude from his gross income in that year is $949.20 ($1,200 times 79.1%). The balance of $250.80 ($1,200 less $949.20) is the amount to be included in gross income. If he instead received only five such payments during the year, he should exclude $395.50 ($500 times 79.1%) of the total amounts received.

If the investment in the contract is an amount of zero or less, no exclusion ratio will be determined, and all amounts received are includible in gross income.

Where the investment in the contract is equal to or greater than the total expected return under the contract, the exclusion ratio will be considered to be 100% and all amounts received will be excludable from the recipient's gross income.

Illustration. The taxpayer, a 64-year-old male, files his return on a calendar year basis and has a life expectancy of 15.6 years on June 30, 1961, the annuity starting date of a contract which he purchased for $20,000. The contract provides

[59] Regulations Section 1.72–2(b).

for variable annual payments for his life. He receives a payment of $1,000 on June 30, 1962, but receives no other payment until June 30, 1964. He excludes the $1,000 payment from his gross income for the year 1962 since this amount is less than $1,324.50, the amount determined by dividing his investment in the contract ($20,000) by his life expectancy adjusted for annual payments, 15.1 (15.6 minus 0.5), as of the original annuity starting date. He may elect, in his return for the taxable year 1964, to redetermine amounts to be received as an annuity under his contract as of June 30, 1963. For the purpose of determining the extent to which amounts received in 1964 or thereafter will be considered amounts received as an annuity (to which a 100% exclusion ratio will apply) he will add $118.63 to the $1,324.50 originally determined to be received as an annuity under the contract, making a total of $1,443.13. This is determined by dividing the difference between what was includible in 1962 and 1963, $2,649 (2 times $1,324.50) and what he actually received in those years ($1,000) by his life expectancy adjusted for annual payments, 13.9 (14.4 minus 0.5), as of his age at his nearest birthday (66) on the first day of the first period for which he received an amount as an annuity in the taxable year of the election (June 30, 1963). The result, $1,443.13, is excludable in that year and each year thereafter as an amount received as an annuity to which the 100% exclusion ratio applies. It will be noted that in this illustration the taxpayer received amounts less than the excludable amount in two successive years and deferred making his election until the third year, and thus was able to accumulate the portion of the investment in the contract allocable to each taxable year to the extent he failed to receive that portion in both years. Assuming that he received $1,500 in the taxable year of his election, he would include $56.87 in his gross income and exclude $1,443.13 for that year.

If the taxpayer chooses to make the election referred to above, he must file with his return a statement that he elects to make a redetermination of the amounts excludable from gross income under his annuity contract. He must supply (1) the original annuity starting date and his age on that date, (2) the date of the first day of the first period for which he received an amount in the current taxable year, (3) the investment in the contract originally determined (as adjusted for any refund feature, and (4) the aggregate of all amounts received under the contract between the date indicated in (1) and the day after the date indicated in (2) to the extent these amounts were excludable from gross income. He must include in gross income any amounts received during the taxable year for which the return is made in accordance with this redetermination.

Expected Return—One Life. If a contract provides that one annuitant is to receive a fixed monthly income for life, the expected return is determined by multiplying the total of the annuity payments to be received annually by a multiple shown in Table I of Regulations Section 1.72–9 under the age (as of the annuity starting date) and sex of the measuring life, which is usually the annuitant's. (The multiple tables also are reproduced in Internal Revenue Service Publication No. 76 (Rev. 11–56).) Thus, where a male purchases a contract providing for an immediate annuity of $100 per month for his life and, as of the annuity starting date (in this case, the date of purchase), the annuitant's age at his nearest birthday is 66, the expected return is computed as follows:

Monthly payment of $100 × 12 = annuity payment of.........	$ 1,200
Multiple shown in Table I, male, age 66........................	14.4
Expected return ($1,200 × 14.4)................................	$17,280

If payments are to be made quarterly, semiannually, or annually, an adjustment of the applicable multiple shown in Table I of the regulations may be required. A further adjustment may be required where the interval between the annuity starting date and the date of the first payment is less than the interval between future payments. Neither adjustment shall be made, however, if the payments are to be made more frequently than quarterly. The amount of the adjustment, if any, is to be found in accordance with the following table:

If the number of whole months from the annuity starting date to the first payment date is........	0–1	2	3	4	5	6	7	8	9	10	11	12
And payments under the contract are to be made:												
Annually	+0.5	+0.4	+0.3	+0.2	+0.1	0	0	−0.1	−0.2	−0.3	−0.4	−0.5
Semiannually	+0.2	+0.1	0	0	−0.1	−0.2						
Quarterly	+0.1	0	−0.1									

Thus, for a male, age 66, the multiple found in this table adjusted for quarterly payments the first of which is to be made one full month after the annuity starting date, is 14.5 (14.4 + 0.1); for semiannual payments the first of which is to be made six full months from the annuity starting date, the adjusted multiple is 14.2 (14.4 — 0.2); for annual payments the first of which is to be made one full month from the annuity starting date, the adjusted multiple is 14.9 (14.4 + 0.5). If the annuitant in the example shown in subparagraph (1) of this paragraph were to receive an annual payment of $1,200 commencing 12 full months after his annuity starting date, the amount of the expected return would be $16,680 ($1,200 times 13.9 (14.4 minus 0.5)).

If the contract provides for fixed payments to be made to an annuitant until death or until the expiration of a specified limited period, whichever occurs earlier, the expected return of such temporary life annuity is determined by multiplying the total of the annuity payments to be received annually by the multiple shown above for the age (as of the annuity starting date) and sex of the annuitant and the nearest whole number of years in the specified period. For example, if a male annuitant, age sixty (at his nearest birthday), is to receive $60 per month for five years or until he dies, whichever is earlier, the expected return under such a contract is $3,456, computed as follows:

Monthly payments of $60 × 12 months = annual payment of.....	$ 720
Multiple shown in Table IV of the regulations for male, age 60, for term of 5 years..........	4.8
Expected return for 5-year temporary life annuity of $720 per year ($720 × 4.8)	$3,456

If the contract provides for payments to be made to an annuitant for his lifetime, but the amount of the annual payments is to be decreased after the expiration of a specified limited period, the expected return is computed by considering the contract as a combination of a whole life annuity for the smaller amount plus a temporary life annuity for an amount equal to the difference between the larger and the smaller amount. For example, if a male annuitant, age sixty, is to receive $150 per month for five years or until his earlier death, and is to receive $90 per month for the remainder of his lifetime after such five years, the expected return is computed as if the annuitant's contract consisted of a whole life annuity for $90 per month plus a 5-year temporary life annuity of $60 per month. In such circumstances, the expected return is computed as follows:

Monthly payments of $90 × 12 months = annual payment of.....	$ 1,080
Multiple shown in Table I of the regulations for male, age 60.....	18.2
Expected return for whole life annuity of $1,080 per year.........	$19,656
Expected return for 5-year temporary life annuity of $720 per year (as found in subparagraph (3) of the regulations)..........	3,456
Total expected return	$23,112

If payments are to be made quarterly, semiannually, or annually, an appropriate adjustment of the multiple found in Table I of the regulations for the whole life annuity should be made as mentioned above.

If the contract described in the last paragraph provided that the amount of the annual payments to the annuitant were to be increased (instead of decreased) after the expiration of a specified limited period, the expected return would be computed as if the annuitant's contract consisted of a whole life annuity for the larger amount minus a temporary life annuity for an amount equal to the difference between the larger and smaller amount. Thus, if the annuitant described were to receive $90 per month for five years or until his earlier death, and to receive $150 per month for the remainder of his lifetime after such five years, the expected return would be computed by subtracting the expected return under a 5-year temporary life annuity of $60 per month from the expected return under a whole life annuity of $150 per month. In such circumstances, the expected return is computed as follows:

Monthly payments of $150 × 12 months = annual payment of....	$ 1,800
Multiple shown in Table I of the regulations (male, age 60)......	18.2
Expected return for annuity for whole life of $1,800 per year......	$32,760
Less: Expected return for 5-year temporary life annuity of $720 per year (as found in subparagraph (3) of the regulations).....	3,456
Net expected return....................................	$29,304

If payments are to be made quarterly, semiannually, or annually, an appropriate adjustment of the multiple found in Table I of the regulations for the whole life annuity should be made.

Expected Return—Joint and Survivor and Joint Annuities. In the case of a joint and survivor annuity contract involving two annuitants which provides the first annuitant with a fixed monthly income for life and, after the death of the first annuitant, provides an identical monthly income for life for a second annuitant, the expected return shall be determined by multiplying the total amount of the payments to be received annually by the multiple obtained from Table II of Regulations Section 1.72–9 under the ages (as of the annuity starting date) and sexes of the living annuitants. For example, a husband purchases a joint and survivor annuity contract providing for payments of $100 per month for life, and, after his death, for the same amount to his wife for the remainder of her life. As of the annuity starting date his age at his nearest birthday is 70 and that of his wife at her nearest birthday is 67. The expected return is computed as follows:

Monthly payments of $100 × 12 months = annual payment of....	$ 1,200
Multiple shown in Table II of the regulations (male, age 70; female, age 67)	19.7
Expected return ($1,200 × 19.7)..............................	$23,640

If payments are to be made quarterly, semiannually, or annually, an appropriate adjustment of the multiple found in Table II of the regulations should be made in accordance with paragraph (a)(2).

If a contract of the type described in subparagraph (1) provides that a different (rather than an identical) monthly income is payable to the second annuitant, the expected return is computed in the following manner. The applicable multiple in Table II of the regulations is first found as in the example in subparagraph (1). The multiple applicable to the first annuitant is then found in Table I of the regulations as though the contract were for a single life annuity. The multiple from Table I of the regulations is then subtracted from the multiple obtained from Table II of the regulations and the resulting multiple is applied to the total payments to be received annually under the contract by the second annuitant. The result is the expected return with respect to the second annuitant. The portion of the expected return with respect to payments to be made during the first annuitant's life is then computed by applying the multiple found in Table I of the regulations to the total annual payments to be received by such annuitant under the contract. The expected returns with respect to each of the annuitants separately are then aggregated to obtain the expected return under the entire contract.

Illustration. A husband purchases a joint and survivor annuity providing for payments of $100 per month for his life and, after his death, payments to his wife of $50 per month for her life. As of the annuity starting date his age at his nearest birthday is 70 and that of his wife at her nearest birthday is 67.

Multiple from Table II of the regulations (male, age 70; female, age 67)	19.7
Multiple from Table I of the regulations (male, age 70)	12.1
Difference (multiple applicable to second annuitant)	7.6
Portion of expected return, second annuitant ($600 × 7.6)	$ 4,560
Portion of expected return, first annuitant ($1,200 × 12.1)	14,520
Expected under the contract	$19,080

The expected return thus found, $19,080, is to be used in computing the amount to be excluded from gross income. Thus, if the investment in the contract in this example is $14,310, the exclusion ratio is $\frac{\$14,310}{\$19,080}$, or 75%. The amount excludable from each monthly payment made to the husband is 75% of $100, or $75, and the remaining $25 of each payment received by him shall be included in his gross income. After the husband's death, the amount excludable by the second annuitant (the surviving wife) would be 75% of each monthly payment of $50, or $37.50, and the remaining $12.50 of each payment shall be included in her gross income. The same method is used if the payments are to be increased after the death of the first annuitant. Thus, if the payments to be made until the husband's death were $50 per month and his widow were to receive $100 per month thereafter until her death, the 7.6 multiple in the above example would be applied to the $100 payments, yielding an expected return with respect to this portion of the annuity contract of $9,120 ($1,200 times 7.6). An expected return of $7,260 ($600 times 12.1) would be obtained with respect to the payments to be made the husband, yielding a total expected return under the contract of $16,380 ($9,120 plus $7,260). If payments are to be made quarterly, semiannually, or annually, an appropriate adjustment of the multiples found in Tables I and II of the regulations should be made.

If a contract provides for the payment of life annuities to two persons during their respective lives and, after the death of one (regardless of which goes first), provides that the survivor will receive for life both his own annuity payments and the payments made formerly to the deceased person, the expected return will be determined as though there were two joint and survivor annuities under the same contract, in the following manner. First, the multiple appropriate to the ages (as of the annuity starting date) and sexes of the annuitants involved will be found in Table II of the regulations and adjusted, if necessary, according to the table on page 12·18. Second, the multiple so found will be applied to the sum of the payments to be made each year to both annuitants. The result is the expected return for the contract as a whole.

Employee Contributions Recoverable in Three Years. There is a special rule as to the treatment of amounts received as an annuity by an employee (or by the beneficiary of an employee). This special rule applies only in the event that (1) at least part of the consideration paid for the contract is contributed by the employer and (2) the aggregate amount receivable as an annuity under this contract by the employee (or by his beneficiary if the employee died before any amount was received as an annuity under the contract) within the 3-year period beginning on the date on which an amount is first received as an annuity equals or exceeds the total consideration deemed to be contributed by the employee as of that date as reduced by all amounts previously received and excludable from the gross income of the recipient under the applicable income tax law.

In this event, all amounts received as an annuity under the contract will be excluded from gross income until the total of the amounts excluded under prior income tax laws equals or exceeds the consideration deemed contributed by the employee. The excess, if any, and all amounts received by a recipient thereafter (whether or not received as an annuity) will be fully included in gross income. If the aggregate amount receivable as an annuity under the contract within three years from the date on which an amount is first received as an annuity will not equal or exceed the consideration deemed contributed by the employee, computed as of that date, the special rule will not apply to amounts received as an annuity under the contract, and the general rules will apply.

The aggregate of the amounts receivable as an annuity within the prescribed 3-year period will be the total of all annuity payments anticipatable by an employee (or a beneficiary of any employee, if the employee died before any amount was received as an annuity) under the contract as a whole.

Exempt Organizations. An annuity purchased by an exempt religious, charitable, or educational organization for its employees is taxed to an employee when he receives annuity payments *after* retirement, contrary to the general rule that taxes the employee at the time the employer pays the premium if the employee has a nonforfeitable right to the payment or contract. But this deferral of taxability applies only to the extent of an employee's *exclusion allowance;* that is, a figure obtained by multiplying 20% of annual compensation by his years of service, and dividing this by that part of the employer's cost of the annuity that had been excluded from the employee's income for prior years.[60]

If an employee's right under an annuity contract purchased by an exempt organization changes from forfeitable to nonforfeitable rights, the value of the contract on the date of the change is income to the employee, to the extent that this value is attributable to amounts contributed by the employer after 1957.

Annuities Starting Prior to 1954. A taxpayer's investment in an annuity contract for purposes of the exclusion ratio consists of what he paid for the contract minus the amounts he had excluded under the law existing prior to 1954. Under the 1939 Code, the amount included in gross income was a figure not in excess of 3% of the aggregate premiums or consideration paid for the annuity. As soon as the aggregate premiums paid for the annuity, the entire amount received thereafter in each taxable year had to be included in gross income.

Illustration. An individual bought in 1949, for $50,000 consideration, a life annuity, payable in annual installments of $5,000. For the calendar year 1952, he would be required to include in gross income $1,500 of the $5,000 received during that year (3% of $50,000), $3,500 being exempt. If he should live long enough to receive exempt amounts totaling $50,000, then total amounts he received thereafter under the annuity contract would be included in gross income.

Supplementary Material

A. Suggested Reading.

Irving V. Brunstrom, "The Life Insurance, Endowment and Annuity Features of the 1954 Code," *TAXES—The Tax Magazine,* November, 1954, Vol. XXXII, #11, p. 866.

Baxter K. Richardson, "Key Man Life Insurance," *Journal of the State Bar of California,* November–December, 1956, Vol. XXXI, #6, p. 525.

[60] I.R.C. Section 403(a)(1).

James J. Convery, "Income Tax Problems Relating to Life Insurance," *Proceedings of the New York University Thirteenth Annual Institute on Federal Taxation* (Albany: Matthew Bender & Co., Inc., 1955), p. 233.

Robert J. Lawthers, "The Fragile Mark of the Small Corporation," *The Journal of the American Society of Chartered Life Underwriters*, Winter, 1957, Vol. XII, #1, p. 4.

Bertram Harnett, *Taxation of Life Insurance* (Englewood Cliffs, N.J.: Prentice-Hall, Inc., 1957).

K. Martin Worthy, "Federal Taxation Affecting Life Insurance," *TAXES—The Tax Magazine,* October, 1958, Vol. XXXVI, #10, p. 737.

Paul D. Seghers, "Federal Income Tax Problems—Fire and Casualty Insurance," *National Insurance Buyer,* July, 1957, Vol. IV, #4, p. 8.

Robert L. Merritt, "How the Proceeds of Use and Occupancy, or Business Interruption, Insurance Are Taxed," *TAXES—The Tax Magazine,* May, 1958, Vol. XXXVI, #5, p. 306.

B. Leading Cases.

Taxation of beneficiary of life insurance proceeds. *United States v. Supplee-Biddle Hardware Co.*, 265 U.S. 189 (1924).

Need for key man insurance. *The Emeloid Co., Inc. v. Commissioner,* 189 F.2d 230 (3d Cir., 1951).

Are premiums dividends to covered shareholders? *Prunier et al. v. Commissioner,* 248 F.2d 818 (1st Cir., 1957).

C. Questions.

1. A corporation took out a policy on the life of its president. When he died, the corporation collected the face amount of the policy. Is this taxable income to the corporation? Would your answer be different if the insured were a merchandise creditor?
2. An old established organization, the M Corporation, took out an insurance policy on the life of its president. The corporation paid the premiums, but the president was permitted to name the beneficiary, and he chose his wife. (a) Does the corporation get a tax deduction for the premiums? (b) Should gross income of anyone reflect the amount of the premiums?
3. An individual on the cash basis pays $600 for fire insurance premiums for three years, as the rate was less than three times the single-year premiums. May he deduct the entire $600 in the year of payment?
4. A corporation takes out an insurance policy on the life of its treasurer. The company pays the premiums and is the beneficiary. Does the treasurer derive any taxable income?
5. A businessman takes out insurance on his life, the policy being payable to him or his estate. Is the premium deductible as business expense?
6. An individual purchased an annuity contract in 1957. In 1960, he exchanged it for another contract, whereunder the annual payments by the insurance company would be smaller but would be guaranteed to him or to his wife for at least ten years. Is the exchange taxable?
7. A trucking company found its liability insurance costs were so high that it was decided not to renew the policies. Instead, the trucker set up an annual reserve for claims equal to what had been the premiums. The insurance company's overhead and profits were eliminated, it was believed. Are the annual reserve provisions deductible?

8. An individual takes out an insurance policy on his life. Subsequently he gives the policy to his wife, but he continues to pay the premiums. The insurance company pays a $300 dividend. To whom is this taxable? Would your answer be different if, instead of being a stock company, the carrier was a mutual?
9. A department store carried use and occupancy insurance; and, after a fire loss, $50,000 was paid by the insurance company. What is the tax status of the payment? Would your answer be different if the loss had been of capital assets?
10. Cain collects the face amount of a policy that had been taken out on the life of his brother, Abel. (a) Is this taxable income to Cain? (b) Would your answer be different if Cain previously had purchased from Abel a policy that the latter had taken out on his own life?
11. In 1960, an individual's yacht was sunk in a storm, and he deducted a casualty loss. In 1961, his insurance company reimbursed him for the full amount of his loss. How is the reimbursement treated for tax purposes? Would your answer be different if loss and reimbursement were in the same taxable year?
12. A wealthy man discovers that the cash surrender value of a certain insurance policy on his life would increase to the extent of $5,000 a year, and if he borrowed money to buy this additional policy, it would cost him only $4,000 ($20,000 interest on a bank loan, deductible from his gross income at his 80% bracket to the extent of $16,000). Is this a valid deduction for tax purposes?
13. On January 1, 1960, an individual purchased for $17,836 an installment refund annuity contract of $1,000 per annum. He was 63 years of age on the annuity starting date. (a) What is the value of the refund? (b) What is the proportionate part of each annuity payment that is to be excluded from gross income? (Assume the actuarial factor to be 5.170.)
14. A male annuitant, age sixty, is to receive $150 per month for five years or until his earlier death, and is to receive $90 per month for the remainder of his lifetime after these five years. What is the expected return? (Assume the multiple for his age is 18.2.)
15. In 1945, an individual contracted for an annuity to be paid to him beginning December 31, 1960. In 1945 and in each successive year until 1960, he paid a premium of $5,000. Assuming he received no payments of any kind under the contract until the date on which he received the first annual payment as an annuity (December 31, 1960), what is his investment in the contract as of the annuity starting date, December 31, 1959?
16. Upon the death of her husband, the insured, his wife elected a settlement option under which she was to receive $5,000 per year for her life while the daughter would receive $5,000 per year for ten years. On this date, the discounted value of the settlement to the wife was $60,000, and to the daughter, $35,000. The wife had a life expectancy of ten years. What annual exclusion from gross income would be made, respectively, by the wife and by the daughter?
17. An individual, 65 years of age on the annuity starting date, had purchased an annuity for payments to him of $1,000 per annum for life. The multiple on the actuarial tables is 15.5. If he had paid $12,000 for the contract, what is the annual exclusion?

13

LOSSES: BAD DEBTS; CASUALTIES; DEMOLITION

Bad Debts

General. Deduction is allowed for a debt which becomes worthless during the taxable year.[1] But the debts of political parties may not be claimed as a deduction, except by banks.[2]

A debt may not be deductible at any time as a bad debt unless it had value when acquired.[3] Thus, a bona fide loan may not exist where advances are made to a person who is insolvent at the time; there is a strong presumption that the advances were intended to be gifts.[4]

A debt is "a specific sum of money, which is due or owing from one person to another, and denotes not only the obligation of the debtor to pay, but the right of the creditor to receive and enforce payment."[5] But advances made with no reasonable prospect or expectation of repayment do not create a debt.[6] "It is also clear that, for purposes of the federal tax statute, even though the parties have intended to create a debt, the courts will not recognize it as such as against the taxing power if they have failed to create a binding obligation."[7]

Worthless debts arising from unpaid wages, salaries, rents, and similar items of taxable income will not be allowed as a deduction unless the income represented by these items has been included in gross income for the year for which the bad debt deduction is sought to be made or for a previous year. Thus, a cash basis taxpayer could not get a bad debt deduction if a fee were not paid to him.

[1] I.R.C. Section 166(a).
[2] I.R.C. Section 271.
[3] *Eckert v. Burnet,* 283 U.S. 140 (1931).
[4] *Estelle Pardee Erdman,* T.C. Memo., Docket ##4699–4700, entered January 25, 1946.
[5] *J. S. Cullinan,* 19 B.T.A. 930 (1930).
[6] *American Cigar Co. v. Commissioner,* 66 F.2d 425 (2d Cir., 1933).
[7] *Gilbert et al. v. Commissioner,* 248 F.2d 399 (2d Cir., 1957).

Reality of Debt. A bad debt deduction is not allowed merely because the debtor refuses to pay.[8] Nor is deduction allowed where one pays the debts of another because of a sense of moral obligation.[9] But see "Guarantors," below.

Where a corporation has bond indebtedness far in excess of the amount of its stock, and bonds and stock are held by substantially the same persons, it may be held that the bonds do not really represent a debt, being merely a mislabeled stock. In such a situation, a bad debt deduction would not be allowed were the obligor to become unable to make payment.

If stockholders make advances to their corporation, the circumstances of the transaction may indicate that a loan with the intention of repayment had not been made. In such a situation, the so-called advance will be treated as a contribution to capital.

Advances to relatives are surrounded by an aura of suspicion. But if such advances had been made in the past, and had been repaid, the debt may be accepted as genuine.

If a taxpayer cancels a debt in consideration of the debtor's agreement to make all of his future purchases from the taxpayer, there is no deduction for bad debt. The transaction was not gratuitous and is classified as a capital expenditure.[10]

Business and Nonbusiness Bad Debts. All bad debts of a corporation are regarded as *business bad debts.* Bad debts of taxpayers other than corporations may be business or nonbusiness.[11]

Business bad debts are of two types: (1) debts which become worthless in the course of a trade or business of the taxpayer and (2) any debt which is either created in the course of the taxpayer's trade or business or is acquired by him in the course thereof without regard to the relationship of the debt to a trade or business of the taxpayer at the time that the debt becomes worthless.

A business bad debt must be connected with the taxpayer's personal business. A business bad debt can arise even out of an isolated transaction, so long as it is closely related to the taxpayer's trade or business.[12]

Illustration. A, an individual engaged in the grocery business and making his tax returns on the calendar year basis, extends credit on an open account to B in 1960.

[8] *Philip C. Hughes et al.,* T.C. Memo., Docket #25313, entered March 7, 1951.
[9] *W. A. Dallmeyer,* 14 T.C. 1282 (1950).
[10] I.T. 1828, II-2 CB 157.
[11] I.R.C. Section 166(d).
[12] *Robert Cluett, 3d et al.,* 8 T.C. 1178 (1947).

(1) In 1961, A sells the business, but retains the claim against B. The claim becomes worthless in A's hands in 1962. A's loss is not controlled by the nonbusiness debt provisions. Inasmuch as the original consideration was advanced by A in his trade or business, the loss is treated as a business bad debt.

(2) In 1962, A sells the business to C, but sells the claim against B to the taxpayer, D. The claim becomes worthless in D's hands in 1962. D's loss is a nonbusiness bad debt, even though the original consideration was advanced by A in his trade or business, inasmuch as the debt was not related to any trade or business of D either at the time he acquired it or at the time it became worthless.

(3) In 1962, A dies, leaving the business (including the accounts receivable) to his son C, the taxpayer. The claim against B becomes worthless in C's hands in 1962. C's loss is a business bad debt. While C did not advance any consideration for the claim or acquire it in carrying on his trade or business, it was a debt the loss from the worthlessness of which was incurred in the taxpayer's trade or business.

(4) In 1961, A dies, leaving the business to his son, C, but leaving the claim against B to another son, D, the taxpayer. The claim against B becomes worthless in D's hands in 1962. D's loss is a nonbusiness bad debt, even though the original consideration was advanced by A in his trade or business, inasmuch as the debt was not related to any trade or business of D either at the time he acquired it or at the time it became worthless.

(5) In 1961, A dies and while his executor, C, is carrying on the business, the claim against B becomes worthless in 1962. The loss sustained by A's estate is not a nonbusiness bad debt inasmuch as the debt was acquired in connection with a trade or business of A's estate, and it was also related to that trade or business at the time it became worthless.

(6) In 1961, A, in liquidating the business, attempts to collect the claim against B but finds that it has become worthless. A's loss is not a nonbusiness bad debt, inasmuch as a loss incurred in liquidating a trade or business is related to it at the time the debt became worthless.

Wholly worthless nonbusiness bad debts of a taxpayer other than a corporation are treated as short-term capital losses and are not deductible as bad debts. No deduction of any kind may be claimed for a partially worthless nonbusiness bad debt.

Ascertainment of Worthlessness. The taxpayer's belief with respect to collectibility and his faith in the debtor's integrity or intentions are not a basis for determining worthlessness within the meaning of the statute. The only test is whether the debt actually becomes worthless within the taxable year claimed.[13]

Where the surrounding circumstances indicate that a debt is worthless and uncollectible, and that legal action to enforce payment would in all probability not result in the satisfaction of execution on a judgment, a showing of these facts is sufficient evidence of the worthlessness of the debt for the purpose of the deduction. Bankruptcy is generally considered an indication of the worthless-

[13] *Watson v. Fahs,* 120 F. Supp. 424 (D.C., Fla., 1954).

ness of at least a part of an unsecured and unpreferred debt. In bankruptcy cases, a debt may become worthless before settlement in some instances, and in others only when a settlement in bankruptcy has been made. In either case, the mere fact that bankruptcy proceedings instituted against the debtor are terminated in a later year, confirming that the debt is worthless, will not authorize shifting the deductions to this later year.

A taxpayer's forbearance in the collection of a debt does not affect his right to claim its deduction on the ground of worthlessness.[14]

It is not necessary to wait until every conceivable contingency of payment has been exhausted to write off a bad debt. "The taxing act does not require the taxpayer to be an incorrigible optimist." [15] A bad debt may be deducted without foreclosure or even a showing that no more could be obtained from the debtor.[16] A creditor was allowed a bad debt deduction even though, because his brother was a supplier to the debtor, insolvency was not forced. Here the taxpayer had investigated the value of the indorsements, and his close connection with the business gave him the necessary information so that he could draw "a fair and honest conclusion." [17] A bad debt deduction was allowed where it was shown that the debtor was no longer what he once had been.[18]

That there may be partial recovery is immaterial.[19] Nor is it material that recovery *might* be possible.[20]

"It is not necessary to be 'an incorrigible optimist,' as stated by the court in *United States v. S. S. White Dental Mfg. Co., supra,* but at the same time a taxpayer is not permitted to be a stygian pessimist." [21]

Burden of Proof. The taxpayer has the burden of showing that the debt became bad in the taxable year. *How* this proof is demonstrated is up to the taxpayer. The finding of the Internal Revenue Service that a deduction of a bad debt as worthless is improper is *prima facie* correct, and the burden is upon the taxpayer to show by a preponderance of evidence that the Government's finding is in-

[14] *C. J. Reuter et al.,* T.C. Memo., Docket ##22658 and 22838, entered March 30, 1951.

[15] *United States v. S. S. White Dental Manufacturing Co. of Pennsylvania,* 274 U.S. 398 (1927).

[16] *Ruppert v. United States,* 22 F. Supp. 428 (Ct. Cl., 1938).

[17] *Clark v. Commissioner,* 85 F.2d 623 (3d Cir., 1936).

[18] *Lauriston Investment Co. v. Commissioner,* 89 F.2d 327 (9th Cir., 1937).

[19] *Rhodes v. Commissioner,* 100 F.2d 966 (6th Cir., 1939).

[20] *Pantex Oil Corp.,* T.C. Memo., Docket #19843, entered December 19, 1949.

[21] *Ruppert v. United States,* 22 F. Supp. 428 (Ct. Cl., 1938).

correct.[22] This evidence may concern the financial status of the debtor, his health (if an individual), the value of collateral. It is enough evidence of worthlessness where it can be shown that action to collect would probably not result in payment of any part of the debt.

There must be financial evidence of the inability of the debtor to pay the debt during the taxable year, if the debt had value at the beginning of the year.[23] It is not enough to show that a debt was worthless at the end of the taxable year; it must also be shown that the debt was *not* worthless at the start of this taxable year.

The running of the statute of limitations does not extinguish a debt or render it worthless, but merely provides the debtor with an affirmative defense which may be pleaded in an action instituted against him for the collection of a debt.[24]

Bankruptcy or curtailed activities do not establish worthlessness, which is only established when the debtor's condition deteriorates so that repayment cannot be expected.[25]

Guarantors. A taxpayer other than a corporation may deduct from gross income the amount of a loss suffered through payment during the taxable year of part or all of his obligation as a guarantor, endorser, or indemnitor of a noncorporate obligation. In order to obtain an ordinary loss, the taxpayer must establish that the proceeds of the loan were used in the trade or business of the borrower and that the obligation of the borrower, to the person to whom the taxpayer made payment in discharge of his guarantor's obligation, was worthless at the time of the payment (without regard to the guaranty, endorsement, or indemnity). The term "guarantor, endorser, or indemnitor" includes not only those persons having collateral obligations as guarantors or endorsers, but also those persons having direct obligations as indemnitors.[26]

The payment by the taxpayer of such an obligation will result in the treatment of the payment as a debt becoming worthless during the taxable year. Thus, a taxpayer who makes only a partial payment in discharge of his obligation as a guarantor (the other portion of the original debt having been collected from the borrower) may treat this payment as being a partially worthless debt if he can establish that the remaining obligation of the borrower to the person to whom the taxpayer makes payment was worthless at the time of this payment.

[22] *Quinn v. Commissioner,* 111 F.2d 372 (5th Cir., 1940).
[23] *C. C. Cooke,* T.C. Memo., Docket #20004, entered September 13, 1951.
[24] *Commissioner v. Burdette,* 69 F.2d 410 (9th Cir., 1934).
[25] *Giles E. Bullock et al.,* 26 T.C. 276 (1956).
[26] I.R.C. Section 166(f).

Illustration. G is a guarantor of an obligation of a debtor, D, an individual, to C, the proceeds of which were used in D's trade or business. D defaults on his obligation. G makes payment in discharge of his obligation as guarantor at a time when the obligation of the borrower to C is worthless. G may claim a business bad debt deduction.

Illustration. G is a guarantor of an obligation of D, an individual, to C, the proceeds of which were used in D's trade or business. D pays a portion of the obligation but defaults on the remainder. G makes payment, in discharge of his obligation as guarantor, of the remaining unpaid portion of the debt at a time when the obligation of the borrower as to this unpaid balance is worthless. G may claim a business bad debt deduction for the remaining portion of the debt which he pays in discharge of his obligation.

Illustration. G is a guarantor of an obligation of D, an individual, to C, the proceeds of which were used for D's personal use. D defaults on the obligation. G makes payment in discharge of his obligation as guarantor for the entire amount of the debt. Assuming that G is not regularly engaged in the business of lending money, G may not take a business bad debt deduction because the proceeds of the loan were not used in D's trade or business.

Worthless Securities. Deductions for bad debts are not allowed taxpayers, other than banks, with respect to debts evidenced by a security.[27] For this purpose, "security" means (1) a share of stock in a corporation; (2) a right to subscribe for, or to receive, a share of stock in a corporation; or (3) a bond, debenture, note, or certificate, or other evidence of indebtedness, issued by a corporation or by a government or political subdivision thereof, with interest coupons or in registered form.[28]

Securities of Affiliate. Ordinary rather than capital loss may be taken upon securities of an affiliated corporation by a domestic corporation. In order to take advantage of this provision the taxpayer (1) must own directly at least 95% of each class of stock of the affiliated corporation and (2) more than 90% of the total gross receipts of the affiliated corporation during all the taxable years in which it has been in existence must have been from sources other than royalties, rents (except those from employees), dividends, interest (except on deferred purchase price of operating assets sold), annuities, and gains from sales or exchanges of stocks and securities.[29] Capital loss may not be converted into ordinary loss by the acquisition of additional securities in a corporation solely for the purpose of bringing the holders of the taxpayer up to the minimum stock ownership requirement.[30]

[27] I.R.C. Section 166(c).
[28] I.R.C. Section 165(g)(2).
[29] I.R.C. Section 165(g)(3).
[30] *Hunter Manufacturing Corp.*, 21 T.C. 424 (1953).

Treatment of Bad Debts. Bad debts may be treated in either of two ways: (1) by a deduction from income in respect of debts which become worthless in whole or in part or (2) by a deduction from income of an addition to a reserve for bad debts. A taxpayer filing his first return may select either method, subject to the Commissioner's approval upon examination of the return. If the method selected is approved, it must be followed in returns for all subsequent years except as permission may be granted by the Commissioner to change to another method. Application for permission to change the method of treating bad debts must be made at least 30 days prior to the close of the taxable year for which the change is to be effective.

The basis for determining the amount of the bad debt deduction is the adjusted basis provided in Section 1011 of the Code for determining the loss from the sale or other disposition of property.[31]

Method (1) above, known as the specific charge-off method, involves the deduction of specific bad debts which become either wholly or partially worthless during the taxable year. *Wholly worthless debts* can be deducted only in the return filed for the taxable year in which total worthlessness occurs. The amount deducted must not include any amount deducted in any prior taxable year. No actual charge-off on the books is required in support of a bad debt deduction for a totally worthless debt, but an actual charge-off is required for a partially worthless debt. Thus, if a debt claimed to be totally worthless (which was not charged off on the books) is later determined by the Internal Revenue Service to be only partially worthless, no deduction for partial worthlessness would be allowed; no charge-off on the books had been made. This could be avoided if a taxpayer made a practice of charging off on the books both totally and partially worthless debts.

Partially worthless debts may be deducted to the extent actually charged off on the books during the taxable year. The taxpayer is not required annually to charge off and to deduct partially worthless debts. He may defer the charge-off to a later year when the accumulated partial worthlessness is greater and then deduct the larger amount in the year charged off. If the Internal Revenue Service disallows the claimed deduction for a partial bad debt in the year it is charged off, the original charge-off (unless reversed on the books) permits the taxpayer to obtain the deduction for the partial bad debt in any subsequent taxable year in which partial worthlessness can be proved.

[31] I.R.C. Section 166(b).

Method (2) above, known as the reserve method, involves the deduction of a reasonable addition to a reserve for bad debts, in lieu of a deduction for the specific bad debts. Debts which become wholly or partially worthless are charged against the reserve and are not themselves deducted from gross income. A reasonable reserve is determined in the light of the facts in each particular case; it varies as between classes of business and with conditions of business prosperity. A reasonable addition to the reserve is based primarily upon the total amount of debts outstanding as of the close of the taxable year, those arising currently as well as those arising in prior taxable years, and the total amount of the existing reserve. If subsequent realizations upon outstanding debts prove to be more or less than estimated at the time of the creation of the existing reserve, the amount of the excess or the inadequacy in the existing reserve must be reflected in the determination of the reasonable addition necessary in the taxable year.

Illustration. The proprietor of a retail clothing store files his returns on the calendar year basis. He had been using the specific charge-off method until 1960, when he was granted permission by the Commissioner to change to the reserve method for 1961 and subsequent years. His books disclose the following information:

Year	Notes and Accounts Receivable at End of Year	Bad Debt Losses	Bad Debt Recoveries
1956	$ 3,500	$ 500	
1957	3,700	700	$ 50
1958	3,400	500	75
1959	3,600	425	
1960	3,800	750	50
Five-year total	$18,000	$2,875	$175
Average	3,600	575	35
1961	3,900	500	

The amount to be credited to the reserve for bad debts would be computed as follows:

(1) Average net bad debt losses ($575 minus $35) is: $540.

(2) Divide $540 by average receivables of $3,600, equals 15%.

(3) 15% of $3,900, receivables at end of year, is $585.

(4) $585 is the balance which should be in the reserve at the close of the year.

(5) The $500 bad debt loss in 1961 is charged to the reserve, thus causing a debit balance. To bring this up to a credit balance of $585 at the end of the year, the taxpayer may add $1,085 to his reserve and claim a bad debt deduction for this amount on his return.

Interest, discount, and other receivables which have not been reported in income may not be considered in determining the annual addition to the reserve for bad debts.

The method used must be adhered to consistently. A combination of specific charge-offs and a reserve is not permissible. If a new business desires to use the reserve method of computing bad debts, it will, of course, have no bad debt experience to use to establish a bad debt ratio or percentage. In that event, the experience of like businesses of similar size may be substituted until such time as the new business has acquired sufficient experience of its own. The most commonly used methods of setting up a bad debt reserve are (1) percentage of sales proving to be uncollectible or (2) percentage of receivables proving to be uncollectible.

Recovery of Bad Debts. Under the specific charge-off method, the recovery of a bad debt which had been deducted in a prior taxable year must be included in gross income in the year of recovery. But income attributable to the recovery during any taxable year of bad debts (and certain other items) is excluded from gross income to the extent of the *recovery exclusion* with respect to these items. This exclusion rule applies as well to such items as prior taxes, delinquency amounts, and war losses, but does not include depreciation, depletion, amortization, or amortizable bond premiums.[32] (An example of a delinquency amount is interest on delinquent taxes.)

Recovery exclusion means an amount equal to the portion of the bad debts and all other items subject to the rule of exclusion which, when deducted or credited for a prior taxable year, did not result in a reduction of income tax. This is sometimes referred to as the tax benefit rule. The items covered are known as *Section 111 items.* If a bad debt previously was charged against a reserve, it was not deducted; and it is, therefore, not considered a Section 111 item.

Recoveries result from the receipt of amounts in respect of the previously deducted or credited Section 111 items, such as from the collection or sale of a bad debt. Care should be taken in the case of bad debts which were treated as only partially worthless in prior years to distinguish between the item described in Section 111 (that is, the part of the debt which was deducted) and the part not previously deducted, which is not a Section 111 item and is considered the first part collected. The collection of the part not deducted is not considered a "recovery." In the case of a bad debt deducted in part for two or more prior years, each such deduction of a part of the debt is considered a separate Section 111 item. A recovery with respect to this debt is considered first a recovery of those items (or portions thereof) resulting from the debt, for which there are recovery exclusions. If there are recovery exclusions for two or more

[32] I.R.C. Section 111.

items resulting from the same bad debt, these items are considered recovered in the order of the taxable years for which they were deducted, beginning with the latest. The recovery exclusion for any such item is determined by considering the recovery exclusion with respect to the prior year for which the item was deducted as being first used to offset all other applicable recoveries on the year in which the bad debt is recovered.

For the year of any recovery, the Section 111 items which were deducted or credited for one prior year are considered as a group and this recovery is considered separately from recoveries of any items which were deducted or credited for other years. This recovery is excluded from gross income to the extent of the recovery exclusion with respect to this group of items as (1) determined for the original year for which these items were deducted or credited and (2) reduced by the excludable recoveries in intervening years on account of all Section 111 items for the original year.

The tax benefit is not restricted to the year of the bad debt deduction. If a bad debt deduction creates or increases the amount of a net operating loss deduction in any other year (see Chapter 14), the recovery is taxable to the extent that the bad debt deduction reduced taxes in any year.

Illustration. A single individual with no dependents has for his 1961 taxable year the following income and deductions:

		With Deduction of Section 111 Items		Without Deduction for Section 111 Items
Gross income		$25,000		$25,000
Less: Deductions:				
Depreciation	$20,000		$20,000	
Business bad debts and taxes	6,300			
Personal exemption	600	26,900	600	20,600
Taxable income or (loss)		$(1,900)		$ 4,400
Adjustment for nonbusiness deductions of taxpayers other than corporations		600		
Net operating loss		$(1,300)		

The full amount of the net operating loss of $1,300 is carried back and allowed as a deduction for 1959. The aggregate of the Section 111 items for 1961 is $6,300 (bad debts and taxes). The recovery exclusion on account of Section 111 items for 1961 is $600, determined by reducing the $6,300 aggregate of the Section 111 items by $5,700; that is, the sum of (1) the difference between the amount of the taxable income for 1961 computed without regard to the Section 111 items ($4,400) and the amount of the taxable income for 1961 (not less than zero) computed by taking these items into account and (2) the amount of the net operating loss ($1,300) which caused the reduction in tax for 1959 by reason of the carryback provision. If, in 1963, the taxpayer recovers $400 of the bad debts, all of the recovery is excluded from the income by reason of the recovery exclusion of $600 determined for the original year 1961. If, in 1964, the taxpayer recovers an additional $300 of bad debts, only $200 is excluded from gross income. That is, the recovery exclusion of $600 determined for the original year 1961 is reduced by the $400 recovered in 1963, leaving a balance of $200 which is used in 1964. The balance of the amount recovered in 1964, $100 ($300 less $200) is included in gross income for 1964.

Where a taxpayer uses the reserve method, Section 111 may not be used in the case of recoveries of bad debts previously charged against a reserve.

Carryovers. Under certain circumstances, the successor corporation in a tax-free reorganization continues certain tax attributes of the predecessor corporation. For instances when this is the case, see Chapter 14.

If the predecessor corporation transfers to the successor corporation the right to recover bad debts, prior taxes, and delinquency amounts previously deducted or credited by the predecessor, then successor will include in its income the amounts that would have been includible by the predecessor pursuant to Section 111, above.[33]

Special Period of Limitation. Ordinarily, the statute of limitations for assessment of income tax is three years; see full discussion of this subject in Chapter 26. But if a claim for credit or refund relates to an overpayment of income tax on account of a bad debt deduction or a loss from the worthlessness of a security, then in lieu of the regular statute of limitations the period is seven years from the date on which the return should have been filed (without regard to any extension in time for filing).[34]

Compromises. A compromise of a debt when the debtor cannot pay is a bad debt.[35]

Foreclosures. In a foreclosure, mortgaged or pledged property may be sold for less than the amount of the debt. The portion of the indebtedness remaining unsatisfied after this sale may be wholly or partially uncollectible. Then the mortgagee or pledgee may deduct this amount, to the extent that it constitutes capital or represents an item previously included in gross income. This is a bad debt for the year in which it has become wholly worthless or is charged off as partially worthless. In addition, if the creditor buys in the mortgaged or pledged property, loss or gain is realized measured by

[33] I.R.C. Section 381(c)(12).
[34] I.R.C. Section 6511(d).
[35] I.T. 3121, 1937-2 CB 138.

the difference between the amount of those obligations of the debtor which are applied to the purchase or bid price of the property and the fair market value of the property. The fair market value of the property is presumed to be the amount for which it is bid in by the taxpayer in the absence of clear and convincing proof to the contrary. The fair market value of the property at the date of acquisition is the basis for determining gain or loss on a subsequent disposition of the property.

The following illustrations show types of mortgage adjustments:

	(1)	(2)	(3)
Mortgage indebtedness	$10,000	$10,000	$10,000
Purchase or bid price of creditor	10,000	5,000	5,000
Amount of bad debt deduction	None	$ 5,000	$ 5,000
Obligations of debtor applied to bid price	$10,000	5,000	5,000
Fair market price of property	5,000	5,000	8,000
Capital gain or (loss)	$(5,000)	None	$ 3,000

Collateral. When a debt is secured by collateral, the debt is not completely worthless as long as the security has some value.[36] A bad debt deduction is allowed in the amount of the difference between the debt and the value of the collateral.[37]

If the collateral also becomes worthless, deduction for the debt is in the year of the collateral's becoming worthless.[38]

Casualties

General Rule. A casualty loss is to be claimed as a deduction in the year of incurrence, whether or not that is most convenient taxwise. Ordinarily a casualty loss is deductible in full, to the extent that it is not compensated for by insurance or otherwise.[39]

In the case of individuals, casualty losses of property used for *personal purposes* are computed differently from losses of *business property* or *property used for the production of income.* The two types of losses are given separate treatment. The amount of the deduction allowable for a casualty loss of personal or nonbusiness property is the difference between the value of the property immediately before the casualty and its value immediately after the casualty, but not in excess of the cost or adjusted basis of the property, reduced by any insurance or other compensation received or recoverable.

[36] *Old Colony Trust Associates v. Hassett,* 150 F.2d 179 (1st Cir., 1945).
[37] *The Murchison National Bank v. Grissom,* 50 F.2d 1056 (4th Cir., 1931).
[38] *E. L. Thomas,* 6 B.T.A. (1927).
[39] I.R.C. Section 165.

(a) Value Before Casualty	(b) Value After Casualty	(c) Loss in Value, (a) Minus (b)	(d) Cost or Other Basis	(e) Insurance or Other Compensation Received or Recoverable	(f) Allowable Casualty Loss Deduction, Lesser of (c) or (d) Minus (e)	(g) Taxable Gain, (e) Minus (d)	(h) Remaining Tax Basis, (d) Plus (g) Minus Sum of (e) and (f)
(1) $15,000....	$11,000	$ 4,000	$10,000	$ 3,000	$ 1,000	$ 0	$6,000
(2) $15,000....	3,000	12,000	10,000	0	10,000	0	0
(3) $ 5,000....	2,000	3,000	10,000	3,000	0	0	7,000
(4) $15,000....	1,000	14,000	10,000	3,000	7,000	0	0
(5) $19,000....	10,000	9,000	5,000	8,000	0	3,000	0
(6) $18,000....	0	18,000	10,000	12,000	0	2,000	0

What Is a Casualty? The loss may be from "fire, storm, shipwreck, or other casualty, or from theft." "Generally, 'other casualty' has been confined by the courts to events having the characteristic of being sudden, unexpected and unusual. . . . This has the practical advantage of confining personal losses to somewhat dramatic settings which are susceptible to identification and verification by the administrative authorities."[40] Examples are:

Loss from the freezing of water pipes in a residence during the absence of the occupant.[41]

Loss occasioned by the bursting of a boiler in a heating plant of a residence.[42]

Loss due to an extensive gradual vertical sinking of land caused by a subterranean disturbance.[43]

Damages to trees on residential property caused by a sleet and ice storm.[44]

Damage to household goods and an automobile from storms encountered while the articles were being shipped by sea.[45]

Casualty is distinguished from what ordinary foresight and prudence could guard against or prevent.

The loss may be the direct or the proximate result of a casualty. The court found no reason to determine whether an automobile accident was occasioned by faulty driving over an icy road or to subsequent freezing of the motor.[46]

Damages resulting from a collision which is caused by the faulty driving of either driver are casualty losses, provided the collision was not caused by the taxpayer's *willful* negligence. Drunken driving, for instance, is regarded by the Internal Revenue Service

[40] *W. W. Bercaw,* T.C. Memo., Docket #7263, entered January 21, 1947.
[41] *Seward City Mills,* 44 B.T.A. (1939).
[42] I.T. 2231, IV-2 CB 53.
[43] *Harry Johnston Grant,* 30 B.T.A. 1028 (1935).
[44] *Whipple v. United States,* 25 F.2d 520 (D.C., Mass., 1928).
[45] *Leland Webb,* 1 B.T.A. 759 (1926).
[46] *Shearer v. Anderson,* 16 F.2d 995 (2d Cir., 1927).

as a case of willful negligence. Faulty driving, however, is not in itself willful negligence.

Termite damage is not a casualty loss. "That word denotes an accident, a mishap, some sudden invasion by a hostile agency; it excludes the progressive deterioration of property through a steadily operating cause." [47] (There is not even a deduction for long-termite loss.) Nor was there a deductible casualty loss when worms ate the piles on which a home had rested.[48]

Time of Deduction. Casualty losses are deductible only in the taxable year in which sustained, and not in any succeeding taxable year, regardless of whether the damages are actually repaired in the year the casualty occurred. In this respect, a loss is sustained during the taxable year if it is a completed fact, fixed by identifiable events from which it can be determined that a loss in fact has been sustained.

The Internal Revenue Service claims that the above rule applies even though insurance recovery is not made during the year in which the loss occurred or even though suit filed for recovery of damages is not finally decided until a later year. "In such case, you should compute your loss by deducting from the total loss the estimated amount of recoverable insurance, or other recoverable compensation, and deduct the loss so determined in the year the casualty occurred. If subsequent events demonstrate that this estimate was substantially inaccurate, an amended return should be filed correcting the mistake. If such a correction results in an overpayment of tax, the amended return or a claim for refund (Form 843) should be filed. . . ." [49]

But it has been held that where the insurance company neither admitted nor settled a claim until a year subsequent to the loss, the unreimbursed portion was a deduction in the year of the settlement.[50] Loss similarly may be deferred where there is reasonable doubt as to the collectibility of insurance.[51]

If the amount of the loss cannot be determined before the due date for the filing of the tax return, an extension of time for filing should be obtained from the District Director of Internal Revenue. Or an amended return should be filed within the statutory period. See Chapter 26.

[47] *Fay v. Helvering,* 120 F.2d 253 (2d Cir., 1941).
[48] *Matheson v. Commissioner,* 54 F.2d 537 (2d Cir., 1931).
[49] *Internal Revenue Service Publication* No. 155.
[50] *Charles F. Jeffrey et al.,* T.C. Memo., Docket #30918, entered May 30, 1953.
[51] *Commissioner v. Harwick,* 184 F.2d 835 (5th Cir., 1950).

Proof. No loss deduction is allowed in the absence of proof that there was a loss in the taxable year. The fact that something was missing did not establish that there was a theft (casualty) loss.[52] No deduction is allowed in the absence of proof of basis.[53] Deduction is disallowed when the year of the casualty cannot be proved.[54]

The taxpayer should be prepared to prove:

(1) The nature of the casualty and when it occurred.

(2) That the loss was the result of the casualty.

(3) That he is the owner of the property. Members of an incorporated club were assessed their pro rata shares of a casualty sustained by the club, but a member could not claim his assessment as a deduction, inasmuch as the corporation and not she owned the property.[55]

(4) The cost or other adjusted basis of the property, evidenced by purchase contract, deed, etc. Improvements should be supported by checks, receipts, etc.

(5) Depreciation allowed or allowable, if any.

(6) Values before and after casualty. Pictures and appraisals before and after the casualty are pertinent evidence.

(7) The amount of insurance or other compensation received, including the value of repairs, restoration, and cleanup provided without cost by disaster relief agencies.

Sentimental Value. Sentimental value is not a factor in determining the amount of the loss suffered. The loss must, in general, relate to the market value of the property damaged or stolen. Thus, the loss from the destruction, damage, or theft of a family portrait, heirloom, or keepsake must be based on the loss of its intrinsic value, apart from any attached sentimental value.

Extent of Destruction. Where business property is completely destroyed, the deductible loss is the excess of the depreciated cost or other adjusted basis of the property over the total of any salvage value, insurance, or other compensation received or recoverable.

In a partial destruction, the deductible loss is the percentage of the depreciated cost or other basis which the *value of the destroyed portion* is of the *value of the entire property,* reduced by any insurance or other compensation received or recoverable. The entire property consists of the total of the portion destroyed and the por-

[52] *Mildred Bauman (Malley)*, T.C. Memo., Docket #25298, entered January 12, 1951.

[53] *Rufus K. Steele,* T.C. Memo., Docket #17096, entered August 11, 1948.

[54] *Evans v. Commissioner,* 235 F.2d 586 (8th Cir., 1956).

[55] *West v. United States,* 163 F. Supp. 739 (D.C., Pa., 1958).

tion not destroyed; but property, such as a building, does not include the value of the land.

The value of the destroyed portion is the difference between the value of the property immediately before and immediately after the casualty. These values should be ascertained by competent appraisals.

Illustration. A taxpayer owned a building used in his trade or business, with a cost basis of $50,000. Exclusive of the land, the building had a depreciated (adjusted) basis of $30,000 when it was partially destroyed by storm. The value immediately before the storm was $60,000 and the value immediately after was $45,000. The percentage of the portion destroyed ($15,000) to the entire property before the loss ($60,000) is 25%. Applying this percentage of the adjusted basis of $30,000, there is a deductible loss of $7,500, decreased by any insurance or other recovery.

A formula may be used in the case of partial destruction of an asset. Where A is the adjusted basis for computing loss, B is the fair market value before the casualty, F is the fair market value after the casualty, and R is any recovery, then

$$\text{Deductible loss} = \frac{A(B-F)}{B} - R$$

Estate Tax Limitation. No casualty loss may be deducted on an income tax return if, at the time the return is filed, this loss has been claimed for estate tax purposes on the estate tax return. The taxpayer must attach to his income tax return a statement that the loss had not been claimed on an estate tax return and that the right to file such a claim on an estate tax return is waived by the taxpayer.[56]

Demolition Loss

In general, deduction is allowed for the voluntary removal or demolition of old buildings, the scrapping of old machinery, equipment, etc., incident to renewals and replacements. When a taxpayer buys real estate upon which is located a building which he proceeds to raze with a view to erecting thereon another building, it will be considered that the taxpayer has sustained no deductible loss by reason of the demolition of the old building, and no deductible expense on account of the cost of the removal. It will be presumed that the value of the real estate, exclusive of old improvements, is equal to the purchase price of the land and building plus the cost of removing the useless building.

[56] I.R.C. Section 165(c)(3).

Supplementary Material

A. Suggested Reading.

Don J. Summa, "The Present Status of Bad Debts," *Proceedings of the New York University Sixteenth Annual Institute on Federal Taxation* (Albany: Matthew Bender & Co., Inc., 1958), p. 1958.

Robert S. Holzman, "Tax Consequences of a Loss," *Insurance Law Journal,* December, 1957, #419, p. 734.

James S. Eustice, "Cancellation of Indebtedness and the Federal Income Tax: A Problem of Creeping Confusion," *Tax Law Review,* January, 1959, Vol. XIV, #2, p. 225.

Alfred J. McDowell, "Casualty Losses," *Proceedings of the New York University Seventeenth Annual Institute on Federal Taxation* (Albany: Matthew Bender & Co., Inc., 1959), p. 627.

B. Leading Cases.

What is a debt? *American Cigar Co. v. Commissioner,* 66 F.2d 425 (2d Cir., 1933).

Degree of optimism required of creditor. *United States v. S. S. White Dental Manufacturing Co. of Pennsylvania,* 247 U.S. 398 (1927).

C. Questions.

1. A cash basis accountant billed a client for $250 for an audit but the client meanwhile failed. Is the accountant entitled to a bad debt deduction for the unpaid amount?
2. Julius lent money to his wife, Calpurnia, so that she could settle all of her outstanding household bills. She had expected to make repayment out of the commission on a casual sale of real estate she thought she could make; but the deal was not consummated, and she had no funds. How should Julius treat the loan for tax purposes?
3. A vendor ascertained that certain receivables were uncollectible. Must they be written off on the books in order to justify a tax deduction?
4. An individual borrowed $10,000 from a bank, giving as collateral a corporate bond with a value of that amount. The individual lost all of his money and prospects, at a time when the bond was worth $7,500. How will the bank treat the transaction for tax purposes?
5. Harry owned a goatskin baseball that was said to have been given to his great-great-grandfather by Abner Doubleday. It was stolen. Will the Internal Revenue Service recognize a deductible loss of the $10,000 claimed?
6. Early in 1961, a calendar year retailer read in a trade association credit report that one of his customers was unable to honor his financial commitments. The retailer thereupon wrote off a receivable as bad. By the end of 1961, the customer had repaid 80% of the original indebtedness. Is any bad debt deduction possible for 1961? Would your answer be different if the repayments were in 1962?
7. A creditor strongly believed that his debtor could not repay a certain loan; but as a bad debt deduction would be more valuable to the creditor in 1962 than in 1961, he carefully refrained from demanding payment or even looking into the debtor's financial condition until

1962, when the latter unquestionably was bankrupt. In what year, if any, is the bad debt deductible?

8. An individual pledged a certain sum to a political party, but he lost his money before making any payments. Is the political party allowed a bad debt deduction?
9. A manufacturer's chief customer refused to pay a particular invoice on the grounds that the shipment was defective. To avoid friction with a good account, the manufacturer charged off the item as a bad debt by reason of the fact that it would not be collected. Will the Internal Revenue Service agree?
10. P Corporation owned all of the stock of S Corporation, all of the income of which was from sales. S Corporation failed, and its securities were worthless. How will P treat the S securities it owns for tax purposes?
11. When Junior went into business at age sixteen, his father, Senior, advanced $2,000 for the purpose. The business was not successful, to put it negatively, and Junior lost all of his savings. Could Senior deduct the $2,000 as a bad debt?
12. The home of a manufacturer of fire extinguishers was destroyed by fire in 1961. He claimed no casualty loss in that year, as he expected the loss would be reimbursed fully by his insurance company; but in 1963 he learned that, because of a technicality, the insurance company was not liable. In what year is the loss deductible?
13. An individual purchased an old building and the land on which it stood for $27,500. Almost immediately he tore down the building and proceeded to erect a new structure, at a cost of $40,000. Is he entitled to a deduction for a loss on the value of the old building? What is the basis of the land in his hands?
14. Is a tax-exempt organization entitled to a bad debt deduction for pledged moneys that were not paid because of an insolvency?
15. A corporation lent money to an employee, who was unable to make repayment. Is this a nonbusiness bad debt as far as the corporation is concerned?
16. A highly successful public relations counselor was sent to prison for six months for contempt of Congress. While he languished in durance vile, a note that he had signed became due; and as the debtor was in prison, the creditor wrote off the item as a bad debt. Will the Internal Revenue Service acquiesce?
17. An individual, who had a cold, made copious use of disposable tissues that he kept on a night table next to his bed. The next day, the maid threw away the contents of the waste basket; and it was not until a later hour that he missed the diamond ring that had been on the night table (along with the tissues) when he retired. Is this a casualty loss?
18. Gregory Gull endorsed the note of his brother-in-law for $1,000. Later that same taxable year, the note became due; and as the brother-in-law could not pay it, Gull had to pay. Is he entitled to a deduction and, if so, what kind? Would your answer be different if the endorsement arose in a transaction connected with Gull's trade or business?
19. A damsel's home, which cost her $3,600, was partially destroyed by fire. The value of the home immediately before the fire was $6,000, and the value immediately afterward was $2,000. She collected $2,400 from the insurance company. What was her casualty loss?

20. A dealer files his returns on a calendar year basis. He had been using the specific charge-off method until 1960, when he was granted permission by the Internal Revenue Service to change to the reserve method for 1961 and subsequent years. His books disclose the following information:

Year	Receivables at End of Year	Bad Debt Losses	Bad Debt Recoveries
1956	$17,500	$ 500	0
1957	18,500	700	$ 50
1958	17,000	500	75
1959	18,000	425	0
1960	19,000	750	50
Five-year total	$90,000	$2,875	$175
Average	18,000	575	35
1961	19,500	500	0

How much should be credited to the reserve for bad debts?

14

CARRYBACKS AND CARRYOVERS

The income tax, as has been noted previously, is computed upon the basis of a specific period—the taxable year. In general, each year stands on its own feet, unaffected by what happens in any other period. This can create unfortunate results. If, over a period of years, a business has a loss in only one year, tax is paid for every year of profit, with no offset for the year of loss, with the result that there is an *economic loss* even though no recognizable tax loss. Assuming that actual gain for the period and taxable gain for the period were the same, the taxpayer actually would be out of pocket the amount of the loss, inasmuch as taxable income for a year is never less than zero.

Another inequity about treating each taxable year as an entity unrelated to other years may be seen in the case of capital losses. An individual may not deduct a net capital loss to a greater extent than $1,000 a year; a corporation may not deduct a net capital loss at all. So if there is a capital loss in one year and a capital gain in the other, there would be a nondeductible loss in one year and a taxable gain in the other.

In order to provide for certain important situations where losses of a particular year would be wasted if reference could not be made to other years, Congress created the concept of the carryover. Under stipulated facts, a *net operating loss* may be carried *back* to reduce (or to wipe out) past losses, and to the extent that the loss is not thus utilized, there may be a carry *forward* of the loss as an offset to future profits. Capital losses may be carried forward as an offset against future capital gains.

Carrybacks were first provided for in the Revenue Act of 1918.

Net Operating Loss Deduction

In brief, a net operating loss is the excess of allowable deductions over gross income, with certain adjustments.[1] There are three steps

[1] I.R.C. Section 172(c).

to be taken in the ascertainment of the net operating loss deduction for any taxable year:

(1) Compute the net operating loss for any preceding or succeeding taxable year from which a net operating loss may be carried over or carried back.

(2) Compute the net operating loss carryovers to this taxable year from the preceding taxable years and the net operating loss carrybacks from the succeeding taxable years.

(3) Add the net operating loss carryovers and carrybacks in order to determine the net operating loss deduction for the taxable year.

The computation of a net operating loss is not quite the same for corporations and for individuals. The two main differences concern the adjustments necessary in determining a net operating loss and the adjustments to taxable income in determining carrybacks or carryovers.

Corporate Net Operating Loss. The starting point is taxable income (actually, *loss*) per the tax return, with these adjustments:

(1) No deduction is allowed for any net operating loss carryover or carryback from another year.

(2) No deduction is allowed for partially tax exempt interest.

(3) No deduction is allowed for the special deduction allowed to Western Hemisphere trade corporations. See Chapter 2.

(4) The 85% deduction for dividends received is allowed to that extent without regard to the provision which otherwise limits it to 85% of taxable income. The dividends received deduction is limited to 85% of taxable income, which would mean zero in the case of a corporation with a loss. But where there is a net operating loss, the limitation does not apply.

(5) The deduction for dividends paid on certain preferred stock of public utilities is not limited to a specified percentage of taxable income otherwise imposed.

Illustration. For the calendar year 1961 a corporation has gross income of $400,000 and total allowable deductions of $375,000, exclusive of any net operating loss deduction and exclusive of any deduction for dividends received or paid. In 1961 the corporation received $100,000 in dividends from domestic corporations. These dividends are included in the $400,000 gross income. The corporation likewise received $50,000 of partially tax-exempt interest in 1961 for which a deduction is allowed. This interest is included in both the $400,000 gross income and the $375,000 total deductions. The corporation has no other deductions subject to special treatment under the carryover provisions. On the basis of these facts, the corporation has a net operating loss for the year 1961 of $10,000, computed as follows:

Deductions for 1961	$375,000
Plus: Deduction for dividends received, computed without regard to the limitation of 85% of income (85% of $100,000)	85,000
Total	$460,000
Less: Deduction with respect to partially tax-exempt interest	50,000
Deductions as modified for carryover purposes	$410,000
Less: Gross income for 1961 (including $100,000 dividends and $50,000 partially tax-exempt interest)	400,000
Net operating loss for 1961	$ 10,000

Losses of a corporation in process of liquidation may be carried back.[2] It is not necessary that the business of the corporation be the same in the loss year and in the year to which the loss is carried back.[3]

Individual's Net Operating Loss. In the case of an individual or any taxpayer other than a corporation, the starting point is taxable income (which may be a loss). The following adjustments are then made:

(1) No deduction is allowed for a net operating loss carryover or carryback from any year.

(2) The deduction for capital losses cannot exceed the amount of capital gains included in gross income. Furthermore, nonbusiness capital losses are deductible only to the extent of nonbusiness capital gains, even though the taxpayer has an excess of business capital gains over business capital losses.

(3) There may not be taken into account the 50% deduction from gross income for the excess of a net long-term capital gain over a net short-term capital loss.

(4) No deduction is allowed for personal exemptions.

(5) Nonbusiness deductions may not exceed nonbusiness income. Any gain or loss on the sale or other disposition of property which is used in the taxpayer's trade or business and which is of a character that is subject to depreciation, or real estate used in the taxpayer's trade or business, is considered as trade or business income for this purpose. Salaries and wages received are regarded as trade or business income. Any deduction claimed for a casualty loss is considered as being attributable to the trade or business. This is true even though it involves nonbusiness property.

Illustration. An individual operates a retail clothing business. He began operations of his business in 1960, and had a net operating loss of $185 for that year.

[2] *Justice Motor Corp. v. McGowan,* 97 F. Supp. 570 (D.C., N.Y., 1951).

[3] *Acampo Winery & Distilleries, Inc.,* 7 T.C. 629 (1946).

He had no taxable income for 1958 and 1959. During the taxable year 1961 he had the following income and deductions:

INCOME

Salary earned as part-time helper in garage (salary is treated as business income)	$ 875
Interest on savings	425
Net long-term capital gain on sale of machinery	2,000
Total income	$3,300

DEDUCTIONS

Net operating loss carryover from 1960	$ 185
Net loss from business (gross receipts $66,000 minus expenses $72,000)	6,000
Net short-term capital loss on sale of stock	500
Casualty loss on business property not held more than 6 months	200
Deductions for excess of net long-term capital gains over net short-term capital loss (50% of $1,500)	750
Personal exemption	600
Itemized deductions on tax return	560
Total deductions	$8,795
Deductions exceeded income by	$5,495

But to arrive at the net operating loss, these adjustments must be made:

Deductions minus income		$5,495
(1) Eliminate the net operating loss carryover from 1960	$185	
(2) Eliminate the 50% deduction for net long-term capital gain	750	
(3) Eliminate the net short-term capital loss	500	
(4) Eliminate the personal exemption	600	
(5) Eliminate the excess of nonbusiness deductions (itemized deductions, $560) over nonbusiness income (interest, $425)	135	
Total adjustments to net loss		2,170
Net operating loss for 1961		($3,325)

Sequence of Carrybacks and Carryovers. In order to compute the net operating loss deduction, the taxpayer must first determine the part of any net operating losses for any preceding or succeeding taxable years which are carryovers or carrybacks to the taxable year in issue. A net operating loss must be carried back to the third preceding taxable year from which it was sustained. Any amount of the loss not used to offset income for the third preceding year must be carried to the second preceding year, then to the first preceding year. Where the loss is not entirely used to offset taxable income in the third, second, and first preceding years, the balance may be carried to the next five years in order of their occurrence.

Illustration. An individual had a net operating loss for 1961 of $40,000. His taxable income (after necessary adjustments) in the other years is as follows:

Year		Carryback or Carryover	Adjusted Taxable Income	Unused Carryback or Carryover
1958	Third preceding year	$40,000	$ 3,000	$37,000
1959	Second preceding year	37,000	5,000	32,000

Year		Carryback or Carryover	Adjusted Taxable Income	Unused Carry-back or Carryover
1960	First preceding year........	32,000	500	31,500
1961	Net operating loss year			
1962	First succeeding year........	31,500	7,000	24,500
1963	Second succeeding year......	24,500	3,800	20,700
1964	Third succeeding year........	20,700	10,700	10,000
1965	Fourth succeeding year......	10,000	6,000	4,000
1966	Fifth succeeding year........	4,000	2,500	1,500

The $1,500 carryover remaining at the end of 1966 may not be used in 1967 nor any other year.

If there is more than one net operating loss to be carried to the same taxable year, the loss from the earlier year is applied first. The sum of the net operating loss carrybacks and carryovers represents the *net operating loss deduction* for the taxable year. If the sum of all the net operating losses carried to a particular year is greater than the amount needed to absorb all the income for that year, the earliest loss is considered to be used first.

A fractional part of a year which is treated as a taxable year is a preceding or a succeeding taxable year for the purpose of determining the first, second, etc., preceding or succeeding taxable year. Thus, if a calendar year corporation is incorporated on December 1, 1959, a carryback from 1961 only has thirteen months in which to be absorbed rather than twenty-four.

In determining the amount of any operating loss carryback or carryover to any taxable year, the necessary computations involving any other taxable year must be made under the law applicable to the other taxable year.

Joint Returns. If a husband and wife, making a joint return for any taxable year, did not make a joint return for any of the taxable years involved in the computation of a carryback or carryover to the taxable year for which the joint return is filed, the separate net operating loss carryover or carryback is a joint net operating loss carryback or carryover to that taxable year. If a husband and wife making a joint return for a taxable year made a joint return for each of the taxable years involved in the computation of a net operating loss carryback or carryover to that taxable year, the joint net operating loss carryback or carryover to that taxable year is computed in the same manner as the net operating loss carryback or carryover of an individual, but upon the basis of the joint net operating losses and the combined taxable income of both spouses.

If a husband and wife making separate returns for a taxable year make a joint return for any, or all, of the taxable years involved in the computation of a net operating loss carryback or carryover to that taxable year, the separate net operating loss carryback or carryover of each spouse to the taxable year is computed in the standard manner, with the following modifications:

(1) The net operating loss of each spouse for a taxable year for which a joint return was made will be deemed to be that portion of the joint net operating loss which is attributable to the gross income and deductions of that spouse, gross income and deductions being taken into account to the same extent that they are taken into account in computing the joint net operating loss.

(2) The taxable income of a particular spouse for any taxable year which is subtracted from the net operating loss of that spouse for another taxable year in order to determine the amount of that loss which may be carried back or carried over to still another taxable year is deemed to be, in a case in which this taxable income was reported in a joint return, the sum of the following:

(A) That portion of the combined taxable income of both spouses for that year for which the joint return was made which is attributable to the gross income and deductions of the particular spouse, gross income and deductions being taken into account to the same extent that they are taken into account in computing the combined taxable income, and

(B) That portion of the combined taxable income which is attributable to the other spouse; but, if this other spouse sustained a net operating loss in a taxable year beginning on the same date as the taxable year in which the particular spouse sustained the net operating loss from which the taxable income is subtracted, then this portion will first be reduced by the net operating loss of the other spouse.[4]

Statement Required. Each taxpayer claiming a net operating loss deduction for any taxable year must file with his tax return for that year a concise statement setting forth the amount of the net operating loss deduction claimed and all material and pertinent facts relative to the claim, including a detailed schedule showing the computation of the net operating loss deduction.

Refund Based on Carryback. If a net operating loss is carried back one or two years, a refund of part or all of the tax paid at such time is in order. Refund of this tax may be obtained in either of two ways: (1) a refund claim on Form 843 may be filed prior to the running of the statute of limitations. See Chapter 26. (2) An amended tax return may be filed for the year to which the loss is

[4] Regulations Section 1.172-7.

carried back, showing a recomputation that results in a lesser tax. But even under (2), a refund claim should be filed protectively. If an individual files an amended return, the net operating loss deduction should be claimed on a separate Schedule C of Form 1040, even though the taxpayer had no other business income or deductions for that year.

But a more rapid process than a standard refund claim form is available in the case of a loss carryback. This is sometimes referred to as a *quickie* claim. A taxpayer who is entitled to a loss carryback may file an application for a tentative adjustment. This application must be filed on or after the date of filing the return for the year of the loss, but not later than twelve months from the end of that taxable year.[5] A corporation uses Form 1139 for this purpose; an individual, Form 1045. The Internal Revenue Service will ordinarily act on this application within a period of ninety days from the date it is filed.

The amount of the adjustment with respect to the tax is limited to the decrease in tax as previously determined which results from the net operating loss carryback and the effect of this carryback upon any items taken into account in computing the tax previously determined. This decrease must be determined on the basis of the items reflected in the computation of the tax as previously determined. Accordingly, items must be taken into account only to the extent that they were reported in the return or were reflected in amounts assessed (or collected without assessment) as deficiencies, or in amounts which were abated, credited, refunded, or otherwise repaid, prior to the time of filing the application. Deductions (except the charitable contributions deduction) which are limited, for example, by taxable income are to be recomputed on the basis of the taxable income as affected by the carryback. Thus, an individual with medical expenses that are deductible only to the extent that they exceed 3% of adjusted gross income would have to adjust his medical expense deduction for the year to which the loss is carried back.

In general, the tax previously determined will be the tax shown on the return as filed, increased by any amounts assessed (or collected without assessment) as deficiencies prior to the date of filing the application and decreased by any amounts abated, credited, refunded, or otherwise repaid prior to that date.

Illustration. An individual has a net operating loss in 1961 of $8,000; he had no other carryovers or carrybacks. No adjustments are required under the facts of the case. The net operating loss deduction for 1959 was also $8,000. Adjusted

[5] I.R.C. Section 6411.

gross income in 1959 was $12,000 and taxable income was $8,160. Itemized deductions amounted to $3,240, which included $840 for medical expenses and $2,400 for contributions. He had one personal exemption of $600. The recomputation of taxable income and tax liability is as follows:

Adjusted gross income as shown on 1959 return		$12,000.00
Less: Net operating loss deduction from 1961		8,000.00
Adjusted gross income after carryback		$ 4,000.00
Less: Itemized deductions:		
Contributions ($2,800 actually paid but allowable only to extent of 20% of adjusted gross income without regard to carryback)	$2,400	
Medical expenses ($1,200 actually paid but allowable only to extent in excess of 3% of adjusted gross income as adjusted after carryback)	1,080	
Total	$3,480	
Personal exemption	600	$ 4,080.00
Taxable income after carryback		0.00
Tax liability after carryback		0.00
Taxes paid on 1959 return		$ 2,014.40
Amount of refund of 1959 taxes		$ 2,014.40

Partnerships. A partnership is not allowed to claim a net operating loss deduction, but a partner may use his proportionate share of the partnership's loss to arrive at his individual net operating loss.

Extension of Time for Corporations Expecting Carrybacks. Ordinarily, a taxpayer can obtain the benefit of a loss carryback only by filing a claim for refund or an application for a tentative carryback adjustment after the close of the year from which a net operating loss arises. But a corporation (no other taxpayer gets similar treatment) expecting at the close of the taxable year a net operating loss carryback from the next succeeding year may file during this following year a statement supporting the expected loss. The filing of this statement on Form 1138 extends the time for payment of all or part of any tax for the taxable year immediately preceding the year of the expected loss.[6]

The time for payment of the tax for the immediately preceding taxable year is automatically extended upon the filing of the statement of the expected loss carryback. The extension is effective until the last day of the month in which expires the time (including any extensions of time to file) for filing the return for the taxable year of the loss. If before that date the corporation files an application on Form 1139 for a tentative carryback adjustment (the abovementioned *quickie*), the extension will continue until the date on which the Internal Revenue Service notifies the corporation that

[6] I.R.C. Section 6164.

its application for the adjustment is allowed or disallowed in whole or in part.

Interest. The carryback of a net operating loss does not affect the computation of interest on any income tax for the period commencing with the last date prescribed for the payment of this tax and ending with the last day of the taxable year in which the loss occurs. For example, if the carryback of a net operating loss to a prior taxable period eliminates or reduces a deficiency in income tax for that period, the full amount of the deficiency will nevertheless bear interest at the rate of 6% per annum from the last date prescribed for payment of the tax until the last day of the taxable year in which the loss occurred. Interest will continue to run beyond the last day on any portion of the deficiency which is not eliminated by the carryback.[7]

Where an extension of time for payment of income tax has been granted to a corporation expecting a carryback, interest is payable at the rate of 6% per annum on the amount of the unpaid tax from the last date prescribed for payment without regard to this extension.

Where there has been an allowance of an overpayment attributable to a net operating loss carryback and all or part of this allowance is later determined excessive, interest will be computed on the excessive amount from the last day of the year in which the net operating loss arose until the date on which the repayment of this excessive amount is received.

Termination of Estate or Trust. If, on the final termination of an estate or trust, a net operating loss carryover would be allowable to the estate or trust in a subsequent year, the carryover is allowable to the beneficiaries succeeding to the property of the estate or trust.[8]

If, on the termination of an estate or trust, this entity has for its last taxable year deductions (other than personal exemptions and contributions) in excess of gross income, the excess is allowable as a deduction to the beneficiaries succeeding to the property of the estate or trust. The deduction is allowed only in computing taxable income; it is not allowed in computing adjusted gross income. The deduction is allowable only in the taxable year of the beneficiary in which or with which the estate or trust terminates, whether the year of termination of the estate or trust is of normal duration or is a short taxable year.

[7] I.R.C. Section 6601(e).
[8] I.R.C. Section 642(h).

Illustration. A trust distributes all of its assets to the sole beneficiary and terminates on December 31, 1960. As of that date it had excess deductions (for example, because of corpus commissions on termination) of $18,000. The beneficiary, who reported on the calendar year basis, could claim the $18,000 as a deduction for 1960. But if the deduction, when added to his other deductions, exceeds his gross income, the excess may not be carried over to 1961 or subsequent years.

Unused Capital Losses

Any taxpayer sustaining a net capital loss may carry over this loss to each of the five succeeding years and treat it in each of these five years as a short-term capital loss to the extent not allowed as a deduction against any net capital gains of any taxable years intervening between the taxable year in which the net capital loss was sustained and the taxable year to which carried. There is no carryback, as with net operating losses. The unused capital loss carryover is thus applied in each succeeding taxable year to offset any net capital gain in these succeeding years. The amount of the net capital loss carryover may not be included in computing a new net capital loss of a taxable year which can be carried forward to the next five succeeding taxable years.[9]

Illustration. An individual with one personal exemption had the following transactions:

1959		
Taxable income (exclusive of capital transactions and personal exemption)		$ 1,100
Taxable income for limitation purposes		$ 1,100
Excess of capital losses over gains	$50,500	
Amount of loss deductible		1,000
Taxable income (exclusive of exemption)		$ 100
Less: Personal exemption		600
Taxable income (after deducting exemption)		None
Net capital loss carryover ($50,500 − $1,000)	$49,500	
1960		
Taxable income (exclusive of capital transactions and personal exemption)		$ 900
Taxable income for limitation purposes		$ 900
Excess of capital gains over losses (without carryover)		20,000
Taxable income (exclusive of exemption)		$20,900
Capital loss carryover from 1959	$49,500	
Amount of loss deductible ($20,000 + $900)		20,900
Taxable income		None
Balance of net capital loss carryover from 1959 ($49,500 − $20,900)	$28,600	
1961		
Taxable income (exclusive of capital transactions and personal exemption)		$30,600
Taxable income for limitation purposes		$30,600
Excess of capital gains over losses (without carryover)		24,000
Taxable income (exclusive of exemption)		$54,600

[9] I.R.C. Section 1212.

1961—*Continued*

Capital loss carryover from 1959	$28,600	
Amount of loss deductible ($24,000 + $1,000)		25,000
Taxable income (before deducting exemption)		$29,600
Less: Personal exemption		600
Taxable income		$29,000
Balance of net capital loss carryover from 1959 ($28,600 − $25,000)	$ 3,600	

Husband and Wife. If a husband and wife making a joint return for any taxable year made separate returns for the preceding taxable year any net capital loss carryover of each spouse from this preceding taxable year may be carried forward to the taxable year as a short-term capital loss to the extent allowed by the general carryover rule.

If a joint return was made for the preceding taxable year, any net capital loss carryover from this preceding year must be allocated to the spouses on the basis of their individual net capital losses which gave rise to the carryover, and the net capital loss carryover so allocated to each spouse may be carried forward by each to the taxable year as a short-term capital loss to the extent provided in the general rule.

If separate returns are made both for the taxable year and the preceding taxable year, any net capital loss carryover of each spouse may be carried forward by that spouse to the taxable year as a short-term capital loss to the extent provided by the general rule.

Illustration. If H and W, husband and wife, make a joint return for 1960, having made separate returns for 1959 on which H had a net capital loss of $3,000 and W had a net capital loss of $2,000, in their joint return for 1960 they would have a short-term capital loss of $5,000 (the sum of their separate net capital loss carryovers from 1959), allowable to the extent provided in the general rule. If, on the other hand, they make separate returns in 1960 following a joint return in 1959 in which their net capital loss was $5,000 (allowable $3,000 to H and $2,000 to W), the carryover of H as a short-term capital loss for the purpose of his 1960 separate return would be $3,000 and that of W for her separate return would be $2,000, each allowable to the extent provided by the general rule.

Termination of Estate or Trust. An unused capital loss of an estate or trust which terminates may be utilized by the beneficiaries succeeding to the property as a carryover, to the extent that the estate or trust could have made use of the carryover had not termination occurred. This is similar to the rule as to net operating losses and is in fact provided for in the same section of the Code.[10]

Treatment of Two or More Carryovers. If there are two or more carryovers, the oldest one must be applied first before the others are utilized.

[10] I.R.C. Section 642(h).

Corporate Reorganizations

When a tax-free corporate reorganization takes place, the philosophy is that the successor corporation is the same as the predecessor for tax purposes, if it is substantially the same corporation. See Chapter 17. Therefore, any tax privileges, elections, or similar characteristics will carry over from the transferor to the transferee. This rule applies to (1) the complete liquidation of a subsidiary (unless the subsidiary's stock had been purchased within two years for the purpose of getting the subsidiary's assets in liquidation) and (2) to a tax-free acquisition of property solely for the transferee's voting stock in a reorganization, such as a statutory merger, consolidation, or "mere change in identity, form, or place of organization."[11] The rule as to carryovers in reorganization does not apply to partial liquidations or to divisive or other reorganizations not mentioned in the preceding sentence.

There are eighteeen types of carryover in the case of the successor corporation in a corporate reorganization of the types specified. Each of these types refers to an item or tax attribute of the predecessor corporation which is to be taken into account by the successor corporation as of the close of the date of the reorganization. The following are the carryovers involved. No other type of item may be carried forward:

(1) Net operating loss.

(2) Earnings and profits (cumulative). Earnings and profits (including a deficit in earnings and profits) of the predecessor become the earnings and profits of the successor corporation.

Illustration. A parent corporation, P, completely liquidates within three years a subsidiary corporation, S, the stock of which had been acquired five years previously. Any earnings and profits of S are added to those of P. Thus, in appraising the amount of earnings and profits that P has available for distribution as a taxable dividend, the earnings and profits of S are taken into account.

(3) Capital loss carryover.

(4) Method of accounting. The successor corporation must use the method of accounting used by the predecessor, unless different methods were used by several predecessors, or by the predecessor and the successor. If different methods were used, the method or combination of methods used must be in accordance with the regulations of the Secretary of the Treasury.

(5) Inventories. The inventory will be used by the successor on the same basis on which this inventory was used by the predecessor,

[11] I.R.C. Section 381.

unless a different method or basis is approved by the Secretary of the Treasury.

(6) Method of computing depreciation allowance. The successor corporation will step into the predecessor's tax shoes in computing depreciation on assets acquired from the predecessor.

(7) Installment methods. Ordinarily, any installment obligations held by a corporation will be deemed to mature if the corporation liquidates. But in the case of a corporate reorganization of the types described above, the successor will treat installment obligations of the predecessor as though they were those of the successor.

(8) Amortization of bond discount or premium. If the successor corporation assumes liability for bonds of the predecessor issued at a discount or premium, the former will be treated as the latter after the date of reorganization for purposes of determining the amount of amortization allowable or includible with respect to this discount or premium.

(9) Treatment of certain expenses deferred by the election of the predecessor corporation. The successor corporation will be entitled to deduct, as if it were the predecessor, expenses deferred as exploration and development expenditures, if the predecessor had so elected.

(10) Contributions to pension plans, employees' annuity plans, and stock bonus and profit-sharing plans. The successor corporation will be treated as though it were the predecessor for the purpose of obtaining a deduction for employee benefit plans of the type described.

(11) Recovery of bad debts, prior taxes, or delinquency amounts. If the successor corporation is entitled to the recovery of bad debts, prior taxes, or delinquency amounts previously deducted or credited by the predecessor, the former will include in its income such amounts as would have been includible by the latter under the recovery rule of Section 111. See Chapter 13.

(12) Involuntary conversions. The successor corporation will be treated as the predecessor would have been when property of the latter involuntarily converted is replaced by the former.

(13) Dividend carryover to personal holding companies. The successor corporation is treated as though it were the predecessor. For explanation of *dividend carryover to personal holding companies,* see Chapter 16.

(14) Indebtedness of certain personal holding companies. The successor corporation is considered to be the predecessor for the purpose of getting the special deduction for payment of certain indebtedness incurred before 1934. This is discussed under "Personal Holding Companies" in Chapter 16.

(15) Certain obligations of the predecessor corporation. If the successor (1) assumes an obligation of the predecessor which, after the reorganization, gives rise to a liability and (2) this liability if paid or accrued by the predecessor, would have been deductible in computing its taxable income, then the successor will be entitled to deduct the items.

(16) Deficiency dividend of personal holding company. If the successor pays a deficiency dividend with respect to the predecessor, the latter will be entitled to the deficiency dividend deduction. This is discussed under "Personal Holding Companies" in Chapter 16.

(17) Percentage depletion on extraction of ores or minerals from the waste or residue of prior mining. The successor corporation will be treated as the predecessor for the purpose of determining the deduction.

(18) Charitable contributions in excess of prior years' limitation. Contributions made in the taxable year ending on the date of the reorganization and the prior taxable year by the predecessor in excess of the amount allowable as a tax deduction in those years may be deductible by the successor corporation in its first two taxable years which begin after the date of the reorganization.

Special Limitations on Net Operating Loss Carryovers

A loss carryover is something of value, for it may reduce subsequent income that otherwise would be taxable. To the uninitiated, "The idea that a loss is an 'asset' is a little hard to grasp." [12] But a corporation with a loss carryover has something of value: a means of reducing the income of an acquiring company. In order to prevent this, the Internal Revenue Code has provided the Internal Revenue Service with several weapons.

Purchase of Corporation and Change in Its Trade or Business. Net operating loss carryovers will not be allowed where a corporation is purchased and this company changes its trade or business, if this corporation falls within *each* of the following three conditions: [13]

(1) One or more of the ten largest unrelated stockholders must own, at the end of the taxable year, a percentage of the fair market value of the outstanding stock which is at least fifty *percentage points* more than that person or persons owned at either the be-

[12] *Alprosa Watch Corp.*, 11 T.C. 240 (1948).
[13] I.R.C. Section 382(a).

ginning of the taxable year or the prior taxable year. This condition will not be applicable unless the ten largest stockholders own at least 50% of the fair market value of the outstanding stock and, even then, will only be applicable if one or more of these ten persons has increased the percentage of the fair market value of the outstanding stock he or they owned by at least fifty percentage points during the period specified.[14] An increase of fifty percentage points does not mean the same thing as a 50% increase. Thus, a stockholder who owns 4% of the fair market value of the stock and who increases his ownership to 6% has had a 50% increase in ownership but only a two percentage point increase. The constructive ownership rules apply; that is, a person is deemed to own the shares owned by his immediate relatives.

(2) The increase of fifty percentage points must be caused by a purchase by the person who has the increase or by a decrease in the amount of outstanding stock, but not a decrease resulting from redemption to pay death taxes (a subject that is covered in Chapter 17). The statute is worded so as to prevent avoidance of the limitation through the purchase of an interest in a corporation, partnership, or trust owning stock in the corporation with the net operating loss carryover. An increase in percentage of stock owned resulting from a purchase by some other person, a tax-free reorganization, a gift, or a devise is not counted in determining whether the fifty percentage point increase has been reached.

(3) If the corporation has not continued to carry on a trade or business substantially the same as that conducted immediately before any change in the percentage ownership of the fair market value, the third condition is met. The change in percentage ownership refers to an increase that would be counted under (1) and (2) in determining whether fifty percentage point increase has been reached. If, as a result of such an increase, the corporation shifts from one type of business to another, discontinues any except a minor portion of its business, changes its location, or otherwise fails to carry on substantially the same trade or business as was conducted before the increase, then the condition in (3) is met.

Change of Ownership as a Result of a Reorganization. A net operating loss carryover may not be used where one corporation acquires a loss corporation without giving up at least a 20% share to the stockholders of the loss corporation. If the stockholders of the loss corporation receive less than a 20% interest in the successor corporation, the net operating loss carryover is reduced. The amount

[14] I.R.C. Section 382(b).

of the reduction is the percentage obtained by subtracting from 100% an amount equal to five times the percentage interest going to the loss corporation's stockholders.

Illustration. L Corporation has a net operating loss carryover to 1961 of $100,000 and assets valued at approximately 4% of the value of the assets of P Corporation. P merged into L in a statutory merger on December 31, 1960. P's stockholders own, as the result of the reorganization, 96% of the fair market value of L's outstanding stock, and L's stockholders now own 4% of the fair market value. The reduction applies, because the stockholders of the loss corporation owned only a 4% interest in the successor corporation. The 4% would be multiplied by five to give 20%, and this amount would be subtracted from 100% to give the percentage of reduction, 80%, of the carryover.

Acquisitions Made To Evade or To Avoid Income Tax. Another section of the Code permits the Internal Revenue Service to disallow an amount otherwise constituting a deduction, credit, or other allowance. For this disallowance to apply, the principal purpose for which an acquisition was made must have been the evasion or avoidance of income tax by securing the benefit of a deduction or other allowance which the person or corporation would not otherwise enjoy.[15]

The types of transaction at which this section was primarily aimed are:

(1) Use of the carryover and carryback of net operating losses.

(2) Use of the deficit of an acquired corporation to reduce affiliated company income on a consolidated return. See Chapter 27.

(3) Use of the basis of the transferor in a tax-free reorganization by the transferee for computation of loss or depreciation.

(4) Use of an acquired corporation to permit companies filing consolidated returns to revert to a separate return basis.

(5) Use of the capital loss carryover of an acquired company, to which will be transferred assets to be disposed of as offsetting capital gains.

The Government does not have the full burden of proving that there was no purpose of evasion or avoidance in cases where the consideration paid in acquiring control of another corporation, or corporate property, is substantially disproportionate to the sum of the adjusted basis of the property and the tax benefits not otherwise available. There is a statutory presumption that the principal purpose was evasion or avoidance of tax in case of a substantially disproportionate purchase price. But the taxpayer has the opportunity of proving that tax avoidance was not the principal purpose of the acquisition.

[15] I.R.C. Section 269.

The presumption that income tax evasion or avoidance was contemplated was successfully refuted where it could be shown that an acquisition was for these business reasons: (1) to reduce manufacturers' excise taxes, (2) to secure additional customers who otherwise would not be available, (3) to increase volume and to reduce costs, and (4) to spread the risk of a hazardous business.[16]

But the presumption could not be offset by the taxpayer's contention that it had not anticipated unduly large profits, nor had it known whether the acquired companies would continue to operate at a loss. There was no evidence that the acquiring corporation did not expect the losses to continue. The purchaser had not seen the books of the loss companies prior to acquisition and had made no inquiries as to potential financial success to the former owners.[17]

Supplementary Material

A. Suggested Reading.

Charles N. Whitehead, "Net Operating Loss Deductions," *Proceedings of the Fifth Annual Tulane Annual Tax Institute* (Indianapolis: The Bobbs-Merrill Co., Inc., 1956), p. 148.

Godfrey W. Welsch, "Planning To Get Full Tax Benefit from an Operating Loss Deduction," *Journal of Taxation,* February, 1958, Vol. VIII, #2, p. 88.

Theodore Berger, "Purchase of Loss Companies: Code Section 382(a)," *TAXES—The Tax Magazine,* November, 1954, Vol. XXXIII, #11, p. 876.

John G. Gemmill, "Loss Corporations," *TAXES—The Tax Magazine,* February, 1958, Vol. XXXVI, #2, p. 105.

B. Leading Cases.

Change of business of corporation. *Alprosa Watch Corp.,* 11 T.C. 240 (1948).

Loss of carryover. *American Pipe & Steel Corporation v. Commissioner,* 243 F.2d 125 (9th Cir., 1957).

What are acceptable reasons? *Contract Battery Manufacturing Company v. Tomlinson,* D.C., Fla., 1958.

Business purpose. *WAGE, Inc.,* 19 T.C. 249 (1952).

C. Questions.

1. May an unused capital loss carryover of a corporation be used to reduce income from operations of the subsequent years?
2. An Associated Press dispatch from London dated July 2, 1946, quoted *Pravda* as saying that the carryback law "acquires extreme significance. It results in the fact that the Government compensates corporations for losses caused by strikes and therefore it actually finances

[16] *Contract Battery Manufacturing Co. v. Tomlinson,* — F. Supp. — (D.C., Fla., 1958).

[17] *Elko Realty Corp.,* 29 T.C. 1012 (1958).

the capitalist monopolies in their struggles against workers." Discuss this point of view.

3. In 1960, a corporation had income of $40,000. When the return for 1961 is filed, a loss of $25,000 is shown. But $6,000 of the 1960 tax has not been paid as yet. What, if anything, may be done to avoid a payment of this installment?
4. P, a parent corporation, liquidated S Corporation, all of the stock of which it owned. P took the S assets, including machinery and equipment. Will P apply its own depreciation methods and rates to these assets, or S's?
5. T & G, a partnership, had a loss from operating a business of $60,000 in 1961. Income from the business was $75,000 in 1960. How is the carryback handled?
6. A taxpayer had a loss for 1961. Inasmuch as the 1959 returns recently had been audited, and there was no income for 1960, may the taxpayer use the 1961 loss entirely for carryover purposes?
7. A Revenue Agent assessed a deficiency for a taxpayer's 1961 return. In 1962, the taxpayer had an operating loss, which, when carried back to 1961, would wipe out the tax deficiency. Inasmuch as the deficiency is canceled, is interest owing on the 1961 underpayment?
8. The S Corporation had a net capital loss of $10,000 in 1961. Inasmuch as the corporation expected to liquidate at the start of 1962, may the loss be carried back against capital gains of the preceding year?
9. A taxpayer used the calendar year basis for five years, then in 1961 switched to a fiscal year ending March 31. A return for the short period January 1, 1961, to March 31, 1961, had to be filed, which showed a loss of $100,000. Assuming taxable income for each of the preceding five years of $40,000, what is the amount of the carryback to each year?
10. A calendar year taxpayer had a net operating loss for 1961 of $50,000. There was taxable income of $25,000 in each of the preceding four years. What alternatives are available for tax purposes? Give the appropriate date of each alternative.
11. A taxpayer's return for 1960 was audited, and a closing agreement was signed with the Commissioner of Internal Revenue, finalizing the settlement. Will a 1962 operating loss be carried back to a year closed by this agreement?
12. An individual had income or losses as follows:

1960	$20,000	1965	($60,000 loss)
1961	$30,000	1966	$75,000
1962	($80,000 loss)	1967	$56,000
1963	$40,000	1968	$21,000
1964	$25,000	1969	($14,000 loss)

Applying carrybacks and carryovers, what is the taxable income of each year?

13. A corporation had $500,000 gross income and $625,000 of allowable expenses from its business. It also received $150,000 in dividends from domestic corporations. Compute the net operating loss, if you please.
14. An individual had a casualty loss deduction of $25,000 as the result of the complete destruction by fire of his residence. He had salary of

$14,000, traveling expenses on a trip for his employer of $200, net long-term capital gains of $1,800 (before the 50% reduction for excess of net long-term capital gains over net short-term capital losses). He had other nonbusiness deductions of $700. Was there a net operating loss for the year? If so, compute it.

15. A taxpayer had net operating losses in the calendar years 1960 and 1961 of $3,000 and $5,000, respectively. His adjusted taxable income in 1958 is $2,500. What is the carryover into 1959?
16. A calendar year taxpayer incurred net operating losses of $13,000 in 1960 and $7,000 in 1961. Taxable income in 1958 was $6,000 after deducting $1,500 for the excess of net long-term capital gain over net short-term capital loss, and $1,800 for personal exemptions. There were no other carrybacks or carryovers. What is the net operating loss deduction for 1958? What is the net operating loss deduction for 1959?
17. A jeweler had a net operating loss for the calendar year 1961 of $16,000 that he carried back to 1958. His taxable income for 1958 was $12,000 and was computed with a deduction for capital losses of $1,000. His personal exemption was $1,200. What is the amount of the net operating loss from 1961 which he may carry back to 1959, after applying it against 1958 income?

15

SPECIAL TAX TREATMENT FOR INDIVIDUALS

In most respects, the income tax law applies to *taxable events.* The nature of the taxpayer is not the decisive factor. Thus, "The term 'person' shall be construed to mean and include an individual, a trust, estate, partnership, association, company or corporation." [1] But for a number of purposes, an individual sustains individualized tax treatment because he is an individual. It is the purpose of this chapter to discuss those areas where an individual is not treated in the same manner as are other taxpayers.

Joint Returns. Under most circumstances, a husband and wife are permitted to file joint income tax returns. See Chapter 24. This privilege is open only to individuals.[2]

Adjusted Gross Income. Certain deductions of an individual are geared to an item on the personal income tax return known as *adjusted gross income.* Adjusted gross income is used as the basis for the determination of the following:

(1) The optional tax if adjusted gross income is less than $10,000. See Chapter 24.

(2) The amount of the standard deduction. See Chapter 24.

(3) The limitation on the amount of the deduction for charitable contributions. See Chapter 9.

(4) The limitation on the amount of the deduction for medical and dental expenses, to be discussed later in this chapter.

(5) In certain cases, the limitation on the deduction for expenses of care of certain dependents under Section 214 of the Code. See Chapter 24.

Adjusted gross income means gross income (see Chapter 4) minus the following deductions:

(1) Deductions attributable to a trade or business carried on by

[1] I.R.C. Section 7701(a).
[2] I.R.C. Section 6013(a).

the taxpayer, if this trade or business does not consist of the performance of services by the taxpayer as an employee.

(2) Trade and business deductions of employees of the following types:

(A) Reimbursement of expenses paid or incurred by the taxpayer in connection with the performance by him of services as an employee, under a reimbursement or other expense allowance arrangement with his employer.

(B) Expenses for travel, meals, and lodgings while away from home, paid or incurred by the taxpayer in connection with the performance by him of services as an employee.

(C) Transportation expenses paid or incurred by the taxpayer in connection with the performance by him of services as an employee.

(D) Expenses which are attributable to a trade or business carried on by the taxpayer, if this trade or business consists of the performance of duties by him as an employee and if this trade or business is to solicit, away from the employer's place of business, business for the employer. This applies only to full-time salesmen. Except for meals, these expenses are deductible even though the salesman is not away from home; he may not deduct the cost of meals, unless he is traveling away from home. A person is not an outside salesman if his principal duties are in the nature of service or delivery.

(3) If for any taxable year the net long-term capital gain exceeds the net short-term capital loss, 50% of the amount of this excess is a deduction from gross income.[3]

(4) Losses from sales or exchanges of property.

(5) Deductions attributable to rents and royalties which relate to property held for the production of income.

(6) Deduction and depletion in the case of a life tenant of property, or an income beneficiary of property held in trust, or an heir, legatee, or devisee of an estate.[4]

Expenses paid or incurred by an employee which are deductible from gross income in computing taxable income and for which he is reimbursed by the employer under an express agreement for reimbursement or pursuant to an expense allowance arrangement may be deducted from gross income in computing adjusted gross income. Where an employee is reimbursed by his employer in an amount less than his total expense, and the reimbursement is in-

[3] I.R.C. Section 1202.

[4] I.R.C. Section 62.

tended to cover all types of deductible expenses, expenses (other than those described in (B), (C), and (D), above) are taken into account in computing adjusted gross income in an amount which bears the same ratio to the amount of the reimbursement as the total amount of deductible expenses computed without those described in (B), (C), and (D) bears to the total amount of deductible expenses, including those described in (B), (C), and (D).[5]

Illustration. An employee, who is not an outside salesman, received a salary of $20,000 and an expense allowance of $1,200 in a certain taxable year. He expended $800 for travel, meals, and lodging while away from home, $500 for local transportation expenses, and $300 for the entertainment of customers. His adjusted gross income is computed as follows:

Salary	$20,000		
Expense allowance	1,200		
Gross income		$21,200	
Less: Travel—meals and lodgings while away from home	$ 800		
Transportation expense	500		
Reimbursed expenses *	225	1,525	
Adjusted gross income			$19,675

* The amount of the reimbursement allocable to entertainment expenses is:

Travel, meals, and lodging while away from home	$ 800	
Transportation expense	500	
Expenses deductible in arriving at adjusted gross income (whether or not reimbursed)	1,300	
Entertainment expense	300	
Total expenses	$1,600	
Deductible for adjusted gross income: 300/1,600 × $1,200 (expense allowance)		$225

Contributions. An individual may deduct charitable contributions as defined in Section 170(c) of the Code, as discussed in Chapter 9. Except in the case of the unlimited deduction discussed in that chapter, the deduction is limited in any taxable year to 20% of the individual's adjusted gross income, or 30% of adjusted gross in the case of contributions to (1) a church or a convention or association of churches, (2) an educational organization, or (3) a hospital or to a medical research organization directly engaged in the continuous active conduct of medical research in conjunction with a hospital, if during the calendar year in which the contribution is made this organization is committed to spend the contributions for this research before January 1 of the fifth calendar year which begins after the date this contribution is made.[6]

[5] Regulations Section 1.62–1(f)(1).
[6] I.R.C. Section 170(b)(1).

Medical, Dental, Etc., Expenses. An individual may take a limited deduction for payments for certain medical and dental expenses (including expenses for medicine and drugs). Except in the case of decedents (see below), a deduction is allowable only to individuals and only with respect to medical expenses actually paid during the taxable year, regardless of when the incident or event which occasioned the expenses occurred and regardless of the method of accounting employed by the taxpayer in making his income tax return. Thus, if the medical expenses are incurred but not paid during the taxable year, no deduction for these expenses will be allowed for that year.[7]

For medical expenses paid (including expenses paid for medicine and drugs) to be deductible, they must be for medical care of the taxpayer, his spouse, or a dependent of the taxpayer. They must not be compensated for by insurance or otherwise.

Where either the taxpayer or his spouse has attained the age of 65 before the end of the taxable year, the 3% limitation (see below) on the deduction for medical expenses does not apply with respect to expenses for the medical care of the taxpayer or his spouse.

Amounts paid for medicine and drugs are to be taken into account in computing the allowable deduction for medical expenses paid during the taxable year only to the extent that the aggregate of these amounts exceeds 1% of the adjusted gross income for the taxable year. Thus, if the aggregate of the amounts paid for medicine and drugs exceeds 1% of adjusted gross income, the excess is added to other medical expenses for the purpose of computing the medical expense deduction.

The medical expense deduction is the amount by which the expenditure exceeds 3% of the taxpayer's adjusted gross income for the year of the payment. There is a ceiling for the allowable deduction. The maximum deduction allowable for medical expenses paid in any one taxable year is the lesser of:

(1) $2,500 multiplied by the number of exemptions allowed, exclusive of the exemptions for a taxpayer or spouse attaining the age of 65 and exclusive of the additional exemption for a taxpayer who is blind or a spouse who is blind. These additional deductions are discussed in Chapter 24.

(2) $5,000, if the taxpayer is single, not the head of a household, and not a surviving spouse. The second and third of these characterizations are discussed in Chapter 24.

(3) $10,000, if the taxpayer is married and files a joint return with his spouse, or is the head of a household or a surviving spouse.

[7] I.R.C. Section 213.

If a taxpayer is 65 or older and is disabled, or if his spouse meets these qualifications, and if the spouse does not file a separate return, the maximum medical expense deduction is $15,000. If both spouses are 65 or older and disabled, the maximum deduction on a joint return is $30,000. But only $15,000 may be taken into account for medical payments of any one individual taxpayer or spouse. An individual is considered to be disabled if he is unable to engage in any substantial gainful activity by reason of any medically determinable physical or mental impairment which can be expected to result in death or to be of long-continued and indefinite duration.[8]

Illustration. A husband and wife make a joint return for the calendar year and were allowed five exemptions (exclusive of those because of age or blindness), one for each taxpayer and three for their dependents. Adjusted income for the husband and wife during the taxable year was $40,000. They paid during the year $12,500 for medical care, no part of which is compensated for by insurance or otherwise. The deduction allowable for the taxable year is $10,000, computed as follows:

Payments for medical care in the taxable year..................	$12,500
Less: 3% of $40,000 (adjusted gross income)...................	1,200
Excess of medical expenses over 3% of adjusted gross income..	$11,300
Allowable deduction ($2,500 × 5 exemptions, but not in excess of $10,000)	$10,000

Expenses for medical care of a deceased taxpayer which are paid out of his estate during the 1-year period beginning with the day after the date of his death arc treated as paid by the taxpayer at the time the medical services were rendered. But no credit or refund of tax will be allowed for any taxable year for which the statutory period for filing a claim has expired. See Chapter 26. If this deduction is claimed on the income tax return of a decedent, there must be a waiver of the right to claim the deduction on the estate tax return for the decedent.[9]

The term "medical care" includes the diagnosis, cure, mitigation, treatment, or prevention of disease. Expenses paid for "medical care" include those paid for the purpose of affecting any structure or function of the body, for accident or health insurance, or for transportation primarily for and essential to medical care. Amounts paid for hospitalization insurance, for membership in an association furnishing cooperative or so-called free-choice medical service, or for group hospitalization and clinical care are expenses paid for medical care. But premiums paid by a taxpayer under an insurance contract which provides reimbursement for loss of earnings due to

[8] I.R.C. Section 213(g).
[9] I.R.C. Section 213(d)(2)(A).

accident or illness do not constitute amounts expended for medical care. In the case of a policy providing reimbursement for both loss of earnings and medical expenses, only the pro rata portion of the premium payments which is properly attributable to the coverage for medical expenses will constitute an expense paid for medical care.[10]

A capital expenditure for a permanent improvement or betterment of property is not deductible as an expenditure for medical care, even though it may have some relation to medical care. Thus, the cost of a swimming pool, the addition of an elevator, or a first-floor bedroom and bath to a house for the benefit of a person unable to climb stairs, the installation of an oil burner to alleviate an allergy to coal, etc., would not be deductible. But the cost of a reclining chair purchased by a taxpayer with a cardiac condition on his doctor's advice qualifies as a medical deduction if it is not generally used as an article of furniture.[11]

Expenses paid for transportation primarily for and essential to the rendition of the medical care are expenses paid for medical care. But an amount allowable as a deduction for "transportation primarily for and essential to medical care will not include the cost of any meals and lodgings while away from home receiving medical treatment. Thus, if a physician prescribes that a taxpayer go to a warm climate in order to alleviate a specific chronic ailment, the cost of meals and lodging while there would not be deductible. On the other hand, if the travel is undertaken merely for the general improvement of a taxpayer's health, neither the cost of the transportation nor the cost of meals and lodging would be deductible. "[M]any expenses, such as the cost of vacations, though undoubtedly highly and directly beneficial to the general health, or athletic club expenses by means of which an individual keeps physically fit, are not deductible because they fall within the category of personal or living expenses. To be deductible as medical expense, there must be a direct or proximate relation between the expense and the diagnosis, cure, mitigation, treatment, or prevention of disease or the expense must have been incurred for the purpose of affecting some structure or function of the body." [12]

To qualify as "medical expense," the payee need not be a physician. Thus, payments to a Christian Science practitioner may be deductible.[13] Amounts paid to qualified psychologists come within

[10] *Drayton Heard et al.*, 30 T.C. 1093 (1958).
[11] Revenue Ruling 58–155, I.R.B. 1958–15, 12.
[12] *Edward A. Havey*, 12 T.C. 409 (1949).
[13] Revenue Ruling 55–261, 1955–1 CB 307.

the meaning of medical care, and thus are deductible within the limits of the Code.[14]

The cost of special education, training, and treatment afforded a mentally retarded child in an institution is deductible. The total cost of meals, lodging, and ordinary education that is furnished to a mentally retarded child attending a special school is deductible only if his condition is such that the resources of the institution for alleviating the mental or physical handicap is a principal reason for the child's presence there. It is immaterial whether medical care is furnished in a public or private residence.[15]

Sick Pay

This subject is treated in Chapter 4.

Personal Injuries

Compensation for personal injuries is discussed in Chapter 4.

Losses

This subject is treated in Chapter 13.

Alimony

Alimony payments, including payments of temporary alimony, are generally deductible by the husband if the payments are required to be included in the income of the wife. For convenience, the payee spouse will be referred to in this section as the "wife" and the spouse from whom she is divorced or separated as the "husband." The rules and principles will apply with equal force to the converse.

Income. In the case of divorce or legal separation, the wife must include in her gross income all periodic payments (whether or not made at regular intervals) received by her after a decree of divorce or of separate maintenance. These periodic payments must be made in discharge of a legal obligation imposed upon or incurred by the husband because of the marital or family relationship under a court order or decree divorcing or legally separating the husband and wife or a written instrument incident to this divorce status or legal separation status.[16]

[14] Revenue Ruling 143, 1953–2 CB 129.
[15] Revenue Ruling 58–280, I.R.B. 1958–23, 13.
[16] I.R.C. Section 71.

Where the husband and wife are separated and living apart and do not file a joint income tax return for the taxable year, the wife must include in her gross income all periodic payments (whether or not made at regular intervals) received by her pursuant to a written separation agreement executed after December 16, 1954. The periodic payments must be made under the terms of the written separation agreement after its execution and because of the marital or family relationship. These payments are includible in the wife's gross income whether or not the agreement is a legally enforceable instrument. Moreover, if the wife is divorced or legally separated subsequent to the written separation agreement, payments made under this agreement continue to be taxed in this manner.

Where the husband and wife are separated and living apart and do not file a joint income tax return, the wife must include in her gross income all periodic payments (whether or not made at regular intervals) received by her after August 16, 1954, from her husband under any type of court order or decree entered after March 1, 1954, requiring the husband to make the payments for her support or maintenance. It is not necessary for the wife to be legally separated or divorced from her husband under a court order or decree; nor is it necessary for the order or decree for support to be for the purpose of enforcing a written separation agreement.

Periodic payments are includible in the wife's income only for the taxable year in which received by her. As to these amounts, the wife is to be treated as if she makes her income tax returns on the cash method, regardless of whether she normally makes her returns on the accrual method. But, if the periodic payments are made by an estate or trust, these payments are to be included in the wife's taxable year in which they are includible according to the rules as to income of estates and trusts, whether or not the payments are made out of the estate or trust income.

In the case of divorce or legal separation, the wife must include in gross income all periodic payments (whether or not made at regular intervals) attributable to property transferred, in trust or otherwise, and received by her after a decree of divorce or of separate maintenance. This property must have been transferred in discharge of a legal obligation imposed upon or incurred by the husband because of the marital or family relationship under a decree of divorce or separate maintenance or under a written instrument incident to divorce or legal separation status. Where the spouses are separated and living apart, and do not file a joint return, the wife must include in her income all periodic payments which are attributable to property transferred, in trust or otherwise, under a written separation agreement executed after August 16, 1954. The property must be transferred because of the marital or family relationship.

The full amount of periodic payments received under a decree of divorce or separate maintenance, a written separation agreement, or a decree for support must be included in the wife's gross income, regardless of the source of the payments. Thus, it is immaterial whether these payments are attributable to property in trust; to life insurance, endowment, or annuity contracts; or to any other interest in property or are paid directly or indirectly by the husband from his income or capital. If the husband pays medical expenses of the wife under a decree or agreement, and the payments qualify as periodic payments, the wife must include them in her gross income; but to the extent that they are allowable deductions as medical expenses, she may deduct them.

Child support is not alimony. Payments which have been specified as support for minor children are not includible in the wife's gross income. This applies even though the payments are made through a probation officer. When payments are required for both alimony and child support, and the payments made are less than the amount called for in the decree or agreement, these lower payments are first considered as support for the children before any amount is considered as alimony for the wife. If the portion of periodic payments for the support of minor children is not identifiable from the court decree or separation agreement, the entire amount is includible in the wife's income.

Illustration. In the taxable year, in accordance with the terms of a divorce decree, a husband paid his divorced wife $350 a month, $200 of which was for the support of their minor children, as specified in the decree. Total payments for the year were $4,200. The wife is required to include $1,800 in her income as alimony. The $2,400 paid for support of the children is not reportable by the wife. But it is counted as support furnished by the husband in determining who is entitled to the dependency deduction for the children. See Chapter 24.

In general, installment payments discharging a part of an obligation the principal sum of which is in terms of money or property, specified in the decree, instrument, or agreement, are not considered "periodic payments" and, therefore, are not to be included in the wife's income. But an exception is made in cases where this principal sum, by the terms of the decree, instrument, or agreement, may be or is to be paid over a period ending more than ten years from the date of the decree, etc. In such cases, the installment payment is considered a periodic payment, but only to the extent that the installment payment (or sum of the installment payments) received during the wife's taxable year does not exceed 10% of the principal sum. This 10% limitation applies to installment payments made in advance but does not apply to delinquent installment payments for a prior taxable year of the wife, made during her taxable year.

Where payments under a decree, instrument, or agreement are to be paid over a period ending ten years or less from the date of the decree, etc., these payments are not installment payments discharging a part of an obligation the principal sum of which is, in terms of money or property, specified in the decree, etc. Such payments are considered periodic payments only if the following two conditions are met:

(1) The payments are subject to any one or more of the contingencies of death of either spouse, remarriage of the wife, or change in the economic status of either spouse, and

(2) The payments are in the nature of alimony or an allowance for support.

Payments meeting the above requirements are considered periodic payments regardless of whether—

(1) The contingencies described above are set forth in the terms of the decree, instrument, or agreement, or are imposed by local law, or

(2) The aggregate amount of the payments to be made in the absence of the occurrence of the contingencies described above is explicitly stated in the decree, etc., or may be calculated from the face of the decree, etc., or

(3) The total amount which will be paid may be calculated actuarially.

The following items are not included in the wife's gross income:

(1) Lump-sum cash settlements required by a decree, etc. Such a settlement is not a periodic payment.

(2) Any payment that is not required by the decree, etc., inasmuch as the payment is not made in discharge of a legal obligation.

(3) Any payment made by the husband without legal obligation after the wife remarries.

(4) Any payment that is required by the decree, etc., that does not arise out of the marital relationship, such as a repayment of a loan to the wife.

(5) Any payment made before the decree or agreement or any payments of so-called alimony accruing before a decree, etc., and paid subsequently, inasmuch as the payment is not incident to the decree, etc.

Deductions. The payor of alimony (the husband, in all of the examples and text in this discussion) is allowed a tax deduction for periodic payments in the nature of, or in lieu of, alimony or an allowance for support actually paid by the taxpayer during his taxable year, if the amount was required to be included in his former wife's gross income.[17] This deduction is available only to the paying spouse. It is not allowed to an estate, trust, corporation, or any other person who may pay the alimony obligation of the obligor spouse. Nor is the obligor spouse allowed a deduction for any periodic payment includible in the income of the spouse or former spouse, if that payment is attributable to property transferred in discharge of his obligation and which is not includible in his gross income.

Illustration. Pursuant to the terms of a decree of divorce, the husband transferred securities in trust for the benefit of his wife, which transfer fully discharged all of his obligations to her. The periodic payments made by the trust to the wife must be included in her gross income. These payments are not includible in his income and, therefore, they are not deductible from his income.

Nonresident Aliens

The subject of personal service income of nonresident aliens is treated in Chapter 22.

Income Earned Abroad

The tax treatment of income earned abroad by citizens or residents of the United States is treated in Chapter 22.

Personal Residence

Special tax treatment afforded to disposition of one's personal residence under certain circumstances is dealt with in Chapter 6.

Child Care Expense

An individual may be entitled to deduct expenses paid for the care of certain dependents where the care is for the purpose of enabling the taxpayer gainfully to be employed. These expenses are referred to as "child care" expenses. The deduction may not exceed $600 for any taxable year (regardless of the number of dependents for whose care the expenses are paid) and is allowed only for ex-

[17] I.R.C. Section 215.

penses incurred while the taxpayer is gainfully employed or in active search of gainful employment. The employment which is the cause of the incurring of the expenses may, however, consist of services either within or without the home of the taxpayer. Self-employment qualifies as employment for this purpose.[18]

Taxpayers Who May Qualify for the Deduction. This deduction is allowed only to a woman or a widower.

(1) *A widower.* The deduction is allowed for expenses paid by a taxpayer who is a widower at the time the expenses are incurred. The term "widower" includes (A) a man whose wife has died and who has not remarried, (B) a man who is divorced from his wife and has not remarried, and (C) a man who is legally separated from his wife under a decree of legal separation.

(2) *A married woman whose husband is capable of self-support.* If the expenses are paid by a woman (A) who is married at the time the expenses are incurred, (B) whose husband at that time is incapable of self-support because he is mentally defective or physically disabled, and (C) who is not divorced or legally separated at the end of the taxable year, the deduction is allowed, but only if she files a joint income tax return with her husband for the taxable year in which the expenses are paid. Further, the amount otherwise deductible must be reduced by the amount, if any, by which the combined adjusted gross income of the taxpayer and her spouse exceeds $4,500 for the taxable year in which the expenses are paid. The amount otherwise deductible is the amount expended for the child's care or $600, whichever is lesser.

(3) *A married woman whose husband is incapable of self-support.* The deduction is allowed without regard to the limitations described in (2), above, for expenses paid by a married woman whose husband is incapable of self-support because he is mentally defective or physically disabled at the time the expenses are incurred. Where the husband is capable of self-support for part of a taxable year, the child care expenses incurred for that part will be treated under (2), above.

(4) *A single woman.* The deduction is also allowed without regard to the limitations described in (2), above, for expenses paid by a woman who is unmarried at the time the expenses are incurred, or who is, at the close of her taxable year, legally separated from her husband under a decree of divorce or of separate maintenance.

A wife who was separated from her husband was allowed to claim both the dependency credit (see Chapter 24) and the child care

[18] I.R.C. Section 214.

deduction on her own return, where she furnished more than half of the support of the child.[19]

Determination of Status. If child care expenses are incurred in one taxable year and paid in another, the status of a taxpayer will be determined as of the year in which the expenses are incurred, and not when the expenses are paid.

Computation of Deduction. The deduction for child care expenses is allowable only with respect to those expenses actually paid during the taxable year regardless of when the event which occasioned the expenses occurred and regardless of the method of accounting employed by the taxpayer in making his income tax return. If child care expenses are incurred but not paid during the taxable year, no deduction can be taken for that year.

Illustration. The taxpayer was a widower during the taxable year until September 1, when he remarried. He paid $50 each month for child care expenses. He may take into account only the expenses paid during the year which were incurred while he was unmarried. Inasmuch as the expenses were $400 ($50 per month from January to August, inclusive), the amount of the deduction is $400. If he had paid $100 per month, the deduction would be limited to $600, although the expenses incurred while he was unmarried amounted to $800.

Illustration. A husband and wife were married during the entire taxable year. The wife paid $900 for child care expenses incurred during the year. The combined adjusted gross income of husband and wife for the year was $5,000. The allowable deduction is $100 ($600, the maximum deduction allowable, reduced by $500, the excess of adjusted gross income of $5,000 over $4,500). The deduction of $100 is allowable only if the husband and wife made a joint return.

Illustration. During the taxable year, a woman paid $50 each month for child care expenses. She was unmarried until April 1, and was married for the remainder of the year. Her husband was capable of self-support, and the combined adjusted gross income of husband and wife was $4,700. They made a joint return for the taxable year. The total deduction allowable to her is $400, computed as follows: $150 as expenses incurred while she was a single woman and $250 as expenses incurred while she was married; the $250 is arrived at by taking the amount expended while she was married, $450, and reducing it by $200 (the excess of adjusted gross income, $4,700 over $4,500).

Dependents. The deduction is allowed only for expenses paid for the care of an individual who (for the taxable year of the taxpayer in which the expenses are incurred) is a dependent of the taxpayer for whom an exemption is allowed under Section 151; see Chapter 24. Furthermore, the dependent, at the time the expenses are incurred, must be either (1) under the age of twelve years or (2) physically or mentally unable to care for himself. The deduction

[19] *Paul Lustig et al.*, 30 T.C. #94 (1958).

under (1) is allowed even though the dependent is not a child or stepchild of the taxpayer. It is not necessary that the dependent be permanently disabled in order for the amount expended for his care to be deductible. But the mere fact that the disability, whether temporary or permanent, renders him incapable of self-support does not necessarily mean that he is incapable of self-care.

Payments to a Dependent. No deduction is allowed for expenses paid to an individual for whom the taxpayer is allowed (for the taxable year in which the expenses are paid) an exemption under Section 151 (see Chapter 24).

Illustration. The taxpayer, a working widow, supports her mother and is entitled to claim her as a dependent. Consequently, she may not deduct amounts paid to the mother for the care of the taxpayer's children.

Deductible Expenses. In order for an expense to be deductible, it must meet three conditions: (1) the expense must be for the care of a dependent, (2) it must be for a dependent's care while the taxpayer is gainfully employed or in search of gainful employment, and (3) the expense must be for the purpose of enabling the taxpayer gainfully to be employed.

Expenses for the care of a dependent are those for the primary purpose of assuring the dependent's well-being and protection. It does not include all benefits which may be bestowed upon him. Thus, amounts expended to provide food, clothing, or education are not, in themselves, amounts expended for "care" so as to be deductible. But where the manner of providing care is such that the expense which must be incurred includes payments for other benefits which are inseparably a part of the care, the full amount of the expense will be considered to be incurred for care. Thus, the full amount paid to a nursery school will be considered to be for the care of the child, even though the school also furnishes lunch, recreational activities, and other benefits.

Even if an expense is incurred for the care of a dependent, it is not deductible unless it is incurred for the purpose of permitting the taxpayer gainfully to be employed.

An expense which may constitute a deductible medical expense may also constitute a deductible child care expense. In such a case, that part of the amount for which a deduction is allowed as child care expense will not be treated as a medical expense. But where an amount is treated as a medical expense, it will not be allowed as a child care expense.

Illustration. A single woman pays $720 during the taxable year for the care of her child, who suffers from infantile paralysis. It is assumed that the expenses are of a nature which qualify as medical expenses. It is also assumed that these expenses are for the purpose of permitting her gainfully to be employed. Her adjusted gross income for the taxable year is $5,000. She is allowed a deduction of $600 for child care expenses. The balance of the expenses, or $120, she treats as medical expenses. But this amount does not exceed 3% of her adjusted gross income and is thus not allowable as a medical expense deduction.

Farmers

Farmers are subject to the same general rules of taxation as are other taxpayers. Special rules applicable to farmers are treated in this division.

The wage-earners' reporting form (Form 1040A, discussed in Chapter 23) may not be used by farmers; this form is used by individuals whose income is solely from wages, and, perhaps, a small amount of dividends and interest. Such also is the case with Form 1040W. But as an appendage to the regular tax return (Form 1040) farmers may use Schedule F, on which will be entered all farm income and deductions in order to arrive at net farm profit or loss, which is carried forward to the regular income tax form. Schedule F is used whether the taxpayer is on the cash or the accrual method.

Income To Be Reported. Sales or trades of livestock, whether raised or purchased, if held primarily for sale, produce ordinary farm income. If sold, the amount of money received must be shown. If traded, the fair market value of the property, plus any money received, must be shown.

Sales and trades of livestock, held for draft, breeding, or dairy purposes, and held for twelve months or more from the date of acquisition sometimes result in ordinary gains or losses and sometimes result in capital gains and losses, depending upon the circumstances.[20] Also, if property is destroyed, stolen, seized, requisitioned, or condemned, in whole or in part, and other property or money (including insurance proceeds and condemnation awards) is received in payment, it may give rise to ordinary gain or loss or capital gain or loss. See Chapter 13.

In the case of produce raised or purchased by the taxpayer, he must include in income the fair market value of any property or services received from the sale or exchange.

A taxpayer who receives a loan from the Commodity Credit Corporation may, at his election, include the amount of this loan in his gross income for the taxable year in which the loan is received, instead of in the year when the commodity is finally sold.[21] No

[20] I.R.C. Section 1231.
[21] I.R.C. Section 77.

formal permission is required. An election is made by including the amount of the loan in income in the year it is received and attaching a statement to the return indicating that the election was made. But once a return is filed on this basis, all such succeeding loans must be reported as income in the year received unless permission is obtained from the Internal Revenue Service to make a change.

If Commodity Credit loans are reported as income in the year the loan is received, then in the year the commodity is sold there must be reported as additional income any amount received in excess of the loan.

Rents received in crop shares must be reported in income in the year in which the crop shares are reduced to money or the equivalent, whether the cash or the accrual method is used.

All Government payments (such as those for approved conservation practices) must be included in gross income, whether received in cash or in materials, such as fertilizer or lime. Payments received under the Soil Bank Act for reducing crop acreage below acreage allotments or base acreage must be included in gross income. Likewise included are payments received under the Soil Bank Act to cover the cost of establishing conservation practices and the annual rental on acreage placed in the conservation reserve.

Patronage dividends received from cooperatives (whether in cash, stock certificates, revolving fund certificates, or any other form) generally should be included in farm income in the year received.[22] Patronage dividends arising from purchases of nonbusiness items should not be included in income. Dividends which result from the purchase of capital assets or depreciable property used in the business are not to be included in income, but the cost of the items purchased must be reduced accordingly. If patronage dividends are received in document form in prior years which should have been included in income in the year received, but were not, or if deductible expenses were not reduced by the amount of the dividend, an amended return should be filed for any year not yet closed by the statute of limitations (see Chapter 26); the dividends should then be included in income for that year. But if the statute of limitations has expired and cash or other property is received in a later year in redemption of the document, the taxpayer should report this cash or property in income in the year received.

Other farm income might include soil and gravel sales, sod sales, gasoline tax refunds (inasmuch as farm vehicles may not have been used on a road, for the cost or upkeep of which road a part of the

[22] I.R.C. Section 522.

gasoline tax applies), income from rights of way, proceeds of insurance on growing crops, and prizes won on farm livestock or products at county fairs, etc.

Farm Business Expenses. Any farmer who operates a farm for profit is entitled to deduct all his ordinary and necessary expenses of carrying on the business of farming. The farm must be operated for profit and there must be a reasonable expectation of profit.[23]

Deductions include expense of labor, repairs and maintenance (if the expenditures do not add to the value or prolong the life of property), fertilizers and lime, property taxes, premiums on insurance on farm properties, interest on farm mortgages, farm rent, depreciation on farming implements and buildings, penalties paid for marketing crops in excess of farm marketing quotas, insect sprays and dusts, trucking, tying materials, and containers.

Capital Expenditures. There are three definite periods in the life of a farm, ranch, orchard, or grove. These are (1) the preparatory period, (2) the development period, and (3) the productive period.

Expenditures made during the preparatory period in establishing a farm, etc., may not be deducted. They must be capitalized (that is, added to the cost). Typical preparatory expenditures (including material and labor costs) which must be capitalized are the costs of clearing brush, trees, and stumps; leveling and conditioning land; trees and the planting of trees; drilling and equipping wells; building irrigation canals and ditches; laying irrigation pipes; installing drain tile; straightening creek beds; constructing earthen, masonry, or concrete tanks, reservoirs, or dams; building roads.

During the development period, a taxpayer may capitalize his expenditures which are incident to current operations, or he may deduct them as current expenses. Expenditures of a capital nature, however, may not be deducted in any stage, unless they are for soil or water conservation. Among the expenditures which may be capitalized *or* deducted during the development period are the cost of the upkeep, taxes, water for irrigation, fertilizer, controlling undergrowth, and cultivating and spraying of trees.

When the farm, etc., reaches its productive period, a taxpayer loses the option he had during the development period. The business is now a full-fledged operating business, and ordinary and necessary expenses cannot be capitalized. Instead, these expenses should be

[23] *George W. Cutting et al.*, T.C. Memo., Docket ##12682 and 111970-1, entered December 18, 1947.

deducted each year, when they are incurred (if an accrual basis is used) or when they are paid (if a cash basis is used).[24]

Farm Inventories. If an accrual method is used, opening and closing inventories must be taken into account. All unsold items on hand at the close of the taxable year which are held for sale or for use as feed, seed, etc. are to be included in inventory. Examples are:

(1) Farm products (whether raised or purchased), such as grain, hay, ensilage, concentrates, cotton, tobacco, and other crops held for sale or for feed.

(2) All livestock raised or purchased and held primarily for sale.

(3) Supplies, unless only small amounts are on hand. Growing or standing crops are not included.

Livestock held for draft, dairy, or breeding purposes (and not primarily for sale) may be capitalized and depreciated, or they may be included in inventory. If they are included, no deduction may be taken for depreciation. A consistent practice must be followed.

Inventories may be valued on the basis of cost; cost or market, whichever is lower; farm price method; or unit-livestock-price method (for valuing livestock inventories only).

Under the *farm price method,* each item (whether raised or purchased) is valued at the market price less the estimated direct cost of disposition. Market price means the current price at the nearest market in the quantity usually sold. Cost of disposition includes brokers' commissions, freight, hauling to market, and other marketing costs. If this method is employed, it must be used for the entire inventory, except that livestock may be inventoried on the unit-livestock-price method.

Under the *unit-livestock-price method,* the livestock is grouped or classified according to kind and age. A standard unit price is used for each animal within a class or group. Unit prices assigned to animals should be such as to account for the costs of production. A reasonable approximation of costs of production will be accepted.

Illustration. A farmer determined that it costs him $25 to produce a calf and $15 each year to raise the calf to maturity. The following classifications and unit prices are selected to value the inventory of raised livestock:

Calves	$25
Yearlings	40
Two-year-olds	55
Mature animals	70

Once the unit prices and classifications have been established, they may not be changed without the permission of the Internal Revenue Service.

[24] Mimeograph 6030, 1948–2 CB 45.

If this method is used, all livestock raised, regardless of whether held for sale or for breeding, dairy, or draft purposes, must be included in the inventory. Livestock purchased primarily for sale must also be included in the inventory. Livestock purchased for breeding, dairy, or draft purposes may be included in inventory or treated as assets subject to depreciation. Either practice may be adopted, but then it must be followed consistently.

Animals purchased after maturity should be inventoried or capitalized at their purchase price. If the animals purchased are not mature at the time of purchase, the cost should be increased at the end of each year by the same amount that is added each year to the inventory of raised animals of the same classification. But no increase is made in the year of purchase if the animal is purchased during the last 6 months of the taxable year.

Persons in the Armed Forces

Basically, individuals in the armed forces are subject to the same tax treatment as are civilians. This division will deal with exceptions.

Compensation received by a member of the armed forces for service in a combat area is exempt from income tax.[25] But no combat area has existed within the meaning of this act since January 31, 1955, when combat in Korea was proclaimed at end.[26]

Payments made by employers during the military service of an employee are taxable income to the recipient.[27]

It has been held that "commutation of quarters and rental value of quarters occupied by officers of the army are not taxable income, since the government furnishes the quarters as part of the military establishment." [28] This rule has been extended to those under the rank of commissioned officer.[29]

The cost of uniforms is a personal expense, although the uniforms only can be worn on certain occasions.[30] No deduction is allowed for such items as gold lace, gilt buttons, and cap devices; but the cost of corps devices, epaulets, and company bars is deductible.[31] The cost of laundering uniforms is not deductible.[32]

[25] I.R.C. Section 112.

[26] Executive Order 10585, January 1, 1955.

[27] Press Release No. 140.

[28] *Jones v. United States,* 60 Ct. Cl. 552 (1925).

[29] Ruling by Timothy C. Mooney, Deputy Commissioner of Internal Revenue, December 31, 1942.

[30] I.T. 1937, III-1 CB 200.

[31] I.T. 1965, III-1 CB 201.

[32] I.T. 1903, III-1 CB 200.

Allowances for uniforms are not taxable.[33]

If an individual dies while in active service in the armed forces, and his death occurs while serving in a combat zone or at any place as a result of wounds, disease, or injury incurred while in a combat zone, his tax liability for the taxable year ending on the date of his death, and for any prior taxable year ending on or after the first day he served in a combat zone after June 24, 1950, is canceled; any tax so collected (regardless of the date of collection) will be refunded.[34]

Personal Residence. Under certain circumstances, gain on the sale of an individual's principal residence will not be taxed; specifically, if the full proceeds are reinvested in the acquisition of another principal residence within a stipulated period.[35] See Chapter 6.

In the case of members of the armed forces, the running of the standard 1-year period after the sale of the old residence in the case of the purchase of a new residence, or the 18-month period after the sale in the case of the construction of a new residence, is suspended during any time of service on extended active duty during an induction period.

Illustration. If the taxpayer is on extended active duty with the army from January 1, 1959, to December 31, 1961, and if he sold his old residence on January 1, 1959, the latest date on which the taxpayer may use a new residence constructed by him and have any part of the gain on the sale of the old residence not recognized is January 1, 1963, the date four years after the date of sale of the old residence.

This suspension covers not only the armed forces service of the taxpayer but if the taxpayer and his same spouse used both the old and the new residences as their principal residence, then the extension applies in like manner to the time the taxpayer's spouse is on extended active duty with the armed forces.

Compensation

For a discussion of the compensation of individuals, see Chapter 11.

Related Parties

A consideration of the extent to which losses between individuals who are related will be disallowed will be found in Chapter 27.

[33] I.T. 3603, 1943 CB 69.
[34] I.R.C. Section 692.
[35] I.R.C. Section 1034.

Supplementary Material

A. Suggested Reading.

Arthur I. Hemmings, "Deductions for the Individual Taxpayer," *Proceedings of the Tulane Seventh Annual Institute on Federal Taxation* (Indianapolis: The Bobbs-Merrill Co., Inc., 1958), p. 614.

Arthur J. Lempert, "Who Can Deduct a Business Expense?" *Tax Law Review,* May, 1956, Vol. XI, #4, p. 433.

Reinhold Groh, "Medical Deductions for Aging, Disabled Taxpayers," *TAXES—The Tax Magazine,* April, 1959, Vol. XXXVII, #4, p. 335.

John P. Hodgkin, "Medical Expenses," *The Encyclopedia of Tax Procedures* (Englewood Cliffs, N.J.: Prentice-Hall, Inc., 1956), p. 1481.

Harry M. Halstead, "Taxation of Farmers: Accounting Methods, Records and Returns," *The Practical Lawyer,* November, 1955, Vol. I, #7, p. 57.

Robert S. Holzman, "Our Army of Taxpayers: The Armed Forces," *TAXES—The Tax Magazine,* March, 1943, Vol. XXI, #3, p. 138.

Alan L. Gornick, "How To Make Arrangements Before and After a Separation or Divorce," *The Encyclopedia of Tax Procedures* (Englewood Cliffs, N.J.: Prentice-Hall, Inc., 1956), p. 1324.

B. Questions.

1. Is there any practical significance to an individual whether he shows an item as a deduction *for* or *from* gross income?
2. The president of a corporation travels to another city to discuss a problem with a customer. To set a good example to his staff, the president does not charge his company but pays the expenses out of his own pocket. (This is a hypothetical situation, of course.) Is this a deduction for adjusted gross income as far as he is concerned?
3. The business of a certain industrialist is manufacturing paint. He sells some Government bonds that he owns at a loss of $1,000. Is this a deduction for adjusted gross income?
4. An elderly Westerner becomes ill, and he summons an Indian medicine man, without professional schooling or instruction of any kind. Are the amounts paid to the medicine man deductible as medical expense? Would your answer be the same if the patient derived no benefit from the treatment?
5. The chief accountant of a company is entitled to eat in his firm's cafeteria, without charge for his meals. Occasionally, he has to go to a governmental agency in the same city about some technical question. Is he entitled to a deduction for adjusted gross income for his meals away from his place of business?
6. Harry and Wilma were married in 1956. In 1961, as a result of an argument with Wilma, Harry incurred injuries which rendered him incapable of self-support until September 1. The adjusted gross income of Harry and Wilma for the year was $4,700. She paid $60 each month for child care expenses. How much of a child care deduction is she entitled to in this taxable year?
7. An unemployed individual, hearing that men with his particular talents were being employed in a city two thousand miles away, traveled there. After a few days, he secured a position. Are his expenses

for travel, room, and board in search of what developed into employment deductible as expenses attributable to business?

8. A divorce decree in 1959 provided that Herbert was to pay Wilhelmina $20,000 each year for the next five years, beginning with the date of the decree, and then $5,000 each year for the next ten years. How much of what Wilhelmina receives is includible in her gross income for each year?
9. An individual on a calendar year basis makes a pledge on December 15, 1960, to give $100 to Alma Mater. He makes payment on January 12, 1961. In what year is the deduction allowed if he is on (a) the cash method or (b) the accrual method?
10. A sergeant, a United States soldier on duty in Germany, married the buxom daughter of the mayor of a community there. May he and his bride file a joint return?
11. A calendar year individual, who is on the cash basis, undergoes an operation in November, 1961. The surgeon submits a bill in December. The bill is paid the following January. Assuming the amount falls within the permissible limits, in what year is the deduction allowed? Would your answer be the same if the bill had been rendered and paid in January?
12. Humphrey and Willa were married for ten years when he died on October 1. The combined adjusted gross income of the spouses was $4,800. Willa paid $50 per month for child care expense throughout the entire year. (a) How much of a child care expense is she entitled to if she files a separate return? (b) If a joint return is filed on behalf of Willa and her deceased husband, what is the allowable deduction?
13. A demonstrator of lightweight kitchenware received a salary of $20,000 and an expense allowance of $1,200 for the taxable year. He spent $800 for travel, meals, and lodging while away from home; $500 for local transportation expenses; and $300 for the entertainment of customers. What is his adjusted gross income?
14. Under a divorce decree, Hugo agreed to pay Wanda $400 monthly, provided his income remained at least as high as it then was. When he failed to make payments, Wanda sued for the $10,000 then owing to her, and collected. How much could Hugo deduct as alimony in the year that he made the payment?
15. An individual had adjusted gross income in 1960 of $10,000. During that year he had allowable medical expenses of $1,000 and spent less than $100 for medicines and drugs. He claimed the following deduction:

Total expenses paid in 1960........................	$1,000
Less: 3% of adjusted gross income.................	300
Allowable deduction	$ 700

In 1961, he collected $400 insurance as reimbursement for part of his 1960 medical expenses. Had he collected the insurance in 1960, his deduction for medical expenses would have been only $300. How is the $400 reimbursement treated for tax purposes?

16. A donor has adjusted gross income of $8,000. He makes contributions totaling $1,500 to churches, tax-exempt schools, and hospitals,

as well as $1,000 to a variety of other qualified organizations. What is the contributions deduction?

17. A man and his wife, who have a dependent, make a joint return for 1960. The husband was 65 on September 1. During the year, the family pays the following medical expense bills: (a) $200 for doctors and $100 for medicines and drugs for themselves; (b) $300 for doctors and hospital expenses and $50 for medicines and drugs for the dependent. What is the allowable medical expense deduction?
18. A single individual, with no dependents, had $5,000 in medical expenses in 1960, when his adjusted gross income was $8,000. He took the maximum allowable deduction of $2,500, the amount by which medical expenses exceeded 3% of adjusted gross income. In 1961, he collected $1,000 insurance as reimbursement for part of his medical expenses of the previous year. How much of this $1,000 is taxable?
19. In the previous question, what would your answer be if the 1961 reimbursement had been $3,000?
20. A pharmacist reported the following for the taxable year:

Gross profit on sales		$17,500
Expenses:		
Salaries	$9,000	
Rent	2,700	
Heat, light, and air-conditioning	1,400	
Other expenses	900	14,000
Net operating profit		$ 3,500
Gain on sale of refrigerator		$ 350
Fire loss on store building		1,200
Net operating loss carryover from previous year		1,000

What are the net earnings from self-employment for the purpose of the self-employment tax?

16

SPECIAL TAX TREATMENT FOR CORPORATIONS

What Is a Corporation?

"The term 'corporation' includes associations, joint-stock companies, and insurance companies."[1] Thus, for tax purposes, there may be treated as corporations certain entities which, in fact, are not corporations. And for certain tax purposes, not every corporation is treated as a corporation. A foreign corporation will not be treated as a corporation in the sense that it may be a party to a tax-free corporate reorganization (see Chapter 17) unless, before the transaction, "it has been established to the satisfaction of the Secretary or his delegate that such exchange is not in pursuance of a plan having as one of its principal purposes the avoidance of Federal income taxes."[2]

If a corporation is formed merely to serve as a device for escaping taxation, it will not be recognized as a corporation. "[T]he term 'corporation' will be interpreted to mean a corporation which does some 'business' in the ordinary meaning; and . . . escaping taxation is not 'business' in the ordinary meaning."[3] "Such a corporation might be in some contexts a 'corporation'; but words are chameleons, which reflect the color of their environment, and in a tax statute 'corporation' could not have been so intended."[4]

Association or Corporation. Sometimes the question arises as to whether a certain entity is to be treated for tax purposes as an association taxable as a partnership (that is, the partners are taxed; see Chapter 18) or as a corporation. The problem arises when the entity has certain attributes of an association and certain attributes of a corporation. The Supreme Court recognized the following fea-

[1] I.R.C. Section 7701(a)(3).

[2] I.R.C. Section 367.

[3] *National Investors Corp. v. Hoey,* 144 F.2d 466 (2d Cir., 1944).

[4] *Commissioner v. National Carbide Corp. et al.,* 167 F.2d 304 (2d Cir., 1948), *aff'd,* 336 U.S. 422 (1949).

tures of an enterprise that is to be regarded as a corporation for tax purposes:

(1) A corporation, as an entity, holds the title to the property embarked in the corporate undertaking.

(2) Corporate organization furnishes the opportunity for a centralized management through representatives of the members of the corporation.

(3) Security of the enterprise from termination or interruption by the death or withdrawal of participating interests.

(4) Corporate organization facilitates the transfer of beneficial interests without affecting the continuity of enterprise.

(5) The corporate organization permits the limitation of personal liability of participants to the property embarked in the undertaking. If the organization in question more nearly resembles an association, or a corporation, it will be taxed as such.[5]

In some cases, the controlling question is not the similarity in form to corporate organizations, but rather the purpose of the alleged association, trust, etc.[6]

Election To Be Taxed as Corporation

Certain proprietorships and partnerships may elect to be taxed as domestic corporations, while still conducting the business of the enterprise as a proprietorship or partnership.[7] "The term 'domestic' when applied to a corporation or partnership means created or organized in the United States or under the law of the United States or of any State or Territory." [8]

An election to be taxed as a corporation must be made not later than sixty days after the close of the taxable year to which the election is first applicable by the proprietor or all the partners having an interest in the enterprise at any time on or after the first day of the taxable year, up to and including the date of election. This requirement includes any owners of the enterprise who may have sold their interests prior to the date of the election.[9] If in a year subsequent to the year of the election there is a change of ownership requiring another election (see below), then all persons owning an interest in the enterprise from the beginning of that year until and including the date of the election must file an election in order to continue to have the enterprise taxed as a corporation.

[5] *Morrissey v. Commissioner,* 296 U.S. 344 (1935).
[6] *Helvering v. Washburn,* 99 F.2d 478 (8th Cir., 1938).
[7] I.R.C. Section 1361.
[8] I.R.C. Section 7701(a)(4).
[9] I.R.C. Section 1361(a).

Qualifications. In order for the enterprise to be taxed as a corporation, this enterprise may not be owned by more than fifty individual taxpayers. If a partnership owns an interest in a partnership as to which an election is to be made, all of the partners of the owning partnership must be individuals and their number must be added to the other partners of the electing partnership in determining the number of partners.

No proprietor or partner having more than a 10% interest in an electing enterprise can be an owner of another proprietorship or have more than a 10% interest in another partnership, either of which is taxable as a domestic corporation.

Illustration. Should an individual have an interest of 10% or less in a partnership taxed as a corporation, he may elect to have his proprietorship taxed as a corporation. But if he should own a proprietorship taxed as a corporation, he would be unable to make the election for another proprietorship, or for a partnership in which he has more than a 10% interest.

No proprietor or partner in an enterprise electing to be taxed as a corporation may be either a nonresident alien or a foreign partnership. (For explanation of these terms, see Chapter 22.)

The enterprise must be either one in which capital is a material income-producing factor, or 50% or more of the gross income of the enterprise consists of earnings derived from trading as a principal or from brokerage commissions derived from selling real property, stock, securities, or commodities for others.

Limitations. The enterprise is to be considered a corporation in all respects for purposes of income taxes, except as to (1) the tax on self-employment income and (2) corporate reorganizations. A proprietor or partner of an enterprise taxed as a corporation may not participate as an employee in any qualified pension or profit-sharing plan of the business.

Effect of Election. The election is binding on the enterprise and its owners as long as the original proprietor, or electing partners who own more than an 80% interest, continue to conduct the business in an unincorporated form. In any year in which the ownership of the proprietorship is changed, or the original electing partners no longer own more than 80% of the partnership, the election is revoked, unless the proprietor or partners make a new election.

Other Rules. There is excluded from the income of the enterprise any income classified as personal holding company income (a subject discussed later in this chapter). Any income so excluded is to be taxed directly to the proprietor or partners; deductions attributable to this income will be similarly treated.

A deduction is allowed for salaries only for those payments to a proprietor or partners which are commensurate with the value of services actually rendered.

All distributions, other than distributions in liquidation (see Chapter 17) made with respect to a proprietorship or partnership income (except distributions of personal holding company income and compensation) will be treated as a distribution made by a corporation to a shareholder and will be taxable as a dividend distribution to the extent of the earnings and profits of the enterprise.

Election To Be Taxed as Individuals

A *small business corporation,* as defined in the following paragraph, may, with the consent of all of its shareholders, elect not to be taxed on its income.[10]

For this purpose, a *small business corporation* means a domestic corporation which is not a member of an affiliated group (to be defined in Chapter 27) and which does not—

(1) Have more than ten shareholders;

(2) Have as a shareholder a person (other than an estate) who is not an individual;

(3) Have a nonresident alien as a shareholder; and

(4) Have more than one class of stock.

An *electing* small business corporation is one which has made the election under I.R.C. Section 1372.[11]

An election may be made only with respect to a taxable year beginning after December 31, 1957, and ending after September 2, 1958. The election is effective for the taxable year of the corporation for which it is made and for all succeeding taxable years unless it is terminated (see below). The taxable income of an electing small corporation, to the extent that it exceeds dividends distributed in money out of earnings and profits of the taxable year, is taxed directly to the shareholders to the extent that it would have constituted a dividend if it had been distributed on the last day of the corporation's taxable year.

Making an Election. A corporation makes the election by filing Form 2553, together with a statement of the consent of each shareholder. This form is filed with the District Director of Internal Revenue with whom the tax return is to be filed either (1) during the first calendar month of the taxable year or (2) during the

[10] I.R.C. Section 1372.
[11] I.R.C. Section 1371.

calendar month preceding it. The election is valid only if all persons who are shareholders on the first day of the corporation's taxable year, or on the day of election, whichever is later, consent. Shareholder consent is in the form of a statement signed by the stockholders.

An election will terminate if any person who was not a shareholder on the first day of the first taxable year for which the election is effective, or on the day on which the election is made (whichever is later), becomes a shareholder and does not consent to the election. The termination becomes effective for the taxable year of the corporation in which this person becomes a shareholder and for all subsequent years. A consent by a new shareholder must be filed within a period of thirty days beginning on the day on which he becomes a new shareholder.

An election may be revoked by the corporation (with the consent of all its shareholders) for any taxable year of the corporation after the first taxable year for which the election is effective. A consent of all the shareholders must accompany this revocation. The revocation, if made before the close of the first month of the corporation's taxable year, will be effective for the taxable year in which the revocation is made and for all succeeding taxable years of the corporation. If the revocation is made after the close of the first month of the corporation's taxable year, the revocation will be effective for the taxable year of the corporation following.

Return of Electing Small Business Corporation. Every electing small business corporation must make a return for each taxable year for which the election is effective.

Net Operating Loss. A net operating loss of an electing small business corporation is allowed as a deduction from gross income of the shareholders. Each person who is a shareholder at any time during a taxable year of the corporation in which it has a net operating loss will be allowed as a deduction from gross income, for his taxable year in which or with which the taxable year of the corporation ends, an amount equal to his portion of the corporation's net operating loss. A shareholder's pro rata share of the corporation's net operating loss is the sum of the portions of the corporation's daily net operating loss attributable on a pro rata basis to the shares held by him on each day of the taxable year; the corporation's daily net operating loss is this net operating loss divided by the number of days in the taxable year. But a shareholder's portion of the net operating loss cannot exceed the sum of (1) the adjusted basis of his stock, determined as of the close of the corporation's taxable year (or, in respect of the stock sold or otherwise disposed of during this taxable year, as of the day before the day of sale or other disposition) and (2) the adjusted basis of any indebtedness of the corporation to the shareholder, determined in the same manner as the date in (1).[12]

Distributions of Electing Small Business Corporations. The amount includible in the gross income of a shareholder as dividends from an electing small business corporation during any taxable year of the corporation will be treated as a long-term capital gain to the extent of the shareholder's pro rata share of the excess of the corporation's net long-term capital gain over its net short-term capital loss for that year. But this excess may not exceed the corporation's taxable income for the year.[13] This amount includible in the gross income of a shareholder as dividends from an electing small business corporation may not be the basis for a dividends received credit.

Any dividend received by a shareholder from an electing small business corporation may be apportioned by the Secretary of the Treasury between shareholders who are members of this shareholder's family; this refers to the taxpayer's spouse, ancestors, lineal descendants, and any trusts for the primary benefit of these persons.

Adjustment to Basis of Stock of, and Indebtedness Owing, Shareholders. The basis of a shareholder's stock in an electing small business corporation is increased by the amount that he must pick up in his income as a dividend. The basis of his stock will be reduced (but not below zero) by an amount equal to his portion of the corporation's operating loss for any taxable year attributable to this stock.

The basis of any indebtedness of an electing small business corporation to a shareholder will be reduced (but not below zero) by the amount of the shareholder's portion of the corporation's net operating loss for any taxable year. But this adjustment will be limited to the extent that this amount exceeds the adjusted basis of his stock.[14]

Reduction for Undistributed Taxable Income. The accumulated earnings and profits of an electing small business corporation as of the close of its taxable year are reduced to the extent that any of its undistributed taxable income for that year is included in the gross income of the shareholders.[15] But there is no reduction of earnings and profits for any amount which is not allowable to

[12] I.R.C. Section 1374.
[13] I.R.C. Section 1375.
[14] I.R.C. Section 1376.
[15] I.R.C. Section 1377(a).

the corporation as a deduction in computing its taxable income.

The earnings and profits, and the accumulated earnings credit, are not affected by a net operating loss.

In determining the amount of the net operating loss of any corporation, there will be disregarded the net operating loss for any taxable year for which the corporation is an electing small business corporation.

Small Business Investment Companies

The Small Business Investment Act of 1958 was designed to make equity capital and long-term credit more readily available for small business corporations. *Small business investment companies* are authorized to provide equity capital to small business concerns through the purchase of convertible debentures. Small business investment companies, as defined, are private companies with a paid-in capital and surplus of at least $300,000. The governmental Small Business Administration is authorized to make loans to these companies of up to $150,000 through the purchase of subordinated debentures.

Small business investment companies are allowed an ordinary loss deduction, rather than a capital loss deduction, on losses realized on the convertible debentures (including stock received pursuant to the conversion privilege) acquired in connection with the supplying of long-term equity-type capital for small business concerns. This loss deduction includes losses due to worthlessness, as well as those arising from the sale or exchange of the security.[16]

Taxpayers investing in the stock of these investment companies are also allowed an ordinary loss deduction, rather than a capital loss allowance, on losses arising from the worthlessness, or from the sale, of this stock.

These investment companies are allowed a deduction for 100% of the dividends received from taxable domestic corporations rather than the 85% deduction generally allowed corporate taxpayers.

Ordinary loss treatment on the stock of small business investment companies is allowed for losses which would otherwise be considered capital losses.[17]

Special Deductions for Corporations

A corporation, in computing its taxable income, is allowed as deductions the following items:

(1) Partially tax-exempt interest. Interest on certain obligations

[16] I.R.C. Section 1242.
[17] I.R.C. Section 1242.

of the United States, or governmental instrumentalities, is exempt from normal tax; see Chapter 4.[18]

(2) Dividends received deduction. A corporation is allowed a deduction for dividends received from a taxable domestic corporation; the deduction ordinarily amounts to 85% of the dividends so received. Dividends on the preferred stock of a public utility are not included. Only *dividends* are covered; for example, savings bank interest, even if denominated dividends, is not included. The deduction may not exceed 85% of taxable income, computed without regard to the net operating loss deduction, the dividends received deduction, or the dividends paid deduction. In the case of a small business investment company operating under the Small Business Investment Act of 1958, there will be allowed as a deduction an amount equal to 100% of dividends from taxable domestic corporations, other than dividends on preferred stock of a public utility company.[19]

As mentioned earlier in this chapter (see page **16·7**), small business investment companies are entitled to a dividends received deduction of 100% for dividends received from domestic taxable corporations.

(3) A deduction is allowed for dividends received on certain preferred stock of public utility corporations. But the distributing corporation must have been allowed a deduction under Section 247 of the Code.[20]

(4) Dividends received from a foreign corporation are allowed as a deduction if the foreign corporation (1) was subject to Federal income tax for an uninterrupted period of not less than thirty-six months ending with the close of the foreign corporation's taxable year in which the dividends are paid (or, if the corporation existed for only a shorter period, then for the full period of existence). Furthermore, the foreign corporation must have derived 50% or more of its gross income from sources within the United States in this period.[21]

(5) A deduction is provided for dividends paid during the taxable year by certain public utility corporations on certain preferred stock. This deduction is an amount equal to the product of a specified fraction times the lesser of (1) the amount of the dividends paid during the taxable year by a public utility on its preferred stock or (2) the taxable income of the public utility for the taxable year

[18] I.R.C. Section 242.
[19] I.R.C. Section 243.
[20] I.R.C. Section 244.
[21] I.R.C. Section 245.

without benefit of the dividends paid deduction of Section 247. The specified fraction for any taxable year is the fraction the numerator of which is 14 and the denominator of which is the sum of the corporation normal and surtax rates.[22]

(6) Organizational expenses. A corporation may elect to treat its organizational expenditures as deferred expenses. At the time of the election, a corporation must select a period of not less than sixty months, beginning with the month in which it began business, over which it will amortize its organizational expenditures. These expenditures are those which are directly incident to the creation of the corporation. They must be chargeable to the capital account of the corporation and of a character which, if expended incident to the creation of a corporation having a limited life, would be amortizable over such life.[23]

Illustrations. Legal services incident to the organization of a corporation, such as drafting the corporate charter, by-laws, minutes of organizational meetings, terms of original stock certificates, and the like; necessary accounting services; expenses of temporary directors and of organizational meetings of directors or stockholders; and fees paid to the state of incorporation.

Issuance of Stock or Securities

Stock. No gain or loss is recognized to a corporation on the receipt of money or other property in exchange for its stock, including treasury stock.[24]

Bonds. If bonds are issued by a corporation at their face value, the corporation realizes no gain or loss. If the corporation purchases any of these bonds at a price in excess of the issuing price or face value, this excess is a deductible expense for the taxable year. If the corporation purchases any of the bonds at a price less than the issuing price or face value, the excess is gain or income for the taxable year.

Where bonds are issued by a corporation after February 28, 1913, at a premium, the net amount of this premium is gain or income which should be amortized over the life of the bonds. If the corporation purchases any of these bonds at a price in excess of the issuing price minus any amount of premium already returned as income, the excess minus any amount of premium already returned as income is a deductible expense for the taxable year. But if the corporation purchases any of the bonds at a price less than the issuing price

[22] I.R.C. Section 247.
[23] I.R.C. Section 248.
[24] I.R.C. Section 1032.

minus any amount of premium already returned as income, the excess, minus any amount of premium already returned as income, over the purchase price is gain or income for the taxable year. The rule operates in reverse in the case of bonds issued by a corporation at a *discount*.[25]

Banks

Taxation of Banks. A bank is subject to the customary corporate taxes. This refers to mutual savings banks, building and loan associations, and cooperative banks not having capital stock represented by shares.[26]

While the general principles for determining the taxable income of a corporation are applicable to the organizations named in the preceding sentence, there are special rules (to be discussed below) concerning (1) bad debts; (2) additions to reserves for bad debts; (3) dividends paid by banking corporations; (4) deductions for amounts paid to, or credited to the accounts of, depositors or holders of withdrawable accounts as dividends; and (5) repayment of certain loans.

(1) A bank is allowed an ordinary deduction for a debt which has become worthless in whole or in part and which is evidenced by a security issued by any corporation (including governments and their political subdivisions). Capital loss treatment will not be required if the taxpayer is a bank and owns at least 80% of each class of stock of another bank.[27]

(2) A bank as defined in the first sentence of this section, instead of deducting from gross income specific debts which have become worthless, may deduct amounts credited to a reserve for bad debts. The addition to the bad debt reserve is any amount determined by the taxpayer which does not exceed the lesser of:

(A) The amount of its taxable income for the taxable year, computed without regard to this reserve and without regard to any section providing for a deduction the amount of which is dependent upon the amount of taxable income (the most common example is contributions, which are limited to 5% of the corporation's income), or

(B) The amount by which 12% of the total deposits or withdrawable accounts of its depositors at the close of the year exceeds the sum of its surplus, undivided profits, and reserves at the beginning of the taxable year.

[25] Regulations Section 39.22(a)–17.
[26] I.R.C. Section 581.
[27] I.R.C. Section 582.

Illustration. A bank, which keeps its books on the calendar year basis, has surplus, reserves, and undivided profits of $800,000 as of January 1 of the taxable year and total deposits or withdrawable accounts of $10,000,000 as of December 31 of that year. During the year, the bank credits $30,000, as required by a Federal agency, to a Federal insurance reserve for the sole purpose of absorbing losses. Likewise, it credits $25,000, as permitted by state statute, to another reserve fund for the purpose of absorbing losses. In that year, the bank charges $5,000 against its bad debt reserve for losses sustained during the taxable year. The bank's taxable income for the year is $200,000, computed without regard to a bad debt reserve addition or any amounts geared to taxable income. Upon the basis of these facts, the amount by which 12% of the total deposits or withdrawable accounts at the close of the taxable year exceeds the sum of the bank's surplus, undivided profits, and reserves at the beginning of the taxable year is $400,000 (12% of $10,000,000 minus $800,000). Therefore, the bank may deduct as an addition to the bad debt reserve an amount that does not exceed $200,000 (the lesser of $200,000 or $400,000). The $30,000 credited to the reserve as required by a Federal agency and the $25,000 credited to the reserve as permitted by state statute are regarded as amounts credited to a reserve for bad debts account; thus, the bank can credit an additional $145,000 ($200,000 minus $55,000) to a general reserve for bad debts account at any time during the taxable year. The loss of $5,000 charged to the bad debt reserve during the taxable year does not affect the amount of the deduction to the bad debt reserve. It is of significance only in determining the surplus, undivided profits, and reserves of the bank as of the first date of the following year.

(3) Any national banking association, bank, or trust company organized under the laws of any state, territory, or possession of the United States, or the Canal Zone, or any other banking corporation engaged in the business of industrial banking and under the supervision of a state banking department or of the Comptroller of the Currency, or any incorporated domestic insurance company may deduct from gross income any dividend (not in liquidation) paid within the taxable year to the United States or one of its instrumentalities, on preferred stock of the corporation owned by the United States or the instrumentality. The amount allowable as a deduction under this heading will reduce the deduction for dividends paid.[28]

(4) A bank as defined in the first paragraph of this section may deduct from gross income amounts which during the taxable year are paid to or credited to the accounts of depositors or holders of accounts, as dividends on their deposits or withdrawable accounts, if these amounts paid or credited are withdrawable on demand subject only to customary notice of intention to withdraw.[29] This deduction is applicable to the taxable year in which amounts credited as dividends become withdrawable by the depositor or holder of an

[28] I.R.C. Section 583.
[29] I.R.C. Section 591.

account, subject only to customary notice of intention to withdraw. Thus, amounts credited as dividends as of the last day of the taxable year which are not withdrawable by depositors or holders of accounts until the following business day are deductible in the year subsequent to the taxable year in which they were credited.

(5) A bank as defined in the first paragraph of this section may deduct amounts paid during the taxable year in repayment of loans made before September 1, 1951, by the United States or a wholly-owned instrumentality thereof, or by any mutual fund established under the laws of any state.[30]

Any amount allowed as a deduction for dividends paid by a bank is not eligible for the dividends received deduction where a corporation is the recipient.[31]

Life Insurance Companies

The tax treatment of life insurance companies was adopted in 1959 for the calendar year 1958 and subsequent years. There is a three-phase tax base for these companies: the first is on a portion of investment income; the second is on one-half of underwriting income; and the third is on the remaining half of the underwriting income to the extent it is distributed to stockholders or certain other conditions exist. There is a separate, flat 25% tax on net long-term capital gain (in excess of net short-term capital loss).[32]

Investment Income. The Phase One portion of the tax base represents the life insurance company's share of the investment income less investment expenses. The portion of the investment income which is taxable to the life insurance company is computed as follows: determine the proportion of income needed for policyholder requirements, and then divide all items of income (including tax-exempt income and intercorporate dividends received) between the policyholder and the company in this ratio. Thus, only the life insurance company's share of each of these items is taken into account.

Illustration. If the ratio were 75 to 25 between the policyholders and the company, only 25% of the investment income would be taken into account in computing the company's taxable investment income. From this remaining 25% there would be deducted the portion of the tax-exempt interest and intercorporate dividends received deduction contained in this share.

Gain from Operations. The Phase Two portion of the tax base represents 50% of the excess of total net income from all sources

[30] I.R.C. Section 592.
[31] I.R.C. Section 243(b).
[32] I.R.C. Section 802.

over taxable investment income. This might be referred to an investment gain. It consists of mortality and loading savings; that is, savings resulting from fewer deaths than had been predicted by the mortality tables, as well as reduced expenses of servicing policies. This underwriting income also includes a portion of investment income which is not taxed under Phase One (attributable to the difference between using the company's own required rate rather than its average earning rate as in Phase One). But the mortality and loading savings are the important aspects of this Phase Two tax base. If there is an underwriting gain from these sources, half of this income is added to the Phase One tax base.

If there is an underwriting loss, however, the entire loss is deducted from the taxable investment income as otherwise determined under Phase One. But an underwriting loss may not be used to reduce the tax base to the extent that it consists of policyholder dividends in excess of $250,000.

Other Underwriting Income. The Phase Three portion of the tax base is intended to provide that underwriting gains made available to shareholders will be subject to the full payment of tax. Thus, this phase is concerned with that part of underwriting income which under Phase Two is not added to the tax base. This amount, which has not previously been taxed, is added to the tax base of the insurance company when there is distributed to shareholders a part of that income (less the tax on it), when the accumulated untaxed income exceeds certain limitations, when the company elects to be taxed on that income, or when for a specified period of time the company no longer qualifies as an insurance company. Generally, however, distributions first may be made to the shareholder with respect to the amounts which have been taxed currently without subjecting the company to a Phase Three tax.

Foreign Life Insurance Companies

A foreign life insurance company carrying on life insurance business within the United States (if with respect to its United States business it would qualify as a life insurance company under the Internal Revenue Code) is taxed on its United States business in the same manner as a domestic life insurance company.[33]

There is a special rule where the surplus of a foreign life insurance company which is held in the United States is less than the minimum figure (an amount which the average domestic life insur-

[33] I.R.C. Section 819.

ance company would have maintained with respect to its total insurance liabilities). In such a case, the amount of the policy and other contract liability requirements and the amount of the required interest are reduced. The amount of the reduction is determined by multiplying the excess of the minimum figure over the surplus held in the United States by the company's current earning rate. The "minimum figure" is obtained by multiplying the company's total insurance liabilities on United States business for the year by a percentage proclaimed by the Secretary of the Treasury as being applicable to that year. This percentage is based on data with respect to domestic life insurance companies that the Secretary regards as representative. This percentage is computed by use of the following ratio:

$$\frac{\text{Assets minus total insurance liabilities}}{\text{Total insurance liabilities}}$$

Insurance Companies (Other Than Life or Mutual)

Regular corporate income taxes are imposed on the taxable income of every insurance company (other than a life or mutual insurance company), mutual marine insurance company, and mutual fire insurance company exclusively issuing either perpetual policies or policies for which the sole premium charged is a single deposit which (except for such deduction of underwriting costs as may be provided) is refundable on cancellation or expiration of the policy.[34] Foreign insurance companies (other than a life or mutual insurance company), foreign mutual marine insurance companies, and foreign mutual fire insurance companies as mentioned in the previous sentence are not subject to this rule if they do not carry on an insurance business within the United States. Instead, they are taxable as other foreign corporations. See Chapter 22.

Mutual Insurance Companies

Mutual insurance companies [35] (other than a life or marine insurance company or a fire insurance company subject to the tax imposed by Section 831, above, and other than an interinsurer or reciprocal underwriter) are subject to whichever tax is the greater of:

(1) If taxable income (before deduction for partially tax-exempt interest) is over $3,000, a normal tax of 25% of taxable income, or

[34] I.R.C. Section 831.
[35] I.R.C. Section 821.

50% of the amount by which taxable income exceeds $3,000, whichever is the lesser, plus a surtax of 22% of taxable income (before deduction for partially tax-exempt interest) in excess of $25,000, or

(2) If the gross amount of gross investment income and net premiums, minus dividends to policyholders, minus interest on Government obligations, exceeds $75,000, a tax equal to 1% of the amount so computed, or 2% of the excess of the amount so computed over $75,000, whichever is the lesser.[36]

Gross investment income is the sum of (1) gross income from (A) interest, dividends, rents, and royalties; (B) the entering into of any lease, mortgage, or other instrument or agreement from which the insurance company derives interest, rents, or royalties; (C) the alteration or termination of any instrument or agreement mentioned in (B); and (D) capital gains and (2) the gross income during the taxable year from any trade or business (other than an insurance business) carried on by the insurance company, or by a partnership of which the insurance company is a partner.[37]

Interinsurers and Reciprocal Underwriters. Mutual insurance companies which are interinsurers or reciprocal underwriters (other than a life or a marine insurance company or a fire insurance company subject to Section 831) have a special form of tax.[38]

Tax-exempt Insurance Companies

Included among tax-exempt organizations are mutual insurance companies or associations other than life or marine (including interinsurers and reciprocal underwriters) if the gross amount received during the taxable year from gross investment income items (defined above) other than capital gains does not exceed $75,000.[39]

Farmers' Cooperatives

Special tax treatment may be afforded to farmers' cooperative marketing and purchasing associations. Cooperative associations engaged in the marketing of farm products for farmers, fruit growers, livestock growers, dairymen, etc., and turning back to the producers the proceeds of the sales of their products, less the necessary operating expenses, on the basis of either the quantity or the value of the products furnished by them, are exempt from income tax except

[36] I.R.C. Section 821(a)(2).
[37] I.R.C. Section 822(b).
[38] I.R.C. Section 821(b).
[39] I.R.C. Section 501(c)(15).

as otherwise provided in Section 522 of the Code.[40] If the proceeds of the business are distributed in any other way than on a proportionate basis, the association is not exempt. In other words, nonmember patrons must be treated the same as members insofar as the distribution of patronage dividends is concerned.

An association which has capital stock will not be denied exemption for that reason if (1) the dividend rate is fixed at not to exceed the legal rate of interest in the state of incorporation or 8% per annum, whichever is greater, on the value of the consideration for which the stock was issued and (2) substantially all of the stock (except as noted in the next sentence) is owned by producers who market their products or purchase their supplies and equipment through the association. Any ownership of stock by others than the actual producers must be satisfactorily explained in the association's application for exemption.

Tax Treatment. Farmers' cooperatives are subject to tax. But special rules apply in the computation of taxable income of organizations of this type.

(1) Amounts paid as dividends during the taxable year upon the capital stock of the cooperative are deductible from the association's gross income.[41]

(2) Amounts allocated during the taxable year to patrons with respect to the association's income not derived from patronage are allowed as a deduction, whether or not the income was derived during the taxable year and whether the amounts are paid in cash, merchandise, capital stock, revolving fund certificates, retain certificates, certificates of indebtedness, letters of advice, or in some other manner that discloses to each patron the dollar amount allocated to him. For this purpose, allocations made after the close of the taxable year and on or before the fifteenth day of the ninth month following the close of the taxable year are considered as made on the last day of the taxable year to the extent that these allocations are attributable to income derived during the taxable year or during years prior to the taxable year.[42]

Regulated Investment Companies

Definition. A regulated investment company is any domestic corporation (other than a personal holding company) which is (1) registered at all times during the taxable year under the Investment Company Act of 1940 as amended either as a management

[40] I.R.C. Section 521.
[41] I.R.C. Section 522(b)(1)(A).
[42] I.R.C. Section 522(b)(1)(B).

company or a unit investment trust, or (2) a common trust fund or similar fund excluded by Section 3(c)(3) of the Investment Company Act of 1940 from the definition of "investment company" and not included in the definition of "common trust fund." [43]

Even though it satisfied the other requirements, a corporation will not be considered to be a regulated investment company for the taxable year unless it elects to be one for that year, or an election was made for a previous taxable year which began after 1941. This election is made by the taxpayer by computing income as a regulated investment company in its return for the first taxable year for which the election is applicable. No other method of making the election is permitted. An election once made is irrevocable for the taxable year and all succeeding taxable years.

Gross Income Requirement. Two tests must be met: (1) at least 90% of the corporation's gross income for the taxable year must be derived from dividends, interest, and gains from the sale or other disposition of stock or securities and (2) less than 30% of its gross income must have been derived from the sale or other disposition of stock or securities held for less than three months.

Diversification of Investments. At the close of each quarter of the taxable year, at least 50% of the value of the total assets of the taxpayer corporation must be represented by one or more of the following: (1) cash and cash items, including receivables; (2) Government securities; (3) securities of other regulated investment companies; or (4) securities (other than those described in (2) and (3)) of any one or more issuers which meet the following limitations: (A) The entire amount of the securities of the issuer owned by the taxpayer corporation is not greater in value than 5% of the value of the total assets and (B) the entire amount of the securities of the issuer owned by the taxpayer corporation does not represent more than 10% of the outstanding voting securities of the issuer.

Furnishing of Capital to Development Corporations. In the case of a regulated investment company which furnishes capital to development corporations, an exception is made to the rule relating to the diversification of investments. The investment company may include the value of any securities of an issuer (whether or not the investment company owns more than 10% of the outstanding voting securities of the issuer) if at the time of the latest acquisition of any securities of the issuer the basis of all such securities in the hands of the investment company does not exceed 5% of the value of the total assets of the investment company at that time.

[43] I.R.C. Section 851.

Taxation of Regulated Investment Companies. The special rules as to taxability will be denied unless (1) the deduction for dividends paid for the taxable year (computed without regard to capital gains dividends) is equal to at least 90% of its investment company taxable income (determined without regard to capital gains dividends) and (2) the company keeps all records prescribed for a regulated investment company. If a regulated investment company does not meet the requirements, it will be taxed as an ordinary corporation.

Normal tax and surtax are payable on the investment company taxable income, as defined in the following paragraph. There also is a tax of 25% on the excess, if any, of the net long-term capital gain over the sum of net short-term capital loss and the deduction for capital gains dividends paid.

Investment company taxable income is taxable income of the investment company, with these adjustments:

(1) The excess, if any, of the net long-term capital gain over the net short-term capital loss is excluded.

(2) The net operating loss deduction is not allowed.

(3) The special deductions allowed to corporations are not deductible, except for organizational expenses.

(4) The dividends paid deduction is allowed, but it is computed without regard to capital gains dividends.

(5) Taxable income is computed without annualization for a short period.[44]

A capital gain dividend is any dividend or part thereof which is designated by a regulated investment company as a capital gain dividend in a written notice mailed to its shareholders not later than thirty days after the close of its taxable year. If the aggregate amount so designated with respect to the taxable year (including capital gains dividends paid after the close of the taxable year in accordance with an election to be discussed below) is greater than the excess of the net long-term capital gain over the net short-term capital loss of the taxable year, the portion of each distribution which will be a capital gain dividend will be only that proportion of the amount so designated which this excess bears to the total amount so designated.

Illustration. A regulated investment company making its returns on the calendar year basis advises its shareholders by written notice mailed December 30 that of a distribution of $500,000 made December 15 of that year, $200,000 constituted a capital gain dividend, amounting to $2 per share. It was later discovered that an error had been made in determining the excess of the net long-term capital gain over the net short-term capital loss of the taxable year

[44] I.R.C. Section 852.

and that this excess was $100,000 instead of $200,000. In this case each shareholder would have received a capital gain dividend of $1 per share instead of $2 per share.

A shareholder receiving dividends from a regulated investment company must include these dividends in gross income for the taxable year in which they are received. Ordinarily, shareholders who receive capital gain dividends in respect of the capital gains of an investment company treat such dividends as gains from the sale or exchange of capital assets held for more than six months. But where the shares were held by a shareholder for less than 31 days, then any loss on the sale or exchange of these shares will (to the extent of the amount so treated as a long-term capital gain) be treated as long-term capital loss.

Earnings and Profits of a Regulated Investment Company. Earnings and profits of a regulated investment company for any taxable year (but not the accumulated earnings and profits) are not reduced by any amount which is not allowable as a deduction in computing its taxable income for the taxable year. Thus nondeductible losses do not reduce its current earnings and profits.

Limitations Applicable to Dividends Received from a Regulated Investment Company. A capital gain dividend may not be considered a dividend for the purpose of the dividends received deduction, the dividends received credit, or the dividend exclusion.[45]

Where the aggregate dividends received during the taxable year by a regulated investment company are less than 75% of its gross income for the taxable year, only that portion of the dividend paid by the regulated investment company which bears the same ratio to the amount of the dividend paid as the aggregate dividends received by the regulated investment company, during the taxable year, bear to its gross income for that year (computed without regard to gains from the sale or other disposition of stocks or securities) may be treated as a dividend for purposes of the dividends received deduction, credit, or exclusion.[46]

Dividends Paid After Close of Taxable Year. A regulated investment company may elect to treat a dividend paid by the time of filing its return (including any extension to file) as having been paid during the taxable year. This rule is applicable only if the entire amount of the dividend is actually distributed to the shareholders in the 12-month period following the close of the taxable

[45] I.R.C. Section 854(a).
[46] I.R.C. Section 854(b).

year and not later than the date of the first regular dividend payment made after this declaration. The election must be made in the return filed by the company for the taxable year. The election is made by treating the dividend to which this election applies as a dividend paid during the taxable year in computing its investment company taxable income, or if the dividend to which this election applies is to be designated by the company as a capital gain dividend, in computing the amount of capital gain dividends paid during that taxable year.[47]

Disposition of Shares at a Loss. With respect to shares of stock of regulated investment companies acquired after 1957, if sales are made by the taxpayer at a loss, and the stock was held for more than 31 days, the loss is a long-term capital loss, to the extent of the capital gain dividend on this stock.[48]

Personal Holding Companies

The personal holding company tax may be imposed against domestic and foreign corporations, and likewise against an affiliated group of corporations filing a consolidated tax return. The purpose of this tax is to require corporations otherwise vulnerable to the steep personal holding company tax to make distributions to shareholders. The mechanism is to impose the tax upon subject corporations which do *not* make such distributions. This is more than a tax matter. In many quarters, corporations of the type that meet the personal holding company tests are believed to be detrimental to the economy. Many persons believe that corporations should not be able to accumulate funds which, after all, belong to the shareholders and which would be taxed to the shareholders were there a distribution.

But the philosophy or psychology of the personal holding company tax has no relationship to the imposition of the tax. The tax is automatic. If the conditions called for by the statute are met, the tax must be paid, regardless of why earnings were accumulated or why a distribution was not made.

Exceptions. The following are not included in the term "personal holding company":

(1) A tax-exempt corporation.
(2) A bank.
(3) A life insurance company.

[47] I.R.C. Section 855.
[48] I.R.C. Section 852(b).

(4) A surety company.
(5) A foreign personal holding company.
(6) Certain licensed personal finance companies under state supervision.
(7) Certain lending companies.
(8) Certain loan or investment corporations.
(9) Certain finance companies.
(10) A foreign corporation, if (A) its gross income from sources within the United States is less than 50% of its total gross income from all sources and (B) all of its stock outstanding during the last half of the taxable year is owned by nonresident alien individuals, whether directly or indirectly through other foreign corporations.[49]
(11) Small business investment companies.

Personal Holding Company Requirements. A corporation is classified as a personal holding company only if *both* of the following tests are met:

(1) At some time during the last half of the taxable year, more than 50% in value of the outstanding stock of the corporation is owned, directly or indirectly, by or for not more than five individuals.

(2) At least 80% of the total gross income of the corporation for the taxable year is personal holding company income, as defined below.[50]

As to (1), the constructive rules of stock ownership apply; that is, an individual is deemed to own the shares owned by his spouse, ancestors, lineal descendants, brothers, and sisters. Under certain circumstances, an organization or trust may be treated as an individual for this purpose. Shares of stock which may be acquired by reason of an option are considered to be constructively owned by the individual having the option to acquire this stock. Outstanding securities of a corporation that are convertible into stock of the corporation (whether or not convertible during the taxable year) are considered as outstanding stock of the corporation.

As to (2), *personal holding company income* means the portion of the gross income which consists of the following classes of income: dividends; interest; royalties (other than mineral, oil, or gas); annuities; gains from the sale or exchange of stock or securities; gains from future transactions in commodities; income from estates and trusts (including gain derived by the corporation from the sale or other disposition of any interest in an estate or trust); income from personal service contracts; compensation for the use of property (if at any time during the taxable year 25% or more in value

[49] I.R.C. Section 542.
[50] I.R.C. Section 542.

of the outstanding stock of the corporation is owned, directly or indirectly, by or for an individual entitled to the use of the property); rents; and mineral, oil, or gas royalties. As to rents, if they constitute 50% or more of the gross income of the corporation, they will not be considered personal holding company income. As to mineral, oil, or gas royalties, if (1) the aggregate amount of these items constitutes 50% or more of the gross income of the corporation for the taxable year and (2) the aggregate amount of deductions allowable as trade or business expenses (other than compensation for personal services rendered by the shareholders) equals 15% or more of the corporation's gross income, then these royalties will not be considered personal holding company income.

Basis of Tax. The personal holding company tax, where applicable, is imposed upon *undistributed personal holding company income*. This is taxable income less the deduction for dividends paid, with the adjustments mentioned in the following paragraph.[51]

Federal income taxes accrued in the taxable year are allowed as a deduction (but not the accumulated earnings tax or the personal holding company tax). Deduction is allowed for income taxes paid to a foreign country or United States possession, but no foreign tax credit is allowed. Charitable contributions are allowed, with the limitations applicable to individuals rather than to corporations; but this 20% or 30% deduction is deemed to be sufficiently liberal so that there is no carryover of excess charitable contributions.[52] The special deductions allowed to corporations generally are disallowed. The net operating loss deduction is not allowed, except that of the preceding taxable year; this deduction does not include the dividends received deduction or other special deductions that are not allowed in computing undistributed personal holding company income. There is allowed as a deduction the excess of the net long-term capital gain for the taxable year over the net short-term capital loss, minus the taxes attributable to this excess. A deduction may be taken for amounts used or irrevocably set aside to pay or to retire indebtedness incurred before 1934. Expenses and depreciation applicable to property of the taxpayer are allowed, but not in an amount in excess of the aggregate amount of the rent or other compensation received for the use of, or the right to use, the property, unless the Commissioner is satisfied that the amounts received were the highest obtainable. The amount of a lien in favor of the United States is allowed as a deduction.

[51] I.R.C. Section 545.
[52] I.R.C. Section 545(b).

Income is not annualized if the period is less than a full year.[53]

Dividends Paid Deduction. Personal holding company income is reduced by the sum of (1) the dividends paid during the taxable year, (2) the consent dividends for the taxable year, and (3) the dividend carryover.

The amount of any distribution will not be considered as a dividend for this purpose unless it is pro rata, with no preference to any share of stock as compared with other shares of the same class, and with no preference as to one class of stock as compared with another.[54] Dividends paid in liquidation of a corporation may be included.

A dividend paid after the close of a taxable year and on or before the fifteenth day of the third month following the close of that year will be treated as paid during the taxable year.[55]

A consent dividend is one where a shareholder agrees to include in his own gross income certain amounts as though the corporation actually had paid these amounts in the form of a distribution.[56] The shareholder must file his agreement to be taxed on the unpaid amount on Form 972.

A dividend carryover is the excess of the dividends paid in the two preceding years over the undistributed personal holding company income for these years.[57]

The Tax. Tax is imposed on the first $2,000 of undistributed personal holding company income at the rate of 75%. A tax of 85% is imposed on amounts in excess of $2,000.

Deficiency Dividends. If a Revenue Agent determines that a corporation is liable for personal holding company tax, the corporation may obtain an additional deduction for a dividend distribution that could wipe out the tax. This is known as a *deficiency dividend.* It must be paid on or within 90 days after the date of the deficiency determination.[58]

Foreign Personal Holding Companies

The subject of foreign personal holding companies is discussed in Chapter 22.

[53] I.R.C. Section 546.
[54] I.R.C. Section 562.
[55] I.R.C. Section 563.
[56] I.R.C. Section 565.
[57] I.R.C. Section 564.
[58] I.R.C. Section 547.

Tax on Accumulated Earnings

The tax on accumulated earnings has the objective of forcing corporations to pay dividends; but unlike the personal holding company tax, it is not automatic. Earnings retained for the *reasonable* needs of the business are not the basis for a tax. Thus, the accumulated earnings tax may properly be regarded as a tax on *hoarding.*

Coverage. The tax may be imposed upon any corporation formed or availed of for the purpose of avoiding the income tax with respect to its shareholders, or the shareholders of any other corporation, by permitting earnings and profits to accumulate instead of being divided or distributed. Exceptions are personal holding companies, foreign personal holding companies, and tax-exempt corporations.[59] Especially vulnerable is the holding or investment company. As to other corporations, "the fact that the earnings and profits of a corporation are permitted to accumulate beyond the reasonable needs of the business shall be determinative of the purpose to avoid the income tax with respect to shareholders, unless the corporation by the preponderance of the evidence shall prove to the contrary."[60] But as to the holding or investment company, "The fact that any corporation is a mere holding or investment company shall be prima facie evidence of the purpose to avoid the income tax with respect to shareholders."[61]

Rates of Tax. The tax, when applicable, is at the rate of 27½% of the accumulated taxable income not in excess of $100,000, plus 38½% of the accumulated taxable income in excess of $100,000.

Imposition of the Tax. The accumulated earnings tax, where applicable, is imposed upon accumulated taxable income, which is the taxable income of the corporation after applying the *minus adjustments* to be listed in the next sentence, minus the sum of the dividends paid deduction and the accumulated earnings credit. The minus adjustments are: Federal income taxes and income, war profits, and excess profits taxes of foreign countries and possessions of the United States (to the extent not allowable as a deduction in arriving at taxable income) which accrued during the taxable year; charitable contributions to the extent that they had been disallowed under the percentage limitations; losses from sales or exchanges of

[59] I.R.C. Section 532.
[60] I.R.C. Section 533(a).
[61] I.R.C. Section 533(b).

capital assets which are disallowed as deductions in arriving at taxable income; the excess of net long-term capital gain over net short-term capital loss, minus the taxes attributable to this excess; and a special deduction ordinarily allowed to bank affiliates. Minus adjustments are not allowed for the special deductions allowed to corporations in general (except organizational expenses); the net operating loss deduction; the capital loss carryover.

The *accumulated earnings credit* may take one of several forms. In the case of a corporation other than a mere holding or investment company, the credit is the reasonably retained portion of the year's earnings minus the excess of the net long-term capital gain over net short-term capital loss as reduced by the tax on this excess. Retained earnings are computed after the dividends paid deduction (including dividends paid within 75 days of the close of the taxable year). But there is a minimum credit: the amount by which $100,000 exceeds the accumulated earnings and profits at the close of the previous taxable year. In the case of a corporation which is a mere holding or investment company, the accumulated earnings credit is the amount (if any) by which $100,000 exceeds the accumulated earnings and profits at the close of the preceding taxable year.

Burden of Proof. A corporation may, upon receipt of a notice of proposed deficiency of accumulated earnings tax, file a statement of the grounds (together with sufficient facts to indicate the basis for the statement) on which the corporation relies to establish the reasonableness of the accumulation. If the taxpayer submits the statement within the proper time, the burden of proof will be on the Government as to whether the accumulation is in excess of the reasonable needs of the business. If the taxpayer does not file such a statement within 30 days of the notice, the taxpayer must bear the burden of proof.[62]

Reasons for Retention of Earnings. A corporation may retain its earnings for such needs as expansion, modernization, the going into related lines of endeavor, the desire to become independent of banks, the presence of unusual hazards, the conditions of a depression, the need to finance suppliers or customers, the desire to acquire storage or trucking facilities, the desire to improve credit standing. Reasonable grounds for retention were not found where a corporation wanted to go into a different line of endeavor, to lend money to

[62] I.R.C. Section 534.

shareholders, to make investments unrelated to the business, or to provide for vague contingencies.

Consolidated Returns

Corporations of an affiliated group have the privilege of making a consolidated income tax return for the taxable year in lieu of separate returns. See Chapter 27.

Supplementary Material

A. Suggested Reading.

Harold M. Somers, "The Place of the Corporation Income Tax in the Tax Structure," *National Tax Journal,* September, 1952, Vol. V, #3, p. 279.

William J. Shultz, "Economic Effects of a Corporate Income Tax," *TAXES—The Tax Magazine,* November, 1943, Vol. XXI, #11, p. 598.

Sidney I. Roberts and Herbert A. Alpert, "Subchapter S: Semantic and Procedural Traps in Its Use; Analysis of Dangers," *Journal of Taxation,* November, 1959, Vol. X, #1, p. 2.

James F. Fish, Jr., "Pseudo-Corporations," *L.R.B. & M. Journal,* October–December, 1958, Vol. XXXIX, #4, p. 1.

Bruce H. Greenfield, "Personal Holding Company Dangers and How To Meet Them," *Proceedings of the New York University Thirteenth Annual Institute of Federal Taxation* (Albany: Matthew Bender & Co., Inc., 1955), p. 823.

Robert S. Holzman, *The Tax on Accumulated Earnings* (New York: The Ronald Press Co., 1956).

B. Leading Cases.

Purpose of corporation. *National Investors Corp. v. Hoey,* 144 F.2d 466 (2d Cir., 1944). *National Carbide Corp. et al. v. Commissioner,* 336 U.S. 422 (1949).

What is a corporation? *Morrissey v. Commissioner,* 296 U.S. 344 (1935).

C. Questions.

1. Why should a partnership elect to be taxed as a corporation?
2. May the Internal Revenue Service require a partnership to be taxed as a corporation?
3. A personal holding company had distributed all of its income for the taxable year, except for $25,000 that was being retained to acquire the stock of a competitor. Assuming that this is a sound business purpose, is the corporation still subject to the personal holding company tax?
4. A man owned 25 shares of the stock of the Diareses Corporation. His wife owned 20 shares. Her brother owned 15 shares. He also owned 60% of the stock of the Tilda Corporation, which owned 10 shares of Diareses. His cousin owned a Diareses bond that was convertible

into 10 shares of stock. How many shares does he own, directly and constructively?

5. A small business corporation has taxable income of $100,000 in a year in which an election is made. During the year it distributes $80,000 in cash among its ten equal stockholders. The undistributed taxable income is $20,000. What is the tax status of the shareholders?
6. In order to minimize his personal liability arising from damage claims, an individual in the construction business incorporated his venture. May he still be taxed as an individual rather than as a corporation?
7. On July 1, 1961, Strephon, a patron of a cooperative association, purchases a tractor for use in his farming business from the association for $2,200. The tractor has an estimated useful life of five years and an estimated salvage value of $200. Strephon files his tax return on a calendar year basis and claims depreciation on the tractor for 1961 in the amount of $200 pursuant to his use of the straight line method at the rate of $400 per year; he ignores the accelerated first year method. On July 1, 1962, the cooperative association allocates to him with respect to his purchase of the tractor a dividend of $300 in cash. How will he reduce his depreciation allowance with respect to the tractor for 1962 (and subsequent taxable years)?
8. An electing small business corporation which has four equal shareholders has taxable income and current earnings and profits of $80,000 for the taxable year. It has an excess of $100,000 of net long-term capital gain over net short-term capital loss for the taxable year. The corporation distributes $100,000 in cash during the taxable year, $25,000 to each shareholder, all of which is treated as a dividend, as the corporation had a substantial amount of accumulated earnings and profits at the beginning of the taxable year. How much, if anything, will be treated as long-term capital gain in the hands of the shareholders?
9. The Squirrel Corporation had taxable income of $103,000 for the taxable year, of which $3,000 is the excess of net long-term capital gain of $12,000 over a net short-term capital loss of $9,000. The $9,000 net short-term capital loss includes a capital loss carryover of $5,000. For the purpose of the accumulated earnings tax, what is the capital gains adjustment as reduced by the tax on the adjustment?
10. A corporation of which Vachislava was the sole stockholder was an electing small business corporation for the calendar years 1959, 1960, and 1961. For its taxable year 1959, it had a net operating loss of $10,000. For its taxable year 1960 it has undistributed taxable income of $50,000. Assuming that Vachislava properly included in her gross income the undistributed taxable income of the corporation for 1960, what is her share of the corporation's undistributed taxable income as of December 31, 1960?
11. Continuing the previous problem, the corporation on January 1, 1961, made a distribution to Vachislava of $20,000 of her share of the corporation's undistributed taxable income. For 1961, the corporation has a net operating loss of $40,000. What is the nature of the distribution to Vachislava insofar as she is concerned?
12. An investment company at the close of a particular quarter of the taxable year has its assets invested as follows:

	Per Cent
Cash	10
Government securities	35
Securities of First Corporation	7
Securities of Second Corporation	12
Securities of Third Corporation	15
Securities of Fourth Corporation	21
Total	100

Does it qualify as a regulated investment company?

13. The Yankee Corporation of Delaware owned a minority interest in the Zklsjg Corporation, a foreign company that was not a foreign personal holding company. The Yankee Corporation received $17,000 in dividends in its calendar year 1961 from Zklsjg. Zklsjg had been subject to United States income tax since February 1, 1959, and 50% of its gross income had been from United States sources during the period. Is Yankee entitled to the dividends received deduction?
14. Corporations I, II, and III constitute an affiliated group of corporations which files a consolidated return for the calendar year 1961. Corporations IV and V are wholly owned subsidiaries of Corporation I and derive no gross income from sources outside of the consolidated group. Corporation I, the common parent, has gross income in the amount of $250,000 for the taxable year 1961. Of this gross income, $200,000 consists of dividends received from Corporations II and III. The remaining $50,000 was derived from sources outside of the affiliated group, $40,000 of which represents personal holding company income. May Corporations I, II, and III file a consolidated return so as to avoid the personal holding company tax on any one corporation individually?
15. A corporation elects to be classified as a small business corporation. For the calendar year 1960 it has a net operating loss of $10,000. There were ten equal shareholders until July 1, when Epsilon, a shareholder, sold his stock to Omicron, an existing shareholder. What deduction does each shareholder have for the year by virtue of the corporation's net operating loss?
16. A wife owns all of the stock of P Corporation, which in turn owns all of the stock of S Corporation. S Corporation in turn owns all of the stock of the SS Corporation. Does her husband constructively own any of the stock of the SS Corporation?
17. The T Corporation, which is not a mere holding or investment company, has accumulated earnings and profits in the amount of $75,000 as of December 31, 1960; it has earnings and profits for the taxable year ending December 31, 1961, in the amount of $100,000 and has a dividends paid deduction in the amount of $30,000 so that the earnings and profits for the taxable year which are retained in the business amount to $70,000. Assume that it has been determined that the earnings and profits for the taxable year which may be retained for the reasonable needs of the business amount to $55,000 and that a deduction has been allowed for long-term capital gains less taxes in the amount of $5,000. What is the accumulated earnings credit for the taxable year ended December 31, 1961? For the purpose of this com-

putation, do NOT take into account the minimum accumulated earnings credit.

18. A, B, C, and D are the owners of all of the stock of a certain corporation, which makes its income tax returns on a calendar year basis. With the consent of all of the shareholders, the corporation on July 15, 1960, declared a dividend of $5 a share payable in cash on August 1 to A. On September 15, it declared a dividend of $5 a share payable in cash on October 1 to B, C, and D. What allowance for dividends paid for the taxable year 1960 is permitted to the corporation with respect to the dividends paid on August 1 and October 1, 1960?

17

TAX-FREE EXCHANGES AND CORPORATE REORGANIZATIONS

Tax-free Exchanges

It is a general rule of taxation that gain or loss will be recognized upon the sale or exchange of property. The following types of transaction are exceptions to this general rule:

(1) Exchange of property held for productive use or investment.

(2) Exchange of its stock by a corporation for money or other property.

(3) Involuntary conversions. See Chapter 6.

(4) Sale or exchange of personal residence. See Chapter 6.

(5) Certain exchanges of insurance policies. This subject was treated in Chapter 12.

Property Held for Productive Use or Investment. No gain or loss is recognized if property held for productive use in trade or business or for investment is exchanged solely for property of a like kind to be held either for productive use in trade or business or for investment. Property held for productive use in trade or business may be exchanged for property held for investment. Similarly, property held for investment may be exchanged for property held for productive use in trade or business.[1]

Property held for productive use in trade or business or for investment does not include stock in trade or other property held primarily for sale, nor stocks, bonds, notes, choses in action, certificates of trust or beneficial interest, or other securities or evidences of indebtedness or interest. The exclusions thus listed cannot be enlarged, and hence the statute applies only to the items specifically listed. Thus, no loss was sustained from the transfer of a membership in a Chamber of Commerce for another membership of a similar nature.[2]

[1] I.R.C. Section 1031.
[2] *Wyman & Co.*, 8 B.T.A. 408 (1927).

The words "like kind" have reference to the nature or character of the property and not to its grade or quality. One kind or class of property may not be exchanged for property of a different kind or class. The fact that any real estate involved is improved or unimproved is not material, for that fact relates only to the grade or quality of the property and not to its kind or class. Unproductive real estate held by one other than a dealer for future use or future realization of the increment in value is held for investment and not primarily for sale. But the "like kind" requirement is broadly construed where actual business is involved. Thus, an exchange of a truck for a passenger automobile may be made if the use to which they are put is the same, and unimproved real estate may be exchanged tax-free for improved real estate provided the taxpayer is not a dealer.

The exchange of an undivided fractional oil, gas, and other mineral interest in one county for overriding royalty and mineral interests in and to oil in and under named leasehold estates in another county was a tax-free transaction. "[T]he exchange here of mineral interests for mineral interests was not an exchange of property of unlike kind merely because one of the mineral interests was of indefinite, the other of definite duration." [3]

The fact that the parties did not contemplate a tax-free exchange is immaterial. If the facts of the transaction coincide with the statutory definition of a tax-free exchange, the provisions as to no gain or no loss apply.[4]

Boot. For obvious mathematical reasons, an exchange of property may involve some adjustment in terms of dollars; that is, one party to the exchange or the other may pass money or something else to equalize the values. This is referred to as *boot,* a term which may be more easily understood if one thinks of the original phraseology: cash to boot. Boot is the consideration in connection with an exchange in addition to that which may be exchanged tax-free. The *giving* of boot does not involve the giver in tax consequences.[5] But the *receiving* of boot may require tax adjustments.

If the taxpayer receives other property in addition to what he may receive tax-free in an exchange, then (1) the gain, if any, to the taxpayer will be recognized in an amount not in excess of the sum of the money and the fair market value of the other property, but (2) the loss, if any, to the taxpayer from this exchange will not be recognized to any extent.

[3] *Fleming et al. v. Campbell,* 205 F.2d 549 (5th Cir., 1953).
[4] *W. D. Haden Co. v. Commissioner,* 165 F.2d 588 (5th Cir., 1948).
[5] *George E. Hamilton,* 30 B.T.A. 160 (1934).

Illustration. An individual, who is not a dealer in real estate, in 1960 exchanges real estate held for investment, which he had purchased in 1946 for $5,000, for other real estate (to be held for productive use in trade or business) which has a fair market value of $6,000, and $2,000 in cash. The gain from the transaction is $3,000, but is recognized only to the extent of the cash received of $2,000.

Illustration. An individual acquired a new truck for use in his business. He is allowed $1,800 for his old truck on a trade-in and had to pay an additional $1,900 in cash. His old truck, after depreciation allowances, had an adjusted basis of $1,700. The basis of the new truck is the adjusted basis of the truck at the time of the trade plus the additional cash paid out, or $3,600. If he had sold the old truck for $1,800 to another party and then purchased the new truck for $3,600, he would have had a taxable gain of $100 (the selling price of $1,800 less the adjusted basis of the old truck of $1,700). The basis of the new truck would then be what he paid for it.

Illustration. An individual exchanged a boat (used in his business), having an adjusted basis of $8,000, for another boat to be used in his business, as well as land to be held for investment and $500 cash. The fair market value of the boat and the land received is $5,000 and $1,500, respectively. There is a nonrecognized loss of $1,000 on the transaction, and the basis of the respective properties received is as follows:

Adjusted basis of boat transferred	$8,000
Less: Cash received	500
Total basis of the properties received (to be allocated)	$7,500

The basis of $7,500 is allocated to the land received at its fair market value of $1,500, and the remainder of $6,000 is the basis of the boat acquired.

The amount of any liabilities of the taxpayer assumed by the other party to the exchange (or of any liabilities to which the property exchanged by the taxpayer is subject) is to be treated as money received by the taxpayer upon the exchange, whether or not the assumption resulted in a recognition of gain or loss to the taxpayer under the law applicable to the year in which the exchange was made.

Illustration. A, an individual, owns an apartment house which has an adjusted basis in his hands of $500,000, but which is subject to a mortgage of $150,000. On September 1 of the taxable year, he transfers the apartment house to B, receiving in exchange therefor $50,000 in cash and another apartment house with a fair market value on that date of $600,000. The transfer to B is made subject to the $150,000 mortgage. A realizes a gain of $300,000 on the exchange, computed as follows:

Value of property received	$600,000
Cash	50,000
Liabilities subject to which old property was transferred	150,000
Total consideration received	$800,000
Less: Adjusted basis of property transferred	500,000
Gain realized	$300,000

Under the statute, $200,000 of the $300,000 gain is recognized. The basis of the apartment house acquired by A upon the exchange is $500,000, computed as follows:

Adjusted basis of property transferred		$500,000
Less: Amount of money received:		
Cash	$ 50,000	
Amount of liabilities subject to which property was transferred	150,000	200,000
Difference		$300,000
Plus: Amount of gain recognized upon the exchange		200,000
Basis of property acquired upon the exchange		$500,000

Exchange of Stock for Property. The disposition by a corporation of shares of its own stock (including treasury stock) for money or other property does not give rise to taxable gain or deductible loss to a corporation regardless of the nature of the transaction or the facts and circumstances involved.[6] For example, the receipt by a corporation of the subscription price of shares of its stock upon their original issuance gives rise to neither taxable gain nor deductible loss, whether the subscription or issue price be equal to, in excess of, or less than, the par or stated value of the stock. Also, the exchange or sale by a corporation of its own shares for money or other property does not result in taxable gain or deductible loss, even though the corporation deals in these shares as it might in the shares of another corporation. A transfer by a corporation of shares of its own stock (including treasury stock) as compensation for services is considered as a disposition by the corporation of these shares for money or other property. But this nonrecognition of gain or loss does not apply to the acquisition by a corporation of shares of its own stock unless the corporation acquires these shares in exchange for shares of its own stock (including treasury stock).[7]

Corporate Reorganizations

The doctrine of nonrecognition of immediate gain or loss upon statutory reorganization stems from the philosophy that business enterprise has a nonstatic character. Changes must be made, or should be made. Adjustments are necessary because of human and economic factors. These changes would be discouraged, or perhaps prevented entirely, if a tax accrued at the time of reorganization, when in actual fact there had been a mere change in form, and profits were merely on paper.

Thus, the reorganization provisions were passed to expedite mergers, consolidations, divisive reorganizations, and the reshuf-

[6] I.R.C. Section 1032.

[7] I.R.C. Section 311, to be discussed below.

fling of capital structure. The Government, in its unique position as tax collector, is a major stockholder in every profit-making corporation; and it is definitely to the Government's interest to see that reorganizations are effected if they will enable the corporations to effect operating economies or other legitimate undertakings that will result in higher taxable incomes—and hence higher revenues for the Treasury Department. The Government probably loses nothing by permitting tax-free reorganizations; for if a high tax would result, in most instances the reorganization simply would not be undertaken, and the tax thus would not be paid anyway.

There is also this practical consideration: if a transaction is deemed taxable and yet the taxpayer has received nothing that is more than a paper profit, where is he going to get the money to pay the tax? A transaction should be taxed upon its completion; a reorganization is a *continuing* matter upon which no tax can be justified economically until the completion of the transaction. "The recognized purpose and scheme of the reorganization provisions is to omit from tax a change in form and to postpone the tax until there is a change in substance or a realization in money." [8]

Thus, the theory of the corporate reorganization is the same as that of the tax-free exchange: if what is surrendered is *substantially* the same as what is received in exchange (regardless of the form), the new asset (property, stock) is deemed to take the place of the old. Hence, there is no gain or loss upon the disposition, because fictionally no disposition has taken place.

But inasmuch as corporate reorganizations are used so frequently as a means of tax avoidance or evasion, the taxpayer has the burden of proving that his transaction is in fact what the Code had in mind. A transaction for no purpose other than to escape taxation may be disregarded by the Internal Revenue Service.

What Is a Corporate Reorganization? A corporate reorganization means:

(1) A statutory merger or consolidation. *Statutory* means in this sense a transaction in accordance with the law of the state that granted a corporation its charter. Thus, if the law of the state of incorporation does not permit mergers, there cannot be a statutory merger for the purpose of a corporate reorganization under Federal tax law.

Illustration. If Corporation A merges into Corporation B in accordance with the law of the state or states of incorporation, B being the continuing corporation, there has been a statutory merger. If Corporations C and D transfer their assets

[8] *Morley Cypress Trust et al.*, 3 T.C. 84 (1944).

and liabilities to Corporation E in accordance with state law, there has been a statutory consolidation.

(2) The acquisition of one corporation, in exchange solely for all or a part of its voting stock, of stock of another corporation. But immediately after the acquisition, the acquiring corporation must have control of the other corporation, whether or not control had been held immediately before the acquisition.

Illustration. F Corporation gives 10% of its voting stock for 85% of the voting stock of G Corporation. How much (if any) of the G stock had been held by F Corporation prior to this transaction is immaterial.

(3) The acquisition by one corporation, in exchange solely for all or a part of its voting stock (or in exchange solely for all or a part of the voting stock of another corporation which is in control of the acquiring corporation), of substantially all of the properties of another corporation. But in determining whether the exchange is solely for stock, the assumption by the acquiring corporation of a liability of the other, or the fact that property acquired is subject to a liability, will be disregarded.

Illustration. H Corporation gives 10% of its voting stock for 98% of the properties of I Corporation.

(4) A transfer by a corporation of all or a part of its assets to another corporation if immediately after the transfer the transferor, or one or more of its shareholders (including persons who were shareholders immediately before the transfer), or any combination thereof, is in control of the corporation to which the assets are transferred.

Illustration. J Corporation transfers all of its assets to K Korporation, and immediately after the transfer J Corporation owns 20% of the stock of K Korporation while stockholders of J own 80% of the stock of K.

(5) A recapitalization.

Illustration. L Corporation has $100,000 in debentures outstanding in addition to common stock. In order to eliminate fixed charges for interest, and to reduce the cost of money (the debentures had a 6% interest rate), the corporation replaces the debentures with 1,000 shares of $100 par value 5% preferred stock.

(6) A mere change of identity, form, or place of organization, however effected.[9]

Illustration. An insurance company held a charter from the state of New Jersey. Because of what seemed to the stockholders to be an unfavorable decision as to state franchise taxes of domestic corporations, a Delaware corporation was formed, to which all of the assets and liabilities of the New Jersey corporation

[9] I.R.C. Section 368.

were transferred in return for all of the stock of the Delaware corporation. Thereupon, the Delaware shares were distributed by the New Jersey corporation to its own stockholders, who returned their New Jersey shares to the corporation for cancellation; and the New Jersey corporation was liquidated.

Control as used in the reorganization definition means the ownership of stock possessing at least 80% of the total combined voting power of all classes of stock entitled to vote and at least 80% of the total number of shares of all other classes of stock of the corporation.[10]

Distributions by Corporations—Effects on Recipients. Where the shareholder is not a corporation, the amount of any distribution of earnings will be the amount of money received plus the fair market value of the other property received. If the shareholder is a corporation, the amount of any distribution is the amount of money received plus the lesser of (1) the fair market value of the other property received or (2) the adjusted basis (in the hands of the distributing corporation immediately before the distribution) of the other property received. This latter amount is increased by the amount of gain to the distributing corporation which is recognized under I.R.C. Section 311(b) (relating to distributions of Lifo inventory; see below) or under Section 311(c) (relating to distributions of property subject to a liability in excess of the adjusted basis of the property; see below).[11]

The amount of any distribution as determined in the previous paragraph is reduced (but not below zero) by (1) the amount of any liability of the corporation assumed by the shareholder in connection with the distribution and (2) the amount of any liability to which the property received by the shareholder is subject immediately before, and immediately after, the distribution, whether or not the distributing corporation remains liable in either case.

Illustration. If an individual shareholder received from a corporation a distribution of property having a fair market value of $1,000 subject immediately before and immediately after the distribution to a liability of $700, the amount of the distribution will be $300.

That portion of a distribution which is a dividend is included in the gross income of the recipient. That portion of the distribution which is not a dividend will first be applied against the adjusted basis of the stock as a reduction. To the extent that the portion of the distribution which is not a dividend exceeds the adjusted basis of the stock, this portion will be treated as gain from the sale or

[10] I.R.C. Section 368(c).
[11] I.R.C. Section 301(b)(1).

exchange of property. That portion of the distribution which exceeds the adjusted basis of the stock but which is out of increase in value accrued before March 1, 1913, is exempt from tax.

The basis of property received in a distribution is the fair market value of this property if the shareholder is not a corporation. But if the shareholder is a corporation, the basis of the property is the lesser of (1) the fair market value of the property or (2) the adjusted basis (in the hands of the distributing corporation immediately before the distribution) of this property. The basis will be increased in the amount of gain to the distributing corporation which is recognized under Section 311(b) or (c), which will be discussed below.

Illustration. On the first day of the taxable year, an individual shareholder of X Corporation purchased property from that corporation for $20. The fair market value of that property was $100, and its basis in the hands of X Corporation was $25. The amount of the distribution is $80. If the shareholder were a corporation, the amount of the distribution would be $5, the excess of the basis of the property in the hands of X Corporation over the amount received therefor. The basis of this property to a corporate shareholder would be $25. If the basis of the property in the hands of X Corporation were $10, a corporate shareholder would not receive a distribution. The basis of this property to a corporate shareholder would be $20. Whether or not the shareholder is a corporation, the excess of the amount paid over the basis of the property in the hands of X Corporation ($20 over $10) would be a taxable gain to X Corporation.

Distributions in Redemption of Stock. The redemption of stock by a corporation may be treated as a dividend to the extent of the corporation's earnings and profits (actual and imputed). But there are three conditions, the satisfaction of any one of which will entitle the redemption to be treated as capital gain or loss, rather than a dividend.

(1) If the redemption is not essentially equivalent to the distribution of a taxable dividend. Should the transaction by its nature properly be characterized as a sale of stock by the redeeming shareholder to the corporation?

Illustration. In a year when a corporation had substantial earnings, no cash dividend was declared, but there was a tax-free stock dividend. The following year, the stock which had been issued as a dividend was redeemed in cash. No contraction of the corporation's activities or business had occurred in the year of the redemption. The redemption would be treated as a distribution essentially equivalent to a dividend.

(2) If there is a substantially disproportionate redemption of stock. But this rule will not apply unless immediately after the redemption the shareholder owns less than 50% of the total combined voting power of all classes of stock entitled to vote. A distribution

will be substantially disproportionate with respect to a shareholder (and every shareholder is treated on an individualized basis) only if the ratio which the voting stock owned by him after the redemption bears to all the voting stock at that time is less than 80% of the ratio which the voting stock he owned immediately before the redemption bears to all the voting stock at that time.

Illustration. Corporation M has outstanding 400 shares of common stock, of which A, B, C, and D (all unrelated) each owns 100 shares or 25%. No stock is considered constructively owned by these shareholders. Corporation M redeems 55 shares from A, 25 shares from B, and 20 shares from C. For the redemption to be disproportionate as to any shareholder, he must own after the redemption less than 20% (80% of 25%) of the 300 shares then outstanding. After the redemptions, A owns 45 shares (19%), B owns 75 shares (25%), and C owns 80 shares (26⅔%). The distribution is disproportionate only with respect to A.

(3) If the distribution is in complete redemption of all the stock of a corporation owned by a shareholder. This rule must be read in conjunction with provisions relating to constructive ownership of stock. Stock owned by members of the family of the distributee will not be attributed to him immediately after the distribution in redemption, if the distributee himself has no interest in the corporation, including but not limited to an interest as officer, director, or employee other than an interest as a creditor, provided that the distributee does not acquire such an interest (except by bequest or inheritance) within ten years from the date of the distribution in redemption. An individual will be barred from capital gains treatment on the redemption of all his stock in a corporation, if he has given or sold part of his stock to members of his family within the preceding ten years, unless the stock so sold or given to the other members of his family is redeemed in the transaction in which his stock is redeemed.[12]

Redemptions of Stock To Pay Death Taxes. When a shareholder (particularly one in a closely held corporation) dies, the problem exists as to who will buy his stock from his estate or beneficiaries. It is quite likely that no outside party will know enough about the corporation to buy the shares. Furthermore, the infusion of new interests into the corporation may make for irreconcilable differences with the existing management and shareholders. The best solution in numerous instances would be to have the corporation buy up the shares of a decedent. Yet, were money to flow from the corporation to a shareholder, these funds (particularly if they had originated as corporate earnings) might appear to be

[12] I.R.C. Section 302.

equivalent to dividends. The Code provides relief from this danger of taxability as dividends by declaring that the redemption of stock to pay death taxes will not be regarded as dividends, if certain requirements can be met.

The amount of the distribution which will not be treated as a dividend may equal the estate, inheritance, legacy, and succession taxes (including any interest collected as a part of these taxes) that are imposed because of the decedent's death. Similarly treated is the amount of the funeral and administration expenses allowed as deductions to the estate.[13]

The distribution must be within ninety days after the expiration of the date of the statute of limitations for the assessment of the Federal estate tax. Subject to the provisions of the following sentence, the redemption period may not exceed three years and ninety days from the date set for the filing of the estate tax return. But if a petition for redetermination of a deficiency in the estate tax has been filed with the Tax Court within the time permitted by law (see Chapter 26), the rule of Section 303 will apply to amounts distributed at any time before the expiration of sixty days after the decision of the Tax Court becomes final.

The stock of a corporation will qualify for this special treatment either if (1) the value of the stock for estate tax purposes comprises more than 35% of the value of the *gross* estate of the decedent or (2) the value comprises more than 50% of the decedent's *taxable* estate. Stock of two or more corporations will be treated as stock of a single corporation for this purpose to the extent that (with respect to each of the corporations) more than 75% in value of the outstanding stock is includible in the gross estate.

Illustration. The estate of a decedent presents the following facts:

Gross estate	$1,500,000
Taxable estate	750,000

Stock of Corporations Includible in Gross Estate	Value of Stock Includible in Gross Estate	Percentage of Ownership of Stock Includible in Gross Estate
Corporation A	$300,000	50
Corporation B	300,000	100
Corporation C	250,000	100

Corporations B and C, but not A, would be treated as stock of a single corporation for the purpose of this rule. A redemption of the stock of Corporation A would not meet the percentile requirements, inasmuch as the value of the stock includible in the gross estate is less than 35% of the gross estate ($525,000) and also less than 50% of the taxable estate ($375,000). In the case of Corporations

[13] I.R.C. Section 303.

B and C, a redemption of the stock of either would qualify inasmuch as the value of both corporations treated as a single corporation includible in the gross estate ($550,000) exceeds 35% of the gross estate ($525,000) and also exceeds 50% of the taxable estate ($375,000).

Redemption Through Use of Related Corporations. In any case in which one or more persons who are in control of each of two corporations sell the stock of one of the corporations to another of these corporations, the proceeds of this sale will be considered to be an amount distributed in redemption of the stock of the corporation which purchased the stock. The stock thus acquired will be treated as a contribution to the capital of the acquiring corporation made by the shareholder, and accordingly will take as its basis the basis in the hands of the shareholder.[14]

Illustration. Corporation X and Corporation Y each have outstanding 100 shares of common stock. One-half of the stock of each corporation is owned by an individual, A, and one-half by another individual, B, who is unrelated to A. A sells 40 shares of Corporation X stock (which has an adjusted basis to him of $10,000) to Corporation Y for $50,000. After the sale, A is considered as owning:

(1) 10 shares directly.
(2) 45 shares constructively inasmuch as, by virtue of his 50% ownership of Y, he constructively owns 50% of the 40 shares owned directly by Y, and 50% of the 50 shares attributed to Corporation Y because they are owned by Y's shareholder, B.

Inasmuch as A, after the sale, owns a total of more than 50% of the voting power of all the outstanding stock of Corporation X, the transfer is not "substantially disproportionate" as to him as provided in Section 302 of the Code. Under these facts, Section 302 is not applicable and the entire $50,000 is treated as a dividend to A to the extent of the earnings and profits of Corporation Y. The basis of the Corporation X stock to Corporation Y is $10,000, its adjusted basis to A. The amount of $10,000 is added to the basis of the stock of Corporation Y in the hands of A.

For the purposes of Section 304, "control" means the ownership of stock possessing at least 50% of the total combined voting power of all classes of stock entitled to vote, or at least 50% of the total value of shares of all classes of stock. It is possible under this definition for four unrelated stockholders to be in control of a corporation; that is, two stockholders may own 50% of the total combined voting power and two shareholders own 50% of the total value of the shares.

If a person is in control (within the meaning of the previous sentence) of a corporation which in turn owns at least 50% of the total combined voting power of all stock entitled to vote of another corporation, or owns at least 50% of the total value of the shares of

[14] I.R.C. Section 304.

stock of another corporation, this person will be deemed to be in control of this other corporation.

Illustration. If an individual owns 50% of the total combined voting power of A Corporation, which in turn owns 50% of the total combined voting power of B Corporation, this individual will be deemed to be in control of B Corporation.

Distributions by Corporations—Effects on Distributing Corporations

The general rule is that no gain or loss will be recognized to a corporation on a distribution with respect to its stock of stock or stock rights or property. The fact that the property distributed has appreciated or depreciated in value over its adjusted basis to the distributing corporation will not be significant. But this rule applies only when distributions are made to shareholders *as* shareholders, rather than, for example, as creditors; and there are two exceptions to this general rule.

Exceptions to General Rule. That may be immediate tax consequences to the distributing corporation when assets distributed to shareholders consist of (1) Lifo inventory or (2) assets with a liability in excess of their adjusted basis.[15]

(1) If a corporation inventorying goods under the last-in, first-out method (see Chapter 7) distributes what are defined in the next paragraph as "inventory assets," then the amount of gain determined in accordance with the second following paragraph will be treated as gain to the corporation recognized from the sale of these inventory assets.

"Inventory assets" mean stock in trade of the corporation, or other property of a kind which would properly be included in the inventory of the corporation if on hand at the close of the taxable year. "Inventory amount" means, in the case of inventory assets distributed during a taxable year, the amount of these inventory assets determined as if the taxable year closed at the time of this distribution.

The amount of the gain is the amount by which (1) the "inventory amount" of the assets determined under a method of cost other than the Lifo method exceeds (2) the "inventory amount" of these assets determined under the Lifo method. As to (1), the retail method of valuing inventories will be used if that is the corporation's regular method; otherwise, the lower of cost or market method will be used.

[15] I.R.C. Section 311.

Illustration. A manufacturing corporation using the Lifo method distributes 200 units of its inventory assets to its shareholders on November 15. Immediately before the distribution, the corporation held 300 identical inventory units at the following basis determined by reference to the value computed by using the Lifo method and the value computed by using the Fifo method, in the order of acquisition:

	Number of Units	Basis Lifo	Number of Units	Basis Fifo
(a)	100	$1,000	100	$4,000
(b)	100	2,000	50	2,500
(c)	50	1,000	50	2,500
(d)	50	2,000	100	6,000

The amount includible in income is $4,000, computed as follows:

Inventory before distribution under Fifo method (a), (b), (c), and (d)	$15,000	
Inventory under Fifo method immediately after distribution (d)	6,000	
Difference (Fifo basis of inventory distributed)		$ 9,000
Inventory before distribution under Lifo method (a), (b), (c), and (d)	$ 6,000	
Inventory under Lifo method immediately after distribution (a)	1,000	
Difference (Lifo basis of inventory distributed)		5,000
Amount includible in income		$ 4,000

(2) Where property is distributed to a shareholder with respect to his stock and this property is either subject to a liability or the shareholder assumes a liability of the corporation in connection with the distribution, and the amount of this liability exceeds the adjusted basis (in the hands of the distributing corporation) of this property, gain will be recognized. The amount of the gain will be an amount equal to the excess of the liability over the adjusted basis as if the property had been sold at the time of the distribution by the corporation.

Illustration. If property which is a capital asset having an adjusted basis to the distributing corporation of $100 and a fair market value of $1,000 (but subject to a liability of $900) is distributed to a shareholder, this distribution is taxable (as long- or short-term capital gain, as the case may be) to the corporation to the extent of the excess of the liability ($900) over the adjusted basis ($100), or $800. If the property subject to a liability were not a capital asset in the hands of the distributing corporation, the gain would be taxable as ordinary income.

Effect on Earnings and Profits. The general rule is that if distributions are in cash, the cumulative earnings of the distributing corporation are decreased by the amount of this cash; and if the distribution is in an obligation of the distributor, the earnings are decreased by the principal amount of the obligation. If the distribution is in property, the amount of the decrease is by the adjusted basis of this property. This rule is applicable whether the property has appreciated or depreciated in value.[16]

There must be an upward adjustment of earnings and profits where appreciated inventory assets are distributed. If "inventory assets" (to be defined in the next sentence) are distributed and if the fair market value exceeds the basis, then the corporate earnings are to be increased by the amount of this excess and are to be decreased by the lesser of the fair market value or the earnings and profits so increased; but the required adjustments may not serve to create a deficit in earnings and profits. "Inventory assets" for this purpose are (1) those items normally included in inventory and property held primarily for sale to customers and (2) unrealized receivables or fees from sales or exchanges of assets other than inventory assets. Unrealized receivables or fees means rights to payments for assets other than capital assets or rights to payment for services.

Illustration. A corporation distributes property to its sole stockholder with a value of $10,000 and a basis of $5,000. It has $12,500 in earnings and profits. The reduction in earnings and profits by reason of this distribution is $5,000. Such is the reduction even though the amount of $10,000 is includible in the income of the shareholder (other than a corporation) as a dividend.

Illustration. The facts are the same as in the preceding illustration, except that the property has a basis of $15,000 and the earnings and profits of the corporation are $20,000. The reduction in earnings and profits is $15,000. Such is the reduction even though only the amount of $10,000 is includible in the income of the shareholder as a dividend.

Other adjustments are made in the earnings and profits of the distributing corporation if gain is recognized because of (1) the distribution of property subject to a liability in excess of the adjusted basis of the asset or (2) the distribution of Lifo inventories. There is no adjustment for other distributions that do not represent gain; for example, receipt of tax-free distributions by a corporation will have no effect upon its earnings and profits.

Partial Liquidation

A comparison of dividends or distributions in complete and in partial liquidation will indicate the different effects of each. A dividend in complete liquidation is effected by a single distribution or by a series of distributions pursuant to a plan of complete liquidation. With respect to the distributor, the distribution is considered

[16] I.R.C. Section 312.

payment in exchange for his stock, and it must be reported with other capital gains and losses insofar as the distribution is made out of earnings accumulated after February 28, 1913. With respect to a dividend in partial liquidation, there is a complete cancellation of a part of the stock of the distributor. The distribution may be chargeable to capital, and the distribution may likewise extend to earnings. The recipient of the distribution treats the dividend as payment in exchange for his stock, to be reported as taxable gain or deductible loss. Should the distribution be considered to be essentially equivalent to a dividend, earnings will be charged with the distribution, and capital will be charged with any amount by which accumulated earnings fall short of the distribution. The recipient will pay tax on this dividend (after credits and exclusions) to the extent that it represents earnings accumulated after February 28, 1913.

The definition of partial liquidation includes the concept of corporate contraction; that is, a genuine contraction of the business results in partial liquidation.[17]

Corporate Liquidations—Effects on Recipients

The general rule is that amounts distributed in liquidation (complete or partial) will be treated as in payment for the stock of a shareholder. Such distributions will not be treated as dividends.[18]

Complete Liquidation of Subsidiary Corporations. The general rule is that no gain or loss will be recognized on the receipt by a corporation of property distributed in *complete* liquidation of another corporation.[19] For this rule to apply, the corporate shareholder must own at least 80% of the subsidiary's stock. Gain or loss to the minority shareholders, or to an individual shareholder, will be subject to the ordinary rules as to gain or loss. The rule applies only if complete liquidation is to be completed under a plan within three years from the close of the taxable year during which is made the first of the series of distributions under this plan.

The corporate parent must be the owner of stock possessing at least 80% of the total combined voting power of all classes of stock entitled to vote and the owner of at least 80% of the total number of shares of all other classes of stock (except nonvoting stock which is limited and preferred as to dividends).

[17] *Joseph W. Imler,* 11 T.C. 836 (1948).
[18] I.R.C. Section 331.
[19] I.R.C. Section 332.

If, at the time of its liquidation, a subsidiary corporation is indebted to its parent corporation, no gain or loss will be recognized to the subsidiary because of the transfer of property in satisfaction of the indebtedness.

Under the general rule, not only is there no gain or loss to the parent upon the liquidation of the subsidiary; the basis of the assets in the hands of the subsidiary carries over to the parent. But under certain circumstances, the basis of the subsidiary's assets in the hands of the parent corporation will be the parent's cost of acquiring the subsidiary's stock.[20] This special rule applies at the election of the parent corporation, but only if these conditions are met: (1) the distribution must be made pursuant to a plan of liquidation not more than two weeks after the acquisition of an 80% stock interest in the subsidiary and (2) this stock interest must have been acquired by purchase during a period of not more than twelve months.

Qualified Electing Shareholders. Under specified conditions, a *qualified electing shareholder* may receive property which has appreciated in value from a liquidating corporation without the recognition of gain on this appreciation.[21] This option is not available to a corporation that owns more than a 50% stock interest in the liquidating corporation; such a shareholder is known as an *excluded* corporation. All other shareholders are divided into two groups: (1) shareholders other than corporations and (2) corporate shareholders. As to (1), the provision only applies if written elections have been filed by noncorporate stockholders who at the time of the adoption of the plan owned at least 80% of the stock owned other than by corporations. As to (2), the provision applies only if written elections have been filed by corporate shareholders (other than an excluded corporation) which owned at least 80% of the stock (excluding the number of shares owned by individuals and an excluded corporation).

In the case of individual distributees who are qualified electing shareholders, to the extent gain is realized, any earnings and profits are treated as dividends, and the cash (or stock or securities acquired by the distributor after 1953) is taxed as capital gain. In the case of a qualified electing shareholder that is a corporation, tax is imposed at capital gains rates on the greater of (1) its share of the earnings of the liquidating corporation or (2) cash (or stock and securities acquired by the distributor after 1953).

[20] I.R.C. Section 334.
[21] I.R.C. Section 333.

Corporate Liquidations—Effects on Corporation

The general rule is that no gain or loss is recognized to a corporation on the distribution of property in partial or complete liquidation, except in the case of disposition of installment obligations.[22] The fact that the property distributed has appreciated or depreciated will in no way alter this rule that no gain or loss will be recognized to the distributor.

Tax on Sale of Corporate Property by Shareholders. If property owned by a corporation is sold by the shareholders, who had obtained this property as a liquidating dividend from a corporation, the question exists as to who should be taxed upon this sale. Were the shareholders only acting as agents for the corporation in the transaction? The answer depends upon the question of who had been primarily responsible for the negotiations that ultimated in the sale: corporation or shareholders.[23]

But a special rule exists for the mitigation of this requirement. If a corporation adopts a plan of complete liquidation and, within the 12-month period beginning on the date of the adoption of the plan, disposes of all the corporate assets (less assets retained to meet claims) in complete liquidation, then no gain or loss will be recognized to the corporation from the sale or exchange by it of property within this 12-month period.[24] No provision is made for anything less than a complete liquidation.

This privilege does not apply to inventory (unless sold or exchanged to one person in one transaction). Nor does it apply to a collapsible corporation, or to any transaction where there is a carryover of the subsidiary's basis to the parent corporation.

Collapsible Corporations

A collapsible corporation is a device which has been used to convert ordinary income into long-term capital gain by use of a temporary corporation. In other words, the corporation was formed for the purpose of dissolving (collapsing) it or otherwise disposing of it.

Sales or exchanges of stock of a collapsible corporation, or distributions in liquidation of such a corporation, or other distributions to the extent that they exceed the basis of the stock in the hands of

[22] I.R.C. Section 336.
[23] *Commissioner v. Court Holding Co.,* 324 U.S. 331 (1945).
[24] I.R.C. Section 337.

the shareholders, may be treated by the Internal Revenue Service as ordinary income rather than capital gain.[25] This provision applies in the case of a corporation engaged in building and otherwise meeting the tests of a collapsible corporation, if a distribution is made of the proceeds of a loan in excess of the adjusted basis of the property by which the loan is secured.

A collapsible corporation is defined in the Code as a corporation formed or availed of principally for (1) the manufacture, construction, or production of property, (2) the purchase of property which, in the hands of the corporation, is classified as "Section 341 assets," or (3) the holding of stock in a corporation so formed or availed of, with a view to (A) the sale or exchange of stock by its shareholders, or a distribution to its shareholders, prior to the realization by the corporation manufacturing, constructing, producing or purchasing the property of a substantial part of the taxable income to be derived from this property and (B) the realization by the shareholders of gain attributable to this property.

The term "Section 341 assets" means property held for a period of less than three years. It refers to inventory, unrealized receivables, and property used in the trade or business (such as realty or machinery); but it does not include property used in the trade or business which produced items included as Section 341 assets; for example, inventory produced by the taxpayer's own machinery.

A corporation will be presumed to be a collapsible corporation if the fair market value of its Section 341 assets is (1) 50% or more of the fair market value of its total assets and (2) 120% or more of the adjusted basis of these Section 341 assets. For this purpose, fair market value of the total assets does not include cash, obligations which are capital assets in the hands of the corporation, and stock in any other corporation. If either of the conditions mentioned in this paragraph is not met, however, there will be no presumption that the corporation is not a collapsible corporation.

Illustration. A corporation, filing its income tax returns on the accrual basis, on July 31 owned assets with the following fair market values: cash, $175,000; note receivable held for investment, $130,000; stocks of other corporations, $545,000; rents receivable, $15,000; and a building constructed by the corporation two years ago and held thereafter as rental property, $750,000. The adjusted basis of the building on that date was $600,000. The only debt outstanding was a $500,000 mortgage on the building. On July 31, the corporation liquidated and distributed all of its assets to its shareholders. In computing whether the fair market value of the Section 341 assets (only the building) is 50% or more of the fair market value of the total assets, the cash, note receivable, and stocks of other corporations are not taken into account in determining the value of the total

[25] I.R.C. Section 341.

assets, with the result that the fair market value of the total assets was $765,000 ($750,000 building plus $15,000 rents receivable). Therefore, the value of the building is 98% of the total assets ($750,000 divided by $765,000). The value of the building is also 125% of the adjusted basis of the building ($750,000 divided by $600,000). In view of the above facts, there arises a presumption that the corporation is a collapsible corporation.

Exceptions. Collapsible corporation treatment does not apply to any shareholder owning less than 5% in value of the outstanding stock of the corporation. A further limitation is that Section 341 will apply to the gain recognized during a taxable year upon the stock in a collapsible corporation only if more than 70% of this gain is attributable to Section 341 assets; if more than 70% of the gain is so attributable, then all of the gain is subject to the severe tax treatment; while if 70% or less of the gain is so attributable, then none of the gain is subject to this section of the Code. The section does not apply to that portion of the gain of a shareholder that is realized more than three years after the actual completion of the manufacture, construction, production, or purchase of the property to which that portion is attributable.

Collapsible corporation treatment does not apply where the unrealized appreciation in ordinary income assets does not exceed 15% of the corporation's net worth, unless sales of stock are made to the corporation, or by a person with a stock interest greater than 20% to a related person. Ordinary income assets for this purpose mean inventory and other property, such as intangibles.

Liquidation of Foreign Personal Holding Companies

If a liquidating distribution is made by a foreign personal holding company with respect to which a United States group (see Chapter 22) existed within a defined statutory period, the distribution will be deemed to be in payment for the stock, any resultant gain being treated as a short-term capital gain.[26]

Corporate Organizations and Reorganizations

Transfer to Controlled Corporation. No gain or loss is recognized if property is transferred to a corporation by one or more persons solely in exchange for stock or securities in that corporation and immediately after the exchange that person or persons are in control of the corporation; that is, the holders of 80% or more of the stock. For the purposes of this section, stock or securities issued for services are not considered as issued in return for property.[27]

[26] I.R.C. Section 342.
[27] I.R.C. Section 351.

Exchanges of Stock and Securities in Certain Reorganizations. Securities may only be received tax-free in an amount not in excess of the principal amount of the securities surrendered. If securities in any greater amount are received, the fair market value of the excess amount is treated as other property; that is, it is taxable as *boot*. Likewise, if securities are received and no securities are surrendered, those received are treated as other property.[28]

Distribution of Stock and Securities of a Controlled Corporation. Distributions of stock may be tax-free without any exchange in certain cases. It is not necessary that there be a reorganization in connection with the distribution of stock of a controlled corporation. The distribution of stock of a controlled corporation need not be on a pro rata basis. The distributing corporation may retain stock and securities of a controlled corporation, providing stock constituting control (80%) is distributed, and it is established to the satisfaction of the Secretary of the Treasury that it is not pursuant to a plan having as one of its principal purposes the avoidance of Federal income tax.[29]

For purposes of determining the taxable nature of part of the exchange or distribution, stock in a controlled corporation acquired by purchase within five years of its distribution is treated as other property.

In order to have a tax-free distribution of stock in a controlled corporation, the distributing corporation and the controlled corporation must be engaged immediately after the distribution in the active conduct of a trade or business. If the stock of more than one controlled corporation is distributed, each of the corporations must meet this requirement.

The Spin-off Family. A spin-off occurs when a part of the assets of a corporation is transferred to a new corporation and the stock in the latter is distributed to the shareholders of the original corporation without surrender by the shareholders of stock in the distributing corporation.

Illustration. An existing company, A, transfers assets to a new company, B, in return for all of the B stock. A then distributes the B stock to the A stockholders.

A split-up occurs when a single existing corporation is replaced by two or more new corporations, the stock in the new corporations being distributed to the shareholders of the existing corporation, which is completely liquidated.

[28] I.R.C. Section 354.
[29] I.R.C. Section 355.

Illustration. C Corporation transfers certain of its assets to D Corporation for D stock. The balance of the C assets goes to E Corporation for E stock. C assigns the D and E stock to the C stockholders in exchange for their own (C) stock; then C is liquidated.

A split-off occurs when part of the assets of a corporation is transferred to a new corporation and the stock in the latter is distributed to the shareholders of the original corporation in consideration of a surrender by the shareholders of part of the stock in the distributing corporation.

Illustration. F Corporation transfers certain of its assets to G Corporation for G stock. F assigns the G stock to its (F's) stockholders for part of their stock.

Receipt of Additional Compensation. Where a recapitalization or other type of corporate reorganization occurs, a shareholder may receive money or other property (boot) in addition to the stock or securities which may be received without recognition of gain. The transaction as a whole is not disqualified, but the boot is subject to tax under I.R.C. Section 356. A dividend is taxed only to the extent of the boot received which is not in excess of the particular shareholder's gain.

Illustration. If a shareholder surrenders stock which had a basis of $100 in his hands in a recapitalization and receives in exchange stock which has a value of $50 and a bond with a value of $75, the entire amount of the bond would be considered as boot but only $25 would be subject to tax, inasmuch as this is the amount of his gain realized on the transaction.

Where securities (bonds) are exchanged for securities, no gain or loss is recognized where the securities received are in the same principal amount as the securities surrendered. Where the principal amount of securities received and surrendered varies, this rule is applied to so much of the principal amount of the bonds received as is equal to the amount surrendered.

Illustration. If a shareholder surrenders a bond in the principal amount of $150 in exchange for a bond in the principal amount of $200, the exchange is treated as if there had been a tax-free exchange of a bond in the principal amount of $150 for a bond of identical principal amount and the receipt of an additional bond in the principal amount of $50. The fair market value of this $50 would be taken into account in determining whether there had been a receipt of taxable boot.

Effects on Corporations

Nonrecognition of Gain or Loss to Corporations. No gain or loss is recognized if a corporation a party to a reorganization exchanges property, in pursuance of the plan of reorganization, solely for stock or securities in another corporation a party to the reorganization.[30]

[30] I.R.C. Section 361.

Basis to Corporations. If property is acquired by a corporation in connection with a transfer to a controlled corporation, or as paid-in surplus or as a contribution to capital, then the basis to the transferee will be the same as it would be in the hands of the transferor, increased by any amount of gain recognized to the transferor on the transfer.[31]

If property is transferred to a corporation by persons other than shareholders in their capacity as shareholders, the basis of property (other than money) to the corporation is zero. If money is contributed, the basis of any property acquired with this money during the twelve months' period beginning on the day the contribution is received will be reduced by the amount of the contribution. The excess (if any) of the amount of this contribution over the amount of the reduction of basis will be applied in reduction of the basis of any other property held by the corporation.

Insolvency Reorganizations

Nonrecognition of gain or loss is provided upon certain exchanges made in connection with the reorganization of an insolvent corporation. This does not apply to railroad corporations.[32]

For the purpose of an insolvency reorganization, the term "reorganization" is not controlled by the exact language of the definition of a reorganization in Section 368, as given earlier in this chapter. But certain basic requirements, implicit in the statute, which are essential to a reorganization under Section 368, are likewise required here; for example, there must be a genuine reorganization as distinguished from a liquidation and sale of property to either new or old interests supplying new capital and discharging the obligations of the old corporation.

If an exchange would be within the provisions of the statute were it not for the fact that the consideration for the transfer of the property of the insolvent corporation consists in part of *boot,* then, if this boot, received by the corporation is distributed by it pursuant to the plan of reorganization, no gain to the corporation will be recognized; this distribution may be to shareholders or creditors who have taken over the corporation's property. No loss from the exchange will be recognized.

No gain or loss will be recognized if, pursuant to the plan of reorganization, stock or securities in the insolvent corporation are ex-

[31] I.R.C. Section 362.
[32] I.R.C. Section 371.

changed solely for stock or securities in a corporation organized or made use of to effectuate the plan.

If, as a result of a transaction described in Section 371, above, the property of an insolvent corporation is transferred, in pursuance of a plan of reorganization, to a corporation organized or made use of to effectuate the plan, the basis of this property in the hands of the acquiring corporation is the same as it would be in the hands of the insolvent corporation, increased in the amount of gain recognized upon this transfer under the law applicable to the year in which the transfer was made. In any such case, basis will not be scaled down in respect of any indebtedness canceled pursuant to the plan of reorganization under which the transfer was made.[33]

Carryovers

Carryovers in certain corporate reorganizations are treated in Chapter 14.

Formalities

Corporate reorganizations are an exception to a general rule: that disposition of property occasions taxable gain or deductible loss. Because reorganizations are an exception, the taxpayer has the burden of proof of showing that his transaction should not be treated under the general rule. This involves an extremely elaborate body of formalities. The necessary reorganization forms must be submitted in the manner prescribed by the Code or regulations. The price of failure to abide by the formalities may be loss of the advantages of a corporate reorganization.

Not only is it necessary for the taxpayer to show that his transaction is one covered by the *language* of the statute. He must also show that his transaction is one covered by the *spirit* of the law. The transaction must be one that the law contemplated.[34]

Supplementary Material

A. Suggested Reading.

Robert S. Holzman, *Corporate Reorganizations—Their Federal Tax Status* (New York: The Ronald Press Co., 1956).

John Dane, Jr., "The Case for Nonrecognition of Gain in Reorganization Exchanges," *TAXES—The Tax Magazine,* April, 1958, Vol. XXXV, #4, p. 244.

[33] I.R.C. Section 372.

[34] *Gregory v. Helvering,* 293 U.S. 465 (1935).

Waymon C. Peavy, "Corporate Organizations and Reorganizations," *Journal of Accountancy,* August, 1956, Vol. CII, #2, p. 36.

Jerome R. Hellerstein, "Mergers, Taxes, and Realism," *Harvard Law Review,* December, 1957, Vol. LXXI, #2, p. 254.

Matthew F. Blake, "Taxes and Mergers," *Journal of Accountancy,* July, 1956, Vol. CII, #1, p. 27.

Walter G. Schwartz, "Acquisition of Stock in Another Corporation in Order to Acquire Assets," *Proceedings of the University of Southern California School of Law Ninth Annual Tax Institute* (Albany: Matthew Bender & Co., Inc., 1957), p. 45.

Lawrence J. Seidman, "Divide To Conquer?" *Illinois Certified Public Accountant,* Autumn, 1957, Vol. XX, #1, p. 27.

Samuel Mirandy, "Stock Redemptions—Some Current Aspects," *The New York Certified Public Accountant,* December, 1956, Vol. XXVI, #12, p. 724.

John H. Alexander and William B. Landis, Jr., "Bail-Outs and the Internal Revenue Code of 1954," *Yale Law Journal,* June, 1956, Vol. LXV, #7, p. 909.

M. R. Schlesinger, "Tax Traps and Disasters in the Ubiquitous and Uncoordinated Attribution Rules," *Journal of Taxation,* May, 1958, Vol. VIII, #5, p. 271.

B. Leading Cases.

What is a reorganization? *Fairfield Steamship Corporation v. Commissioner,* 157 F.2d 321 (2d Cir., 1946).

What is a recapitalization? *Helvering v. Southwest Consolidated Corporation,* 315 U.S. 194 (1942).

Corporate purpose. *Gregory v. Helvering,* 293 U.S. 465 (1935).

Who makes the sale? *Commissioner v. Court Holding Co.,* 324 U.S. 331 (1945).

Partial liquidation. *Joseph W. Imler,* 11 T.C. 836 (1948).

C. Questions.

1. In order to save brokerage fees and commissions, the owner of land used for a filling station exchanged the property for similar property in another part of the city. The new property was worth $10,000 less than the adjusted basis of the old. Is the loss recognized for tax purposes?
2. A corporation upon its formation issued $100 par value stock. What is the gain or loss to the corporation if the stock is sold to investors for (a) $100, (b) $102, or (c) $96?
3. An individual transfers property having a basis in his hands of $20,000 but subject to a mortgage of $50,000 to a corporation controlled by him. Is he subject to any tax?
4. Real estate (held for investment purposes) with an adjusted basis of $5,000 is exchanged for other real estate (also to be held for investment purposes), a truck, and $1,000 in cash. The fair market value at the time of the exchange of the other real estate is $2,500 and of the truck, $1,900. (a) What is the gain or loss on the exchange? (b) What is the basis of the properties received?
5. An industrial tycoon, j.g., transferred property with a basis in his hands of $20,000 to a corporation that he controlled. In addition to

stock in the corporation, with a fair market value of $16,000, he received $10,000 in cash, and the corporation assumed a mortgage of $5,000 on the property. What was his gain or loss? How much of this is recognized for tax purposes?

6. P Corporation owns all of the stock of S Corporation. S is liquidated within a 3-year period, all of the S assets going to P. The assets have an adjusted basis in S's hands of $40,000; the fair market value at the time of the liquidation was $50,000. The S stock had cost P $45,000. Does P have any gain or loss on the liquidation? What is the basis of the assets in P's hands?
7. If, in the preceding problem, P had liquidated S within two years of the acquisition of this stock, and the stock had been purchased by P in a 6-month period, may P elect to give the S assets a different basis?
8. A corporation owned a ship. On February 1, after vain efforts to sell the vessel, the corporation was liquidated, the ship going to the stockholders as a distribution in liquidation. On April 18, the stockholders sold the ship to unrelated parties. May the Internal Revenue Service tax the resultant profit to the corporation? Would your answer be the same if the corporation actually had found the buyer in January and discussions about price had been instituted by the corporation?
9. Senior and Junior (father and son) organized a corporation with 100 shares of common stock. Senior transferred property worth $80 in exchange for 20 shares of stock, while Junior transferred property worth $20 to the corporation in exchange for 80 shares of stock. Is gain or loss recognized to any of the parties to the transaction?
10. Property with a value of $100 was distributed by a corporation to its shareholders. The corporation had only $75 of earnings and profits from which the distribution could be made. (a) What is taxable to the shareholders? (b) If the property had cost the corporation $50, how much will earnings and profits be reduced?
11. A truck with an adjusted basis of $3,000 is exchanged for a new smaller truck having a fair market value of $2,200, plus $1,000 in cash. (a) What is the recognized gain or loss? (b) What is the basis of the new truck?
12. A corporation owned assets which had appreciated in value in the amount of $50,000. The corporation was liquidated in one calendar month in 1961, and the five equal shareholders (all individuals) elected to be treated as qualified electing shareholders. There were accumulated earnings of $7,500 and the corporation had cash of $6,000 and stock and securities acquired after 1953 in the amount of $4,000; each shareholder had a basis for his stock of $12,000. How are liquidating distributions to be reported for tax purposes by each of the shareholders?
13. If one of the individual shareholders had not filed an election, what would the tax treatment be to (a) him and (b) the other shareholders? Would your answer be the same if two of the shareholders had not filed an election?
14. In the second preceding question, if all of the shareholders were corporations, what would your answer be?
15. Ralph Reel, the owner of a movie theatre with an adjusted basis of $35,000 and a fair market value of $29,000, exchanged it for a bowling

alley with a basis in the hands of the original owner of $18,000 and a fair market value of $30,000. What is Reel's recognized gain or loss?

16. P Corporation has owned all of the shares of S Corporation for six years. P decides to distribute the S stock to its own (P) shareholders. Will the P shareholders be taxed? Would your answer be different if the P shareholders were obliged to relinquish any of their P stock upon receipt of S shares?
17. The Croesus Corporation purchased securities for $80,000. Three years later, when the securities were worth $90,000, they were distributed as a dividend to the shareholders. Does the distributing corporation have any gain to report? Would your answer be different if, instead of securities, we were talking about an inventory that was carried on the cost basis?
18. First Corporation had assets worth $100,000 and $10,000 in liabilities. Second Corporation acquires $98,000 worth of assets subject to a liability of $10,000. In exchange for these assets, Second transfers its own voting stock, assumes the $10,000 liability, and pays $8,000 in cash. Is the transaction a reorganization in view of the fact that part of First's assets were acquired for cash? Would your answer be the same if the assets of First Corporation, worth $100,000, were subject to $50,000 in liabilities?
19. Under a plan of reorganization, the Corpulent Corporation transferred (a) $25,000 par value of its new preferred stock and $20,000 principal amount of its new debentures to bondholders on a pro rata basis in exchange for (b) $40,000 principal amount of old debentures of the company. Are there any tax consequences to the parties? Would your answer be different if the corporation had exchanged what was listed in (a) for what was listed in (b)?
20. A corporation had inventories that had cost $50,000 with a present fair market value of $75,000. Its other assets were furniture and fixtures with a fair market value of $10,000 and $5,000 in cash. Twelve persons each owned eight of the 100 shares; the remaining stock was owned by a poor but unhappy bachelor. Two years after incorporation, the shareholders collectively sold their stock to another corporation for an aggregate gain of $30,000. Discuss the taxability of the gain insofar as each shareholder is concerned.

18

PARTNERSHIPS—I

Partnership Income and Loss

What Is a Partnership? For Federal income tax purposes, the term "partnership" includes a syndicate, group, pool, joint venture, or other unincorporated organization through or by means of which any business, financial operation, or venture is carried on, and which is not a corporation or a trust or estate within the meaning of the Internal Revenue Code.[1] The term "partnership" is broader in scope than the common law meaning of partnership and may include groups not commonly called partnerships. A joint undertaking merely to share expenses is not a partnership. For example, if two or more persons jointly construct a ditch merely to drain surface waters from their properties, they are not partners for tax purposes. Mere co-ownership of property which is maintained, kept in repair, and rented or leased does not constitute a partnership. Tenants in common may be partners if they actively carry on a trade, business, financial operation, or venture and divide the profits. For example, a partnership exists if co-owners of an apartment building lease space and in addition provide services to the occupants either directly or through an agent.[2]

Under certain conditions, an unincorporated organization may be excluded from the application of all or a part of the partnership provisions. Such an organization must be availed of for investment purposes only and not for the active conduct of a business, or for the joint production, extraction, or use of property, but not for the purpose of selling services or property produced or extracted. The members of the organization must be able to compute their income without the necessity of computing partnership taxable income. Any syndicate, group, pool, or joint venture which is classifiable as an association, or any group operating under an agreement which creates an organization classifiable as an association, does not fall within these provisions.[3]

[1] I.R.C. Section 761.
[2] Regulations Section 1.761-1.
[3] I.R.C. Section 761.

Where the participants in the joint purchase, retention, sale, or exchange of investment property (1) own the property as co-owners, (2) reserve the right separately to take or to dispose of their shares of any property acquired or retained, and (3) do not actively conduct business or irrevocably authorize some other person acting in a representative capacity to purchase, sell, or exchange the investment property, although each separate participant may delegate authority to purchase, sell, or exchange his share of the investment property for a period of not more than a year, the group may be excluded from the partnership rules.

The status of a so-called partnership under state laws is not controlling for Federal tax purposes.[4]

The chief test of whether a claimed partnership is to be recognized as such is *reality*.[5] To hold that "Individuals carrying on business in partnership" include persons who contribute nothing during the tax period would violate the first principle of income taxation: that income must be taxed to him who earns it.[6]

Family Partnerships. A family partnership is one whose members are closely related through blood or marriage. The family, for this purpose, includes only husband or wife, ancestors, and lineal descendants, and any trusts for the primary benefit of these persons. Brothers and sisters are not included.

In the case of family partnerships, it is obvious that the tests of reality must be applied with special care. A partnership is created "when persons join together their money, goods, labor, or skill for the purpose of carrying on a trade, profession, or business and where there is a community of interest in the profits and losses." [7] "The question is not whether the services or capital contributed by a partner are of sufficient importance to meet some objective standard . . . but whether, considering all the facts—the agreement, the conduct of the parties in execution of its provisions, their statements, the testimony of disinterested parties, their respective abilities and capital contributions, the actual control of income and the purposes for which it is used, and any other facts throwing light on their true intent—the parties in good faith and acting with a business purpose intended to join together in the present conduct of the enterprise." [8] Thus, when a certified public accountant claimed

[4] *Burk-Waggoner Oil Association v. Hopkins,* 269 U.S. 110 (1925).
[5] *Eckhard v. Commissioner,* 182 F.2d 547 (10th Cir., 1950).
[6] *Lucas v. Earl,* 281 U.S. 111 (1930).
[7] *Commissioner v. Tower et al.,* 327 U.S. 280 (1946).
[8] *Commissioner v. Culbertson,* 337 U.S. 733 (1949).

his son as a partner the day after the latter was born, the partnership lacked substance.[9]

The Supreme Court took pains to point out that it never said that the donee of an intrafamily gift could never become a partner through investment of the capital in the family partnership. "The fact that transfers to members of the family group may be mere camouflage does not, however, mean that they invariably are."[10]

Generally, where capital is a material income-producing factor and the family member acquired his capital interest in a bona fide transaction, he is a partner, provided he actually owns the partnership interest and he is vested with dominion and control over it. This rule applies even if the interest was acquired by gift or purchase from another family member. If capital is not a material income-producing factor, the family member will still be recognized as a partner provided he contributes substantial or vital services.[11]

Capital is a *material income-producing factor* if a substantial portion of the gross income of the business is due to the use of capital, as when substantial inventories or investments in plant, machinery, or equipment are required. Capital is *not a material income-producing factor* where the income of the business consists principally of fees, commissions, or other compensation for personal services performed by members or employees of the partnership.

A capital interest in a partnership means an interest in the assets of the partnership which is distributable to the owner of the capital interest upon his withdrawal from the partnership or upon liquidation of the partnership. The mere right to share in the earnings and profits is not a capital interest in the partnership.

The distributive share of a family member whose capital interest is created by gift is includible in his gross income, where capital is a material income-producing factor, subject to these conditions:

(1) The donee's share is to be determined by allowance of reasonable compensation for services rendered to the partnership by the donor.

(2) The portion of the income allocated to the donee must be no greater than the share allocated to the donor in proportion to their respective interests.

An interest purchased by one member of a family from another member of the family is considered as created by gift for purposes of these conditions.

[9] *Tinkhoff v. Commissioner,* 120 F.2d 564 (7th Cir., 1941).
[10] *Commissioner v. Culbertson, supra.*
[11] I.R.C. Section 704(4).

Illustration. The profits of a partnership, in which the father sold a 50% interest to his son, amounted to $60,000 in the taxable year. The alleged sale is considered to have been a gift. Capital is a material income-producing factor, and the son performed little service for the partnership. Reasonable compensation for services rendered by the father is $26,000, which must be allowed to the father. The son's share of the profits cannot exceed $17,000 in that year.

Taxability. A partnership as such is not taxable.[12] Partners are liable for income tax only in their separate capacities. The partnership must file an income tax return, regardless of the amount of the income (or loss); but this is only for informational purposes, so that the Internal Revenue Service may ascertain whether each partner picks up his proper share of the income and expenses of various categories.

Each partner is required to take into account in his return his distributive share, whether or not distributed, of each class or item of partnership income, gain, loss, deduction, or credit. Thus, in determining his income tax, each partner must take into account his distributive share of:

(1) Short-term capital gains and losses.

(2) Long-term capital gains and losses.

(3) Gains and losses from sales or exchanges of so-called Section 1231 assets (relating to certain property used in a trade or business and involuntary conversions).

(4) Charitable contributions.

(5) Dividends with respect to which there is provided a credit or deduction, or an exclusion. See Chapter 8.

(6) Taxes paid or accrued to foreign countries and to possessions of the United States.

(7) Partially tax-exempt interest on obligations of the United States. But if the partnership elects to amortize premiums on bonds, the amount received on these obligations by the partnership is reduced by the amortizable bond premium applicable to the obligations.

(8) Other items of income, gain, loss, deduction, or credit. This includes recoveries of bad debts, prior taxes, and delinquency amounts; gains and losses from wagering transactions; soil and water conservation expenditures; nonbusiness expenses; medical and dental expenses; expenses for care of certain dependents; alimony payments; amounts representing taxes and interest paid to cooperative housing corporations; intangible drilling and development costs; exploration expenditures; and any items of income, gain, loss, deduction, or credit subject to a special allocation under

[12] I.R.C. Section 701.

the partnership agreement which differs from the allocation of partnership taxable income or loss generally.

(9) Taxable income or loss, exclusive of items requiring separate computation under Items (1) to (8), above.[13]

The character in the hands of a partner of any item of income, gain, loss, deduction, or credit described in Items (1) to (8), above, will be determined as if the item were realized directly from the source from which realized by the partnership or incurred in the same manner as incurred by the partnership.

Where it is necessary to determine the amount or character of the gross income of a partner, his gross income will include his distributive share of the gross income of the partnership.

If separate returns are made by a husband and wife domiciled in a community property state, and only one spouse is a member of the partnership, the part of his or her distributive share of any item listed in (1) to (9), above, which is community property, or which is derived from community property, should be reported by each spouse in equal proportions.

Taxable Income of Partnership. Even though a partnership is not a taxpayer, it is necessary to compute income, so that each partner's pro rata share of partnership income may be carried to the individual partner's return. The items described in categories (1) to (8) under the previous heading must be shown separately on the partnership return. The partnership also is required to compute and to state separately in its return the total of all other items of gross income (not separately stated) over the total of all other allowable deductions (not stated separately), which total, of course, may result in a loss if deductions exceed income. The partnership may not take as a deduction any of the following:

(1) The standard deduction allowed to individuals. See Chapter 24.

(2) The deduction for personal deductions allowed to individuals. See Chapter 24.

(3) Taxes paid or accrued to foreign countries or to possessions of the United States. Each partner's distributive share of these taxes is accounted for by him separately on his own return.

(4) Charitable contributions. Each partner reflects on his own return his distributive share of partnership contributions.

(5) Any net operating loss deduction. See Chapter 14.

(6) Certain personalized deductions allowed to individuals who itemize their deductions, such as expenses for the production of in-

[13] I.R.C. Section 702.

come, medical expenses, expenses for the care of certain dependents, alimony payments, and amounts representing taxes and interest paid to cooperative housing corporations.

(7) The deduction for capital gains and the deduction for capital loss carryover. See Chapter 14.[14]

Partnership Elections. Any elections (except Item (3) under the previous heading) affecting the computation of income derived from a partnership must be made by the partnership rather than by the partners. All partnership elections are applicable to all partners equally, but any election made by a partnership does not apply to any partner's nonpartnership interests.

Distributive Shares. In general, a partner's distributive share of any item or class of items, gain, loss, deduction, or credit of the partnership will be determined by the partnership agreement.[15] But there are the following exceptions:

(1) If the partnership agreement makes no specific provision for the manner of sharing one or more items or classes of items, a partner's distributive share of these items will be determined in accordance with the provisions of the agreement for the division of the general profits or losses. If the principal purpose of any provision in the partnership agreement determining a partner's distributive share of a particular item is to avoid or to evade Federal income tax, the provision will be disregarded and the distributive shares of that item will be determined in accordance with the general rule of the preceding sentence.

(2) Where property actually has been contributed by a partner to a partnership (so as to become partnership property as among the partners and not merely property subject to the claims of partnership creditors), there are certain alternatives in determining the partners' distributive share of these items in order to account for appreciation or diminution in value of the property contributed which took place *before* the property was contributed to the partnership. When the partnership agreement is silent as to the treatment of contributed property, then depreciation, depletion, or gain or loss will be treated in the same manner as though these items arose with respect to property purchased by the partnership. For example, if a partner contributes to a partnership property with an adjusted basis less than its value at the time of contribution, the gain upon the sale of this property by the partnership will be taxable to each of the partners in accordance with his distributive share

[14] I.R.C. Section 703.
[15] I.R.C. Section 704.

of gains as though the property had been purchased by the partnership. Depreciation on contributed property will also be allocated among the partners without regard to which partner contributed the property.

Illustration. A and B form an equal partnership. A contributes property worth $1,000 with an adjusted basis of $400. B contributes $1,000 in cash. The basis of A's partnership interest is $400. The basis of B's interest is $1,000. If the contributed property depreciates at an annual rate of 10%, the partnership will have an annual depreciation deduction of $40, which results in a deduction of $20 in computing each partner's distributive share of partnership income. Thus, at the end of the first year, the basis of the contributed property will be $360. If the partnership has no operating income or deductions, each partner will have a loss of $20. A's basis for his interest will be $380 ($400, the original basis of his interest, reduced by the loss of $20). B's basis for his interest will be $980 ($1,000 less $20).

Illustration. If the property is sold in the second year of partnership operations for $900, the partnership gain will be $540 ($900, the amount realized, less the basis of $360). Each partner's share of the $540 gain will be $270. Assuming that the partnership engaged in no other transactions that year, each partner will have a capital gain of $270 from the partnership to report. A's basis for his interest will then be $650 (the basis of $380 increased by the gain of $270). B's basis will be $1,250 (the basis of $980 increased by the gain of $270). If the partnership is then liquidated, and its assets consisting of $1,900 in cash are distributed to the partners pro rata, A will have a capital gain of $300 ($950, the amount received, less $650, the basis of the interest). B will have a capital loss of $300 (the excess of B's basis, $1,250, over the amount received, $950).

If the partners so provide in the partnership agreement, depreciation, depletion, or gain or loss with respect to contributed property may be allocated among the partners in a manner which takes into account all or any portion of the difference between the adjusted basis and the fair market value of contributed property at the time of contribution. The allocation may apply to all contributed property or to specific items.

Illustration. Assume that partners A and B, in the illustration above, agree to attribute the potential gain represented by the difference between the basis and the fair market value of the property contributed by A to the contributor. Inasmuch as B, who contributed $1,000 in cash, has, in effect, purchased an undivided half-interest in the property for $500, and inasmuch as the property depreciates at an annual rate of 10%, B should be entitled to a deduction of $50 per year. But as the partnership is allowed only $40 per year (10% of $400), no more than this amount may be allocated to B. Therefore, the partners agree that the $40 deduction for depreciation is to be allocated $40 to B and $0 to A, the contributor. At the end of the first year, the basis of the contributed property will be $360. As the $40 deduction is allocated entirely to B, if the partnership has no operating income or deductions, A will have no gain or loss, and B will have a loss of $40. A's basis for his interest will remain $400. B's basis for his interest will be $960 ($1,000, the original basis of his interest, reduced by the loss of $40).

(3) Where undivided interests in property are contributed by the partners to the partnership, then depreciation, depletion, and gain or loss with respect to this property will be determined in the same manner as though these undivided interests continued to be held by the partners outside of the partnership. This provision is applicable only in the absence of a partnership agreement providing otherwise, and only with respect to property contributed to a partnership by all of its partners. The relative interests of the partners in the property prior to contribution must be in the same ratio as their interests in the capital and profits of the partnership after the contribution.

Illustration. A and B are tenants in common owning undivided one-half interests in real estate consisting of a factory and the land on which the factory is situated. They each contribute their respective undivided interests in the real estate to a partnership in which the profits are to be divided equally, and the assets are to be divided equally on dissolution. It is immaterial whether this contribution is expressly made in exchange for interests in a partnership, or whether a partnership is held to exist by virtue of the joint conduct of a business by A and B. A's basis for his undivided interest is \$4,000, of which \$1,000 is allocable to the land and \$3,000 to the factory. B's basis for his undivided interest is \$10,000, of which \$3,000 is allocable to the land and \$7,000 to the factory. The partnership agreement contains no provision as to the allocation of depreciation or as to the allocation of gain or loss on a sale of property by the partnership. The factory depreciates at a rate of 5% a year. The annual depreciation allowance to the partnership of \$500 (5% of \$10,000) will be allocated between the partners by allowing A a deduction of \$150 (5% of \$3,000, his basis for the factory) and by allowing B a deduction of \$350 (5% of \$7,000, his basis for the factory). At the end of the first year of partnership operations, A's basis for his undivided interest in the factory would be \$2,850 (\$3,000 less \$150), and B's basis would be \$6,650 (\$7,000 less \$350). If the partnership, at the end of the first year's operation, sells the factory and land for \$20,000, each partner's share of the gain would be computed as follows: Inasmuch as A's share of the proceeds is \$10,000, and his basis for the contributed property is \$3,850 (\$1,000 for the land and \$2,850 for the factory), his capital gain from the sale is \$6,150. Inasmuch as B's share of the proceeds also is \$10,000, and his basis in the contributed property is \$9,650 (\$3,000 for the land and \$6,650 for the factory), his capital gain is \$350.

Limitation on Partnership Loss. A partner's distributive share of partnership loss (ordinary or capital) will be allowed only to the extent of the adjusted basis (before reduction by current year's losses) of a partner's interest in the partnership at the end of the partnership taxable year in which the loss occurred. Any excess of this loss over the basis will be allowed as a deduction at the end of the partnership year in which the excess is repaid. The repayment by the partner of the excess loss increases the basis of his interest at the end of the partnership year in which this excess is repaid. The repayment by the partner of this excess loss increases the basis of his interest so that deduction of the loss cannot possibly decrease his basis below zero.

Illustration. A partner has a basis of $50 for his interest, and his distributive share of partnership loss is $100. His distributive share of the loss is limited to $50, thereby decreasing the basis of his interest to zero. The remaining $50 loss would not be recognized, unless he makes a further contribution of $50. If, however, he repays the $50 loss to the partnership out of his share of partnership income for the following year, then the additional $50 loss will be recognized at the end of the year in which this repayment is made.

Taxable Years of Partner and Partnership

Year in Which Income Is Includible. A partner must include in his income his distributive share of partnership items, plus any guaranteed salary or interest payments, which are received or accrued from the partnership for any partnership year ending *within or with* his taxable year.[16]

Illustration. A partner reports his income for a calendar year, while the partnership of which he is a member reports its income for a fiscal year ending May 31. During the partnership taxable year ending May 31, 1961, he received guaranteed payments of $1,200 for services and for the use of capital. Of this amount, $700 was received by him between June 1 and December 31, 1960, and the remaining $500 was received by him between January 1 and May 31, 1961. The entire $1,200 he received is includible in his taxable income for the calendar year 1961 (together with his distributive share of partnership items for the partnership taxable year ending May 31, 1961).

Addition or Change in Taxable Year. The taxable year of a partnership is determined as though the partnership were a taxpayer. A newly formed partnership may adopt a taxable year which is the same as the taxable year of all of its principal partners (or the same as the taxable year to which all of the partners are concurrently changing) without securing prior approval from the Commissioner, or it may adopt a calendar year without securing such prior approval if all its principal partners are not on the same taxable year. In any other case, a newly formed partnership must secure prior approval from the Commissioner for the adoption of a taxable year.

An existing partnership may not change its taxable year without securing approval from the Commissioner, unless all its principal partners have the same taxable year to which the partnership changes, or unless all its principal partners concurrently change to that taxable year. A partner may not change his taxable year without securing prior approval from the Commissioner.

[16] I.R.C. Section 706.

A principal partner, for this purpose, is a partner having an interest of 5% or more in partnership profits or capital.

Application for a change in a taxable year must be filed on Form 1128. Where prior approval is required, the applicant must establish a business purpose (one that is not primarily avoiding or evading of taxes) to the satisfaction of the Commissioner.

Closing of Partnership Year. The closing of a partnership taxable year or a termination of a partnership for Federal income tax purposes is not necessarily governed by the "dissolution," "liquidation," etc. of a partnership under state or local law. The taxable year of a partnership does not close as the result of the death of a partner, the entry of a new partner, the liquidation of a partner's entire interest in the partnership, or the sale or exchange of a partner's interest in the partnership, except (1) in the case of a termination of a partnership or (2) a partner who retires or sells his interest in a partnership.

(1) In the case of termination, the partnership taxable year closes for all partners as of the date of termination.

(2) A partnership taxable year closes with respect to a partner who sells or exchanges his entire interest in a partnership, and with respect to a partner whose entire interest is liquidated. But a partnership taxable year with respect to a partner who dies does not close prior to the end of the partnership taxable year, or the time when the partner's interest (held by his estate or other successor) is liquidated, sold, or exchanged, whichever is earlier.

In the case of a sale, exchange, or liquidation of a partner's entire interest in a partnership, the partner must include in his taxable income for his taxable year within or with which his membership in the partnership ends his distributive share of partnership items, plus any guaranteed items, for his partnership taxable year ending with the date of the sale, exchange, or liquidation. In order to avoid an interim closing of the partnership books, a partner's share of distributive items may, by agreement among the partners, be estimated by taking his pro rata part of the amount of these items he would have included in his taxable income had he remained a partner until the end of the partnership taxable year.

If a partner dies, however, his estate or other successor in interest will report in its return his distributive share of the partnership income items for the partnership year in which he died.

Illustration. If the partnership and the partners all file on the basis of a calendar year, and one of the partners dies on June 10, 1961, none of the income of the partnership for 1961 will be reported in the final return of the deceased partner but all of it will be included in the return of the partner's estate or other successor in interest. But if the partnership year terminates with his death, his share of income for that year will be included in his final return.

If a partner sells or exchanges a part of his interest in a partnership, or if the interest of a partner is reduced, the partnership taxable year continues to its normal end. In this case, the partner's distributive share of items which he is required to include in his taxable income will be determined by taking into account his varying interests in the partnership during the partnership taxable year in which the sale, exchange, or reduction of interest occurred.

The transfer of a partnership interest by gift does not close the partnership taxable year with respect to the donor. But the income up to the date of the gift that is attributable to the donor's interest will be allocated to him.

Transactions Between Partner and Partnership

A partner who engages in a transaction with a partnership other than in his capacity as a partner is treated as if he were not a member of the partnership with respect to that transaction; that is, the partner ordinarily is considered as being an entity separate from the partnership. Such in general is the case when there are loans by the partnership to the partner, or vice versa; sales of property by the partner to the partnership, or vice versa; the rendering of services by the partnership to the partner, or vice versa. Where a partner retains the ownership of property but allows the partnership to use this separately owned property for partnership purposes (for example, to obtain credit), the transaction is treated as one between a partnership and a partner not acting in his capacity as a partner. But transfers of money or property by a partner to a partnership as contributions, or transfers of money or property by a partnership to a partner as distributions, are not transactions covered by this rule.[17] "In all cases, the substance of the transaction will govern rather than its form."[18]

Transactions with Controlled Partnerships. Losses will not be allowed where they result from a sale or exchange of property (other than an interest in the partnership) between a partnership and a

[17] I.R.C. Section 707.
[18] Regulations Section 1.707-1.

partner who owns, directly or indirectly, more than 50% of the capital interest or profits interest in this partnership. Nor is a loss allowed on a sale or exchange of property, directly or indirectly, between two partnerships in which the same persons own, directly or indirectly, more than 50% of the capital or profits interests. But if one of the purchasers subsequently sells the property, any gain realized will be taxable only to the extent that it exceeds the loss previously disallowed.

Gains are treated as ordinary income in the event of a sale or exchange of property between a partner and a partnership, or between two partnerships where more than 80% of the interest in the partnership or partnerships is owned by the same person or persons, if the property in the hands of the transferee immediately after the transfer is depreciable property or *other property not a capital asset.* The *italicized* phrase includes (but is not limited to) trade receivables, inventory, and depreciable or real property used in the trade or business.

Ownership of an interest in partnership capital or profits is determined from the facts in each case.

Guaranteed payments are payments made by a partnership to one of its partners for services or for the use of capital. These payments are considered as payments made to a person who is not a partner, to the extent that they are determined without regard to the income of the partnership. These payments are taxed to the partner either as salary or interest and are deductible by the partnership as a business expense. The payments must be reported in the partner's individual return as ordinary income for his taxable year with or within which ends the partnership taxable year in which the payments were paid or accrued.

Illustration. Under the terms of a partnership agreement, a partner is entitled to a fixed annual salary of $10,000 without regard to the income of the partnership. His distributive share is 10%. After deducting the guaranteed payment, the partnership has $50,000 in ordinary income. He must include $15,000 as ordinary income in his income tax return for his taxable year within or with which the partnership taxable year ends ($10,000 guaranteed payment plus $5,000 distributive share).

A partner who receives guaranteed payments for a period during which he is absent from work because of personal injuries or sickness is not entitled to exclude these payments from gross income; they are not *wages* for this purpose. Similarly, a partner who receives guaranteed payments is not regarded as an employee of the partnership for the purposes of withholding tax at the source, deferred compensation plans, etc.

Continuation of Partnership

An existing partnership is considered as continuing if it is not terminated. The general rule is that a partnership is considered as terminated only if—

(1) No part of any business, financial operation, or venture of the partnership continues to be carried on by any of its partners in a partnership, or

(2) Within a 12-month period there is a sale or exchange of 50% or more of the total interest in partnership capital and profits.

In addition, there are two special rules:

(1) In the case of the merger or consolidation of two or more partnerships, the resulting partnership is considered the continuation of any merging or consolidating partnership whose members own an interest of more than 50% in the capital and profits of the resulting partnership.

Illustration. Partnership WA, in whose capital and profits W and A each own a 50% interest, and partnership VE, in whose capital and profits V and E each own a 50% interest, merge on September 30, and form partnership WAVE. Each partner is on a calendar year basis, as is partnership WA; while partnership VE is on a fiscal year ending June 30. After the merger, W and A each has a 30% interest in capital and profits, and V and E each has a 20% interest. Inasmuch as W and A together own an interest of more than 50% in the capital and profits of WAVE, this partnership is considered a continuation of partnership WA and will continue to file returns on a calendar basis. Inasmuch as V and E own an interest of less than 50% in the capital and profits of WAVE, the taxable year of the partnership VE closes as of September 30, the date of the merger, and VE is terminated as of that date. WAVE is required to file a return for the taxable year commencing with the January 1 of the year in which the merger took place, indicating thereon that until September 30, it was partnership WA. Partnership VE is required to file a return for its final taxable year, July 1 through September 30, the date of the merger.

(2) In the case of a division of a partnership into two or more partnerships, the resulting partnerships (other than any resulting partnership the members of which had an interest of 50% or less in the capital and profits of the prior partnership) is considered a continuation of the prior partnership.[19]

Illustration. Partnership FAIL is in the real estate and insurance business. F owns a 40% interest, while A, I, and L each owns a 20% interest in the capital and profits of the partnership. The partnership and the partners report their income on a calendar year basis. They agree to separate the real estate and insurance businesses as of November 1, and to form two partnerships: partnership FA to take over the real estate business and partnership IL to take over

[19] I.R.C. Section 708.

the insurance business. Inasmuch as members of the resulting partnership FA owned more than a 50% interest in the capital and profits of partnership FAIL (F, 40%, and A, 20%), partnership FA is considered a continuation of FAIL. Partnership FA is required to file a return for the calendar year, indicating thereon that until November 1 it was partnership FAIL. Partnership VE will be required to file a return for the taxable year it adopts.

Supplementary Material

A. Suggested Reading.

Houstin Shockey and Henry W. Sweeney, *Tax Effects of Operating as a Corporation or Partnership* (Englewood Cliffs, N.J.: Prentice-Hall, Inc., 1957).

Benjamin Harrow, "New Taxation of Partnerships," *How To Work with the Internal Revenue Code of 1954* (New York: Federal Tax Forum, Inc., 1954).

Charles B. E. Freeman, "Partnership Formation and Sale or Transfer Under the 1954 Code," *Tax Law Review*, November, 1955, Vol. XI, #1, p. 1.

Harry Janin, "Partners and Partnerships," *Journal of Accountancy*, September, 1956, Vol. CII, #3, p. 47.

William B. Wood, "Tax Problems of Partnerships," *Journal of Accountancy*, February, 1959, Vol. CVII, #2, p. 33.

B. Leading Cases.

What is a partnership? *Commissioner v. Culbertson*, 337 U.S. 733 (1949).
Intention. *Commissioner v. Tower*, 327 U.S. 280 (1946).
Family partnership. *Lusthaus v. Commissioner*, 327 U.S. 293 (1946).

C. Questions.

1. May a corporation elect to be taxed as a partnership?
2. Articles of partnership are obtained under the laws of a certain state. Is this a valid partnership for Federal income tax purposes?
3. Under the laws of a certain state, a certified public accountant may not take as a partner a person who is not so certified. But Charles, C.P.A., formed a partnership with David, who had not passed the state's examinations. Both men worked with equal effectiveness. May the Internal Revenue Service regard this as a partnership for tax purposes? May the alleged partners argue that this could not be a partnership for Federal tax purposes in view of the state law?
4. An individual is a 20% partner in a partnership with income of $100,000 in the taxable year. (a) How much does he include in his gross income? (b) If the partnership makes no distribution, how will he pay tax on the amount in (a)?
5. A partnership earns $2,000 in interest from City of Milwaukee bonds. Discuss the tax aspects of this interest insofar as the parties are concerned.
6. What is the purpose of a family partnership? How does it differ from other partnerships?
7. An attorney performed a considerable amount of work in setting up a partnership in the soft drink bottling field. He arranged for fran-

chises and drew up numerous contracts. Alpha contributed $25,000 to the partnership in cash; Beta contributed $30,000 in equipment; Gamma donated $35,000 in real estate. The attorney was given a 25% interest in return for his services. Are the persons equal partners for Federal income tax purposes in the absence of an agreement to the contrary?

8. Phi, Gamma, and Delta form a partnership and are equal partners. Phi uses the calendar year basis; Gamma, a fiscal year ending June 30; and Delta, a fiscal year ending August 31. Is there any restriction on the fiscal year that the partnership must use? Assuming a calendar year is adopted, in which taxable year will each of the partners report his share of the 1961 profits?
9. In 1960, its first year, a partnership reported a loss on its manufacturing operation of $5,000. May this be carried forward against 1961 manufacturing profits of $11,000?
10. Senior gives Junior, his son, a graduation present of $10,000 in cash when the latter is graduated from State University, and Junior at once invests the money in a partnership with Senior. The family business is the operation of a retail candy store. Will the Internal Revenue Service recognize this partnership for tax purposes? Would your answer be different if the enterprise were a law office?
11. An individual is requested to make a substantial contribution to a charity in which he is interested. What tax factors should determine whether he makes the contribution personally or has it made by a partnership in which he has a 50% interest?
12. A partnership, Beta Gamma Sigma, derives $25,000 profit from sales activities. It makes contributions of $6,000 to a church. (a) What deduction may the partnership take? (b) Partner Beta (one of three equal partners) has adjusted gross income before contributions (including his partnership share) of $20,000, and he makes contributions (all to his church) of $2,000. What is his total deductible contribution? (c) Partner Gamma's equivalent amounts are $30,000 and $9,000. What is his deductible contribution? Partner Sigma's equivalent amounts are $25,000 and $500. What is his deductible contribution?
13. Delta, Kappa, and Epsilon form a partnership to conduct a securities business. The partnership agreement provides that 10% of the profits will be shared equally. As to the remainder, Delta will get the profits from stocks; Kappa, from bonds; and Epsilon, from rights and warrants. Will the Internal Revenue Service honor this allocation for tax purposes?
14. An individual sells property used in his trade or business (Section 1231 assets) to a partnership in which he has a 90% interest. Is the resultant gain ordinary or capital?
15. A partner sells securities to a partnership in which he has a 60% interest. His loss is $5,000. How is this treated for tax purposes? Would your answer be different if his interest were 50%?
16. At the end of the partnership taxable year, 1961, the partnership had a loss of $20,000. The distributive share of this loss to one of the partners was $10,000. The adjusted basis of his interest in the partnership (not taking into account his distributive share of this loss) was $6,000. Assume that at the end of the partnership taxable year

1962, the partnership has no taxable income or loss, but owes $8,000 to a bank for money borrowed. (a) How much of the 1961 loss may be deducted by the partner referred to? (b) What is the basis of his partnership interest at the end of 1962?

17. Rather than impair the credit standing of their partnership by a distribution, the partners agree to invest surplus partnership funds in an equal dollar amount of municipal bonds and corporate stock. The partners further agree that Partner One is to receive all the interest income and gain or loss from tax-exempt bonds, while Partner Two is to receive all the dividend income and gain or loss from corporate stock. Is this arrangement valid for tax purposes?
18. A partner selling his partnership interest on June 30, 1961, has a basis for his interest of $5,000. His pro rata share of partnership income and gain up to that date is $15,000. He sells his interest for $20,000. (a) When does his partnership year close? (b) What gain or loss does he report?
19. East and West form an equal partnership. East contributes $1,000 cash and West contributes inventory with an adjusted basis to him of $800 and a fair market value of $1,000. (a) What is the basis of the inventory to the partnership? (b) If the inventory is sold during the year for $1,100, and there is no provision in the partnership agreement for treatment of contributed properties, what is the distributive share of each partner of the gain or loss on the inventory?
20. A partner is to receive 30% of partnership income as determined before taking into account any guaranteed payments, but not less than $10,000. The income of the partnership is $60,000. (a) To how much is this partner entitled? (b) If the partnership had income of $20,000 instead of $60,000, what would your answer be?
21. An individual has a taxable year ending December 31 and is a member of a partnership, the taxable year of which ends on June 30. He dies on October 31, 1960. His estate adopts a taxable year ending October 31. (a) What will be covered by the return of the decedent for the period January 1 to October 31, 1960? (b) What will happen to the remainder of his distributive share?

19

PARTNERSHIPS—II

Partnership Interests and Basis

Gain or loss is not recognized to a partner or to partnership upon the contribution of property (including installment obligations) to the partnership in exchange for an interest in the partnership.[1] This rule applies to a partnership in the process of formation or to a partnership which is already formed and operating. But the rule does not apply to a transaction between a partnership and a partner not acting in his capacity as a partner. Rather than contributing property to a partnership, a partner may sell property to the partnership or may retain the ownership of property and allow the partnership to use it. "In all cases, the substance of the transaction will govern, rather than its form." [2] Thus, if the transfer of property by the partner to the partnership results in the receipt by the partner of money or other consideration, including a promissory obligation fixed in amount and time for payment, the transaction will be treated as a sale or exchange rather than as a contribution.

Basis of Partner's Interest

General Rule. The determination of the adjusted basis of a partnership interest is ordinarily made as of the end of a partnership taxable year. This year-end determination is necessary, for example, in ascertaining the extent to which a partner's distributive share of partnership losses may be allowed. But where there has been a sale or exchange of all or a part of a partnership interest, or a liquidation of a partner's entire interest in a partnership, the adjusted basis of his interest should be determined as of the date of this event. The adjusted basis of a partner's interest in a partnership is determined without regard to any amount shown in the partnership's books as the partner's "capital," "equity," or similar account.

[1] I.R.C. Section 721.
[2] Regulations Section 1.721-1(a).

Illustration. A contributes property with an adjusted basis to him of $400 (and a value of $1,000) to a partnership. B contributes $1,000 in cash. While under their agreement each may have a "capital account" in the partnership of $1,000, the adjusted basis of A's interest is only $400, while B's interest is $1,000.[3]

Original Basis of Partner's Interest. The original interest of a partner in a partnership is determined under either of two conditions: (1) contributions to a partnership or (2) transfers of partnership interests.

(1) The basis to a partner of a partnership interest acquired by a contribution of property (including money) to the partnership is the amount of money contributed plus the adjusted basis at the time of the contribution of any property contributed.[4] If the acquisition of an interest in partnership capital results in taxable income to a partner, this income constitutes an addition to the basis of the partner's interest. If the contributed property is subject to indebtedness or if liabilities of the partner are assumed by the partnership, the basis of the contributing partner's interest is reduced by the portion of the indebtedness assumed by the other partners, inasmuch as the partnership's assumption of his indebtedness is treated as a contribution of money to the partner. Conversely, the assumption by the other partners of a portion of the contributor's indebtedness is treated as a contribution of money by them.

Illustration. An individual acquired a 20% interest in a partnership by contributing property which had an adjusted basis to him of $8,000, and which was subject to a mortgage of $4,000. Payment of the mortgage was assumed by the partnership. The adjusted basis of his interest would be $4,800, computed as follows:

Partner's adjusted basis of the property contributed	$8,000
Less: Portion of mortgage assumed by other partners which must be considered as a distribution of money to the individual (80% of $4,000)	3,200
Basis of the individual's partnership interest	$4,800

Illustration. If, in the above illustration, the property contributed by the individual was subject to a mortgage of $12,000, the adjusted basis of his partnership interest would be zero, and the excess of the mortgage assumed by the other partners over his basis ($9,600 less $8,000) would be a capital gain to him.

(2) The basis of an interest in a partnership acquired other than by contribution depends upon the manner of acquisition.[5] Thus, the basis of a purchased interest will be its cost. The basis of a partnership interest acquired from a decedent is the fair market value of the interest at the date of his death (or, at the executor's

[3] I.R.C. Section 705.
[4] I.R.C. Section 722.
[5] I.R.C. Section 742.

election, the value one year thereafter), increased by his estate's or other successor's share of partnership liabilities (if any) on that date, and reduced to the extent that this value is attributable to items constituting income in respect of a decedent.

Adjustments to Original Basis. The original basis of a partner's interest in a partnership is *increased* by any further contributions to the partnership and by the sum of the partner's distributive share for the taxable year and prior taxable years of:

(1) Taxable income of the partnership.

(2) Tax-exempt receipts of the partnership.

(3) The excess of the deductions for depletion over the basis of the depletable property.

The basis is *decreased* (but not below zero) by distributions from the partnership and by the sum of the partner's distributive share for the taxable year and prior taxable years of:

(1) Partnership losses (including capital losses).

(2) Partnership expenditures which are not deductible in computing taxable income or loss and which are not capital expenditures.[6]

Alternative Rule. In certain cases, the adjusted basis of a partner's interest in a partnership may be determined by reference to his share of the adjusted basis of partnership property which would be distributable upon termination of the partnership. This alternative rule may be used to determine the adjusted basis of his interest where the circumstances are such that he cannot practically apply the general rule or where, from a consideration of all the facts, it is, in the opinion of the Commissioner of Internal Revenue, reasonable to conclude that the result produced will not vary substantially from the result obtainable under the general rule.

Adjustments may be necessary in determining a partner's adjusted basis of a partnership interest under this rule. Adjustments would be required, for example, in order to reflect in his share of the adjusted basis of partnership property any significant discrepancies arising as a result of contributed property, transfers of partnership interest, or distributions of property to the partners.

Basis of Property Contributed to Partnership

The basis to the partnership of property contributed to it by a partner is the adjusted basis of this property to the contributing partner at the time of the contribution. Inasmuch as this property

[6] I.R.C. Section 705.

has the same basis in the hands of the partnership as it had in the hands of the contributing partner, the holding period of the property for the partnership includes the period during which it was held by the partner.[7]

Extent of Recognition of Gain or Loss on Distribution

Recognition of Gain or Loss to Partner. Where money is distributed by a partnership to a partner, no gain is recognized to the partner except to the extent that the amount of money distributed exceeds the adjusted basis of the partner's interest in the partnership immediately before the distribution. This rule is applicable both to current distributions (that is, distributions other than in liquidation of an entire interest) and to distributions in liquidation of a partner's entire interest in a partnership.[8]

Illustration. If a partner with a basis for his interest of $10,000 receives a distribution of cash of $8,000 and property with a fair market value of $3,000, no gain is recognized to him. If $11,000 cash were distributed, gain would be recognized to the extent of $1,000.

No gain is recognized to a distributee partner on a distribution of property (other than money) until he sells or otherwise disposes of this property, except in the case of (1) payments to a retiring partner or a deceased partner's successor in interest (I.R.C. Section 736, discussed below) or (2) unrealized receivables and inventory items.[9]

Advances or drawings of money or property against a partner's distributive share of income are treated as current distributions made on the last day of the partnership taxable year with respect to that partner.

Loss is recognized to the distributee partner only upon the liquidation of his entire interest in the partnership. Loss will be recognized to the partner whose interest is being liquidated to the extent that the basis of his interest exceeds the sum of (1) any money distributed to him and (2) the basis to him of any unrealized receivables and inventory items that are distributed to him. If he receives any property other than that mentioned in (1) or (2), no loss will be recognized.

Illustration. A partner has a partnership interest with an adjusted basis to him of $10,000. He retires from the partnership and receives, as a distribution in liquidation of his entire interest, his share of partnership property. This share

[7] I.R.C. Section 723.
[8] I.R.C. Section 731.
[9] I.R.C. Section 751, discussed below.

is $5,000 cash and inventory with a basis to him of $3,000. He realizes a capital loss of $2,000, which is recognized. Gain or loss on a distribution is considered gain or loss from the sale or exchange of the partnership interest of the distributee partner, that is, capital gain or loss.

Recognition of Gain or Loss to Partnership. A distribution of property (including money) by a partnership to a partner does not result in recognized gain or loss to the partnership. This rule does not apply in the following situations:

(1) Payments to a retiring partner or to a deceased partner's successor in interest.

(2) Unrealized receivables and inventory items.

(3) Distributions which, under I.R.C. Section 751(b), must be treated as a sale or exchange of property between the distributee partner and the partnership.

(4) The receipt by a partner from the partnership of money or property under an obligation to make repayment. This is regarded as a loan. To the extent that this loan is canceled, the obligor partner will be considered to have received a distribution of money or property at the time of cancellation.

(5) A contribution of property to a partnership, if within a short period (A) before or after this contribution other property is distributed to the contributing partner and the contributed property is retained by the partnership, or (B) after the contribution the contributed property is distributed to another partner.

Basis of Distributed Property Other Than Money

Distributions Other Than in Liquidation of a Partner's Interest. The basis of property (other than money) received by a partner in a distribution from a partnership, which is not in liquidation of his entire interest, will be its adjusted basis to the partnership immediately before the distribution. But the basis of the property to the partner may not exceed the basis of his interest in the partnership, reduced by the amount of any money distributed to him in the same transaction.[10]

Illustration. The adjusted basis of a partner's interest in a partnership is $30,000. He receives a current distribution of property, with an adjusted basis of $20,000 to the partnership, and $4,000 cash. The basis of the property in his hands is $20,000. The adjusted basis of the partnership interest is reduced by the distribution to $6,000 ($30,000 less $4,000 cash, less $20,000).

Illustration. The adjusted basis of a partner's interest in a partnership is $10,000. He receives a current distribution of $4,000 cash and property with an

[10] I.R.C. Section 732(a).

adjusted basis to the partnership of $8,000. His basis for the distributed property is limited to $6,000 ($10,000 less $4,000, the cash received). The adjusted basis of his partnership interest is zero.

Distribution in Liquidation. The basis of property received by a partner in complete liquidation of his interest is an amount equal to the adjusted basis of his interest in the partnership, reduced by the amount of any money distributed to him in the same transaction.[11]

Illustration. A partner, with a partnership interest having an adjusted basis to him of $12,000, retires from the partnership and receives cash of $2,000 and real property with an adjusted basis to the partnership of $6,000 and a fair market value of $14,000. The basis of the real property to him is $10,000 (his basis for the partnership interest, $12,000, reduced by $2,000, the cash distributed).

Allocation of Basis Among Properties Distributed to a Partner. Under I.R.C. Section 732(a) or (b), immediately above, the basis to be allocated to properties distributed to a partner must be allocated first to any unrealized receivables and inventory items. But these receivables or inventory items may not take a higher basis in the hands of the partner than their common adjusted basis to the partnership immediately before the distribution, unless (1) this distribution is treated as a sale or exchange or (2) the distributee partner has a special basis adjustment for the distributed property under I.R.C. Section 732(d) (to be discussed below) or under I.R.C. Section 743(b) (which will be discussed subsequently in this chapter). Any basis not allocated to unrealized receivables or inventory items must be allocated to any other properties distributed to the partner in the same transaction, in proportion to the bases of these other properties in the hands of the partnership before distribution.

Illustration. A partner, whose interest in a partnership has an adjusted basis of $15,000, receives as a distribution in liquidation of his entire interest inventory items having a basis to the partnership of $6,000. In addition, he receives cash of $5,000 and two parcels of real property with adjusted bases to the partnership of $6,000 and $2,000, respectively. Basis in the amount of $10,000 ($15,000 basis, less $5,000 cash received) is allocated $6,000 to inventory items, and $3,000 (6,000/8,000 times $4,000) and $1,000 (2,000/8,000 times $4,000), respectively, to the two parcels of real property.

If the adjusted basis to the partnership of the unrealized receivables and inventory items distributed to a partner is greater than the partner's adjusted basis of his interest (reduced by the amount of money distributed to him in the same transaction), the amount of the basis to be allocated to these unrealized receivables and inventory items must be allocated in proportion to the adjusted bases

[11] I.R.C. Section 732(b).

of these properties in the hands of the partnership. If the basis of the partner's interest to be allocated upon a distribution in liquidation of his entire interest is in excess of the adjusted basis to the partnership of the unrealized receivables and inventory items distributed, and if there is no other property distributed to which this excess can be allocated, the distributee partner sustains a capital loss to the extent of the unallocated basis of his partnership interest.

Illustration. A partner, whose interest in a partnership has an adjusted basis to him of $9,000, receives as a distribution in liquidation cash of $6,000, inventory items having an adjusted basis to the partnership of $6,000, and real property having a basis to the partnership of $4,000. The cash payment reduces his basis to $3,000, which is allocated entirely to inventory items. The real property has a basis of zero in his hands. The partnership bases not carried over to him for the distributed properties are lost unless an election under I.R.C. Section 754 (to be discussed later in this chapter) is in effect, requiring the partnership to make a stipulated adjustment in the bases of remaining partnership properties.

Special Partnership Basis to Transferee. A transfer of a partnership interest occurs upon a sale or exchange of an interest or upon the death of a partner. There is a special rule for the determination of the basis of property distributed to a transferee partner who acquired any part of his partnership interest in a transfer with respect to which the election under I.R.C. Section 754 (relating to the optional adjustment to basis of partnership property) was not in effect.[12]

If a transferee partner receives a distribution of property (other than money) from the partnership within two years after he acquired his interest (or any part of it) in the partnership by a transfer with respect to which the election under I.R.C. Section 754 was not in effect, he may elect to treat as the adjusted partnership basis of this property the adjusted basis this property would have if the adjustment provided in I.R.C. Section 743(b) were in effect.

If an election under I.R.C. Section 732(d) is made upon a distribution of property to a transferee partner, the amount of the adjustment with respect to the transferee partner is not diminished by any depletion or depreciation on that portion of the basis of partnership property which arises from the special basis adjustment of this subsection, inasmuch as depletion or depreciation on this portion for the period prior to distribution is allowed or allowable only if the optional adjustment under I.R.C. Section 743(b) is in effect.

If property is distributed to a transferee partner who elects under I.R.C. Section 732(d), and if this property is not the same property which would have had a special basis adjustment, then this special

[12] I.R.C. Section 732(d).

basis adjustment will apply to any like property received in the distribution, provided that the transferee, in exchange for the property distributed, has relinquished his interest in the property with respect to which he would have had a special basis adjustment. This rule applies whether the property in which the transferee has relinquished his interest is retained or disposed of by the partnership.

A transferee partner wishing to make this election must do so with his tax return (1) for the year of the distribution, if the distribution includes any property subject to the allowance for depreciation, depletion, or amortization, or (2) for any taxable year no later than the first taxable year in which the basis of any of the distributed property is pertinent in determining his income tax, if the distribution does not include any of the property mentioned in (1).

A special exception exists when a partnership distributes (1) unrealized receivables or substantially appreciated inventory items in exchange for any part of a partner's interest in other partnership property (including money) or (2) partnership property (including money) other than what is listed in (1) in exchange for any part of a partner's interest in the partnership's unrealized receivables or substantially appreciated inventory items. The distribution will be treated as a sale or exchange of property. In this event, the above rule of I.R.C. Section 732 applies in determining the partner's basis of the property which he is treated as having sold to or exchanged with the partnership (as constituted after the distribution). The partner is considered as having received this property in a current distribution and as having sold or exchanged it immediately afterwards. But I.R.C. Section 732 does not apply in determining the basis of that part of property actually distributed to a partner which is treated as received by him in a sale or exchange. Consequently, the basis of this property is its cost to the partner.

Special Partnership Basis of Distributed Property. In the case of a distribution of property to a partner, the partnership bases of the distributed properties must reflect any increases or decreases to the basis of partnership property which have been made previously under this rule relating to the optional adjustment to basis of undistributed partnership property, in connection with previous distributions.

There is a special rule in the case of a distribution of property to which a partner who acquired any part of his interest in a transfer as to which an election under I.R.C. Section 754 was in effect. This section provides that a partnership may adjust the basis of partnership property if it files a stipulated election. The election applies to all property distributions and transfers of partnership interests taking place in the partnership taxable year for which the election is made and in all subsequent partnership taxable years unless the election is revoked.[13] If this election is made, then (except for the purposes of I.R.C. Section 732(d)), the adjusted partnership bases of the distributed property must take into account, in addition to any adjustment under I.R.C. Section 734(b), the transferee's special basis adjustment for the distributed property under I.R.C. Section 743(b).[14]

Illustration. Partner Y acquired his interest in partnership FRY from a previous partner. Inasmuch as the partnership had made an election under I.R.C. Section 754, a special basis adjustment with respect to Y is applicable to the basis of partnership property. One of the assets of the partnership at the time Y acquired his interest was certain property, which is later distributed to Y in a current distribution. This specific property has an adjusted basis to the partnership of $1,000 and with respect to Y it has a special basis adjustment of $500. Therefore, the adjusted basis of this property to the partnership with respect to Y immediately before its distribution is $1,500. But, if this specific property is distributed to partner F, a nontransferee partner, its adjusted basis to the partnership is only $1,000. In this case, Y's $500 special basis adjustment may shift over to other property.

The basis to be allocated to distributed properties is allocated first to any unrealized receivables and inventory items. If the distributee partner is a transferee of a partnership interest and has a special basis adjustment for unrealized receivables or inventory items, then the partnership adjusted basis immediately prior to the distribution of these items distributed to this partner are determined as follows: If the distributee partner receives his entire share of the fair market value of the inventory items or unrealized receivables of the partnership, the adjusted basis of this distributed property to the partnership takes into account the entire amount of any special basis adjustment which the distributee partner may have for these assets. If the distributee partner receives less than his entire share of the fair market value of partnership inventory items or unrealized receivables, then the adjusted basis of this distributed property to the partnership takes into account the same proportion of the distributee's special basis adjustment for unrealized receivables or inventory items as the value of these items distributed to him bears to his entire share of the total value of all such items of the partnership.

[13] I.R.C. Section 754.

[14] Regulations Section 1.732-2(b).

Basis of Distributee Partner's Interest

In the case of a distribution by a partnership to a partner other than in liquidation of a partner's entire interest, the adjusted basis to that partner of his interest in the partnership must be reduced (but not below zero) by the amount of any money distributed to that partner and by the amount of the basis to him of distributed property other than money.[15]

Optional Adjustment to Basis of Undistributed Partnership Property

A partnership may not adjust the basis of partnership property as the result of a distribution of property to a partner, unless the election provided in I.R.C. Section 754 (relating to optional adjustment to basis of partnership property) is in effect.[16]

Method of Adjustment. Where an election under I.R.C. Section 754 is in effect and a distribution of partnership property is made, whether or not in liquidation of the partner's entire interest in the partnership, the adjusted basis of the remaining partnership assets is to be increased by—

(1) The amount of any gain recognized to the distributee partner and

(2) The excess of the adjusted basis to the partnership immediately before the distribution of any property distributed over the basis of this property to the distributee partner.

Illustration. A partner has a basis of $10,000 for his one-third interest in a partnership. The partnership has no liabilities and has assets consisting of cash of $11,000 and property with a partnership basis of $19,000 and a value of $22,000. He receives $11,000 in cash in liquidation of his entire interest in the partnership. He has a gain of $1,000. If the election under I.R.C. Section 754 is in effect, the partnership basis for the property becomes $20,000 ($19,000 plus $1,000).

Where the election provided in I.R.C. Section 754 is in effect and a distribution is made in liquidation of a partner's entire interest, the partnership must decrease the adjusted basis of the remaining partnership property by—

(1) The amount of loss, if any, recognized to the distributee partner and

(2) The excess of the basis of the distributed property to the distributee over the adjusted basis of such property to the partnership immediately before this distribution.

[15] I.R.C. Section 733.
[16] I.R.C. Section 734.

Illustration. A partner has a basis of $11,000 for his one-third interest in a partnership. Partnership assets consist of cash of $10,000 and property with a basis of $23,000 and a value of $20,000. There are no partnership liabilities. In liquidation of his entire interest in the partnership, he receives $10,000 in cash. He has a loss of $1,000. If the election under I.R.C. Section 754 is in effect, the partnership basis for the property becomes $22,000 ($23,000 less $1,000).

If a transferee partner, in liquidation of his entire partnership interest, receives a distribution of property (including money) with respect to which he has no special basis adjustment, in exchange for his interest in property with respect to which he has a special basis adjustment, and does not utilize his entire special basis adjustment in determining the basis of the distributed property to him, the unused special basis adjustment of the distributee will be applied as an adjustment to the partnership basis of the property retained by the partnership and as to which the distributee did not use his special basis adjustment.

Illustration. Upon the death of his father, S acquires by inheritance a half-interest in a partnership. His partners each has a one-quarter interest. The assets of the partnership consist of $10,000 cash and land used in farming worth $10,000 with a basis of $1,000 to the partnership. Inasmuch as the partnership had made the election under I.R.C. Section 754 at the time of the transfer, S has a special basis adjustment of $4,500 with respect to his undivided half-interest in the real estate. The basis of S's partnership interest is $10,000. S retires from the partnership and receives $10,000 in cash in exchange for his entire interest. Inasmuch as S has received no part of the real estate, his special basis adjustment of $4,500 will be allocated to the real estate, the remaining partnership property, and will increase its basis to the partnership to $5,500.

Character of Gain or Loss on Disposition of Distributed Property

Any gain realized or loss sustained by a partner on a sale or exchange or other disposition of unrealized receivables received by him in a distribution from a partnership is considered to be ordinary gain or loss. Any gain realized or loss sustained by a partner on a sale or exchange of inventory items received in a distribution from a partnership will be considered ordinary gain or loss if these inventory items are sold or exchanged within five years from the date of the distribution by the partnership. The character of any gain or loss from a sale or exchange by the distributee partner of these inventory items is determined as of the date of the sale or exchange by reference to the character of the assets in his hands at that date; that is, inventory items, capital assets, property used in a trade or business, etc.[17]

[17] I.R.C. Section 735.

A partner's holding period for property distributed to him by a partnership includes the period that this property was held by the partnership. But this provision does not apply for the purpose of determining the 5-year period mentioned in the preceding paragraph. If the property has been contributed to the partnership by a partner, then the period that the property was held by that partner must also be included.

Payments to a Retiring Partner or a Deceased Partner's Successor in Interest

When payments are made to a retiring partner or the successor in interest of a deceased partner in return for the complete relinquishment of his interest in the partnership, the payments are allocated between *payments in liquidation* and *other payments.* For income tax purposes, a retired partner or a successor in interest to a deceased partner will be treated as a partner until his interest in the partnership has been completely liquidated.[18]

Payments in Liquidation. Payments in liquidation of the entire interest of a partner, to the extent they are made in exchange for his interest in partnership property, are treated as proceeds from the sale or exchange of the partner's capital interest and result in capital gain or loss, as the case may be, to the recipient. These payments do not include amounts paid for *unrealized receivables,* or *good will* in excess of its basis to the partnership, unless the partnership agreement provides for payments with respect to good will. Generally, the valuation placed by the partners upon a partner's interest in partnership property in an arm's length agreement will be regarded as correct. If this valuation reflects only the partner's net interest in the property (total assets less liabilities), it must be adjusted so that both the value of the partner's interest in property and the basis for his interest take into account his share of partnership liabilities.

Payments made to a retiring partner for his interest in substantially appreciated inventory items constitute ordinary income to the recipient.

The remaining partners' distributive shares are not reduced by payments in exchange for a retired partner's interest in partnership property.

Other Payments. Payments to a retiring partner in liquidation of his interest which are not considered payments for his interest in

[18] I.R.C. Section 736.

partnership property as described above are treated either as a *distributive share* of partnership income or as a *guaranteed payment* irrespective of the length of time over which the payments are to be made. If the amount is determined with regard to partnership income, the payments to the recipient are taxable as a distributive share. If the amount is not determined with regard to partnership income, the amount is treated as guaranteed payment. In either event, the payments are treated as ordinary income to the recipient in the case of a distributive share of a capital gain. These payments are included in income by the recipient for his taxable year with or within which ends the partnership taxable year for which payments are a distributive share or in the year in which the partnership is entitled to deduct these amounts as guaranteed payments.

The remaining partners' distributive shares are reduced by payments in exchange for a retired or deceased partner's interest when these payments are considered as a distributive share or a guaranteed payment.

Recognition and Character of Gain or Loss on Sale or Exchange

General Rule. The sale or exchange of an interest in a partnership will be treated as the sale or exchange of a capital asset, resulting in capital gain or loss measured by the difference between the amount realized and the adjusted basis of the partnership interest.[19] Where the provisions of I.R.C. Section 751 (discussed in the second succeeding paragraph) require the recognition of ordinary income or loss with respect to a portion of the amount realized from this sale or exchange, the amount realized will be reduced by the amount attributable under Section 751 to unrealized receivables and substantially appreciated inventory items, and the adjusted basis of the transferor partner's interest in the partnership will be reduced by the portion of such basis attributable to these unrealized receivables and substantially appreciated inventory items.

The general rule of I.R.C. Section 741 applies whether the partnership interest is sold to one or more members of the partnership or to one or more persons who are not members of the partnership. This section also applies even though the sale of the partnership interest results in the termination of the partnership. Thus, these provisions apply (1) to the transferor partner in a two-man partnership when he sells his interest to the other partner and (2) to all

[19] I.R.C. Section 741.

the members of a partnership when they sell their interests to one or more persons outside the partnership.

Unrealized Receivables and Inventory Items. To the extent that money or property received by a partner in exchange for all or a part of his partnership interest is attributable to his share of the value of partnership unrealized receivables or substantially appreciated inventory items, the money or fair market value of the property received will be considered ordinary income. The remainder of the total amount realized on the sale or exchange of the partnership interest is realized from the sale or exchange of a capital asset.[20] Unrealized receivables and substantially appreciated inventory items are referred to as "Section 751 property."

The term "unrealized receivables" means any rights (contractual or otherwise) for (1) goods delivered or to be delivered (to the extent that this payment would be treated as received for property other than a capital asset) or (2) services rendered or to be rendered, to the extent that income arising from these rights to payment was not previously includible in income under the method of accounting employed by the partnership. These rights must have arisen under contracts or agreements in existence at the time of the sale or distribution, although the partnership may not be able to enforce payment until a later time.

The term "substantially appreciated inventory items" means inventory items where, at the time of the sale or distribution, the fair market value of all the inventory items of the partnership exceeds 120% of the aggregate adjusted basis for this property in the hands of the partnership (without regard to any special basis adjustment of any partner) and, in addition, exceeds 10% of the fair market value of all partnership property other than money. "Inventory items" include (1) stock in trade of the partnership, or property held by the partnership primarily for sale to customers in the ordinary course of the trade or business; (2) any other property of the partnership which, on sale or exchange by the partnership, would be considered other than a capital asset or that type of business property known as "Section 1231 assets" (see Chapter 5); or (3) any other property retained by the partnership which, if held by the partner selling his partnership interest or receiving a distribution, would be considered property described in (1) or (2). Property actually distributed to the partner does not qualify.

Illustration. A partner sold his one-third interest in a partnership. The partnership was on the accrual basis, had no liabilities, and owned the following assets:

[20] I.R.C. Section 751.

	Adjusted Basis	Fair Market Value
Cash	$ 10,000	$ 10,000
Accounts receivable	5,000	2,500
Notes receivable	2,000	2,100
Merchandise on hand	4,000	9,500
Machinery and equipment	80,000	100,000
Total assets	$101,000	$124,100

The *inventory items* (receivables and merchandise) have a total adjusted basis of $11,000 and a fair market value of $14,100. The total value of all assets, other than cash, is $114,100. Inasmuch as the fair market value of the inventory items, $14,100, is more than 120% of the adjusted basis of these items, $11,000, and also more than 10% of all assets other than cash, $114,100, there has been a *substantial appreciation of inventory items*. Thus, the partner realizes ordinary income to the extent of the amount received for his interest in these inventory items. If the amount he receives for his interest in the other assets exceeds the basis of his interest therein, he realizes capital gain to that extent.

Basis of Transferee Partner's Interest

The basis to a transferee partner of an interest in a partnership is determined under the general rules for property.[21] Thus, the basis of a purchased interest will be its cost. The basis of a partnership interest acquired from a decedent is the fair market value of the interest at the date of his death or one year thereafter (if the latter date is chosen by the executor), increased by his estate's or other successor's share of partnership liabilities, if any, on that date, and reduced to the extent that this value is attributable to items constituting income in respect to a decedent (see Chapter 21).

Optional Adjustment to Basis of Partnership Property

General Rule. The basis of partnership property is not adjusted as the result of a transfer of an interest in a partnership, either by sale or exchange or as a result of the death of a partner, unless the election provided by I.R.C. Section 754 (relating to optional adjustments to basis of partnership property) is in effect with respect to the partnership. But whether or not this election is in effect, the basis of partnership property is not adjusted as the result of a contribution of property, including money, to the partnership.[22]

Adjustment to Basis of Partnership Property. In the case of a transfer of an interest in a partnership, either by sale or exchange

[21] I.R.C. Section 742.
[22] I.R.C. Section 743(a).

or as a result of the death of a partner, a partnership as to which the election under I.R.C. Section 754 is in effect must—

(1) Increase the adjusted basis of partnership property by the excess of the transferee's basis for his partnership interest over his share of the adjusted basis to the partnership of all partnership property or

(2) Decrease the adjusted basis of partnership property by the excess of the transferee partner's share of the adjusted basis of all partnership property over his basis for his partnership interest.[23]

The amount of the increase or decrease constitutes an adjustment affecting the basis of partnership property with respect to the transferee partner only. Thus, for purposes of depreciation, depletion, gain or loss, and distributions, the transferee partner will have a special basis for those partnership properties which are adjusted. This special basis is his share of the common partnership basis (that is, the adjusted basis of these properties to the partnership without regard to any special basis adjustments of any transferee) plus or minus his special basis adjustments. A partner's share of the adjusted basis of partnership property is equal to the sum of his interest as a partner in partnership capital and surplus, plus his share of partnership liabilities. Where an agreement with respect to contributed property is in effect, this agreement will be taken into account in determining a partner's share of the adjusted basis of partnership property. Generally, a partner's share of the adjusted basis of partnership property will be the same as his interest in partnership capital and profits.

Illustration. S is a member of a partnership in which the three partners have equal interests in capital and profits. The partnership has made the election under I.R.C. Section 754 relating to the optional adjustment to the basis of partnership property. S sells his interest to B for $22,000. The balance sheet of the partnership at the date of sale shows the following:

ASSETS	Adjusted Basis per Books	Market Value	LIABILITIES AND CAPITAL	Adjusted Basis per Books	Market Value
Cash	$ 5,000	$ 5,000	Liabilities	$10,000	$10,000
Receivables	10,000	10,000	Capital:		
Inventory	20,000	21,000	A	15,000	22,000
Depreciable assets	20,000	40,000	B	15,000	22,000
			C	15,000	22,000
TOTAL	$55,000	$76,000		$55,000	$76,000

The amount of the adjustment under I.R.C. Section 743(b) is the difference between the basis of the transferee's interest in the partnership and his share of the

[23] I.R.C. Section 743(b).

adjusted basis of partnership property. The basis of B's interest is $25,333 (the cash paid for S's interest, $22,000, plus $3,333, B's share of partnership liabilities). B's share of the adjusted basis of partnership property is $18,333, that is, $15,000 plus $3,333. The amount to be added to the basis of partnership property is, therefore, $7,000, the difference between $25,333 and $18,333. This amount will be allocated to partnership properties.

A partner's share of the adjusted basis of partnership basis, under the provisions of I.R.C. Section 743(b), is determined by taking into account the effect of any partnership agreement with respect to contributed property or the effect of the contribution of undivided interests.

Where an adjustment is made to the basis of partnership property subject to depletion, any depletion allowable will be determined separately for each partner, including the transferee partner, based on his interest in this property.

Treatment of Certain Liabilities

Where the liabilities of a partnership are increased, and each partner's share of these liabilities is thereby increased, the amount of each partner's increase will be treated as a contribution of money by that partner to the partnership.[24]

Illustration. A partnership borrows $1,000. If there are two equal partners, the basis of the partnership interest of each is increased by $500, inasmuch as each is considered to have contributed that amount of money to the partnership.

Any increase in a partner's individual liabilities because of the assumption by him of partnership liabilities will also be considered as a contribution of money by him to the partnership.

Where the liabilities of a partnership are decreased, and each partner's share of these liabilities is thereby decreased, the amount of the decrease will be treated as a distribution of money to the partner by the partnership.

Where a partnership assumes the separate liabilities of a partner or a liability to which property owned by this partner is subject, the amount of the decrease in the partner's liabilities is treated as a distribution of money by the partnership to the partner. This reduces the basis of each partner's interest in the amount of his share of the decrease.

Where property subject to a liability is contributed by a partner to a partnership, or distributed by a partnership to a partner, the amount of the liability, to an extent not exceeding the fair market

[24] I.R.C. Section 752.

value of the property at the time of the contribution or distribution, will be considered as a liability assumed by the transferee.

Where there is a sale or exchange of an interest in a partnership, liabilities are treated in the same manner as liabilities in connection with the sale or exchange of property not associated with partnerships.

A partner's share of partnership liabilities is determined in accordance with his ratio for sharing losses under the partnership agreement. In the case of a limited partnership, a limited partner's share of partnership liabilities may not exceed the difference between his actual contribution credited to him by the partnership and the total contribution which he is obligated to make under the limited partnership agreement. But where none of the partners has any personal liability with respect to a partnership liability (as in the case of a mortgage on real estate acquired by the partnership without the assumption by the partnership or any of the partners of any liability on the mortgage), then all partners, including limited partners, are considered as sharing liability in the same proportion as they share profits.

Partner Receiving Income in Respect of a Decedent

All payments considered as distributive shares or guaranteed payments made by a partnership to the estate or other successor in interest of a deceased partner are considered income in respect of a decedent. (For discussion of income in respect of a decedent, see Chapter 21.) The estate or other successor in interest of a deceased partner is considered to have received income in respect of a decedent to the extent that amounts are paid by a third person in exchange for rights to future payments from the partnership as distributive shares or guaranteed payments. When a partner who is receiving payments of this character dies, this rule applies to any remaining payments of this character made to his estate or other successor in interest.[25]

When a partner dies, the entire portion of the distributive share which is attributable to the period ending with the date of his death and which is taxable to his estate or other successor constitutes income in respect of a decedent. This rule applies even though that part of the distributive share for the period before death which the decedent withdrew is not included in the value of the decedent's partnership interest for estate tax purposes.

[25] I.R.C. Section 753.

Rules for Allocation of Basis

A partnership which has elected under I.R.C. Section 754 must adjust the basis of partnership property under the provisions of Section 734(b) (relating to the optional adjustment to the basis of undistributed partnership property) and Section 743(b) (relating to the optional adjustment to the basis of partnership property where a partnership interest is transferred). The amount of the increase or decrease (as determined in those sections) in the adjusted basis of the partnership property must first be divided between (1) capital assets and business property described in I.R.C. Section 1231 and (2) any other property of the partnership. Then, the portion of the increase or decrease allocated to each class is further allocated to the bases of the properties within the class in a manner which will reduce the difference between the fair market value and the adjusted basis of the partnership properties. In the alternative, any increase or decrease may be allocated in any other manner approved by the District Director of Internal Revenue.[26]

If there is an increase in basis to be allocated to partnership assets, this increase must be allocated only to those assets the values of which exceed their bases and in proportion to the difference between the value and basis of each. No increase is to be made to the basis of any asset the adjusted basis of which equals or exceeds its fair market value. If there is a decrease in basis to be allocated to partnership assets, this decrease must be allocated to assets the bases of which exceed their value and in proportion to the difference between the basis and value of each. No decrease may be made to the basis of any asset, the fair market value of which equals or exceeds its adjusted basis.

To the extent that any increase or decrease in the basis to be allocated to partnership properties is attributable to a distribution of capital assets or depreciable assets by the partnership, or to a gain to a transferor of a partnership interest attributable to assets of this character, the adjustment may be made only to partnership capital assets or depreciable assets. To the extent that the increase or decrease is attributable to a distribution of inventory, receivables, or any other property except capital assets or depreciable assets, the adjustment may be made only to the basis of partnership property other than capital assets or depreciable assets.

In a case where the required increase or decrease in basis cannot be made because the partnership owns no property of the character

[26] I.R.C. Section 755.

required to be adjusted, then the adjustment must be made when the partnership acquires property of such a character.

In a case where a decrease in the basis of partnership assets is required and the amount thereof exceeds the basis to the partnership of property of the required character, the basis of this partnership property must be reduced to zero, and the balance of the decrease in basis will be applied to subsequently acquired partnership property of a like character.

Illustration. A partnership has three assets: X, a capital asset with an adjusted basis of $1,000 and a value of $1,500; Y, a depreciable asset with an adjusted basis of $1,000 and a value of $900; and Z, inventory items with an adjusted basis of $700 and a value of $600. A partner sells his interest to an outsider (when an election under I.R.C. Section 754 is in effect) for $1,000 (one-third of $3,000, the total value of partnership assets). The outsider's share of the adjusted basis of partnership property is $900 (one-third of $2,700). Therefore, he has a special basis adjustment of $100 ($1,000 minus $900). This adjustment must be allocated entirely to property X, inasmuch as this allocation will have the effect of reducing the difference between the value and the basis of the asset. Therefore, the outside buyer has a special basis adjustment of $100 with respect to property X, which now has a special basis to him of $1,100. No part of the adjustment is made to depreciable property Y and inventory items Z, inasmuch as any such adjustment would increase the difference between the basis and value of each such asset.

Supplementary Material

A. Suggested Reading.

Arthur B. Willis, Paul Little, and Donald McDonald, "Problems on Death, Retirement, or Withdrawal of a Partner," *Proceedings of the New York University Seventeenth Annual Institute on Federal Taxation* (Albany: Matthew Bender & Co., Inc., 1959), p. 1033.

Earle B. Fowler and James T. Carey, "Income Tax Consequences of Partnership Agreements Under the 1954 Internal Revenue Code," *Kentucky Law Journal*, Spring, 1955, Vol. XLIII, #3, p. 387.

Bernard J. Long, "Selling Partnership Interests and Partnership Property," *The Encyclopedia of Tax Procedures* (Englewood Cliffs, N.J.: Prentice-Hall, Inc., 1956), p. 1120.

Peter J. Repetti, "Death of a Partner," *Proceedings of the New York University Thirteenth Annual Institute on Federal Taxation* (Albany: Matthew Bender & Co., Inc., 1955), p. 921.

Arthur J. Dixon, "Retirement or Death of a Partner," *The New York Certified Public Accountant,* April, 1957, Vol. XXVII, #4, p. 258.

B. Questions.

1. Franz Ferdinand sold his interest in a partnership for $50,000. Partnership assets were marketable securities. The basis for his partnership interest was $40,000. His allocable part of partnership assets at the time of the sale was $43,000. What was his gain or loss? Was it ordinary or capital?

2. Phi and Pi each contribute property to a new partnership that they form. Phi's property has a fair market value of $40,000; Pi's, $60,000. Each had paid $50,000 for his property. What is the gain or loss to each partner and to the partnership? Would your answer be different if the partnership were not a new one?
3. Business was slack. So a partnership distributed the assets representing one phase of its business on a pro rata basis to the partners. One partner received $5,000 in cash, an automobile that had a basis in his hands of $4,000, and inventory that had a basis in his hands of $10,000. The basis of his interest in the partnership prior to the distribution was $15,000. What is his basis after the distribution?
4. Richard Rho sells his interest in a partnership to his partner. Partnership assets were land and buildings formerly used for manufacturing. Is his gain or loss capital or ordinary?
5. Each of three partners (Beta, Theta, and Pi) contributes to a new partnership property that had cost him $50,000. The respective fair market values of the three properties were $40,000, $50,000, and $60,000 at the time of the contributions. Each man is a one-third partner under the articles of partnership. What is the basis of the partnership interest of each man?
6. A partner had a basis of $10,000 for his partnership interest. He received a distribution, other than in liquidation of his interest, of $4,000, in cash, and property with a basis to the partnership of $8,000. What is the basis to him of the distributed property?
7. Mr. Fennimore, a partner in a wholesale grocery firm, had a distributive share in the profits of $15,000 in the taxable year. Instead of cash, the partnership gave him inventories with a fair market value of $16,000. Seven months later, he sold the inventories for $18,000. What is the gain or loss? What is its character (ordinary or capital)? Would your answer be the same if instead of inventories he had received marketable securities?
8. Beaumont retired from the partnership of Beaumont & Fletcher. His basis for his partnership interest is $10,000. He receives $5,000 in cash and also inventory items with a basis to the partnership of $3,000. What is his gain or loss?
9. A partner receives a distribution of unrealized receivables in exchange for his interest in other partnership property. How is this treated for tax purposes by (a) the partnership and (b) the partner referred to?
10. A partner had a truck that was used in the business for five months. The truck was distributed to a partner, who held it for two months and then sold it at a gain. Is this capital gain to him?
11. Clark contributed $20,000 in cash to a partnership, and the other partner, Fisher, contributed depreciable property with a fair market value of $20,000 and an adjusted basis in his hands of $10,000; the property had a 10-year life. (a) What is the partnership's basis for depreciation? (b) If provision had been made in the partnership agreement, may the entire yearly depreciation be allocated to the partner who contributed the cash? (c) If your answer to (b) is Yes, what is Clark's distributive share of assumed partnership income of $2,000, with no deductions other than depreciation?
12. A partner paid $10,000 in cash for his interest in a partnership in 1958. In 1959, after a boiler explosion, he was "assessed" $5,000 by

the partnership, as was each of the other partners (except for one elderly widow). In 1958, his share of the partnership profits was $3,000, of which none was distributed. In 1961, his share of partnership profits was $7,000, $5,000 of which was distributed to him. In 1960, his share of partnership losses was $4,000. What was the basis of his partnership interest at the end of 1961?

13. A partner, Sigma, dies when the balance sheet of his partnership is as follows:

Assets	Adjusted Basis	Market Value	Liabilities and Capital	Adjusted Basis	Market Value
Cash	$ 5,000	$ 5,000	Liabilities	$10,000	$10,000
Receivables	10,000	10,000	Capital:		
Inventory	20,000	21,000	Sigma	12,000	22,000
Depreciable assets	20,000	40,000	Delta	15,000	22,000
			Tau	18,000	22,000
Total	$55,000	$76,000	Total	$55,000	$76,000

All partners share equally in profits. The partnership has made the election to adjust the basis of the partnership assets upon the transfer of a partnership interest. What is the amount of the adjustment?

14. A partner contributes property with a basis of $1,000, subject to a mortgage of $500, to a partnership in exchange for a one-half interest in the partnership. What is the basis of his interest?

15. A partner's adjusted basis for his interest in the partnership is $30,000. In complete liquidation of his interest, he receives, in kind, $10,000 in cash, inventory items having a basis to the partnership of $12,000, and two parcels of real estate having adjusted bases to the partnership of $12,000 and $4,000, respectively. (a) What is the basis of his partnership interest after this transaction? (b) How is this basis allocated among the properties?

16. A personal service partnership has the following balance sheet:

Assets	Adjusted Basis	Market Value	Liabilities and Capital	Adjusted Basis	Market Value
Cash	$13,000	$13,000	Liabilities	$ 3,000	$ 3,000
Receivables	0	30,000	Capital:		
Fixed assets	20,000	23,000	Alekhine	10,000	21,000
			Bottwinnick	10,000	21,000
			Capablanca	10,000	21,000
Total	$33,000	$66,000	Total	$33,000	$66,000

Alekhine retires from the partnership in accordance with an agreement whereby he is to receive $10,000 a year for three years, a total of $30,000, for his partnership interest. What is the value of his capital interest in the partnership?

17. In the previous problem, how will the $10,000 he receives in each of the years be allocated?

20

ESTATES AND TRUSTS—I

Fiduciaries; Simple Trusts; Complex Trusts

What Is a Fiduciary? The term "fiduciary" means a guardian, trustee, executor, administrator, receiver, conservator, or any person acting in any fiduciary capacity for any person.[1] The fiduciary must be acting in a capacity of trust. Thus, a person who merely acts as an agent for others, without the existence of a legal trust, is not a fiduciary.[2] The holding of legal title to property for the benefit of another does not necessarily create a fiduciary relationship; for example, where grandparents made gifts to their minor grandchildren, the parents held title without being fiduciaries, because under state law the minors could not take title.[3] A receiver, trustee in bankruptcy, or assignee for a corporation is not a fiduciary.[4]

"While a trust in personal property may be created by oral agreement, there must be no doubt or uncertainty concerning either the existence or the terms of such a declaration."[5]

Ordinarily, the fiduciary is not personally liable for the income tax of the person whom he represents. If the fiduciary notifies the Secretary of the Treasury of the capacity in which he (the fiduciary) is serving, any tax is collectible from the person, estate, trust, etc., that he represents.[6]

Income Tax Capacities of Fiduciary. The fiduciary may file income tax returns in either of two general categories:

(1) The fiduciary may file whatever return would have been filed by another party, were this party able to file the return himself. The most common example involves a person who has died during the taxable year. The executor or administrator must file the regular income tax return form that the decedent would have filed, had

[1] I.R.C. Section 7701(a)(6).
[2] O.D. 425, 2 CB 198.
[3] Revenue Ruling 55–469, 1955–2 CB 519.
[4] I.R.C. Section 6012(b)(3).
[5] *John A. Cavanagh,* 2 B.T.A. 268 (1926).
[6] I.R.C. Section 6903.

he lived, covering the period from the first day of the taxable year to the date of death. This return is to be distinguished from the *fiduciary* income tax return that must be filed (if the necessary conditions set forth in Chapter 24 are met) for the period from the date of death to the end of the taxable year. A fiduciary income tax return may also be due for each succeeding year that the estate is in process of being administered or wound up.[7]

A fiduciary (including the guardian of a minor and the guardian or committee of an insane person) who has charge of the income of an individual must make a return of income if a return is required for the individual. But this does not apply to a receiver appointed by authority of law in possession of only a part of the individual's property.[8]

(2) The fiduciary may file a fiduciary income tax return (Form 1041) in his capacity as executor or administrator of an estate, or as trustee of a trust.

Estates and Trusts

Gross Income. The gross income of an estate or trust is determined in the same manner as that of an individual. Thus, the gross income consists of all items of gross income received during the taxable year, including:

(1) Income accumulated in trust for the benefit of unborn or unascertained persons or persons with contingent interests;

(2) Income accumulated or held for future distribution under the terms of the will or trust;

(3) Income which is to be distributed currently by the fiduciary to the beneficiaries, and income collected by a guardian of an infant which is to be held or distributed as the court may direct;

(4) Income received by estates of deceased persons during the period of administration or settlement of the estate; and

(5) Income which, in the discretion of the fiduciary, may be either distributed to the beneficiaries or accumulated.[9]

Deductions and Credits. Generally, the deductions and credits allowed to individuals are also allowed to estates and trusts. But there are some special rules, to be discussed later in the following paragraphs, for the computation of certain deductions and for the allocation between the estate or trust and the beneficiaries of stipulated credits and deductions.

[7] I.R.C. Section 6012(b)(1).
[8] I.R.C. Section 6012(b)(2).
[9] I.R.C. Section 641.

An estate or trust is allowed the following credits only to the extent that they are not properly allocable to a beneficiary: partially tax-exempt interest, taxes imposed by foreign countries and by possessions of the United States (see Chapter 22), and dividends received.[10]

Charitable Contributions. Any part of the gross income of an estate or trust which, by the terms of the will or of the instrument creating the trust, (1) is, during the taxable year, paid or permanently set aside for charitable purposes as defined in I.R.C. Section 170(c) or (2) is to be used exclusively for religious, charitable, scientific, literary, or educational purposes, or for the prevention of cruelty to children or animals, or for the establishment, acquisition, maintenance, or operation of a public cemetery not operated for profit, is allowed as a deduction to the estate or trust in lieu of the charitable, etc., contribution allowable to individuals.

Losses. Losses incurred in a trade or business, those incurred in any transaction entered into for profit, and those arising from casualty are deductible for income tax purposes. But the loss is not allowed if, at the time of the filing of the income tax return, the loss has been claimed for estate tax purposes in the estate tax return.[11]

Standard Deduction. Estates and trusts may not take the standard deduction. See Chapter 24.

Net Operating Loss Deduction. The net operating loss deduction is available to estates and trusts generally, with the following exceptions and limitations:

(1) In computing gross income and deductions for the purpose of the net operating loss deduction, a trust must exclude that portion of the income and deductions attributable to the grantor where he and others are treated as substantial owners (a subject to be treated later in the following chapter).

(2) An estate or trust may not, for this purpose, avail itself of the deductions relating to charitable contributions deductions and deductions for distributions.

Depreciation and Depletion. Deduction is allowed, but only to the extent the deductions are not apportioned to beneficiaries.

Amortization of Emergency or Grain Storage Facilities. The rule is that of the preceding paragraph.

[10] I.R.C. Section 642.
[11] I.R.C. Section 165(c).

Termination. The income of an estate of a deceased person is that which is received by the estate during the period of administration or settlement. The period of administration or settlement is the period actually required by the administrator or executor to perform the ordinary duties of administration, such as the collection of assets and the payment of debts, taxes, legacies, and bequests, whether the period required is longer or shorter than the period specified under the applicable local law for the settlement of estates. But the period of administration of an estate cannot be unduly prolonged. If it is, the estate is considered terminated for income tax purposes after the expiration of a reasonable period for the performance by the executor of all the duties of administration.

Generally, the determination of whether a trust has terminated depends upon whether the property held in trust has been distributed to the persons entitled to succeed to the property upon termination of the trust rather than upon the technicality of whether or not the trustee has rendered his final accounting. The winding up of a trust cannot be unduly postponed; and if the distribution of the trust corpus is unreasonably delayed, the trust is considered terminated for income tax purposes after the expiration of a reasonable period for the trustee to complete the administration of the trust.

If, on the final termination of an estate or trust, a net operating loss carryover or a capital loss carryover would be allowable to the estate or trust in a taxable year subsequent to that of the termination but for this termination, the carryover or carryovers are allowed to the beneficiaries succeeding to the property. The first taxable year of the beneficiary to which the loss is carried over is the taxable year of the beneficiary in which or with which the estate or trust terminates. But the last taxable year of the estate or trust (whether or not a short taxable year) and the first taxable year of the beneficiary to which a loss is carried over each constitute a taxable year for purposes of determining the number of years to which a loss may be carried over.

If, on the termination of an estate or trust, the estate or trust has for its last taxable year deductions (other than for personal exemptions and charitable contributions) in excess of the gross income, the excess is allowed as a deduction to the beneficiaries succeeding to the property of the estate or trust. The deduction is allowed only in computing taxable income; it is not allowed in computing adjusted gross income. The deduction is allowable only in the taxable year of the beneficiary in which or with which the estate or trust terminates, whether the year of termination is of normal duration or is a short taxable year.

Allocation. The carryovers and excess deductions referred to in the two preceding paragraphs are allocated among the beneficiaries succeeding to the property according to the share of each in the burden of the loss or deductions. A person who qualifies as a beneficiary succeeding to the property of an estate or trust with respect to one amount and does not qualify with respect to another amount is a beneficiary succeeding to the property of the estate or trust as to the amount with respect to which he qualifies.

Illustration. A decedent's will leaves $100,000 to A, and the residue of his estate equally to B and C. His estate is sufficient to pay only $90,000 to A, and nothing to B and C. There is an excess of deductions over gross income for the last taxable year of the estate or trust of $5,000, and a capital loss carryover of $15,000. A is a beneficiary succeeding to the property of the estate to the extent of $10,000; and inasmuch as the total of the excess of deductions and the loss carryover is $20,000, A is entitled to the benefit of one-half of each item, and the remaining half is divided equally between B and C.

Distributable Net Income

The term "distributable net income" means the taxable income of the estate or trust, with certain modifications. This concept of distributable net income serves the general purpose of limiting the additional deductions allowed to estates and trusts (under I.R.C. Sections 651 and 661, which are discussed below) for amounts paid, credited, or required to be distributed to beneficiaries and also of determining how much of an amount distributed, or required to be distributed, to a beneficiary will be taxed to him. In effect, the concept of distributable net income gives statutory expression to the principle underlying the taxation of estates and trusts; that is, that these separate taxable entities are only conduits through which income flows to the beneficiaries except where income is accumulated by the estate or trust for future distribution. Inasmuch as the distributable net income concept is used to determine the character of amounts distributed to a beneficiary, it is necessary to adjust the taxable income of the estate or trust by adding to it items of trust income which are not includible in the gross income of the estate or trust but which may nevertheless be available for distribution to the beneficiaries. Distributable net income means for any taxable year the taxable income of the estate or trust, computed with seven modifications.

(1) No deduction may be taken for amounts paid, credited, or required to be distributed to beneficiaries.[12]

(2) No deduction is allowed for personal exemptions.

(3) Gains from the sale or exchange of capital assets are excluded from the computation of distributable net income, to the extent that they are allocated to corpus and are not (A) paid or credited to any beneficiary during the taxable year or (B) paid, permanently set aside, or to be used for charitable purposes. The effect of this is to tax capital gains to the estate or trust where the gains must be or are added to principal. But where the gains are actually distributed to the beneficiaries during the taxable year (for example, in the year of termination of the trust) then the gains are included in the computation of distributable net income. Similarly, if capital gains are paid, permanently set aside, or to be used for charitable purposes, so that a charitable deduction is allowed in respect of the gains, they must be included in the computation of distributable net income. Losses from the sale or exchange of capital assets are excluded from the computation of distributable net income except to the extent that they enter into the determination of any net capital gains that are paid, credited, or required to be distributed to a beneficiary. The deduction for capital gains is not taken into account in computing distributable net income. If capital gains are accumulated, and thus excluded from the computation of distributable net income, the deduction for capital gains is available only to the estate or trust. On the other hand, if capital gains are distributed to a beneficiary, they retain their character in the hands of the beneficiary, and he becomes entitled to the deduction for capital gains in respect of the gains.

(4) Exclusively in the case of trusts which distribute current income only, distributable net income is computed without regard to items of gross income constituting extraordinary dividends or taxable stock dividends which the fiduciary, acting in good faith, deems to be allocable to corpus.

Illustration. If a trust instrument should provide that only dividends paid out of corporate earnings accumulated or earned subsequent to the creation of the trust would be available for distribution to the income beneficiaries and that all other dividends should be accumulated for the remaindermen, any dividends which the trustee determines, in good faith, to be allocable to corpus must be excluded from distributable net income in the case of trusts which distribute current income only.

(5) There must be included in the computation of distributable net income the amount of any interest on governmental obligations

[12] I.R.C. Section 643.

which is exempt from tax. This figure is reduced by interest which is nondeductible because it was incurred in connection with the acquisition or carrying of tax-exempt obligations.

(6) In the case of a foreign trust, there must be included in the computation of distributable net income the amount of gross income from sources outside the United States, reduced by any disbursements allocable to this income which are nondeductible because they relate to tax-exempt income.

(7) Distributable net income includes the amount of any dividends received by the estate or trust which were entitled to the partial exclusion of dividends received. See Chapter 8.

If the estate or trust is allowed a deduction under I.R.C. Section 642 for charitable, etc., gifts and contributions, the items of exempt income which are included in the computation of distributable net income must be reduced to the extent that these items of trust income have been paid, permanently set aside, or are to be used for the charitable, etc., purposes. In determining whether amounts of trust income which have been paid, etc., for charitable, etc., purposes include items of tax-exempt income, these amounts are deemed to consist of the same proportion of each class of items entering into the computation of trust income for trust accounting purposes as the total of each class bears to the total of all classes of trust income.

Beneficiary Defined. An heir, legatee, or devisee (including an estate or trust) is a beneficiary. A trust created under a decedent's will is a beneficiary of the decedent's estate. The following persons are treated as beneficiaries:

(1) Any person with respect to an amount used to discharge or to satisfy that person's legal obligation.

(2) The grantor of a trust with respect to an amount applied or distributed for the support of a dependent out of corpus or out of other than income for the taxable year of the trust.

(3) The trustee or co-trustee of a trust with respect to an amount applied or distributed for the support of a dependent out of corpus or out of other than income for the taxable year of the trust.

Trusts Which Distribute Current Income Only

Deduction for Trusts Distributing Current Income Only. For income tax purposes, trusts fall into either of two categories:

(1) A *simple trust* is one the governing instrument of which (A) requires that the trust distribute all of its income currently for

the taxable year and (B) does not provide that any amounts may be paid, permanently set aside, or used in the taxable year for charitable, etc., purposes. The characterization applies only if the trust does not in fact make any distribution other than of current income.[13]

(2) A *complex trust* is any other trust, for reasons that will become painfully obvious in the discussion of I.R.C. Section 661, below.

A trust may be a simple trust for one year and a complex trust for another year. A trust qualifies as a simple trust in a taxable year in which it is required to distribute all its income currently and makes no other distributions, whether or not distributions of current income are in fact made. On the other hand, a trust is not a complex trust by reason of distributions of amounts other than income unless these distributions are in fact made during the taxable year, whether or not they are required in that year.

The determination of whether trust income is required to be distributed currently depends upon the terms of the trust instrument and the applicable *local* law. The fiduciary must be under a duty to distribute the income currently even if, as a matter of practical necessity, the income is not distributed until after the close of the trust's taxable year.

Illustration. Under the terms of the trust instrument, all of the income is currently distributable to A. The trust reports on the calendar year basis and as a matter of practical necessity makes distributions to A of each quarter's income on the fifteenth day of the month following the close of the quarter. The distribution made by the trust on January 15, 1961, of the income for the fourth quarter of 1960 does not disqualify the trust for treatment in 1961 as a simple trust, as the income is required to be distributed currently. But if the terms of a trust require that none of the income be distributed until after the year of its receipt by the trust, the income of the trust is not required to be distributed currently, and the trust is a complex trust.

It is immaterial, for purposes of determining whether all the income is required to be distributed currently, that the amount of income allocated to a particular beneficiary is not specified in the instrument.

A trust does not qualify as a simple trust for any taxable year in which it actually distributes corpus. Thus, a trust which is required to distribute all of its income currently would not qualify in the year of its termination, as in that year actual distributions of corpus would be made.

In computing its taxable income, a simple trust is allowed a deduction for the amount of income which is required under the terms

[13] I.R.C. Section 651.

of the trust agreement to be distributed currently to beneficiaries. If the amount of income required to be distributed currently exceeds the distributable net income, the deduction allowable to the trust is limited to the amount of the distributable net income. For this purpose, the amount of income required to be distributed, or distributable net income, whichever is applicable, does not include items of trust income (adjusted for deductions allocable thereto) which are not included in the gross income of the trust.

Inclusion of Amounts in Gross Income of Beneficiaries of Simple Trusts. Subject to the rules in the two following paragraphs, a beneficiary of a simple trust includes in his gross income for the taxable year the amounts of income required to be distributed to him for that year, whether or not distributed. Thus, the income of a simple trust is includible in the beneficiary's gross income for the taxable year in which the income is required to be distributed currently even though, as a matter of practical necessity, the income is not distributed until after the close of the taxable year of the trust. The term "income required to be distributed currently" includes income required to be distributed currently which is in fact used to discharge or to satisfy any person's legal obligation.[14]

If the amount of income required to be distributed currently to beneficiaries exceeds the distributable net income of the trust, each beneficiary includes in his gross income an amount equivalent to his proportionate share of the distributable net income.

Illustration. If beneficiary A is to receive two-thirds of the trust income and B is to receive one-third, and the income required to be distributed currently is $99,000, A will receive $66,000 and B, $33,000. But if the distributable net income is only $90,000, A will include two-thirds ($60,000) of the sum of his gross income, and B will include one-third ($30,000) in his.

In determining the gross income of a beneficiary, the amounts includible have the same character in the hands of the beneficiary as in the hands of the trust. This refers to exempt income, dividends, foreign income of a foreign trust.

Allocation of Income Items. The amounts which are required to be included in the gross income of a beneficiary are treated as consisting of the same proportion of each class of items entering into the distributable net income of the trust as the total of each class bears to the distributable net income, unless the terms of the trust specifically allocate different classes of income to different beneficiaries, or unless local law requires such an allocation.

[14] I.R.C. Section 652.

Illustration. Under the terms of the governing instrument, beneficiary A is to receive currently one-half of the trust income and beneficiaries B and C are each to receive currently one-quarter. Distributable net income of the trust (after allocation of expenses) consists of dividends of $10,000, taxable interest of $10,000, and tax-exempt interest of $4,000. A will be deemed to have received $5,000 of dividends, $5,000 of taxable interest, and $2,000 of tax-exempt interest. B and C will each be deemed to have received $2,500 of dividends, $2,500 of taxable interest, and $1,000 of tax-exempt interest. But if the terms of the trust specifically allocate different classes of income to different beneficiaries, entirely or in part, or if local law requires such an allocation, each beneficiary will be deemed to have received those items of income specifically allocated to him.

Allocation of Deductions. Items of deduction of a trust that enter into the computation of distributable net income are allocated among the items of income in accordance with these principles:

(1) All deductible items attributable to one class of income (except dividends excluded under I.R.C. Section 116) are allocated to this class. For example, repairs to, taxes on, and other expenses directly attributable to the maintenance of rental property or the collection of rental income are allocated to rental income. If the deductions directly attributable to a particular class of income exceed that income, the excess is applied against other classes of income in the manner provided in (4), below.

(2) The deductions which are not directly attributable to a specific class of income may be allocated to any item of income (including capital gains) included in computing distributable net income, but a portion must be allocated to nontaxable income (except excluded dividends).

Illustration. If the income of a trust is $30,000 (after direct expenses), consisting equally of $10,000 of dividends, tax-exempt interest, and rents, while income commissions amount to $3,000, one-third ($1,000) of the commissions should be allocated to tax-exempt interest, but the balance of $2,000 may be allocated to the rents or dividends in such proportions as the trustee may elect. The fact that the governing instrument or applicable local law treats certain items of deduction as attributable to corpus or to income not included in distributable net income does not affect the allocations.

(3) Examples of expenses which are considered as not directly attributable to a specific class of income are trustee's commissions, the rental of safe-deposit boxes, and state income and personal property taxes.

(4) To the extent that any items of deduction which are directly attributable to a class of income exceed that class of income, they may be allocated to any other class of income (including capital gains) included in distributable net income in the manner provided in (3), above, except that any excess deductions attributable to

tax-exempt income (other than excluded dividends) may not be offset against any other class of income.

Different Taxable Years. If a beneficiary has a different taxable year from the taxable year of the trust, the amount he is required to include in gross income is based on the income of the trust for any taxable year or years ending with or within his taxable year. Income of the trust, however, is determined in accordance with its method of accounting and without regard to that of the beneficiary.

Deduction for Estates and Trusts Accumulating Income or Distributing Corpus

Deduction for Distributions to Beneficiaries. In computing the taxable income of an estate or trust, there is allowed as a deduction for distributions to beneficiaries the sum of (1) the amount of income for the taxable year which is required to be distributed currently and (2) any other amounts properly paid or credited or required to be distributed for that taxable year. But the total amount deductible cannot exceed the distributable net income.[15]

The term "income required to be distributed currently" includes any amount required to be distributed which may be paid out of income or corpus (such as an annuity), to the extent that it is paid out of income for the taxable year.

The term "any other amounts properly paid or credited or required to be distributed" includes all amounts properly paid, credited, or required to be distributed by an estate or trust during the taxable year other than income required to be distributed currently. Thus, the term includes the payment of an annuity to the extent it is not paid out of income for the taxable year, and a distribution of property in kind. Where the income of an estate or trust may be accumulated or distributed in the discretion of the fiduciary, or where the fiduciary has a power to distribute corpus to a beneficiary, a discretionary distribution would qualify under (2), above.

The terms "income required to be distributed currently" and "any other amounts properly paid or credited or required to be distributed" also include any amount used to discharge or to satisfy any person's legal obligation. These terms do not include amounts required to be paid by a decedent's estate pursuant to a court order as an allowance under local law for the support of the decedent's widow or other dependent for a limited period during the adminis-

[15] I.R.C Section 661.

tration of the estate, except to the extent these amounts are payable out of and chargeable to income under the order of local law.

If property is paid, credited, or required to be distributed in kind—

(1) No gain or loss is realized by the trust or estate (or the other beneficiaries) by reason of the distribution, unless it is in satisfaction of a right to receive a distribution in a specific dollar amount or in specific property other than that distributed.

(2) In determining the amount deductible by the trust or estate and includible in the gross income of the beneficiary, the property distributed in kind is taken at its fair market value at the time it was distributed, credited, or required to be distributed.

(3) The basis of the property in the hands of the beneficiary is its fair market value at the time it was paid, credited, or required to be distributed, to the extent this value is included in the gross income of the beneficiary. To the extent that the value of the property distributed in kind is not included in the gross income of the beneficiary, its basis in the hands of the beneficiary is governed by the ordinary basis rules applying to property acquired from a decedent or in trust. See Chapter 6.

Character of Amounts Distributed. In the absence of specific provisions in the governing instrument for the allocation of different classes of income, or unless local law requires such an allocation, the amount deductible for distributions to beneficiaries is treated as consisting of the same proportion of each class of items entering into the computation of distributable net income as the total of each class bears to the total distributable net income.

In the application of the rule stated in the preceding paragraph, the items of deduction which enter into the computation of distributable net income are allocated among the items of income which enter into the computation of distributable net income in the same manner as illustrated in the case of a simple trust, above, except that, in the absence of specific provisions in the governing instrument, or unless local law requires a different apportionment, amounts paid, permanently set aside, or to be used for charitable, etc., purposes are first ratably apportioned among each class of items of income entering into the computation of the distributable net income of the estate or trust.

Limitation on Deduction. An estate or trust is not allowed a deduction for any amount which is treated as consisting of any item of distributable net income which is not included in the gross income of the estate or trust.

Illustration. A trust has distributable net income of $20,000, which is deemed to consist of $10,000 of dividends and $10,000 of tax-exempt interest. The trust distributes $10,000 to beneficiary A. The deduction allowable without regard to the limitation amounts to $10,000, consisting of $5,000 of dividends and $5,000 of tax-exempt interest. The deduction actually allowable under the limitation is $4,975, as no deduction is allowable for the $5,000 of tax-exempt interest and the $25 deemed distributed out of the $50 of dividends excluded, these being items of distributable net income which are not included in the gross income of the estate or trust.

Inclusion of Amounts in Gross Income of Beneficiaries of Estates and Trusts Accumulating Income or Distributing Corpus. Gross income of a beneficiary of an estate or complex trust includes the sum of (1) amounts of income required to be distributed currently to him by the estate or trust and (2) all other amounts properly paid, credited, or required to be distributed to him. But the amount so includible may not exceed the beneficiary's proportionate share of the distributable net income. The effect of this limitation is to preserve the conduit principle by providing that all distributions (or amounts required to be distributed) from an estate or trust will be taxable, but not to an extent in excess of the taxable income of the estate or trust (computed without regard to the deductions for distributions and for personal exemptions, and without inclusion of capital gains allocable to corpus). Any distribution is considered a distribution of the trust's or estate's current income to the extent of its taxable income for the year. This principle is similar to the determination of whether a dividend has been distributed; that is, that every distribution made by a corporation is deemed to be out of earnings and profits to the extent thereof and from the most recently accumulated earnings and profits.[16]

In determining what constitutes a beneficiary's proportionate share of the distributable net income of the estate or trust, an *order of priority* has been established. A beneficiary must include in gross income the amount of any income of the estate or trust which is required to be distributed to him currently, whether or not the income is actually distributed to him. This includes an annuity which is required to be paid at all events (either out of income or corpus), but only to the extent that it is satisfied out of income. If the income of the estate or trust which is required to be distributed currently exceeds the distributable net income (computed, for this purpose, without the charitable deduction), then each beneficiary of this income, instead of being taxed on the income required to be distributed to him, is taxed only upon his proportionate part of the distributable net income. This is determined by attributing to him

[16] I.R.C. Section 662(a).

the same fractional part of distributable net income as the amount of trust income required to be distributed currently to each beneficiary bears to the trust income required to be distributed currently to *all* beneficiaries.

Illustration. Under the terms of a trust instrument, $5,000 is to be paid to a charity out of income each year, $20,000 of income is currently distributable to A, and an annuity of $12,000 is to be paid to B out of income or corpus. All expenses are charges against income and capital gains allocable to corpus. During the taxable year the trust had income of $30,000 (after the payment of expenses) derived from taxable income and made the payments to the charity and the distributions to A and B as required by the governing instrument. The amounts treated as distributed currently total $25,000 ($20,000 to A and $5,000 to B). Inasmuch as the charitable contribution is out of income, the amount of income available for B's annuity is only $5,000. The distributable net income of the trust computed without taking into consideration the charitable contributions deduction of $5,000 is $30,000. Inasmuch as the amounts treated as distributed currently of $25,000 do not exceed the distributable net income (as modified) of $30,000, A is required to include $20,000 in his gross income and B is required to include $5,000.

If the estate or trust pays, credits, or is required to distribute to beneficiaries amounts other than income which is required to be distributed currently, these *other amounts* are includible in the gross incomes of the recipient beneficiaries, but only to the extent of each beneficiary's proportionate share of the distributable net income (reduced by the amount of any income required to be distributed currently). This rule does not apply to the following situations:

(1) Any amount which, under the terms of the governing instrument, is properly paid or credited as a gift or bequest of a specific sum of money or of specific property and which is paid or credited all at once or in not more than three installments. For this purpose an amount which can be paid or credited only from the income of the estate or trust is not considered as a gift or bequest of a specific sum of money.

(2) Any amount paid or permanently set aside as a charitable, etc., distribution under I.R.C. Section 642(c).

(3) Any amount paid, credited, or distributed in the taxable year, if I.R.C. Sections 651 or 661 (described above) applied to this amount for a preceding taxable year of an estate or trust because credited or required to be distributed in that preceding taxable year.[17]

Distributable net income, as used in connection with the term "amounts required to be distributed currently," is to be computed

[17] I.R.C. Section 663(a).

without regard to any portion of a charitable deduction allowance which is not attributable to income of the taxable year.[18]

Distributions in First Sixty-five Days of Taxable Year. The fiduciary of a trust may elect to treat distributions within the first sixty-five days of the taxable year of the trust as amounts which were paid or credited on the last day of the preceding taxable year if (1) the trust was in existence prior to 1954; (2) an amount in excess of the income of the immediately preceding taxable year may not (under the terms of the governing instrument) be distributed in any taxable year; and (3) the fiduciary elects on the trust's first tax return to have this section apply.[19]

Supplementary Material

A. Suggested Reading.

Arthur M. Michaelson, *Income Taxation of Estates and Trusts* (New York: The Practising Law Institute, 1955).

Stuart E. White, "Ten-Year Short-Term Trusts—Greatest Tax Relief Measure in Forty-five Years," *The Arthur Andersen Chronicle*, October, 1958, Vol. XVIII, #4, p. 287.

B. Questions.

1. An individual was executor for his mother's estate. Does he have any personal liability for unpaid income taxes of the estate?
2. A fiduciary held business property under a trust agreement. According to the terms, Napoleon was to have the use of the property as long as he lived, as life tenant, after which the property would go to Josephine. Who gets the deduction for depreciation?
3. Under a trust agreement, the fiduciary was directed to distribute all income in the year received by him. A bond held by the trust was called at a figure in excess of the fiduciary's basis. To whom is the gain taxed?
4. An individual who had used the calendar year basis died on June 2, 1960. What income tax returns must be filed on his behalf?
5. A fiduciary was obliged to distribute all the income of a trust currently. He also had the right, in his sole discretion, to invade corpus for the benefit of the beneficiary if current income were insufficient to meet emergency medical needs of the beneficiary; and such was the case in 1961. Is this a simple trust in 1961?
6. An estate had gross income of $50,000. Under the terms of the instrument setting it up, the executor gave $10,000 of the income to three churches. How much of a deduction from gross income is allowed? Would your answer be the same if the instrument had made no specific reference to contributions?
7. Norman Neat, who used the calendar year basis, conveniently died on December 31, 1960. The executor wound up the estate on September

[18] I.R.C. Section 662(b).
[19] I.R.C. Section 663(b).

15, 1961, the final income tax return showing an excess of deductions over income in the amount of $10,000. Deductions included $600 for personal exemptions and $500 for contributions to the Salvation Army. What happens?

8. A trust had income of $100,000, composed of $50,000 of taxable income and $50,000 of tax-exempt income. Distributable net income is $98,000. Of the $2,000 in deductions, $1,000 is attributable to tax-exempt income. All of the income is distributed currently. To how much of a deduction is the trust entitled for distributable amounts?
9. Under the terms of a will, some of the estate's income was to be distributed currently to the decedent's son, some was to be accumulated until such time as the executor saw fit to give it to the decedent's daughter, and some was to be accumulated until the decedent's grandson was 21. Which items are included in the estate's gross income?
10. A fiduciary operated a certain business for the benefit of the beneficiaries. The trust was terminated in 1961, at which time there was a net operating loss carryover of $7,000 from 1959. Is anyone entitled to the deduction? Would your answer be different if just before the termination of the trust the business had been sold by the fiduciary? What would happen if the beneficiaries had sold the business as soon as it was turned over to them?
11. A fiduciary is required to distribute income currently to the beneficiaries, and $10,000 was received in that year. But the fiduciary was low in ready funds, and he persuaded one beneficiary to accept a $1,000 utility bond, with a fair market value of $1,000, in lieu of a check for that amount. If the bond had an adjusted basis in the fiduciary's hands of $900, does the fiduciary have gain to report?
12. The decedent had owned a factory, which the fiduciary continued to run until fire wiped it (the factory) out. On which tax return is the loss shown, income tax, estate tax, or both?
13. The estate of a deceased individual consisted largely of investments, the income from which was to be accumulated for the benefit of his children. Under what circumstances is this income included in the estate's gross income?
14. A fiduciary was under instructions to distribute all income currently, but certain 1960 income was inadvertently retained. When the fiduciary discovered this in 1962, he immediately turned the funds over to the beneficiary. To whom is this overlooked money taxable in each year?
15. A trust, the terms of which require all of its income to be distributed currently, has $10,000 income for the calendar year 1960, of which $2,500 represents income collected in December that the trustee pays to the sole beneficiary in March and April, 1961. How much of a deduction is allowed to the trust for 1960, assuming the amount of income required to be distributed currently does not exceed the distributable net income of the trust for that year? If the beneficiary also is on the calendar year basis, in what year does he report the $10,000?
16. The terms of a trust provide that one-half of its income must be distributed currently to Son, and that the trustee in his discretion may either (1) accumulate the other one-half for Daughter or Sister, (2) distribute the income to designated charities currently, or (3) accumulate the income and pay the accumulations to the designated charities

in subsequent years. In 1961, the trust has $40,000 of taxable income and $10,000 of tax-exempt income. The trustee distributes $25,000 to Son and $50,000 (consisting of both current and accumulated income) to the charities. (a) What is distributable income for 1961? (b) How much is taxable to Son?

17. The terms of a testamentary trust require that one-half of the trust income be distributed currently to the grantor's wife, Winifred, for her life. The remaining trust income, in the trustee's discretion, may either be paid to the grantor's daughter, Deborah, paid to designated charities, or accumulated. The trust is to terminate at Winifred's death, and the principal will then be payable to Deborah. Under the applicable local law, capital gains realized by the trust are allocable to the principal account. The records of the fiduciary show the following for calendar year 1960:

Income from rents	$50,000
Income from dividends of domestic corporations	50,000
Tax-exempt interest on municipal bonds	20,000
Partially tax-exempt interest on United States bonds	10,000
Capital gains (long-term) in excess of capital losses	20,000
Depreciation on buildings	10,000
Administrative expenses and local taxes attributable to rental income	15,000
Administrative disbursements and trustee's commissions allocable to tax-exempt interest	1,000
Other trustee's commissions allocable to income account	2,200
Other trustee's commissions allocable to principal account	1,100

On the basis of the above, the trust income for trust accounting purposes is $111,800. The trustee distributes one-half of the trust income ($55,900) to Winifred and makes discretionary distributions of one-quarter of the income ($27,950) to a charity, and the remaining one-quarter to Deborah. What is the total deduction for distributions?

18. On the basis of the facts in Question 17, what is distributable net income?
19. On the basis of the facts in Question 17, what is the allowable deduction for distributions?
20. On the basis of the facts in Question 17, what is the taxable income of the trust?

21

ESTATES AND TRUSTS—II

Treatment of Excess Distributions by Trusts

General. I.R.C. Sections 665–668 were designed generally to prevent a shift of tax burden to a trust from a beneficiary or beneficiaries. To accomplish this, special rules were provided for treatment of amounts paid, credited, or required to be distributed by a complex trust in any year in excess of distributable net income for that year. This excess distribution is defined as an accumulation distribution, subject to certain limitations. An accumulation distribution is "thrown back" to each of the five preceding years in inverse order. That is, it will be taxed to the beneficiaries of the trust in the year the distribution is made or required, but, in general, only to the extent of the distributable net income of those years which was not in fact distributed. But the resulting tax will not be greater than the aggregate of the taxes that would have been attributable to the amounts thrown back to previous years had they been included in gross income of the beneficiaries in those years. To prevent double taxation, the beneficiaries receive a credit for any taxes previously paid by the trust which are attributable to the excess thrown back. But the beneficiaries are deemed to have received their shares of the tax paid by the trust on this excess. These principles do not apply to an estate.[1]

Definitions. The term "undistributed net income" means for any taxable year the distributable net income of the trust for that year, less (1) the amount of income required to be distributed currently and any other amounts properly paid or credited or required to be distributed to beneficiaries in the taxable year and (2) the amount of taxes imposed on the trust.

Illustration. Under the terms of a trust, $10,000 of income must be distributed currently to A and the trustee has discretion to make additional distributions to A. During the taxable year the trust had distributable net income of $30,100 derived from royalties and the trustee made distributions of $20,000 to A. The taxable income of the trust is $10,000 on which a tax of $2,640 is paid. The undistributed

[1] I.R.C. Section 665.

net income of the trust as of the close of the taxable year is $7,460, computed as follows:

Distributable net income		$30,100
Less: Income currently distributable to A	$10,000	
Other amounts distributed to A	10,000	
Taxes imposed on the trust	2,640	22,640
Undistributed net income		$ 7,460

But the undistributed net income for any year to which an accumulation distribution for a later year may be thrown back may be reduced by accumulation distributions in intervening years and also by any taxes imposed on the trust which are deemed to be distributed by reason of the accumulation distributions. On the other hand, undistributed net income for any year will not be reduced by any distributions in an intervening year which are excluded from the definition of an accumulation distribution or which are excluded as gifts or bequests.

The term "accumulation distribution" for any taxable year means an amount (if in excess of $2,000) by which the amounts properly paid, credited, or required to be distributed for that year exceed the distributable net income of the trust, reduced (but not below zero) by the amount of income required to be distributed currently. In computing the amount of the accumulation distribution, there is taken into account moneys applied or distributed for the support of a dependent (under circumstances to be detailed below) out of corpus or out of other than income for the taxable year and amounts used to discharge or to satisfy any person's legal obligation. If the distribution so computed is $2,000 or less, it is not an accumulation distribution; if the distribution exceeds $2,000, then the full amount is an accumulation distribution. Although amounts properly paid, credited, or required to be distributed do not exceed the income of the trust during the taxable year, an accumulation distribution may result if these amounts exceed distributable net income reduced (but not below zero) by the amount required to be distributed currently.

Illustration. A trustee properly makes a distribution to a beneficiary of $20,000 during the taxable year, of which $10,000 is income required to be distributed currently to the beneficiary. The distributable net income of the trust is $15,000. There is an accumulated distribution of $5,000, computed as follows:

Total distribution		$20,000
Less: Income required to be distributed currently		10,000
Other amounts distributed		$10,000
Distributable net income	$15,000	
Less: Income required to be distributed currently	10,000	
Balance of distributable net income		5,000
Accumulation distribution		$ 5,000

The following items are not regarded as accumulation distributions:

(1) Amounts paid, credited, or required to be distributed to a beneficiary as income accumulated before the birth of this beneficiary or before this beneficiary attains the age of 21;

(2) Amounts properly paid or credited to a beneficiary to meet the emergency needs of the beneficiary;

(3) Amounts properly paid or credited to a beneficiary upon his attaining a specified age or ages if—

(A) The total number of the distributions with respect to that beneficiary cannot exceed four;

(B) The period between each distribution is four years or more; and

(C) On January 1, 1954, these distributions were required by the specific terms of the governing instrument.

The term "taxes imposed on the trust" means the amount of Federal income taxes which are properly allocable to the undistributed portion of the distributable net income. This amount is the difference between the total taxes of the trust for the year and the amount which would have been paid by the trust had all of the distributable net income been distributed. Thus, in determining the amount of taxes imposed on the trust, there is excluded the portion of the taxes paid by the trust which is attributable to items of gross income which are not includible in distributable net income, such as capital gains allocable to corpus.

The term "preceding taxable year" does not include a taxable year to which this part of the Code does not apply.

Accumulation Distribution Allocated to Five Preceding Years. If a trust makes an accumulation distribution in any taxable year, the distribution is included in the beneficiary's taxable income for that year to the extent of the undistributed net income of the trust for the preceding five years. It is therefore necessary to determine the extent to which there is undistributed net income for the preceding five years. For this purpose, an accumulation distribution made in any taxable year is allocated to each of the five preceding taxable years in turn, beginning with the most recent year, to the extent of the undistributed net income of each of these years. Thus, an accumulation distribution is deemed to have been made from the most recently accumulated income of the trust. If, before the application of this so-called "five-year throw-back" rule to an accumulation distribution for the taxable year, there is no undistributed net income for a preceding taxable year, then no portion of the accumulation distribution is deemed distributed on the last day of this preceding taxable year. Thus, if an accumulation distribution is made during the taxable year 1962 and the trust had no undistributed net income for the taxable year 1961, then no portion of the 1962 accumulation distribution is deemed distributed on the last day of 1961.[2]

Illustration. In 1961, a trust, reporting on the calendar year basis, makes an accumulation distribution of $25,000. In 1960, the trust had $7,000 of undistributed net income; in 1959, none; in 1958, $12,000; in 1957, $4,000; in 1956, $4,000. The accumulation distribution will be deemed distributed $7,000 in 1960, none in 1959, $12,000 in 1958, $4,000 in 1957, and $2,000 in 1956.

If an accumulation distribution is deemed to be distributed on the last day of a preceding taxable year and the amount is not less than the undistributed net income for that preceding taxable year, then an additional amount equal to the taxes imposed on the trust for that preceding taxable year is likewise deemed distributed.

Illustration. A trust has taxable income of $11,032 (not including any capital gains) and undistributed net income of $8,000 for the taxable year 1960. The taxes imposed on the trust are $3,032. During the taxable year 1961, an accumulation distribution of $8,000 is made to the beneficiary, which is deemed to have been distributed on the last day of 1960. The taxes imposed on the trust for 1960 of $3,032 are also deemed to have been distributed on the last day of 1960 inasmuch as the 1961 accumulation distribution is not less than the 1960 undistributed net income. Thus, a total of $11,032 will be deemed to have been distributed on the last day of 1960 because of the accumulation distribution of $8,000 made in 1961.

Denial of Refund to Trusts. If an amount is deemed to be an amount paid, credited, or required to be distributed on the last day of a preceding taxable year, the trust is not allowed a refund or credit of the amount of taxes imposed on the trust, which would not have been payable for the preceding taxable year had the trust in fact made the distribution on the last day of that year. But these taxes are allowed as a credit against the tax of the beneficiaries who are treated as having received the distributions in the preceding taxable year. The amount of taxes which may not be refunded or credited to the trust and which are allowed as a credit against the tax of the beneficiaries is an amount equal to the excess of (1) the taxes imposed on the trust for any preceding taxable year (computed without regard to the accumulation distribution for the taxable year) over (2) the amount of taxes for that preceding taxable year which would be imposed on the undistributed portion of the distributable net income of the trust for that preceding taxable year

[2] I.R.C. Section 666.

after the application of the throw-back rule on account of the accumulation distribution determined for the taxable year.[3]

Illustration. In 1960, a trust of which A is the sole beneficiary has taxable income of $20,000 (including capital gains of $5,100 allocable to corpus less a personal exemption of $100), on which a tax of $7,260 is paid. The undistributed portion of distributable net income is $15,000, to which $6,160 of the tax is allocable. The undistributed net income is therefore $8,840 ($15,000 minus $6,160). In 1961, the trust makes an accumulation distribution of $8,840. The total taxes for 1960 attributable to the undistributed net income are deemed distributed, so $15,000 is deemed distributed. The amount of the tax which may not be refunded to the trust and the credit to which A is entitled is the excess of $6,160 over zero, for after the distribution and the application of the throw-back rule, there is no remaining undistributed portion of distributable net income for 1960.

Treatment of Amounts Deemed Distributed in Preceding Years. The total of the amounts treated as having been distributed by the trust on the last day of a preceding taxable year of the trust are included in the gross income of the beneficiary or beneficiaries receiving them. The total of these amounts is includible in the gross income of each beneficiary to the extent the amounts would have been included if the total actually had been paid by the trust on the last day of that preceding taxable year. The total is included in the gross income of the beneficiary for his taxable year in which these amounts are in fact paid, credited, or required to be distributed unless his taxable year differs from the taxable year of the trust. The total of the amounts treated as having been distributed by the trust on the last day of a preceding taxable year of the trust are included in the gross income of the beneficiary even though as of that day he would not have been entitled to receive them had they actually been distributed on that day.

When a trust pays, credits, or is required to distribute to a beneficiary amounts which are excluded from the computation of an accumulation distribution under one of the exceptions mentioned above, the amount includible under the throw-back rule in the gross income of the beneficiaries is first allocated to the beneficiaries and, second, the amount allocable to the beneficiary receiving amounts which are excluded is reduced by the excluded amounts.

The tax attributable to amounts deemed distributed is imposed on the beneficiary for his taxable year in which the accumulation distribution is made unless his taxable year is different from that of the trust. But the tax cannot be greater than the aggregate of the taxes attributable to those amounts had they been included in the gross income of the beneficiary for the preceding taxable year or

[3] I.R.C. Section 667.

years in which they were deemed distributed. The tax liability for the beneficiary for the taxable year is computed in the following manner:

(1) First, compute the amount of tax for the taxable year attributable to the accumulation distributions thrown back ("Section 666 amounts") which are included in the gross income of the beneficiary for the year. The tax attributable to these amounts is the difference between the tax for the taxable year computed with the inclusion of the Section 666 amounts in gross income and the tax computed without including them in gross income.

(2) Next, compute the tax attributable to the Section 666 amounts for each of the preceding taxable years as if they had been included in gross income for those years. The tax attributable to these amounts in each such preceding taxable year is the difference between the tax for such preceding year computed with the inclusion of the Section 666 amounts in gross income and the tax for that year computed without including them in gross income. The tax computation for each preceding year must reflect the taxpayer's marital and dependency status for that year.

(3) The total tax for the taxable year is the tax for that year computed without including the Section 666 amounts, plus—

(A) The amount of the tax for the taxable year attributable to the Section 666 amounts (computed in accordance with (1), above), *or*

(B) The sum of the taxes for the preceding taxable years attributable to the Section 666 amounts (computed in accordance with (2), above),

whichever is the smaller.

Illustration. During the taxable year 1961, $10,000 is deemed distributed under the throw-back rule to a beneficiary, of which $6,000 is deemed distributed by the trust on the last day of 1960 and $4,000 on the last day of 1959. The beneficiary had taxable income (after deductions) from other sources of $5,000 for 1961, $10,000 for 1960, and $10,000 for 1959. The beneficiary's tax liability for 1961 is $4,730, determined as follows:

YEAR 1961

Tax on $15,000 (taxable income including amounts thrown back)	$4,730
Tax on $5,000 (taxable income excluding amounts thrown back)	1,100
Tax attributable to amounts thrown back	$3,630

YEAR 1960

Tax on $16,000 (taxable income including amounts thrown back)	$5,200
Tax on $10,000 (taxable income excluding amounts thrown back)	2,640
Tax attributable to amounts thrown back	$2,560

YEAR 1959

Tax on $14,000 (taxable income including amounts thrown back)..........	$4,260
Tax on $10,000 (taxable income excluding amounts thrown back)..........	2,640
Tax attributable to amounts thrown back..........................	$1,620

Inasmuch as the tax of $3,630 attributable to the amounts thrown back is less than the aggregate of the taxes of $4,180 ($2,560 plus $1,620) determined for the preceding taxable years, the amount of $3,630 is added to the tax ($1,100) computed for 1961 without including the amounts thrown back.

The taxes imposed on a complex trust for a taxable year which would not have been payable by the trust if amounts deemed under the throw-back rule to have been distributed in the year had in fact been distributed in the year are not allowable as a refund to the trust but are allowable as a credit against the beneficiaries' tax.

Grantors and Others Treated as Substantial Owners

The Clifford Rule. Trusts have numerous advantages, tax and otherwise: principal may be safeguarded from inexperienced or greedy persons while the income is being spent, plans may be made to bypass one estate tax (see Chapter 29), principal or income may be devoted to charitable purposes. But the person setting up the trust (the grantor or settlor) cannot obtain the advantages of a trust if he really has not divested himself of the trust property. If the interest he retains in the property, or in its use, or in its possibility of ultimate return to him, is so great that he really has not let go of the property, his transfer in trust may be ignored for tax purposes. Trust income may be taxed to him, even though he never sees it. Trust property may be considered to be his.

"[T]he bundle of rights which he retained was so substantial that respondent cannot be heard to complain that he is the victim of despotic power when for purposes of taxation he is treated as owner altogether." [4]

The classic case on this subject is *Helvering v. Clifford,* 309 U.S. 331 (1940). Mr. Clifford set up a trust, with himself as trustee, for the exclusive benefit of his wife. The life of the trust was to be five years, unless either spouse died earlier. Upon termination of the trust, the corpus would go to him, while the undistributed income and the profits of the investment of such income would go to his wife. During the life of the trust, he could (as trustee) pay over to his wife whatever he deemed desirable. She could not encumber or

[4] *Dupont v. Commissioner,* 289 U.S. 685 (1933).

otherwise anticipate any interest in the trust or its income prior to actual payment to her. The Supreme Court held that as far as his dominion and control were concerned, the trust did not effect any substantial change. "The bundle of rights which he retained was so substantial" that the trust income could be taxed to him. To this day, trusts where the grantor has retained vitally substantial interests are referred to as "Clifford trusts."

Grantors and Others Treated as Substantial Owners. Income of a trust is taxed to the grantor or another person under these circumstances:

(1) If the grantor has retained a reversionary interest in the trust, within time limits set by I.R.C. Section 673. A reversionary interest is an interest that may *revert* to the grantor or other person;

(2) If the grantor or a nonadverse party has certain powers over the beneficial interests under the trust, as defined by I.R.C. Section 674. An adverse party is any person having a substantial beneficial interest in a trust which would be adversely affected by the exercise or nonexercise of a power which he possesses respecting the trust. A trustee is not an adverse party merely because of his interest as a trustee. Ordinarily, a beneficiary will be an adverse party. The interest of a remainderman (the person who gets whatever is left) is adverse to the exercise of any power over the corpus of a trust, but not to the exercise of a power over any income interest preceding his remainder. *A nonadverse party is any person who is not an adverse party;*

(3) If certain administrative powers over the trust exist under which the grantor can or does benefit, in the manner described in I.R.C. Section 675;

(4) If the grantor or a nonadverse party has a power to revoke the trust or to return the corpus to the grantor, in the manner indicated in I.R.C. Section 676; or

(5) If the grantor or a nonadverse party has the power to distribute income to or for the benefit of the grantor, as developed in I.R.C. Section 677.[5]

Income of a trust is taxed to a person other than the grantor (for example, a trustee) to the extent that he has the sole power to vest corpus or income to himself.

The circumstances listed above are deemed not to apply (that is, the *Clifford* rule does not operate) if the income of a trust is taxable to a grantor's spouse as alimony or separate maintenance payments, or as the income of an estate or trust in the case of divorce.

[5] I.R.C. Section 671.

When a grantor or another person is treated as the owner of any portion of a trust, there are included in computing his tax liability those items of income, deduction, and credit against tax attributable to or included in that portion.

Reversionary Interests. A grantor, in general, is treated as the owner of any portion of a trust in which he has a reversionary interest in either the corpus or income if, as of the inception of that portion of the trust, the grantor's interest will or may reasonably be expected to take effect in possession or enjoyment *within ten years* commencing with the date of transfer of that portion of the trust.[6] But the following types of reversionary interests are excepted from the general rule just stated:

(1) A reversionary interest after the death of the income beneficiary of a trust.

(2) A reversionary interest in a charitable trust to the extent that, under the terms of the trust, the income of the portion is irrevocably payable for a period of *at least two years* (commencing with the date of transfer) to a designated beneficiary that is a church or a convention or an association of churches, or to certain stipulated educational organizations or hospitals as defined in I.R.C. Section 170.

Power To Control Beneficial Enjoyment. The grantor is treated as the owner of a portion of a trust if the grantor or a nonadverse party has a power, beyond specified limits, to dispose of the beneficial enjoyment of the income or corpus, whether the power is a fiduciary power, a power of appointment, or any other power. The grantor is treated as the owner in every case in which he or a nonadverse party can affect the beneficial enjoyment of a portion of a trust.[7] But the following powers may be exercisable by any person without causing the grantor to be treated as an owner of a trust:

(1) Powers to apply income to the support of a dependent.

(2) Powers affecting beneficial enjoyment only after a period.

Illustration. If a trust created on January 1, 1961, provides for the payment of income to the grantor's son, and the grantor reserves the power to substitute other beneficiaries of income or corpus in lieu of his son on or after January 1, 1971, the grantor is not treated as the owner of the trust with respect to ordinary income received before January 1, 1971. But the grantor will be treated as an owner on and after that date unless the power is relinquished.

(3) Testamentary powers. A power in any person to control beneficial enjoyment exercisable only by will does not cause a

[6] I.R.C. Section 673.
[7] I.R.C. Section 674.

grantor to be treated as an owner; but this exception does not apply to income accumulated for testamentary disposition by the grantor or to income which may be accumulated for such distribution in the discretion of the grantor or a nonadverse party, or both, without the approval or consent of any adverse party.

(4) Powers to determine beneficial enjoyment of charitable beneficiaries.

Illustration. If a grantor creates a trust, the income of which is irrevocably payable solely to educational or other organizations that qualify under I.R.C. Section 170, he is not treated as an owner although he retains the power to allocate the income among these organizations.

(5) Powers to distribute corpus. If the power is limited by a reasonably definite standard which is set forth in the trust instrument, it may extend to corpus distributions to any beneficiary or beneficiaries (whether income beneficiaries or remaindermen) without causing the grantor to be treated as an owner.

(6) Powers to withhold income temporarily. There is excepted a power which, in general, enables the holder merely to effect a postponement in the time when the ordinary income is enjoyed by a current income beneficiary.

(7) Powers to withhold income during disability. There is an exception for a power which, in general, will permit ordinary income to be withheld during the legal disability of an income beneficiary or while he is under 21.

(8) Powers to allocate between corpus and income. A power to allocate receipts and disbursements between corpus and income, even though expressed in broad language, will not cause the grantor to be treated as an owner.

Administrative Powers. The grantor is treated as the owner of any portion of a trust if under the terms of the trust instrument or circumstances attendant on its operation administrative control is exercisable primarily for the benefit of the grantor rather than the beneficiaries of the trust. If a grantor retains a power to amend the administrative provisions of a trust instrument which is broad enough to permit an amendment causing the grantor to be treated as the owner of a portion of the trust, he will be treated as the owner of the portion from its inception.[8]

Power To Revoke. If a power to revest in the grantor title to any portion of a trust is exercisable by the grantor or a nonadverse party, or both, without the approval or consent of an adverse party, the

[8] I.R.C. Section 675.

grantor is treated as the owner of that portion, except in the case of powers affecting beneficial enjoyment of income only after the expiration of certain periods of time.[9]

Illustration. A grantor is not regarded as the owner with respect to ordinary income if exercise of a power to revest corpus in him cannot affect the beneficial enjoyment of the income received within ten years after the date of transfer of that portion of the trust. It is immaterial for this purpose that the power is vested at the time of the transfer. But the grantor is regarded as an owner after the expiration of the period unless the power is relinquished. Thus, he may be treated as the owner and taxed on all income in the eleventh and succeeding years if exercise of the power can affect beneficial enjoyment of income received in those years.

Income for Benefit of Grantor. A grantor may be treated as the owner of a portion of the trust because he has retained an interest in the income from that portion. He is treated in any taxable year as the owner of a portion of a trust of which the income is, or on the discretion of the grantor or a nonadverse party, may be:

(1) Distributed to the grantor;

(2) Held or accumulated for future distributions to the grantor; *or*

(3) Applied to the payment of premiums on policies of insurance on the life of the grantor, except policies irrevocably payable for a charitable purpose.[10]

Persons Other Than Grantor Treated as Substantial Owner. Where a person other than the grantor of a trust has a power exercisable solely by himself to vest the corpus or income of any portion of a trust in himself, he is treated as the owner of that portion, except as described in the following paragraph. The holder of such a power also is treated as an owner of the trust even though he has partially released or otherwise modified the power so that he can no longer vest the corpus or income in himself, if he has retained such control of the trust as would, if retained by a grantor, subject the grantor to treatment as the owner.[11]

This rule does not apply with respect to a power over income, as originally granted or modified, if the grantor of the trust is treated as the owner. Nor does the rule apply to a power which enables the holder, in the capacity of trustee or co-trustee, to apply the income of the trust to the support or maintenance of a person whom the holder is obligated to support, except to the extent the income is so applied.

[9] I.R.C. Section 676.
[10] I.R.C. Section 677.
[11] I.R.C. Section 678.

Limitation on Charitable Contributions

The unlimited charitable contributions deduction that a trust ordinarily would obtain is, in general, subject to percentage limitations, corresponding to those allowed an individual, under these circumstances:

(1) To the extent that the income is allocable to unrelated business income;

(2) If the trust has engaged in a prohibited transaction;

(3) If income is accumulated for a charitable purpose and the accumulation is (A) unreasonable, (B) substantially diverted to a noncharitable purpose, or (C) invested against the interests of the charitable beneficiaries.[12]

Unrelated business income is defined in the same manner as in the case of a tax-exempt organization. See Chapter 2.

Prohibited transaction is any transaction entered into by a trust holding income or corpus permanently set aside or to be used exclusively for charitable purposes with (1) the creator of the trust, (2) any substantial contributor to the trust, (3) a member of the family (as defined in I.R.C. Section 267, dealing with transactions between related taxpayers—see Chapter 27), or (4) a corporation which the creator or a substantial contributor controls.

Income in Respect of Decedents

The term "income in respect of a decedent" refers to those amounts to which a decedent was entitled as gross income but which were not properly includible in computing his taxable income for the taxable year ending with the date of his death or for a previous taxable year under the method of accounting he employed. The term includes:

(1) All accrued income of a decedent who reported his income by use of the cash receipts and disbursements method;

(2) Income accrued solely by reason of the decedent's death in case of a decedent who reports his income by use of the accrual method; and

(3) Income to which the decedent had a contingent claim at the time of his death.

The term "income in respect of a decedent" also includes the amount of all items of gross income in respect of a *prior decedent,*

[12] I.R.C. Section 681.

if (1) the right to receive this amount was acquired by the decedent by reason of the death of the prior decedent or by bequest, devise, or inheritance from the prior decedent and if (2) the amount of gross income in respect of the prior decedent was not properly includible in computing the decedent's taxable income for the taxable year ending with the date of his death or for a previous taxable year.[13]

Income in respect of a decedent is included in the gross income, for the taxable year when received, of:

(1) The estate of the decedent, if the right to receive the amount is acquired by the decedent's estate from the decedent;

(2) The person who, by reason of the death of the decedent, acquires the right to receive the amount, if this right is not acquired by the decedent's estate from the decedent; or

(3) The person who acquires from the decedent the right to receive the amount by bequest, devise, or inheritance, if the amount is received after a distribution by the decedent's estate of this right. These amounts are included in the income of the estate or of such persons when received by them whether or not they report income on the cash or the accrual method.

The right to receive income in respect of a decedent is treated in the hands of the estate, or by the person entitled to receive the amount by bequest, etc., as if it had been acquired in the transaction by which the decedent (or a prior decedent) acquired the right. It is considered as having the same character it would have had if the decedent (or a prior decedent) had lived and received that amount. Thus, income may preserve its character as long-term capital gain, exempt interest, income attributable to several taxable years (see Chapter 11), etc.

If the right to income in respect of a decedent is transferred, the transferor must include in his gross income for the taxable year in which the transfer occurs the amount of the consideration, if any, received for the right or the fair market value of the right at the time of the transfer, whichever is greater. Thus, upon a sale of such a right by the estate or person entitled to receive it, the fair market value of the right or the amount received upon the sale, whichever is greater, is included in the gross income of the vendor. Similarly, if this right is disposed of by gift, the fair market value of the right at the time of the gift must be included in the gross income of the donor.

If the estate of a decedent or any person transmits the right to income in respect of a decedent to another who is required to include

[13] I.R.C. Section 691.

this income when received in *his* gross income, only the transferee will include the income when received in his gross income.

Supplementary Material

A. Suggested Reading.

James P. Johnson, "Trusts and the Grantor," *TAXES—The Tax Magazine*, December, 1958, Vol. XXXVI, #12, p. 869.

Allen Tomlinson, "How To Handle Income in Respect of a Decedent Under Section 691," *Journal of Taxation*, April, 1957, Vol. VI, #4, p. 250.

Mary E. Lanigan, "Estate and Trust Income," *Journal of Accountancy*, October, 1956, Vol. CII, #4, p. 37.

B. Leading Cases.

"Bundle of rights." *Dupont v. Commissioner*, 289 U.S. 685 (1933).

Retained interest. *Helvering v. Clifford*, 309 U.S. 331 (1940).

C. Questions.

1. How could the fiduciary and a beneficiary conspire to have trust income be paid to the beneficiary at a time when he is in a favorable tax bracket?
2. An individual sets up a trust for the benefit of his daughter. As his health is not too good, he reserves the right to terminate the trust should he be obliged to retire upon his physician's orders. To whom is the trust income taxable?
3. Willa acquired, by bequest from her husband Hubert, the right to receive renewal commissions on life insurance sold by him in his lifetime, which commissions were payable over a period of years. Willa died before having received all of these commissions, and her son inherited the right to receive the remainder of the commissions. In whose gross income must there be reported (a) commissions received by Willa and (b) commissions received by her son?
4. In 1961, because of oversight, the fiduciary of a trust distributed less than the amount available to him. When he discovered what had happened, in 1962, he paid out to the beneficiaries the remaining balance from 1961 of $4,200. Is this subject to the throw-back rule? Would your answer be different if the amount had been $2,000?
5. A man sets up a trust for the benefit of his son, a minor. The trustee, a bank, may determine how much to spend on the lad's education, clothing, allowance, vacation trips, and whatever else seems indicated. How is the trust income to be taxed?
6. An estate had income in the years 1956–1960, inclusive, but no distributions were made to the sole beneficiary (the decedent's widow) until 1961. Describe the application of the 5-year throw-back rule in this situation.
7. A trust had income of $50,000 in the taxable year. There is included in this amount a net profit of $31,000 from the operation of a business. The trustee is required to pay one-half of the trust income to a named

individual and the balance to a specified university. The trustee pays each beneficiary $25,000. How much is the allowable charitable contribution? (Note: A $1,000 specific deduction is allowed in the computation of unrelated business income.)

8. An individual sets up an irrevocable trust for the benefit of his five children, none of whom is a minor. All of the income must be distributed annually, but he reserves the right to say how much each child will receive. Who is taxed on the trust income?
9. William Pitt, Jr., owned and operated a peach orchard. During his lifetime, he sold and delivered 1,000 bushels of peaches to a canner, but he did not receive payment before his death. After Pitt's death, the executor received payment from the canner. He also completed the sale to the canner and transferred to him 1,200 bushels of peaches on hand at Pitt's death and harvested and transferred an additional 1,800 bushels. What part, if any, of the gain from the sale of peaches by Pitt to the canner constitutes income in respect of a decedent when received?
10. An individual sets up a trust for the benefit of his nephew on the day that the latter enters college. The trust is to expire, and the corpus is to revert to the creator upon the boy's being graduated with a bachelor of arts degree. To whom is the trust income taxable?
11. In 1960, a trust paid out $12,000 less than its income. In 1961 the fiduciary, under specific powers conferred by the trust agreement, paid out $5,000 more than the income of that year to one of the beneficiaries, who required major surgery as a result of a rocket collision. Is the $5,000 payment subject to the throw-back rule? Would your answer be different if the fiduciary had had no powers other than to pay income at such time as he deemed appropriate?
12. A trust had income of $50,000 in 1960. Distributions to beneficiaries were made, at the fiduciary's discretion, in the amount of $30,000. The trust paid income tax on $18,000 (undistributed income less allowable deductions). In 1961, a distribution was made to beneficiaries. The Internal Revenue Service labeled this an accumulation distribution and imposed tax on the beneficiaries for 1960 under the throw-back rule. Is the trust entitled to a refund for any portion of the tax that it paid for 1960?
13. A trust is required to distribute currently one-half of its income to Alpheus, and the trustee has full discretionary power to distribute the remaining income to Bettigole or to Gambrelli in whatever amounts he sees fit. The trust had the following amounts of income during its taxable years 1960, 1961, and 1962:

	Royalties	Interest (Taxable)	Interest (Exempt)
1960	$20,000	$10,000	$5,000
1961	15,000	10,000	5,000
1962	25,000	15,000	5,000

In 1960 the trustee distributed only half of the trust income for that year. In 1961 the trustee distributed half of the trust income to Alpheus and $6,000 to Bettigole. In 1962 the trustee distributed half of the trust income to Alpheus, $20,000 to Bettigole, and $10,000 to

Gambrelli. Assuming that the 5-year throw-back rule were not operative, complete the following table:

WITHOUT APPLICATION OF 5-YEAR THROW-BACK RULE

	Included in Alpheus' Gross Income	Included in Bettigole's Gross Income	Included in Gambrelli's Gross Income	Taxable Income of Trust	Tax of Trust	Trust's Undistributed Income
1960					$4,683	
1961					1,780	
1962					None	

14. In the above problem, does the trust have an accumulation distribution in any year?
15. Returning to Problem 13, how much is Alpheus deemed to have received in each year as the result of a throw-back?
16. Returning to Problem 13, how much is Bettigole deemed to have received in each year as the result of a throw-back?
17. Returning to Problem 13, how much is Gambrelli deemed to have received in each year as the result of a throw-back?

22

FOREIGN OPERATIONS

The Pattern

United States citizens and domestic corporations, wherever they are, are subject to United States tax laws. But under certain conditions, income earned abroad by these parties is exempt from Federal taxation, either in whole or in part. Resident alien individuals and foreign corporations are given special treatment, being subject to United States income tax only upon income from sources in the United States.

This chapter deals with the following aspects of the problem:

Subject	*I.R.C. Section*
Earned income of United States citizens.	911
Income from sources within and without the United States.	861 to 863
Nonresident alien individuals.	871 to 874
Foreign partnerships.	875
Alien residents of Puerto Rico.	876
Foreign corporations.	881 to 883
Personal holding companies.	541
Foreign personal holding companies.	551 to 555
Dependents.	152
Joint returns.	6013
Standard optional deduction.	142(b) (1)
Optional tax.	4(d)
Arm's length transactions.	482
Filing date and extensions.	6072
Foreign tax credit.	901 to 905
Closing by Commissioner of taxable year.	6658
Income from sources within U.S. possessions.	931
Dividends received credit.	245
Accumulated earnings tax.	531
Corporate reorganizations.	367
Consolidated returns.	1504(b)
Charitable contributions.	170(c)
Withholding of tax at source.	1441 to 1443
Information returns.	6042 to 6044
Advice to foreign corporations.	6046
Income exempt under treaty.	894

Earned Income of Citizens of the United States

Earned Income from Sources Without the United States. Amounts constituting earned income as defined below are excluded from the gross income of an individual citizen of the United States who establishes to the satisfaction of the Commissioner that he has been a bona fide resident of a foreign country or countries for an uninterrupted period which includes an entire taxable year, if these amounts are (1) from sources without the United States, (2) attributable to this uninterrupted period, and (3) not paid by the United States or any agency or instrumentality thereof. The exemption from tax thus provided is applicable to these amounts that are attributable to that portion of an uninterrupted period of bona fide foreign residence which falls within a taxable year during which the citizen begins or terminates bona fide residence in a foreign country, provided that this period includes at least one entire taxable year. If attributable to an uninterrupted period in respect of which the citizen qualifies for the exemption from tax thus provided, the amounts will be excluded from gross income irrespective of when they are received.[1]

There is no simple one-sentence definition of *bona fide residence.* One's bona fide residence is not necessarily the same thing as one's domicile. A man's domicile, generally, is his fixed and permanent place of abode, the place to which he always returns (or intends to return) when, for any reason, he goes somewhere else. It is quite possible, therefore, for a man to have his domicile in Paducah, Kentucky, and to have a bona fide residence in Seoul, Korea, if his intention ultimately is to return to Paducah. The fact that a man simply goes to Seoul does not automatically make Seoul his bona fide residence. If he goes there as a tourist, or on a short business trip, and then returns to the United States, he has not established bona fide residence in Seoul. But if he goes to Seoul to work for an indefinite period, sets up permanent quarters there for himself and his family, and settles down in the community, so to speak, then probably he has established a bona fide residence in a foreign country, even though ultimately he intends to return to the United States.

The mere fact that the taxpayer's domicile is in the United States does not prevent him from becoming a bona fide resident abroad.[2] There must, nevertheless, appear an intention to establish a resi-

[1] I.R.C. Section 911.
[2] *Swenson v. Thomas,* 164 F.2d 783 (5th Cir., 1947).

dence in the foreign country.[3] "Such items as the degree of social contact with the natives, the facility in language, the presence of family, the establishment of a home, are all important indicia of intention to establish a residence." [4]

The bona fide residence must be for an uninterrupted period which includes an entire taxable year. "Uninterrupted" refers to the bona fide residence proper and not necessarily to the physical presence of the citizen. During the period of bona fide residence in a foreign country (even during the first full year), a man can leave the country for brief and temporary trips back to the United States or elsewhere for vacation or even for business. To preserve his status as a bona fide resident in a foreign country, he must have a clear intention of returning from these trips, without unreasonable delay, to his foreign residence or to a new bona fide residence in another foreign country.

One does not automatically acquire bona fide resident status merely by living in a foreign country or countries for one year. A citizen who goes to a foreign country specifically to work on a particular construction job will not be regarded necessarily as a bona fide resident of that country merely because he works there for one tax year, or even longer. The duration and nature of the job is merely one of the factors to be considered.

Though the period of bona fide foreign residence must be continuous and uninterrupted, once bona fide residence in a foreign country or countries has been established, temporary visits to the United States or elsewhere on vacation or business trips will not necessarily deprive the citizen of his status as a bona fide resident of a foreign country. Whether the individual citizen of the United States is a bona fide resident of a foreign country will be determined largely by the principles of I.R.C. Section 871, to be discussed below, relating to what constitutes residence or nonresidence in the case of an alien individual.

Where any amount is excluded from gross income under this heading, there will be disallowed as deductions any expenses, losses, or other items otherwise deductible (other than personal exemptions) properly allocable to or chargeable against the amounts so excluded from gross income. Thus, travel and entertainment expenses incurred by a United States citizen for the production of earned income in a foreign country where he has been a bona fide resident for several years would not be deductible to any extent. But he could deduct items which are not properly chargeable against or

[3] *Joseph A. McCurnin,* 30 T.C. 143 (1958).
[4] *Lois Kaiser Stierhout,* 24 T.C. 483 (1955).

allocable to excludable income items; for example, medical expenses, real estate taxes on a personal residence, or contributions.

Earned income consists of wages, salaries, or professional fees, and other amounts received as compensation for personal services actually rendered. *Unearned income,* on the other hand, consists of income from business, dividends, rents, gambling gains, interest, capital gains, and certain royalties.

The entire amount received as professional fees is treated as *earned income* if the taxpayer is engaged in a professional occupation, such as a doctor or lawyer, even though he employs assistants to perform part or all of the services, if the patients or clients are his.

Where a taxpayer is engaged in a trade or business (other than in corporate form) in which both personal services and capital are material income-producing factors, a reasonable allowance as compensation for the personal services actually rendered by him will be considered earned income; but the amount treated as earned income may not exceed 30% of his share of the net profits of the trade or business.

Where a corporation is involved, the treatment is different. The entire distribution of profit which the taxpayer receives from the corporation is taxable. The salary which the taxpayer receives from a corporation is considered earned income only if it represents a reasonable allowance as compensation for services rendered to the corporation. If he gets more than what is considered a reasonable salary, the excess is fully taxable.

Earned income which is derived from sources without the United States is not included in gross income solely because it is received *within* the United States. The place of receipt is immaterial.

The term "foreign country" means territory under the sovereignty of a government other than that of the United States. It does not include a possession or territory of the United States.

Amounts constituting earned income are excluded from gross income in the case of an individual citizen of the United States who during any period of *eighteen consecutive months* is present in a foreign country or countries during a total of at least 510 full days, if such amounts are (1) from sources without the United States, (2) attributable to that period, and (3) not paid by the United States or any agency or instrumentality thereof. For purposes of determining this exclusion, the period of presence in a foreign country may include a period prior to the beginning of the taxable year. The amount excluded from gross income may not exceed $20,000 if the 18-month period includes the entire taxable year; if the 18-month period does not include the entire taxable year, the amount excluded from gross income for the taxable year may not exceed an amount which bears the same ratio to $20,000 as the number of days in the part of the taxable year within the 18-month period bears to the total number of days in that year.

The following equation may be used:

$$\frac{\text{Number of days in part of tax year falling within the 18-month period}}{\text{Number of days in tax year of receipt}} \times \$20{,}000 = \text{maximum amount excludable}$$

Illustration. A United States citizen who qualifies for tax exemption under the physical-presence test ends his 18-month period by departing for the United States on September 1, 1961, after spending 244 days on foreign soil during 1961. His salary during that 244-day period was $18,000. He does not get the full $20,000 exemption for 1961 because his 18-month period did not include the entire 1961 tax year; so he uses the formula to determine how much of the $18,000 he earned and received abroad is excludable:

$$\$20{,}000 \times 244 \div 366 = \$13{,}333.33.$$

As he may exclude no more than $13,333.33, he is taxable on $4,666.67 of the $18,000 foreign-earned income in 1961.

The term "full day" means, not any 24-consecutive-hour period, but a continuous period of twenty-four hours commencing from midnight and ending with the following midnight.

Exemption for Certain Allowances. Amounts received by Government civilian personnel stationed outside the continental United States as cost-of-living allowances are excluded from gross income.[5] Amounts received by personnel of the Foreign Service of the United States as allowances or otherwise are likewise excluded.

Form To Be Used. Form 2555 may be used in order to exclude from gross income the income that has been earned abroad.

Tax Based on Income from Sources Within or Without the United States

Income from Sources Within the United States. There are three categories of income: (1) within the United States, (2) without the United States, and (3) partly within and partly without the United States.[6]

Included in (1) are:

(A) Interest received or accrued from the United States, any territory, any political subdivision of a territory, or the District

[5] I.R.C. Section 912.
[6] I.R.C. Section 861.

of Columbia, and interest on bonds, notes, or other interest-bearing obligations of residents of the United States, whether corporate or otherwise, except:

(i) Interest paid on deposits with persons, including individuals, partnerships, or corporations, carrying on the banking business, to persons not engaged in business within the United States.

(ii) Interest received from a resident alien individual, a resident foreign corporation, or a domestic corporation, when it is shown to the satisfaction of the District Director of Internal Revenue that less than 20% of the gross income of the payor has been derived from sources within the United States for the 3-year period ending with the close of the taxable year of the payor which precedes the payment of the interest (or for that part of the period which is applicable).

(iii) Income derived from a foreign central bank of issue from bankers' acceptances.

(B) Dividends from:

(i) A domestic corporation other than one entitled to the benefits of taxpayers doing business with possessions of the United States.

(ii) A foreign corporation unless less than 50% of its gross income for the 3-year period ending with the close of its taxable year preceding the declaration of the dividends, or for that part of the period that it has been in existence, was derived from sources within the United States. Dividends are included only in an amount which bears the same ratio to such dividends as the gross income of the corporation for the period derived from sources within the United States bears to its gross income from all sources.

(C) Compensation for labor or personal services performed in the United States regardless of the residence of the payor, of the place in which the contract for service was made, or the place of payment. But this compensation is not deemed to be from sources within the United States if:

(i) The labor or services are performed by a nonresident alien individual temporarily present in the United States for a period or periods not exceeding a total of 90 days during the taxable year;

(ii) The compensation does not exceed $3,000 in the aggregate; and

(iii) The compensation is for labor or services performed as an employee of, under a contract with (a) a nonresident alien, foreign partnership, or foreign corporation, not engaged in trade or business within the United States, or (b) a domestic corporation, if the labor or services are performed for an office or place of business maintained in a foreign country or in a possession of the United States by that corporation.

(D) Rentals or royalties from property located in the United States or from any interest in that property, including rentals or royalties for the use of, or for the privilege of using, in the United States, patents, copyrights, secret processes and formulas, good will, trade marks, and other like property.

(E) Gains, profits, and income derived from the purchase and sale of personal property is treated as derived entirely from the country in which the property is sold. Thus, gross income from sources within the United States includes gains, profits, and income derived from the purchase of personal property without the United States and its sale within the United States.

From the items of gross income specified in Items (A) to (E), inclusive, as being income from sources within the United States, there will be deducted the expenses, losses, and other deductions properly apportioned or allocated thereto and a ratable part of any other such expenses, etc. The remainder, if any, is included in full as taxable income from sources within the United States. The ratable part is based upon the ratio of gross income from sources within the United States to the total gross income.

Included in (2), that is, income from sources without the United States, are:

(A) Interest other than that specified above as being from sources within the United States.[7]

(B) Dividends other than those derived from sources within the United States.

(C) Compensation for labor or personal services performed without the United States.

(D) Rentals or royalties from property located without the United States or from any interest in such property.

(E) Gains, profits, and income from the sale of real property located without the United States.

(F) Gains, profits, and income derived from the purchase of personal property within the United States and its sale without the United States.

The taxable income from sources *without* the United States is determined on the same basis described above for determining the taxable income from sources *within* the United States.

[7] I.R.C. Section 862.

Included in (3), that is, that category of income which is partly within and partly without the United States, are items of gross income other than those specified in (1) and (2). These items are allocated or apportioned to sources within or without the United States.[8] This refers to gains, profits, and income—

(A) From transportation or other services rendered partly within and partly without the United States;

(B) From the sale of personal property produced (in whole or in part) by the taxpayer within and sold without the United States, or produced (in whole or in part) by the taxpayer without and sold within the United States; or

(C) Derived from the purchase of personal property within a possession of the United States and its sale within the United States.

In the case of gains, profits, and income derived from the sale of personal property derived from the production of personal property in the United States and its sale within a foreign country, or vice versa, the allocation takes the following forms. Where the manufacturer or producer regularly sells part of his output to wholly independent distributors or other selling concerns in such a way as to establish fairly an independent factory or production price, the taxable income attributable to sources within the United States is computed by an accounting which treats the products as sold by the factory or productive department of the business to the distributing or selling department at the independent factory price so established. But where an independent factory or production price has not been established, the allocable taxable income is determined by apportioning one-half according to the ratio of the taxpayer's property in the United States to his total property, and one-half according to the ratio of the taxpayer's gross sales within the United States to his total gross sales.

Special apportionment rules have been provided for transportation service and for telegraph and cable service.

Nonresident Alien Individuals

Tax on Nonresident Alien Individuals. For purposes of the income tax, alien individuals are divided generally into two classes, namely, resident and nonresident aliens. Resident aliens are, in general, taxable the same as citizens of the United States; that is, a resident alien is taxable on income derived from all sources, including sources without the United States. Nonresident aliens are

[8] I.R.C. Section 863.

taxable only on income derived from sources within the United States.[9]

The term "nonresident alien individual" means an individual whose residence is not within the United States, and who is not a citizen of the United States. The term includes a nonresident alien fiduciary.

An alien is presumed to be a nonresident alien; but this presumption may be rebutted by competent proof.

Nonresident alien individuals are divided into four classes for tax purposes:

(1) *Class 1.* Nonresident alien individuals not engaged in trade or business within the United States at any time during the taxable year and receiving in that year an aggregate of not more than $15,400 gross income (determined without regard to the partial exclusion of dividends) from sources within the United States consisting of (A) fixed or determinable annual or periodical income and (B) amounts constituting, or considered to be, gains from the sale or exchange of capital assets.

(2) *Class 2.* Nonresident alien individuals not engaged in trade or business within the United States at any time during the taxable year and receiving in that year an aggregate of more than $15,400 gross income (without regard to the dividends received exclusion) described under Class 1.

(3) *Class 3.* Nonresident alien individuals who at any time during the taxable year are engaged in trade or business within the United States.

(4) *Class 4.* Nonresident alien individuals who are bona fide residents of Puerto Rico during the entire taxable year.

Individuals within Classes 1 to 3, inclusive, are subject to tax as nonresident aliens. Individuals within Class 4 are subject to the standard income tax treatment.

A nonresident alien individual within Class 1 is not subject to the standard income tax treatment but is liable to a flat tax of 30% of the gross amount of his fixed or determinable annual or periodical income, amounts considered to be capital gains, and capital gains less capital losses. (Income is fixed when it is to be paid in amounts definitely predetermined. Income is determinable whenever there is a basis of calculation by which the amount to be paid may be ascertained.[10]) If the nonresident alien has been present in the United States for a period or periods aggregating less than 90 days during the taxable year, net capital gains are limited to those ef-

[9] I.R.C. Section 871.

[10] Regulations Section 1.1441-2(a)(2).

fected during his presence; if he is here for 90 days or more, net capital gains include transactions effected at any time during that year. The alternative tax may not be used.

A person within Class 2 is subject to regular United States income tax on fixed or determinable annual or periodical income from sources within the United States. Deductions are permitted for capital losses allocable to sources within the United States, charitable contributions to domestic organizations, and any other deductions properly allocable to items included in gross income. The tax is computed at regular rates; but if this tax (less the dividends received credit and the credit for partially tax-exempt interest) is less than 30%, 30% will be the tax.[11] A tax treaty may modify this.

A person within Class 3 is subject to the regular Federal income tax on income from sources within the United States. The term "engaged in trade or business within the United States" includes the performance of personal services within that country at any time within the taxable year, but does not include the performance of personal services—

(1) For a nonresident alien individual, foreign partnership, or foreign corporation, not engaged in trade or business within the United States; or

(2) For an office or place of business maintained by a domestic corporation in a foreign country or in a possession of the United States, by a nonresident alien individual temporarily present in the United States for a period or periods not exceeding a total of 90 days during the taxable year and whose compensation for such services does not exceed in the aggregate $3,000.

A person within Class 4 may exclude from his gross income any amounts derived from sources within Puerto Rico, except amounts received for services performed as an employee of the United States or any agency thereof.[12]

Gross Income. The gross income of a nonresident alien individual includes only the gross income from sources within the United States.[13]

Deductions. In computing the taxable income of a nonresident alien individual, the deductions otherwise allowable are allowed only if, and to the extent that, they are connected with sources from within the United States.[14]

[11] I.R.C. Section 871(b).
[12] I.R.C. Section 876.
[13] I.R.C. Section 872.
[14] I.R.C. Section 873.

Allowance of Deductions and Credits. A nonresident alien individual may only receive the benefit of the deductions and credits allowed to him if he files a true and accurate return of his total income from all sources within the United States.[15] Thus, if a District Director of Internal Revenue prepares the return from such information as is available, no credits or deductions are allowed except for withheld taxes.

Partnerships. A nonresident alien individual is deemed to be engaged in trade or business within the United States if the partnership of which he is a member is so engaged.[16]

Foreign Corporations

Tax on Foreign Corporations Not Engaged in Business in the United States. For income tax purposes, foreign corporations are divided into two classes: (1) nonresident foreign corporations and (2) resident foreign corporations. A nonresident foreign corporation is a foreign corporation which is not engaged in trade or business within the United States at any time during the taxable year. A resident foreign corporation is a foreign corporation which, at some time during the taxable year, is engaged in trade or business within the United States.[17]

A foreign corporation, whether resident or nonresident, is taxable only on income derived from sources within the United States. Unless otherwise provided by treaty, a nonresident foreign corporation is not subject to regular Federal tax but pays a flat 30% upon fixed or determinable annual or periodical income and on capital gains from sources within the United States. No deduction is allowed for any loss.

Tax on Resident Foreign Corporations. Except as provided otherwise by treaty, a resident foreign corporation is subject to regular Federal income tax. The taxable income of such a corporation includes only the taxable income from sources within the United States.[18]

A nonresident foreign corporation is not permitted any deductions, inasmuch as the tax is imposed upon the gross amount received from sources within the United States. But allocable deductions are allowed if the corporation is permitted to make such an

[15] I.R.C. Section 874.
[16] I.R.C. Section 875.
[17] I.R.C. Section 881.
[18] I.R.C. Section 882.

election under a tax convention and, in fact, it does make the election.

Exclusions from Gross Income. Earnings of foreign ships or aircraft within the United States may be excluded from gross income to the extent that the foreign country under which registry was granted allows similar treatment to United States craft.[19]

Income exempt under the terms of a tax convention or treaty also is excluded from gross income.

Personal Holding Companies

The personal holding company tax (see Chapter 16) applies to both domestic and foreign corporations.[20] But a foreign corporation will not be classified as a personal holding company if it is a foreign personal holding company, as defined below.

Foreign Personal Holding Companies

There is no tax upon foreign personal holding companies, as there is in the case of personal holding companies in general (see Chapter 16). But the *undistributed foreign personal holding company income* of the former must be included in the manner set forth below in the gross income of their *United States shareholders;* that is, the shareholders who are individual citizens or residents of the United States, domestic corporations, domestic partnerships, and estates or trusts (except estates or trusts the gross income of which includes only income from sources within the United States).[21]

Amount Included in Gross Income. The undistributed foreign personal holding company income is included only in the gross income of the United States shareholders who were shareholders in the company on the last day of its taxable year on which a United States group (to be defined) existed with respect to that company. These United States shareholders, accordingly, are determined by the stock holdings as of the specified time. This rule applies to every United States shareholder who was a shareholder in the company at the specified time, regardless of whether he is included within the United States group.

The United States shareholders must include in their gross income their distributive shares of that proportion of the undistributed foreign personal holding company income for the taxable

[19] I.R.C. Section 883.
[20] I.R.C. Section 541.
[21] I.R.C. Section 551.

year of the company which is equal in ratio to that which the portion of the taxable year up to and including the last day on which the United States group with respect to the company existed bears to the entire taxable year.

The amount which each United States shareholder must return is that amount which he would have received as a dividend if the above-specified portion of the undistributed foreign personal holding company income had in fact been distributed by the foreign personal holding company as a dividend on the last day of its taxable year on which the required United States group existed. The assumed distribution of the required portion of the undistributed foreign personal holding company income must be returned as dividend income by the United States shareholders for their respective taxable years in which or with which the taxable year of the foreign personal holding company ends.

Definition. A foreign personal holding company is any foreign corporation (other than a tax-exempt corporation and certain banking institutions) which meets both of the following requirements with respect to a taxable year:

(1) The *gross income requirement.* At least 60% of its gross income for the taxable year is foreign personal holding company income. But if the corporation has been classified as a foreign personal holding company for any taxable year ending after August 26, 1937, the figure drops to 50%, unless (A) a taxable year has intervened since the last taxable year for which it was so classified, during no part of which the stock ownership requirement specified in (2) exists, or (B) three consecutive years have intervened since the last taxable year for which it was so classified, during each of which its foreign personal holding company income was less than 50% of its gross income.

(2) The *stock ownership requirement.* At some time in the taxable year, more than 50% in value of the outstanding stock of the foreign corporation is owned, directly or indirectly, by or for not more than five individuals who are citizens or residents of the United States (referred to as *the United States group*).[22]

Foreign Personal Holding Company Income. Foreign personal holding company income is the same as personal holding company income (as defined in Chapter 16), with the following exceptions:

(1) The entire amount received as "interest," whether or not treated as rent, is considered to be foreign personal holding company income.

[22] I.R.C. Section 552.

(2) The entire amount received as "royalties," whether or not mineral, oil, or gas royalties, is considered to be foreign personal holding company income.[23]

A foreign personal holding company is not entitled to an excess contributions carryover. Nor does the net operating loss deduction include the dividends received deduction or other special deductions which are not allowed in computing foreign personal holding company income.[24]

Dependents

To qualify as a dependent, an individual must be a citizen or resident of the United States or be a resident of the Canal Zone, the Republic of Panama, Canada, or Mexico at some time during the calendar year in which the taxable year of the taxpayer begins. A resident of the Republic of the Philippines who was born to or legally adopted by the taxpayer in the Philippine Islands before 1956, at a time when the taxpayer was a member of the Armed Forces of the United States, may also be claimed as a dependent if the resident otherwise qualifies as a dependent.[25]

Joint Returns

A joint return may not be made if either the husband or wife at any time during the taxable year is a nonresident alien.[26]

Standard Optional Deduction

The standard deduction (see Chapter 24) is not allowable in the case of a nonresident alien individual.[27] This includes one who enters and leaves the United States at frequent intervals.

Optional Tax

The optional tax (see Chapter 24) does not apply to a nonresident alien individual.[28]

[23] I.R.C. Section 553.
[24] I.R.C. Section 556(a), (b).
[25] I.R.C. Section 152(b).
[26] I.R.C. Section 6013(a).
[27] I.R.C. Section 142(b)(1).
[28] I.R.C. Section 4(d).

Arm's Length Transactions

The Secretary of the Treasury may re-allocate items of income or expense between two or more organizations, trades, or businesses that are owned or controlled directly or indirectly by the same interests, if they deal at less than arm's length. See Chapter 27. This applies whether or not they are organized in the United States.[29]

Filing Date and Extensions

The customary filing dates for income tax returns do not always apply in the case of foreign taxpayers or operations.

The income tax return of a nonresident alien individual must be filed on or before the fifteenth day of the *sixth* month (rather than the fourth) following the close of the taxable year. But such a person must file by the fifteenth day of the fourth month if he has wages subject to withholding.[30]

The income tax return of a domestic corporation or of a foreign corporation having an office or place of business in the United States must be filed on or before the fifteenth day of the third month following the close of the taxable year. But the return of a foreign corporation not having an office or place of business in the United States need not be filed for another two months.[31]

Foreign Tax Credit

Citizens of the United States, domestic corporations, and certain aliens resident in the United States or Puerto Rico may choose to claim a *credit* against Federal income tax (as opposed to the usual *deduction* from gross income) for taxes paid or accrued to foreign countries and possessions of the United States, subject to the following rules:

(1) A citizen of the United States, whether resident or nonresident, may claim a credit for (A) the amount of any income, war profits, and excess profits taxes paid or accrued during the taxable year to any foreign country or possession of the United States and (B) his share of any such tax of a partnership of which he is a member, or of an estate or trust of which he is a beneficiary.

(2) A domestic corporation may claim a credit for (A) the amount of such foreign taxes paid or accrued during the taxable

[29] I.R.C. Section 482.
[30] I.R.C. Section 6072(c).
[31] I.R.C. Section 6072(b).

year to any foreign country or possession of the United States and (B) the taxes *deemed to have been paid.* The italicized phrase will be explained below.

(3) An alien resident of the United States, or an alien individual who is a bona fide resident of Puerto Rico during the entire taxable year, may claim a credit for (A) the amount of any such foreign taxes paid or accrued during the taxable year to any possession of the United States, (B) the amount of any such foreign taxes paid or accrued during the taxable year to any foreign country, if the foreign country of which he is a citizen or subject allows a similar credit to citizens of the United States residing in that country, and (C) his share of any such foreign taxes of a partnership of which he is a member, or of an estate or trust of which he is a beneficiary, paid or accrued during the taxable year, (i) to any foreign country, subject to the equal treatment mentioned in (B) or (ii) to any possession of the United States.[32]

Taxes Deemed To Have Been Paid. In the case of a domestic corporation which owns at least 10% of the voting stock of a foreign corporation from which it receives dividends in any taxable year, the credit for foreign taxes includes the income, war profits, and excess profits taxes deemed to have been paid by the domestic corporation. The amount of taxes deemed to have been paid is determined by taking the same proportion of any such taxes paid or accrued to any foreign country or to any possession of the United States by the foreign corporation, on or with respect to the accumulated profits of the foreign corporation from which these dividends were paid, which the amount of any such dividends received bears to the amount of the accumulated profits. If dividends are received from more than one such foreign corporation, the taxes deemed to have been paid by the domestic corporation are computed separately for the dividends received from each such foreign corporation.

If any foreign corporation (referred to here as the former corporation) owns 50% or more of the voting stock of another foreign corporation (referred to here as the latter corporation) from which it receives dividends in any taxable year, the former corporation will be deemed to have paid that proportion of any income, war profits, and excess profits taxes paid or accrued to any foreign country or to any possession of the United States by the latter corporation, on or with respect to the accumulated profits of the latter corporation from which these dividends were paid, which the amount of these dividends bears to the amount of the accumulated profits. The tax

[32] I.R.C. Section 901.

so deemed to have been paid will then be taken into consideration in determining the amount of income, etc., taxes paid or deemed to have been paid by the former corporation to any possession or foreign country on or with respect to its own accumulated profits from which the dividends were paid by that corporation to the domestic corporation.[33]

Limitation on Credit. The amount of the foreign tax credit may not exceed the same proportion of the tax against which this credit is taken which the taxpayer's taxable income from sources within that country (but not in excess of the taxpayer's entire taxable income) bears to his entire taxable income for the same taxable year.[34] For purposes of computing this limitation, the taxable income in the case of an individual, estate, or trust will be computed without any deduction for personal exemptions.

Where taxes paid or accrued to any foreign country or possession of the United States are more than the amount allowable as a credit, the excess may be carried back for two years and forward for five years.

Income from Sources Within Possessions of the United States

This subject is dealt with in Chapter 2.

Dividends Received Credit

The credit for dividends received from foreign corporations is considered in Chapter 8.

Accumulated Earnings Tax

The accumulated earnings tax (see Chapter 16) applies to every corporation formed for the purpose of avoiding shareholder taxes.[35] But a foreign personal holding company is not subject.

Corporate Reorganizations

A foreign corporation may not be a party to a corporate reorganization (see Chapter 17) unless, before the transaction takes place, it has been established to the satisfaction of the Secretary of

[33] I.R.C. Section 902.
[34] I.R.C. Section 904.
[35] I.R.C. Section 532.

the Treasury that the transaction is not in pursuance of a plan having as one of its principal purposes the avoidance of Federal income taxes.[36]

Consolidated Returns

A foreign corporation may not be included in a consolidated tax return. But in the case of a domestic corporation owning or controlling, directly or indirectly, 100% of the capital stock (exclusive of directors' qualifying shares) of a corporation organized under the laws of Canada or Mexico and maintained solely for the purpose of complying with the laws of that country as to title and operation of property, the foreign corporation may, at the option of the domestic corporation, be treated as a domestic corporation for this purpose.[37]

Charitable Contributions

A charitable contribution for the purpose of allowable deductions is a contribution or gift to a corporation, trust, or community chest, fund, or foundation created or organized in the United States or in any possession thereof, or under the law of the United States, any state or territory, the District of Columbia, or any possession of the United States. An individual may not claim a deduction to a charity created in a foreign country. A corporation may deduct a contribution to a trust, chest, fund, or foundation only if the money or other property is to be used within the United States or any of its possessions.[38]

Withholding of Tax at Source

This subject is treated in Chapter 25.

Information Returns

This subject is treated in Chapter 25.

Advice to Foreign Corporations

Every attorney, accountant, fiduciary, bank, trust company, financial institution, or other person who aids, assists, counsels, or advises in, or with respect to, the formation, organization, or reorganization

[36] I.R.C. Section 367.
[37] I.R.C. Section 1504.
[38] I.R.C. Section 170(c).

of any foreign corporation must, within thirty days, file a report with the Secretary of the Treasury that sets forth the nature of the aid, etc., given.[39] The penalties for failure to comply may be as high as $10,000, or imprisonment for not more than one year, or both. But the privileged nature of attorney and client is not disturbed where a lawyer gives such counsel.

Blocked Income

Where, under limitations placed by a foreign country, income derived abroad cannot be converted into United States dollars (or into assets which can be so converted), a taxpayer subject to Federal taxes may elect to defer the reporting of this income. He may elect to report the income (1) when it *is* convertible into dollars; (2) when it is actually converted into dollars even if contrary to foreign regulations; (3) when the income is used for nondeductible purposes or is disposed of; or (4) when, in the case of a resident alien, he terminates his residence in the United States.[40]

Income Exempt Under Treaty

Income of any kind, to the extent required by any treaty obligation of the United States, is not included in gross income and is exempt from taxation.[41] See page **25·30**.

Supplementary Material

A. Suggested Reading.

Neil F. Phillips, *United States Taxation of Nonresident Aliens and Foreign Corporations* (Toronto: The Carswell Co., Ltd., 1952).

Alexander Cameron, "Tax Considerations in Organizing a Business Abroad," *The Price Waterhouse Review*, September, 1957, Vol. II, #3, p. 44.

William G. Gibbons, *Business Abroad: Study of Law of United States and of Selected Foreign Countries* (Cambridge: Law School of Harvard University, 1957).

Paul D. Seghers, "Tax Advantages in Doing Business Abroad and How To Obtain Them," *Proceedings of the Tulane Second Annual Tax Institute* (New Orleans: Tulane University, 1953), p. 128.

B. Questions.

1. Why is a United States citizen taxed on income that is not earned in this country? What can he do to avoid this?
2. A corporation with a Delaware charter has its factory in West Germany, where substantially all of its executive and sales activities also

[39] I.R.C. Section 6046.
[40] Mimeograph 6475, 1950–1 CB 50.
[41] I.R.C. Section 894.

are conducted. To what extent is income earned by this corporation exempt from United States income tax?

3. A professional musician was deprived of her Austrian citizenship during World War II and never acquired citizenship anywhere; she is "stateless." On a concert tour, she earned $3,000 in the United States and $5,000 elsewhere. To what extent is she subject to United States income tax? Would your answer be different if she owned a home in San Francisco?
4. A nonresident alien individual spent one month's vacation in the United States. During that time he won a TV consolation prize of $15,000 for not knowing what president is buried in Grant's Tomb; he received a check for $1,000 from his father in the old country as allowance; he got $500 interest on State of West Virginia bonds he owned and $400 interest on United States Treasury notes of 1959. How will he be taxed in the United States?
5. A United States citizen has been in Norway as the representative of his New Jersey employer for 505 continuous days. He is injured while engaged on company business and is sent back to Passaic, New Jersey, for two months' medical treatment by the company physician. Is he entitled to tax exemption under the physical presence test in view of the circumstances?
6. Kim, a United States citizen, establishes a permanent residence in India. He invests in a partnership—the Bombay Duck Company, an Indian retail firm. He performs no services whatsoever for the organization. At the end of his tax year, his share of the profits is $80,000. (a) Is this included in his gross income for United States tax purposes? (b) Would your answer be different if he spent his full time in operating the business?
7. A French actress received a contract for $75,000 to make a movie in Hollywood. Because of certain aspects of her personal life, the American producer decided not to make use of her services; but the $75,000 was paid under the contract. Could she successfully argue that this was not income earned in the United States as she never had performed services here?
8. A resident of Nantucket, Massachusetts, made a contribution to a fund for Tibetan refugees. The organization had been chartered in Tibet. Is he entitled to a tax deduction? Would your answer be different if the organization had been formed in the United States? What would your answer be if the donor were a corporation?
9. A United States citizen is the traveling auditor of his American employer. He spends 300 full days in Switzerland and then is ordered to the company's plant in Norway, where he spends 220 continuous days. Does he meet the continuous residence test in view of the fact that he was not in either country for 510 days?
10. On October 1, 1960, a United States citizen accepts a position as production manager for a hopje firm in Holland, where he establishes permanent residence immediately. He uses the calendar year basis. Is any portion of his 1960 income exempt from United States tax?
11. An American chain store organization sent a United States citizen to England to be its representative for the sale of chains. He arrived in Liverpool on November 1, 1960, with his family on indefinite assignment. He intended to live in Liverpool with his family until the com-

pany assigned him a new post, and he established his residence there. On April 1, 1961, he arrived in the United States for consultation with his employer, leaving his family in Liverpool. He returned to England on May 1 and continued to live there. For his calendar year 1961 Federal return will he be able to exclude his income earned in England?

12. Assume the same facts as in the previous problem, except that the representative is transferred back to the United States on December 15, 1961. May he exclude his income earned abroad?
13. An attorney, a British citizen, came to New York to work on a complicated admiralty matter, for which he was paid $15,000 by a United States firm. The attorney paid $2,000 for rental of an office in New York and $5,000 for clerical assistance. How much was his earned income in the United States?
14. In order to create a "foreign atmosphere," a group of United States citizens incorporated their perfume business in France. Actually all of the business and assets were in the United States, except for furniture and fixtures in a showy office for American tourists in Paris. The corporation had $50,000 income in excess of allowable deductions in the taxable year. Will the corporation be able to be taxed as a nonresident foreign corporation?
15. A United States citizen owns a castle in the Kingdom of Graustark, which he rents out. If he qualifies for exclusion of income earned abroad, must he report the rentals as income on his Federal tax return? Would your answer be different if he performed personal services in connection with the production of rent?
16. A United States citizen established a permanent residence in Belgium, where he resided for three years. Which if any of the following items are subject to United States tax: (a) salary earned in Belgium and paid by an employer there; (b) consulting fees earned in Belgium and paid by a New York corporation; (c) consulting fees earned in Belgium but paid through a Philadelphia bank; (d) fees earned from advice rendered to a Chicago firm by mail; (e) fee earned while he was on a vacation trip to Boston; (f) interest on a savings account in Washington; and (g) dividends on stock of a United States corporation, the certificate of which was in a vault in Belgium.
17. A Venezuelan citizen earned $12,000 as a baseball player on the Chicago White Sox team. He was in the United States from March 1 until September 30. Discuss his tax status here. What would happen if he earned an additional $5,000 that was paid to him by a United States syndicate for playing baseball in Cuba in the month of December?
18. A steamship captain, a United States citizen, departed from the United States on June 3, 1960, and arrived in Yemen on the following day. He remained there until he had established a qualifying 18-month period. While there, the captain earned and received a salary of $15,000 for the period from June 5 until December 31, 1960. On how much of his foreign-earned income is he taxed?
19. A husband and wife work in Holland. Both are United States citizens, but only she has lived continuously abroad for more than 510 days. He is employed by the United States Department of Agriculture; she is employed by a Rotterdam pearl merchant. He earns $9,000; she, $25,000. How much of this income must be reported for

Federal income tax purposes? Would your answer be the same whether they file separate or joint returns?

20. A United States citizen works in Iraq for a 26-consecutive-month period from July 1, 1960, to September 1, 1962, except that he spends February, 1961, and February, 1962, on vacation in the United States. Is he entitled to exemption for being outside of the United States for 510 days?

23

PREPARATION AND FILING OF THE TAX RETURN

Who Must File?

If a taxpayer is required to file an income tax return, he is not excused by the fact that forms were not sent to him, or even by the fact that he made diligent effort to get forms from the Internal Revenue Service.

Individuals. An income tax return must be filed for each taxable year by every individual who receives $600 or more of gross income during this taxable year and who is (1) a citizen of the United States (whether residing at home or abroad), (2) a resident of the United States though not a citizen, or (3) an alien bona fide resident of Puerto Rico during the entire taxable year. The return must be filed regardless of the family or marital status of the individual.[1]

But if the individual has attained the age of 65 before the close of his taxable year, the $600 figure becomes $1,200.

Corporations. Every corporation subject to taxation must file a return, even if there is no income.

Partnerships. Every partnership must file a return. This does not apply to a partnership carrying on no business in the United States and deriving no income from sources within the United States.[2]

Estates. A return must be filed for each estate the gross income of which for the taxable year is $600 or more.[3]

Trusts. A return must be filed by every trust that has any taxable income for the taxable year, or that has gross income of $600 or more, regardless of the amount of taxable income.

[1] I.R.C. Section 6012.
[2] I.R.C. Section 6031(d).
[3] I.R.C. Section 6012.

Forms To Be Used

Unlike other taxpayers, an individual may have a choice as to the tax form to be used.

Form 1040A. An individual may use the simplified form, known as 1040A, if his gross income for the taxable year (1) is less than $10,000; (2) consists entirely of remuneration for personal services performed as an employee, dividends, or interest; and (3) does not include more than $200 from dividends, interest, and remuneration for personal services other than wages.[4]

An individual may not use Form 1040A if he:

(1) Has income other than that described in the previous paragraph;
(2) Claims status as head of household;
(3) Claims status as a surviving spouse;
(4) Claims credit for retirement income;
(5) Claims credit for dividends;
(6) Is delinquent in making his return;
(7) Claims exclusion for sick pay;
(8) Does not use the cash method;
(9) Uses a fiscal year;
(10) Paid an estimated tax during the year;
(11) Is subject to the self-employment tax;
(12) Itemizes deductions (or if his spouse itemizes);
(13) Claims travel, transportation, or other expenses; or
(14) Is a nonresident alien.

If Form 1040A is filed and income is under $5,000, the taxpayer need not compute his tax liability, although he may do so if he desires (or is suspicious). The District Director of Internal Revenue will compute the tax from a table. If income is $5,000 or more, the taxpayer must compute his own tax, even if Form 1040A is used.

A joint Form 1040A may be filed by a married couple if the combined income is less than $10,000 and the detailed requirements set forth above are met. If a joint Form 1040A is filed, the taxpayers must compute the tax if combined income is $5,000 or more.

Form 1040W. Used for the first time in 1960 is Form 1040W, an optional short form. An individual may use this form if his income consists of (1) salary and wages regardless of amount, *and* (2) not more than $200 of dividends and interest, *and* (3) no other items of

[4] I.R.C. Section 6012.

income. It was designed for taxpayers who are not eligible to use the punched-card Form 1040A but whose affairs do not require the use of the business and investment schedules on Form 1040. Specifically, the streamlined Form 1040W does not contain schedules for income from business, rents, royalties, capital gains, partnerships, estates, trusts, annuities, etc., or for computing depreciation or the retirement income credit. But Form 1040W may be used for wage and salary earners who wish to take advantage of head of household or surviving spouse status, exclusion for sick pay, exclusion and credit for dividends received (within the limits set in the second sentence of this paragraph), estimated tax payment credit, or itemized deductions (as for contributions, interest payments, medical expenses, and the like).

If Form 1040W is used, the tax table computation available in connection with Form 1040 may be used; that is, where adjusted gross income is less than $5,000. As in the manner of Form 1040, the standard deduction may be used in lieu of itemized deductions.

Form 1040. This must be used by individuals not permitted to use Form 1040A or Form 1040W. It *may* be used by any individual.

Completeness of Tax Return

Before a tax return is filed, the taxpayer must remember that all of the required information, including answers to questions on the tax blank, must be furnished. The gathering of information in the manner required by the form may take far more time and effort than the prepaartion of the return itself. But if all of the required information is not supplied, the tax return may be regarded as "no return." [5]

Reconciliation of Book and Tax Return Items

The taxpayer should be able to trace his income and expenses directly to the tax return; or, stated differently, he should be able to identify the items on his tax return with his records—books, bank statements, checkbooks, etc. If the taxpayer prepares his return directly from his employer's withholding tax statement or information return, and if other items are the same as checkbook, etc., entries, there is no problem. But in many situations, book income and tax return income are quite different. Then a reconciliation should be effected. It *must* be effected in the case of corporations.

The preparation of the tax return thus involves the following considerations: (1) figures per books and per tax returns should be

[5] *Carmichael Tile Co.,* T.C. Memo., Docket #22858, entered April 21, 1950.

reconciled; (2) allowance should be made for items that are treated differently for book and for tax return purposes; (3) items involving other taxable years should be highlighted so that they may receive proper treatment in the other years; and (4) any person who reviews the return should be able to understand readily where each figure was obtained.

A serviceable method is to head up sheets, such as columnar schedules, that are prepared directly from the taxpayer's records. Two sets of adjustments are then made: (1) items that are treated differently for book and for tax purposes and (2) reclassifications to coincide with tax form treatment. The items listed under (2) balance out. Book figures, plus or minus these two sets of adjustments, are thus converted directly into the figures that appear on the tax return.

On the corporation income tax return, the form of reconciliation, given on page 23·5, must be filled in.

Examination of Prior Years' Returns

Before a tax return is prepared, examination should be made of tax returns of prior years and the supporting work sheets. This is necessary for the following reasons:

(1) Ascertainment of elections that have been made. Most tax return elections are binding upon future years' returns.

(2) Maintenance of consistency and uniformity that is required of taxpayers.

(3) Establishment of whether there are carryovers that may be utilized, such as the 5-year carryover of capital loss.

(4) Determination of whether there are years to which carrybacks may be taken, such as net operating losses.

(5) Discovery of transactions of prior periods that might otherwise go unnoted; *e.g.*, amortization of patent expense of fifteen years ago.

Revenue Agents' reports should be examined. For example, upon audit of a prior year's return, a Revenue Agent might have disallowed a certain expenditure, which, the record notes, he permitted as an annual write-off to the extent of 10% per annum.

Supporting Schedules

Completion of the tax return form is only part of the preparation required. Where applicable, supplementary printed schedules should be obtained from the Internal Revenue Service and appended

Schedule M.—RECONCILIATION OF TAXABLE INCOME AND ANALYSIS OF EARNED SURPLUS AND UNDIVIDED PROFITS

1. Earned surplus and undivided profits at end of preceding taxable year (Schedule L).........		**9.** Total distributions to stockholders charged to earned surplus during the taxable year: (a) Cash.......	
2. Taxable income before net operating loss deduction and special deductions (line 24, page 1)....		(b) Stock of the corporation................	
3. Nontaxable interest on:		(c) Other property (Attach schedule)............	
(a) Obligations of a State, Territory, or a possession of the United States, or any political subdivision of any of the foregoing, or the Dist. of Columbia.		**10.** Contributions in excess of 5% limitation...........	
(b) Obligations of the United States issued on or before Sept. 1, 1917; all postal savings bonds.		**11.** Federal income and excess profits taxes...........	
4. Other nontaxable income (Attach schedule)....................		**12.** Income taxes of foreign countries or United States possessions if claimed as a credit in whole or in part on line 6, page 3 Tax Computation.........	
5. Charges against surplus reserves deducted from income in this return (Attach schedule)..........		**13.** Insurance premiums paid on the life of any officer or employee where the corporation is directly or indirectly a beneficiary.........................	
6. Adjustments for tax purposes not recorded on books (Attach sch.)..		**14.** Unallowable interest incurred to purchase or carry tax-exempt interest obligations.................	
7. Sundry credits to earned surplus (Attach schedule)..............		**15.** Excess of capital losses over capital gains..........	
8. Total of lines 1 to 7........		**16.** Additions to surplus reserves (Attach schedule)......	
		17. Other unallowable deductions (Attach schedule)....	
		18. Adjustments for tax purposes not recorded on books (Attach schedule)........................	
		19. Sundry debits to earned surplus (Attach schedule)...	
		20. Total of lines 9 to 19......................	
		21. Earned surplus and undivided profits at end of the taxable year (Schedule L) (Line 8 less line 20)...	

to the basic income tax form; for example, the personal holding company schedule or the schedule of gains and losses from sales or exchanges of property. In addition, schedules have to be prepared for such items as pension expense and depreciation.

Other schedules, not specifically called for by the tax form, are almost certain to be needed, such as losses on abandonments, advances and deposits from customers, allocation of stock dividends and rights, amortization of intangibles, bond discount or premium, capitalized taxes, casualty losses, development expense, election as to capitalization of certain items, installment sales, involuntary conversions, long-term contracts, separate sales of realty acquired as a unit, worthless stock or securities, travel and entertainment expense, legal fees, repairs, and miscellaneous expenses.

Many taxmen believe that it is good policy to anticipate any possible questions that a Revenue Agent might ask. If a Revenue Agent has to call upon a taxpayer for account analyses or to ask a question which might have been answered by a schedule filed with the return, it is quite conceivable that this Agent will think of other (and possibly more embarrassing) questions to ask. But if the return is so complete that he does not have to call to ask that first question, there may be no additional questions.

Even if the taxpayer prefers to submit with his return only those schedules specifically called for, on the theory that it is better never to advance any information, an analysis of all figures should be prepared when the return is made up and *carefully preserved.* Many a tax deduction has been lost because, years later, the supporting details could not be found when the Revenue Agent asked his questions.

The following Treasury forms may be used as adjuncts to Form 1040:

Form	*Description*
2106	Statement of Employee Business Expenses.
2440	Statement to Support Exclusion of Sick Pay.
2441	Statement of Expenses for Care of Children and Certain Other Dependents.
2555	Exclusion of Income Earned Abroad.

Supporting Data

In addition to figures, the taxpayer should keep available for verification purposes any material that might be necessary to support tax return entries. For example, purchase and sale memoranda from brokers is very helpful in verifying capital gain and loss.

In the case of travel and entertainment expense, there should be ticket stubs, brokers' memoranda, hotel bills, accounts with clubs. In the case of write-downs in the value of assets, there should be contemporary correspondence with experts, appraisals, and the like, to show why the figures were selected. Where bad debts have been written off, there should be such substantiation as credit reports, correspondence with banks or attorneys, or court decrees.

Although it is a cardinal principle of United States jurisprudence that a man is innocent until proved guilty, that principle generally does not apply to taxation. A Revenue Agent will not deny the validity of the principle, of course. But he will say: "I cannot conscientiously allow you to take any deduction until you have proved to my satisfaction that you are entitled to it." The result is the same.

Employee business expenses present such an audit problem that the Internal Revenue Service has devised a form solely for this purpose. If an employee is required to travel and to incur business expenses, or to incur transportation, outside salesman, or educational expenses during the taxable year, he is invited to use Form 2106 to help to determine the correct deduction. Travel expenses are listed under these headings: (1) railroad, airplane, boat, etc., fares; (2) meals and lodgings; (3) automobile expenses; (4) other travel expenses. Local transportation expenses and outside salesmen's expenses are called for separately. Another heading is for employee business expenses. Persons claiming a deduction for education expenses must show the name of the educational institution or activity, the reason for undertaking the education, the principal subjects studied, and the degree (if any) for which the taxpayer was a candidate.

Specific Tax Returns

Individual. The principal schedules that an individual might have to append to his tax return are (1) profit or loss from business and (2) gains and losses from sales or exchanges of property. Another schedule that might be required is profit or loss from farming.

A wage-earner is required to attach a copy of his employer's withholding tax statement Form W–2 to page one of the income tax return.

Partnership. The statement of gross income and deductions includes only those items which all of the partners treat in the same manner, subject, of course, to the varying degrees of partnership

Schedule M.—RECONCILIATION OF

	1. Capital account at beginning of year	2. Capital contributed during year	3. Income not included in column 4 plus nontaxable income
(a)...			
(b)...			
(c)...			
(d)...			
(e)...			

interests held. The following items are not included in arriving at the partnership *ordinary* income; they are, however, shown on a separate multicolumned schedule, with each partner being assigned his proper amount: payments to partners—salaries and interest, net short-term gain (or loss) from sale or exchange of capital assets, net long-term gain (or loss) from sale or exchange of capital assets, net gain (or loss) from disposition of business assets, qualifying dividends, partially tax-exempt interest less amortization, contributions, income specially allocated, deductions specially allocated, interest on tax-free covenant bonds, income and profits taxes paid to a foreign country or United States possession, and net earnings from self-employment. A single illustration will show why these items are allocated specifically and individually to each partner. A partner will pick up as a single item his share of the partnership ordinary income. But, in the case of specially allocated items, he must add his share of the partnership figure to the corresponding item on his personal tax return. Thus, in the case of *contributions,* he transfers his share of the partnership contributions to his own tax return and adds it to his own contributions. The combined total will be deducted to the extent that an individual may deduct contributions; that is, to the extent of 20% or 30% (depending upon the nature of the payees) of his adjusted gross income.

In the manner of corporations, but not of individuals, the partnership presents a balance sheet.

The partnership must supply a reconciliation of the partners' capital accounts, given above.

Corporations. As has been mentioned earlier in this chapter, the corporation tax return contains a balance sheet and a surplus reconciliation schedule.

Fiduciaries. In arriving at the taxable income of a fiduciary, a deduction is allowed for distributions to beneficiaries. See Chapter 20.

PARTNERS' CAPITAL ACCOUNTS

4. Ordinary income (or loss) from line 26, page 1	5. Losses not included in column 4, plus unallowable deductions	6. Withdrawals and distributions	7. Capital account at end of year

Beneficiaries' shares of income and credits are listed for each beneficiary under the following headings: (1) amount of income required to be distributed currently; (2) other amounts paid, credited, or otherwise required to be distributed; (3) domestic dividends qualifying for credit; (4) partially tax-exempt interest; (5) income taxable to beneficiaries less amounts reported under (3), (4), (6), (7), and (8); (6) net short-term capital gain; (7) net long-term capital gain; (8) the total of tax-exempt income and foreign income of a foreign trust; (9) Federal income tax paid at the source; (10) income and profits taxes paid to a foreign country or United States possession; (11) depreciation and depletion.

Round Dollar Figures

Figures on income tax returns may be rounded out to the nearest full dollars.[6]

Self-Employment Tax

An individual who reports a profit (or loss) from a business or profession must attach to his income tax return a copy of Schedule C, which contains a profit and loss statement for the enterprise. Attached to this is a computation of the self-employment tax.

Every individual, other than a nonresident alien, having net earnings from self-employment of $400 or more for the taxable year must complete this schedule.[7]

In the case of a husband and wife filing a joint return, the tax on self-employment income is computed on the self-employment income of each spouse, and not on the aggregate of the two amounts. If the net earnings from self-employment of either spouse are less than $400, these net earnings are not subject to the tax on self-

[6] I.R.C. Sections 6102 and 7504.
[7] I.R.C. Section 6017.

employment income, even though they must be shown on the joint return.

The self-employment tax is equivalent in effect to the Federal Insurance Contributions Act tax. But the latter is paid equally by employer and employee, whereas the former is paid only by the self-employed person. The self-employment tax is 50% higher than the tax paid equally by employer and employee. The self-employment tax on the first $4,800 of self-employment income is at these rates:

1960–62	4.50%
1963–65	5.25%
1966–68	6.00%
1968—	6.75%

Burden of Proof

Who Bears the Burden? The filing of a return is only half of the taxpayer's problem. It is equally important to be able to make the items of income and deduction *stick*. It is unrealistic to file a tax return if the items will not stand upon examination by the Internal Revenue Service.

"Once the government has established its case, the defendant remains quiet at his peril." [8]

Unless the Internal Revenue Code or the regulations specify some particular form of proof, it is up to the taxpayer to prove his case in any way that he sees fit. Thus, an individual was allowed to claim business expenses when he produced a diary that referred to the events that were the basis for his claim.[9] But deductions were not allowed to a taxpayer who maintained an account book, as there were no supporting receipts or invoices.[10]

In tax matters, the burden of proof is almost always upon the taxpayer.[11] Of course, the taxpayer has the opportunity of meeting this burden.[12]

In accumulated earnings tax matters, the burden of proof may be shifted to the Secretary of the Treasury if the taxpayer makes a timely statement as to why earnings have been retained.[13]

Where assets are transferred to another party under certain circumstances, the recipient may be faced with *transferee liability*. See Chapter 26. In proceedings before the Tax Court, the Secretary of

[8] *Percifield v. United States,* 241 F.2d 225 (9th Cir., 1957).
[9] *George A. Jacquemot et al.,* T.C. Memo. 1956–198, filed August 28, 1956.
[10] *William Auerbacher et al.,* T.C. Memo. 1956–218, filed September 27, 1956.
[11] *United States v. Rindskopf,* 105 U.S. 418 (1881).
[12] *Dick Brothers, Inc. v. Commissioner,* 205 F.2d 64 (3d Cir., 1953).
[13] I.R.C. Section 534.

the Treasury has the burden of showing that the recipient is liable as a transferee of property of a taxpayer, but the Secretary does not have to show that the taxpayer was liable for the tax.[14] In such a situation, it is sufficient if the Secretary shows that the recipient had received a distribution of assets from an insolvent transferor, or that the distribution rendered the transferor insolvent, or that the transfer was in fraud of creditors.[15]

The Secretary has the burden of proving that fraud exists.[16] Fraud is not to be presumed but must be established by clear and convincing evidence.[17]

What Must Be Proved? Any item which appears on the tax return is subject to proof. This may range from the fact that the taxpayer is married to the date on which the return was mailed to the Internal Revenue Service. A taxpayer claiming a deduction has the burden of bringing himself within the terms of the statute authorizing such relief.[18]

The following are the more common types of situation requiring proof.

A dependency exemption was denied where a taxpayer could not prove that he had provided more than half of the support of a child.[19] The result was similar where there was no proof that a son had contributed more than half of his father's support; the father's cost of living could not be established.[20]

In the absence of any evidence of the amount of the adjusted basis of property destroyed by fire, the basis was deemed to be zero, and no loss resulted.[21]

No loss deduction is allowed until basis is shown.[22]

Where the Federal Republic of Germany makes restitution to persons for property taken by the Nazis, payments which are measured by the value of the property are not taxable income where the taxpayer has not recovered the basis of his property.[23] But he must establish the basis.

Prizes must be reported at retail valuations in the absence of proof that fair market value is a lesser figure.[24]

[14] I.R.C. Section 6902(a).
[15] *Maurice L. Rose et al.,* T.C. Memo. 1958–144, filed July 25, 1958.
[16] *Budd v. Commissioner,* 43 F.2d 509 (3d Cir., 1930).
[17] *Walter M. Ferguson, Jr.,* 14 T.C. 846 (1950).
[18] *New Colonial Ice Company v. Helvering,* 292 U.S. 435 (1934).
[19] *Orlando G. Rodman, Senior,* T.C. Memo. 1958–145, filed July 25, 1958.
[20] *Stanley N. Jankowski,* T.C. Memo. 1958–130, filed July 9, 1958.
[21] *Pasquale Colabella et ux.,* T.C. Memo. 1958–136, filed July 15, 1958.
[22] *Anthony Delsanter et al.,* 28 T.C. 845 (1957).
[23] Revenue Ruling 58–500, I.R.B. 1958–42, 8.
[24] Revenue Ruling 58–347, I.R.B. 1958–28, 27.

Where notes are received as part of the selling price, the taxpayer has the burden of showing that fair market value as established by the Secretary of the Treasury is not to be used.[25]

Although loss on the sale of stock purchased solely in order to get inventory is part of the cost (and not a capital loss), it must be proved that desire to obtain these inventories was the real reason for the stock acquisition.[26]

Where a taxpayer discontinued the use of assets, no deduction was allowed in the absence of proof of the date of acquisition, cost, and probable life of the assets.[27]

No deduction for obsolescence was allowed unless a taxpayer could show that normal depreciation was inadequate to recover the adjusted cost of assets when the useful life was terminated.[28]

Where a Canadian author did not break down the story rights on a United States sale covering both United States and Canadian rights, the full proceeds were taxed here.[29]

A medical expense deduction was not allowed when there was only a widow's statement that a physician had prescribed a special diet for her late husband's hypertension: steak, avocados, pears, grapefruit, and potatoes, cooked in a certain manner three times a day.[30]

Proof may be required that an individual is entitled to the maximum permissible medical expense deduction.[31]

Mere nonuse of property is not enough to establish an abandonment for tax purposes.[32]

Accelerated depreciation was not permitted when extra use of the assets was not proved.[33]

An entertainment expense deduction was not allowed where the taxpayer could not prove that claimed expenses were incurred for business purposes.[34]

No bad debt or loss deduction was allowed on an alleged loan, where no records of the loan were kept by the reputed lender and the so-called borrower's books had been destroyed. The "lender's" canceled checks were not proof that there had been a loan.[35]

[25] *A. & A. Tool & Supply Co. v. Commissioner,* 182 F.2d 300 (10th Cir., 1950).

[26] *McGhee Upholstery Company, Inc.,* T.C. Memo., Docket #39898, entered December 31, 1953.

[27] *Co-operative Foundry Co.,* 2 B.T.A. 888 (1926).

[28] *Southeastern Building Corp. v. Commissioner,* 148 F.2d 879 (5th Cir., 1945).

[29] *Wodehouse v. Commissioner,* 166 F.2d 986 (4th Cir., 1948).

[30] *Eugene Merrick Webb Estate,* 30 T.C., No. 126 (1958).

[31] I.R.C. Section 213(g)(3).

[32] *George G. Ebner et al.,* T.C. Memo. 1958–108, filed June 9, 1958.

[33] *Western Constructing Corporation,* T.C. Memo. 1958–77, filed April 30, 1958.

[34] *Erwin et al. v. Granquist,* 253 F.2d 26 (9th Cir., 1958).

[35] *Rubin Uslander et al.,* T.C. Memo. 1958–212, filed December 15, 1958.

Under a qualified pension plan, the employer may take a deduction not exceeding 5% of the compensation of persons covered by the plan. See Chapter 11. But this amount may be reduced for later years if the Secretary of the Treasury finds that this amount is more than is reasonably necessary to provide the remaining unfunded cost of the plan.[36]

The taxpayer must be able to prove that a loss was sustained as a result of a casualty.[37] "For failure of proof, a taxpayer could not deduct either as a casualty loss or as a traveling expense damage to an automobile muffler and fuel pump allegedly caused by flying stones." [38] The fact that a horse died after eating the lining of a silk hat is not tantamount to saying that the horse died as the result of a casualty; influenza might have been the cause of death, and no casualty loss was allowed.[39]

There was no proof that trees had been killed by drought when an arborist testified that he had examined them after their destruction. He had not seen the trees when they had been alive.[40]

Ordinarily, a casualty loss is not allowed for destruction caused by termites, as there was no "sudden invasion of a hostile agency." [41] But when it could be *proved* that a house had been free of termites when examined by an expert less than a year before the claimed casualty, loss was allowed.[42]

In general, a disposition of property implies taxable gain or deductible loss; but there may be neither in a tax-free corporate reorganization. See Chapter 17. "To sustain this exception, the burden of proof is upon the taxpayer to establish the existence of a plan of reorganization." [43]

The taxpayer has the burden of upsetting the Secretary's use of the net worth method by producing the proper books and records.[44]

The taxpayer has the burden of proving that a delinquency penalty should not be assessed in the case of a late return.[45] See Chapter 26.

[36] I.R.C. Section 404(a)(1)(A).
[37] *Raymond Tank,* 29 T.C. 77 (1958).
[38] *Harry M. Leet,* T.C. Memo. 1955–13, filed January 24, 1955.
[39] *Davis C. McMorran,* 39 B.T.A. 1241 (1939).
[40] *James M. Kemper,* 30 T.C., No. 51 (1958).
[41] *United States v. Rogers et al.,* 120 F.2d 244 (9th Cir., 1941).
[42] *Rosenberg v. Commissioner,* 198 F.2d 46 (8th Cir., 1952).
[43] *United States v. Murdock et ux.,* D.C., Tenn., 1957, aff'd, — F.2d — (6th Cir., 1959).
[44] *Hansen v. Vidal,* 237 F.2d 453 (10th Cir., 1956).
[45] *Andrew Flori,* T.C. Memo. 1955–108, filed April 29, 1955.

Record-keeping Requirements

Every person liable for any tax imposed by this title, or for the collection thereof, shall keep such records, render such statements, make such returns, and comply with such rules as the Secretary or his delegate may from time to time prescribe. "Whenever in the judgment of the Secretary or his delegate it is necessary, he may require any person, by notice served upon such person or by regulations, to make such returns, render such statements, or keep such records, as the Secretary or his delegate deems sufficient to show whether or not such person is liable for tax under this title." [46]

The following are among the situations covered in *Guide To Record Retention Requirements,* May 13, 1958, 23 Federal Register 3165:

Persons Subject to Income Tax, Except Persons Whose Gross Income Consists Solely of Compensation for Personal Services Rendered or Arises Solely from Growing and Selling Products of the Soil. To keep permanent books of account or record, including inventories, as are sufficient to establish the amount of gross income, deductions, credits, and other matters required to be shown in any income tax return. In addition, every organization which is exempt from income tax but is required to file an annual income tax return must keep permanent books of account or records, including inventories, that are sufficient to show specifically the items of gross income, receipts and disbursements, and other required information.

Persons Receiving Any Class of Exempt Income or Holding Property or Engaging in Activities the Income of Which Is Exempt. To keep records that will enable allocation to be made of amounts of each class of exempt income and amounts of items or parts of items allocated to each class.

Persons Engaged in the Production, Purchase, or Sale of Merchandise. To keep a record of inventory conforming to the best accounting practice in the trade or business which clearly reflects income and is consistent from year to year.

Persons Claiming Allowance for Depreciation of Property Used in Trade or Business or Property Held for the Production of Income. To keep records of all factors entering into the computation of depreciation allowances.

[46] I.R.C. Section 6001.

Persons Claiming an Allowance for Depletion. To keep accurate accounts in which will be recorded the cost or other basis of the wasting asset, with all adjustments required.

Persons Making Transfers of Property by Gift. To preserve in their files letters from brokers furnishing quotations, or evidence obtained from officers of issuing companies as to sales, of stocks and bonds which are not listed upon an exchange but are dealt in through brokers, or which have a market. To keep books of account or record necessary to establish the amount of their total gifts.

Persons Making or Receiving Gifts of Property Acquired by Gift After 1920. To preserve and to keep accessible a record of the facts necessary to determine the cost of the property and, if pertinent, its fair market value as of March 1, 1913, to insure a fair and adequate determination of the proper basis.

Corporations Claiming Allowance for Dividends Paid to Shareholders. To keep permanent records necessary (1) to establish that dividends with respect to which the allowance is claimed were actually paid during the taxable year and (2) to supply the information required to be filed with the income tax return of the corporation. To keep canceled dividend checks and receipts obtained from shareholders acknowledging payment.

Persons Who Participate in a Tax-free Exchange in Connection with a Corporate Reorganization. To keep records in substantial form showing the cost or other basis of the transferred property and the amount of stock or securities and other property or money received (including any liabilities assumed upon the exchange, or any liabilities to which any of the properties received were subject), in order to facilitate the determination of gain or loss from a subsequent disposition of the stock or securities and other property received from the exchange.

Executors or Other Legal Representatives. To make and to maintain records showing in detail all deductions, distributions, or other items for which adjustment to basis is required to be made.

Verification of Tax Returns

All income tax returns contain statements to the effect that the returns are made under the penalties of perjury. Except in the case of individuals, the requirement may be made that a return is to be verified by an oath.[47]

[47] I.R.C. Section 6065.

If a return is prepared for a taxpayer by another person for compensation or as an incident to the performance of other services for which compensation is paid, the preparer must so certify the return. This does not refer to a person who provides merely mechanical assistance (such as a typist), nor to an employee.[48]

Each individual (including a fiduciary) must sign the return required to be made by him. A duly authorized agent may have power to sign the return for his principal.[49]

A wife was not liable on a joint return, that she signed, where her uncontradicted testimony was that she signed because of fear of bodily injury at the hands of her husband.[50] Nor was a wife liable for tax on a joint return where she showed that she signed only upon her physician's request to refrain from arguing with her husband because of his heart condition.[51] The November 28, 1955, issue of *Time* magazine made reference to a woman who, suing for divorce, testified that her husband had not spoken to her for eight years, except to ask what her income was when he prepared the joint return.

Corporation returns may be signed by the president, vice-president, treasurer, assistant-treasurer, chief accounting officer, or any other officer duly authorized so to act.[52] Note that this does not include such officers as secretary or chairman of the board, unless there is specific authorization to this effect by the corporation.

The return of a partnership may be signed by any one of the partners.[53]

An unsigned tax return does not start the running of the statute of limitations.[54] In fact, an unsigned return is not regarded as a return at all.[55]

Filing of Returns

Place of Filing. Income tax returns of individuals, estates, and trusts are to be filed with the District Director of Internal Revenue for the district in which is located the legal residence or principal place of business of the person required to make the return. If this person has no legal residence or principal place of business in any

[48] Regulations Section 1.6065–1(b).
[49] I.R.C. Section 6061.
[50] *Paul J. Frederick et al.,* T.C. Memo. 1957–225, filed December 9, 1957.
[51] *Ethel S. Hickey,* T.C. Memo. 1955–149, filed June 13, 1955.
[52] I.R.C. Section 6062.
[53] I.R.C. Section 6063.
[54] *J. S. Deese,* T.C. Memo. 1958–89, filed May 19, 1958.
[55] *Jesse Ullman Reaves,* 31 T.C., No. 72 (1959).

internal revenue district, the return is to be filed with the District Director at Baltimore, Maryland.[56] Corporation income tax returns are to be filed with the district director for the internal revenue district in which is located the principal place of business or principal office or agency of the corporation.

Two exceptions to the previous paragraph may be made:

(1) Income tax returns to be filed with the Director, International Operations Division, Internal Revenue Service, Washington 25, D.C.:

(A) Income tax returns on which any of the tax is to be paid in foreign currency.

(B) Returns of individuals (whether citizens of the United States or possessions thereof, or aliens) outside of the United States, having no legal residence, or principal place of business, in any internal revenue district in the United States.

(C) The income tax return of an estate or trust the fiduciary of which is outside the United States and has no legal residence or place of business in any internal revenue district in the United States.

(D) Income tax returns of foreign corporations having no principal place of business, or principal office or agency in any internal revenue district in the United States.

(2) Exceptional cases:

(A) The Secretary of the Treasury may permit the filing of a return in a district other than the one required.

(B) The Secretary may require any officer or employee of the Internal Revenue Service to file his return in any district selected by the Secretary.

Time of Filing. In general, tax returns are to be filed on or before the fifteenth day of the fourth month following the close of the calendar or fiscal year.[57] That means April 15 is the due date for a return for a calendar year ending the previous December 31.[58] Corporation returns are due not later than the fifteenth day of the third month following the close of the calendar or fiscal year. Returns of nonresident alien individuals (other than those whose wages are subject to withholding) and foreign corporations (other than those having an office or place of business in the United States) are due not later than the fifteenth day of the sixth month following the close of the calendar or fiscal year. Returns of exempt cooperative

[56] I.R.C. Section 6091.
[57] I.R.C. Section 6072.
[58] I.R.C. Section 6072.

associations are due not later than the fifteenth day of the ninth month following the close of the calendar or fiscal year.

In the case of a final return of a decedent, the return is due on the date when it would have been due had not the individual died.

A corporation that has dissolved must file its return not later than the third full month after liquidation.

Extensions for Filing

Extensions for the filing of tax returns may be granted by a District Director of Internal Revenue for a reasonable time, which, except in the case of taxpayers who are abroad, may not be for more than six months.[59] An application for an extension must be in writing, signed. There must be given the desired filing date and the reason for seeking the extension. An agent may sign the application if the taxpayer is unable to do so for reasons of illness, absence, or other good cause. In the case of citizens who are residing or traveling abroad, there is an automatic extension time for filing returns until the fifteenth day of the sixth month following the close of the taxable year.

Corporations may follow the above procedure or use an alternative one. Upon the submission of Form 7004 in duplicate, prior to the due date of the return, a corporation is entitled to an automatic extension of three months.

In the case of any extension of time for filing returns, 6% interest per annum is assessed for any amounts of tax subsequently ascertained to have been payable.

Payment

Estimated Income Tax. The dates for payment of estimated income tax installments are set forth in Chapter 25.

Corporations. Corporations may pay income taxes (other than of estimated taxes) in two installments, due, respectively, on the fifteenth days of the third and sixth months following the close of the taxable year.[60]

Estates of Decedents. A decedent's estate may elect to pay tax in four equal installments, on the due date of the return and quarterly thereafter.

[59] I.R.C. Section 6081.
[60] I.R.C. Section 6152(a).

Extensions for Payment

Extension of time for paying the tax is granted only for undue hardship.[61] Undue hardship is more than financial inconvenience; substantial financial loss must result.[62] Usually, a bond of not more than twice the amount of tax due is required before the due date of payment.

Form 1127 is used to request an extension of time to make payment of tax. District Directors of Internal Revenue may give extensions of up to twelve months.

Form of Payment

Payment of tax may be made by United States notes and certificates of indebtedness.[63] Series E bonds may not be used.

A taxpayer may not stop the Secretary of the Treasury from collecting additional taxes by marking a check, "In full." [64]

Supplementary Material

A. Selected Reading.

Walter M. Jensen, "Proper Working Papers for Tax Return Preparation," *Michigan Certified Public Accountant,* January, 1950, p. 9.

J. L. Boughner, *How To Save Taxes Through Proper Accounting* (New York: Prentice-Hall, Inc., 1954).

Accountants' Handbook, "Taxes," Section 27 (New York: The Ronald Press Co., 1956).

Henry Cassorte Smith, "What Are Adequate Records for the Preparation of Income Tax Returns?" *The Encyclopedia of Tax Procedures* (Englewood Cliffs, N.J.: Prentice-Hall, Inc., 1956), p. 1555.

Robert S. Holzman, "Photography and the Burden of Proof," *TAXES—The Tax Magazine,* February, 1959, Vol. XXXVII, #2, p. 123.

Andrew Kopperud and J. Bruce Donaldson, "Burden of Proof in Accumulated Surplus Cases," *TAXES—The Tax Magazine,* November, 1957, Vol. XXXV, #11, p. 827.

Edward Pesin, "Techniques in Proving a Tax Case," *Proceedings of the New York University Seventeenth Annual Institute on Federal Taxation* (Albany: Matthew Bender & Co., Inc., 1959), p. 37.

Harry Graham Balter, "The Accountant's Responsibility for Working Papers, Books and Records," *TAXES—The Tax Magazine,* May, 1954, Vol. XXXII, #5, p. 415.

Hugh Bickford, *Successful Tax Practice* (New York: Prentice-Hall, Inc., 1950).

[61] I.R.C. Section 6161.
[62] Mimeograph 4303, XIV–1 CB 133.
[63] I.R.C. Section 6312.
[64] *Ray Howard et al.,* T.C. Memo. 1956–219, filed September 27, 1956.

B. Questions.

1. Is it advisable to file a tax return if one is not required to do so?
2. An individual claimed four minor children as dependents. How can he support the deduction if questioned by the Revenue Agent?
3. Do corporations have an automatic extension for filing tax returns?
4. When must income tax returns be filed for each of the following:
   (a) Individual using fiscal year ending August 31.
   (b) Nonresident alien who worked for two months for a manufacturing corporation in Philadelphia.
   (c) Corporation that dissolved on July 17.
   (d) Individual on calendar year basis who died March 19.
   (e) Partnership using calendar year basis.
5. Why is a fiduciary required to file an income tax return if all of the income is currently distributed to beneficiaries?
6. An individual claimed his mother-in-law as a dependent. He is required to show that he paid for more than half of her support; but the tax return form asks for total income of the alleged dependent, and she indignantly refuses to divulge the amount of her modest dividends. What does he do?
7. A simple trust has gross income of exactly $600. Must it file a tax return? Would your answer be different if it were a complex trust?
8. An individual is preparing his tax return but finds that he has no capital gain and loss schedule. He makes the proper computation on the back of an envelope, which he attaches to the tax return that he files. What will happen?
9. An individual converted his residence into a business property, and it was necessary to establish the value of the property at the time of conversion. Realizing this, he engaged a reputable appraiser, who set a value of $35,000. The Internal Revenue Service used its own expert, who placed a value of $28,500 on the property. What value will be used?
10. How long must records be kept in order to support tax returns?
11. A long-standing grudge existed between an individual and the person who was now District Director of Internal Revenue where the individual resided and had his place of business. May he file his return in another district to avoid "incidents"?
12. Under what circumstances may an extension of time for payment of tax be obtained?
13. A theatrical producer spent considerable sums entertaining actors, critics, and other persons whose good will he needed for business purposes. But he kept no record of expenses whatsoever. Will the entire deductions claimed be disallowed?
14. A son, who is single, maintains a home for his fully dependent mother (a widow) and himself. A Revenue Agent learns that she completely dominates him and the home in every respect. May the son claim head of household status under the circumstances?
15. A corporation was incorporated in Delaware. Its factory is in South Carolina. Its executive offices are in New York. Its president and chief stockholder lives in Connecticut. Where is the corporate tax return to be filed?
16. An individual has $1,800 in gross income; but by reason of his five

children, it is obvious that his personal exemptions will exceed his income. Is he obliged to file a tax return?

17. May Form 1040A be used if a joint return is filed?
18. An accountant is preparing a tax return for his client, who expects to be out of the country before the return is completed. The taxpayer is reluctant to sign a blank return. What should be done?
19. An individual sets up an irrevocable trust for the benefit of his wife, and the fiduciary is required to distribute all of the income as soon as it is received. It is apparent that the fiduciary will not be a taxpayer. Must an income tax return be filed by the fiduciary?
20. A long-time bachelor was given some securities as a wedding gift. Subsequently he sold them. He feels that it would be embarrassing to ask the donor how much was paid for the gift; but gain or loss on the sale of securities must be reported. What basis should he use?
21. The Mandalay Road Corporation has income tax liability for its fiscal year ended April 30 of $40,000. By what date or dates must the tax be paid?
22. A taxpayer's store was destroyed by fire. Will the inventory records be accepted by the Internal Revenue Service as proof of the value of the merchandise loss?
23. A man sells property that has been in the family for centuries; an ancestor had purchased it from the Indians for beads. How does he establish basis when he sells the property?
24. An individual receives $8,500 in salary, $150 in dividends from domestic corporations, and $200 in interest from municipal bonds in the taxable year. May he use the simplified form, Form 1040A?
25. Is an individual obliged to sign the tax return that he prepares for another individual?
26. A man claimed a deduction for traveling expenses in connection with his business, and he produced some canceled checks with hotels named as payees. Is this adequate verification of the deduction?
27. If an individual may use either Form 1040 or Form 1040A, on what basis should he decide which to use?
28. An individual has $5,200 in salary and no other income. Is he permitted to use Form 1040?
29. Johann Faust filed a tax return, which later was found to have some fraudulent statements on it. When the Revenue Agent spoke of bringing perjury action, Faust replied that the return had not been sworn to but merely bore his signature. Is he correct?
30. A calendar year individual with $9,000 in salary and no other income was in a hospital in April, and did not file his tax return until April 27. May he use Form 1040A?
31. Kenneth Knox claimed a deduction for a casualty loss to his personal automobile. How can he justify the deduction?

24

TAX COMPUTATIONS AND CREDITS

Individuals

The method of computation of an individual's income tax varies according to whether he uses Form 1040A, Form 1040W, or Form 1040. Who may use Form 1040A and Form 1040W is described in Chapter 23. Any individual may use Form 1040.

Two terms must be understood at this point, regardless of which of the three types of form is used: these terms are *joint return* and *dependent.*

Joint Return. If husband and wife are married on the last day of the taxable year, a single return may be made by them jointly, which generally is called a *joint return.* But this is not possible if at any time during the taxable year either spouse was a nonresident alien, or if the spouses have different taxable years.[1] The same accounting period must be used by each spouse.

Where a joint return is filed, the items of income and deductions for each spouse are aggregated. For tax computation purposes only, half of this income is deemed to be that of each spouse, and tax is computed on half; the tax is then doubled to produce the actual tax. This rather clumsy arithmetic is not necessary, for tables are available (to be presented later in this chapter) for ready computation of the tax on joint returns.

Advantages of filing a joint return:

(1) Under most circumstances, the tax will be lower. This is because of the non-Euclidean mathematics of taxation, which indicates that the sum of the parts is less than the whole. Specifically, where the total income of the spouses is divided in two parts, the top tax bracket on each half is less than the top tax bracket for the whole, and doubling the taxes on the two parts will produce a lower tax than on the whole.

[1] I.R.C. Section 6013.

Illustration.

Taxable Income of	Tax for Single Taxpayer	Tax on Joint Return
$ 4,000	$ 840	$ 800
$12,000	$ 3,400	$ 2,720
$20,000	$ 7,260	$ 5,280
$50,000	$26,820	$20,300

(2) Capital gains of one spouse may be offset by capital losses of the other. A net capital loss is limited (see Chapter 5), but the otherwise unutilized loss of one spouse may reduce the gain of the other.

(3) The exclusion from gross income of interest on the first $5,000 principal amount of partially exempt United States bonds (see Chapter 4) is doubled, if each spouse actually owns at least $5,000 of such bonds.

(4) The $50 dividend exclusion is doubled, if each spouse owns stocks producing at least $50 in dividends.

(5) Business losses of one spouse may be set against gains of the other.

(6) The deduction for contributions may be increased. The deduction for contributions is limited to 20% or 30% (depending on the payee) of adjusted gross income (see Chapter 9). Adjusted gross income was illustrated in Chapter 4, but it may be defined here simply as gross income less the costs of producing that income. The higher the adjusted gross income, the greater is the ceiling on deductible contributions.

(7) Under certain circumstances, the deduction for medical expenses may be increased. Deductible medical expenses are those that exceed 3% of adjusted gross income. See Chapter 4. Thus the smaller the adjusted gross income, the larger the amount of the medical expense deduction, within statutory limits. Ordinarily, the filing of a joint return will produce *higher* adjusted gross income; but under certain circumstances (see Items (2) and (5) above), adjusted gross income on a joint return may be less than on separate returns.

Disadvantages of filing a joint return are:

(1) Only $1,000 net capital loss is allowable.

(2) Medical expenses generally are less, as adjusted gross income customarily is higher on a joint return. See Item (7) above.

(3) Since both parties are expected to sign a joint return, it is not possible to keep one's spouse from knowing his income. This objection can be overcome if the reluctant spouse gets the other one to sign a separate power of attorney, allowing the reluctant spouse to sign on behalf of both parties.

(4) Tax liability is joint and several on a joint return. Each party is liable for the full amount of the tax.

Joint returns may be filed only by persons who were legally married on the last day of the taxable year. Common law marriages are recognized for this purpose if they are recognized by the state in which they are entered into.[2] A Mexican marriage was not valid for joint return purposes where invalid under the laws of California, the state where the couple was domiciled.[3]

A husband and wife may elect to file a joint return even though one of the spouses has no gross income or deductions. For any taxable year with respect to which a joint return has been filed, separate returns may not be made by the spouses after the time for filing the return of either has expired. (See "Statute of Limitations" in Chapter 26.)

If a person dies during a taxable year, a joint return may be made for the survivor and the deceased spouse if the taxable years of the spouses began on the same day and end on different days only because of the death of one spouse. The same is true if both spouses die during the taxable year. There are two limitations: (1) If the surviving spouse remarries before the close of his taxable year, he may not make a joint return with the first spouse who died during that year. (2) The surviving spouse may not make a joint return with the deceased spouse if the taxable year of either spouse is a fractional part of a year because of a change in accounting period.

The general rule is that, in the case of death of one spouse, or of both spouses, the joint return with respect to the decedent may be made only by his executor or administrator. An exception is made whereby, in the case of the death of one spouse, the joint return may be made by the surviving spouse with respect to both him and the decedent if all the following conditions exist:

(1) No return has been made by the decedent for the taxable year in respect of which the joint return is made.

(2) No executor or administrator has been appointed at or before the time of making the joint return; and

(3) No executor or administrator is appointed before the last day prescribed by law for filing the return of the surviving spouse.

If a taxpayer is eligible to file a joint return for the taxable year in which his spouse dies, his return for each of the next two taxable years following the year of the death of the spouse will be treated as a joint return if all three of the following requirements are satisfied:

(1) He has not remarried before the close of the taxable year the return for which is sought to be treated as a joint return, and

[2] Revenue Ruling 58–66, I.R.B. 1958–9, 8.

[3] *Albert Gersten,* 28 T.C. 756 (1958).

(2) He maintains as his home a household which constitutes for the taxable year the principal place of abode as a member of this household of a person who is (whether by blood or adoption) a son, stepson, daughter, or stepdaughter of the taxpayer, and

(3) He is entitled for the taxable year to a dependency deduction with respect to this son, stepson, daughter, or stepdaughter.[4]

Illustration. The taxpayer meets the above requirements for the years 1957 through 1961. The taxpayer, whose wife died during 1956 while married to him, remarried in 1958. In 1959, his second wife died while married to him, and he remained single thereafter. For 1957 he will qualify as a surviving spouse, provided that neither he nor his first wife was a nonresident at any time during 1956 and that she (immediately prior to her death) did not have a taxable year different from that of the taxpayer. For 1958 he does not qualify as a surviving spouse because he remarried before the close of that taxable year. He will qualify as a surviving spouse for 1960 and 1961, provided that neither he nor his second wife was a nonresident alien at any time during 1959 and that she (immediately prior to her death) did not have a taxable year different from his. On the other hand, if the taxpayer, in 1959, was divorced or legally separated from his wife, he will not qualify as a surviving spouse for 1960 or 1961, as he could not have filed a joint return for 1959 (the year in which his second wife died).

Dependent. A *dependent* means any individual described under the following ten categories, more than half of whose support was received from the taxpayer for the calendar year in which the taxable year of the taxpayer begins, provided the gross income of the "dependent" for the calendar year is less than $600. As will be mentioned below, this $600 test may be waived in the case of certain children.

The categories are:

(1) A son or daughter of the taxpayer, or a descendant of either. This includes a legally adopted child.

(2) A stepson or stepdaughter of the taxpayer.

(3) A brother, sister, stepbrother, or stepsister of the taxpayer, whether by the whole or half blood.

(4) The father or mother of the taxpayer, or an ancestor of either.

(5) A stepfather or stepmother of the taxpayer.

(6) A son or daughter of a brother or sister of the taxpayer.

(7) A brother or sister of the father or mother of the taxpayer.

(8) A son-in-law, daughter-in-law, father-in-law, mother-in-law, brother-in-law, or sister-in-law of the taxpayer.

(9) An individual (other than a person who at any time during the taxable year was the taxpayer's spouse) who, for the taxable

[4] I.R.C. Section 2(b).

year of the taxpayer, has as his principal place of abode the home of the taxpayer and is a member of the taxpayer's household.

(10) An individual who—

(A) Is a descendant of a brother or sister of the father or mother of the taxpayer.

(B) For the taxable year of the taxpayer receives institutional care required by reason of a physical or mental disability, and

(C) Before receiving such institutional care, was a member of the same household as the taxpayer.

A dependency exemption may be claimed for a child placed with the taxpayer by an authorized placement agency for legal adoption by him, if the child is a member of his household.

The term "dependent" does not include any individual who is not a citizen of the United States unless he is a resident of the United States, Canada, Mexico, the Canal Zone, or the Republic of Panama. The preceding sentence does not exclude from the definition of "dependent" any child of the taxpayer—

(1) Born to him, or legally adopted by him, in the Philippine Islands before 1956, if the child is a resident of the Republic of the Philippines, and if the taxpayer was a member of the Armed Forces of the United States at the time the child was born to him or legally adopted by him, or

(2) Legally adopted by him, if, for the taxable year of the taxpayer, the child has as his principal place of abode the home of the taxpayer and is a member of the taxpayer's household, and if the taxpayer is a citizen of the United States.[5]

A payment to a wife which is includible in her gross income is not treated as a payment by her husband for the support of any dependent.

Only one exemption is allowed for a wife. None is allowed for a deceased first wife, where the second wife claimed her own exemption on a separate return.[6]

A single individual could not claim a dependency deduction for a woman with whom he lived in adultery. "We are of the opinion that to so construe the statute would in effect ascribe to the Congress an intent to countenance, if not to aid and encourage, a condition not only universally regarded as against good public morals, but also constituting a continuing, wilful, open, and deliberate violation of the laws of the State of Alabama."[7]

[5] I.R.C. Section 152.
[6] *Asa Charles Epps,* 26 T.C. 843 (1956).
[7] *Leon Turniseed,* 27 T.C. 758 (1957).

An individual is not a member of the taxpayer's household if at any time during the taxable year of the taxpayer the relationship between them is in violation of local law.

For purposes of determining whether an individual received more than half of his support from the taxpayer for a given calendar year, there is taken into account the amount of support received from the taxpayer as compared to the entire amount of support which the individual received from all sources, including support which the individual himself supplied. The term "support" includes food, shelter, clothing, medical and dental care, education. Church contributions are included.[8]

An individual may claim a dependency exemption in the case of a child who is under 19 or who is a student, provided the taxpayer has furnished more than one-half of the support of the child for the calendar year in which the taxable year of the claimant begins, even though the child's income for that year may be $600 or more. In determining whether the taxpayer does in fact furnish more than one-half of the support of the child who is a student, a special rule regarding scholarships applies. Amounts received as scholarships for study at an educational institution will not be considered in determining whether the taxpayer furnishes more than one-half the support.

Illustration. A taxpayer has a child who receives a $1,000 scholarship to a certain college for one year. The taxpayer contributes $500, which constitutes the balance of the child's support for that year. The taxpayer may claim the child as a dependent, as the $1,000 scholarship is not counted in determining the support of the child. Amounts received for tuition payments and allowances by a veteran under the provisions of the Serviceman's Readjustment Act of 1944 or the Veterans' Readjustment Assistance Act of 1952 are not amounts received as scholarships.

If no one person contributes more than half the support of an individual, but more than half of his support is contributed by two or more persons combined, each of whom (but for the *support* test) could claim the individual as a dependent, then any *one* of these persons who furnished more than 10% of the support may claim an exemption for the individual. In such a case, each such person, except the person claiming the exemption, must file a written statement on Form 2120 that he will not claim the individual as a dependent for that year.

Illustration. I, an individual who resides with his son, received $1,500 during the calendar year, which constituted his entire support for that year. The source of the $1,500 was as follows:

[8] Revenue Ruling 58–67, I.R.B. 1958–9, 9.

Source	Amount Received	Percentage of Total
Social Security	$ 375	25
N, an unrelated neighbor..........	165	11
B, a brother	210	14
D, a daughter	150	10
S, a son	600	40
Total received by I.........	$1,500	100

B, D, and S are persons each of whom, but for the fact that he did not contribute more than half of the $1,500, could claim I as a dependent. The three together contributed $960, or 64% of the $1,500, and thus, each is a member of the group to be considered as supporting the dependent but for the support test. B and S are the only ones who can meet all of the requirements, and either one could claim I as a dependent provided he attached to his income tax return a written statement signed by the other. Inasmuch as D did not contribute more than 10% of I's support, she is not entitled to claim I as a dependent, nor is she required to file a written statement with respect to her contributions to I. N contributed more than 10% of I's support, but, as he is an unrelated neighbor, he does not qualify.

Form 1040A

Form 1040A is the simplest tax return. It is a tabulating machine card. Who may use Form 1040A is detailed in Chapter 23.

This form may be filed on a joint return basis. If it is, the first names and middle initials of each spouse should appear at Item 1; Social Security numbers appear at Item 2. Item 3 asks about prior years' tax liability. Item 4 asks whether the taxpayer's spouse is filing a separate return.

For Item 5, information is to be copied from the taxpayer's Federal Withholding Tax Statement, Form W–2: wages, tax withheld, employer's name. Space is provided for the names of three employers; if there are more, the information must be supplied on a separate statement. The actual Withholding Statements must be attached, or, if they cannot be supplied, an explanation is required.

At Item 6, enter all other taxable income from dividends (except the first $50 received from domestic corporations), interest, and wages not subject to withholding.

There must be entered at Item 7 the total of Federal income tax withheld and excess Social Security tax (F.I.C.A.), if any; that is, withholding by employers of a total more than required by law.

Item 8 is for reimbursed employee expenses. If the taxpayer has had to account to his employer for business expenses (or where the employer gives the employee a flat allowance for subsistence and mileage of not more than $15 per day and 12½ cents per mile), and the employer pays for them (either by advances or reimbursements

Tax Table for Persons with Incomes Under $5,000, for Use with Form 1040A

To find your tax read down income columns until you find the line covering the total income shown as item 9. Then read across to appropriate column headed by number corresponding to number of exemptions claimed on item 15. Enter tax as item 10.

If your total income is— At least	If your total income is— But less than	And the number of exemptions is— 1	2	3 (If 4 or more there is no tax)	If your total income is— At least	If your total income is— But less than	And the number of exemptions is— 1: And you are— Single or a married person filing separately	2: And you are— Single or a married person filing separately	2: And you are— A married couple filing jointly	3: And you are— Single or a married person filing separately	3: And you are— A married couple filing jointly	4	5	6	7 (If 8 or more there is no tax)
		Your tax is—					Your tax is—								
$0	$675	$0	$0	$0	$2,325	$2,350	$301	$181	$181	$61	$61	$0	$0	$0	$0
675	700	4	0	0	2,350	2,375	305	185	185	65	65	0	0	0	0
700	725	8	0	0	2,375	2,400	310	190	190	70	70	0	0	0	0
725	750	13	0	0	2,400	2,425	314	194	194	74	74	0	0	0	0
750	775	17	0	0	2,425	2,450	319	199	199	79	79	0	0	0	0
775	800	22	0	0	2,450	2,475	323	203	203	83	83	0	0	0	0
800	825	26	0	0	2,475	2,500	328	208	208	88	88	0	0	0	0
825	850	31	0	0	2,500	2,525	332	212	212	92	92	0	0	0	0
850	875	35	0	0	2,525	2,550	337	217	217	97	97	0	0	0	0
875	900	40	0	0	2,550	2,575	341	221	221	101	101	0	0	0	0
900	925	44	0	0	2,575	2,600	346	226	226	106	106	0	0	0	0
925	950	49	0	0	2,600	2,625	350	230	230	110	110	0	0	0	0
950	975	53	0	0	2,625	2,650	355	235	235	115	115	0	0	0	0
975	1,000	58	0	0	2,650	2,675	359	239	239	119	119	0	0	0	0
1,000	1,025	62	0	0	2,675	2,700	364	244	244	124	124	4	0	0	0
1,025	1,050	67	0	0	2,700	2,725	368	248	248	128	128	8	0	0	0
1,050	1,075	71	0	0	2,725	2,750	373	253	253	133	133	13	0	0	0
1,075	1,100	76	0	0	2,750	2,775	377	257	257	137	137	17	0	0	0
1,100	1,125	80	0	0	2,775	2,800	382	262	262	142	142	22	0	0	0
1,125	1,150	85	0	0	2,800	2,825	386	266	266	146	146	26	0	0	0
1,150	1,175	89	0	0	2,825	2,850	391	271	271	151	151	31	0	0	0
1,175	1,200	94	0	0	2,850	2,875	395	275	275	155	155	35	0	0	0
1,200	1,225	98	0	0	2,875	2,900	400	280	280	160	160	40	0	0	0
1,225	1,250	103	0	0	2,900	2,925	405	284	284	164	164	44	0	0	0
1,250	1,275	107	0	0	2,925	2,950	410	289	289	169	169	49	0	0	0
1,275	1,300	112	0	0	2,950	2,975	415	293	293	173	173	53	0	0	0

1, 300	1, 325	116	0	0	2, 975	3, 000	420	298	298	178	178	58	0	0	0
1, 325	1, 350	121	1	0	3, 000	3, 050	427	305	305	185	185	65	0	0	0
1, 350	1, 375	125	5	0	3, 050	3, 100	437	314	314	194	194	74	0	0	0
1, 375	1, 400	130	10	0	3, 100	3, 150	447	323	323	203	203	83	0	0	0
1, 400	1, 425	134	14	0	3, 150	3, 200	457	332	332	212	212	92	0	0	0
1, 425	1, 450	139	19	0	3, 200	3, 250	467	341	341	221	221	101	0	0	0
1, 450	1, 475	143	23	0	3, 250	3, 300	476	350	350	230	230	110	0	0	0
1, 475	1, 500	148	28	0	3, 300	3, 350	486	359	359	239	239	119	0	0	0
1, 500	1, 525	152	32	0	3, 350	3, 400	496	368	368	248	248	128	8	0	0
1, 525	1, 550	157	37	0	3, 400	3, 450	506	377	377	257	257	137	17	0	0
1, 550	1, 575	161	41	0	3, 450	3, 500	516	386	386	266	266	146	26	0	0
1, 575	1, 600	166	46	0	3, 500	3, 550	526	395	395	275	275	155	35	0	0
1, 600	1, 625	170	50	0	3, 550	3, 600	536	404	404	284	284	164	44	0	0
1, 625	1, 650	175	55	0	3, 600	3, 650	546	414	413	293	293	173	53	0	0
1, 650	1, 675	179	59	0	3, 650	3, 700	556	424	422	302	302	182	62	0	0
1, 675	1, 700	184	64	0	3, 700	3, 750	566	434	431	311	311	191	71	0	0
1, 700	1, 725	188	68	0	3, 750	3, 800	575	443	440	320	320	200	80	0	0
1, 725	1, 750	193	73	0	3, 800	3, 850	585	453	449	329	329	209	89	0	0
1, 750	1, 775	197	77	0	3, 850	3, 900	595	463	458	338	338	218	98	0	0
1, 775	1, 800	202	82	0	3, 900	3, 950	605	473	467	347	347	227	107	0	0
1, 800	1, 825	206	86	0	3, 950	4, 000	615	483	476	356	356	236	116	0	0
1, 825	1, 850	211	91	0	4, 000	4, 050	625	493	485	365	365	245	125	5	0
1, 850	1, 875	215	95	0	4, 050	4, 100	635	503	494	374	374	254	134	14	0
1, 875	1, 900	220	100	0	4, 100	4, 150	645	513	503	383	383	263	143	23	0
1, 900	1, 925	224	104	0	4, 150	4, 200	655	523	512	392	392	272	152	32	0
1, 925	1, 950	229	109	0	4, 200	4, 250	665	533	521	401	401	281	161	41	0
1, 950	1, 975	233	113	0	4, 250	4, 300	674	542	530	410	410	290	170	50	0
1, 975	2, 000	238	118	0	4, 300	4, 350	684	552	539	420	419	299	179	59	0
2, 000	2, 025	242	122	2	4, 350	4, 400	694	562	548	430	428	308	188	68	0
2, 025	2, 050	247	127	7	4, 400	4, 450	704	572	557	440	437	317	197	77	0
2, 050	2, 075	251	131	11	4, 450	4, 500	714	582	566	450	446	326	206	86	0
2, 075	2, 100	256	136	16	4, 500	4, 550	724	592	575	460	455	335	215	95	0
2, 100	2, 125	260	140	20	4, 550	4, 600	734	602	584	470	464	344	224	104	0
2, 125	2, 150	265	145	25	4, 600	4, 650	744	612	593	480	473	353	233	113	0
2, 150	2, 175	269	149	29	4, 650	4, 700	754	622	602	490	482	362	242	122	2
2, 175	2, 200	274	154	34	4, 700	4, 750	764	632	611	500	491	371	251	131	11
2, 200	2, 225	278	158	38	4, 750	4, 800	773	641	620	509	500	380	260	140	20
2, 225	2, 250	283	163	43	4, 800	4, 850	783	651	629	519	509	389	269	149	29
2, 250	2, 275	287	167	47	4, 850	4, 900	793	661	638	529	518	398	278	158	38
2, 275	2, 300	292	172	52	4, 900	4, 950	803	671	647	539	527	407	287	167	47
2, 300	2, 325	296	176	56	4. 950	5, 000	813	681	656	549	536	416	296	176	56

or by allowing the employee to use a charge account), the employee may file Form 1040A without showing these items by simply checking the box in Item 8. But if the employer's payments are more than the employee's expenses, Form 1040 must be used.

Item 9 shows the totals of (1) wages and other income and (2) tax withheld.

If the income is $5,000 or more, the taxpayer must compute his own tax; he may do so if the income is less.

The tax table shown above allows about 10% of one's income as deductions which include charitable contributions, interest, taxes, losses, medical expenses, child care expenses, and certain miscellaneous deductions. If a taxpayer's deductions exceed 10% of his income, it will be advantageous to use Form 1040 and to list the deductions. But remember that itemized deductions are susceptible to *proof.*

The taxpayer turns to the table and finds the line that encompasses his income, on a horizontal plane. On the vertical plane, he finds the column that describes his marital status and the number of exemptions to which he is entitled. In general, one exemption is allowed for the taxpayer; one exemption for his spouse if a joint return is made, or if a separate return is made by the taxpayer and his spouse has no gross income for the calendar year in which the taxable year of the taxpayer begins and is not the dependent of another taxpayer for that taxable year; and one exemption for each dependent whose gross income is less than $600. No exemption is allowed for any dependent who has made a joint return with his spouse. The taxpayer may, in certain cases, be allowed an exemption for his dependent child even though the child has gross income of $600 or more. Additional exemptions are allowed for a taxpayer or spouse who has attained the age of 65 and also for a blind taxpayer or blind spouse

Illustration. A taxpayer's income on Item 9 is $4,731.28, and he desires to compute his own tax. He turns to the income range $4,700 to $4,750. If he is filing a joint return with his wife, who has no income or deductions, he follows this line horizontally until it meets the vertical line, "A married couple filing jointly." If he has no dependents, the number of exemptions is two (his wife and himself). At the intersection is the figure $611. This is the tax. If the couple had a 6-year-old son, the number of exemptions would be three, and the tax under three exemptions for a married couple filing jointly would be $491. If there were a second child who qualified as an exemption, the tax under the column for four exemptions would be $371.

If Item 9 shows total income of $5,000 or more, the table cannot be used. Instead, the tax must be computed in the following manner.

A single taxpayer or a married taxpayer filing a separate return uses this tax rate schedule:

If the amount is:

Over	But Not Over	Tax Is
$ 0	$2,000	20% of the amount of income.
$2,000	$4,000	$400, plus 22% of the excess over $2,000.
$4,000	$6,000	$840, plus 26% of the excess over $4,000.
$6,000	$8,000	$1,360, plus 30% of the excess over $6,000.
$8,000	$9,999.99	$1,960, plus 34% of the excess over $8,000.

Married taxpayers filing a joint return use this tax rate schedule:

If the amount of income is:

Over	But Not Over	Tax Is
$ 0	$4,000	20% of the amount of income.
$4,000	$8,000	$800, plus 22% of the excess over $4,000.
$8,000	$9,999.99	$1,680, plus 26% of the excess over $8,000.

If Form 1040A is used and the District Director of Internal Revenue computes the tax, he will advise the taxpayer by mail if additional tax is due. If the taxpayer computes the tax and there is a balance due, the taxpayer must enclose the payment in full with his return. If he is entitled to a refund, it will be mailed to him. A balance of less than $1 need not be paid. Overpayments of less than $1 will not be refunded unless the taxpayer makes a separate application to the District Director.

Form 1040

If a taxpayer has adjusted gross income of less than $5,000 and he elects to use Form 1040 (or is required to use that form), he may choose either of two methods of determining his tax: (1) by itemizing his deductions or (2) by using the standard deduction.

Taxable income consists of adjusted gross income less (1) deductions and (2) the deduction for exemptions. As to (1), the deductions may be itemized. Or, within certain limitations to be detailed below, a flat figure may be taken in lieu of itemized deductions.

Form 1040 lists as itemized deductions the following: contributions, interest, taxes, medical and dental expense, and "other deductions." The statute lists these deductions: trade and business deductions, trade and business deductions of employees, the deduction for long-term capital gains, losses from sale or exchange of property, deductions attributable to rents and royalties, and certain deductions of life tenants and income beneficiaries of property.[9]

[9] I.R.C. Section 62.

Tax Table for Persons with Incomes Under $5,000 Who Elect Not To Itemize Their Deductions, for Use with Form 1040

If total income on line 11, page 1, is— At least	But less than	And the number of exemptions claimed on line 4, page 1, is— 1	2	3 If 4 or more there is no tax
		Your tax is—		
$0	$675	$0	$0	$0
675	700	4	0	0
700	725	8	0	0
725	750	13	0	0
750	775	17	0	0
775	800	22	0	0
800	825	26	0	0
825	850	31	0	0
850	875	35	0	0
875	900	40	0	0
900	925	44	0	0
925	950	49	0	0
950	975	53	0	0
975	1, 000	58	0	0
1, 000	1, 025	62	0	0
1, 025	1, 050	67	0	0
1, 050	1, 075	71	0	0
1, 075	1, 100	76	0	0
1, 100	1, 125	80	0	0
1, 125	1, 150	85	0	0
1, 150	1, 175	89	0	0
1, 175	1, 200	94	0	0
1, 200	1, 225	98	0	0
1, 225	1, 250	103	0	0
1, 250	1, 275	107	0	0
1, 275	1, 300	112	0	0
1, 300	1, 325	116	0	0
1, 325	1, 350	121	1	0

If total income on line 11, page 1, is—		And the number of exemptions claimed on line 4, page 1, is—											
		1 And you are—		2 And you are—			3 And you are—						7
At least	But less than	Single or a married person filing separately	An unmarried head of a household	Single or a married person filing separately	An unmarried head of a household	(*) A married couple filing jointly	Single or a married person filing separately	An unmarried head of a household	(*) A married couple filing jointly	4	5	6	If 8 or more there is no tax
		Your tax is—											
$2, 325	$2, 350	$301	$301	$181	$181	$181	$61	$61	$61	$0	$0	$0	$0
2, 350	2, 375	305	305	185	185	185	65	65	65	0	0	0	0
2, 375	2, 400	310	310	190	190	190	70	70	70	0	0	0	0
2, 400	2, 425	314	314	194	194	194	74	74	74	0	0	0	0
2, 425	2, 450	319	319	199	199	199	79	79	79	0	0	0	0
2, 450	2, 475	323	323	203	203	203	83	83	83	0	0	0	0
2, 475	2, 500	328	328	208	208	208	88	88	88	0	0	0	0
2, 500	2, 525	332	332	212	212	212	92	92	92	0	0	0	0
2, 525	2, 550	337	337	217	217	217	97	97	97	0	0	0	0
2, 550	2, 575	341	341	221	221	221	101	101	101	0	0	0	0
2, 575	2, 600	346	346	226	226	226	106	106	106	0	0	0	0
2, 600	2, 625	350	350	230	230	230	110	110	110	0	0	0	0
2, 625	2, 650	355	355	235	235	235	115	115	115	0	0	0	0
2, 650	2, 675	359	359	239	239	239	119	119	119	0	0	0	0
2, 675	2, 700	364	364	244	244	244	124	124	124	4	0	0	0
2, 700	2, 725	368	368	248	248	248	128	128	128	8	0	0	0
2, 725	2, 750	373	373	253	253	253	133	133	133	13	0	0	0
2, 750	2, 775	377	377	257	257	257	137	137	137	17	0	0	0
2, 775	2, 800	382	382	262	262	262	142	142	142	22	0	0	0
2, 800	2, 825	386	386	266	266	266	146	146	146	26	0	0	0
2, 825	2, 850	391	391	271	271	271	151	151	151	31	0	0	0
2, 850	2, 875	395	395	275	275	275	155	155	155	35	0	0	0
2, 875	2, 900	400	400	280	280	280	160	160	160	40	0	0	0
2, 900	2, 925	405	404	284	284	284	164	164	164	44	0	0	0
2, 925	2, 950	410	409	289	289	289	169	169	169	49	0	0	0
2, 950	2, 975	415	414	293	293	293	173	173	173	53	0	0	0
2, 975	3, 000	420	419	298	298	298	178	178	178	58	0	0	0
3, 000	3, 050	427	426	305	305	305	185	185	185	65	0	0	0

1,350	1,375	125	5	0	3,050	3,100	437	435	314	314	314	194	194	194	74	0	0	0
1,375	1,400	130	10	0	3,100	3,150	447	445	323	323	323	203	203	203	83	0	0	0
1,400	1,425	134	14	0	3,150	3,200	457	454	332	332	332	212	212	212	92	0	0	0
1,425	1,450	139	19	0	3,200	3,250	467	464	341	341	341	221	221	221	101	0	0	0
1,450	1,475	143	23	0	3,250	3,300	476	473	350	350	350	230	230	230	110	0	0	0
1,475	1,500	148	28	0	3,300	3,350	486	482	359	359	359	239	239	239	119	0	0	0
1,500	1,525	152	32	0	3,350	3,400	496	492	368	368	368	248	248	248	128	8	0	0
1,525	1,550	157	37	0	3,400	3,450	506	501	377	377	377	257	257	257	137	17	0	0
1,550	1,575	161	41	0	3,450	3,500	516	511	386	386	386	266	266	266	146	26	0	0
1,575	1,600	166	46	0	3,500	3,550	526	520	395	395	395	275	275	275	155	35	0	0
1,600	1,625	170	50	0	3,550	3,600	536	530	404	404	404	284	284	284	164	44	0	0
1,625	1,650	175	55	0	3,600	3,650	546	539	414	413	413	293	293	293	173	53	0	0
1,650	1,675	179	59	0	3,650	3,700	556	549	424	423	422	302	302	302	182	62	0	0
1,675	1,700	184	64	0	3,700	3,750	566	558	434	432	431	311	311	311	191	71	0	0
1,700	1,725	188	68	0	3,750	3,800	575	567	443	441	440	320	320	320	200	80	0	0
1,725	1,750	193	73	0	3,800	3,850	585	577	453	451	449	329	329	329	209	89	0	0
1,750	1,775	197	77	0	3,850	3,900	595	586	463	460	458	338	338	338	218	98	0	0
1,775	1,800	202	82	0	3,900	3,950	605	596	473	470	467	347	347	347	227	107	0	0
1,800	1,825	206	86	0	3,950	4,000	615	605	483	479	476	356	356	356	236	116	0	0
1,825	1,850	211	91	0	4,000	4,050	625	615	493	489	485	365	365	365	245	125	5	0
1,850	1,875	215	95	0	4,050	4,100	635	624	503	498	494	374	374	374	254	134	14	0
1,875	1,900	220	100	0	4,100	4,150	645	634	513	508	503	383	383	383	263	143	23	0
1,900	1,925	224	104	0	4,150	4,200	655	643	523	517	512	392	392	392	272	152	32	0
1,925	1,950	229	109	0	4,200	4,250	665	653	533	527	521	401	401	401	281	161	41	0
1,950	1,975	233	113	0	4,250	4,300	674	662	542	536	530	410	410	410	290	170	50	0
1,975	2,000	238	118	0	4,300	4,350	684	671	552	545	539	420	419	419	299	179	59	0
2,000	2,025	242	122	2	4,350	4,400	694	681	562	555	548	430	429	428	308	188	68	0
2,025	2,050	247	127	7	4,400	4,450	704	690	572	564	557	440	438	437	317	197	77	0
2,050	2,075	251	131	11	4,450	4,500	714	700	582	574	566	450	448	446	326	206	86	0
2,075	2,100	256	136	16	4,500	4,550	724	709	592	583	575	460	457	455	335	215	95	0
2,100	2,125	260	140	20	4,550	4,600	734	719	602	593	584	470	467	464	344	224	104	0
2,125	2,150	265	145	25	4,600	4,650	744	728	612	602	593	480	476	473	353	233	113	0
2,150	2,175	269	149	29	4,650	4,700	754	738	622	612	602	490	486	482	362	242	122	2
2,175	2,200	274	154	34	4,700	4,750	764	747	632	621	611	500	495	491	371	251	131	11
2,200	2,225	278	158	38	4,750	4,800	773	756	641	630	620	509	504	500	380	260	140	20
2,225	2,250	283	163	43	4,800	4,850	783	766	651	640	629	519	514	509	389	269	149	29
2,250	2,275	287	167	47	4,850	4,900	793	775	661	649	638	529	523	518	398	278	158	38
2,275	2,300	292	172	52	4,900	4,950	803	785	671	659	647	539	533	527	407	287	167	47
2,300	2,325	296	176	56	4,950	5,000	813	794	681	668	656	549	542	536	416	296	176	56

* This column may also be used by a *surviving spouse.*

But a *standard deduction* may be taken in lieu of these itemized deductions and in lieu of the following credits: the credit for tax withheld at the source on nonresident aliens and foreign corporations and on tax-free covenant bonds; the credit for taxes of foreign countries and possessions of the United States; and the credit for partially tax-exempt interest received by individuals.[10] In the case of taxpayers whose adjusted gross income is $5,000 or more, the standard deduction is $1,000 or 10% of adjusted gross income, whichever is the *lesser,* except that in the case of a separate return by a married individual, the maximum standard deduction is $500. In the case of taxpayers whose adjusted gross income is less than $5,000, the table on pages 24·12 and 24·13 has incorporated a standard deduction of about 10% of the adjusted gross income upon which the tax is determined.[11]

In the case of a joint return, there is only one adjusted gross income and only one standard deduction.

Illustration. If a husband has an income of $15,000 and his spouse has an income of $12,000 for the taxable year for which they file a joint return, and they have no deductions allowable for the purpose of computing adjusted gross income, the adjusted gross income is $27,000, and the standard deduction is $1,000 (not $2,000).

An election to take the standard deduction may be made for a taxable year which is less than twelve months on account of the death of the taxpayer.

Use of the standard deduction is easier than itemizing one's deductions. Also, no *proof* is required when the standard deduction is used. But if an individual has deductions and the above-described credits in excess of 10% of adjusted gross income, there is a tax advantage in itemizing.

If an individual elects to use the standard deduction, the tax table, or Form 1040A, and later he finds out that it would have been advantageous to have itemized his deductions, he may do so by filing an amended return within the time prescribed for filing such a return. See Chapter 26.

The table on pages 24·12 and 24·13 is similar in use to the one on pages 24·8 and 24·9, except that there are several computations available to a *head of household.* This term is explained immediately after the following tabular presentations.

If the above table for the standard deduction is not used, the taxpayer computes his tax by using the appropriate rate schedule (I, II, or III, below). Schedule I applies to (1) single taxpayers

[10] I.R.C. Section 36.
[11] I.R.C. Section 141.

who do not qualify for the special rates for head of household or for surviving spouse and (2) married taxpayers filing separate returns. Schedule II applies to married taxpayers filing joint returns and for surviving spouses; it provides the split-income benefits. Schedule III applies to unmarried (or legally separated) taxpayers who qualify as head of household.

Schedule I. (A) SINGLE TAXPAYERS who do not qualify for rates in Schedules II and III, and (B) married persons filing separate returns.

If the amount on line 5, page 2, is:		*Enter on line 6, page 2:*	
Not over $2,000		20% of the amount on line 5.	
Over—	*But not over—*		*of excess over—*
$2,000	—$4,000	$400, plus 22%	—$2,000
$4,000	—$6,000	$840, plus 26%	—$4,000
$6,000	—$8,000	$1,360, plus 30%	—$6,000
$8,000	—$10,000	$1,960, plus 34%	—$8,000
$10,000	—$12,000	$2,640, plus 38%	—$10,000
$12,000	—$14,000	$3,400, plus 43%	—$12,000
$14,000	—$16,000	$4,260, plus 47%	—$14,000
$16,000	—$18,000	$5,200, plus 50%	—$16,000
$18,000	—$20,000	$6,200, plus 53%	—$18,000
$20,000	—$22,000	$7,260, plus 56%	—$20,000
$22,000	—$26,000	$8,380, plus 59%	—$22,000
$26,000	—$32,000	$10,740, plus 62%	—$26,000
$32,000	—$38,000	$14,460, plus 65%	—$32,000
$38,000	—$44,000	$18,360, plus 69%	—$38,000
$44,000	—$50,000	$22,500, plus 72%	—$44,000
$50,000	—$60,000	$26,820, plus 75%	—$50,000
$60,000	—$70,000	$34,320, plus 78%	—$60,000
$70,000	—$80,000	$42,120, plus 81%	—$70,000
$80,000	—$90,000	$50,220, plus 84%	—$80,000
$90,000	—$100,000	$58,620, plus 87%	—$90,000
$100,000	—$150,000	$67,320, plus 89%	—$100,000
$150,000	—$200,000	$111,820, plus 90%	—$150,000
$200,000		$156,820, plus 91%	—$200,000

Schedule II. (A) MARRIED TAXPAYERS filing joint returns, and (B) certain widows and widowers.

If the amount on line 5, page 2, is:		*Enter on line 6, page 2:*	
Not over $4,000		20% of the amount on line 5.	
Over—	*But not over—*		*of excess over—*
$4,000	—$8,000	$800, plus 22%	—$4,000
$8,000	—$12,000	$1,680, plus 26%	—$8,000
$12,000	—$16,000	$2,720, plus 30%	—$12,000
$16,000	—$20,000	$3,920, plus 34%	—$16,000
$20,000	—$24,000	$5,280, plus 38%	—$20,000
$24,000	—$28,000	$6,800, plus 43%	—$24,000
$28,000	—$32,000	$8,520, plus 47%	—$28,000
$32,000	—$36,000	$10,400, plus 50%	—$32,000
$36,000	—$40,000	$12,400, plus 53%	—$36,000
$40,000	—$44,000	$14,520, plus 56%	—$40,000

Schedule II. (A) MARRIED TAXPAYERS filing joint returns, and (B) certain widows and widowers—*Continued.*

If the amount on line 5, page 2, is:		*Enter on line 6, page 2:*		
Not over $4,000		20% of the amount on line 5.		
Over—	*But not over—*			*of excess over—*
$44,000	— $52,000	$16,760,	plus 59%	— $44,000
$52,000	— $64,000	$21,480,	plus 62%	— $52,000
$64,000	— $76,000	$28,920,	plus 65%	— $64,000
$76,000	— $88,000	$36,720,	plus 69%	— $76,000
$88,000	— $100,000	$45,000,	plus 72%	— $88,000
$100,000	— $120,000	$53,640,	plus 75%	— $100,000
$120,000	— $140,000	$68,640,	plus 78%	— $120,000
$140,000	— $160,000	$84,240,	plus 81%	— $140,000
$160,000	— $180,000	$100,440,	plus 84%	— $160,000
$180,000	— $200,000	$117,240,	plus 87%	— $180,000
$200,000	— $300,000	$134,640,	plus 89%	— $200,000
$300,000	— $400,000	$223,640,	plus 90%	— $300,000
$400,000		$313,640,	plus 91%	— $400,000

Schedule III. Unmarried (or legally separated) taxpayers who qualify as HEAD OF HOUSEHOLD.

If the amount on line 5, page 2, is:		*Enter on line 6, page 2:*		
Not over $2,000		20% of the amount on line 5.		
Over—	*But not over—*			*of excess over—*
$2,000	— $4,000	$400,	plus 21%	— $2,000
$4,000	— $6,000	$820,	plus 24%	— $4,000
$6,000	— $8,000	$1,300,	plus 26%	— $6,000
$8,000	— $10,000	$1,820,	plus 30%	— $8,000
$10,000	— $12,000	$2,420,	plus 32%	— $10,000
$12,000	— $14,000	$3,060,	plus 36%	— $12,000
$14,000	— $16,000	$3,780,	plus 39%	— $14,000
$16,000	— $18,000	$4,560,	plus 42%	— $16,000
$18,000	— $20,000	$5,400,	plus 43%	— $18,000
$20,000	— $22,000	$6,260,	plus 47%	— $20,000
$22,000	— $24,000	$7,200,	plus 49%	— $22,000
$24,000	— $28,000	$8,180,	plus 52%	— $24,000
$28,000	— $32,000	$10,260,	plus 54%	— $28,000
$32,000	— $38,000	$12,420,	plus 58%	— $32,000
$38,000	— $44,000	$15,900,	plus 62%	— $38,000
$44,000	— $50,000	$19,620,	plus 66%	— $44,000
$50,000	— $60,000	$23,580,	plus 68%	— $50,000
$60,000	— $70,000	$30,380,	plus 71%	— $60,000
$70,000	— $80,000	$37,480,	plus 74%	— $70,000
$80,000	— $90,000	$44,880,	plus 76%	— $80,000
$90,000	— $100,000	$52,480,	plus 80%	— $90,000
$100,000	— $150,000	$60,480,	plus 83%	— $100,000
$150,000	— $200,000	$101,980,	plus 87%	— $150,000
$200,000	— $300,000	$145,480,	plus 90%	— $200,000
$300,000		$235,480,	plus 91%	— $300,000

Head of Household. An individual receives tax rate treatment that is more favorable than that afforded a single taxpayer if he qualifies as a head of household. This permits approximately half the benefit of a married couple filing a joint return.

A taxpayer is considered as the head of a household if he is not married at the close of his taxable year, is not a surviving spouse, and (1) maintains as his home a household which constitutes for that year the principal place of abode, as a member of his household, at least one of the individuals described in the next paragraph or (2) maintains (whether or not as his home) a household which constitutes for that taxable year the principal place of abode of one of the individuals described in the following paragraph.[12]

(1) Any one of the following persons may qualify the taxpayer as a head of a household: a son, stepson, daughter, or stepdaughter of the taxpayer, or a descendant of a son or daughter of the taxpayer. A legally adopted child is considered the same as a child by blood for this purpose. If any such person is not married at the close of the taxpayer's year, the taxpayer may qualify as the head of a household by reason of that person, even though the person does not qualify as a dependent; *e.g.,* where the taxpayer does not furnish more than one-half of the support of that person. But if the person is married at the close of the taxpayer's taxable year, the taxpayer may qualify as the head of a household only if this person meets the test of a dependent. (2) The taxpayer also is qualified as a head of household by reason of any other person who is a dependent as defined by statute earlier in this chapter. Head of household status is not conferred by virtue of a multiple support agreement, support of an unrelated person, or support of a person receiving institutional care.

The taxpayer must furnish more than half of the cost of maintaining a household for the entire year for at least one relative. Whether the relative must also qualify as his dependent and whether the relative must actually live in the taxpayer's household depends upon the relationship.

(1) The taxpayer's father or mother must qualify as a dependent and must live in a home that the taxpayer maintains for him or her. It is not necessary that the parent live in the same household as the taxpayer. But maintenance of a parent in a home for the aged is not maintaining a household for that parent.

(2) The taxpayer's unmarried child, grandchild, or stepchild must live with him. But it is not necessary that the person qualify as a dependent of the taxpayer.

(3) All other relatives must live with the taxpayer in his household and must also qualify as dependents.

[12] I.R.C. Section 1(b)(2).

Temporary absences for vacation, sickness, school, military service, etc., are disregarded in determining whether a related person actually lives in the taxpayer's household.

Family control is not necessary. As a matter of fact, "head of household" is a term that may properly be used upon a tax return without fear of perjury, even if in fact the person who gives himself this title is shamelessly ordered around by every member of the household.

If the person who enabled the taxpayer to claim status as surviving spouse or head of household died during the year or was born during the year, the taxpayer is considered to have maintained the principal residence for this person if he provided the residence for the entire part of the year the person was alive.

The head of a household must provide more than half the cost of the maintenance. Cost for this purpose includes rent, mortgage interest, taxes, insurance on a dwelling and premises, upkeep and repairs, utilities, domestic help, and food consumed in the home. Cost does not include clothing, education, medical treatment, vacations, life insurance, or transportation.

Form 1040W

This is the optional short form for wages and salary income, regardless of amount, where there is not more than $200 of interest and dividends. It is a combination of Forms 1040A and 1040. Income from wages, salary, dividends, and interest is shown. Deductions and tax computation are in the same manner as on Form 1040.

Personal Exemptions

An individual is allowed a deduction for the following exemptions:

(1) Himself.

(2) His spouse, if—

(A) A joint return is filed or

(B) A separate return is filed and this spouse has no gross income and is not the dependent of another taxpayer.

(3) A second exemption for himself if he has attained age 65.

(4) A second exemption for his spouse if she qualifies under (2) and has attained age 65.

(5) An additional exemption for himself if he is blind. He is deemed blind for this purpose if his central visual acuity does not exceed 20/200 in the better eye with correcting lenses, or the widest

diameter of the visual field subtends an angle no greater than 20 degrees.

(6) An additional exemption for his spouse if she qualifies under (2) and is blind.

(7) An additional exemption for each dependent, as defined earlier in this chapter.

Each of these exemptions is for $600. Except in the case of determination of whether the definition of a dependent is met, the taxpayer's right to an exemption is determined on the last day of his taxable year or on the date of his death, should he die before the end of his taxable year.[13]

Sale or Exchange of Capital Assets

Included with other gross income are capital gains and losses. Short-term capital gains and losses are merged with each other by adding the gains and the losses separately and subtracting one total from the other to obtain the net short-term capital gain or loss. Long-term capital gains and losses are similarly merged with each other to obtain the net long-term capital gain or loss. The total net gain or loss is then determined by merging the net short-term capital gain or loss with the net long-term capital gain or loss. If the net long-term capital gain exceeds the net short-term capital loss, the taxpayer claims a deduction equal to 50% of this excess. If he has no net short-term capital loss, his capital gain deduction is 50% of his net long-term capital gain. If there is a net short-term capital gain, it is included in income at 100%.

Alternative Tax. In case the net long-term capital gain of a taxpayer (other than a corporation) exceeds the net short-term capital loss, there is an *alternative tax* that the taxpayer may elect to use. He should only make this election if a lower tax would result. The alternative tax is the sum of—

(1) A partial tax on the taxable income reduced by an amount equal to 50% of the excess of the net long-term capital gain over the net short-term capital loss, plus

(2) 25% of the excess of the net long-term capital gain over the net short-term capital loss.[14]

Illustration. A single individual has for the taxable year taxable income (exclusive of capital gains and losses) of $99,400. He realizes in that year a gain of $50,000 on the sale of a capital asset held for nineteen months and sustains a loss

[13] I.R.C. Section 151.
[14] I.R.C. Section 1201(b).

of $20,000 on the sale of a capital asset held for five months. He has no other capital gains or losses. Tax is computed as follows:

REGULAR METHOD

Taxable income exclusive of capital gains and losses		$ 99,400
Net long-term capital gain (100% of $50,000)	$50,000	
Net short-term capital loss (100% of $20,000)	$20,000	
Excess of net long-term capital gain over the net short-term capital loss		30,000
		$129,400
Deduction of 50% of excess of net long-term capital gain over the net short-term capital loss		15,000
		$114,400

TAXABLE INCOME

Tax under regular method	$ 80,136

ALTERNATIVE TAX

Taxable income	$114,400
Less: 50% of excess of net long-term capital gain over net short-term capital loss	15,000
Taxable income exclusive of capital gains and losses	$ 99,400
Partial tax (tax on $99,400)	$ 66,798
Plus 25% of $30,000	7,500
Alternative tax	$74,298

As the alternative tax is the lower one, this is the method that should be used.

It is usually to the taxpayer's advantage to use the alternative method if—

(1) Taxable income exceeds $18,000 in the case of a separate return.

(2) Taxable income exceeds $24,000 in the case of a head of household.

(3) Taxable income exceeds $36,000 in the case of a joint return.

In the case of a joint return, the excess of any net long-term capital gain over any net short-term capital loss is to be determined by combining the long-term capital gains and losses and the short-term capital gains and losses of the spouses.

Tax Credits

If the taxpayer itemizes his deductions, the following tax credits may be taken:

The Credit for Foreign Taxes. Form 1116 in support of this credit must accompany the tax return.

Credit for Partially Tax-exempt Interest. This credit is 3% of the partially tax-exempt interest included in gross income. The credit may not exceed the lesser of (1) 3% of taxable income for the taxable year or (2) the amount of tax less the credit for income taxes paid to foreign countries and possessions of the United States and the credit for dividends received.

Other credits allowed are the *dividends received credit* (see Chapter 8) and the *retirement income credit* (see the following paragraphs).

Retirement Income Credit

A credit against the income tax is allowed to an individual who receives in the taxable year what is defined as *retirement income* and who meets certain eligibility requirements. The amount of the credit is determined by multiplying the amount of the retirement income (subject to limitations mentioned below) by the rate of tax applicable to the first $2,000 of taxable income.[15] Thus, if the retirement income is $1,000, the retirement income credit so computed is, at the present rate for the first $2,000 of taxable income, 20% of $1,000, or $200. The credit, however, cannot exceed the tax, reduced by allowable credits.

The amount of retirement income with respect to which the retirement income credit is allowable can in no event exceed $1,200. Thus, where the lowest tax rate is 20%, the maximum credit for an individual cannot exceed $240.

Joint Returns. In the case of a joint return, a separate determination is made with respect to the eligibility of each spouse for the retirement income credit, and (with the exceptions mentioned below) the retirement income credit of each spouse eligible for the credit is separately computed. The retirement income credit is allowable in the case of a joint return on account of the retirement income of each spouse without regard to whether the spouse would be liable for the income tax if a joint return had not been filed.

If retirement income constitutes community property under community property laws, the retirement income credit of each spouse is separately computed by taking into account one-half of these amounts. But, if a joint return is filed, the limitation on the amount of the combined retirement income credit is determined as in the case of any other joint return.

Eligibility. To be eligible for the credit, the taxpayer must have received earned income in excess of $600 during each of any ten calendar years preceding the taxable year. Earned income for this

[15] I.R.C. Section 37.

purpose means wages, salaries, or professional fees, and other amounts received as compensation for personal services actually rendered, but does not include that part of the compensation derived by the taxpayer for personal services rendered by him to a corporation which represents a distribution of earnings or profits rather than a reasonable allowance as compensation for the personal services actually rendered. In the case of a taxpayer engaged in a trade or business in which both personal services and capital are material income-producing factors, a reasonable allowance as compensation for the personal services rendered by the taxpayer (not in excess of 30% of his share of the net profits of the trade or business) will be considered as earned income.[16] Earned income means the entire amount of the income and will not be reduced by an expense connected with the earning of that income.

An individual who is a nonresident alien at any time during the taxable year is not eligible for the retirement income credit for that year.

For purposes of determining eligibility, the ten calendar years must occur before the beginning of the taxable year for which the credit is allowable. The ten calendar years need not immediately precede the taxable year, need not be consecutive, and need not include years subject to the income tax laws.

If a husband or wife dies, the earned income which the deceased spouse received in any calendar year is treated as earned income of the surviving spouse for that calendar year for the purpose of determining the eligibility of the surviving spouse for the retirement income credit. In any case in which the deceased spouse was eligible for the retirement income credit for the taxable year ending with his death, the surviving spouse will be deemed to have received earned income of more than $600 for ten calendar years for the purpose of determining the eligibility of the surviving spouse.

If an individual has married more than once, the status of the individual as a surviving spouse is determined only by reference to his most recent marriage.

Retirement Income. If the taxpayer is under 65, retirement income includes only a pension or annuity received from a public retirement system. Only the taxable portion of the pension or annuity is retirement income in computing the credit.

If the taxpayer is 65 or over before the end of his taxable year, retirement income includes all his taxable income from pensions, annuities, interest, dividends, and rents.

[16] I.R.C. Section 911(b).

Credit Computation. The credit is 20% of the lesser of:

(1) The retirement income received during the year, or

(2) $1,200 minus the total of certain pensions and annuities and earned income. The "certain pensions and annuities" refers to amounts received which are not taxed.

If the taxpayer is under 65, he must reduce the $1,200 in (2) by his earned income received during the year which is in excess of $900. If he is 65 or over but not yet 72, he reduces the $1,200 by his earned income which is in excess of $1,200. If he is 72 or over by the end of the year, he does not reduce the $1,200 regardless of the amount of his earned income.

Illustration. A taxpayer is 67 years old and has met the prior earnings requirement. He had the following income for the taxable year:

Dividends (after $50 exclusion)	$ 240
Railroad retirement pension (nontaxable)	500
Disability benefits under Workmen's Compensation Act (nontaxable)	400
Rental income (gross rents)	600
Purchased annuity ($600 − return of investment of $140)	460
Earned income from odd jobs	1,500

The credit is computed thus:

Retirement income:		
Dividends		$ 240
Rents		600
Annuity		460
Total retirement income		$1,300
But the retirement income is limited to		$1,200
Less: Railroad retirement pension	$500	
Earned income over $1,200 ($1,500 − $1,200)	300	800
Basis for computing credit		$ 400

20% of $400 equals the retirement income credit of $80.

The retirement income credit is only available to persons who have retired. No one else has the time to work it out.

Corporations

Rates of Tax. A corporation may be subjected to two types of income tax.[17] Form 1120 is used.

The normal tax is 30% of taxable income.

The surtax is 22% of taxable income (computed without regard to the deduction, if any, for partially tax-exempt interest) in excess of $25,000. But in certain circumstances, this $25,000 exemption from surtax may be disallowed in whole or in part. See Chapter 14.

[17] I.R.C. Section 11.

Illustration. A domestic corporation has gross income of $86,000 for the taxable year. The gross income includes interest of $5,000 on United States obligations which are partially tax-exempt. Other deductions are $11,000. Tax is computed as follows:

NORMAL TAX

Gross income		$86,000
Deductions:		
Partially tax-exempt interest	$ 5,000	
Other	11,000	16,000
Taxable income		$70,000
Normal tax (30%)		21,000

SURTAX

Taxable income	$70,000
Add: Amount of partially tax-exempt interest deducted in computing taxable income	5,000
Taxable income subject to surtax	$75,000
Less: Exemption from surtax	25,000
Excess of taxable income subject to surtax over exemption	$50,000
Surtax (22%)	11,000

Where a corporation has taxable income in excess of $25,000, a composite tax rate is sometimes used. Take 52% of taxable income and subtract $5,500. But an adjustment for partially tax-exempt interest must be made if such an item is present.

Alternative Tax. In case the net long-term capital gain of any corporation exceeds the net short-term capital loss, an alternative tax may be utilized. The election to use the alternative method is optional with the corporation and should only be used if a lower tax results.

The alternative tax is the sum of (1) a partial tax at normal and surtax rates on taxable income decreased by the amount of the excess of the net long-term capital gain over the net short-term capital loss and (2) an amount equal to 25% of this excess. In the computation of the partial tax, the special deductions (see Chapter 16) will not be recomputed as the result of the reduction of taxable income by the excess of net long-term capital gain over net short-term capital loss.[18]

Illustration. A corporation had taxable income of $20,000, which included:

Long-term capital gain	$6,500	
Long-term capital loss	1,800	
Net long-term capital gain		$4,700
Short-term capital gain	$1,000	
Short-term capital loss	2,700	
Net short-term capital loss		1,700
Excess of net long-term capital gain over net short-term capital loss		$3,000

[18] I.R.C Section 1201(a).

REGULAR METHOD

Normal tax, 30% of $20,000 taxable income	$6,000
Surtax, under $25,000; not applicable	0
Normal and surtax	$6,000

ALTERNATIVE METHOD

Partial tax, 30% of $17,000 ($20,000 − $3,000)	$5,100
Add: 25% of $3,000	750
Alternative tax	$5,850

Fiduciaries

The rates of tax for estates and trusts are the same as for individuals.

The alternative method of capital gain and loss computation is also the same as for individuals.

Interdependent Computations

Some computations require the use of a figure that cannot be known until the Federal income tax is known; but that tax cannot be computed until this aforementioned figure is known. For example, a certain state income tax is deductible in the computation of Federal income tax, and the Federal income tax is deductible in the computation of state income tax. Or a corporate officer may be entitled to a bonus based upon the company's earnings after taxes; but the tax cannot be computed until the amount of the bonus is known.

These computations may be made on the trial-and-error basis; but the computations must be made many times before one arrives at the correct amounts. A much easier method is to use a simultaneous equation, which, however, requires a formula that varies with the facts.

Illustration. A corporation agrees to give its president a bonus of 10% of corporate earnings after profits. The corporation has earnings of $300,000 before the bonus and tax; its tax rate is 52% on income in excess of $25,000, 30% on income below that figure. Thus, the composite tax rate is 52% minus $5,500 (22% on the first $25,000 that is not subject to surtax). Let b stand for bonus, t for tax.

$$\begin{aligned}
b &= 0.10\ (300{,}000 - t) \\
t &= 0.52\ (300{,}000 - b) - 5{,}500 \\
b &= 0.10\ (300{,}000 - [0.52\ (300{,}000 - b) - 5{,}500]) \\
b &= 0.10\ (300{,}000 - [156{,}000 - 0.52b - 5{,}500]) \\
b &= 0.10\ (300{,}000 - [150{,}500 - 0.52b]) \\
b &= 0.10\ (149{,}500 + 0.52b) \\
b &= 14{,}950 + 0.052b \\
0.948b &= 14{,}950
\end{aligned}$$

$$b = 15{,}770.04$$
$$t = 0.52\,(300{,}000 - 15{,}770.04) - 5{,}500$$
$$t = 0.52\,(284{,}229.96) - 5{,}500$$
$$t = 142{,}299.58$$

Proof.

Income before bonus and tax	$300,000.00
Bonus as above	15,770.04
Amount subject to tax	284,229.96
Tax	142,299.58

OR

Income before bonus and tax	$300,000.00
Tax as above	142,299.58
Amount subject to bonus	157,700.42
10% bonus	15,770.04

Supplementary Material

A. Suggested Reading.

Samuel Padgug, "Personal Deductions Under the 1954 Code," *How To Work with the Internal Revenue Code of 1954* (New York: Federal Tax Forum, Inc., 1954), p. 11.

Don V. Harris, Jr., "The Individual Dividends Received Credit and Capital Gains," *TAXES—The Tax Magazine,* August, 1956, Vol. XXXIV, #8, p. 536.

B. Questions.

1. Herman uses the accrual method; his wife, Wanda, uses the cash method. May they file a joint return if both are United States citizens who use the calendar year and itemize deductions?
2. Ronald and Donald jointly maintain their mother, who is without income. Which may claim her as a dependent?
3. An individual filed on a calendar year basis. On January 31, his first wife divorced him. He promptly married a second wife, who died on April 30. On November 1, he married a third wife. None of his wives had any income. On a joint return, how many exemptions may he claim?
4. Harry and his wife, Wilma, file a joint return. He owns stocks that pay $200 in dividends annually; she owns stock that pays $25 in dividends. What is the dividend exclusion and the dividends received credit?
5. A married individual with one dependent has salary of $8,000 and dividends from domestic corporations of $250. What is his tax (a) on Form 1040 and (b) on Form 1040A?
6. A married couple provides free quarters in their home for their son, who is a 30-year-old bachelor. The son pays all of his own expenses, other than his room, and, when he is in the house, his meals. May his father claim head-of-household status on a joint return?
7. A man and his wife have adjusted gross incomes of $10,000 and of $5,000, respectively. He has medical expenses of $800; she, of $200. What is the allowable medical expense deduction on (a) joint return and (b) separate return bases?

8. A single individual, Bernard, with $22,000 in salary permits his sister, Stephanie, and her husband, Helmuth, to live in his house. Stephanie has no income, while Helmuth's salary is $5,000. On the basis of these facts, should Bernard claim head-of-household status or should Helmuth file a joint return?
9. If a wife has a net capital gain and the husband a net capital loss, is a joint return always desirable?
10. A corporation had income of $100,000 and deductions of $28,000. In addition to the above, there was a net long-term capital gain of $15,000 and a net short-term capital loss of $5,000. What is the corporation's tax?
11. An individual fully maintains in his home the following:
    (a) Mother-in-law (whose annual income is $500).
    (b) 22-year-old son who is physically unable to work (his income is zero).
    (c) 17-year-old son (whose income is $2,000, earned while on vacation from high school).
    (d) 20-year-old nephew (whose income is $600).
    (e) 19-year-old niece (whose income is $460). She is a Canadian citizen now residing in the United States.

    Which is a dependent for tax purposes?
12. Sylvester was on a calendar year basis through 1960. In 1961, he received permission to change his accounting period to a fiscal year ended September 30. For 1961, therefore, he was obliged to file a short-period return. His income before deductions and credits was $13,800 for the short period, including $140 in dividends and $180 in partially tax-exempt interest. What is his tax for the short period?
13. Hans has an income of $15,000 and his wife has an income of $12,000 for the taxable year for which they file a joint return. They have no deductions for adjusted gross income. What is the standard deduction?
14. A vigorous 90-year-old laborer maintains in his home a 66-year-old son who has retired and a 68-year-old daughter who is blind. His wife is 89. How many exemptions may he claim on a joint return?
15. The following profit and loss account appeared in the books of the Nonesuch Corporation for the taxable year:

PROFIT AND LOSS ACCOUNT

Account		Debit	Credit
Gross sales			$1,840,000
Sales returns and allowances		$ 20,000	
Cost of goods sold		1,520,000	
Interest income:			
From banks	$10,000		
On state bonds	5,000		15,000
Proceeds from life insurance on corporate officer			6,000
Bad debt recoveries (no deduction previously made for tax purposes)			3,500
Insurance premiums on life of corporate officers (corporation is beneficiary of policies)		9,500	
Compensation of officers		40,000	
Salaries and wages		28,000	
Repairs		800	

PROFIT AND LOSS ACCOUNT—*Continued*

Account		Debit	Credit
Taxes		$ 10,000	
Contributions:			
Charitable	$11,500		
Other	500	12,000	
Interest paid (on loan to purchase tax-exempt bonds)		850	
Depreciation		5,200	
Loss on securities		3,600	
Net profit per books		214,550	
Totals		$1,864,500	$1,864,500

Earned surplus was analyzed and the following appeared in this account on the books of the corporation:

EARNED SURPLUS ACCOUNT

Item	Debit	Credit
Opening balance		$ 225,000
Net profit per books		214,550
Reserve for contingencies	$ 10,000	
Income tax accrued for taxable year	106,144	
Dividends paid during taxable year	76,000	
Refund of income tax for prior period		18,000
Closing balance	265,406	
Total	$ 457,550	$ 457,550

Prepare the surplus reconciliation, Schedule M.

16. A corporation had gross income for the taxable year of $86,000. The gross income included $5,000 on United States obligations of a partially tax-exempt character. Other deductions totaled $11,000. What is the income tax?
17. An individual has taxable income of $70,000 (exclusive of net capital gain). He is filing a separate return. During the year he had a net long-term capital gain of $16,000 and a net short-term capital loss of $6,000. Compute his tax on both the regular and alternative methods.
18. Oliver, who was eligible for the retirement income credit, was 68 at the close of the taxable year. He received as his only income during the year $800 of interest and $1,700 as compensation for personal services rendered by him during the year. What is his retirement income credit?

25

WITHHOLDING TAXES AND DECLARATION OF ESTIMATED TAX

There are several types of withholding of tax; but in the vast majority of all instances, *withholding* is considered to refer to that phase of the pay-as-you-go method of income tax collection that applies to individuals.

Pay-As-You-Go

Pay-as-you-go is a technique that may be applied in two stages. The objective is to make a taxpayer current in his income tax payments; that is, he pays tax at the time that he earns income, rather than when the income tax return is filed; the tax may be paid, at least in part, more than a year before the return is filed. This technique generally is regarded as being advantageous to the Government: (1) taxes are collected as rapidly as possible, with benefits in the form of saved interest (money does not have to be borrowed to anticipate later collections) and (2) there is greater certainty of receipt if the taxpayer does not have generous time to disappear or to lose his money. But there is also an advantage to the taxpayer: he is not faced with a huge tax bill all at one time. If the taxpayer really keeps current, he pays his taxes as the income is earned or at least in the same quarter that the income is earned. This helps his tax planning and also avoids the dire consequences of suddenly interrupted income out of which tax payments for prior periods were supposed to have been made. Appropriate are the familiar arguments about the virtues of compulsory saving.

Individuals covered by the withholding requirements are subjected to withholding of tax by stipulated payors. If the payors do not deduct the equivalent of the full tax that is due, the balance is payable by quarterly declarations of estimated tax. Corporations, if tax liability is in excess of $100,000, are subject to the latter process only; there is no withholding tax.

Individuals—Withholding

Who Is Covered? Withholding of tax may be required in the case of (1) payment of wages for covered employment (2) by employers (3) to employees if (4) the wages are in excess of (5) the withholding exemptions.[1]

Wages. The term "wages" means all remuneration for services performed by an employee for his employer unless specifically exempted. See "Exemptions," below.

In general, the medium in which payment is made is immaterial. Pensions and retirement pay are customarily regarded as wages subject to withholding, unless the payments are taxable as annuities. Amounts paid specifically (either as advances or reimbursements) for traveling or other bona fide ordinary and necessary expenses incurred or reasonably expected to be incurred in the business of the employer are not wages and are not subject to withholding. Amounts of so-called "vacation allowances" paid to an employee constitute wages. Dismissal payments are wages. The value of any meals or lodging furnished to an employee by his employer is not subject to withholding if the value of these items is excludable from the employee's gross income.

Exemptions. The term "wages" does not include any remuneration for services performed by an employee for his employer which is specifically excepted. The exception attaches to the remuneration for services performed by an employee and not to the employee as an individual; that is, the exception applies only to the remuneration in an excepted category. Payments of the following types are excepted:

(1) For fees paid to a public official: notaries public, clerks of courts, sheriffs, etc., for services rendered in the performance of their official duties. But salaries paid to governmental officials by governmental agencies or instrumentalities are subject to withholding.

(2) For active service as a member of the Armed Forces of the United States during a month when he is entitled to exclude combat pay from his gross income in accordance with I.R.C. Section 112. See Chapter 4.

(3) For agricultural labor, as defined in detail in I.R.C. Section 3121(g).

[1] I.R.C. Section 3401.

(4) For domestic service in a private home, local college club, or local chapter of a college fraternity or sorority.

(5) For services not in the course of the employer's trade or business performed in any calendar quarter by an employee, unless the *cash* remuneration is $50 or more and the recipient is regularly employed for this service.

(6) For services by a citizen or resident of the United States for a foreign government or an international organization.

(7) For services performed by a nonresident alien individual.

(8) For services for an employer (other than the United States or any of its agencies) if performed by a United States citizen if it is (A) excludable from gross income as amounts earned abroad, or (B) subject to withholding tax by a foreign country or United States possession, or (C) performed in a possession of the United States (except Puerto Rico) and constitutes at least 80% of the remuneration paid him that year by the employer, or (D) reasonable to believe that the employee will be a bona fide resident of Puerto Rico for the full year.

(9) For services performed by a minister of a church, or by a member of a religious order, in the exercise of his duties.

(10) For services performed by a newsboy under 18 years of age.

(11) For services by individuals who sell periodicals at retail at a fixed price, compensation being the excess of this price over cost.

(12) For services not in the course of the employer's trade or business, where payment is made in a form other than cash.

(13) For payments to or for an employee or his beneficiary from a qualified employee trust (except for services) or an annuity plan.[2]

If a portion of the remuneration paid by an employer to his employee for services performed during a payroll period of not more than 31 consecutive days constitutes wages, and the remainder does not constitute wages, all the remuneration paid during this period will be treated alike; that is, either all is included as wages or all is excluded. If one-half or more of the employee's time in the employ of a particular employer in a payroll period is spent in performing services the remuneration for which constitutes wages, then all the remuneration paid the employee for services performed in that payroll period constitutes wages; if less than one-half of the employee's time is spent in performing services the remuneration for which constitutes wages, then none of the compensation will be deemed wages.[3]

[2] I.R.C. Section 3401(a).

[3] Regulations Section 31.3402(e)-1.

Employee. The term "employee" includes every individual performing services if the relationship between him and the person for whom he performs such services is in the legal relationship of employer and employee.

The amount must be in connection with the employer-employee relationship. Thus, payments to an independent contractor are not subject to withholding; for example, payments to a public stenographer, a certified public accountant acting on his own behalf, a broker who will perform identical services for anyone requesting his aid, etc. In determining whether a person is an employee, the general test is whether the person for whom the services are performed has the right to control and direct the individual who performs the services, not only as to the result to be accomplished by the work, but also as to the details and means by which the result is accomplished. It is not necessary that the employer actually direct or control the manner in which the services are performed; it is sufficient if he has the right to do so. The right to discharge is also an important factor indicating that the person possessing that right is the employer. Other factors characteristic of an employer, but not necessarily present in every case, are the furnishing of tools and the furnishing of a place to work to the individual who performs the services.[4]

A partner is not an employee. Consequently, payments to him are not subject to withholding tax. But executives of a corporation are employees, subject to withholding.

Employer. The term "employer" means any person for whom an individual performs or performed any service, of whatever nature, as an employee. It is not necessary that the services be continuing at the time the wages are paid in order that the status of employer exist.

Withholding Exemption. The number of exemptions to which an employee is entitled depends upon his status as single or married, old age, blindness, number of dependents, exemptions claimed by his spouse.[5] Exemptions are one each for the following: the taxpayer, an additional one if he is 65 or over, an additional one if he is blind, an additional one for his spouse (unless she is claiming this exemption on her own exemption certificate), an additional one if the spouse is 65 or over (with the same qualification), an additional one if the spouse is blind (with the same qualification), an additional one for each dependent. Dependents are defined for

[4] Regulations Section 31.3401(c)-1(b).
[5] I.R.C. Section 3402(f)(1).

purposes of the income tax in Chapter 24. Exemptions are claimed on a certificate designated as Form W-4, which must be filed with the employer not later than the date on which employment begins. If the employee refuses to present the certificate, the number of exemptions to which he is entitled must be zero. For example, an employee may not wish to have his employer or his fellow-employees know anything about his family situation. An employee may properly understate the number of exemptions to which he is entitled, but there are penalties for overstatement. Thus, an employee may deliberately understate the number of his exemptions, so that the withholding tax will be large, with the objective of reducing the amount of tax payable in excess of amounts withheld.

The employee is required to notify his employer within ten days of the time that the number of exemptions affecting the taxable year is reduced; for example, if a child that presumably would have been claimed as a dependent has now gone to work and presumably will provide for more than half of her own support during that year. The employee *may* advise the employer if the number of exemptions affecting the taxable year is increased.[6]

Where a change in exemptions will affect the next calendar year, the employee must notify the employer by December 1 of the year in which the change occurs, unless the change takes place in December, in which event notification must take place within ten days.

The employer must put the change in effect on the January 1 or July 1 that follows the notification of a change, although he may make the change sooner.[7]

Payroll Period. The term "payroll period" means the period of service for which a payment of wages is ordinarily made to an employee by his employer. It is immaterial that the wages are not always paid at regular intervals.

An employee can have but one payroll period with respect to wages paid by any one employer. Thus, if an employee is paid a regular wage for a weekly payroll period and in addition he is paid supplemental wages (*e.g.*, bonuses) determined with respect to a different period, the payroll period is the weekly payroll period. The computation of tax on supplemental wage payments will be discussed below.

The term "miscellaneous payroll period" means a payroll period other than a daily, weekly, biweekly, semimonthly, monthly, quarterly, semiannual, or annual payroll period.

[6] Regulations Section 31.3402(f)(2)-1.
[7] Regulations Section 31.3402(f)(3)-1.

Methods of Computing Withholding Tax. The employer has available two methods of determining the amount to be withheld. He need not follow a consistent method, and he may switch from one to the other as often and to the extent that he chooses. These are the percentage method and the wage bracket method.

Under the *percentage method,* the following table is used:

Payroll Period	Amount of One Withholding Exemption
Weekly	$ 13.00
Biweekly	26.00
Semimonthly	28.00
Monthly	56.00
Quarterly	167.00
Semiannual	333.00
Annual	667.00
Daily or miscellaneous (per day of such period)	1.80

Withholding is at the rate of 18%, computed in the following manner:

(1) Determine the amount of one withholding exemption for the particular payroll period from the above table.

(2) Multiply the amount thus determined by the number of exemptions claimed by the employee.

(3) Subtract the amount just obtained from the employee's wages.

(4) Multiply the difference by 18%.

Illustration. These steps may be shown in the following example. An employee has a weekly payroll period for which he is paid $75, and he has in effect a withholding exemption certificate claiming three exemptions. Under the percentage method, the employer would thus withhold tax:

(1) Amount of one withholding exemption	$13.00
(2) Multiply by number of exemptions claimed	× 3
Total withholding exemption	$39.00
(3) Total wage payment	$75.00
Less: Amount determined in (2), above	39.00
Balance subject to tax	$36.00
(4) Tax at 18% to be withheld	6.48

If there is an established payroll period (other than daily or miscellaneous), as shown on the percentage method withholding table, the amount of one withholding exemption is determined by referring to the line applicable to that payroll period without reference to the time the employee is actually engaged in the performance of services during that period. Thus, even if an employee works only forty hours during a semimonthly payroll period, he will be entitled to an exemption of $28 for each exemption claimed.

If wages are paid for a period which is not a payroll period, the withholding exemption allowable for each payment will be the exemption allowable for a miscellaneous payroll period containing a number of days (including Sundays and holidays) equal to the number of days (also including Sundays and holidays) in the period for which wages are paid.

Illustration. An individual is hired by a contractor to perform services in connection with a building project. The individual has two withholding exemptions. Wages of $9 per day are to be paid when the project is completed. The project is completed in twelve consecutive days, at the end of which the worker is paid wages of $90 for ten days' services performed during the period. The amount of the withholding exemption allowable for the 12-day period is $43.20 (12 × (2 × $1.80)). Tax should be withheld on $46.80 ($90 minus $43.20).

If wages are paid to an employee without regard to any particular period (*e.g.*, commissions paid to a salesman upon completion of a sale), the withholding exemption is measured by the number of days (including Sundays and holidays) which have elapsed, beginning with the latest of the following dates:

(1) The first day after the last payment of wages to the employee by the employer in the calendar year, or

(2) The date on which the employee's employment began in the calendar year, or

(3) January 1 of the calendar year,

and ending with (and including) the date on which the wages are paid.

Illustration. On April 2, EE is employed by ER to sell real estate on a commission basis, commissions to be paid upon consummation of sales. EE claims one withholding exemption. On May 21 of the same year, EE receives a commission of $300. Again, on June 16, EE receives a commission of $400. The amount of the withholding exemption for the commission paid on May 21 is $90 ($1.80 × 50). The amount of the withholding exemption paid on June 16 is $46.80 ($1.80 × 26).

If the payroll period, other period, or elapsed time where wages are paid without regard to any period, is less than one week, the employer may elect to compute the withholding tax as if the total of the wages paid to the employee during the calendar week were paid for a weekly payroll period. The employer may only make this election if he is the only employer for whom the employee works for wages during this week; the employee must furnish a written statement to that effect, agreeing to notify the employer of any other compensation within ten days after the beginning of this additional employment.

Illustration. EE works for ER on four consecutive days in a calendar year, for which he is paid $36. EE claims two withholding exemptions. ER elects to use the weekly withholding exemption and obtains the necessary statement from EE. The amount of the withholding exemption allowable is \$26 ($2 \times$ \$13).

Under the *wage bracket method* of withholding, separate tables are provided for weekly, biweekly, semimonthly, monthly, and daily or miscellaneous payroll periods.[8] See pages 25·9 to 25·18.

The wage bracket withholding tables for established payroll periods other than daily or miscellaneous should be used in determining the tax to be withheld for that period without reference to the time the employee is actually engaged in the performance of services during this payroll period.

Illustration. An employee has a weekly payroll period, and his wages are at the rate of \$1.20 per hour. He is entitled to two withholding exemptions. During a certain payroll period, he works thirty hours and earns \$36. Although he worked only thirty hours during the weekly payroll period, the wage bracket withholding table for a weekly payroll period should be used in determining the tax to be withheld. Under this table it will be found that \$2.00 is the amount of tax to be withheld.

If wages are paid for a period which is not a payroll period, the amount to be withheld will be the amount applicable in the case of a miscellaneous payroll period containing a number of days (including Sundays and holidays) equal to the number of days (also including Sundays and holidays) in the period for which the wages are paid.

Illustration. An individual is hired by a contractor to perform services in connection with a construction project. The individual claims two withholding exemptions. Wages of \$9 per day are to be paid at the end of the project. The project is completed within twelve days, at the end of which time he is paid wages of \$90 for ten days' services performed during this period. Withholding tax is determined by dividing the amount of the wages (\$90) by the number of days in the period (12), the result being \$7.50. The amount of tax to be withheld according to the table for a miscellaneous payroll period is \$8.40 ($12 \times$ \$0.70).

The treatment for wages paid without regard to any period, and where the period or elapsed time is less than one week, is comparable to what has been described previously for the percentage method of withholding.

Supplemental wage payments are treated in the same manner under both of the withholding methods.[9] This includes bonuses, commissions, and overtime pay, paid for the same or a different period, or without regard to a particular period. The supplemental payments, if paid at the same time as wages for a payroll period, will be added to the regular wages, and withholding tax will be

[8] I.R.C. Section 3402(c).
[9] Regulations Section 31.3402(g)–1.

If the payroll period with respect to an employee is **Weekly:**

And the wages are—		And the number of withholding exemptions claimed is—										
At least	But less than	0	1	2	3	4	5	6	7	8	9	10 or more
		The amount of income tax to be withheld shall be—										
$0	$13	18% of wages	$0	$0	$0	$0	$0	$0	$0	$0	$0	$0
13	14	$2.40	.10	0	0	0	0	0	0	0	0	0
14	15	2.60	.30	0	0	0	0	0	0	0	0	0
15	16	2.80	.50	0	0	0	0	0	0	0	0	0
16	17	3.00	.70	0	0	0	0	0	0	0	0	0
17	18	3.20	.80	0	0	0	0	0	0	0	0	0
18	19	3.30	1.00	0	0	0	0	0	0	0	0	0
19	20	3.50	1.20	0	0	0	0	0	0	0	0	0
20	21	3.70	1.40	0	0	0	0	0	0	0	0	0
21	22	3.90	1.60	0	0	0	0	0	0	0	0	0
22	23	4.10	1.70	0	0	0	0	0	0	0	0	0
23	24	4.20	1.90	0	0	0	0	0	0	0	0	0
24	25	4.40	2.10	0	0	0	0	0	0	0	0	0
25	26	4.60	2.30	0	0	0	0	0	0	0	0	0
26	27	4.80	2.50	.20	0	0	0	0	0	0	0	0
27	28	5.00	2.60	.30	0	0	0	0	0	0	0	0
28	29	5.10	2.80	.50	0	0	0	0	0	0	0	0
29	30	5.30	3.00	.70	0	0	0	0	0	0	0	0
30	31	5.50	3.20	.90	0	0	0	0	0	0	0	0
31	32	5.70	3.40	1.10	0	0	0	0	0	0	0	0
32	33	5.90	3.50	1.20	0	0	0	0	0	0	0	0
33	34	6.00	3.70	1.40	0	0	0	0	0	0	0	0
34	35	6.20	3.90	1.60	0	0	0	0	0	0	0	0
35	36	6.40	4.10	1.80	0	0	0	0	0	0	0	0
36	37	6.60	4.30	2.00	0	0	0	0	0	0	0	0
37	38	6.80	4.40	2.10	0	0	0	0	0	0	0	0
38	39	6.90	4.60	2.30	0	0	0	0	0	0	0	0
39	40	7.10	4.80	2.50	.20	0	0	0	0	0	0	0
40	41	7.30	5.00	2.70	.40	0	0	0	0	0	0	0
41	42	7.50	5.20	2.90	.50	0	0	0	0	0	0	0
42	43	7.70	5.30	3.00	.70	0	0	0	0	0	0	0
43	44	7.80	5.50	3.20	.90	0	0	0	0	0	0	0
44	45	8.00	5.70	3.40	1.10	0	0	0	0	0	0	0
45	46	8.20	5.90	3.60	1.30	0	0	0	0	0	0	0
46	47	8.40	6.10	3.80	1.40	0	0	0	0	0	0	0
47	48	8.60	6.20	3.90	1.60	0	0	0	0	0	0	0
48	49	8.70	6.40	4.10	1.80	0	0	0	0	0	0	0
49	50	8.90	6.60	4.30	2.00	0	0	0	0	0	0	0

***Weekly** payroll period—Continued*

And the wages are—		And the number of withholding exemptions claimed is—										
At least	But less than	0	1	2	3	4	5	6	7	8	9	10 or more
		The amount of income tax to be withheld shall be—										
$50	$51	$9.10	$6.80	$4.50	$2.20	$0	$0	$0	$0	$0	$0	$0
51	52	9.30	7.00	4.70	2.30	0	0	0	0	0	0	0
52	53	9.50	7.10	4.80	2.50	.20	0	0	0	0	0	0
53	54	9.60	7.30	5.00	2.70	.40	0	0	0	0	0	0
54	55	9.80	7.50	5.20	2.90	.60	0	0	0	0	0	0
55	56	10.00	7.70	5.40	3.10	.80	0	0	0	0	0	0
56	57	10.20	7.90	5.60	3.20	.90	0	0	0	0	0	0
57	58	10.40	8.00	5.70	3.40	1.10	0	0	0	0	0	0
58	59	10.50	8.20	5.90	3.60	1.30	0	0	0	0	0	0
59	60	10.70	8.40	6.10	3.80	1.50	0	0	0	0	0	0
60	62	11.00	8.70	6.40	4.10	1.70	0	0	0	0	0	0
62	64	11.30	9.00	6.70	4.40	2.10	0	0	0	0	0	0
64	66	11.70	9.40	7.10	4.80	2.50	.20	0	0	0	0	0
66	68	12.10	9.80	7.40	5.10	2.80	.50	0	0	0	0	0
68	70	12.40	10.10	7.80	5.50	3.20	.90	0	0	0	0	0
70	72	12.80	10.50	8.20	5.90	3.50	1.20	0	0	0	0	0
72	74	13.10	10.80	8.50	6.20	3.90	1.60	0	0	0	0	0
74	76	13.50	11.20	8.90	6.60	4.30	2.00	0	0	0	0	0
76	78	13.90	11.60	9.20	6.90	4.60	2.30	0	0	0	0	0
78	80	14.20	11.90	9.60	7.30	5.00	2.70	.40	0	0	0	0
80	82	14.60	12.30	10.00	7.70	5.30	3.00	.70	0	0	0	0
82	84	14.90	12.60	10.30	8.00	5.70	3.40	1.10	0	0	0	0
84	86	15.30	13.00	10.70	8.40	6.10	3.80	1.50	0	0	0	0
86	88	15.70	13.40	11.00	8.70	6.40	4.10	1.80	0	0	0	0
88	90	16.00	13.70	11.40	9.10	6.80	4.50	2.20	0	0	0	0
90	92	16.40	14.10	11.80	9.50	7.10	4.80	2.50	.20	0	0	0
92	94	16.70	14.40	12.10	9.80	7.50	5.20	2.90	.60	0	0	0
94	96	17.10	14.80	12.50	10.20	7.90	5.60	3.30	.90	0	0	0
96	98	17.50	15.20	12.80	10.50	8.20	5.90	3.60	1.30	0	0	0
98	100	17.80	15.50	13.20	10.90	8.60	6.30	4.00	1.70	0	0	0
100	105	18.50	16.10	13.80	11.50	9.20	6.90	4.60	2.30	0	0	0
105	110	19.40	17.00	14.70	12.40	10.10	7.80	5.50	3.20	.90	0	0
110	115	20.30	17.90	15.60	13.30	11.00	8.70	6.40	4.10	1.80	0	0
115	120	21.20	18.80	16.50	14.20	11.90	9.60	7.30	5.00	2.70	.40	0
120	125	22.10	19.70	17.40	15.10	12.80	10.50	8.20	5.90	3.60	1.30	0
125	130	23.00	20.60	18.30	16.00	13.70	11.40	9.10	6.80	4.50	2.20	0
130	135	23.90	21.50	19.20	16.90	14.60	12.30	10.00	7.70	5.40	3.10	.80
135	140	24.80	22.40	20.10	17.80	15.50	13.20	10.90	8.60	6.30	4.00	1.70
140	145	25.70	23.30	21.00	18.70	16.40	14.10	11.80	9.50	7.20	4.90	2.60
145	150	26.60	24.20	21.90	19.60	17.30	15.00	12.70	10.40	8.10	5.80	3.50
150	160	27.90	25.60	23.30	21.00	18.70	16.40	14.10	11.70	9.40	7.10	4.80
160	170	29.70	27.40	25.10	22.80	20.50	18.20	15.90	13.50	11.20	8.90	6.60
170	180	31.50	29.20	26.90	24.60	22.30	20.00	17.70	15.30	13.00	10.70	8.40
180	190	33.30	31.00	28.70	26.40	24.10	21.80	19.50	17.10	14.80	12.50	10.20
190	200	35.10	32.80	30.50	28.20	25.90	23.60	21.30	18.90	16.60	14.30	12.00
		18 percent of the excess over $200 plus—										
$200 and over		36.00	33.70	31.40	29.10	26.80	24.50	22.20	19.80	17.50	15.20	12.90

If the payroll period with respect to an employee is **Biweekly:**

And the wages are—		And the number of withholding exemptions claimed is—										
At least	But less than	0	1	2	3	4	5	6	7	8	9	10 or more
		The amount of income tax to be withheld shall be—										
$0	$26	18% of wages	$0	$0	$0	$0	$0	$0	$0	$0	$0	$0
26	28	$4.90	.20	0	0	0	0	0	0	0	0	0
28	30	5.20	.60	0	0	0	0	0	0	0	0	0
30	32	5.60	1.00	0	0	0	0	0	0	0	0	0
32	34	5.90	1.30	0	0	0	0	0	0	0	0	0
34	36	6.30	1.70	0	0	0	0	0	0	0	0	0
36	38	6.70	2.00	0	0	0	0	0	0	0	0	0
38	40	7.00	2.40	0	0	0	0	0	0	0	0	0
40	42	7.40	2.80	0	0	0	0	0	0	0	0	0
42	44	7.70	3.10	0	0	0	0	0	0	0	0	0
44	46	8.10	3.50	0	0	0	0	0	0	0	0	0
46	48	8.50	3.80	0	0	0	0	0	0	0	0	0
48	50	8.80	4.20	0	0	0	0	0	0	0	0	0
50	52	9.20	4.60	0	0	0	0	0	0	0	0	0
52	54	9.50	4.90	.30	0	0	0	0	0	0	0	0
54	56	9.90	5.30	.70	0	0	0	0	0	0	0	0
56	58	10.30	5.60	1.00	0	0	0	0	0	0	0	0
58	60	10.60	6.00	1.40	0	0	0	0	0	0	0	0
60	62	11.00	6.40	1.70	0	0	0	0	0	0	0	0
62	64	11.30	6.70	2.10	0	0	0	0	0	0	0	0
64	66	11.70	7.10	2.50	0	0	0	0	0	0	0	0
66	68	12.10	7.40	2.80	0	0	0	0	0	0	0	0
68	70	12.40	7.80	3.20	0	0	0	0	0	0	0	0
70	72	12.80	8.20	3.50	0	0	0	0	0	0	0	0
72	74	13.10	8.50	3.90	0	0	0	0	0	0	0	0
74	76	13.50	8.90	4.30	0	0	0	0	0	0	0	0
76	78	13.90	9.20	4.60	0	0	0	0	0	0	0	0
78	80	14.20	9.60	5.00	.40	0	0	0	0	0	0	0
80	82	14.60	10.00	5.30	.70	0	0	0	0	0	0	0
82	84	14.90	10.30	5.70	1.10	0	0	0	0	0	0	0
84	86	15.30	10.70	6.10	1.50	0	0	0	0	0	0	0
86	88	15.70	11.00	6.40	1.80	0	0	0	0	0	0	0
88	90	16.00	11.40	6.80	2.20	0	0	0	0	0	0	0
90	92	16.40	11.80	7.10	2.50	0	0	0	0	0	0	0
92	94	16.70	12.10	7.50	2.90	0	0	0	0	0	0	0
94	96	17.10	12.50	7.90	3.30	0	0	0	0	0	0	0
96	98	17.50	12.80	8.20	3.60	0	0	0	0	0	0	0
98	100	17.80	13.20	8.60	4.00	0	0	0	0	0	0	0
100	102	18.20	13.60	8.90	4.30	0	0	0	0	0	0	0
102	104	18.50	13.90	9.30	4.70	.10	0	0	0	0	0	0
104	106	18.90	14.30	9.70	5.10	.40	0	0	0	0	0	0
106	108	19.30	14.60	10.00	5.40	.80	0	0	0	0	0	0

Income Tax Withholding Tables—*Continued*

***Biweekly** payroll period—Continued*

And the wages are—		And the number of withholding exemptions claimed is—										
At least	But less than	0	1	2	3	4	5	6	7	8	9	10 or more
		The amount of income tax to be withheld shall be—										
$108	$110	$19.60	$15.00	$10.40	$5.80	$1.20	$0	$0	$0	$0	$0	$0
110	112	20.00	15.40	10.70	6.10	1.50	0	0	0	0	0	0
112	114	20.30	15.70	11.10	6.50	1.90	0	0	0	0	0	0
114	116	20.70	16.10	11.50	6.90	2.20	0	0	0	0	0	0
116	118	21.10	16.40	11.80	7.20	2.60	0	0	0	0	0	0
118	120	21.40	16.80	12.20	7.60	3.00	0	0	0	0	0	0
120	124	22.00	17.30	12.70	8.10	3.50	0	0	0	0	0	0
124	128	22.70	18.10	13.40	8.80	4.20	0	0	0	0	0	0
128	132	23.40	18.80	14.20	9.60	4.90	.30	0	0	0	0	0
132	136	24.10	19.50	14.90	10.30	5.70	1.00	0	0	0	0	0
136	140	24.80	20.20	15.60	11.00	6.40	1.80	0	0	0	0	0
140	144	25.60	20.90	16.30	11.70	7.10	2.50	0	0	0	0	0
144	148	26.30	21.70	17.00	12.40	7.80	3.20	0	0	0	0	0
148	152	27.00	22.40	17.80	13.20	8.50	3.90	0	0	0	0	0
152	156	27.70	23.10	18.50	13.90	9.30	4.60	0	0	0	0	0
156	160	28.40	23.80	19.20	14.60	10.00	5.40	.70	0	0	0	0
160	164	29.20	24.50	19.90	15.30	10.70	6.10	1.50	0	0	0	0
164	168	29.90	25.30	20.60	16.00	11.40	6.80	2.20	0	0	0	0
168	172	30.60	26.00	21.40	16.80	12.10	7.50	2.90	0	0	0	0
172	176	31.30	26.70	22.10	17.50	12.90	8.20	3.60	0	0	0	0
176	180	32.00	27.40	22.80	18.20	13.60	9.00	4.30	0	0	0	0
180	184	32.80	28.10	23.50	18.90	14.30	9.70	5.10	.50	0	0	0
184	188	33.50	28.90	24.20	19.60	15.00	10.40	5.80	1.20	0	0	0
188	192	34.20	29.60	25.00	20.40	15.70	11.10	6.50	1.90	0	0	0
192	196	34.90	30.30	25.70	21.10	16.50	11.80	7.20	2.60	0	0	0
196	200	35.60	31.00	26.40	21.80	17.20	12.60	7.90	3.30	0	0	0
200	210	36.90	32.30	27.70	23.10	18.40	13.80	9.20	4.60	0	0	0
210	220	38.70	34.10	29.50	24.90	20.20	15.60	11.00	6.40	1.80	0	0
220	230	40.50	35.90	31.30	26.70	22.00	17.40	12.80	8.20	3.60	0	0
230	240	42.30	37.70	33.10	28.50	23.80	19.20	14.60	10.00	5.40	.80	0
240	250	44.10	39.50	34.90	30.30	25.60	21.00	16.40	11.80	7.20	2.60	0
250	260	45.90	41.30	36.70	32.10	27.40	22.80	18.20	13.60	9.00	4.40	0
260	270	47.70	43.10	38.50	33.90	29.20	24.60	20.00	15.40	10.80	6.20	1.50
270	280	49.50	44.90	40.30	35.70	31.00	26.40	21.80	17.20	12.60	8.00	3.30
280	290	51.30	46.70	42.10	37.50	32.80	28.20	23.60	19.00	14.40	9.80	5.10
290	300	53.10	48.50	43.90	39.30	34.60	30.00	25.40	20.80	16.20	11.60	6.90
300	320	55.80	51.20	46.60	42.00	37.30	32.70	28.10	23.50	18.90	14.30	9.60
320	340	59.40	54.80	50.20	45.60	40.90	36.30	31.70	27.10	22.50	17.90	13.20
340	360	63.00	58.40	53.80	49.20	44.50	39.90	35.30	30.70	26.10	21.50	16.80
360	380	66.60	62.00	57.40	52.80	48.10	43.50	38.90	34.30	29.70	25.10	20.40
380	400	70.20	65.60	61.00	56.40	51.70	47.10	42.50	37.90	33.30	28.70	24.00
		18 percent of the excess over $400 plus—										
$400 and over		72.00	67.40	62.80	58.20	53.50	48.90	44.30	39.70	35.10	30.50	25.80

If the payroll period with respect to an employee is **Semimonthly:**

And the wages are—		And the number of withholding exemptions claimed is—										
At least	But less than	0	1	2	3	4	5	6	7	8	9	10 or more
		The amount of income tax to be withheld shall be—										
$0	$28	18% of wages	$0	$0	$0	$0	$0	$0	$0	$0	$0	$0
28	30	$5.20	.20	0	0	0	0	0	0	0	0	0
30	32	5.60	.60	0	0	0	0	0	0	0	0	0
32	34	5.90	.90	0	0	0	0	0	0	0	0	0
34	36	6.30	1.30	0	0	0	0	0	0	0	0	0
36	38	6.70	1.70	0	0	0	0	0	0	0	0	0
38	40	7.00	2.00	0	0	0	0	0	0	0	0	0
40	42	7.40	2.40	0	0	0	0	0	0	0	0	0
42	44	7.70	2.70	0	0	0	0	0	0	0	0	0
44	46	8.10	3.10	0	0	0	0	0	0	0	0	0
46	48	8.50	3.50	0	0	0	0	0	0	0	0	0
48	50	8.80	3.80	0	0	0	0	0	0	0	0	0
50	52	9.20	4.20	0	0	0	0	0	0	0	0	0
52	54	9.50	4.50	0	0	0	0	0	0	0	0	0
54	56	9.90	4.90	0	0	0	0	0	0	0	0	0
56	58	10.30	5.30	.30	0	0	0	0	0	0	0	0
58	60	10.60	5.60	.60	0	0	0	0	0	0	0	0
60	62	11.00	6.00	1.00	0	0	0	0	0	0	0	0
62	64	11.30	6.30	1.30	0	0	0	0	0	0	0	0
64	66	11.70	6.70	1.70	0	0	0	0	0	0	0	0
66	68	12.10	7.10	2.10	0	0	0	0	0	0	0	0
68	70	12.40	7.40	2.40	0	0	0	0	0	0	0	0
70	72	12.80	7.80	2.80	0	0	0	0	0	0	0	0
72	74	13.10	8.10	3.10	0	0	0	0	0	0	0	0
74	76	13.50	8.50	3.50	0	0	0	0	0	0	0	0
76	78	13.90	8.90	3.90	0	0	0	0	0	0	0	0
78	80	14.20	9.20	4.20	0	0	0	0	0	0	0	0
80	82	14.60	9.60	4.60	0	0	0	0	0	0	0	0
82	84	14.90	9.90	4.90	0	0	0	0	0	0	0	0
84	86	15.30	10.30	5.30	.30	0	0	0	0	0	0	0
86	88	15.70	10.70	5.70	.70	0	0	0	0	0	0	0
88	90	16.00	11.00	6.00	1.00	0	0	0	0	0	0	0
90	92	16.40	11.40	6.40	1.40	0	0	0	0	0	0	0
92	94	16.70	11.70	6.70	1.70	0	0	0	0	0	0	0
94	96	17.10	12.10	7.10	2.10	0	0	0	0	0	0	0
96	98	17.50	12.50	7.50	2.50	0	0	0	0	0	0	0
98	100	17.80	12.80	7.80	2.80	0	0	0	0	0	0	0
100	102	18.20	13.20	8.20	3.20	0	0	0	0	0	0	0
102	104	18.50	13.50	8.50	3.50	0	0	0	0	0	0	0
104	106	18.90	13.90	8.90	3.90	0	0	0	0	0	0	0
106	108	19.30	14.30	9.30	4.30	0	0	0	0	0	0	0
108	110	19.60	14.60	9.60	4.60	0	0	0	0	0	0	0

***Semimonthly** payroll period—Continued*

And the wages are—		And the number of withholding exemptions claimed is—										
At least	But less than	0	1	2	3	4	5	6	7	8	9	10 or more
		The amount of income tax to be withheld shall be—										
$110	$112	$20.00	$15.00	$10.00	$5.00	$0	$0	$0	$0	$0	$0	$0
112	114	20.30	15.30	10.30	5.30	.30	0	0	0	0	0	0
114	116	20.70	15.70	10.70	5.70	.70	0	0	0	0	0	0
116	118	21.10	16.10	11.10	6.10	1.10	0	0	0	0	0	0
118	120	21.40	16.40	11.40	6.40	1.40	0	0	0	0	0	0
120	124	22.00	17.00	12.00	7.00	2.00	0	0	0	0	0	0
124	128	22.70	17.70	12.70	7.70	2.70	0	0	0	0	0	0
128	132	23.40	18.40	13.40	8.40	3.40	0	0	0	0	0	0
132	136	24.10	19.10	14.10	9.10	4.10	0	0	0	0	0	0
136	140	24.80	19.80	14.80	9.80	4.80	0	0	0	0	0	0
140	144	25.60	20.60	15.60	10.60	5.60	.60	0	0	0	0	0
144	148	26.30	21.30	16.30	11.30	6.30	1.30	0	0	0	0	0
148	152	27.00	22.00	17.00	12.00	7.00	2.00	0	0	0	0	0
152	156	27.70	22.70	17.70	12.70	7.70	2.70	0	0	0	0	0
156	160	28.40	23.40	18.40	13.40	8.40	3.40	0	0	0	0	0
160	164	29.20	24.20	19.20	14.20	9.20	4.20	0	0	0	0	0
164	168	29.90	24.90	19.90	14.90	9.90	4.90	0	0	0	0	0
168	172	30.60	25.60	20.60	15.60	10.60	5.60	.60	0	0	0	0
172	176	31.30	26.30	21.30	16.30	11.30	6.30	1.30	0	0	0	0
176	180	32.00	27.00	22.00	17.00	12.00	7.00	2.00	0	0	0	0
180	184	32.80	27.80	22.80	17.80	12.80	7.80	2.80	0	0	0	0
184	188	33.50	28.50	23.50	18.50	13.50	8.50	3.50	0	0	0	0
188	192	34.20	29.20	24.20	19.20	14.20	9.20	4.20	0	0	0	0
192	196	34.90	29.90	24.90	19.90	14.90	9.90	4.90	0	0	0	0
196	200	35.60	30.60	25.60	20.60	15.60	10.60	5.60	.60	0	0	0
200	210	36.90	31.90	26.90	21.90	16.90	11.90	6.90	1.90	0	0	0
210	220	38.70	33.70	28.70	23.70	18.70	13.70	8.70	3.70	0	0	0
220	230	40.50	35.50	30.50	25.50	20.50	15.50	10.50	5.50	.50	0	0
230	240	42.30	37.30	32.30	27.30	22.30	17.30	12.30	7.30	2.30	0	0
240	250	44.10	39.10	34.10	29.10	24.10	19.10	14.10	9.10	4.10	0	0
250	260	45.90	40.90	35.90	30.90	25.90	20.90	15.90	10.90	5.90	.90	0
260	270	47.70	42.70	37.70	32.70	27.70	22.70	17.70	12.70	7.70	2.70	0
270	280	49.50	44.50	39.50	34.50	29.50	24.50	19.50	14.50	9.50	4.50	0
280	290	51.30	46.30	41.30	36.30	31.30	26.30	21.30	16.30	11.30	6.30	1.30
290	300	53.10	48.10	43.10	38.10	33.10	28.10	23.10	18.10	13.10	8.10	3.10
300	320	55.80	50.80	45.80	40.80	35.80	30.80	25.80	20.80	15.80	10.80	5.80
320	340	59.40	54.40	49.40	44.40	39.40	34.40	29.40	24.40	19.40	14.40	9.40
340	360	63.00	58.00	53.00	48.00	43.00	38.00	33.00	28.00	23.00	18.00	13.00
360	380	66.60	61.60	56.60	51.60	46.60	41.60	36.60	31.60	26.60	21.60	16.60
380	400	70.20	65.20	60.20	55.20	50.20	45.20	40.20	35.20	30.20	25.20	20.20
400	420	73.80	68.80	63.80	58.80	53.80	48.80	43.80	38.80	33.80	28.80	23.80
420	440	77.40	72.40	67.40	62.40	57.40	52.40	47.40	42.40	37.40	32.40	27.40
440	460	81.00	76.00	71.00	66.00	61.00	56.00	51.00	46.00	41.00	36.00	31.00
460	480	84.60	79.60	74.60	69.60	64.60	59.60	54.60	49.60	44.60	39.60	34.60
480	500	88.20	83.20	78.20	73.20	68.20	63.20	58.20	53.20	48.20	43.20	38.20
		18 percent of the excess over $500 plus—										
$500 and over		90.00	85.00	80.00	75.00	70.00	65.00	60.00	55.00	50.00	45.00	40.00

If the payroll period with respect to an employee is **Monthly:**

And the wages are—		And the number of withholding exemptions claimed is—										
At least	But less than	0	1	2	3	4	5	6	7	8	9	10 or more
		The amount of income tax to be withheld shall be—										
$0	$56	18% of wages	$0	$0	$0	$0	$0	$0	$0	$0	$0	$0
56	60	$10.40	.40	0	0	0	0	0	0	0	0	0
60	64	11.20	1.20	0	0	0	0	0	0	0	0	0
64	68	11.90	1.90	0	0	0	0	0	0	0	0	0
68	72	12.60	2.60	0	0	0	0	0	0	0	0	0
72	76	13.30	3.30	0	0	0	0	0	0	0	0	0
76	80	14.00	4.00	0	0	0	0	0	0	0	0	0
80	84	14.80	4.80	0	0	0	0	0	0	0	0	0
84	88	15.50	5.50	0	0	0	0	0	0	0	0	0
88	92	16.20	6.20	0	0	0	0	0	0	0	0	0
92	96	16.90	6.90	0	0	0	0	0	0	0	0	0
96	100	17.60	7.60	0	0	0	0	0	0	0	0	0
100	104	18.40	8.40	0	0	0	0	0	0	0	0	0
104	108	19.10	9.10	0	0	0	0	0	0	0	0	0
108	112	19.80	9.80	0	0	0	0	0	0	0	0	0
112	116	20.50	10.50	.50	0	0	0	0	0	0	0	0
116	120	21.20	11.20	1.20	0	0	0	0	0	0	0	0
120	124	22.00	12.00	2.00	0	0	0	0	0	0	0	0
124	128	22.70	12.70	2.70	0	0	0	0	0	0	0	0
128	132	23.40	13.40	3.40	0	0	0	0	0	0	0	0
132	136	24.10	14.10	4.10	0	0	0	0	0	0	0	0
136	140	24.80	14.80	4.80	0	0	0	0	0	0	0	0
140	144	25.60	15.60	5.60	0	0	0	0	0	0	0	0
144	148	26.30	16.30	6.30	0	0	0	0	0	0	0	0
148	152	27.00	17.00	7.00	0	0	0	0	0	0	0	0
152	156	27.70	17.70	7.70	0	0	0	0	0	0	0	0
156	160	28.40	18.40	8.40	0	0	0	0	0	0	0	0
160	164	29.20	19.20	9.20	0	0	0	0	0	0	0	0
164	168	29.90	19.90	9.90	0	0	0	0	0	0	0	0
168	172	30.60	20.60	10.60	.60	0	0	0	0	0	0	0
172	176	31.30	21.30	11.30	1.30	0	0	0	0	0	0	0
176	180	32.00	22.00	12.00	2.00	0	0	0	0	0	0	0
180	184	32.80	22.80	12.80	2.80	0	0	0	0	0	0	0
184	188	33.50	23.50	13.50	3.50	0	0	0	0	0	0	0
188	192	34.20	24.20	14.20	4.20	0	0	0	0	0	0	0
192	196	34.90	24.90	14.90	4.90	0	0	0	0	0	0	0
196	200	35.60	25.60	15.60	5.60	0	0	0	0	0	0	0
200	204	36.40	26.40	16.40	6.40	0	0	0	0	0	0	0
204	208	37.10	27.10	17.10	7.10	0	0	0	0	0	0	0
208	212	37.80	27.80	17.80	7.80	0	0	0	0	0	0	0
212	216	38.50	28.50	18.50	8.50	0	0	0	0	0	0	0
216	220	39.20	29.20	19.20	9.20	0	0	0	0	0	0	0
220	224	40.00	30.00	20.00	10.00	0	0	0	0	0	0	0
224	228	40.70	30.70	20.70	10.70	.70	0	0	0	0	0	0
228	232	41.40	31.40	21.40	11.40	1.40	0	0	0	0	0	0
232	236	42.10	32.10	22.10	12.10	2.10	0	0	0	0	0	0
236	240	42.80	32.80	22.80	12.80	2.80	0	0	0	0	0	0

***Monthly** payroll period—Continued*

And the wages are—		And the number of withholding exemptions claimed is—										
At least	But less than	0	1	2	3	4	5	6	7	8	9	10 or more
		The amount of income tax to be withheld shall be—										
$240	$248	$43.90	$33.90	$23.90	$13.90	$3.90	$0	$0	$0	$0	$0	$0
248	256	45.40	35.40	25.40	15.40	5.40	0	0	0	0	0	0
256	264	46.80	36.80	26.80	16.80	6.80	0	0	0	0	0	0
264	272	48.20	38.20	28.20	18.20	8.20	0	0	0	0	0	0
272	280	49.70	39.70	29.70	19.70	9.70	0	0	0	0	0	0
280	288	51.10	41.10	31.10	21.10	11.10	1.10	0	0	0	0	0
288	296	52.60	42.60	32.60	22.60	12.60	2.60	0	0	0	0	0
296	304	54.00	44.00	34.00	24.00	14.00	4.00	0	0	0	0	0
304	312	55.40	45.40	35.40	25.40	15.40	5.40	0	0	0	0	0
312	320	56.90	46.90	36.90	26.90	16.90	6.90	0	0	0	0	0
320	328	58.30	48.30	38.30	28.30	18.30	8.30	0	0	0	0	0
328	336	59.80	49.80	39.80	29.80	19.80	9.80	0	0	0	0	0
336	344	61.20	51.20	41.20	31.20	21.20	11.20	1.20	0	0	0	0
344	352	62.60	52.60	42.60	32.60	22.60	12.60	2.60	0	0	0	0
352	360	64.10	54.10	44.10	34.10	24.10	14.10	4.10	0	0	0	0
360	368	65.50	55.50	45.50	35.50	25.50	15.50	5.50	0	0	0	0
368	376	67.00	57.00	47.00	37.00	27.00	17.00	7.00	0	0	0	0
376	384	68.40	58.40	48.40	38.40	28.40	18.40	8.40	0	0	0	0
384	392	69.80	59.80	49.80	39.80	29.80	19.80	9.80	0	0	0	0
392	400	71.30	61.30	51.30	41.30	31.30	21.30	11.30	1.30	0	0	0
400	420	73.80	63.80	53.80	43.80	33.80	23.80	13.80	3.80	0	0	0
420	440	77.40	67.40	57.40	47.40	37.40	27.40	17.40	7.40	0	0	0
440	460	81.00	71.00	61.00	51.00	41.00	31.00	21.00	11.00	1.00	0	0
460	480	84.60	74.60	64.60	54.60	44.60	34.60	24.60	14.60	4.60	0	0
480	500	88.20	78.20	68.20	58.20	48.20	38.20	28.20	18.20	8.20	0	0
500	520	91.80	81.80	71.80	61.80	51.80	41.80	31.80	21.80	11.80	1.80	0
520	540	95.40	85.40	75.40	65.40	55.40	45.40	35.40	25.40	15.40	5.40	0
540	560	99.00	89.00	79.00	69.00	59.00	49.00	39.00	29.00	19.00	9.00	0
560	580	102.60	92.60	82.60	72.60	62.60	52.60	42.60	32.60	22.60	12.60	2.60
580	600	106.20	96.20	86.20	76.20	66.20	56.20	46.20	36.20	26.20	16.20	6.20
600	640	111.60	101.60	91.60	81.60	71.60	61.60	51.60	41.60	31.60	21.60	11.60
640	680	118.80	108.80	98.80	88.80	78.80	68.80	58.80	48.80	38.80	28.80	18.80
680	720	126.00	116.00	106.00	96.00	86.00	76.00	66.00	56.00	46.00	36.00	26.00
720	760	133.20	123.20	113.20	103.20	93.20	83.20	73.20	63.20	53.20	43.20	33.20
760	800	140.40	130.40	120.40	110.40	100.40	90.40	80.40	70.40	60.40	50.40	40.40
800	840	147.60	137.60	127.60	117.60	107.60	97.60	87.60	77.60	67.60	57.60	47.60
840	880	154.80	144.80	134.80	124.80	114.80	104.80	94.80	84.80	74.80	64.80	54.80
880	920	162.00	152.00	142.00	132.00	122.00	112.00	102.00	92.00	82.00	72.00	62.00
920	960	169.20	159.20	149.20	139.20	129.20	119.20	109.20	99.20	89.20	79.20	69.20
960	1,000	176.40	166.40	156.40	146.40	136.40	126.40	116.40	106.40	96.40	86.40	76.40
		18 percent of the excess over $1,000 plus—										
$1,000 and over		180.00	170.00	160.00	150.00	140.00	130.00	120.00	110.00	100.00	90.00	80.00

If the payroll period with respect to an employee is a
Daily Payroll Period *or a*
Miscellaneous Payroll Period:

And the wages divided by the number of days in such period are—		And the number of withholding exemptions claimed is—										
		0	1	2	3	4	5	6	7	8	9	10 or more
At least	But less than	The amount of income tax to be withheld shall be the following amount multiplied by the number of days in such period—										
$0	$2.00	18% of wages	$0	$0	$0	$0	$0	$0	$0	$0	$0	$0
2.00	2.25	$0.40	.05	0	0	0	0	0	0	0	0	0
2.25	2.50	.45	.10	0	0	0	0	0	0	0	0	0
2.50	2.75	.45	.15	0	0	0	0	0	0	0	0	0
2.75	3.00	.50	.20	0	0	0	0	0	0	0	0	0
3.00	3.25	.55	.25	0	0	0	0	0	0	0	0	0
3.25	3.50	.60	.30	0	0	0	0	0	0	0	0	0
3.50	3.75	.65	.30	0	0	0	0	0	0	0	0	0
3.75	4.00	.70	.35	.05	0	0	0	0	0	0	0	0
4.00	4.25	.75	.40	.10	0	0	0	0	0	0	0	0
4.25	4.50	.80	.45	.15	0	0	0	0	0	0	0	0
4.50	4.75	.85	.50	.15	0	0	0	0	0	0	0	0
4.75	5.00	.90	.55	.20	0	0	0	0	0	0	0	0
5.00	5.25	.90	.60	.25	0	0	0	0	0	0	0	0
5.25	5.50	.95	.65	.30	0	0	0	0	0	0	0	0
5.50	5.75	1.00	.70	.35	.05	0	0	0	0	0	0	0
5.75	6.00	1.05	.75	.40	.05	0	0	0	0	0	0	0
6.00	6.25	1.10	.75	.45	.10	0	0	0	0	0	0	0
6.25	6.50	1.15	.80	.50	.15	0	0	0	0	0	0	0
6.50	6.75	1.20	.85	.55	.20	0	0	0	0	0	0	0
6.75	7.00	1.25	.90	.60	.25	0	0	0	0	0	0	0
7.00	7.25	1.30	.95	.60	.30	0	0	0	0	0	0	0
7.25	7.50	1.35	1.00	.65	.35	0	0	0	0	0	0	0
7.50	7.75	1.35	1.05	.70	.40	.05	0	0	0	0	0	0
7.75	8.00	1.40	1.10	.75	.45	.10	0	0	0	0	0	0
8.00	8.25	1.45	1.15	.80	.50	.15	0	0	0	0	0	0
8.25	8.50	1.50	1.20	.85	.50	.20	0	0	0	0	0	0
8.50	8.75	1.55	1.20	.90	.55	.25	0	0	0	0	0	0
8.75	9.00	1.60	1.25	.95	.60	.30	0	0	0	0	0	0
9.00	9.25	1.65	1.30	1.00	.65	.35	0	0	0	0	0	0
9.25	9.50	1.70	1.35	1.05	.70	.35	.05	0	0	0	0	0
9.50	9.75	1.75	1.40	1.05	.75	.40	.10	0	0	0	0	0
9.75	10.00	1.80	1.45	1.10	.80	.45	.15	0	0	0	0	0
10.00	10.50	1.85	1.50	1.20	.85	.55	.20	0	0	0	0	0
10.50	11.00	1.95	1.60	1.30	.95	.60	.30	0	0	0	0	0
11.00	11.50	2.05	1.70	1.35	1.05	.70	.40	.05	0	0	0	0
11.50	12.00	2.10	1.80	1.45	1.15	.80	.45	.15	0	0	0	0
12.00	12.50	2.20	1.90	1.55	1.20	.90	.55	.25	0	0	0	0

INCOME TAX WITHHOLDING TABLES—*Continued*

***Daily or Miscellaneous** payroll period—Continued*

And the wages divided by the number of days in such period are—		And the number of withholding exemptions claimed is—										
		0	1	2	3	4	5	6	7	8	9	10 or more
At least	But less than	The amount of income tax to be withheld shall be the following amount multiplied by the number of days in such period—										
$12.50	$13.00	$2.30	$1.95	$1.65	$1.30	$1.00	$0.65	$0.30	$0	$0	$0	$0
13.00	13.50	2.40	2.05	1.75	1.40	1.05	.75	.40	.10	0	0	0
13.50	14.00	2.50	2.15	1.80	1.50	1.15	.85	.50	.15	0	0	0
14.00	14.50	2.55	2.25	1.90	1.60	1.25	.90	.60	.25	0	0	0
14.50	15.00	2.65	2.35	2.00	1.65	1.35	1.00	.70	.35	0	0	0
15.00	15.50	2.75	2.40	2.10	1.75	1.45	1.10	.75	.45	.10	0	0
15.50	16.00	2.85	2.50	2.20	1.85	1.50	1.20	.85	.55	.20	0	0
16.00	16.50	2,95	2.60	2.25	1.95	1.60	1.30	.95	.60	.30	0	0
16.50	17.00	3.00	2.70	2.35	2.05	1.70	1.35	1.05	.70	.40	.05	0
17.00	17.50	3.10	2.80	2.45	2.10	1.80	1.45	1.15	.80	.45	.15	0
17.50	18.00	3.20	2.85	2.55	2.20	1.90	1.55	1.20	.90	.55	.25	0
18.00	18.50	3.30	2.95	2.65	2.30	1.95	1.65	1.30	1.00	.65	.35	0
18.50	19.00	3.40	3.05	2.70	2.40	2.05	1.75	1.40	1.05	.75	.40	.10
19.00	19.50	3.45	3.15	2.80	2.50	2.15	1.80	1.50	1.15	.85	.50	.20
19.50	20.00	3.55	3.25	2.90	2.55	2.25	1.90	1.60	1.25	.90	.60	.25
20.00	21.00	3.70	3.35	3.05	2.70	2.35	2.05	1.70	1.40	1.05	.75	.40
21.00	22.00	3.85	3.55	3.20	2.90	2.55	2.25	1.90	1.55	1.25	.90	.60
22.00	23.00	4.05	3.70	3.40	3.05	2.75	2.40	2.10	1.75	1.40	1.10	.75
23.00	24.00	4.25	3.90	3.55	3.25	2.90	2.60	2.25	1.95	1.60	1.25	.95
24.00	25.00	4.40	4.10	3.75	3.40	3.10	2.75	2.45	2.10	1.80	1.45	1.10
25.00	26.00	4.60	4.25	3.95	3.60	3.25	2.95	2.60	2.30	1.95	1.65	1.30
26.00	27.00	4.75	4.45	4.10	3.80	3.45	3.15	2.80	2.45	2.15	1.80	1.50
27.00	28.00	4.95	4.60	4.30	3.95	3.65	3.30	3.00	2.65	2.30	2.00	1.65
28.00	29.00	5.15	4.80	4.45	4.15	3.80	3.50	3.15	2.85	2.50	2.15	1.85
29.00	30.00	5.30	5.00	4.65	4.30	4.00	3.65	3.35	3.00	2.70	2.35	2.00
		18 percent of the excess over $30 plus—										
$30.00 and over		5.40	5.05	4.75	4.40	4.10	3.75	3.45	3.10	2.75	2.45	2,10

10-DAY AND 28-DAY PAYROLL PERIODS: Wage-bracket withholding tables for 10-day and 28-day payroll periods are not included in this circular. A 10-day table (I.R.S. Publication No. 35) and a 28-day table (I.R.S. Publication No. 36) are available at the office of the District Director of Internal Revenue and will be supplied on request. There is also available a weekly withholding table combining income tax and Social Security employee tax. (I.R.S. Publication No. 192.)

computed upon the total. But if the supplemental payment is not made at the same time as a regular wage payment, then the supplemental wages will be added for withholding tax purposes to the wages paid or to be paid within the same calendar year for the last preceding payroll period or for the current payroll period.

Illustration. EE is employed as a salesman at a monthly salary of $100 plus commissions on sales made during the month. He claims one withholding exemption. During January he earns $275 in commissions, which together with the salary of $100 is paid on February 10. Under the wage bracket method, the amount of withholding tax may be found on the table for a monthly payroll period. The tax will be $57.00.

Illustration. EE is employed at a salary of $3,000 per year, paid semimonthly on the fifteenth day and the last day of each month, plus a bonus and commission determined at the end of each 3-month period. He claims four withholding exemptions. The bonus and commission for the 3-month period ending on March 31 amount to $250, which is paid on April 10. Under the wage bracket method, withholding tax on the total of $250 bonus and $125 last preceding semimonthly wage payment, or $375, is $46.60. Since tax of $2.70 was withheld on the semimonthly wage payment of $125, the amount to be withheld on April 10 is $43.90.

If supplemental wages are paid and the tax has been withheld on the employee's regular wages, the employer may determine the tax to be withheld from supplemental wages by applying 18% without allowance for exemptions, without reference to any regular payment of wages.

Amounts of so-called "vacation allowances" are subject to withholding as though they were regular wage payments made for the period covered by the vacation. If the vacation allowance is paid in addition to the regular wage payment for that period, the supplemental payments rules will apply to the vacation allowance.[10]

Additional Withholding. In addition to the tax that must be deducted, the employer and the employee may agree in writing that an additional amount will be withheld from the latter's wages.[11] The purpose is to enable the employee to build up a larger credit for withheld taxes.

Individuals—Declarations of Estimated Tax

Even if an individual has been subjected to withholding tax, the rate was only 18%, whereas the combined normal and surtax rates start at 20%, which covers but the first $2,000 of taxable income. Furthermore, persons who are not employees (such as self-employed

[10] Regulations Section 31.3402(g)-1.
[11] Regulations Section 31.3402(e)-1.

people and investors) have no tax withheld from their income. In order to put everyone on a current tax payment basis, declarations of estimated tax (with a corollary payment of tax when indicated) must be filed by persons where income tax payments are not satisfied in a substantial way by withholding tax.

Who Must Make a Declaration? A return must be filed by all United States citizens or residents; nonresident aliens subject to withholding tax on wages if residents of Canada, Mexico, or Puerto Rico; and every nonresident alien who has been or expects to be a resident of Puerto Rico during the entire taxable year if the following requirements are met:

(1) Where more than $100 is not subject to withholding, if estimated gross income exceeds $600 times the number of exemptions, plus $400.

(2) Where $100 or less is not subject to withholding, if estimated gross income exceeds these amounts:

Status	
Single	$ 5,000
Married (not entitled to file joint declaration)	5,000
Married (entitled to file joint declaration)	10,000
Surviving spouse	10,000
Head of household	10,000 [12]

Illustration. A married individual with two dependent children makes his return on the calendar year basis. Neither his wife nor his children have any source of income. He is engaged in the practice of a profession and has gross income of $600 from it for January and February. He reasonably expects that his gross income from his profession will continue to average $300 each month throughout the year and that he will have no income from any other source. Since he has gross income which can reasonably be expected to exceed $2,800 ($2,400 for four exemptions plus $400), and the income does not constitute wages subject to withholding, he is required to file a declaration of estimated tax.

A husband and wife may file a joint declaration if they are married on the last day of the taxable year, even though they are not living together. Such a declaration, however, may not be filed if either spouse is a nonresident alien, or if the spouses had different taxable years. Even if a joint declaration is made, separate income tax returns may be filed; in this case, the payments already made may be allocated as the spouses decide. But if they cannot agree as to the division, the portion of the payments to be allocated to a spouse will be that portion of the estimated tax paid that the tax shown on his separate income tax return bears to the total tax shown on the separate returns of both spouses.[13]

[12] I.R.C. Section 6015.

[13] Regulations Section 1.6015(b)-1(b).

To determine whether a declaration is required, the test is applied to each spouse. If one has more than $100 not subject to withholding and the number of exemptions is a consideration, each spouse is entitled only to his own exemption. Consequently, neither spouse may take into account the exemptions of the other if the latter is reasonably expected to have gross income.

Date of Declaration. An individual required to make a declaration must file it by the fifteenth day of the fourth month of the year covered by the estimate; that is, a person on a calendar year basis would file his estimate of 1960 tax liability not later than April 15, 1960.[14] The declaration is to be filed on the following dates if the requirements necessitating the submission of the declaration are first met at later periods:

After or	*Before*	*Filing Date*
April 1	June 2	June 15
June 1	September 2	September 15
September 1	January 1	January 15 of following year[15]

If an individual has at least two-thirds of his total estimated gross income from farming, he may file his declaration within fifteen days after the close of his year in lieu of the above quarterly dates.[16]

Where an individual has a fiscal year, the above dates are modified; that is, April 1 becomes the first day of the fourth month following the close of the year.

If an individual is not required to file a declaration during the taxable year (that is, he does not meet the requirements until after September 1), he will be deemed to have met the requirements provided he files his income tax return by the following January 15 with payment in full. The corresponding dates are February 15 for farmers and the fifteenth day of the month following the close of the year for fiscal basis taxpayers.[18]

Payment of Estimated Tax. For calendar basis individuals, the following prevails:

Declaration Filed *After*	*but Before*	*Dates of Payment of Installments of Estimated Tax*
	April 15	One-fourth each by June 15, September 15, and January 15 of the following year.

[14] I.R.C. Section 6073.
[15] Regulations Section 1.6073–1(a).
[16] Regulations Section 1.6073–1(b).
[17] Regulations Section 1.6073–3(a).
[18] I.R.C. Section 6015(f).

Declaration Filed *After*	*but Before*	*Dates of Payment of Installments of Estimated Tax*
April 15	June 16	One-third each by September 15 and January 15 of the following year.
June 15	September 16	One-half each at time of filing declaration and by January 15 of the following year.
September 15		In full at time of filing declaration.

If any amendment of a declaration is filed, the remaining installments (if any) will be modified ratably to reflect the amendment.[19]

Amendments. When he makes his declaration of estimated tax, an individual must take into account the then existing facts and circumstances, as well as those reasonably to be anticipated insofar as they relate to prospective gross income, allowable deductions, and estimated credits for the full year. But circumstances change. Accordingly, an individual may file an amended declaration; but only one amended declaration may be filed for each quarter of the year. This may be accomplished by using a new Form 1040–ES, marked "Amended." Or the individual may utilize the blank form that is printed on the back of the bill received for an installment of estimated tax.

Penalties. A person receiving most of his revenue from salary or from fixed income should not have difficulty in making a reasonable estimate. But the self-employed person or anyone with unpredictable income will have to make careful estimates. Subject to certain exceptions that will be noted, there is a penalty for substantial underpayments of estimated tax. This penalty will be imposed whether or not there was reasonable cause for the underpayment.

The penalty is 6% per annum on the difference between the amount paid and 70% (66⅔% in the case of farmers) of the amount which should have been paid. The charge, which is computed for each installment date, runs until the amount is paid or until the filing date of the tax return, whichever is earlier.[20]

Illustration. An individual (other than a farmer) shows a tax liability of $40,000 on his income tax return for 1960. He has paid a total of $20,000 in equal installments of $5,000 during the year through withholding tax and declarations. Inasmuch as the amount of prepaid tax in each quarter is less than one-quarter of 70% of the final tax liability, the charge is applicable for each quarter and would be computed as follows:

[19] I.R.C. Section 6153.
[20] I.R.C. Section 6654.

Tax liability	$40,000
70% of tax liability	28,000
One-quarter of 70%	$ 7,000
Deduct quarterly prepayment	5,000
Under payment	$ 2,000
Additional charge:	
1st quarter—6% of $2,000 for 365 days (4/15/60–4/15/61)	120
2d quarter—6% of $2,000 for 304 days (6/15/60–4/15/61)	100
3d quarter—6% of $2,000 for 212 days (9/15/60–4/15/61)	70
4th quarter—6% of $2,000 for 90 days (1/15/61–4/15/61)	50
Total	340

The underpayment is presumed to apply equally to each quarterly installment. Sometimes, however, an installment will have been computed accurately on the basis of information then known, but a substantial amount of unforeseen income was received in a later quarter. The taxpayer then has the opportunity of avoiding penalty for periods prior to that of the additional income. If he believes that the penalty should not apply to all four quarters, he should attach to his income tax return a copy of Form 2210, which allocates income to each quarter on an individualized basis.[21]

Payment may be avoided for underpayment of any installment of estimated tax if there has been paid by the due date of the installment the smallest of the following figures:

(1) The tax for the preceding year (if it was a full one);

(2) A tax based upon income of the preceding year, with rates and exemptions of the taxable year;

(3) 70% (66⅔% for farmers) of a tax computed by annualizing income for the taxable year prior to the month when the installment is due; or

(4) 90% of a tax computed on the actual taxable income for the months in the taxable year ending before the month in which the installment is due.[22]

It is desirable to avoid this penalty, as it is not deductible for tax purposes. The most simple mechanism is to pay the same tax as last year's, inasmuch as any overpayment may be obtained by filing a refund claim; or if the taxpayer wishes to avoid a claim, he may use the overpayment as a credit against his tax for the following year. Another possibility is to file an amended estimate by January 15 of the following year, revising the estimate downward, so that there will not be an indicated overpayment on the final income tax return. That overpayment sometimes is unfortunate psychologically; a Revenue Agent may try to find some deduction to disallow, so that a refund will not have to be paid to the taxpayer.

[21] Regulations Section 1.6654–1(b).
[22] I.R.C. Section 6654(d).

There is no penalty for underpayment of estimated tax for the current year, when the return for the prior year reflects no taxable income because of a net operating loss carryover.[23]

Corporations

There is no withholding tax for corporations. A declaration of estimated tax may be required.

Who Must File a Declaration? Every corporation subject to the income tax law (including unincorporated business enterprises electing to be taxed as corporations under Section 1361) must file a declaration of estimated tax if its income tax can reasonably be expected to exceed $100,000.[24] "Estimated tax" means the excess of the amount estimated as corporate income tax liability exceeds any estimated credits. Thus, if it is believed that a corporation's tax will be $105,000, but there will be an allowable foreign tax credit of $10,000, no declaration will have to be filed.[25]

A declaration is filed on Form 1120–ES.

A declaration is required where the taxable year is less than twelve months, unless the short year is a period of less than nine months, or the period is of nine or more months but less than twelve and the requirements for filing are not met until the last month of the short year.[26] If the short year results from a change in accounting period, that income must be annualized in order to see whether it exceeds $100,000.[27]

Filing the Declaration. The declaration of estimated tax, where applicable, must be filed by the fifteenth day of the ninth month of the taxable year. Thus, a calendar year corporation would ordinarily file a declaration by September 15 for its tax of that year. But if a corporation meets the requirements for filing at a date after the last day of the eighth month but before the first day of the twelfth month, the declaration must be filed by the fifteenth day of the twelfth month. Where the requirements are not met until the first day of the twelfth month, no declaration need be filed.[28]

Illustration. A calendar year corporation is not subject to the filing of a declaration until November 30. The declaration must be filed by December 15.

[23] Revenue Ruling 58–369, I.R.B. 1958–29, 28.
[24] I.R.C. Section 6016.
[25] Regulations Section 1.6016–1(c)(2).
[26] Regulations Section 1.6016–4(a).
[27] Regulations Section 1.6015–4(b).
[28] Regulations Section 1.6074–1(a).

A declaration filed by the fifteenth day of the twelfth month may be amended by that fifteenth day through the mechanism of filing an amended return.

Payments. If the taxable year of the corporation ends before December 31, 1959, 40% of the estimated tax must be prepaid; the figure is 50% where the taxable year ends on or after December 31, 1959.[29] The estimated tax as used here means the full tax estimated, less a $100,000 credit and less any other anticipated credits.[30] Where a corporation files its estimate by the fifteenth day of the ninth month of the taxable year, the percentage of the estimated tax required is payable in two equal installments, one at the time of filing the declaration and one by the fifteenth day of the twelfth month of that year. If the declaration is filed after the fifteenth day of the ninth month, the required estimated tax is payable in full by the fifteenth day of the twelfth month.[31]

Where an amended declaration is filed, the second installment will be ratably modified to reflect the change in the estimated tax by reason of the amendment.

Illustration. A corporation on the calendar year basis filed a declaration on September 15, 1960, reporting an estimated tax (after credits) in the amount of $20,000. The first installment of $5,000 (25% of $20,000) accompanied the declaration. The corporation then filed an amended declaration on December 15, 1960, showing an estimated tax of $30,000. Inasmuch as $5,000 already had been paid, a payment now must be made in the amount of $10,000, computed as follows:

Required amount of estimated tax which must be paid for calendar year 1960 (50% of $30,000)..................	$15,000
Amount paid with original estimate (25% of $20,000)....	5,000
Balance to accompany amended declaration...........	$10,000

Had the amended declaration been filed on December 10, 1960, then only the balance of the first installment ($2,500) otherwise due on September 15 would have had to be paid with the declaration and the installment required to be paid by December 15, 1960, would be $7,500.

Substantial Underpayment of Tax. With certain exceptions to be mentioned below, there is an addition to the tax in the case of an underpayment of estimated tax by a corporation. This addition to the tax is imposed whether or not there was a reasonable cause for the underpayment. The amount of the underpayment for any installment date is the excess of—

(1) 70% of the tax shown on the return for the taxable year or, if no return was filed, 70% of the tax for that year, multiplied by

[29] I.R.C. Section 6154.
[30] I.R.C. Section 6016(b).
[31] I.R.C. Section 6154(b).

the percentage of the estimated tax which is required to be paid, and divided by the number of installment dates prescribed for the taxable year, over

(2) The amount, if any, of the installment paid on or before the last day prescribed for the payment.[32]

The amount of the addition is determined at the rate of 6% per annum upon the underpayment of any installment of estimated tax from the date this installment is required to be paid until the fifteenth day of the third month following the close of the taxable year, or the date this underpayment is paid, whichever is earlier. The term "tax" means the excess of the actual tax over $100,000 and the credits against the tax.

Illustration. A corporation using the calendar year basis reported on its declaration for the taxable year an estimated tax in the amount of $50,000. It made payments of $2,500 each on September 15 and December 15 of the taxable year. On the following March 15, the corporation filed its final income tax return showing a tax liability of $200,000. As the amount of each of the two installments paid by the last date prescribed for payment was less than 5% of 70% of the tax shown on the return, the addition to the tax is applicable and is computed as follows:

(1) Tax as defined ($200,000 minus $100,000, with no credits allowable)	$100,000
(2) 70% of Item (1)	70,000
(3) Amount of estimated tax required to be paid on each installment date (5% of $70,000)	3,500
(4) Deduct amount paid on each installment date	2,500
(5) Amount of underpayment for each installment date (Item (3) minus Item (4))	$ 1,000
(6) Addition to the tax:	
First installment—period 9/1 to 3/15	$ 30
Second installment—period 12/15 to 3/15	15
Total	$ 45

Exceptions. The addition to the tax will not be imposed for any underpayment of any installment of estimated tax if, on or before the date prescribed for payment of the installment, the total amount of all payments of estimated tax made equals or exceeds the amount which would have been required to be paid on or before that date if the estimated tax were the least of the following amounts—

(1) The tax shown on the return for the preceding taxable year, provided that the preceding taxable year was a year of twelve months and a return showing the liability for tax was filed for that year;

[32] I.R.C. Section 6655.

(2) An amount equal to a tax determined on the basis of the tax rates for the taxable year but otherwise on the basis of the facts shown on the return for the preceding taxable year and the law applicable to that year, in the case of a corporation required to file a return for that preceding taxable year;

(3) An amount equal to 70% of the tax determined by placing on an annual basis the taxable income for either the first six months or the first eight months of the taxable year (whichever results in no addition being imposed), in the case of the installment required to be paid by the fifteenth day of the ninth month, or for either the first nine months or the first eleven months of the taxable year (whichever results in no addition being imposed), in the case of the installment required to be paid by the fifteenth day of the twelfth month. The taxable income so determined is placed on an annual basis by—

(A) Multiplying it by 12, and

(B) Dividing the result by the number of months in the taxable year for which the taxable income was so determined.

(4) In the case of a taxpayer whose taxable income consists of 52 or 53 weeks, special rules apply.[33]

If there has been an underpayment of estimated tax as of the installment date prescribed for its payment and the taxpayer believes that one or more of the above exceptions precludes the assertion of the addition to the tax, there should be attached to the income tax return for the taxable year a Form 2220 showing the applicability of any exception upon which the taxpayer relies.

Tax-free Covenant Bonds

At one time, corporations that issued bonds were obliged to withhold tax on a portion of the interest which was paid to bondholders. In order to make its bonds more salable, some corporations agreed to pay the full interest without any deduction for taxes; that is, the bond contained a covenant under which the corporation assumed the tax payment.

The law since has been changed. But in the case of interest upon bonds or other corporate obligations containing a tax-free covenant that were issued before January 1, 1934, the obligor is still required to withhold a tax of 2% of the interest. This covers payments on bonds owned by individuals, partnerships, or foreign corporations not engaged in trade or business within the United States. If the

[33] Regulations Section 1.6655–2(a)(4), (5).

liability assumed by the issuing corporation does not exceed 2% of the interest, then the deduction and withholding is at the rate of 30% where bonds are owned by nonresident alien individuals, a partnership not engaged in trade or business within the United States if composed in whole or in part of nonresident aliens, and a foreign corporation not engaged in trade or business within the United States.[34]

If the owners of the obligations are not known to the payor, the rate of withholding is 30%.

No withholding is required in the case of a citizen or resident if he filed with the withholding agent by February 1 of the following year a signed notice in writing claiming the benefit of the deduction for personal exemptions. Form 1000 is used for this purpose.

The corporate obligor customarily advises applicable bondholders of the amount of tax that was paid under the covenant. Taxpayers who own these bonds and who itemize their deductions are entitled to a credit of the amount of income tax paid by the corporation. The credit for the tax paid at the source should be entered on Line 8(b), page 2 of Form 1040. The bondholder is not required to include this payment of interest for him by the corporation in his gross income.[35]

Withholding of Tax on Nonresident Aliens and Foreign Corporations

Subject to exceptions to be noted below, there is a 30% withholding tax in the case of specified items of income (to the extent that these items constitute gross income from sources within the United States) paid to a nonresident alien individual, a nonresident partnership composed in whole or in part of nonresident alien individuals, or a nonresident foreign corporation. This 30% rate is reduced by various treaties, as summarized in the chart that appears below. For purposes of this section, "nonresident alien individual" includes an alien resident of Puerto Rico.[36]

The specified items of income are interest (except interest on deposits with persons carrying on the banking business paid to persons not engaged in business in the United States), dividends, rent, salaries, wages, premiums, annuities, compensations, remunerations, emoluments, or other fixed or determinable annual or periodi-

[34] I.R.C. Section 1451.
[35] Regulations Section 1.1451–1(f).
[36] I.R.C. Section 1441.

cal gains, profits, and income, and amounts which are considered to be gains from the sale or exchange of capital assets.

Exceptions. No deduction or withholding is required in the case of—

(1) Dividends of foreign corporations unless (A) the corporation is engaged in trade or business within the United States and (B) more than 85% of the gross income of the corporation for the 3-year period ending with the close of its taxable year preceding the declaration of these dividends (or for that part of the period that the corporation has been in existence) was derived from sources within the United States.

(2) The nontaxable portion of corporate distributions.

(3) Dividends paid by a China Trade Act corporation.

(4) Dividends paid to a shareholder whose status is not definite.

(5) Accrued interest on sale of bond between interest dates.

(6) Compensation for personal services of a nonresident alien individual who enters and leaves the United States at frequent intervals if he is a resident of Canada or Mexico and is engaged in agricultural labor.

Special Tax Treaties. Under tax treaties, exemptions from, or reduced rates of, United States tax require individualized treatment. The table on page 25·30 has been confined to dividends, interest, royalties, and real estate rentals, which, with few exceptions, include practically all income subject to withholding of tax in the case of nonresident aliens and nonresident foreign corporations.[37]

The reduced rates in the case of dividends (other than those with respect to which the rate of 5% is claimed) is applicable at the source in every case in which the address of the stockholder on the records of the disbursing entity paying the dividend (or on those of the domestic agent receiving this dividend on behalf of the nonresident alien individual or nonresident foreign corporation) is in the foreign country concerned. The reduced rate of 5% is applicable only where the Commissioner of Internal Revenue determines, and so notifies the paying corporation, that the reduced rate applies.

Supplementary Material

A. Suggested Reading.

Jay O. Kramer, "Estimated Income and Expense in the Tax Law," *TAXES—The Tax Magazine,* November, 1954, Vol. XXXII, #11, p. 906.

[37] Revenue Ruling 57–391, 1957–2 CB 606.

SPECIAL TAX TREATIES

Country	Dividends	Interest [1]	Royalties	Real Estate Rentals and Natural Resource Royalties
Australia	15% [4]	NE	E [2,3]	NE [8]
Belgium	15% [3]	15% [3]	E [3]	NE [8]
Canada	15% [3,5]	15% [3]	15% [3,12]	15 [3,9]
Denmark	15% [3,5]	E [3]	E [3]	NE [8]
Finland	15% [3,5]	E [3]	E [3]	NE [8]
France	15% [3,16]	15% [3,16]	E [3]	NE [8]
Germany	15% [3,14]	E [3,15]	E [3]	NE [8]
Greece	NE	E [3,6]	E [3,11]	NE [8]
Honduras	NE	E [3]	E [3]	NE [8]
Ireland	15% [4,5]	E [4,6]	E [4]	15% [4,8]
Italy	15% [3,5]	NE	E [3]	NE [8]
Japan	NE	15% [3]	15% [3]	NE [8]
Netherlands	15% [3,5]	E [3,7]	E [3]	NE [8]
Netherlands Antilles	15% [3,5]	E [3,7]	E [3]	NE [8]
New Zealand	15% [3,6]	NE	NE [10]	NE [10]
Norway	NE	E [3]	E [3]	NE [8]
South Africa	NE	NE	NE	NE [8]
Sweden	10% [13]	NE	E [13]	NE
Switzerland	15% [3,5]	5% [3]	E [3]	NE [8]
United Kingdom	15% [4,5]	E [4,6]	E [4]	15% [4,8]

DEFINITIONS:

E = Exempt.
NE = Not exempt. Tax to be withheld at the statutory rate prescribed by sections 1441 and 1442 of the Internal Revenue Code of 1954.

REFERENCES:

1 Except interest on tax-free covenant bonds issued before January 1, 1934, as to which the obligor has assumed liability for tax greater than 2% of such interest.
2 Copyright royalties only.
3 Applicable if no permanent establishment in United States.
4 Applicable if no permanent establishment in United States and subject to United Kingdom (or Irish or Australian) tax.
5 The rate is 5% on dividends paid by domestic subsidiary corporation subject to prescribed conditions.
6 Does not apply to interest paid by controlled corporation.
7 Does not apply to interest paid by controlled corporation nor to interest on mortgages secured on real estate.
8 Recipient may elect to be subject to tax on a net basis by filing Form 1040B.
9 Recipient may elect to be subject to tax on a net basis but only on real property by filing Form 1040B.
10 No exemption except motion picture film rentals; net basis tax elective (on filing Form 1040B) on real property rentals, natural resource royalties, and industrial royalties (other than film rentals).
11 Does not apply to motion picture film rentals or royalties.
12 Copyright royalties are exempt from tax and withholding provided the taxpayer has no permanent establishment in the United States.
13 Applicable whether or not engaged in trade or business in the United States.
14 Applies only if the German company deriving dividend owns at least 10% of voting stock of the domestic corporation paying dividend. (Reduced rate is confined to dividends paid by a corporation of one country to a *corporation* of the other country. The 30% Code rate applies to *individual* recipients.)
15 Not applicable to interest on debts secured by mortgages on farms, timberlands, or real property used wholly or partly for housing purposes.
16 Supplemental Convention of June 22, 1956, finalized June 13, 1957.

Carroll F. Lewis, "Declaration of Estimated Income Tax and Tax Payment Schedule for Corporations," *How To Work with the Internal Revenue Code of 1954* (New York: Federal Tax Forum, Inc., 1954), p. 375.
R. C. Wetterhall, "How To Avoid Penalties in Estimating Taxes," *Journal of Accountancy,* April, 1956, Vol. CI, #4, p. 34.

B. Questions.

1. May a taxpayer, by posting a bond, avoid the payment of estimated income tax?
2. How may an individual with a salary of $50,000 per annum avoid the payment of estimated income taxes? May he avoid the filing of a declaration of estimated tax?
3. When is the declaration of estimated tax by a fiduciary due?
4. S and C, a partnership, pays a salary to each of the principal partners. Is this subject to withholding?
5. A partnership elects to be taxed as a corporation. Is the salary of a partner subject to withholding?
6. A corporation reasonably estimates that it will have tax liability for 1960 of $105,000. No allowable credits against the tax are anticipated. Is a declaration of estimated tax required? If a foreign tax credit of $10,000 is anticipated, would your answer be different?
7. An individual supports three children and both of his parents. If he has no income except salary, what must his estimated gross income be before he is required to file a declaration of estimated tax?
8. In which of the following situations is withholding of wages required:
   (a) Juror's fees in a case of long duration.
   (b) Salary of chef in a fraternity house.
   (c) Payment to bartender occasionally employed by a sales office for parties to out-of-town buyers. The bartender averaged $15 a week for this function.
   (d) Payments to a German chemist on a monthly basis for advice that he rendered by mail to a manufacturer in Massachusetts.
   (e) Salary received by a clergyman from a lumber company for holding services in a camp in an obscure point in the Rockies.
9. A corporation hired a married employee on March 1. On July 15, he becomes a father. As of what date will the new withholding exemption be effected?
10. An individual has a fiscal year ending on June 30, 1961. When must he file a declaration of estimated tax?
11. A woman (who was not a farmer) filed her return for the calendar year 1960 on April 15, 1961, showing a tax of $30,000. The requirements for filing were first met after April 1 and before June 2, 1960, and a total of $18,000 of estimated tax was paid in three equal installments of $6,000 on each of the three prescribed installment dates. What addition to tax, if any, is required, and on what date or dates?
12. A carpenter, who worked out of his own home, worked for anyone who asked for his services, although he did refuse new orders from persons he deemed "too fussy." Most of his work was done for one warehouseman, who frequently needed special racks and loading platforms. Are the carpenter's receipts subject to withholding?
13. Junior works for his father, Senior. Junior does not file an exemption certificate on Form W-4, as Senior knows jolly well how many de-

pendents Junior has—in fact, Senior really supports most of them. May Senior recognize all of these dependents for withholding tax purposes insofar as Junior's salary is concerned?

14. A corporation on the calendar year basis filed a declaration on September 15, reporting an estimated tax in the amount of $20,000. The first installment of $1,000 (5% of $20,000) accompanied the declaration. On December 15, the corporation filed an amended declaration, showing an estimated tax of $30,000. How much will the payment be that accompanies the amended declaration? Would your answer be the same if the amended declaration had been filed on December 10?
15. A single individual on the calendar year basis was employed from the beginning of 1956 and for several years prior thereto at an annual salary of $6,000. He filed his declaration for 1961 on September 15 of that year. How much of his estimated tax is due at that time?
16. An individual estimates that his gross income for the taxable year will be $6,000, including $105 in dividends from domestic corporations. Will he be required to make a declaration of estimated tax if (a) he is single, with no dependents; (b) if he is married and eligible to file a joint return, with one child; or (c) if he is married, with one child, and eligible to file a joint return, although he has every reason to believe that he and his wife will file separate returns; or (d) married to a nonresident alien, with one dependent in this country?
17. In the preceding problem, would any of your answers be different if dividends from domestic corporations were $200?
18. An individual is paid at the rate of $6,000 per year. If he is paid on a monthly basis, and has two withholding exemptions, what is the amount of withholding tax on (a) the percentage method and (b) the wage bracket method?
19. Mr. Peters has three withholding exemptions. What is the amount of withholding for April if he is paid $100 a week (there are four pay days that month) and receives a bonus of $200 in that month? Use (a) the percentage method and also (b) the wage bracket method.

26

PROCEDURE

Audit

The Chances. When he prepares his return, a taxpayer may ponder over the possibility of an audit. In certain instances, the amount of a figure or the treatment of an item may be decided upon by the taxpayer in the light of what he believes to be the audit possibility. In other words, he may be taking a calculated risk.

But as has been mentioned previously, the return is made under the penalty of perjury. There are various monetary (and worse) penalties, as will be detailed in this chapter.

In an address before the Pennsylvania Society of Certified Public Accountants in 1958, the then Commissioner of Internal Revenue made some official statements as to the audit possibilities facing a given taxpayer.

A survey indicated that three out of four returns filed were correct, technically and mathematically; and of the remainder, tax changes from a detailed audit were insignificant in a substantial percentage of cases. "The problem, then, is to identify the returns that do justify audit, and to concentrate our available manpower in this productive area."

Every return is checked arithmetically. Verification of wages is accomplished through the W–2 forms which the taxpayer attaches to his return. About 70% of the taxpayers use the standard deductions. Only in the remaining 30% of the returns is closer examination indicated. The returns selected for examination are not chosen by lot as one out of every ten or any such figure, nor is a certain letter of the alphabet selected each year. Returns selected for examination may be identified by type of return, by type of business or occupation, by size of income, or by type of error. Certain types of return are given particular attention. "Examples are personal or business returns reporting adjusted gross income above certain designated levels; or combinations of personal service and business income above certain levels. Further selection for audit may be made on the basis of such factors as substantial income reported from sources not subject to withholding; or income from professions or business which deal largely in cash; or returns from such enterprises that local experience has demonstrated to be error-prone; or returns presenting unusual dependency exemption claims; or proportionately large deductions."

Method of Assessment. The assessment is made by recording the liability of the taxpayer in the office of the appropriate District Director of Internal Revenue.[1] This is automatic. But a supplemental assessment may be made "whenever it is ascertained that any assessment is imperfect or incomplete in any material respect." [2]

Audit. A tax deficiency is not to be confused with errors in arithmetic. If an error in arithmetic involves an underpayment, it is merely called to the taxpayer's attention and his remittance is awaited; if an overpayment is involved, a check is mailed. A *deficiency* means the excess of the tax over the sum of the amount shown as the tax by the taxpayer upon his return and the amounts previously assessed (or collected without assessment) as a deficiency; but this sum must first be reduced by the amount of rebates made.[3]

The Secretary of the Treasury may fix the time and place for a tax examination or audit in a reasonable manner.[4] An *office audit* may be conducted by correspondence or by having the taxpayer appear in person with his records. A *field audit* may be made by having an examining officer (a Revenue Agent) go to the taxpayer's home or place of business to check his books and records. The Secretary may examine any person having custody of books of account relating to the business of the person liable for tax and may require testimony under oath.[5] The Secretary may enter, in daytime, any building or place where items subject to tax are made, produced, or kept. He may enter at night if the premises are open at night.[6]

A taxpayer claimed ill health as a reason for not answering an administrative summons to testify as to his tax liability. The court found that this was no defense. His health was not so poor as to prevent him from having daily conferences with his counsel about tax matters.[7]

[1] I.R.C. Section 6203.
[2] I.R.C. Section 6204.
[3] I.R.C. Section 6211.
[4] I.R.C. Section 7605.
[5] I.R.C. Section 7602.
[6] I.R.C. Section 7606.
[7] *Duffy v. Brody,* 147 F. Supp. 897 (D.C., Mass., 1957).

After the Revenue Agent has completed his examination, he will discuss with the taxpayer his findings concerning a proposed deficiency or overassessment. If the taxpayer agrees with the proposed changes, he should then execute Form 870 or other appropriate agreement form, which will be offered to him by the Revenue Agent; this waives the restrictions on the assessment and collection of the whole or any part of the deficiency.[8] Interest will not be imposed on this deficiency for the period beginning immediately after the thirtieth day after its filing.[9] But if the taxpayer does not agree with the Agent, the latter will furnish a statement of the proposed tax adjustment and will tell the taxpayer of his right to an informal conference at the office of the District Director. If the taxpayer does not request an informal conference within ten days, the Revenue Agent will proceed with the completion of his report, a copy of which will be mailed to the taxpayer by the District Director under cover of a *30-day letter* (to be discussed below) that states the action proposed to be taken.

Informal Conference. The informal conference is conducted by the Revenue Agent's group supervisor or a designated conferee. Oaths are not administered, and no stenographic transcript is taken. The taxpayer may appear on his own behalf, or he may be represented by his attorney or accountant if these representatives are licensed to practice before the Treasury Department. Regardless of whether he is so licensed, the person who prepared a tax return under question may represent the taxpayer at this conference. The official conducting this conference then prepares a report that is subject to review in the Audit Division of the District Director's office.

If the taxpayer does not agree with the conference report, he will receive a written copy of this report with a 30-day letter.

30-Day Letter. The report of the examining agent, as approved after review, recommends one of four determinations:

(1) Acceptance of the return as filed and closing of the case.

(2) Assertion of a given deficiency or additional tax.

(3) Allowance of a given overassessment, with or without a claim for refund, credit, or abatement.

(4) If a claim for refund, credit, or abatement has been filed and has been found wholly lacking in merit, denial of the claim.

If any one of the last three determinations is made (except a full allowance of a claim in respect of any tax), unless the taxpayer has

[8] I.R.C. Section 6213(d).
[9] I.R.C. Section 6601(d).

previously agreed with the finding by signing an agreement form, the District Director issues a preliminary or 30-day letter. This is a form letter which states the determination proposed to be made. It is accompanied by a copy of the Revenue Agent's report explaining the basis of the proposed determination. It suggests to the taxpayer that if he concurs in the recommendation, he indicate his agreement by executing and returning the enclosed form of waiver or acceptance. The preliminary letter also advises the taxpayer that if he disagrees with the proposed determination, he may file a written protest under oath within thirty days (from the date of the letter) stating the grounds for his disagreement and may have a hearing in the Appellate Division of the region if requested. Failure by the taxpayer to make any response within thirty days will result in the issuance of a statutory notice of deficiency or other appropriate action, such as the issuance of a notice of adjustment or the denial of a claim.

If the taxpayer chooses to file a protest against the proposed determination set forth in the 30-day letter, his protest should be filed in triplicate in the District Director's office and, following the review of the protest, the case will be referred to the Appellate Division. The taxpayer will also be accorded a conference in the Appellate Division if he requests it.

Appellate Division. Each region of the Internal Revenue Service has an Appellate Division, which has complete jurisdiction of every income tax case after the issuance of the statutory notice of deficiency. But the Appellate Division may not (1) make or approve a settlement in any case docketed in the Tax Court, except with the concurrence of regional counsel of the Internal Revenue Service; (2) eliminate the ad valorem fraud or negligence penalty in any case not docketed in the Tax Court, except with the concurrence of regional counsel; or (3) act in any case in which criminal prosecution has been recommended, unless and until disposition has been made of the criminal aspects of the matter.

Proceedings before this division are informal. The taxpayer does not need to have counsel authorized to practice before the Treasury Department; and there are no transcripts or sworn testimony. Of course, the taxpayer may be represented by counsel if he desires.

If the Appellate Division of any region determines in any case that there is an overassessment (of taxes, penalties, or interest) exceeding $100,000, this determination is subject to review by the Office of the Chief Counsel.

Notice and Demand for Tax. In general, the District Director gives notice to each person liable for unpaid tax after the making of an assessment of a tax. This notice must be given as soon as possible and within sixty days. But failure to give notice within sixty days does not invalidate the notice.[10]

If any tax is assessed prior to the last date prescribed for payment of the tax, the District Director will not demand that this tax be paid before the last date, except where he believes that collection would be jeopardized by delay.

90-Day Letter. Before a deficiency may be assessed, a statutory notice of deficiency (commonly called a "90-day letter") must be sent to the taxpayer by registered mail, unless he waives this restriction on assessment. He may then file a petition for a redetermination of the proposed deficiency with the Tax Court of the United States within 90 days from the date of the mailing of the statutory notice. If the notice is addressed to a person outside the states of the Union and the District of Columbia, the 90 days is extended to 150. In other words, the taxpayer has the right in respect of these taxes to contest any proposed deficiency before an independent tribunal prior to assessment or payment of the deficiency. Unless the taxpayer waives the restrictions on assessment and collection after the date of the mailing of the statutory notice, no assessment or collection of a deficiency (not including the correction of a mathematical error) may be made in respect of these taxes until the expiration of the applicable period or if a petition is filed with the Tax Court, until the decision of that court has become final; that is, until no further appeal is possible. If, however, the taxpayer makes a payment with respect to a deficiency, the amount of that payment may be assessed. If the taxpayer fails to file a petition with the Tax Court within the applicable period, the deficiency will be assessed upon the expiration of the period, and notice and demand for payment will be mailed to him by the District Director. If the taxpayer files a petition with the Tax Court, the entire amount redetermined as the deficiency by a final decision of the Tax Court will be assessed and is payable upon notice and demand from the District Director.

There are no restrictions on the assessment and collection of the amount of any deficiency determined by the Tax Court, and a petition for review of the court's decision will not stay the assessment and collection of the deficiency so determined, unless on or before the time the petition for review is filed the taxpayer files with the

[10] I.R.C. Section 6303.

Tax Court a bond in a sum fixed by the court not exceeding twice the portion of the deficiency in respect of which the petition for review is filed. No part of an amount determined as a deficiency but disallowed as such by a decision of the Tax Court which has become final may be assessed or collected by levy or by proceeding in a court with or without assessment.[11]

The Commissioner of Internal Revenue sent a 90-day letter to a taxpayer, care of the taxpayer's sister, with whom he had lived prior to going to the Federal penitentiary at Terre Haute for tax evasion. The Government could not institute proceedings for tax collection, as notification had not been sent (as required by law) to the taxpayer's last-known address. The Commissioner knew the taxpayer's address was really care of the jail, for the Commissioner had sent him there.[12]

Offers in Compromise. The Commissioner of Internal Revenue may compromise any civil or criminal case arising under the Internal Revenue laws prior to reference to the Department of Justice for prosecution or defense.[13] An offer in compromise of taxes, interest, or penalty may be based upon either inability to pay the tax or doubt as to liability. Offers in compromise are submitted on Form 656, properly executed, and are accompanied by a financial statement on Form 433.

Closing Agreements. The Internal Revenue Service may enter into a written agreement with the taxpayer in respect of any tax for any taxable period. This agreement will be final and conclusive, except upon a showing of fraud, or upon misrepresentation of a material fact.[14]

Closing agreements may refer to tax liability, or they may provide a determination of any fact. But the Commissioner will only agree to signing such a form if it is determined that the Government "will sustain no disadvantage through consummation of such an agreement."[15]

Form 866, "Agreement as to Final Determination of Tax Liability," or Form 906, "Closing Agreement as to Final Determination Covering Specific Matters," is used.

Jeopardy Assessments. If the District Director believes that the assessment or collection of a tax will be jeopardized by delay, he may

[11] Regulations Section 601.103.
[12] *Barack v. United States*, D.C., Mo., 1956.
[13] I.R.C. Section 7122.
[14] I.R.C. Section 7121.
[15] Regulations Section 601.202(a).

assess the tax immediately, together with interest and other additional amounts provided by law, despite the regular assessment dates specified in I.R.C. Section 6213(a). A jeopardy assessment does not deprive the taxpayer of his right to file a petition with the Tax Court.[16]

To stay collection, the taxpayer may file with the District Director a bond equal to the amount for which the stay is desired.

Litigation

There are two main streets through which a taxpayer may take his case to the United States court system if he is not satisfied with the treatment that he gets from the Internal Revenue Service.

(1) Before paying the tax, he may file a petition with the Tax Court.

(2) He may pay the tax and then file a refund claim. If the claim is disallowed, he may sue for refund of the tax, regardless of the amount involved, in a United States District Court or in the Court of Claims.

Tax Court. The Tax Court (which formerly was known as the Board of Tax Appeals) is not a part of the Treasury Department but is an independent court. It has its own rules of practice, which differ in material respects from those followed by other tribunals.[17]

A petition to the Tax Court must be filed within the 90-day period stated in the deficiency notice. The hearing, if granted, will be held in the city elected by the taxpayer.

A copy of the petition to the Tax Court will be served on the Commissioner of Internal Revenue, who has 60 days in which to file an answer. If the Commissioner's answer contains nothing but an admission or denial of the facts stated in the petition, the taxpayer need not reply; but if new issues are raised, the taxpayer has 45 days after the mailing of this answer in which to admit or to deny the allegations. If the taxpayer fails to answer adequately, the court may grant a motion by the Commissioner for a judgment in accordance with his claims.

Before a Tax Court hearing takes place, the taxpayer may have another conference with Internal Revenue Service officials to try to arrive at a settlement without trial. If the hearing is held, the burden is on the taxpayer to disprove any findings in the 90-day letter.

[16] I.R.C. Section 6851.

[17] *Rules of Practice, Tax Court of the United States,* as published by the Government Printing Office.

After the hearing is over, the taxpayer may be required to prepare and to file a brief containing arguments and citations of similar cases in support of his contention. The Tax Court may approve the finding of a deficiency, or it may conclude that there was none, or that there is an overpayment. Often the ruling will conclude with these words: "Decision will be entered under Rule 50." This means that the tax is to be recomputed. Each side may file its proposed computation for consideration of the court. But if only one party does so, the court will accept that recomputation.

If the Tax Court rules against the taxpayer, and he wishes to appeal to the Court of Appeals, he must file a bond with the Tax Court to prevent assessment of deficiency.

District Court. Some tax cases (a very small minority) have their first hearing in a United States District Court, or, very occasionally, in the Court of Claims. The District Court may have to be used because the tax already has been paid and a suit is necessary for refund purposes. Sometimes a District Court is selected because after examining the results of past litigations involving similar issues, the taxpayer believes that he will find here a more sympathetic climate for his particular case than in the Tax Court. This practice is referred to as "tribunal shopping." But with increasing frequency, taxpayers are bringing their cases to a District Court because of the opportunity of having a trial by jury. A jury is available in the District Court upon the request of either party.[18]

Taxpayers or their counsel sometimes like to have a case tried before a jury because of the fact that any jury is almost certain to contain at least one businessman. A businessman is apt to feel that members of his calling will be more sympathetic to one of their fellows who seems to have gotten into the toils of some governmental rule that no ordinary person knows anything about.

Court of Appeals. Within three months after a decision by the Tax Court, the unsuccessful party may file a petition with the Court of Appeals for the jurisdiction where the return was filed or, if no return was filed, with the Court of Appeals for the District of Columbia. Similar appeal may be made after an unsuccessful verdict by the District Court.

Supreme Court. The party that is unsuccessful in the Court of Appeals may appeal to the United States Supreme Court. The procedure is to file an application for a writ of certiorari. If the Supreme Court wishes to hear the case (*e.g.*, if there is a substantial

[18] 28 U.S.C. 2402.

Federal question involved or if there is a conflict between various Courts of Appeals), certiorari will be granted. If the Supreme Court does not wish to hear an appeal, it will deny certiorari. "Cert. den." is a reference in a citation that, inasmuch as the Supreme Court would not take the appeal, the judgment of the Court of Appeals automatically is final.

Petition for a writ of certiorari (that is, calling up records of the lower court) must be filed with the Supreme Court within ninety days after the entry of the judgment or decree. The high court may, for good cause, allow an additional time not exceeding sixty days.

Unlike the procedure in some of the states, the title "United States *Supreme* Court" means what it says.

Collection of Assessments

Levy and Distraint. If a taxpayer neglects or refuses to pay any tax within ten days after notice and demand for its payment, the District Director may collect by levy on the taxpayer's property.[19] Levy may be made by serving a notice of levy on any person in possession of, or obligated with respect to, property or rights to property subject to levy, such as receivables, bank accounts, evidences of debt, securities, and accrued salaries, wages, commissions, and other compensation.

No suit for the purpose of restraining the assessment or collection of any Internal Revenue tax may be maintained in any court, except to restrain the assessment or collection of taxes during the period within which the assessment or collection of deficiencies in these taxes is prohibited.[20]

Property taken under authority of any revenue law of the United States may not be replevined.[21]

Liens. The Government's claim for taxes is a lien on the taxpayer's property. This lien is not valid as against any mortgagee, pledgee, purchaser, or judgment creditor until notice has been filed by the District Director.[22] Even if he has filed notice, the lien is not valid with respect to certain securities as against any mortgagee, pledgee, or purchaser of these securities, for an adequate and full consideration in money or money's worth, who is without notice or knowledge of the existence of the lien. A valid lien generally con-

[19] I.R.C. Section 6331.
[20] I.R.C. Section 7421.
[21] 28 U.S.C. 2463.
[22] I.R.C. Section 6321.

tinues until the liability is satisfied or becomes unenforceable by reason of lapse of time.[23]

Suit Against Taxpayer. Any portion of a tax refund erroneously made by the Government may be recovered by civil action brought in the name of the United States.[24] The suit must be begun within two years after the making of the refund, except that suit may be brought at any time within five years from the making of the refund if it appears that any portion was induced by fraud or misrepresentation of a material fact.[25]

Claims for Refund

After payment of a tax, a taxpayer may, within the applicable period of limitations, contest the assessment by filing with the District Director a claim for refund of all or any part of the amount paid, except with reference to certain taxes determined by the Tax Court, the decision of which has become final. If the claim is allowed, the overpayment of tax and allowable interest thereon will be credited against other liabilities of the taxpayer, or will be refunded to him. Generally, if the claim for refund is rejected in whole or in part, the taxpayer is notified of the rejection by registered mail. He may then bring suit in the District Court or Court of Claims for recovery of the tax. Suit may not be commenced before the expiration of six months from the date of filing of the refund claim, unless a decision is rendered thereon within that time, nor after the expiration of two years from the date of mailing by registered mail to the taxpayer of a notice of the disallowance of the part of the claim to which the suit relates. The 2-year period of limitation for bringing suit may be extended for whatever period is agreed upon in a properly executed Form 907.[26]

Full payment of an assessed tax is a condition precedent to the right to sue the Government for a refund.[27]

A refund claim must be filed by the taxpayer within three years from the time the return was filed or two years from the time the tax was paid, whichever is later. If no return was filed, the claim must be filed within two years from the time the tax was paid.[28]

If the claim was filed by the taxpayer during the 3-year period prescribed in the previous paragraph, the amount of the credit or

[23] I.R.C. Section 6322.
[24] I.R.C. Section 7405.
[25] I.R.C. Section 6532(b).
[26] I.R.C. Section 6532(a).
[27] *Flora v. United States,* 357 U.S. 28 (1958).
[28] I.R.C. Section 6511(a).

refund may not exceed the portion of the tax paid within the period immediately preceding the filing of the claim, equal to three years plus the period of any extension of time for filing the return. If the claim was not filed in that 3-year period, the amount of the credit or refund may not exceed the portion of the tax paid within the three years immediately preceding the filing of the claim.

Where the filing date has been extended, the period for filing a refund claim may not expire before six months after the expiration of the extended period.

7-Year Period of Limitation. In lieu of the 3-year period customarily operative, the time is seven years with respect to bad debts and worthless securities.

Carrybacks. In the case of net operating loss carrybacks, there is substituted for the 3-year rule that period which ends with the expiration of the fifteenth day of the fortieth month (or thirty-ninth month, in the case of a corporation) following the end of the taxable year of the net operating loss which results in the carryback, or the period covered by a special agreement, whichever is later.

Foreign Tax Credit. The 3-year rule is replaced by a 10-year limit in the case of a foreign tax credit allowed by statute or treaty.

A refund claim is filed on Form 843. Where an individual has died, there is Form 1310, "Statement of Claimant to Refund Due on Behalf of Deceased Taxpayer." For forms to be used in the case of "quickie claims" for carrybacks, see Chapter 14.

No refund or credit in excess of $100,000 may be made until after the expiration of thirty days from the date a report is made and is submitted to the Joint Committee on Internal Revenue Taxation.[29]

Peril of Refund Claim. A taxpayer does not know whether or not his return will be audited. If his return will be audited in any event, the filing of a refund claim will have no significance. But in the case of a person whose return otherwise would not be audited, the filing of a refund claim represents a risk; it is a virtually certain invitation to the Internal Revenue Service to make an examination.

An audit may be a matter of concern even to the most careful taxpayer. He will have to devote time to the process. He may have items disallowed, despite their legitimacy, because he cannot furnish *proof*.

[29] I.R.C. Section 6405(a).

Statute of Limitations

The amount of any income tax must be assessed within three years after the return was filed.[30] If a return is filed before its due date, it will be considered to have been filed on the last date set by the statute.

This three-year rule does not apply in the following cases:

(1) In the case of a false or fraudulent return, there is no statute of limitations. Such also is the case where there was a willful attempt to evade tax, or where no return was filed.

(2) If the taxpayer omits from gross income an amount properly includible therein which is in excess of 25% of the amount of gross income stated in the return, the 3-year period becomes six years. The 6-year statute did not apply where basis was overstated; this was an error in reporting an item disclosed on the return, not an omission of income.[31] Where a taxpayer made a full disclosure of his "position" with respect to his gross income on his tax return (a disclosure that would arrest the attention of the Internal Revenue Service upon its examination of his return), but has not included the amount involved as taxable, the regular 3-year statute of limitations applies.[32]

(3) Where the assessment period was extended by agreement, the tax may be assessed at any time prior to the expiration of the period agreed upon.

(4) Where a request for prompt assessment has been made by the taxpayer, the tax must be assessed or court proceedings to collect the tax begun within eighteen months after the request, but not after the expiration of three years after the return was filed.

(5) In the case of a personal holding company that fails to file the necessary personal holding company schedule, the limitation period is six years.

(6) Where a taxpayer has sold his principal residence and acquires another one, the statute of limitations does not expire before the expiration of three years from the date the Secretary of the Treasury is notified as to the replacement status.[33]

If a taxpayer determines in good faith that it is a trust or partnership and files a return as such, and if the taxpayer subsequently is deemed to be a corporation, the return as filed will be deemed to be

[30] I.R.C. Section 6501.

[31] *The Colony, Inc. v. Commissioner,* 357 U.S. 28 (1958).

[32] *Lawrence et ux. v. Commissioner,* — F.2d — (9th Cir., 1958).

[33] I.R.C. Section 1034(j).

the return of the corporation. A similar rule exists where an organization believes that it is an exempt organization and files accordingly, where in fact it was a taxable organization.[34]

Transferee Liability

For the purpose of transferee liability, the term "transferee" includes an heir, legatee, devisee, distributee of an estate of a deceased person, the shareholder of a dissolved corporation, the assignee or donee of an insolvent person, a party to a reorganization, and all other classes of distributees. Tax against the transferee of property is collected in the same manner and subject to the same provisions and limitations as in the case of a deficiency.[35] The period of limitation, in the case of an initial transferee, is one year after the expiration of the period of limitation against the transferor. In the case of a transferee of a transferee, the period is one year after the period of limitation against the preceding transferee, or three years after the expiration of the limitation for assessment against the original transferor, whichever is earlier.

A transferee is liable for tax only when he receives assets from a transferor who was insolvent at the time of the transfer, or was rendered insolvent by the transfer. The Internal Revenue Service has the burden of proving that a taxpayer had received a distribution of assets from an insolvent transferor, or that the distribution rendered the transferor insolvent, or that the transfer was in fraud of creditors.[36]

No transferee liability will be imposed on the proceeds of a life insurance policy, if under state law the proceeds are exempt from creditors' claims.[37] But where there had been an assessment before the decedent's death, the Government's lien was a charge against the property before the beneficiary received it; and the Government's lien was not extinguished.[38]

Interest

Interest at the rate of 6% runs from the due date of the tax until payment is made, or to the date of notice and demand if paid within ten days from the date thereof, in the case of any amount of tax

[34] I.R.C. Section 6501(g).
[35] I.R.C. Section 6901.
[36] *Maurice L. Rose et al.,* T.C. Memo. 1958–144, filed July 25, 1958.
[37] *Commissioner v. Stern,* 357 U.S. 39 (1958).
[38] *United States v. Bess,* 357 U.S. 51 (1958).

which is not paid on the due date.[39] Failure to pay estimated taxes as required is not covered by this rule.[40] See Chapter 25.

The due date for payment of tax is determined without regard to any extension of time, and interest continues to run during the period of the extension and for any further period during which the tax remains unpaid.

The following rules are provided for determining the due date of installment payments:

(1) In the case of any portion of the tax not shown on the return, the due date is deemed to be the due date of the first installment.

(2) In the case of unpaid installments of tax shown on the return, the due date is the date fixed for payment of the installment.

(3) If any installment is not paid when due and a notice and demand for subsequent installments is issued, the due date of the subsequent installments is the date of notice and demand.

In cases where, by reason of jeopardy, payment is demanded before the due date otherwise prescribed, interest will not begin to run prior to the prescribed due date.

If a waiver of restrictions, Form 870, on the assessment of a deficiency has been filed, but notice and demand is not issued within thirty days after the filing of the waiver, interest will not be imposed on the deficiency for the period beginning after this thirtieth day and ending with the date of notice and demand.

Interest is not paid on unpaid interest.[41]

Overpayments. Interest is paid to the taxpayer on overpayments at the rate of 6% per annum. In the case of a credit, interest runs from the date of the overpayment to the due date of the amount against which the credit is taken. In the case of refunds, interest runs from the date of the overpayment to a date (to be determined by the Secretary of the Treasury) preceding the date of the refund check by not more than thirty days, whether or not the check is accepted by the taxpayer.[42]

Interest arising from a carryback is not allowed for any period before the close of the year in which the loss occurred.

Tentative Net Operating Loss Carryback Adjustments. Interest rules applicable to tentative net operating loss carryback adjustments are as follows:

[39] I.R.C. Section 6601(a).
[40] I.R.C. Sections 6153 and 6154.
[41] Revenue Ruling 54–426, 1954–2 CB 39.
[42] I.R.C. Section 6611.

(1) Where unpaid original tax for the year being adjusted is abated by reason of a net operating loss carryback, interest will be charged from the due date of the tax, or the respective due dates of unpaid installments, to the last day of the loss year. According to the usual rule, if payment of the original tax was deferred and the tax is not extinguished by the loss carryback, 6% interest will be charged from the due date until the tax is paid.

(2) Where there is an additional tax which is not to be paid by reason of the allowance of a tentative carryback adjustment, additional interest should be charged on the tax only (or on the tax and penalty, if penalty was assessed) and not on interest previously assessed, from the date of notice and demand to the last day of the loss year. If interest on a deficiency had been charged to a date beyond the last day of the loss year, adjustment should be made to the last day of the loss year. If the tentative carryback adjustment does not extinguish all of the additional tax, payment of which had been deferred, additional interest should be charged on the unpaid portion from the date of notice and demand to the date of payment.

(3) If the tax for the year being adjusted has been paid and becomes an overpayment by reason of the allowance of a tentative carryback adjustment, and such overpayment is applied as a credit to unpaid original tax for another year or another type of tax, interest shall be charged on such unpaid original tax from the due date, or the respective due dates of unpaid installments, to the last day of the loss year. However, if the overpayment is applied as a credit to additional tax, additional interest should be charged from the date of notice and demand to the date of the schedule.[43]

Penalties

Taxpayers, and at times their advisors, may become subject to a variety of penalties because of acts which they perform or fail to perform, or do belatedly, or advise others to do or not to do. A survey of the coverage of these penalties should serve as a guide to what may be avoided.

Failure To File Tax Return. Unless it is shown that the failure is due to reasonable cause and not to willful neglect, there will be added to the tax 5% if the failure is for not more than one month, with an additional 5% for each additional month or fraction during which the failure continues, not exceeding 25% in the aggregate.[44]

[43] Revenue Ruling 56–668, 1956–2 CB 961.
[44] I.R.C. Section 6651.

Failure To File Certain Information Returns. In the case of each failure to file certain returns, unless it is shown that the failure is due to reasonable cause and not willful neglect, there must be paid by the person failing to file the statement the amount of $1 for each statement not filed; but the total amount imposed upon the delinquent for all such failures during the calendar year may not exceed $1,000. The statements referred to relate to information at the source, payments of corporate dividends, returns of brokers, and information returns with respect to income tax withheld.[45]

Failure To Pay Tax. If any part of the underpayment of income, estate, and gift taxes is due to negligence or intentional disregard of rules and regulations, but without intent to defraud, there will be a penalty of 5%.

If any part of the underpayment is due to fraud, there will be a 50% penalty.[46]

Failure To Pay Estimated Income Tax. In the case of any underpayment by an individual, the penalty will be 6% per annum on the amount of the underpayment.[47]

A similar penalty will be imposed for failure by a corporation to pay its estimated income tax.[48]

Failure To Make Deposit of Taxes. Unless it is shown that the failure is due to reasonable cause and not to willful neglect, the following penalties will be imposed upon any person who fails to make a required deposit of withheld taxes with a government depositary on time: 1% of the underpayment if the failure is for not more than one month, with an additional 1% for each additional month or fraction thereof during which the failure continues, not exceeding 6% in the aggregate.[49]

Bad Checks. There will be imposed upon the person who tenders a worthless check or money order in payment of taxes a penalty of 1% of the amount of the check, with a minimum $5 fine.[50] But it is difficult to think of a less likely person to whom to tender a bad check than the Director of Internal Revenue.

Addition to Tax in Case of Jeopardy. If a taxpayer violates or attempts to violate the provisions relating to termination of a taxable year, there will be a penalty of 25% of the tax or deficiency.[51]

[45] I.R.C. Section 6652.
[46] I.R.C. Section 6653.
[47] I.R.C. Section 6654.
[48] I.R.C. Section 6655.
[49] I.R.C. Section 6656.
[50] I.R.C. Section 6657.
[51] I.R.C. Section 6658.

Willful Violation of the Tax Law. Any person required to collect, truthfully account for, and pay over a tax who willfully fails to perform this duty, or who willfully attempts in any manner to evade or to defeat the tax or its payment, will (in addition to other penalties that may be imposed) be liable to a penalty equal to the total amount of the tax evaded, or not collected, or not accounted for and paid over.[52]

Upon conviction, this person may be fined not more than $10,000, or imprisoned not more than five years, or both.[53]

Any person who willfully attempts in any manner to evade or to defeat the tax will, upon conviction, incur similar fines and penalties.[54]

Any person required to pay any estimated tax or tax, or to make a return other than for estimated income tax, or to keep any records, or to supply any information, who willfully fails to do so, will, upon conviction, be fined not more than $10,000, or imprisoned not more than one year.[55]

Any person who willfully makes and subscribes any return, statement, or other document, which contains or is verified by a written declaration that it is made under the penalties of perjury, and which he does not believe to be true as to every material matter, will, upon conviction, be fined not more than $5,000, or imprisoned not more than three years, or both.[56]

Similarly treated is any person who willfully aids or assists in, or procures, counsels, or advises the preparation or presentation of any matter arising under the Internal Revenue laws which is fraudulent, whether or not the fraud is with the knowledge or consent of the person authorized to present the return or document.

Any person who willfully delivers or discloses to the Secretary of the Treasury any list, return, account, statement, or other document (known by him to be fraudulent as to any material matter) will be fined not more than $1,000, or imprisoned not more than one year, or both.[57]

Income Tax Statements for Employees. In addition to criminal penalties, any person who is required to furnish employees with withholding tax statements but who willfully furnishes a false or fraudulent statement, or who willfully fails to furnish a statement in the time and manner required, will be subject to a $50 penalty.[58]

[52] I.R.C. Section 6672.
[53] I.R.C. Section 7202.
[54] I.R.C. Section 7201.
[55] I.R.C. Section 7203.
[56] I.R.C. Section 7206.
[57] I.R.C. Section 7207.
[58] I.R.C. Section 6674.

Upon conviction, the person required to furnish this information will be fined for each offense not more than $1,000, or imprisoned not more than one year, or both.[59]

Any individual required to supply information to his employer as to withholding exemption who willfully supplies false or fraudulent information, or who willfully fails to supply information thereunder which would require an increase in tax to be withheld, is subject to a fine of not more than $500, or imprisonment of not more than one year, or both.[60]

Aid to Foreign Corporations. Every accountant, attorney, fiduciary, financial institution, or other person who aids, assists, counsels, or advises as to the formation, organization, or reorganization of any foreign corporation must, within thirty days, make an information return as to this advice, etc.[61] The penalties for failure to comply are stated under Section 7203 (see footnote 55). But the confidential nature of lawyer-client discussions need not be violated.

Sundry Offenses. Whenever it appears to the Tax Court that proceedings before it had been instituted by the taxpayer merely to delay the payment of tax, damages in an amount not in excess of $500 will be assessed.[62]

Any person who, being duly summoned to appear to testify, or to appear and to produce books, accounts, records, memoranda, or other papers, neglects to comply with the terms of the summons will be subject to a fine of not more than $1,000 upon conviction, or imprisonment of not more than one year, or both.[63]

False statements relating to tax that are made to purchasers or lessees are covered by Section 7211.

Any attempts to interfere with the administration of Internal Revenue laws will constitute an offense, punishable upon conviction by a fine of not more than $5,000, or imprisonment of not more than three years, or both. If the offense is committed only by threats of force, the maximum penalties will be, respectively, $3,000 and/or one year.[64]

Offenses by government employees, such as unauthorized disclosures of information, are covered by Sections 7213 and 7214.

[59] I.R.C. Section 7204.
[60] I.R.C. Section 7205.
[61] I.R.C. Section 6046.
[62] I.R.C. Section 6673.
[63] I.R.C. Section 7210.
[64] I.R.C. Section 7212.

Fraud

Several of the above penalties involve *fraud.* It has been noted previously that where there is fraud, the statute of limitations does not run; and a closing agreement obtained through a fraudulent representation is not binding upon the Government.

Fraud is "actual, intentional wrong doing and the intent required is the specific purpose to evade a tax believed to be owing. Mere negligence does not establish either." [65] Fraud "implies bad faith, intentional wrong doing and a sinister motive. It is never imputed or presumed and courts should not sustain findings of fraud upon circumstances which at most create only suspicion." [66]

The reason for the fraud is immaterial if there was a willful intent to evade taxes. Thus, an individual could not escape liability despite his testimony that he had concealed income merely because he had been kidnapped by the underworld and did not want his true income known.[67] Fraud penalties could not be avoided even though the taxpayer testified "that he had told his accountant to make it appear that his income was less than it actually was, not for the purpose of evading taxes but merely to mislead his wife." [68]

Where income per the tax returns was less than on the books, it was argued on behalf of a deceased taxpayer that he merely had used poor judgment and that the poorly disguised action was evidence of a mental lapse. The fact that the fraud was not a clever one did not change its character, observed the court. "We may comment that anyone attempting to defraud the United States shows *ipso facto* a certain lack of judgment regardless of his mental acuteness." [69]

Fraud may take an almost endless variety of forms. But "There is hardly a more routine badge of income tax fraud than a double set of books." [70]

Informants' Fees

Payments to informers are authorized for detecting and bringing to trial and punishment persons who are guilty of violating the Internal Revenue laws.[71] Persons who claim such rewards from the

[65] *Mitchell v. Commissioner,* 118 F.2d 308 (5th Cir., 1941).
[66] *Davis v. Commissioner,* 184 F.2d 86 (10th Cir., 1950).
[67] *John Factor,* T.C. Memo. 1958–94, filed May 23, 1958.
[68] *John D. Helvey et al.,* T.C. Memo. 1956–123, filed May 22, 1956.
[69] *Clinton H. Martin Estate,* T.C. Memo. 1959–20, filed January 30, 1959.
[70] *Masters v. Commissioner,* 243 F.2d 335 (3d Cir., 1957).
[71] I.R.C. Section 7623.

Secretary of the Treasury should make application on Form 211. Relevant facts should be stated on the form, which, after execution, should be forwarded to the District Director for the district where the informer lives or, alternatively, to the Commissioner of Internal Revenue, Washington 25, D.C.

Sundry Considerations

Disclosure of Tax Return Information. The adversary of a taxpayer in a lawsuit may be able to see the latter's tax return. Such was the case where it was necessary to establish whether alleged damages sustained by a professional wrestler had impaired his earning capacity.[72]

Unreasonable Search. In general, a taxpayer is obliged to show a Revenue Agent whatever pertinent information is requested. But there is a limit. I.R.C. Section 7506(b) ". . . spares the *taxpayer* from unnecessary examinations or investigations. . . . I believe the privilege was undoubtedly designed to spare the taxpayer harassment from time consuming examinations."[73]

Supplementary Material

A. Suggested Reading.

R. P. Hertzog, "Administrative and Procedural Changes in the New Code," *TAXES—The Tax Magazine,* November, 1954, Vol. XXXII, #11, p. 855.

Sherwin T. McDowell, "Traps in Refund Claims and Filing Returns," *Proceedings of the New York University Sixteenth Annual Institute on Federal Taxation* (Albany: Matthew Bender & Co., Inc., 1958), p. 485.

Robert S. Holzman, "Should You Use a Jury?" *TAXES—The Tax Magazine,* May, 1958, Vol. XXXVI, #5, p. 301.

Harry Graham Balter, *Fraud Under Federal Tax Law* (Chicago: Commerce Clearing House, Inc., 1953).

Elmer L. Irey, *The Tax Dodgers* (New York: Greenberg, 1948).

B. Leading Cases.

Fraud. *Mitchell v. Commissioner,* 118 F.2d 308 (5th Cir., 1941).
Davis v. Commissioner, 184 F.2d 86 (10th Cir., 1950).

C. Questions.

1. Is it to the taxpayer's advantage to have his tax returns audited?
2. Is it necessary for a taxpayer to be represented by an attorney in disputes with the Internal Revenue Service?
3. Angus MacDonald, an elderly agriculturist, failed to pay his taxes, and the Government obtained a lien against his farm. The farm had been

[72] *Karllson v. Wolfson et al.,* D.C., Minn., 1956.
[73] *Schulman et al. v. Dunlap et al.,* 105 F. Supp. 104 (D.C., N.Y., 1952).

pledged by the taxpayer as security for a bank loan. How does this lien affect the status of the bank?

4. May a taxpayer request a prompt assessment of his tax return? Why would he want to make such a request?
5. Discuss the tax aspects of a jeopardy assessment.
6. If a taxpayer itemizes his deductions instead of using the standard deduction, are the chances greater that there will be a tax audit?
7. A physicist filed his tax return on April 15, 1959, for calendar year 1958. On September 1, 1960, the return was audited and a proposed deficiency was found. The taxpayer received a 30-day letter dated October 1. If he did nothing, what happens? If he receives a 90-day letter on November 15, by what date must he take action? What happens if he does nothing?
8. Under what circumstances may it be advisable for a taxpayer to have a controversy tried before a jury? How can he secure a jury trial?
9. A taxpayer was advised by his accountant that a certain tax had been overpaid. How does the taxpayer recover it? Discuss the time element involved.
10. For calendar year 1960, an association honestly believed it was a partnership and filed a partnership return on April 15, 1961. In 1962, the Internal Revenue Service insisted that the organization actually was a corporation and, hence, a corporate return was due and had to be filed. Is any interest involved?
11. A Revenue Agent examined a tax return and proposed to assess a deficiency. He requested the taxpayer to sign an agreement to accept the findings on Form 870. What does the taxpayer gain by doing so? Are there any disadvantages?
12. Under what circumstances may a tax deficiency be compromised? Why would the Government entertain such an offer?
13. A bookkeeper was ordered by his department head to prepare details of an imaginary business trip to give to a Revenue Agent. The bookkeeper was reluctant; but to refuse would have meant the loss of his job. The Revenue Agent was not fooled. What are the penal consequences, if any, to (a) the bookkeeper, (b) the department head, and (c) the corporation for which they worked?
14. If a taxpayer believes that the Internal Revenue Service will not relax its position on a proposed tax deficiency and that the issue will have to be litigated, is there anything that he can do to get the matter before the courts quickly?
15. A businessman was told by his accountant that the profit on a certain sale was $5,000 if the facts of a complicated transaction proved to be precisely what a junior clerk had related from memory. The businessman never got around to checking the facts. Subsequently a Revenue Agent established that the transaction had not been as described, and a tax deficiency was asserted. Who, if anyone, may be involved in a fraud action?
16. A taxpayer filed his return for calendar year 1960 on April 15, 1961, showing gross income of $10,000. (a) When does the statute of limitations run? (b) Would your answer be different if an examination by a Revenue Agent showed that gross income actually was $15,000?
17. In the preceding question, what would your answer be to (a) if the return had been filed on April 10? On May 10?

18. Mr. Walters effected a casual sale of realty in his taxable year 1960. His accountant suggested that the transaction not be reported, as it had been for cash, with no records; and Walters followed this curious advice. Subsequently a Revenue Agent discovered that $8,000 in profit had not been reported. What are the penalties, if any, that apply to (a) the taxpayer and (b) the accountant? Would your answer to (b) be different if the accountant had given his advice gratuitously?
19. If, in the previous problem, Walters had left the handling of all of his affairs to the accountant, and if Walters had had no knowledge of how the transaction had been handled, would your answer be the same?
20. The Calypso Corporation filed its income tax return on March 15, 1961, for the calendar year 1960 with an indicated tax liability of $1,000. Half of this was paid on March 15, 1961, the balance on June 15. Subsequently, upon audit, the correct tax liability was found to be $900. How is interest on the overpayment to be computed?
21. Cato gave certain property to his son. Actually, the father was made insolvent by the gift, as his liabilities now exceeded his assets, and he could not pay the last installment of his income tax of the preceding year. Is Cato the younger responsible to any extent for his father's unpaid taxes?
22. If, in the preceding question, Cato the elder had made the gift on August 27, 1959, and both he and his son were on the calendar year basis, what is the last date by which the Government may proceed against either party?
23. The Sine Qua Non Corporation filed an income tax return for the calendar year 1958 on March 15, 1959, disclosing a tax liability of $50,000, and elected to pay the tax in installments. On October 15, 1960, a deficiency in the amount of $10,000 was assessed and was paid in equal installments on November 15 and November 26, 1960. On April 15, 1961, it was determined that the correct tax liability for 1958 was only $35,000. How is interest computed on the overassessment?

27

TRANSACTIONS WITH RELATED PARTIES

There is no reason why a person may not carry on transactions with a related party. But if a transaction with a party under common control is carried on at less than arm's length, the Secretary of the Treasury may reshuffle items of income or deduction to arrive at the result that would have obtained had the parties been dealing on the same basis that unrelated parties would have utilized. In the case of transactions with relatives of certain specified degrees of relationship, losses will not be recognized for tax purposes, even if the transactions are carried on at arm's length. In certain instances, capital gains treatment is not allowed to transactions between parties where there is a specified relationship.

But sometimes an affiliated corporation may be used to advantage by means of the consolidated return technique.

Arm's Length Transactions

General. Where there is a transaction between unrelated parties, it may be assumed that each party will bargain for his own best interest; and the resultant price or other consideration will be a fair one. But where parties under common control engage in a transaction, it is highly possible that the price will be rigged; that is, one party or the other will be deliberately allowed a price or charge so that on the whole matter, there will be a tax saving. For example, a person in a high tax bracket will sell to a party under common control who is in a lower tax bracket at such a price that the profit will be derived by the party who pays the lower tax.

But the Secretary of the Treasury has the authority to prevent that sort of thing. In the case of two or more organizations, trades, or businesses (whether or not incorporated, whether or not organized in the United States, and whether or not affiliated) which are owned or controlled directly or indirectly by the same interests, the Secretary of the Treasury may distribute, apportion, or allocate gross income, deductions, credits, or allowances between these parties if he determines that this action is necessary in order to prevent evasion of taxes or clearly to reflect the income of the parties.[1]

The Secretary *may* reallocate items of income or expense between entities under common control; he does not have to do so. Thus, in consecutive years, taxpayers under common control may be subjected to a reallocation in one year but not in the other. A taxpayer may be subject to reallocation, while his competitor (who conducts operations in precisely the same manner) is not. The fact that nothing has happened upon past tax audits is no guaranty that nothing will happen the next time.

Control. *Control* does not exist where there is a half-interest.[2] Where two unrelated corporations each owned 50% of the stock of a third corporation, there was not sufficient control for the Secretary to effect a reallocation.[3] The rules of constructive ownership of stock do not apply.[4]

What Is Allocable. The Secretary may not create income to reallocate, where no such income does in fact exist. If a corporation borrows from a controlled affiliate under a contract calling for interest, the fact that the borrowing continues after the note expires does not mean that interest is still required; without the note, there was no interest liability.[5] Where a corporation borrowed from another company under common control against noninterest-bearing demand notes, the accruing of income by the Internal Revenue Service was not justified.[6]

The Secretary may not take the position that a taxpayer *might* have made a different arrangement with a party where there is common control.[7] By a reallocation, the Secretary may not create a result that would not have come about in an arm's length transaction.[8]

Although income may not be attributed where none exists, deductions may be.[9]

Notification. The Secretary must do more than merely state in a deficiency notice that a reallocation is being made. The taxpayer

[1] I.R.C. Section 482.
[2] *Q. I. Roberts et al.*, T.C. Memo., Docket ##15773–5, January 19, 1949.
[3] *Lake Erie and Pittsburgh Railroad Co.*, 5 T.C. 558 (1945).
[4] *A. G. Nelson Paper Co., Inc.*, T.C. Memo., Docket #1553, entered August 30, 1944.
[5] *Tennessee-Arkansas Gravel Co. v. Commissioner*, 112 F.2d 508 (6th Cir., 1940).
[6] *Smith-Bridgman & Co.*, 16 T.C. 287 (1951).
[7] *Stevens Brothers et al.*, 24 T.C. 953 (1955).
[8] *Motor & Industrial Finance Corp. v. Scofield*, D.C., Texas, 1955.
[9] *Southern College of Optometry, Inc.*, T.C. Memo., Docket #10556, entered March 31, 1947.

can hardly shoulder his burden if he does not know which transaction or group of transactions the Secretary has determined to have resulted in distortions of true taxable income.[10] But if the Secretary shows a factual basis which supports the allocations proposed, the taxpayer has the burden of proof of showing that the allocation should not be allowed.[11] Allocation is not always a problem that can be solved with mathematical exactitude; it may be sufficient if the method employed by the taxpayer seems not unreasonable.[12]

Intent. The Secretary may effect an allocation even if there was no attempt at tax evasion or even avoidance. The allocation may be proper in any situation where income cannot be clearly reflected without it.[13]

Transactions between parties under common control may be subject to allocation if the dealings are at less than arm's length; that is a factual question which may be justified or shown to be the result of mitigating circumstances. But such explanations cannot even be made if there was no reason for having the separate entities. The motivation may not even have been sound; that is immaterial if the parties actually believed in the validity of the reason.[14]

The Measure of Arm's Length. When transactions are engaged in with parties under common control and with others, it is not difficult to see whether an arm's length consideration was used. Where the terms given to outsiders cannot be demonstrated because nonexistent or otherwise, the consideration may be determined by a qualified third party. Thus, where property is to be sold, an independent appraiser may establish the price. If part of the property rented from an outside party is rented to a party under common control, an allocation on a space basis may be made. A certified public accountant may make an allocation.[15] An arrangement between companies under common control was accepted as being at arm's length because it was a continuation of an agreement made before the companies were under common control.[16]

Consequences of a Reallocation. If the Secretary makes a reallocation, unfortunate consequences may result.

[10] *Commissioner v. Chelsea Products, Inc.*, 197 F.2d 620 (3d Cir., 1952).
[11] *The Friedlander Corporation*, 25 T.C. 70 (1955).
[12] *Motors Securities Corporation*, T.C. Memo., Docket #31656, entered October 30, 1952.
[13] *Central Cuba Sugar Co. v. Commissioner*, 198 F.2d 214 (2d Cir., 1952).
[14] *Polak's Frutal Works, Inc. et al.*, 21 T.C. 953 (1954).
[15] *Reynolds v. Cooper*, 64 F.2d 644 (10th Cir., 1933).
[16] *L. E. Shunk Latex Products, Inc. et al.*, 18 T.C. 940 (1952).

(1) A deduction may be transferred from an income company to a deficit company, where it would be wasted.

(2) Income might be allocated to one party, the tax returns of which are still open, while the corresponding deduction might be given to an entity whose tax returns are closed by the statute of limitations. See Chapter 26.

(3) Allocation of additional income to a corporation may greatly complicate its financial affairs in such matters as dividend payments, bonus and other compensation plans, and perhaps even a major price policy.

(4) The accumulated earnings tax (see Chapter 16) might be involved, were a corporation retroactively to learn that its earnings for a past year were higher than could be justified by reasonable needs for retention.

(5) If a corporation's income is retroactively reduced by an allocation, the company may have paid dividends in the face of impaired surplus, an action which might subject the directors to penal action in some states.

(6) If the Secretary finds that an individual's income is in part to be allocated to his corporation, this amount may be regarded as equivalent to a taxable dividend.

Areas Where Allocation Is Possible. The Secretary may make an allocation in such instances as these:

(1) A taxpayer sells to another party under common control certain assets, and the Secretary determines that the gain or loss should be reported in an amount different from that reported by the parties.

(2) A taxpayer renders a service to a party under common control, but the fee is modified by the Secretary, as in the case of a parent company (a manufacturer) which makes a sale to a subsidiary (a selling company).

(3) Two companies are under common control, and the same persons serve as officers of both companies. Executive compensation, administrative overhead, rent of office facilities, advertising expenses, and other costs might be reshuffled by the Secretary between the entities.

What To Do. If the Secretary proposes to make an allocation, the most satisfactory course is to show that the parties under common control actually are dealing at arm's length; that is, on the same basis that they would deal with outsiders. Failing this, it may be possible to demonstrate that although the parties were dealing at less than arm's length, there was reason for the arrangement.

(1) A related party was given a lower price than were outsiders, because the former was buying in larger quantities than were outsiders and made unusually fast returns of shipping cases that were in short supply.[17]

(2) A party under common control was charged with a smaller fee than was charged to outsiders, because actual services rendered to the affiliate were less than those related to outsiders.[18]

(3) Less than normal prices were satisfactory where it was necessary for the payor (a related party) to become financially established.[19]

Losses, Expenses, and Interest with Respect to Transactions Between Related Taxpayers

General. Except in cases of distributions in corporate liquidations (see Chapter 17), no deduction is allowed for losses arising from direct or indirect sales or exchanges of property between persons who, on the date of the sale or exchange, are within one of these relationships:

(1) Members of a family. The family of an individual includes for this purpose only his brothers and sisters, spouse, ancestors, and lineal descendants;

(2) An individual and a corporation, more than 50% in value of the outstanding stock of which is owned, directly or indirectly, by or for this individual;

(3) Two corporations more than 50% in value of the outstanding stock of each of which is owned, directly or indirectly, by or for the same individual, if either of these corporations in the taxable year preceding the sale or exchange was a personal holding company or a foreign personal holding company;

(4) A grantor and a fiduciary of any trust;

(5) A fiduciary of a trust and a fiduciary of another trust, if the same person is a grantor of both trusts;

(6) A fiduciary of a trust and a beneficiary of that trust;

(7) A fiduciary of a trust and a beneficiary of another trust, if the same person is a grantor of both trusts;

(8) A fiduciary of a trust and a corporation more than 50% in value of the outstanding stock of which is owned, directly or indirectly, by or for the trust or by or for a person who is a grantor of the trust; or

[17] *Barq's Bottling Co.*, T.C. Memo., Docket #6758, entered June 21, 1946.
[18] *Joseph Harris, Inc.*, T.C. Memo., Docket #5637, entered June 5, 1946.
[19] *Roy J. Champayne et al.*, 26 T.C. 634 (1956).

(9) A person and a tax-exempt organization which is controlled directly or indirectly by this person or (if this person is an individual) by members of his family.[20]

A taxpayer is not allowed a deduction for trade or business expenses otherwise deductible for expenses for production of income, or for interest otherwise deductible—

(1) If, at the end of the taxpayer's taxable year within which these items are accrued by the taxpayer or at any time within two and a half months thereafter, both the taxpayer and the payee are persons within any one of the nine relationships specified above and

(2) If the payee is on the cash receipts and disbursements method of accounting with respect to these items of gross income for his taxable year in which or with which the taxable year of accrual by the debtor-taxpayer ends; and

(3) If, within the taxpayer's taxable year within which these items are accrued by the taxpayer and two and a half months after the close thereof, the amount of these items is not paid and is not otherwise (under the rules of constructive receipt) includible in the gross income of the payee.

Illustration. An individual is the owner of an interest-bearing note of a corporation, all the stock of which he owned on the last day of his taxable year (December 31, 1960). Both the individual and the corporation use the calendar year basis. The individual uses the cash basis; the corporation, the accrual. The corporation does not pay interest on its note to the individual during 1960 or within two and a half months after the close, nor does it credit any interest to his account in such a manner that it is subject to his unqualified demand and thus is constructively received by him. The corporation claims a deduction for 1960 for the interest accruing on the note for that year. Inasmuch as the individual is on the cash basis, he does not report any interest for 1960. The corporation is not allowed the interest deduction for 1960 or, for that matter, for any other year, as the interest accrued only for 1960 and yet was disallowed for that year.

Amount of Gain Where Loss Previously Disallowed. If a taxpayer acquires property by purchase or exchange from a transferor who, on the transaction, sustained a loss not allowable as a deduction by reason of the relationship between the parties, then any gain realized by the taxpayer on a sale or other disposition of the property after 1953 will be recognized only to the extent that the gain exceeds the amount of this loss that is properly allocable to the property sold or otherwise disposed of by the taxpayer.

Illustration. A husband sells to his wife for $500 certain corporate stock with an adjusted basis for determining loss to him of $800. The loss of $300 is not allowable to him. The wife later sells his stock for $1,000. Although her realized gain is $500 ($1,000 minus $500, her basis), her recognized gain is only $200, the

[20] I.R.C. Section 267.

excess of the realized gain of $500 over the loss of $300 not allowable to the husband. In determining capital gain or loss, her holding period commences on the date of the sale by the husband to her. If the facts were the same except that she later sold her stock for $300 instead of $1,000, her recognized loss is $200 and not $500, as the rule applies only to the nonrecognition of gain, and does not affect basis.

This rule is also applicable to a sale or other disposition of property by a taxpayer when the basis of this property in the taxpayer's hands is determined directly or indirectly by reference to other property acquired by the taxpayer from a transferor through a sale or exchange in which a loss sustained by the transferor was not allowable. Therefore, the rule applies to a sale or other disposition of property after a series of transactions if the basis of the property acquired in each transaction is determined by reference to the basis of the property transferred, and if the original property was acquired in a transaction in which a loss to a transferor was not allowable.

Illustration. A husband sells to his wife for $5,500 certain farm land, with an adjusted basis for determining loss to him of $8,000. The loss of $2,500 is not allowable to him. The wife exchanges the farm land, held for investment purposes, with an unrelated individual for two city lots, also held for investment purposes. The basis of the city lots in the wife's hands ($5,500) is a substituted basis determined by reference to the farm land. Later she sells the city lots for $10,000. Although her realized gain is $4,500 ($10,000 minus $5,500), her recognized gain is only $2,000, the excess of the realized gain of $4,500 over the loss of $2,500 not allowable to her husband.

The benefit of the rule is available only to the original transferee but does not apply to any original transferee (such as a donee) who acquired the property in any manner other than by purchase or exchange.

Motivation. The motivation or intent of the parties is immaterial if the conditions making for disallowance of loss between related parties fall within the language of the Internal Revenue Code. The disallowance of loss is automatic, and there are no mitigating circumstances. Unlike the tax on accumulated earnings, this is not a matter out of which a taxpayer may talk his way.

Gain from Sale of Certain Property Between Related Parties

It was noted in Chapter 5 that gain on the sale of depreciable property used in the taxpayer's trade or business, if held for more than six months, may be treated as long-term capital gain, even though by definition depreciable property is not a capital asset. But any gain from the sale or exchange of depreciable property between a husband and wife or between an individual and a controlled corporation will be treated as ordinary income. Thus, any gain recognized to the transferor from a sale or exchange after May 3, 1951, directly or indirectly, between a husband and wife or between an individual and a controlled corporation, of property which, in the hands of the transferee, is property of a character subject to a depreciation allowance will be considered as ordinary income.[21]

For the purpose of this section, a corporation is controlled when more than 80% in value of all outstanding stock is beneficially owned by the taxpayer, his spouse, and his minor children and grandchildren; this includes legally adopted children and their children. The rule applies whether property is transferred from a corporation to a shareholder or from a shareholder to a corporation.

Leases

If improvements are made on leased property, the general rule is that depreciation is taken over the shorter of (1) the remaining life of the asset or (2) the life of the lease, including, as a rule, any optional renewal periods. Where, however, the lessor and lessee are related parties, depreciation is taken only over the life of the asset. For this purpose, "related party" is as defined earlier in this chapter in I.R.C. Section 267, except that "80% or more" is substituted for "more than 50%" as stated in that section.[22]

Nonbusiness Bad Debts

In the case of a nonbusiness bad debt (see Chapter 13), a short-term capital loss is allowed rather than a deduction; this refers to debts not originally created or acquired in the taxpayer's trade or business.[23] Where a loan is made to a relative, the transaction may be regarded by the Internal Revenue Service as being of this character. The question may arise as to whether a transaction with a relative should beget a bad debt deduction at all; perhaps there was no intention or expectation that the loan be repaid.[24] Loans to one's children are particularly suspect.[25]

[21] I.R.C. Section 1239.
[22] I.R.C. Section 178.
[23] I.R.C. Section 166(d)(2).
[24] *Griffiths v. Commissioner,* 70 F.2d 946 (7th Cir., 1934).
[25] *Montgomery v. United States,* 23 F. Supp. 130 (Ct. Cl., 1938).

Economic Benefits

If a stockholder derives any economic benefits from a corporation, these may be deemed to be distributions essentially equivalent to dividends, to the extent of the corporation's accumulated earnings. Similarly, if an employee gets economic benefits from his employer, the amounts are apt to be regarded as compensation. See Chapter 11.

Employment of Relatives

The taxpayer has the burden of proving that amounts paid to relatives as compensation are reasonable.[26]

Family Partnerships

This subject is treated in Chapter 18.

Dependents

This subject is treated in Chapter 24.

Redemption of Stock by Affiliated Corporation

The operation of I.R.C. Section 304 is discussed in Chapter 17.

Tax on Accumulated Earnings

In general, a corporation is not justified in retaining earnings because of the needs of related corporations. The business of an affiliated corporation is not considered to be the business of the taxpayer for this purpose.[27] But the retention may be deemed to be proper if the taxpayer demonstrably would suffer if the affiliate were not protected from insolvency.[28]

Constructive Receipt

A person may not avoid taxability by arranging to have income otherwise payable to him be assigned to someone else, who gener-

[26] *J. Gordon Gaines, Inc.*, T.C. Memo., Docket ##24662 and 29056, entered March 2, 1951.
[27] *Keck Investment Co.*, 29 B.T.A. 143 (1933).
[28] *Mellbank Corp.*, 38 B.T.A. 1108 (1938).

ally is a relative. "It is well established that earned income is taxable to those who earn it, notwithstanding a contractual disposition after it is received." [29] An anticipatory assignment of income is no more effective.[30]

Consolidated Tax Returns

An *affiliated group* of corporations has the privilege of making a consolidated income tax return in lieu of separate returns. This privilege is given, however, upon the condition that all corporations which have been members of the affiliated group at any time during the taxable year for which the return is made consent to the regulations applicable to that year. The making of the consolidated return is considered as consent.[31]

Affiliated Group. The term "affiliated group" means one or more chains of *includible corporations* connected through stock ownership with a common parent corporation which is an includible corporation if—

(1) Stock possessing at least 80% of the voting power of all classes of stock and at least 80% of each class of the nonvoting stock of each of the includible corporations (except the common parent corporation) is owned directly by one or more of the other includible corporations; and

(2) The common parent corporation owns directly stock possessing at least 80% of the voting power of all classes of stock and at least 80% of each class of the nonvoting stock of at least one of the other includible corporations.

For this purpose, the term "stock" does not include nonvoting stock which is limited and preferred as to dividends.

Includible Corporation. The term "includible corporation" means any corporation except—

(1) A tax-exempt corporation;

(2) An insurance company subject to taxation as such (although two or more such companies may be included in a return of insurance companies);

(3) A foreign corporation, except when a wholly owned foreign corporation was organized under the laws of Canada or Mexico and is maintained solely for the purpose of complying with the laws of such country as to title and operation of property;

[29] *Comer v. Davis*, 107 F.2d 355 (5th Cir., 1939).
[30] *Lucas v. Earl*, 281 U.S. 111 (1930).
[31] I.R.C. Section 1501.

(4) A corporation carrying on business within possessions of the United States under I.R.C. Section 931 (see Chapter 2);

(5) A corporation organized under the China Trade Act (see Chapter 2);

(6) A regulated investment company (see Chapter 16);

(7) An unincorporated business enterprise subject to tax as a corporation (see Chapter 16); and

(8) A small business corporation as defined in I.R.C. Section 1371(b) which elects to have its corporate income taxed directly to the shareholders (see Chapter 16).

The consolidated income tax return must include every includible corporation which is a member of the affiliated group. No corporation which is connected by stock ownership with an affiliated group of includible corporations through a nonincludible corporation may be included in the consolidated return of that group. In no case may be consolidated return be filed by subsidiary corporations as an affiliated group unless the common parent corporation through which the subsidiaries are connected is a member of the group. For instance, there will not be recognized as an affiliated group two domestic industrial corporations, the common parent corporation of which is a regulated investment company.

Duration of Election. The filing of *separate* returns does not constitute a binding election for future years. But if a consolidated return is filed, a consolidated return also must be filed for each subsequent taxable year during which the affiliated group remains in existence unless—

(1) A corporation (other than a corporation created or organized, directly or indirectly, by a member of the group) becomes a member of the group during any subsequent taxable year, or

(2) The Internal Revenue Code or the regulations are amended in such a manner that the filing of a consolidated return is less advantageous to affiliated groups *as a class.* Thus, it was ruled that the election was revived as a result of the Technical Changes Act of 1958.[32] *Or*

(3) The Commissioner of Internal Revenue grants permission to switch back to separate returns prior to the time of making the consolidated return.

Advantage of Filing a Consolidated Return. Whether it is advantageous to file a consolidated tax return generally depends upon the arithmetic of the situation. The following factors would make

[32] Revenue Ruling 58–471, I.R.B. 1958–39, 96.

the filing of a consolidated return by an affiliated group advantageous:

(1) One or more of the corporations may be operating at a loss. By filing a consolidated return, this loss will offset income of the other companies.

(2) All intercompany transactions are eliminated on a consolidated return. If Company A sells to an affiliate, Company B, in one taxable year, but B has not yet sold the product to an outside party by the end of the year, there will be a profit to be shown by A, even though the corporate group actually had not disposed of the asset.

(3) Dividends from domestic corporations are eligible for the 85% dividends received deduction under the circumstances mentioned in Chapter 16. But 15% of the dividends still would be taxable. On a consolidated return, however, none of the dividends would be taxed, as all intercompany items are eliminated.

(4) One or more corporations in an affiliated group might be vulnerable to the accumulated earnings tax or to the personal holding company tax. But the filing of a consolidated return might eliminate the hazard, for the tax (if any) would be assessed on the consolidated return. *Consolidated* reasons for retention of earnings might eliminate the danger of the first tax; *consolidated* gross income might mean that the personal holding company tax would not apply.

(5) Corporations are not entitled to any deduction for net capital losses. But on a consolidated return, capital losses of one corporation might be set against capital gains of other corporations.

But there might be disadvantages in filing a consolidated return:

(1) If a consolidated return is filed, the resultant income tax is increased by 2% of the consolidated taxable income of the affiliated group of consolidated corporations.[33] When a consolidated return is filed, surtax is imposed upon the entire consolidated taxable income. This is in addition to the surtax otherwise imposed with respect to taxable income which exceeds $25,000.[34]

(2) If a consolidated return is filed, a binding election has been made to continue filing consolidated returns in the future. But three methods of avoiding the consequences of a permanent election have been mentioned above.

(3) If a consolidated return is filed in order to absorb the loss of one or more corporations, the possibility of such corporations using the net operating loss carryback or carryover (see Chapter 14) is lost. It should be determined mathematically whether it is better

[33] I.R.C. Section 1503.

[34] Revenue Ruling 58–246, I.R.B. 1958–21, 30.

to file a consolidated return or to make use of the net operating loss technique.

(4) On a consolidated return, there is but *one* surtax exemption and *one* minimum accumulated earnings credit.

An election of a tax-option corporation terminates automatically if the corporation becomes a member of an affiliated group.

Making a Consolidated Return. The parent corporation files a regular corporate income tax return for the group. Each subsidiary must file Form 1122, consenting to the consolidated return regulations and authorizing the common parent to make the return. The common parent must file Form 851, an affiliations schedule.

Change in Affiliated Group During Taxable Year. A consolidated return, in general, includes the income of all of the affiliated companies for the entire taxable year. Corporations that are formed, added to the group, or eliminated from the group report their income for that portion of the year when they were part of the group. Separate returns may be required for that part of the year when a corporation was not part of the consolidated group.

Liability. Each member of the group is severally liable for the tax and any deficiency.

Tax Computation. The consolidated taxable income is the combined taxable income of all affiliated corporations—

(1) Minus the sum of—

(A) Any consolidated net operating loss deduction.

(B) Any consolidated Section 1231 net loss; that is, losses from involuntary conversions and from sales or exchanges of property subject to the provisions of Section 1231 (see Chapter 5).

(C) Any consolidated charitable contribution deduction, but not in excess of 5% of the consolidated taxable income without the contributions deduction, any special deductions for corporations other than organizational expense, any consolidated net operating loss carrybacks, and any deduction for Western Hemisphere trade corporations.

(D) Any consolidated dividends received deduction.

(E) Any consolidated Western Hemisphere trade corporation deduction.

(F) Any consolidated soil and water conservation expenditures, but not in excess of 25% of the gross income derived from farming during the taxable year.

(G) Any consolidated deduction for dividends paid on certain preferred stock of public utilities.

(2) Plus any consolidated net capital gain.

(3) Minus, in the case of an affiliated group including as members one or more corporations taxable as insurance companies, the combined additional capital loss deductions of these corporations (but in an amount not in excess of the consolidated net capital loss).

Apportionment of Consolidated Loss. If an affiliated group filing a consolidated return sustains a consolidated net operating loss and if there are included as members of this group one or more corporations which made separate returns, or joined in a consolidated return filed by another affiliated group, either in a preceding taxable year or in a succeeding one, the portion of the consolidated net operating loss attributable to the corporations severally will be determined. The portion will be determined in an amount proportionate to the net losses (capital net losses and ordinary net losses alike) of those affiliated corporations having net losses, to the extent that the losses were taken into account in the computation of the consolidated net operating loss.

A comparable rule exists in the case of consolidated net capital loss.

Allocation of Tax Liability. The tax liability of a consolidated group will be allocated among the members of the group in accordance with whichever of the following methods the group elects in its first consolidated return for that taxable year:

(1) The tax liability will be apportioned among the members of the group in accordance with the ratio which that portion of the consolidated taxable income attributable to each member of the group having taxable income bears to the consolidated taxable income.

(2) The tax liability of the group will be allocated to the several members of the group on the basis of the percentage of the total tax which the tax of that member if computed on a separate return would bear to the total amount of the taxes for all members of the group so computed.

(3) The tax liability of the group (excluding the tax increases arising from the consolidation) will be allocated on the basis of the contribution of each member of the group to the consolidated taxable income of the group. Any tax increases from the consolidation will be distributed to the several members in direct proportion to the reduction in tax liability resulting to these members from the filing of the consolidated return as measured by the difference between their tax liabilities determined on a separate return basis and their tax liabilities (determined without the 2% increase for

the consolidated return privilege) based on their contributions to the consolidated taxable income.

(4) The tax liability of the group will be allocated in accord with any other method selected by the group with the approval of the Commissioner of Internal Revenue.[35]

Supplementary Material

A. Suggested Reading.

Robert S. Holzman, *Arm's Length Transactions* (New York: The Ronald Press Co., 1958).

Robert Anthoine, "Transactions Between Related Taxpayers," *Proceedings of the Tulane Fifth Annual Tax Institute* (Indianapolis: The Bobbs-Merrill Co., Inc., 1956), p. 269.

Seymour Mintz, "Tax Disallowance of Loss on Sales Between Related Companies or Individuals," *Miami Law Quarterly*, 1950, Vol. IV, p. 277.

Morton F. Swift, "Why the Consolidated Return?" *Illinois Certified Public Accountant*, Spring, 1958, Vol. XX, #3, p. 25.

———, "The Consolidated Return," *TAXES—The Tax Magazine*, August, 1958, Vol. XXXVI, #8, p. 583.

B. Leading Cases.

Evils aimed at. *Alpha Tank & Sheet Metal Mfg. Co. v. United States*, 116 F. Supp. 721 (Ct. Cl., 1953).

What is arm's length? *Wilhelmina Dauth et al.*, 42 B.T.A. 1181 (1940).

Situations covered. *Simon J. Murphy Co. et al. v. Commissioner*, 231 F.2d 639 (6th Cir., 1956).

C. Questions.

1. "Any transaction between parties under common control is subject to reallocation by the Secretary of the Treasury." Is this statement true?
2. When the Internal Revenue Service seeks to reallocate items of income or expense between parties under common control, who has the burden of proof?
3. A United States and a French corporation was each owned by the same interests in the same proportions. The Internal Revenue Service sought to reallocate a portion of the profit on a sale between the corporations. Is the argument valid that the Service may not intervene where one of the parties is a foreign corporation not subject to the Internal Revenue Code?
4. The president of a corporation owned 51% of its stock. He sold to the corporation certain land that he had used for a filling station which he also owned. The transaction resulted in a tidy profit of $23,000 for him. Is this capital gain?
5. Is it possible to resist a reallocation by the Internal Revenue Service when parties under common control admittedly are dealing at less than arm's length?
6. Beta sells property to his grandmother, Gamma, at a loss of $5,000. She later sells the property to her sister, Sigma, at cost. Sigma sells

[35] I.R.C. Section 1552.

the property to an outsider at a profit of $7,000. How much is the recognized gain or loss to Beta, Gamma, and Sigma, respectively?

7. Partners in a textile manufacturing enterprise formed a corporation, shares of which went to the partners in the same proportions as their partnership equities. Are transactions between corporation and partnership subject to reallocation if conducted at less than arm's length? If such transactions are at less than arm's length, may the corporation insist on a reallocation even if the Internal Revenue Service does not propose it?
8. A parent corporation was in existence for years prior to the time that the company formed a subsidiary corporation. The companies were engaged in the same line of work, and the function of the subsidiary was to handle the more hazardous operations, so that if there were financial loss, all of the assets of the enterprise would not be endangered. May the Internal Revenue Service reallocate all of the income to the parent corporation on the ground that the subsidiary corporation serves no purpose except to reduce taxes?
9. Two corporations are 100% owned by the same interests in the same proportions. One corporation performs services for the other, at a fee set by the person who is general manager of both corporations. He chooses a fee arbitrarily, and the Internal Revenue Service seeks to effect a reallocation; but evidence discloses that the fee approximates what outsiders had been paying. Is a reallocation by the Internal Revenue Service possible? Would your answer be different if the fee were not equivalent to the rate charged to outsiders?
10. R, O, and T Corporations were all owned by the same persons in the same proportions; but the corporations were in different lines of manufacturing endeavor and had absolutely no contact with each other. R had some property that was no longer needed, and the property was listed with a broker for sale. O, which required such property, purchased it at a price above market. May the Internal Revenue Service reallocate a portion of this profit? If the property were made available by R to T, may the Internal Revenue Service charge intercompany rent at the going rates?
11. An individual sold property below market to a corporation that he controlled. At the same time, he sold similar property at the same price to an unrelated corporation. Is either transaction subject to reallocation by the Internal Revenue Service?
12. An individual owned property, which was sold by a county official for nonpayment of property taxes. The purchaser was a corporation owned by the same delinquent individual. Will the loss he sustained on the sale be recognized for tax purposes?
13. The officers of the Hammerklavier Corporation charged a service fee to the Waldstein Corporation, which was under common control, for processing a product. The officers believed that the fee charged was reasonable; but a Revenue Agent showed that similar processing was available elsewhere at a much lower figure. May the Internal Revenue Service make a reallocation in the face of total absence of wrongful purpose?
14. As a result of a transaction between two parties under common control, the taxes paid to the Government were reduced. On these facts alone is a reallocation permitted to the Internal Revenue Service?

15. An individual sold property at fair market value to his sister. He had a loss on the transaction. How is this loss treated for tax purposes?
16. Two men owned all of the stock of Corporation I. Their wives owned all of the stock of Corporation II. Is a reallocation by the Internal Revenue Service possible where a transaction is at less than arm's length?
17. Mr. Barry, a cash basis taxpayer, is the majority stockholder of the Pond Corporation, which is on the accrual basis. A Christmas bonus was authorized for him on December 24, but it was not paid until the following April 1, his birthday. In which year will the corporation get the deduction? In which year will he report the income?
18. Which of the following corporations may be included in a consolidated income tax return to be filed by A Corporation?
    (a) A Corporation owns 80% of the stock of B Corporation.
    (b) B Corporation owns all of the stock of C Corporation.
    (c) A Corporation owns all of the voting common stock of D Corporation and 50% of the preferred stock.
    (d) A Corporation owns all of the stock of E Corporation, a Mexican company that was formed to comply with local laws in Chihuahua as to ownership of property.
    (e) B Corporation owns all of the stock of F Corporation, a French company.
    (f) D Corporation owns all of the stock of G Corporation.
    (g) The stockholders of A Corporation individually own all of the stock of H Corporation.
19. A and B, who are brothers-in-law, each owns 50% of the stock of a corporation. A sells assets to the corporation at a loss. Will the loss be recognized for tax purposes, assuming the price represented fair market value?
20. The president of a corporation owns 20% of the stock. The remainder of the shares are widely held, with no one else owning as much as 1% of the stock. To all practical intent and purpose, he controls the corporation. Is a transaction between him and the corporation subject to reallocation if it is at less than arm's length?
21. Two corporations under common control were audited by a Revenue Agent for 1959 and 1960, and the intercompany arrangement, while examined, was not disturbed. A different Revenue Agent made the examination for 1961 and he sought to reallocate certain items. It was argued on behalf of the taxpayers that the arrangement already had been approved on audit and could not be upset now. Who is correct?
22. P Corporation owned all of the stock of S Corporation. P permits S to use the parent's general accounting office, warehouse, and trucks without charge. May the Internal Revenue Service reallocate a fair value for such facilities as intercompany rent?
23. Hendrick has an automobile that is used exclusively in his business, a sole proprietorship. He sells the car at a gain to his wife one year later. Is this a long-term capital gain?

28

BUYING AND SELLING TECHNIQUES

A number of techniques is available in the conduct of business affairs from a tax point of view. Sometimes it seems to be desirable to spread the reporting of income over a period of years in order to avoid "bunching." It might seem attractive to use such mechanisms as the sale and lease-back, or percentage rentals, or a lease with option to purchase. These and other alternative methods of carrying on business transactions are discussed in this chapter.

When property is sold, the full sales price is not always received in the year of sale. A taxpayer may not want to pay tax on sales proceeds before he receives them; in fact, he may never receive the proceeds, even though he has paid tax upon them. To provide relief in this situation, a taxpayer may elect under certain circumstances to spread profits from sales over the years during which payments are received. These sales may be classified in two categories: (1) sales on the installment plan and (2) deferred-payment sales not on the installment plan.

Installment Sales

The installment method of reporting income recognizes that each collection from the buyer consists of two elements: (1) a *return of cost* and (2) a *profit* on the sale. The seller may apportion his collections between these two elements, including in gross income only that portion which constitutes profit.

Sales Subject to Installment Treatment. The installment method may be used for the following types of sale:

(1) The sale of personal property by a dealer who is regularly engaged in the sale of personal property on the installment plan, regardless of the selling price or the amount collected in the year of sale.

(2) A casual or incidental sale of personal property for a price of more than $1,000, where collections, if any, in the year of sale do not exceed 30% of the selling price.

(3) The sale of real estate, regardless of the amount of the sale, where the collections, if any, in the year of sale do not exceed 30% of the selling price.[1]

Income on an installment sale is reported for tax purposes by use of a *gross profit percentage.* The gross profit percentage for any sale is the per cent that the gross profit to be realized is of the total *contract price.*

Illustration. If property is sold at a contract price of $2,000 and there is a gross profit of $500, the gross profit percentage is 25% ($500 divided by $2,000). Thus, 25% of each payment collected on the sale (including the down payment) is profit and must be included in gross income for the tax year in which collected. This percentage, once determined, remains the same throughout the period for which installment payments on the sale are received, and need not be redetermined each year.

Definitions. Several terms require special examination.

Payments *in the year of sale* include not only the down payment but also all other cash payments and property (other than evidences of indebtedness of the buyer) received in that year.

Selling price is the entire cost of the property to the buyer. It includes cash, carrying charges, the fair market value of other property conveyed to the seller, and any debt assumed or paid by the buyer.

Contract price is the purchaser's equity in the property. It is generally the amount to be received by the seller and is equal to the selling price when no debts are involved. If the selling price is payable partly in cash and partly on time, secured by a purchase money mortgage from the buyer to the seller, the selling price is the contract price. Often, however, the property is encumbered by a mortgage which the buyer assumes as part of the purchase price. When this occurs, two situations are possible:

(1) Where the mortgage assumed by the buyer does not exceed the seller's cost or other basis of the property, the contract price is equal to the sale price, less the amount of the loan, as the difference is all that the seller will collect directly from the buyer.

(2) Where the mortgage assumed by the buyer exceeds the seller's cost or other basis of the property, the seller has, in effect, recovered his entire basis plus an additional amount. The excess of the mortgage over the seller's basis is, in effect, an additional collection made on the sale of the seller's equity in addition to collections made or to be made from the buyer, and this excess

[1] I.R.C. Section 453.

should be included both in the contract price and in the payments received in the year of sale.

Expenses. Deductible expenses are not allocated to the years in which the profits from the sales of a particular year are to be returned as income. They must be deducted in the tax year in which they are paid or incurred.

Gross Profits Percentages. Collections in a taxable year are subjected to the gross profits ratio of the year in which occurred the sale, payments for which are now being collected.

Illustration. The records of a dealer in installment property show the following:

Year	Installment Sales	Gross Profit	Gross Profit Percentage
1959..............	$100,000	$ 42,000	42%
1960..............	280,000	120,400	43%
1961..............	300,000	123,000	41%

In computing his gross profit on his 1961 return, the dealer must take into account collections of payments on prior years' installment sales as follows:

Year of Sale	1961 Collections on Sales	Gross Profit Percentage	1961 Gross Profit
1959..............	$ 25,000	42%	$ 10,500
1960..............	190,000	43%	81,700
1961..............	160,000	41%	65,600
Total to be included in 1961 return......			$157,800

Change from Accrual Method. Were it not for a special rule, a taxpayer using the accrual method would have a duplicate tax should he shift from the accrual method to the installment method. In the year of sale, he would have included the amount of the sale in his gross income on the accrual method; if he had switched to the installment by the time of collection, he would have to apply his gross profits percentage of the year of sale to the amount collected against that sale, even though it already had been included in his gross income. But a special adjustment is provided to the extent that the gross profit for the same item sold is included in income twice. The adjustment is in the form of a reduction in tax for the year in which the profit is included the second time. The reduction is the amount of the tax attributable to the profit reported in the prior year but not in excess of the tax attributable to the profit in the year in which it is included the second time.

Illustration.

	First Year	Second Year	Third Year (Year of Change)
Gross profit from installment sales (receivable in five installments)	$100,000	–	$ 20,000 [1]
		$ 50,000	10,000 [2]
			20,000 [3]
Other income	80,000	200,000	150,000
Gross income	$180,000	$250,000	$200,000
Deductions	60,000	50,000	50,000
Taxable income	$120,000	$200,000	$150,000
Assuming a tax rate of	30%	50%	40%
Tax would be	$ 36,000	$100,000	$ 60,000

[1] From first-year sales.
[2] From second-year sales.
[3] From third-year sales.

COMPUTATION OF ADJUSTMENT

First-Year Item

In third year—

Tax attributable to first-year item.......... $\frac{\$20,000}{\$200,000} \times$ $ 60,000

(A) Tax attributable to second inclusion of gross profit from first year is .... $ 6,000

In first year—

Tax attributable to prior inclusion.......... $\frac{\$20.000}{\$180,000} \times$ $ 36,000

(B) Tax attributable to original inclusion is.......... $ 4,000
Adjustment in respect of first-year item is the lesser of (2) or (B), or $ 4,000

Second-Year Item

In third year—

Tax attributable to second-year item.......... $\frac{\$10,000}{\$200,000} \times$ $ 60,000

(C) Tax attributable to second inclusion of gross profit from second year is .... $ 3,000

In second year—

Tax attributable to prior inclusion.......... $\frac{\$10,000}{\$250,000} \times$ $100,000

(D) Tax attributable to original inclusion is.......... $ 4,000
Adjustment in respect of second-year item is lesser of (C) or (D), or .... $ 3,000

The tax for the third year would be reduced by $4,000 plus $3,000, a total of $7,000. The tax would then be $53,000 in the third year.

Repossessions. When a buyer defaults on his contract and a seller repossesses the property, either through a voluntary surrender by the buyer or through foreclosure, the result to the seller may be a gain, a bad debt, or other loss.

Where mortgaged property is sold for less than the amount of the debt, whether to the creditor or another purchaser, and the portion of indebtedness remaining unsatisfied after the sale is wholly or partially uncollectible, the creditor may deduct the uncollectible amount as a bad debt for the taxable year in which it becomes wholly worthless or is charged off as partially worthless. In such a case, the bad debt deduction is further limited to the amount of the indebtedness which constitutes capital or represents an item the income of which has been reported by the creditor. But, in the case of a foreclosure, the creditor is not entitled to any deduction for a bad debt unless it is clearly shown that the debtor remained liable for the unpaid portion of the debt after the property was sold.

In addition to a bad debt, gain or loss is realized if there is a difference between the amount of the obligations of the debtor applied to the purchase or bid price of the property and the fair market value of the property, if the creditor buys in the property, provided the obligations surrendered constitute capital or represent items the income of which has been reported by the creditor. But the fair market value of the property is presumed to be the amount for which it is bid in by the creditor in the absence of clear and convincing proof to the contrary. If the creditor subsequently sells the property thus acquired, the basis for determining gain or loss is the fair market value of the property at the date of acquisition.

Where the purchaser defaults in his payments, gain or loss to the seller upon repossession is the difference between (1) the fair market value of the property repossessed and (2) the basis in the hands of the seller of the obligations of the purchaser which are satisfied or discharged upon the repossession, or are applied by the seller to the purchase or bid price of the property, with proper adjustment for any other amounts realized or costs incurred in connection with the repossession. The basis in the hands of the seller of the obligations of the purchaser thus satisfied, discharged, or applied upon the reacquisition of the property is the excess of the face value of the obligations over the income which would be reported if the obligations were paid in full.

If the property is repossessed in connection with a sale reported on the installment method, the repossession gain or loss is of the same character as the gain or loss on the original sale.

Illustration.

Fair market value of property repossessed by dealer		$450
Basis in hands of the dealer of the obligations of the purchaser at the time of repossession:		
Selling price of the property	$500	
Less: Payments made on contract	180	

Face value of obligations at time of repossession.........	$320	
Less: Income which would have been reported if the obligations had been paid in full, $320 times 20% (mark-up at the time of original sale)...........................	64	256
Taxable gain (ordinary income)................................		$194

The property should be included in inventory at $450.

Disposition of Installment Obligations. Gain or loss will result when installment obligations are satisfied at other than face value or when they are disposed of by the vendor. These gains or losses are considered as resulting from the sale or exchange of the property in respect of which the installment obligations were received.

If the obligations are satisfied at other than face value or are sold or exchanged, the gain or loss is measured by the difference between the basis of the obligations and the amount realized. If the obligations are distributed, transmitted, or disposed of other than by sale or exchange, the gain or loss is measured by the difference between the basis of the obligations and their fair market value at the time of the distribution, transmission, or disposition.

The basis of an installment obligation is the excess of the face value of the obligation over the income which would be reportable were the obligation paid in full.

Illustration. A vendor sells for $20,000 certain property that he had acquired in a prior taxable year for $10,000. In the year of the sale the seller received $5,000 in cash and the purchaser's notes for the remainder of the selling price, or $15,000, payable in subsequent years. In a later taxable year, before the purchaser made any further payments, the seller sold the notes for $13,000 cash:

Selling price of property (also contract price)..................	$20,000
Cost of property...	10,000
Total profit	$10,000
Percentage of profit, or proportion of each payment returnable as income, $10,000 ÷ $20,000, or 50%.	
Face value of notes..	$15,000
Amount of income reportable if the notes were paid in full, 50% of $15,000	7,500
Excess of face value of notes over amount of income reportable if the notes were paid in full..................................	$ 7,500

Deferred Payment Sales

If the requirements mentioned above for reporting sales on the installment plan cannot be met, gain from the sale is reported in the year of sale, whether the cash or accrual method is used. But a seller may elect to report on the deferred payment sales method. Under this method, the sales price takes into account any cash plus the fair market value of the buyer's obligations and other property received as consideration by the seller. The obligations of the buyer received by the seller are considered the equivalent of cash to the extent of their fair market value.

The profit realized at the time of sale is the excess of the sale price (including the purchaser's obligations at their fair market value and reduced by the costs, if any, of making the sale) over the adjusted basis of the property. Thus, if there is a gain, the return of capital is accomplished in the year of the sale and that entire capital is offset against the proceeds realized in order to arrive at the profit reportable in the year of sale.

Illustration. Certain real estate was sold for $50,000, payable $40,000 down and the balance over a period of five years at $2,000 a year, plus 4% interest. The balance payable was represented by the purchaser's note, which had a fair market value of 75% of its face value. A commission of 5%, or $2,500, was paid to a broker for negotiating the sale. The real estate cost the seller $25,000 and was held by him for more than six months.

Computation of profit:		
Selling price		$50,000
Less: Commission		2,500
Selling price less commission		$47,500
Adjusted basis of property		25,000
Profit to be realized		$22,500
Profit recognized in year of sale:		
Cash		$40,000
Market value of note (75% of $10,000)		7,500
Total realized in year of sale		$47,500
Less: Commission	$ 2,500	
Cost of property	25,000	27,500
Profit recognized in year of sale		$20,000

The $20,000 may be a capital gain. But as collections are made on the note, the amount by which each collection exceeds its proportionate valuation is included in the seller's return as ordinary income. In this illustration, 25% of each principal payment received on the $10,000 note would be reported as ordinary income in year of collection. The interest on the note also would be ordinary income.

Repossessions. In the case of deferred sales not on the installment plan, bad debts are treated in the same manner as described above for installment sales.

Gain or loss upon repossession of real property is figured by one of two methods, dependent upon whether the seller (1) retained title to the property or (2) transferred title to the purchaser.

(1) Where the seller retained title and the purchaser defaults in any of his payments, if the seller repossesses the property, gain or loss to the seller for the year in which the property is repossessed is measured by the difference between:

(A) The entire amount of the payments received on the contract and retained by the seller, plus the fair market value at the time of repossession of fixed improvements placed on the property by the purchaser, and

(B) The sum of the profits previously returned as income in connection with the transaction and an amount representing what would have been a proper adjustment for exhaustion, wear and tear, obsolescence, amortization, and depletion of the property during the period the property was in the hands of the purchaser had not the sale been made.

The basis of property reacquired, where the seller retained title, is the original basis at the time of the sale, plus the value at the time of repossession of any fixed improvements placed on it by the purchaser. The basis of the property must be reduced by an amount equal to the depreciation the seller would have been entitled to during the period the property was held by the purchaser, had not the sale been made.

(2) Where the seller did not retain title and the purchaser defaults in any of his payments, if the seller repossesses the property, the method of determining gain or loss to the seller depends upon whether the reconveyance is voluntary or involuntary.

If the seller accepts a *voluntary* reconveyance of the property in partial or full satisfaction of the unpaid portion of the purchase price, the receipt of the property so reacquired, to the extent of its fair market value at that time (including the fair market value of fixed improvements placed on the property by the purchaser) is considered as the receipt of payment on the obligations satisfied. Thus, if the fair market value of the property reacquired is greater than the basis of the obligations of the purchaser so satisfied, the excess constitutes ordinary income. But if the value of the property reacquired is less than the basis of these obligations, the difference may be deducted as a bad debt if wholly uncollectible or charged off as partially uncollectible. If the obligations satisfied are securities which are capital assets, any gain or loss resulting from the transaction is capital.

If the reconveyance is *involuntary,* gain or loss is the difference between:

(1) The amount of the obligations of the purchaser which are applied to the purchase or bid price of the property (to the extent that these obligations constitute capital or represent an item the income of which has been included by him in gross income), and

(2) The fair market value of the property (which, however, is presumed to be the amount for which it is bid in by the taxpayer in the absence of clear and convincing proof to the contrary).

Any portion of the obligation not applied to the purchase or bid price may be deducted as a bad debt.

The basis of property reacquired, where the seller transferred title, is the fair market value of the property at the time of reacquisition.

Long-term Contracts

If a taxpayer is engaged in a building, installation, or construction activity that requires more than one year to complete, he may, with the permission of the Commissioner of Internal Revenue, use the long-term contract method. Gross income from the contract is reported either by (1) the percentage of completion method or (2) the completed contract method. This method may not be used for contracts involving the mere sale of completed property.

Percentage of Completion Method. Under the percentage of completion method, the taxpayer reports as gross income that part of the contract price representing the percentage of the contract which was completed during the taxable year. He deducts from this gross income all expenditures made during the taxable year on account of the contract, taking into account materials and supplies on hand at the beginning and end of the taxable year for use in connection with the work under the contract, but not yet so applied. The tax return for the year should be accompanied by a certificate of an architect or engineer showing the percentage of the work completed during the year.

Illustration. On May 1, 1960, a builder contracted to construct an edifice for $100,000. On December 31 of that year, his engineer certified that the contract was 35% completed. After taking into consideration the inventories of materials and supplies on hand, he found he had expended $28,000 on his contract in 1960. When the building was completed and accepted in August, 1961, he had spent $80,000 to complete the contract. Under the percentage of completion method, he had a gross income from his contract of $35,000 to report in his 1960 return. He could deduct $28,000 in his 1960 return, the amount spent to complete 35% of the contract. The balance of the contract price, $65,000, and the balance of the expenses, $52,000, are reported in his 1961 return.

Completed Contract Method. Under the completed contract method, the taxpayer reports gross income from the contract in the year the contract is completed and accepted, even though he may have received a part or all of the contract payment in a prior year. He also defers until the year of completion all deductions properly allocable to the contract.

Illustration. A contractor using the completed contract method started the construction of a building in 1960 and finally completed his contract, which was accepted, in 1962. His expenses, allocated to the job, were $50,000 during 1960, $90,000 during 1961, and $30,000 during 1962. He received $80,000 during 1960, $100,000 during 1961, and $35,000 during 1962 as payments from the contract. His income tax returns for 1960 and 1961 will show no income or expenses attributable to this particular contract. His income tax return for 1962 will disclose the total income and expenses of this job, and will reflect his profit of $45,000 from this contract.

Long-term Compensation

This subject is discussed in Chapter 11.

Installment Buying

The treatment of interest when property is purchased on the installment plan is considered in Chapter 9.

Sale and Lease-back

The sale and lease-back involves an arrangement under which the owner of property sells it to another person; according to the plan, the property is then leased back from the new owner by the original owner. Certain aspects of this technique do not involve taxation. The original owner is able to improve his balance sheet position by converting fixed assets into cash. He may circumvent provisions in bond indentures, stock issues, bank credit agreements, etc., against borrowing; that is, he raises funds without having to borrow. He may be able to obtain the full value of his property in cash—perhaps more than market value—whereas a loan would only produce a part (70%, for example) of fair worth.

But there are also some important tax advantages, to be detailed below.

The mechanics of the sale and lease-back are simple. If property is sold for *more* than its value, the purchaser has sustained an economic loss. This loss is equated by having the original owner, who is now the tenant, pay more than the property in rent than the going rate. Ignoring the interest factor, the excess purchase price paid by the buyer is the same as the excess rental that the tenant will pay over the period of the lease. If property is sold for *less* than its value, the purchaser has received an economic benefit; and the new tenant will pay less rent than the going rate. If property is sold at fair market value, the rental will be the going rate.

The lease is generally for a long period of years.

The tax aspects are these:

(1) The original owner of the property may sell appreciated-value assets without recognition of taxable gain. Thus, if the assets are sold at adjusted book value, there will be no gain to tax. And appreciated-value assets may well be sold at cost or adjusted book value, to create the situation of having low rent to pay in the future.

(2) The original owner of the property may sell property for less than adjusted book value, in order to create a tax loss. Such a loss will be recognized for tax purposes if there was a business purpose in making the sale.[2]

(3) The original owner of the property, who is now the tenant, will be able to deduct the full rent that he pays on property used for business or nonbusiness purposes. If he had retained the property, he would have been able to take depreciation only on depreciable property. Thus, the greater proportion of the property that is represented by land, the greater the tax advantage of the sale and lease-back.

In most sale and lease-back arrangements, the property is sold for more or less than its fair market value. That would create a situation where the Internal Revenue Service could step in and reallocate the income or deductions of the parties under the arm's length provision of the Internal Revenue Code.[3] Or the loss might be denied because the transaction was between related parties.[4] See Chapter 27.

Regardless of the divergence of terms from what would prevail if a sale and lease-back were not involved, the transaction can be justified if the two parties are not under common control, nor are they related, and if each is selfishly bargaining for his own best interest. A taxpayer "would be entitled to deduct rent if it had sold its property in an arm's length transaction to a buyer having adverse interests and then had leased it back at a fair rental." [5] But such may not be the case when the parties to such an arrangement are under common control.[6]

Gift and Lease-back

Under a gift and lease-back arrangement, a person *gives* property to someone else and then leases it back. But this technique generally is dangerous; for one is not likely to give property to

[2] *Standard Envelope Manufacturing Co.*, 15 T.C. 41 (1950).
[3] I.R.C. Section 482.
[4] I.R.C. Section 267.
[5] *Riverpoint Lace Works, Inc.*, T.C. Memo. 1954–39, filed May 13, 1954.
[6] *Shaffer Terminals, Inc. v. Commissioner*, 194 F.2d 539 (9th Cir., 1952).

another person unless there is present, at least presumptively, a degree of family relationship or control. A gift and lease-back may not involve a bona fide transfer of property that would affect taxable income of the donor.[7]

Percentage Rentals

Sometimes, instead of paying a flat or sliding scale rental, landlord and tenant will agree that the rent will be a stipulated percentage of the tenant's sales, gross receipts, or comparable figure. In certain years, it is apparent, the rent paid may be considerably more or less than the rent that would have been paid under a standard lease arrangement. The tenant may like such an arrangement because when business is good, he can afford to pay a substantial rental, whereas when business is poor, the rent bill automatically is cut. This is a generally recognized type of lease. But where landlord and tenant are under common control, or are relatives, the legitimacy of the arrangement may be suspect. If the transaction was one that would have been entered into by an outsider dealing at arm's length, the relationship of the parties is not significant.[8] But a seemingly innocuous percentage rental may spell out an actual charge that is excessive.[9] This is particularly true if the parties realized in advance that because of a monopoly situation, receipts would be unusually high.[10]

Rent with Option To Buy

The owner of property may agree with a person who wishes to make use of the assets that this property will be rented, the tenant to have the option of purchasing the assets at any time; if the option is availed of, any rental payments made up to that point will be considered as part of the cost and will be applied to the purchase price. The arrangement, while legitimate in itself, may be misused for tax purposes. The so-called tenant may really be buying the property on a long-term installment basis. If it was the tenant's intention to make payments of purchase price in the guise of annual rentals, no rent deduction will be allowed even if the property is to be used for business or nonbusiness purposes; the payments will be regarded as capital expenditures for a period of

[7] *White v. Fitzpatrick,* 193 F.2d 398 (2d Cir., 1951).
[8] *Ray's Clothes, Inc.,* 22 T.C. 1332 (1954).
[9] *Abe Wender,* T.C. Memo. 1956–81, filed April 10, 1956.
[10] *Herbert Davis et al.,* 26 T.C. 49 (1956).

years. But if the tenant really was paying rent because he did not know as yet whether he actually would acquire the property, payments claimed as rent on tax returns for years prior to the time the option was exercised will not be disturbed. "If payments are large enough to exceed the depreciation and value of the property and thus give the payor an equity in the property, it is less of a distortion of income to regard the payments as purchase price and allow depreciation on the property than to offset the entire payment against the income of one year." [11] Rent was not allowed as a deduction where payments were found to have been installments on equipment purchases.[12]

In the absence of compelling factors indicating a different intent, it will be presumed that a conditional sales contract was intended if the total of the rental payments and any option payable approximates the price at which the asset could have been acquired by purchase at the time of entering into the agreement, plus interest and/or carrying charges. If the sum of the specified "rentals" over a relatively short part of the expected useful life of the asset approximates the price at which the asset could have been acquired by purchase at the time of entering into the agreement, plus interest and/or carrying charges on this amount, and the lessee may continue to use the equipment for an additional period approximating its remaining useful estimated life for relatively nominal payments, it may be assumed that the parties have entered into a sale contract, even though a passage of title is not expressly provided in the agreement.[13]

Where property was rented, with the tenant to have the option of acquiring it for $1 at the termination of the lease, no rent deduction was allowed. The rental charge of $10,750 for the year was entirely disproportionate to the $1 purchase price.[14]

Assignment of Right to Future Income

For a long time it had been believed that the assignment of rights to future income for a lump-sum payment involved capital gain. But it is now held that the consideration is taxable as ordinary income if it "seems essentially a substitute for what would otherwise be received at a future time as ordinary income." [15]

[11] *Chicago Stoker Corp.*, 14 T.C. 441 (1950).
[12] *Western Contracting Corporation*, T.C. Memo. 1958–77, filed April 30, 1958.
[13] Revenue Ruling 55–540, 1955–2 CB 39.
[14] *Quartzite Stone Co.*, 30 T.C., #47 (1958).
[15] *Commissioner et al. v. P. G. Lake, Inc. et al.*, 356 U.S. 260 (1958).

Sale of a Business in Bulk

When a going business is sold, "it is to be comminuted into its fragments, and these are to be separately matched against the definition" of capital or ordinary assets.[16] The parties should bargain and ultimately agree as to that part of the total consideration that is to be allocated to capital assets and to ordinary assets. In general, what the parties to the contract agree to will be controlling.[17] But where there is evidence to show that the allocation as between capital and ordinary assets is other than what the contract says, the agreement is not binding upon the Internal Revenue Service.[18] No agreement between the parties as to what is capital asset "could affect their character." [19]

Tax-free Exchange

Property held for productive use in trade or business or for investment may be exchanged without recognition of gain or loss for property of like kind; that is, property of the same general character which is not necessarily identical as to grade or quality.[20] Thus, where a taxpayer has property which has appreciated in value, he may dispose of it without recognition of gain by exchanging it for like property. See Chapter 17. If there is such an exchange, there is no recognition of gain or loss, even if the parties had not planned the transaction as a tax-free exchange and even if they were unaware of the implications.[21]

Where a taxpayer has property which has depreciated in value, he may find it to his interest to sell the property in order to establish a loss for tax purposes. Then other property may be purchased with the proceeds.

Identification of Property Sold

If a seller has several lots of an item (stocks, grain, etc.), it is presumed that the property he sells first is the property that he acquired first. But the vendor may not wish to have this "Fifo" rule apply. In that case, he must identify the lot that he intends to

[16] *Williams v. McGowan,* 152 F.2d 570 (2d Cir., 1946).
[17] *Fraser v. Nauts,* D.C., Ohio, 1925.
[18] *Particelli Estate,* T.C. Memo., Docket # #25439–40, entered February 20, 1952.
[19] *Glenmore Securities Corporation v. Commissioner,* 62 F.2d 780 (2d Cir., 1933).
[20] I.R.C. Section 1031.
[21] *W. D. Haden Company v. Commissioner,* 165 F.2d 588 (5th Cir., 1948).

sell. This may be done in several ways. The broker or other party making the sale may be given the specific property that is to be sold. The property may be identified by serial numbers or other identifying factors. The order of sale may make reference to "the property which I acquired on May 27, 1938."

Establishment of Intent

Taxability of a transaction may depend upon the seller's intent, either in entering upon the transaction or in the holding of an asset.

Losses are only allowed in the case of an individual if incurred in a trade or business or "incurred in any transaction entered into for profit . . ." [22]

An asset is not included in the capital asset classification if "held by the taxpayer primarily for sale to customers in the ordinary course of his trade or business." [23]

An individual may take a deduction for ordinary and necessary expenses paid or incurred during the taxable year "for the management, conservation, or maintenance of property held for the production of income . . ." [24]

Supplementary Material

A. Suggested Reading.

Robert S. Holzman, "How To Buy and Sell Real Estate, Business Property, and Business Assets," *Proceedings of the New York University Sixth Annual Institute on Federal Taxation* (Albany: Matthew Bender & Co., Inc., 1948), p. 383.

T. Hartley Pollock, "General Outline of Tax Considerations in Sales Decisions," *The Encyclopedia of Tax Procedures* (Englewood Cliffs, N.J.: Prentice-Hall, Inc., 1956), p. 919.

Harvey Greenfield and Frank K. Griesinger, *Sale Leasebacks and Leasing in Real Estate and Equipment Transactions* (New York: McGraw-Hill Book Co., Inc., 1958).

Willard J. Lassers, "Does a Lease-Back Save You Money?" *TAXES—The Tax Magazine,* April, 1954, Vol. XXXII, #4, p. 279.

A. H. Cohen, *Long Term Leases—Problems of Taxation, Finance and Accounting* (Ann Arbor, Mich.: University of Michigan Press, 1954).

L. J. Desmond, "Sales of Property Under the Deferred Payment Method," *TAXES—The Tax Magazine,* January, 1954, Vol. XXXII, #1, p. 40.

Robert L. Taylor, "Tax Relief for Income Attributable to Several Years," *TAXES—The Tax Magazine,* October, 1956, Vol. XXXVI, #10, p. 701.

[22] I.R.C. Section 165(c)(2).
[23] I.R.C. Section 1221(1).
[24] I.R.C. Section 212(2).

B. Questions.

1. If a sale is effected in one manner so as to produce a smaller amount of tax than is effected in the standard manner of the trade, may the Internal Revenue Service insist on the tax consequences of this standard pattern?
2. A dealer made a casual sale of property for $10,000, with a down payment of $1,000. The transaction resulted in a loss. May this be reported on the installment plan?
3. A Revenue Agent informed a credit jeweler that he would have to use the installment method on his tax returns, as that was standard practice in the industry. Will the jeweler be obliged to use this method?
4. A builder has a contract for the construction of a building. The contract was executed June 27, 1961, and provides for payment of $180,000 for the structure, which is to be completed November 15, 1962. Construction was begun by the builder on July 1, 1961. He uses the calendar year basis. On December 31, 1961, the architect certified that 25% of the work was completed. How much gross income will the builder report for 1961? How will he handle expenditures made that year in connection with the contract?
5. Over a 5-year period, a dealer determined that his gross profit percentage on installment sales averaged 22%. May he use this 22% for his future years?
6. A manufacturer (a sole proprietor) sells his business for $100,000. Included are inventories, receivables, fixed assets, and good will. How will the $100,000 be apportioned to the assets?
7. A dealer in installment property had gross profit ratios as follows: 1957, 31%; 1958, 29%; 1959, 26%; 1960, 28%; 1961, 30%. In 1961, his collections were as follows from sales in the years indicated: 1957, $18,000; 1958, $20,000; 1959, $25,000; 1960, $32,000; 1961, $10,000. What gross profit is to be reported for 1961?
8. A dealer made a casual sale on April 1 for $10,000, taking 10% down payment and notes for $3,000 due October 1 and each anniversary thereof. The first note was paid when due. May the transaction be reported on the installment plan? Would your answer be different if the first note had not been paid until six months after it was due?
9. Legion, an individual, purchased property for $50,000, the seller taking $40,000 in cash and a $10,000 mortgage on the property. On March 1, 1961, Legion sold the property for $60,000, including $10,000 in cash and the assumption of the mortgage (now $8,000) by the new purchaser. The balance is payable in notes for $2,000 each, payable every six months beginning September 1, 1961. Legion is on the calendar year basis.
   (a) May the transaction be reported on the installment basis?
   (b) What is the selling price?
   (c) What are the payments in the year of sale?
   (d) What is the contract price?
10. In 1960, Docile Corporation sold a piece of unimproved real estate for $20,000. The corporation acquired the property in 1948 at a cost of $10,000. During 1960, the corporation received $5,000 cash and vendee's notes for the remainder of the selling price, or $15,000, payable in subsequent years. In 1962, before the vendee made any further

payments, the corporation sold the notes for $13,000 in cash. The corporation makes its returns on the calendar year basis. How much income is to be reported for 1962?

11. Assume, in the previous problem, that Docile Corporation instead of selling the notes, distributed them in 1962 to its shareholders as a dividend. The fair market value of the notes at the time of distribution was $14,000. What is the taxable income to be reported for 1962?
12. The owner of a commercial building leased it to a restaurant corporation at an annual rental of $5,000 plus one-fifth of 1% of gross receipts. In 1961, the rent thus derived totaled $31,000. Rents for comparable properties on a flat-rate basis averaged $20,000. Will the transaction be interfered with by the Internal Revenue Service? Would your answer be different if the restaurant corporation were owned by the same party as the commercial building?
13. A corporation in the retail clothing industry decided to sell its building and lease it back for a period of years. The property had an adjusted basis of $200,000 and a fair market value of $280,000. The corporation sold the property to an unrelated investor for $200,000 and leased the premises back for $18,000 a year. What are the tax consequences to the corporation?
14. If, in the preceding question, the property had been sold for $350,000 and leased back for $32,000 a year, what are the tax consequences?
15. If, in the second preceding question, the property had been sold for $100,000 and leased back for $12,000 a year, what are the tax consequences?
16. As a result of an advertisement a piano teacher sold his old piano to a buyer for $3,000, accepting cash for $1,000 and $500 notes for the balance, one payable every six months.
    (a) May this be treated by the seller as an installment sale?
    (b) Is there any other manner in which the sale may be spread over a period of years? If so, describe it. Assume the teacher is on a calendar year basis and made the sale on January 1; the piano had a basis for tax purposes of $2,400.
17. In the preceding problem, assume the notes were only worth 80% of face value. Would your answer be different?
18. Cellers sells property to Byer on the installment plan for $10,000, payable $2,000 at the time of sale and $2,000 each year on the anniversary thereof. The property had an adjusted basis to Cellers of $9,000. After $4,000 in all had been paid, Byer went bankrupt, and Cellers took back the property, which then had a fair market value of $7,000. What are the tax consequences to Cellers in the year of default and repossession?
19. A contractor built a bridge for a municipality for $200,000. At the end of the first taxable year, 1960, the contract was ascertained to be 40% completed. Expenditures made in that year on the contract were $20,000, taking into account inventories of materials and supplies on hand. At the end of 1961, the contract was certified to be 60% completed, and expenditures on the same basis as in the preceding sentence were $35,000. In 1962, the bridge was completed; expenditures in that year were $25,000. How much is income in each year on the percentage of completion method?

20. The owner of an office building signed a contract in 1956 to rent the structure to a tenant for $40,000 a year for thirty years. At any time, the tenant was permitted to buy the building for $200,000, in which event all rent payments to date would be treated as installments of purchase price. In 1961, after five years' rentals had been paid, the tenant exercised his option to purchase the edifice. In what year does the sale take place for tax purposes? What is the cost to the new owner? How are the rent payments for 1956–1961 to be treated?
21. An individual sold 200 shares of corporate stock for $20,000, of which $15,000 was paid in cash and $5,000 was covered by the purchaser's notes having a fair market value of 90% of face. The note was payable in four equal installments of $1,250 beginning January 1 of the following year. The stock cost $13,000 and was held for more than six months. What is his gain or loss on the transaction?

29

TAX PLANNING

Legitimacy

There is nothing legally or morally reprehensible about tax planning. "Where for legitimate business purposes, a person has a choice of conducting his business transactions without tax liability, such a liability does not arise simply because it would have arisen if another process had been chosen."[1] The fact that a transaction might have resulted in a tax if achieved in another manner is not important. "Income tax liability must be determined by what actually takes place rather than by what might have taken place."[2]

In a celebrated dissent, Judge Learned Hand declared: "Over and over again courts have said that there is nothing sinister in so arranging one's affairs as to keep taxes as low as possible. Everybody does so, rich or poor; and all do right, for nobody owes any public duty to pay more than the law demands: taxes are enforced exactions, not voluntary contributions. To demand more in the name of morals is mere cant."[3]

A purpose to minimize or to avoid taxation is not an illicit motive.[4] But if a transaction is planned with a view to minimizing taxes, it will be subjected to careful examination. "Admittedly, and we have so found as a fact, the transaction was carried out in this particular form in order to minimize the tax thereon. Where transactions are carried out in that manner, we should scrutinize the transaction carefully in order to determine whether the statute has been strictly complied with."[5]

Theory of Tax Planning. Tax planning generally is a matter of alternatives. A course of action may take one of several forms. The selection may be made on the basis of the respective tax consequences. "This transaction might have been consummated in either

[1] *Commissioner v. Kolb,* 100 F.2d 920 (9th Cir., 1938).
[2] *J. Hampton Hoult et al.,* 24 B.T.A. 79 (1932).
[3] *Commissioner v. Newman,* 159 F.2d 848 (2d Cir., 1947).
[4] *Granite Trust Co. v. United States,* 238 F.2d 670 (1st Cir., 1956).
[5] *The Coca-Cola Co. v. United States,* 47 F. Supp. 109 (Ct. Cl., 1942).

one of three forms, and while substantially the same result would have been achieved by either, the tax liability might have been different. . . . In our opinion this conduct of the petitioners is not subject to adverse criticism. The avoidance of tax liability prior to its incurrence is an entirely different thing from evasion of tax liability after it is definitely incurred. If a transaction is carried out in such form as to avoid or reduce tax liability, it is not subject to legal censure, provided the method adopted is legal. . . . In the absence of fraud, it is immaterial that the method of effecting the transfer here in question was adopted by these petitioners for the express purpose of avoiding taxes." [6]

Tax planning, then, is legitimate in concept. Such planning involves the arrangement of one's affairs so that, when the transactions actually take place, the tax impact will be less than if the transaction had taken place in another manner.

The Pattern

Reduced to essential elements, there are few types of tax planning. But the variations on each theme are virtually without limit. The pattern of tax planning may be set up thus:

Income.	Not taxable.
	Partially taxable.
	Taxable at preferential rates.
	Taxable over a period of years.
	Taxable to plural entities.
	Taxable to persons in lower tax brackets.
	Ownership.
	Form of organization.
Expenses.	Fully deductible.
	Partially deductible.
	Deductions from adjusted gross income.
	Deductions that are tied to adjusted gross income.
	Deduction in the year most suitable.
	Deductions where there is an alternative method of treatment.
	Creating deductions.
	Utilization of deduction of another person.
	Deductions to gain other objectives.

Disposition of property.
Importance of records.
Traps to be avoided.

[6] *Georgia Savings Bank & Trust Company,* 28 B.T.A. 1152 (1940).

The ingenuity of taxpayers is boundless. The following examples of tax planning are illustrative, not complete.

Income

Not Taxable. Interest from the bonds of states and their political subdivisions is excluded from the definition of gross income. See Chapter 4.

Under certain circumstances, income earned abroad is not taxable; *e.g.,* where an individual has been outside of the United States for either of two stipulated periods. Income of nonresident alien individuals and of nonresident foreign corporations is not included in gross income if various tests are met. Special foreign treaties exempt named classifications of income. See Chapter 22.

What is received in a tax-free corporate reorganization may not be subject to tax. Individual shareholders (*e.g.,* qualified electing shareholders) may elect to have tax-free receipts. See Chapter 17.

When a tax-free exchange has taken place, that which is received is nontaxable. See Chapter 17.

The proceeds of an involuntary conversion may be tax-free. See Chapter 5.

Various types of fringe benefit do not constitute income to the recipient. See Chapter 11.

Income may be that of a tax-exempt organization. See Chapter 2.

If a person holds property that has appreciated in value, neither he nor anyone else may pay income tax on the appreciation; if he holds the property until he dies, the person who acquires this property by bequest or by devise gets the property with a basis that is (at the election of the executor or administrator) the value at the date of death or one year thereafter (or the value at any intervening date of disposition). See Chapter 6. Thus, the appreciation never has been subjected to income tax.

Partially Taxable. Interest from certain obligations of the United States is partially taxable. See Chapter 4.

In the case of the proceeds of an involuntary conversion, income may be taxable to a limited extent only. See Chapter 6.

In the case of a tax-free corporate reorganization or a tax-free exchange (Chapter 17), part of what is received may be included in gross income. This is discussed under heading of "boot."

Annuities and pensions may beget income that is subject to tax within certain limitations. See Chapters 11 and 12.

Taxable at Preferential Rates. The most common example of income that may be taxed at an alternative rate, if that produces a lower tax, concerns capital gains. Factors to be appraised in determining whether the gain is capital (that is, the gains from the disposition of capital assets, or assets that are so treated) include "the intent of the taxpayer, the general history of the property involved, the purpose of the acquisition, holding, and disposition of the property; the method of the acquisition and use; the lapse of time between the acquisition and sale; the general conduct of the operation, the number, frequency, and continuity of transactions, the activities of the taxpayer in promoting sales, soliciting customers, conducting a sales campaign, or advertising the property to attract purchasers." [7]

The selection of the *holding period* of the asset may determine the tax result. See Chapter 5.

Certain assets, although not capital assets by definition, may be given capital asset treatment under certain circumstances. See Chapter 5.

The form of doing business can govern the applicable tax rates; *e.g.*, as an individual, as a corporation, or as a single or multiple trust.

Taxable over a Period of Years. If the requisite tests can be met, income may be reported on the installment plan, or as a deferred sale not on the installment plan, or under the long-term contract method. See Chapter 28.

Income that is earned over a period of 36 months or more may qualify for the preferential treatment afforded to long-term compensation. See Chapter 11.

Where substantial contingencies or conditions have been placed upon income, there may be nothing to include in gross income until an element of certainty has been established. See Chapter 4.

Taxable to Plural Entities. An individual may proliferate his income by making bona fide gifts of income-producing properties to his relatives, dependents, or other persons, including charitable organizations. The fruit is taxed to the tree on which it grew. See Chapter 1.

The concept of *estate planning* is generally related to the idea of spreading one's income and properties. Many factors, tax and otherwise, are involved in estate planning; but it may be noted at this point that the subject is concerned with the disposition of an individual's properties (including, of course, income-producing

[7] *Fort Wentworth Corporation v. United States,* D.C., Ga., 1958.

properties) according to a custom-tailored plan, while the individual lives and at the time of his death (or subsequently).

Illustration. An individual realizes that any property which he owns at the time of his death will be included in his gross estate. That can mean *estate tax*. He therefore disposes of some of this property during his lifetime. Property that he thus gives away may be exempt from the *gift tax* either because (1) the donor has not yet used up his specific exemption for gift tax or (2) it is within his annual exclusion for gift tax purposes. Even if a gift is taxable, the rates are only about 75% of the estate tax rates.

Illustration. An individual would like to have his wife get the income from certain properties, should he die first; but he learns that if he leaves the property to his spouse, it may never reach his children. She may lose the property by mismanagement or may will it to a subsequent husband. Thus, her present husband sets up a trust, to which he transfers the property in question to hold in trust for his wife, the income to be paid as long as she lives. Upon her death, the trust would terminate and the property, under the terms of the original declaration of trust, would go to the children. In addition to nontax advantages, two sets of estate taxes have been eliminated: the tax upon the husband's property (technically, upon the *disposition* of it) upon his death and that upon his wife upon her death.

Estate planning is planned to meet the needs of individual taxpayers and their families or other persons. There may be a careful integration between income, estate, and gift taxes, with savings possible in each area.

The use of plural entities may be helpful to corporations. If the business activities of a company may be separated between several corporations, each of which has a business reason for a separate existence, these tax advantages are possible: (1) no one corporation may be subject to surtax, despite the size of total income of the enterprise; (2) there may be several surtax exemptions; (3) there may be several minimum accumulated earnings credits. See Chapter 16.

The use of plural entities may be helpful when trusts are used. A multiple trust arrangement may attain the objectives of a single trust but will allow several entities each to have an exemption; likewise, the income will be taxed at lower rates if it is spread between several taxpayers.

Taxable to Persons in Lower Tax Brackets. A person (including a corporation) may reduce the total impact of the income tax by having some of his income assigned to, or earned by, a person who is in a lower tax bracket. Thus, a man might take steps so that commissions he otherwise might earn would be earned by his son, who was in a lower tax bracket; or a corporation might arrange to have certain transactions carried on by an affiliate that was in a lower tax bracket. Of course, any arrangements between related parties are controlled by the rules peculiar to this subject. See Chapter 27. See also the concept about taxing the fruit to the tree on which it grew in Chapter 1.

Ownership. An asset should be recorded in the type of ownership that most nearly approaches the optimum tax condition under the circumstances—tenancy in common, joint tenants, etc. See Chapter 1.

Form of Organization. Income treatment may depend upon whether the taxpayer is set up as a sole proprietor, partnership, corporation, foreign corporation, etc.

Expenses

The classification of expenses might determine the extent, if any, to which deduction may be taken for tax purposes.

Fully Deductible. It is to the taxpayer's interest to see that expenses are fully deductible. This means that—

(1) They are not related to the production of nontaxable income. See Chapter 4.

(2) They are not regarded as unreasonable. See Chapter 9.

(3) They are not capital losses. See Chapter 5.

(4) They are not disallowed to any extent because they result from transactions with related parties. See Chapter 27.

(5) They are not allocable in whole or in part to principal.

(6) They are not treated as nondeductible expenses of nonresident aliens. See Chapter 22.

(7) They are not regarded as part of a tax-free exchange. See Chapter 17.

(8) They are not disqualified because of statutory provisions, such as the wash sales proviso. See Chapter 6.

(9) They are not limited or disallowed because of failure of proof. See Chapter 23.

Deductions for Adjusted Gross Income. It may be to an individual's interest to endeavor to have an item classified as a deduction *for* adjusted gross income rather than a deduction *from* adjusted gross income. If an item may be deducted in the former category, this deduction may be in addition to the optional deduction or standard deduction that is in lieu of all *other deductions.* See Chapter 24.

Deductions That Are Tied to Adjusted Gross Income. Sometimes a taxpayer may legitimately control the time of reporting items of income or expense. See Chapter 4. Then he should consider the effect upon items that relate to adjusted gross income.

Illustration. An individual has medical expenses sufficiently high to allow him a medical expense deduction for the taxable year. The lower the amount of adjusted gross income, the higher is the allowable medical expense deduction, for the deduction is the amount whereby medical expenses exceed 3% of adjusted gross income. See Chapter 15.

Illustration. An individual has substantial charitable contributions in the taxable year. It may be that he will lose some of the charitable contribution deduction, which is limited to 20% or 30% (depending upon the nature of the payee) of adjusted gross income. See Chapter 9. Then a larger amount of adjusted gross income will produce a larger tax deduction.

Deduction in the Year Most Suitable. Sometimes there is a choice as to the year in which a deduction will be taken. Typical examples are: business bad debts which become partially worthless; charitable contributions by accrual basis corporations; write-offs for loss on abandonments; admission of liability.

If a taxpayer can take a deduction in any one of several years (*e.g.*, the cost of painting an office), the deduction should be planned for the year when it is most desirable. Perhaps the taxpayer will want to take the deduction in a year when tax rates are particularly high, or when income is unusually large. Or the taxpayer might want to take a business expense in a year when there is a loss, in order to increase the amount of loss carryback or carryover. An arithmetical decision may have to be made: Is it better to reduce taxable income *this* year or to take a deduction in a year when a loss may be carried backward or forward to a year when the tax rate is higher?

Deduction Where There Is an Alternative Method of Treatment. There may be valid reasons for not closing a transaction until a subsequent period. In general, there is no loss until there is a closed transaction.

A taxpayer may have a choice as to whether he should repair a damaged piece of equipment or buy a new one. The cost of a repair is deductible. See Chapter 9. A new piece of equipment will have to be capitalized. But perhaps it will be advantageous to take the deduction over a period of subsequent years, via depreciation, when the taxpayer expects to be in a higher tax bracket.

The choice of a depreciation method (see Chapter 10) will determine the amount of deduction for a particular year. Is it advantageous to get fast initial write-offs? Or is it advisable to spread the deduction equitably over the useful life of the asset?

In negotiating a lease, the tenant may consider whether he wants to have a flat rental as a deduction or whether it would be advantageous to use a percentage rental, so that in years of high income there will be a greater tax deduction.

Valuation of inventory on the Lifo basis may provide a hedge against rising prices. See Chapter 7.

When securities or other assets of like kind are sold, the tax treatment will depend upon identification of the particular assets sold. Where the taxpayer has several items, or lots of item, of similar nature, the ordinary rules of first in, first out will apply, unless the taxpayer specifically identifies what he desires to have sold. Thus, there may be tax advantages in having a second lot of assets sold before the first one: the basis may be higher, so that there is less gain to report.

If a loss is possible, the taxpayer should consider whether other factors of the transaction make it advisable to forgo the loss by having the transaction treated as a tax-free exchange or a tax-free corporate reorganization (Chapter 17). The same is true in the case of an involuntary conversion or the disposition of one's principal residence (Chapter 6). It is within the taxpayer's power to cast the transaction (here, the replacement purchase) in the desirable form to have gain, partial gain or loss, or loss.

Is it desirable, in lieu of ordinary depletion, to take statutory depletion? See Chapter 10.

If a taxpayer pays items such as salaries on a contingency basis, a higher deduction may be possible in those years when a higher deduction is most desirable; that is, when profits are highest.

A sale may be made under a contract of sale, rather than a sales contract, if there are advantages in having the transaction be reported in a different year (Chapter 26) or with a different holding period (Chapter 8).

The taxpayer may have a choice as to whether he will take a foreign tax as a deduction or as a foreign tax credit. See Chapter 22.

Creation of Deductions. A taxpayer owning property on which there is modest depreciation or (as in the case of land) none at all may create a deduction by engaging in a sale and lease-back transaction. Such a transaction may also result in a deductible loss. See Chapter 14.

If a person purchases property for use in his business, the cost is not deductible but is recoverable over the life of the asset (assuming there is a depreciable asset) as depreciation. But a lease will convert this property to an expense item.

There are various ways of getting a tax deduction for contributions.

Illustration. An individual may set up an irrevocable trust for the benefit of a religious, charitable, or educational organization; *e.g.*, his alma mater. The contract provides for the transfer of money, securities, or other property to a trustee, to pay the entire income from the trust fund to the grantor for life, and to a secondary beneficiary (if one survives the grantor) for life. Under the contract, the trust will terminate upon the decease of the last survivor of the grantor and the secondary beneficiary, and the principal and any undistributed income will become a part of the general funds of the institution. The grantor will be entitled to deduct the present value of the remainder interest in what he transfers to the trustee in computing his taxable income for the year of the transfer. He will not realize gain or loss upon transfer of the property to the trust even though the property has appreciated in value since the date of acquisition by the grantor.[8] Inasmuch as the grantor under the agreement has retained a life interest in the income of the trust, he will be deemed to remain the owner of a portion of the trust; but to the extent that the current net income of the trust which is payable to the grantor or secondary beneficiary consists of tax-exempt interest, the income will be tax-exempt in the hands of the recipient. Capital gain realized on the sale of the property contributed to the trust will not be taxable to the grantor if it is added to the principal for future distribution to the remainderman (the institution). The capital gain will be includible in gross income of the trust. But the trust will be entitled to a deduction with respect to any capital gain which is paid to, or permanently set aside for the use of, the institution.

An individual is not entitled to a deduction for the rent that he pays on an apartment that he rents for personal purposes. But if he invests in the stock of a cooperative apartment house corporation in which he lives, a portion of what he pays as monthly "upkeep" or "carrying charges" may be deductible; that is, he may deduct that portion of property taxes and mortgage interest that is allocable to that proportion of the total represented by his investment. See Chapter 9.

Utilization of Deduction of Another Person. Under certain circumstances, losses or deductions of a corporation may be utilized by a successor, via the carryover route. See Chapter 14.

Deduction To Gain Other Objectives. A taxpayer may be entitled to a deduction that will be, in effect, a substantial subsidy in the cost of what the taxpayer would like to do.

Illustration. A corporation would like to provide retirement benefits for employees after long service, but the cost of such a program might be very expensive. If the plan is entitled to treatment as a qualified pension plan (see Chapter

[8] Revenue Ruling 55–275, C.B. 1955–1, 295.

11), the corporation is entitled to a tax deduction. If the corporation is in the 52% tax bracket, the Government is subsidizing 52% of the cost of the plan. Where the employees have no vested rights until after a long period of years (which may extend to the actual retirement date), the employer establishes an economic hold over veteran employees, who, very likely, would never think of leaving under their own power.

Similarly, in the form of allowable deductions, the Government may be paying a substantial cost of advertising campaigns, refurbishing an office, and the like.

Disposition of Property

Corporate-owned Property. If a corporation has appreciated-value property, what is in effect a double tax results should the corporation make the sale; shareholders also will be taxed when they receive dividends representative of their shares of the profit. Perhaps the property should go to the shareholders (1) as a distribution in liquidation or (2) as a dividend in kind. Under (1), the corporation will not have tax attributed to it if the requirements of I.R.C. Section 337 are met. See Chapter 17. Tax will not be so attributed under either (1) or (2) if the stockholders *primarily* negotiate the sale.

Insolvent Corporations. Liquidation of an insolvent corporation may result in the loss of valuable carrybacks or carryovers.[9] See Chapter 14.

If assets are to be disposed of, consideration should be given as to who the seller should be: insolvent corporation, stockholders, bondholders or other creditors, or successor corporation.

During the period of insolvency, decision should be made as to what is more important: to obtain a deductible loss for the present owners of the enterprise or to preserve the old basis of the assets for the new enterprise.

If it is desired to have a deductible loss, assets should be sold to outsiders and not transferred in reorganization.

Importance of Records

Tax planning may be *offensive* or *defensive*. Offensive planning is exemplified by the techniques and procedures mentioned in the chapter up to this point; that is, steps that the taxpayer may take in order to have income or deduction consequences follow a course

[9] I.R.C. Section 381.

of action. Defensive planning involves steps to protect the tax return as filed.

The essence of defensive tax planning is good records. No matter how legitimate a transaction may be, how meticulous the figures, how faithful to the letter and spirit of the Internal Revenue Code, the taxpayer still has the burden of proving his contention. See Chapter 23. Good records support the tax return and justify what has been done. A few examples will illustrate this point:

(1) Gain or loss on the disposition of assets requires the establishment of cost or other basis of the particular asset believed to have been disposed of and also the realization. Had other assets of similar type been held? Was any part of the original purchase price to have been allocated to other assets?

(2) A transaction is claimed to have been effected for a business purpose, not for the purpose of dodging taxes. Can a business purpose be established, one that demonstrably existed when the transaction was cast in the form it took? If the taxpayer was a corporation, may this purpose be buttressed by an appropriate notation in the corporate minutes? Are any other contemporary records available as evidence?

(3) A taxpayer sold all, or a substantial part, of his assets for a bulk price. Is it possible to establish what part of this consideration is to be allocated to inventory, depreciable property, intangibles, realty? The tax treatment will depend upon the proof of this allocation.

Traps

Tax planning is valueless, or downright expensive, if a course of action leads to consequences that do not beget the desired result. Generally, the worst consequence is fraud: a transaction is effected in a certain mold, which a court finds was the result of willful intent to violate a Federal statute.

But other consequences can be unpleasant and expensive. Examples:

(1) A corporation effects a recapitalization from preferred stock to bonds in order to get an interest deduction. But receipt of the bonds is deemed to be a taxable dividend to the shareholders; the corporation loses the interest deduction because the debentures are deemed to be really the old stock in another form; and the corporation, because its income was increased retroactively by the disallowed deduction, runs into difficulties with the accumulated earnings tax.

(2) An individual sells stock to unrelated parties in order to establish a tax loss. But he reacquires substantially the same stock within thirty days, and his loss is disallowed as a wash sale. See Chapter 6. Meanwhile, he may be involved with a negligence penalty and several years' interest.

(3) An individual has property which has depreciated in value. He cannot use this property in his business any longer; but in order to save brokerage commissions, he trades the property for other property instead of selling it. This is a tax-free exchange, and the loss is not recognized for tax purposes. See Chapter 17.

(4) An individual has property which has depreciated in value. The only interested party is his brother. The would-be seller establishes what is unquestionably an arm's length price by selling a few units of the same type of property to an outsider. Loss on the sale to his brother is disallowed under I.R.C. Section 267, even though loss on a similar sale to an outsider at the same time is recognized. See Chapter 27.

(5) Shares of a corporation are sold in order to get capital gains treatment. But collapsible corporation treatment is imposed, and ordinary income results. See Chapter 17.

Other common traps to be avoided are constructive receipt of income and constructive ownership of stock. See Chapter 1. Apparently unrelated actions, perhaps in different taxable years, may be treated as phases of a single step transaction. See Chapter 1.

Any tax return election that is binding (and virtually every such election *is* binding) may be a trap. An election is made that saves a certain amount of tax the first year. But in the second and all subsequent years, the consequences of the election are that higher tax is due than if the election had not been made. The Commissioner of Internal Revenue will not agree to a change. What spelled good sense (and dollars) in one year proved to be poor tax planning in the long run.

In a course in taxation, it may seem self-defeating for a book to suggest that nontax considerations may be more important than tax considerations. But that is sometimes the case. Examples:

(1) A wealthy individual, in order to reduce his income tax, transfers some income-producing properties as a bona fide, irrevocable gift to his son, who is in a much lower tax bracket. Subsequently the son marries; and when Junior and his bride are killed in an automobile accident, the properties all go to the wife's relatives. Subsequently the wealthy father loses his once-prosperous business. The assets that he had transferred to save taxes cannot support him in his penurious old age.

4

(2) An individual, in order to reduce taxes, claims that his wife is a member of a family partnership. She is not; but he argues his case so persuasively that the partnership is recognized. Subsequently there is a divorce or separation, and, as a partner, she claims her share of the partnership assets and business. It is too late for him to change his position. His original contention had satisfied the Secretary of the Treasury. The wife was satisfied. Everyone was satisfied, except the individual who had thought up a perfectly executed plan.

On that dismal theme, this book comes to an end.

Supplementary Material

A. Suggested Reading.

Sydney A. Gutkin and David Beck, *Tax Avoidance vs. Tax Evasion* (New York: The Ronald Press Co., 1958).

John S. Pennell, "Tax Planning at the Time of Incorporation," *TAXES—The Tax Magazine,* December, 1957, Vol. XXXV, #12, p. 927.

Jerome R. Hellerstein, "Planning the Corporation," *Proceedings of the Tulane Seventh Annual Tax Institute* (Indianapolis: The Bobbs-Merrill Co., Inc., 1958), p. 416.

Robert Merritt, "Basic Tax Considerations Upon the Purchase of a Corporate Business," *Tax Planners Quarterly,* March, 1957, Vol. I, #1, p. 75.

Samuel F. Mirandy, "Tax Planning for the Corporate Official," *Lybrand Journal,* 1959, Vol. XL, #1, p. 50.

Reuel L. Olson and R. L. Gradeshar, *Saving Income Tax by Short Term Trusts* (Englewood Cliffs, N.J.: Prentice-Hall, Inc., 1956).

Harry J. Rudick, "The Problem of Personal Income Tax Avoidance," *Law and Contemporary Problems,* Spring, 1940, Vol. VII, #2, p. 243.

G. L. Cohen, "Transfers and Leasebacks to Trusts: Tax and Planning Considerations," *Virginia Law Review,* January, 1957, Vol. XLIII, #1, p. 31.

Robert Emerson Potts, "A Psychologist Looks at Estate Planning," *The Journal of the American Society of Chartered Life Underwriters,* Fall, 1956, Vol. X, #4, p. 303.

B. Leading Case.

Right to save taxes. *Gregory v. Helvering,* 293 U.S. 465 (1935).

C. Questions. (These are not necessarily based on this chapter.)

1. Where a transaction would produce a lower tax if handled in a certain manner, is tax avoidance involved should this alternative manner be followed?
2. What is the practical difference between tax avoidance and tax evasion?
3. What are the advantages of spreading income among several entities? Are there limitations to the extent that a taxpayer may do this? What are the disadvantages?

4. An individual purchased bonds of a municipality because, unlike railroad bonds, the interest is tax-exempt. Is this tax avoidance or evasion?
5. How may property that has appreciated in value be disposed of without recognition of taxable gain?
6. An individual has invested most of his wealth in the stock of a corporation, which he controls. He is concerned about who will buy the stock and pay the proceeds to his wife when he dies. What would you suggest?
7. How may a taxpayer correlate his rental deduction and the productivity of the property?
8. An individual believes that as long as he works, he will not need the income from his investments; but upon his retirement in fifteen years, he will need the investment income to add to his modest pension. How may he avoid paying any income tax on investment income until he retires?
9. How may the year of taxability of a sale be controlled by a contract of sale?
10. A merchant buys out the business of a well-established tradesman and pays a specific sum for the latter's promise not to compete with him. How may a tax deduction be gotten for this payment? Does the seller have taxable income?
11. A taxpayer is aware that increasing scarcities of merchandise have caused inventory prices to rise considerably. Sale of goods is the corporation's chief income-producing factor. What tax procedure seems indicated?
12. How may ordinary income be converted into capital gain? Is this advisable?
13. If a corporation is involved in a tax-free reorganization, but management wants to take advantage of a loss that would be denied in a tax-free reorganization, what should be done to insure the deductibility of this loss?
14. How may a loyal alumnus of a college create tax benefits for his Alma Mater without tax cost to himself? How may he regard gifts to the college as tax boons to himself?
15. How may long-term income be spread over a period of years? Is this advisable?
16. A corporate group has been filing consolidated income tax returns for several years. The election is expensive, as a deficit company formerly in the group has now been liquidated. What should be done?
17. To what extent may a taxpayer control the time of deduction of a bad debt?
18. How may a corporation's capital structure determine its income tax liability?
19. There are various sections of the tax law that were designed to prevent an individual from gaining tax advantages in transactions with persons with specified degrees of relationship. Is there anything to prevent such transactions with trusted friends?
20. If a contract is hedged with various contingencies, may the tax consequences of a transaction be controlled as to time?
21. An individual is in an 80% tax bracket. How can he limit the tax payable upon the business that he operates as a sole proprietorship?

22. An individual has equipment used in his business, a sole proprietorship. Some of the assets could be disposed of at a gain; some, at a loss. How should he plan the disposition of these assets?
23. A corporation has assets that have appreciated in value. To what extent may tax liability be avoided by distributing these assets to the shareholders, who are in lower tax brackets?
24. How can proper identification of what is sold control the taxability of a transaction?
25. If interest from municipal bonds is tax-exempt, why should not a taxpayer place his entire investment funds in such securities?
26. How may the proceeds of a sale be spread over several tax years?
27. How does the choice of parties with whom transactions are carried on determine the taxability of a transaction?
28. How does the form of property ownership determine the taxability of income from that property?
29. An individual owns shares, at a very low basis, in a small corporation. A large corporation wishes to acquire these shares. How may he dispose of his stock without payment of tax on the appreciation?
30. An accrual-basis taxpayer makes a sale, but it does not wish to pay tax on the sale until payment is received. What may be done?
31. Hendrick and Wilhelmina, who are married, file on the calendar year basis, using the cash method. On January 1, Hendrick dies. Is there any reason why his executor, a trust company, would not desire to have a joint return filed for the year of death?
32. How can an employer make employment financially more satisfactory to an employee without subjecting the latter to income taxes?
33. How may a taxpayer relate the depreciation deduction to actual usage of his depreciable assets?
34. A taxpayer had capital losses in 1956, and in 1961 the unused carryover will expire. What action should be taken to prevent the wasting of the carryover in 1961?
35. The principal shareholders of a corporation are disturbed that, should one of their number die, his widow or estate might sell the decedent's stock to raise money to pay the death taxes, with the result that undesirable outsiders might be brought into the company. Or the heirs might force the liquidation of the corporation to get cash for their stock. How may this be prevented?
36. Late in 1961, a corporation on the accrual basis plans to make contributions to a charity, but it is not certain as yet whether the deductions will be more advantageous in 1961 or 1962. What steps may be taken to retain a choice as to the year of deduction?

Appendix

FEDERAL INCOME TAX FORMS

Form 1040A **U. S. INDIVIDUAL INCOME TAX RETURN (Less than $10,000 total income)** **1959**

Please use this preaddressed card.

1. Check and correct any information already printed in this box.

2. Your Social Security No. Wife's Social Security No.

3. If you owe any Federal tax for years before 1959, enter here the Internal Revenue District where the account is outstanding ______

4. If married, is your wife (husband) filing separately? . . . . ☐ Yes ☐ No
If "yes," write her (his) name

5. WAGES SHOWN ON FORMS W-2 AND OTHER INCOME		INCOME TAX WITHHELD	EMPLOYER'S NAME. Where employed. Write (W) before name of each of wife's employers
If total income (item 9) is $10,000 or more, OR if other income (item 6) is over $200, you must use Form 1040.	$	$	
6. INTEREST, DIVIDENDS, AND OTHER WAGES — Yours		7. Total income tax withheld	8. If you had an expense allowance or charged expenses to your employer, see instruction 8 and check here ☐ if appropriate.
6. — Wife's			
9. TOTAL INCOME →	$	$	Enclose Forms W-2, Copy B. If your income was $5,000 or more, you must compute your tax. However, if your income was less than $5,000, you may have the Internal Revenue Service compute your tax by omitting items 10, 11, and 12. *If you compute your own tax,* ← *pay balance (item 11) in full with return to your District Director.*
10. Enter tax from Tax Table or from tax computation schedule →			
11. If item 10 is larger than item 7, enter **balance due** →			
12. If item 7 is larger than item 10, enter **refund** →			List your exemptions and SIGN on other side.

U. S. TREASURY DEPARTMENT ● INTERNAL REVENUE SERVICE (OVER) **PLEASE DO NOT BEND, PIN OR TEAR THIS CARD**

13. EXEMPTIONS FOR YOURSELF AND WIFE

Check blocks which apply. Check for wife if she had no income OR if her income is included in this return.

			Enter number of exemptions checked →
(a) Regular $600 exemption	☐ Yourself	☐ Wife	
(b) Additional $600 exemption if 65 or over at end of 1959	☐ Yourself	☐ Wife	
(c) Additional $600 exemption if blind at end of 1959	☐ Yourself	☐ Wife	

14. EXEMPTIONS FOR YOUR CHILDREN AND OTHER DEPENDENTS (List below)

NAME ▶ Enter figure 1 in the last column to right for each name listed (Give address if different from yours)	Relationship	ANSWER ONLY FOR DEPENDENTS OTHER THAN YOUR CHILDREN: Months lived in your home. If born or died during year also write "B" or "D"	Did dependent have gross income of $600 or more?	Amount YOU furnished for dependent's support. If 100% write "ALL"	Amount furnished by OTHERS including dependent	
				$	$	→
						→
						→
						→
						→
						→

15. Enter total number of exemptions listed in items 13 and 14 above →

SIGN → HERE

I declare under the penalties of perjury that to the best of my knowledge and belief this is a true, correct, and complete return.

(Your signature) (Date) (If this is a joint return, wife's signature) (Date)

● If this is a joint return, BOTH HUSBAND AND WIFE MUST SIGN even if only one had income.

FORM **1040W**

U.S. Treasury Department
Internal Revenue Service

U.S. INDIVIDUAL INCOME TAX RETURN—1959

Optional Short Form for Wages and Salary Income and Not More Than $200 of Interest and Dividends

• Attach Check or Money Order Here •

Name ______________________________
(PLEASE PRINT. If this is a joint return of husband and wife, use first names and middle initials of both)

Home address ______________________________
(Number and street or rural route)

____
(City, town, or post office) (Postal zone number) (State)

Your Social Security Number	Occupation	Wife's Social Security Number	Occupation

INCOME

1. Wages, salaries, bonuses, tips, other compensation, and excess of expense allowances. (See instructions, page 3)

Employer's Name	Where Employed (City and State)	(a) Income Tax Withheld	(b) Wages, etc.
		$	$

2. Totals ....
3. Excludable "Sick Pay" if included in line 1 (See instructions, page 3 and attach statement)....
4. Subtract line 3 from line 2..
5. (a) Total dividends $________ less exclusion of $________ ....Balance
   (b) Interest (If total of lines (a) and (b) is over $200, use Form 1040) ....
6. Total of lines 4 and 5..

Check if Unmarried "Head of Household" ☐, or "Surviving Widow or Widower" with dependent child ☐. (See instructions, p. 4)

• Forms W-2 Here •

TAX TABLE COMPUTATION

If line 6 is less than $5,000 and you do not itemize personal deductions:
- •List your exemptions in Schedule A on page 2. •Find your tax in the table on page 8 of instructions. •Check proper box and enter tax on line 11. •Omit lines 7 through 10.....

● Attach Copy B of

TAX RATE SCHEDULE COMPUTATION

7. If your deductions are itemized, check here ☐ and enter total from Schedule B.............
If your deductions are not itemized and line 6 is $5,000 or more, enter the smaller of 10 percent of line 6 or $1,000 ($500 if a married person filing a separate return).................
8. Subtract line 7 from line 6 ....
9. Multiply $600 by total number of exemptions claimed on line 3, Schedule A, page 2, and enter here.
10. Subtract line 9 from line 8 ....
Figure your tax on this amount by using the appropriate tax rate schedule on page 7 of instructions and enter the tax on line 11.

TAX DUE OR REFUND

11. Total tax. Check whether figured from Tax Table ☐, or Tax Rate Schedule ☐ ....
12. Payments and Credits
(a) Tax withheld (line 2(a) above). Attach Forms W-2, Copy B...
(b) Payments and credits on 1959 Declaration of Estimated Tax...
District Director's office where paid ____________
(c) Dividends received credit (See instructions, page 4)..........

If either you or your wife worked for more than one employer, see page 3 of instructions **TOTAL**→

13. If your tax (line 11) is larger than your payments (line 12), enter the **BALANCE DUE** here→
Pay in full to "Internal Revenue Service." If less than $1.00, file return without payment.
14. If your payments (line 12) are larger than your tax (line 11), enter the **OVERPAYMENT** here→
15. Amount of line 14 to be (a) Credited on 1960 estimated tax $________, (b) Refunded $________

Did you receive an expense allowance or reimbursement, or charge expenses to your employer? .. ☐ Yes ☐ No
If "Yes," did you submit an itemized accounting of expenses to your employer? (See page 3, instructions.) ☐ Yes ☐ No

Is your wife (husband) filing a separate return for 1959? ☐ Yes ☐ No
If "Yes," enter the name and do not claim the exemption on this return.

If you owe any Federal tax for years before 1959, enter here the Internal Revenue District where the account is outstanding.

County in which you live→

I declare under the penalties of perjury that this return (including any accompanying schedules and statements) has been examined by me and to the best of my knowledge and belief is a true, correct, and complete return. If the return is prepared by a person other than the taxpayer, his declaration is based on all the information relating to the matters required to be reported in the return of which he has any knowledge.

Sign here____

(Taxpayer's signature and date) (If this is a joint return, BOTH HUSBAND AND WIFE MUST SIGN) (Wife's signature and date)

____

(Signature of preparer other than taxpayer) 16—75395-1 (Address) (Date)

SCHEDULE A.—EXEMPTIONS (See page 5 of instructions)

Page 2

1. Exemptions for yourself and wife

Check blocks which apply. Check for wife only if all of her income is included in this return, or if she had no income.

(a) Regular $600 exemption.......................... ☐ Yourself ☐ Wife
(b) Additional $600 exemption if 65 or over at end of 1959.. ☐ Yourself ☐ Wife
(c) Additional $600 exemption if blind at end of 1959..... ☐ Yourself ☐ Wife

Enter number of exemptions checked →

2. Exemptions for your children and other dependents (List below)

→ If an exemption is based on a multiple-support agreement of a group of persons, attach the declarations described on page 5 of instructions.

NAME ▶ Enter figure 1 in the last column to right for each name listed (Give address if different from yours)	Relationship	ANSWER ONLY FOR DEPENDENTS OTHER THAN YOUR CHILDREN: Months lived in your home. If born or died during year also write "B" or "D"	Did dependent have gross income of $600 or more?	Amount YOU furnished for dependent's support. If 100% write "ALL"	Amount furnished by OTHERS including dependent	
				$	$	→
						→
						→
						→
						→
						→
						→
						→

3. Enter the total number of exemptions claimed on lines 1 and 2 ....

SCHEDULE B.—ITEMIZED DEDUCTIONS—If You DO NOT Use Tax Table or Standard Deduction

If Husband and Wife (Not Legally Separated) File Separate Returns and One Itemizes Deductions, the Other Must Also Itemize

State to whom paid. If necessary write more than one item on a line or attach additional sheets. Please put your name and address on any attachments.

Contributions		

	Total paid but not to exceed 20% of line 6, page 1, except as described on page 5 of instructions....	$
Interest		
	Total interest	
Taxes		
	Total taxes	
Medical and dental expense (If 65 or over, see instructions, page 6)	Submit itemized list. Do not enter any expense compensated by insurance or otherwise. 1. Total cost of medicine and drugs .... $ 2. 1 percent of line 6, page 1 .... 3. Subtract line 2 from line 1 .... 4. Other medical and dental expenses .... 5. Total of lines 3 and 4........ 6. Enter 3 percent of line 6, page 1........ $ 7. Allowable amount (excess of line 5 over line 6). (See instructions, page 6, for limitations)....	
Other Deductions (See page 6 of instructions and attach information required)		
	Total	
	TOTAL DEDUCTIONS (Enter here and on line 7, page 1)........	$

U.S. GOVERNMENT PRINTING OFFICE 16—75395-1

● ATTACH CHECK OR MONEY ORDER HERE ●

FORM **1040**

U.S. Treasury Department
Internal Revenue Service

U. S. INDIVIDUAL INCOME TAX RETURN—1959

or Other Taxable Year Beginning ______________, 1959, Ending ______________, 19____
(PLEASE TYPE OR PRINT)

Name ____
(If this is a joint return of husband and wife, use first names and middle initials of both)

Home address ____
(Number and street or rural route)

____
(City, town, or post office) (Postal zone number) (State)

Your Social Security Number	Occupation	Wife's Social Security Number	Occupation

Exemptions

1. Check blocks which apply. Check for wife only if all of her income is included in this return, or if she had no income.
   - (a) Regular $600 exemption .... ☐ Yourself ☐ Wife
   - (b) Additional $600 exemption if 65 or over at end of taxable year. ☐ Yourself ☐ Wife
   - (c) Additional $600 exemption if blind at end of taxable year..... ☐ Yourself ☐ Wife

   Enter number of exemptions checked → ____
2. List first names of your children who qualify as dependents; give address if different from yours. ____________ ____________ ____________ **Enter number of children listed** → ____
3. Enter number of exemptions claimed for other persons listed at top of page 2.......... ____
4. Enter the total number of exemptions claimed on lines 1, 2, and 3.......... ____

● FORMS W-2 HERE ●

Income

5. Enter all wages, salaries, bonuses, commissions, tips, and other compensation before payroll deductions (including any excess of expense account or similar allowance paid by your employer over your ordinary and necessary business expenses. See instructions, pp. 5–6.)

Employer's Name	Where Employed (City and State)	(a) Wages, etc.	(b) Income Tax Withheld
		$	$
	Enter totals here →	$	$

6. Less: Excludable "Sick Pay" in line 5 (See instructions, page 7. Attach required statement.)... ____
7. Balance (line 5 less line 6).......... $____
8. Profit (or loss) from business from separate Schedule C.......... ◆ ____
9. Profit (or loss) from farming from separate Schedule F.......... ◆ ____

If the social security tax (FICA) withheld from wages exceeded $120 because you or your wife had more than one em-

● ATTACH COPY B OF

Tax due or refund

10. Other income (or loss) from page 3 **(Dividends, Interest, Rents, Pensions, etc.)** . ______ | ployer, see instructions, page 5.

11. Adjusted Gross Income (sum of lines 7, 8, 9, and 10) . . . . ♦ $______

● **Check if unmarried "Head of Household"** ☐**, or "Surviving Widow or Widower" with dependent child** ☐. **(See instructions pp. 7-8)**

12. TAX on income on line 11. (If line 11 is under $5,000, and you do not itemize deductions, use Tax Table on page 16 of instructions to find your tax and check here ☐. If line 11 is $5,000 or more, or if you itemize deductions, compute your tax on page 2 and enter here the amount from line 9, page 2). $______

If income was all from wages, omit lines 13 through 16

13. (a) Dividends received credit from line 5 of Schedule J. . . . . $______

(b) Retirement income credit from line 12 of Schedule K. . . . ______

14. Balance (line 12 less line 13). . . . . $______

15. Enter your self-employment tax from separate Schedule C or F. . . . . ______

16. Sum of lines 14 and 15. . . . . $______

17. (a) Tax withheld (line 5 above). Attach Forms W–2, Copy B. . . . . $______

(b) Payments and credits on 1959 Declaration of Estimated Tax (See page 8, instructions.) ● ______ $______

District Director's office where paid ______

18. If your tax (line 12 or 16) is larger than your payments (line 17), enter the **BALANCE DUE** here ⟶ $______
Pay in full with this return to "Internal Revenue Service." If less than $1.00, file return without payment.

19. If your payments (line 17) are larger than your tax (line 12 or 16), enter the **OVERPAYMENT** here ⟶ $______
If less than $1.00, the overpayment will be refunded only upon application.

20. Amount of line 19 to be: (a) Credited on 1960 estimated tax $______; (b) Refunded $______

Did you receive an expense allowance or reimbursement, or charge expenses to your employer? . ☐ Yes ☐ No (See page 6, instructions.)
If "Yes," did you submit an itemized accounting of expenses to your employer? . . . . ☐ Yes ☐ No

County in which you live.	Is your wife (husband) filing a separate return for 1959? ☐ Yes ☐ No. If "yes," enter her (his) name and do not claim the exemption on this return.	If you owe any Federal tax for years before 1959, enter here the Internal Revenue District where the account is outstanding.

I declare under the penalties of perjury that this return (including any accompanying schedules and statements) has been examined by me and to the best of my knowledge and belief is a true, correct, and complete return. If the return is prepared by a person other than the taxpayer, his declaration is based on all the information relating to the matters required to be reported in the return of which he has any knowledge.

Sign here______

(Taxpayer's signature and date) (If this is a joint return, BOTH HUSBAND AND WIFE MUST SIGN) (Wife's signature and date)

______ ______ ______

(Signature of preparer other than taxpayer) (Address) (Date)

o70—16—75313-1

Form 1040—1959 **EXEMPTIONS FOR PERSONS OTHER THAN YOUR WIFE AND CHILDREN** Page 2

Name	Relationship	Months lived in your home. If born or died during year also write "B" or "D"	Did dependent have gross income of $600 or more?	Amount YOU furnished for dependent's support. If 100% write "All"	Amount furnished by OTHERS including dependent
				$	$

Enter on line 3, page 1, the number of exemptions claimed above.

→ If an exemption is based on a multiple-support agreement of a group of persons, attach the declarations described on page 5 of instructions.

ITEMIZED DEDUCTIONS—IF YOU DO NOT USE TAX TABLE OR STANDARD DEDUCTION

If Husband and Wife (Not Legally Separated) File Separate Returns and One Itemizes Deductions, the Other Must Also Itemize

State to whom paid. If necessary write more than one item on a line or attach additional sheets.

Please put your name and address on any attachments.

Contributions		
	Total paid but not to exceed 20% of line 11, page 1, except as described on page 8 of instructions. . . .	$
Interest		
	Total interest	
Taxes		
	Total taxes	

Medical and dental expense

(If 65 or over, see instructions, page 10)

Submit itemized list. Do not enter any expense compensated by insurance or otherwise

1. Cost of medicines and drugs IN EXCESS of 1 percent of line 11, page 1 .... $
2. Other medical and dental expenses ....
3. Total .... $
4. Enter 3 percent of line 11, page 1 ....
5. Allowable amount (excess of line 3 over line 4). (See instructions, page 10, for limitations.) ....

Other Deductions

(See page 10 of instructions and attach information required)

Total

TOTAL DEDUCTIONS (Enter here and on line 2 of Tax Computation, below).......... $

TAX COMPUTATION—IF YOU DO NOT USE THE TAX TABLE

1. Enter Adjusted Gross Income from line 11, page 1 .... $
2. If deductions are itemized above, enter total of such deductions. If deductions are not itemized ***and line 1, above, is $5,000 or more,*** enter the smaller of 10 percent of line 1 or $1,000 ($500 if a married person filing a separate return)..........
3. Balance (line 1 less line 2)..........
4. Multiply $600 by total number of exemptions claimed on line 4, page 1 ....
5. Taxable Income (line 3 less line 4)..........
6. Tax on amount on line 5. Use appropriate tax rate schedule on page 15 of instructions. Do not use Tax Table on page 16..........
7. If you had capital gains and the alternative tax applies, enter the tax from separate Schedule D ....
8. Tax credits. If you itemized deductions, enter:
   - (a) Credit for income tax payments to a foreign country or U. S. possession (Attach Form 1116)..... $
   - (b) Tax paid at source on tax-free covenant bond interest and credit for partially tax-exempt interest.....
   - (c) Total.......... **Enter here** →
9. Enter here and on line 12, page 1, the amount shown on line 6 or 7 less amount claimed on line 8(c)... $

c70—16—75313-1 GPO

IF INCOME WAS ALL FROM SALARIES AND WAGES, TEAR OFF THIS PAGE AND FILE ONLY PAGES 1 AND 2

Schedule A.—INCOME FROM DIVIDENDS (Income from Savings (Building) and Loan Associations and Credit Unions should be entered as interest in Schedule B)

	Amount	
1. Name of qualifying corporation declaring dividend (See instructions, page 11): (Indicate by (H), (W), (J) whether stock is held by husband, wife, or jointly)		
	$	
2. Total	$	
3. Exclusion of $50 (If both husband and wife received dividends, each is entitled to exclude not more than $50 of his (her) own dividends)		
4. Excess, if any, of line 2 over line 3. Enter here and on line 1, Schedule J	$	
5. Name of nonqualifying corporation declaring dividend:		
6. Enter total of lines 4 and 5		$

Schedule B.—INCOME FROM INTEREST (This includes interest credited to your account)

Name of payer	Amount	Name of payer	Amount
	$		$
		Enter total here→	

Schedule D Summary.—GAINS AND LOSSES FROM SALES OR EXCHANGES OF PROPERTY

1. From sale or exchange of capital assets (from separate Schedule D) ....
2. From sale or exchange of property other than capital assets (from separate Schedule D) ....

Schedule E.—INCOME FROM PENSIONS AND ANNUITIES (See instructions, page 12)

1. Investment in contract .... $______
2. Expected return .... $______
3. Percentage of income to be excluded (line 1 divided by line 2) .... %
4. Amount received this year .... $______
5. Amount excludable (line 4 multiplied by line 3) ....
6. Taxable portion (excess of line 4 over line 5) ......

Part II.—Where your employer has contributed all or part of the cost and your contribution will be recovered tax-free within three years.
If your cost was fully recovered in prior years or if you did not contribute to the cost, enter the total amount received in line 5 omitting lines 1 through 4.

1. Cost of annuity (amounts you paid) . . $______
2. Cost received tax-free in past years . . ______
3. Remainder of cost (line 1 less line 2) . . $______
4. Amount received this year .... $______
5. Taxable portion (excess, if any, of line 4 over line 3) . .

Schedule G.—INCOME FROM RENTS AND ROYALTIES

1. Kind and location of property	2. Amount of rent or royalty	3. Depreciation (explain in Sch. I) or depletion	4. Repairs (attach itemized list)	5. Other expenses (attach itemized list)
	$	$	$	$
1. Totals	$	$	$	$

2. Net income (or loss) from rents and royalties (column 2 less sum of columns 3, 4, and 5) ....

Schedule H.—OTHER INCOME

1. Partnerships (name and address) ______
2. Estates or trusts (name and address) ______
3. Other sources (state nature) ______

Total income (or loss) from above sources (Enter here and on line 10, page 1) .... $

Form 1040—1959

Page 4

IF INCOME WAS ALL FROM SALARIES AND WAGES, TEAR OFF THIS PAGE AND FILE ONLY PAGES 1 AND 2

Schedule I.—EXPLANATION OF DEDUCTION FOR DEPRECIATION CLAIMED IN SCHEDULE G

1. Kind of property (if buildings, state material of which constructed). Exclude land and other nondepreciable property	2. Date acquired	3. Cost or other basis	4. Depreciation allowed (or allowable) in prior years	5. Method of computing depreciation	6. Rate (%) or life (years)	7. Depreciation for this year

Schedule J.—DIVIDENDS RECEIVED CREDIT (See instructions, page 14)

1. Amount of dividends on line 4, Schedule A .... $
2. Tentative credit (4 percent of line 1) ....

LIMITATION ON CREDIT

3. Tax shown on line 12, page 1, plus amount, if any, shown on line 8(b), page 2 ....
4. 4 percent of taxable income ....

Taxable Income Means:
(a) If tax is computed on page 2, the amount shown on line 5, page 2.
(b) If Tax Table is used, the amount shown on line 11, page 1, less 10 percent thereof, and less the deduction for exemptions ($600 multiplied by the number of exemptions claimed on line 4, page 1).

5. Dividends received credit. Enter here and on line 13(a), page 1, the smallest of the amounts on line 2, 3, or 4, above .... $

Schedule K.—RETIREMENT INCOME CREDIT (See instructions, page 14)

This credit does not apply
1. If you received pensions or annuities of $1,200 or more from Social Security or Railroad Retirement;
2. If you are under 65 years of age and had "earned income" of $2,100 or more; OR
3. If you are 65 or over and under 72, and had "earned income" of $2,400 or more.

If separate return, use column B only. If joint return, use column A for wife and column B for husband →	A	B
Did you receive earned income in excess of $600 in each of any 10 calendar years before the taxable year 1959? Widow or widowers see instructions, page 14	☐ Yes ☐ No	☐ Yes ☐ No

If answer above is "Yes" in either column, furnish all information below in that column.

	Column A		Column B	
1. Retirement income for taxable year:				
(a) **For taxpayers under 65 years of age:** Enter only income received from pensions and annuities under public retirement systems and included in line 11, page 1, of this return	$		$	
(b) **For taxpayers 65 years of age or older:** Enter total of pensions and annuities, interest, and dividends included in line 11, page 1, and gross rents included in column 2, Schedule G, page 3, of this return				
LIMITATION ON RETIREMENT INCOME				
2. Maximum amount of retirement income for credit computation	$ 1,200	00	$ 1,200	00
3. Deduct:				
(a) Amounts received in taxable year as pensions or annuities under the Social Security Act, the Railroad Retirement Acts, and certain other exclusions from gross income				
(b) Earned income received in taxable year: (This line does not apply to persons 72 years of age or over)				
(1) Taxpayers under 65 years of age, enter amount in excess of $900				
(2) Taxpayers 65 or over and under 72, enter amount in excess of $1,200				
4. Total of lines 3(a) and 3(b)				
5. Balance (line 2 minus line 4)				
6. Line 5 or line 1, whichever is smaller				
7. Tentative credit (20 percent of line 6)				

8. Total tentative credit on this return (total of amounts on line 7, columns A and B)		
LIMITATION ON RETIREMENT INCOME CREDIT		
9. Amount of tax shown on line 12, page 1		
10. Less: Dividends received credit from line 5, Schedule J, above		
11. Balance (line 9 less line 10)		
12. Retirement income credit. Enter here and on line 13(b), page 1, the amount on line 8 or line 11, whichever is smaller	$	

U. S. GOVERNMENT PRINTING OFFICE c70—16—75313-1

SCHEDULE C (Form 1040)

U. S. Treasury Department—Internal Revenue Service

PROFIT (OR LOSS) FROM BUSINESS OR PROFESSION

(Compute Social Security Self-Employment Tax on Page 3)

1959

Attach this schedule to your Income Tax Return, Form 1040 — Partnerships, Joint Ventures, Etc., Must File On Form 1065

For Calendar Year 1959, or other taxable year beginning ________, 1959, and ending ________, 19

Name as shown on page 1, Form 1040 ________

If you had more than one business, or husband and wife had separate businesses, a separate page 1 of Schedule C must be completed for each business.

A. Principal business activity: ________ (Retail trade, wholesale trade, lawyer, etc.) ________ (Principal product or service)
(See instructions, page 2)

B. Business name: ________ **C.** Employer's Identification Number: ________

D. Business location: ________ (Number and street or rural route) ________ (City or post office) ________ (State)

1. Total receipts $________, less allowances, rebates, and returns $________		$________
2. Inventory at beginning of year	$________	
3. Merchandise purchased $________, less any items withdrawn from business for personal use $________	________	
4. Cost of labor (do not include salary paid to yourself)	________	
5. Material and supplies	________	
6. Other costs **(explain in Schedule C–2)**	________	
7. Total of lines 2 through 6	$________	
8. Inventory at end of year	________	
9. **Cost of goods sold** (line 7 less line 8)		________
10. **Gross profit** (line 1 less line 9)		________

OTHER BUSINESS DEDUCTIONS

11. Salaries and wages not included on line 4 (exclude any paid to yourself)	$________	
12. Rent on business property	________	
13. Interest on business indebtedness	________	

C

14. Taxes on business and business property ....

15. Losses of business property **(attach statement)** ....

16. Bad debts arising from sales or services..........

17. Depreciation **(explain in Schedule C-1)**..........

18. Repairs **(explain in Schedule C-2)** ....

19. Depletion of mines, oil and gas wells, timber, etc. **(attach schedule)**..........

20. Amortization **(attach statement)**..........

21. Other business expenses **(explain in Schedule C-2)**..........

22. Total of lines 11 through 21..........

23. Net profit (or loss) (line 10 less line 22). Enter here; on line 24, page 3; and on line 8, page 1, Form 1040. . $

Schedule C-1. EXPLANATION OF DEDUCTION FOR DEPRECIATION CLAIMED ON LINE 17

1. Kind of property (if buildings, state material of which constructed). Exclude land and other nondepreciable property	2. Date acquired	3. Cost or other basis	4. Depreciation allowed (or allowable) in prior years	5. Method of computing depreciation	6. Rate (%) or life (years)	7. Depreciation for this year
		$	$			$

Schedule C-2. EXPLANATION OF LINES 6, 18, AND 21

Line No.	Explanation	Amount	Line No.	Explanation	Amount
		$			$

COMPUTATION OF SOCIAL SECURITY SELF-EMPLOYMENT TAX
(See Instructions—Page 4)

▶ **If you had wages of $4,800 or more which were subject to the deduction for social security, do not fill in this page.**
▶ **Complete only one page 3; if you had more than one business, combine profits (or losses) from all of your businesses on this page.**
▶ **Each self-employed person must file a separate schedule. See instructions, page 4, for joint returns and partnerships.**

NAME OF SELF-EMPLOYED PERSON (as shown on social security card)

24. Net profit (or loss) shown on line 23, page 1 **(Enter combined amount if more than one business)**	$			
25. Add to net profit (or subtract from net loss) losses of business property shown on line 15, page 1				
26. Total (or difference)			$	
27. Net income (or loss) from excluded services or sources included on line 26 (See "Exclusions," page 4)				
Specify excluded services or sources				
28. Net earnings (or loss) from self-employment—				
(a) From business (line 26 less any amount on line 27)			$	
(b) From partnerships, joint ventures, etc. (other than farming)				
(c) From service as a minister, member of a religious order, or a Christian Science practitioner. Enter only if you elect Social Security coverage by filing Form 2031 (See instructions, page 4).				
(d) From farming reported on line 12 or 13, separate Schedule F (Form 1040)				
29. Total net earnings (or loss) from self-employment reported on line 28. Enter here and on line 6 below. **(If line 29 is under $400, you are not subject to self-employment tax. Do not fill in rest of page.)**			$	
30. The largest amount of combined wages and self-employment earnings subject to social security tax is	$ 4,800	00		
31. Total wages, covered by social security, paid to you during the taxable year. (For "Covered" wages see "F. I. C. A. Wages" box on Form W-2.) Enter here and on line 7, below				

32. Balance (line 30 less line 31) .... $

33. Self-employment income—line 29 or 32, whichever is smaller. Enter here and on line 8, below............ $

34. Self-employment tax—take 3¾% of the amount on line 33. (You can do this by multiplying the amount on line 33 by .0375.) Enter this amount here and on line 15, page 1, Form 1040 .... $

Important.—The amounts reported on the form below are for your social security account. This account is used in figuring any benefits, based on your earnings, payable to you, your dependents, and your survivors. Fill in each item **accurately** and **completely**, but do not detach.

SCHEDULE SE (Form 1040)
U. S. Treasury Department
Internal Revenue Service

U. S. REPORT OF SELF-EMPLOYMENT INCOME 1959

For Crediting to Your Social Security Account

1. Indicate year covered by this return (even though income was received only in part of year):
☐ Calendar year 1959 ☐ Other taxable year beginning ______________, 1959, ending ______________
If less than 12 months, was short year due to (a) ☐ Death, or (b) ☐ Change in accounting period, or (c) ☐ Other.

2. BUSINESS ACTIVITIES SUBJECT TO SELF-EMPLOYMENT TAX (Grocery Store, Restaurant, etc.)

3. BUSINESS ADDRESS (Number and Street, City or Post Office, Postal Zone Number, State)

4. SOCIAL SECURITY ACCOUNT NUMBER OF PERSON NAMED IN ITEM 5 BELOW ➔

5. PRINT OR TYPE NAME OF SELF-EMPLOYED PERSON AS SHOWN ON SOCIAL SECURITY CARD
PRINT OR TYPE HOME ADDRESS (Number and Street or Rural Route)
(City or Post Office, Postal Zone Number, State)

PLEASE DO NOT WRITE IN THIS SPACE

6. ENTER TOTAL EARNINGS FROM SELF-EMPLOYMENT SHOWN ON LINE 29 ABOVE.. $

7. ENTER WAGES, IF ANY, SHOWN ON LINE 31 ABOVE...... $

8. ENTER AMOUNT SHOWN ON LINE 33 ABOVE............ $

SE

o48—16—75307-1 GPO

SCHEDULE D (Form 1040)

U. S. Treasury Department—Internal Revenue Service

GAINS AND LOSSES FROM SALES OR EXCHANGES OF PROPERTY

Attach this schedule to your Income Tax Return, Form 1040

1959

For Calendar Year 1959, or other taxable year beginning , 1959, and ending , 19

Name and Address as shown on page 1 of Form 1040

(I) CAPITAL ASSETS

Short-Term Capital Gains and Losses—Assets Held Not More Than 6 Months

a. Kind of property (if necessary, attach statement of descriptive details not shown below)	b. Date acquired (mo., day, yr.)	c. Date sold (mo., day, yr.)	d. Gross sales price (contract price)	e. Depreciation allowed (or allowable) since acquisition or March 1, 1913 (attach schedule)	f. Cost or other basis and cost of subsequent improvements (if not purchased, attach explanation)	g. Expense of sale	h. Gain or loss (column d plus column e less sum of columns f and g)
1.							$

2. Enter your share of net short-term gain (or loss) from partnerships and fiduciaries.........

3. Enter unused capital loss carryover from 5 preceding taxable years **(Attach statement)**.........

4. Net short-term gain (or loss) from lines 1, 2, and 3......... $

Long-Term Capital Gains and Losses—Assets Held More Than 6 Months

a.	b.	c.	d.	e.	f.	g.	h.
5.							$

6. Enter the full amount of your share of net long-term gain (or loss) from partnerships and fiduciaries.........

7. Net long-term gain (or loss) from lines 5 and 6......... $

8. Combine the amounts shown on lines 4 and 7, and enter the net gain (or loss) here . . . . . . $

9. If line 8 shows a GAIN—Enter 50 percent of line 7 or 50 percent of line 8, whichever is smaller. **(Enter zero if there is a loss or no entry on line 7)** . . . . . .

10. Deduct line 9 from line 8. Enter balance here and on line 1, Schedule D Summary on page 3 of Form 1040 . . . . . . $

11. If line 8 shows a LOSS—Enter here and on line 1, Schedule D Summary, Form 1040, the **smallest** of the following: (a) the amount on line 8; (b) taxable income computed without regard to capital gains and losses and the deduction for exemptions; or (c) $1,000 . . . . . . $

COMPUTATION OF ALTERNATIVE TAX.—Use only if the net long-term capital gain exceeds the net short-term capital loss, or if there is a net long-term capital gain only, and you are filing (a) a separate return with taxable income exceeding $18,000, or (b) a joint return, or as a surviving husband or wife, with taxable income exceeding $36,000, or (c) as a head of household with taxable income exceeding $24,000.

12. Enter the amount from line 5, page 2, of Form 1040 . . . . . . $

13. Enter amount from line 9 above . . . . . .

14. Balance (line 12 less line 13) . . . . . . $

15. Enter tax on amount on line 14 (Use applicable tax rate schedule on page 15 of Form 1040 Instructions) . . . . . . $

16. Enter 50 percent of line 13 . . . . . .

17. Alternative tax (line 15 plus line 16). If smaller than amount on line 6, page 2, Form 1040, enter this alternative tax on line 7, page 2, Form 1040 . . . . . . $

(II) PROPERTY OTHER THAN CAPITAL ASSETS

a. Kind of property (if necessary, attach statement of descriptive details not shown below)	b. Date acquired (mo., day, yr.)	c. Date sold (mo., day, yr.)	d. Gross sales price (contract price)	e. Depreciation allowed (or allowable) since acquisition or March 1, 1913 (attach schedule)	f. Cost or other basis and cost of subsequent improvements (if not purchased, attach explanation)	g. Expense of sale	h. Gain or loss (column d plus column e less sum of columns f and g)
1.							$

2. Enter your share of non-capital gain (or loss) from partnerships and fiduciaries . . . . . .

3. Net gain (or loss) from lines 1 and 2. Enter here and on line 2, Schedule D Summary on page 3 of Form 1040 . . . . $

c59—16—75306-1

SCHEDULE F (Form 1040)	U. S. Treasury Department—Internal Revenue Service **SCHEDULE OF FARM INCOME AND EXPENSES** (Compute Social Security Self-Employment Tax on page 3) Attach this schedule to your Income Tax Return, Form 1040	**1959**

For Calendar Year 1959, or other taxable year beginning , 1959, and ending , 19

Name and Address as shown on page 1, Form 1040

FARM INCOME FOR TAXABLE PERIOD—CASH RECEIPTS AND DISBURSEMENTS METHOD

(Report receipts from sale of livestock held primarily for sale in the applicable column below. Do not include other sales of livestock such as those held for draft, breeding, or dairy purposes; report such sales on Schedule D (Form 1040))

SALES OF LIVESTOCK AND PRODUCE RAISED						OTHER FARM INCOME	
Kind	Quantity	1. Amount	Kind	Quantity	2. Amount	Items	3. Amount
Cattle		$	Dairy products		$	Mdse. rec'd for produce	$
			Eggs			Machine work	
Horses			Meat products			Breeding fees	
Mules			Poultry, dressed			Wood and lumber	
Sheep			Wool			Other forest products	
Swine			Honey			Agricultural program payments	
Poultry			Sirup and sugar				
Bees			Other (specify):			Patronage dividends, rebates or refunds	
Grain							
Hay						Other (specify):	
Cotton							
Tobacco							
Vegetables							
Fruits and nuts							
Total of Columns 1, 2, and 3. Enter here and on line 1 of summary below							$

SALES OF PURCHASED LIVESTOCK AND OTHER PURCHASED ITEMS

a. Description	b. Date acquired	c. Amount received	d. Cost or other basis	e. Profit (or loss)

F

		$	$	$
Total (enter on line 2 of summary below)				$

FARM EXPENSES FOR TAXABLE YEAR (See Instructions)

(Do not include personal or living expenses or expenses not attributable to production of farm income, such as taxes, insurance, repairs, etc., on your dwelling)

Items	1. Amount	Items	2. Amount	Items	3. Amount
Labor hired	$	Veterinary, medicine	$	Freight, trucking	$
Feed purchased		Gasoline, fuel, oil		Amortization	
Seed, plants purchased		Storage, warehousing		Conservation expenses	
Machine hire		Taxes		Other farm expenses (specify):	
Supplies purchased		Insurance			
Repairs, maintenance		Farm interest			
Breeding fees		Utilities			
Fertilizers, lime		Rent of farm, pasturage			

Total of Columns 1, 2, and 3. Enter here and on line 4 of summary below (cash method) or line 6, page 2 (accrual method) $

SUMMARY OF INCOME AND DEDUCTIONS—CASH RECEIPTS AND DISBURSEMENTS METHOD

1. Sale of livestock and produce raised and other farm income	$		**4.** Farm expenses (from above)	$	
2. Profit (or loss) on sale of purchased livestock and other purchased items			**5.** Depreciation (from page 2)		
			6. Other farm deductions (specify):		
3. Gross Profits*	$		**7.** Total Deductions	$	

8. Net farm profit (or loss) (line 3 minus line 7). Enter here and on line 9, page 1, Form 1040. Make your computation of self-employment income and the self-employment tax on page 3 of this schedule. $

* Use this amount for optional method of computing net earnings from self-employment. (See line 13, page 3.)

c59—16—75309-1

DEPRECIATION (See Instructions) **Page 2**

(Do not include property you and your family occupy as a dwelling, its furnishings, and other items used for personal purposes)

1. Kind of property (if buildings, state material of which constructed). Exclude land and other nondepreciable property	2. Date acquired	3. Cost or other basis	4. Depreciation allowed (or allowable) in prior years	5. Method of computing depreciation	6. Rate (%) or life (years)	7. Depreciation for this year
		$	$			$
Total (enter on line 5 of summary on page 1 (cash method) or line 7, below (accrual method))						$

FARM INCOME FOR TAXABLE PERIOD—ACCRUAL METHOD

(Do not include sales of livestock held for draft, breeding, or dairy purposes; report such sales on Schedule D (Form 1040), and omit them from "On hand at beginning of year" column)

Description (Kind of livestock, crops, or other products).	On hand at beginning of year		Purchased during year		Raised during year	Consumed or lost during year	Sold during year		On hand at end of year	
	Quantity	Inventory value	Quantity	Amount paid	Quantity	Quantity	Quantity	Amount received	Quantity	Inventory value

		$		$				$		$
Totals		$ (Enter on line 3)		$ (Enter on line 4)				$ (Enter on line 1(b))		$ (Enter on line 1(a))

SUMMARY OF INCOME AND DEDUCTIONS—ACCRUAL METHOD

1(a). Inventory of livestock, crops, and products at end of year	$		**6.** Farm expenses (from page 1)	$	
(b). Sales of livestock, crops, and products during year			**7.** Depreciation (from above)		
(c). Other farm income (specify):			**8.** Other farm deductions (specify):		
2. Total	$				
3. Inventory of livestock, crops, and products at beginning of year $					
4. Cost of livestock and products purchased during year					
5. Gross profits (line 2 minus the sum of lines 3 and 4)*	$		**9.** Total Deductions	$	
10. Net farm profit (or loss) (line 5 minus line 9). Enter here and on line 9, page 1, Form 1040. Make your computation of self-employment income and the self-employment tax on page 3 of this schedule.				$	

*Use this amount for optional method of computing net earnings from self-employment. (See line 13 page 3.)

c59—16—75309-1

COMPUTATION OF SOCIAL SECURITY SELF-EMPLOYMENT TAX ON FARM EARNINGS
(For social security)
(See instructions—Page 4)

▶ If you had wages of $4,800 or more which were subject to the deduction for social security, do not fill in this page.
▶ Each self-employed person must file a separate schedule. See instructions, page 4, for joint returns and partnerships.
▶ If you had net earnings from self-employment from both farm and nonfarm sources, fill in only lines 11 and 12 (line 13, if applicable), and use separate Schedule C to compute your self-employment tax. Net farm earnings from self-employment should be entered on line 28(d) of separate Schedule C (Form 1040).

NAME OF SELF-EMPLOYED PERSON (as shown on social security card)

CHOICE OF METHODS.—A farmer must report his net farm earnings for self-employment tax purposes. Net earnings may be computed under the optional method (line 13, below) by a farmer (1) whose GROSS profits are $1,800 or less, or (2) whose GROSS profits are more than $1,800 and NET profits are less than $1,200. If your GROSS profits from farming are not more than $1,800 and you elect to use the optional method, you need not complete lines 11 and 12.

11. Net farm profit (or loss) from:
(a) Line 8, page 1 (cash method), or line 10, page 2 (accrual method) .... $
(b) Farm partnerships ....

12. Net earnings from self-employment from farming. Total of line 11 (a) and (b) .... $

Computation Under Optional Method

13. If gross profits from farming (see note below) are:
(a) Not more than $1,800, enter two-thirds of the gross profits ....
(b) More than $1,800 and the net farm profit is less than $1,200, enter $1,200 .... } $

NOTE.—Gross profits from farming are the total of the gross profits on line 3, page 1 (cash method), or line 5, page 2 (accrual method), plus the distributive share of gross profit from farm partnerships as explained on page 4.

If line 12 (or line 13, if used) is under $400, do not fill in rest of page.

Computation of Social Security Self-Employment Tax

14. The largest amount of combined wages and self-employment earnings subject to social security tax is .... $ 4,800 | 00

15. Total wages, covered by social security, paid to you during the taxable year. (For "Covered" wages see "F. I. C. A. Wages" box on Form W-2.) Enter here and on line 7, below .... $

16. Balance (line 14 less line 15) .... $

17. Self-employment income. Enter here and on line 8 below your choice of **EITHER:**
(a) REGULAR METHOD.—The smaller of line 12 or 16 ....
(b) OPTIONAL METHOD.—The smaller of line 13 or 16 .... $

18. Self-employment tax—take $3\frac{3}{4}\%$ of the amount on line 17. (You can do this by multiplying the amount on line 17 by .0375.) Enter this amount here and on line 15, page 1, Form 1040 .... $

Important.—The amounts reported on the form below are for your social security account. This account is used in figuring any benefits, based on your earnings, payable to you, your dependents, and your survivors. Fill in each item **accurately** and **completely**, but do not detach.

SCHEDULE SE (Form 1040)
U. S. Treasury Department
Internal Revenue Service

U. S. REPORT OF SELF-EMPLOYMENT INCOME
For Crediting to Your Social Security Account

1959

1. Indicate year covered by this return (even though income was received only in part of year):
☐ Calendar year 1959 ☐ Other taxable year beginning ________ 1959, ending ________.
If less than 12 months, was short year due to (a) ☐ Death, or (b) ☐ Change in accounting period, or (c) ☐ Other.

2. FARM ACTIVITIES SUBJECT TO SELF-EMPLOYMENT TAX (Raising livestock, custom harvesting, etc.)

3. FARM ADDRESS (Rural Route, Post Office, State)

4. SOCIAL SECURITY ACCOUNT NUMBER OF PERSON NAMED IN ITEM 5 BELOW ➔

5. PRINT OR TYPE NAME OF SELF-EMPLOYED PERSON AS SHOWN ON SOCIAL SECURITY CARD

PRINT OR TYPE HOME ADDRESS (Number and Street, or Rural Route)

(City or Town, Postal Zone Number, State)

PLEASE DO NOT WRITE IN THIS SPACE

6. IF YOU USE THE OPTIONAL METHOD, CHECK HERE ☐ AND ENTER THE AMOUNT FROM LINE 13. OTHERWISE ENTER AMOUNT FROM LINE 12....

7. ENTER WAGES, IF ANY, FROM LINE 15 ABOVE.. $

8. ENTER AMOUNT FROM LINE 17 ABOVE.. $

S E

c59—16—75309—1 U. S. GOVERNMENT PRINTING OFFICE

FORM **1041**

U. S. Treasury Department
Internal Revenue Service

U. S. FIDUCIARY INCOME TAX RETURN

(FOR ESTATES AND TRUSTS)
FOR CALENDAR YEAR

or other taxable year beginning............, 1959
and ending............, 19...

1959

Do not write in space below

PLEASE TYPE OR PRINT PLAINLY

Name of Estate or Trust. Check Whether Estate ☐, Simple Trust ☐, Complex Trust ☐

Name, Address, and Title of Fiduciary

Simple trusts are not required to fill in the schedules on page 4. They need complete only the lines and schedules on pages 1, 2, and 3 that apply to them. See page 2 of instructions.

Line and Instruction No.

INCOME

1. Dividends (Enter full amount before exclusion)............
2. Interest on bank deposits, notes, corporation bonds, etc............
3. Interest on tax-free covenant bonds upon which a Federal income tax was paid at source............
4. Interest on Government obligations, etc............
5. Income from partnerships and other fiduciaries **(See Instruction 5)**............
Name and address ....
6. Gross rents and royalties............
7. Gross profit (or loss) from trade or business............
8. (a) Net gain (or loss) from sale or exchange of capital assets (from line 10, Schedule D)............
(b) Net gain (or loss) from sale or exchange of property other than capital assets (from line 19, Schedule D)............
9. Other income **(State nature of income)**............
10. Total income (lines 1 to 9, inclusive)............

DEDUCTIONS

11. Interest (Explain in Schedule A)............
12. Taxes (Explain in Schedule A)............

13. Fiduciary's portion of depreciation (Schedule B) and depletion. Explain depletion		
14. Charitable deduction (line 9, Schedule F)		
15. Other deductions authorized by law (Explain in Schedule A)		
16. Total (lines 11 to 15, inclusive)		
17. Line 10 minus line 16. (Complex trusts and estates enter this amount on line 1 in Schedule G, also)		
18. Deduction for distributions to beneficiaries		
19. Adjustment of dividend exclusion (not to exceed $50) **(See Instruction 19)**		
20. Federal estate tax attributable to income in respect of a decedent (Fiduciary's share)		
21. Long-term capital gain deduction. Enter 50% of line 11 (e), Schedule D		
22. Exemption (Trusts see instructions; $600 for an estate)		
23. Total (lines 18 to 22, inclusive)		
24. Taxable income of fiduciary (line 17 minus line 23)		

COMPUTATION OF TAX

25. Tax on amount on line 24 **(See Tax Rate Schedule in Instruction 25)**		
26. If alternative tax is applicable, enter the tax from line 17, Schedule D		
27. Fiduciary's share of foreign tax credit **(Attach Form 1116)**		
28. Fiduciary's share of credit for tax paid at source on tax-free covenant bond interest		
29. Fiduciary's share of dividends received credit (line 7, Schedule E)		
30. Fiduciary's share of credit for partially tax-exempt interest		
31. Credit for tax deemed paid on undistributed capital gains of regulated investment companies		
32. Tax previously paid, or withheld **(See Instruction 32 and attach explanation)**		
33. Total of lines 27 to 32, inclusive		
34. Balance of tax or overpayment (subtract line 33 from line 25 or line 26, whichever is applicable)		

SIGNATURE AND VERIFICATION (See General Instruction E)

I declare under the penalties of perjury that this return (including any accompanying schedules and statements) has been examined by me and to the best of my knowledge and belief is a true, correct, and complete return. If the return is prepared by a person other than the fiduciary, his declaration is based on all the information relating to the matters required to be reported in the return of which he has knowledge.

(Signature of fiduciary or officer representing fiduciary) (Date)

(Signature of preparer other than fiduciary) 16—75405-1 (Address) (Date)

Page 2

Schedule A.—EXPLANATION OF DEDUCTIONS CLAIMED ON LINES 11, 12, and 15, PAGE 1 (See Instruction 33)

Line No.	Explanation	Amount	Line No.	Explanation	Amount

Schedule B.—EXPLANATION OF DEDUCTION FOR DEPRECIATION (See Instruction 34)

1. Kind of property (if buildings, state material of which constructed). Exclude land and other nondepreciable property.	2. Date acquired	3. Cost or other basis	4. Depreciation allowed (or allowable) in prior years	5. Method of computing depreciation	6. Rate (%) or life (years)	7. Depreciation for this year
1.						

2. Total depreciation..........

3. Total fiduciary's portion. Enter here and on line 13, page 1..........

Schedule C.—BENEFICIARIES' SHARES OF INCOME AND CREDITS (Estates and complex trusts, see Instruction 35)

1. Name of each beneficiary (Designate nonresident aliens, if any)	2. Address (Where return of beneficiary is filed in another internal revenue district, specify district, if known)
(a)	
(b)	
(c)	
(d)	

Continuation of Schedule C

	3. Amount of income required to be distributed currently	4. Other amounts paid, credited, or otherwise required to be distributed	5. Domestic dividends qualifying for credit	6. Partially tax-exempt interest included in amount on line 4, page 1	7. Income taxable to beneficiaries less portion reportable in cols. 5, 6, 8, 9 and 10
(a)					
(b)					
(c)					
(d)					
Totals					

Continuation of Schedule C

	8. Net short-term capital gain	9. Net long-term capital gain (100%)	10. Tax-exempt income, and foreign income of a foreign trust (enter total only)	11. Federal income tax paid at source (2% of line 3, page 1, less line 28, page 1)	12. Income and profits taxes paid to a foreign country or United States possession	13. Depreciation and depletion
(a)						
(b)						
(c)						
(d)						
Totals						

ADDITIONAL INFORMATION REQUIRED

1. Was an income tax return (Form 1041) filed for the preceding year? ☐ Yes ☐ No.
If answer is "Yes," to which District Director's office was it sent? ....

2. Date trust was created or, if an estate, date of decedent's death ....

3. If copy of will or trust instrument and statement required under General Instruction "H" have been previously furnished, do not file again but enter date and place where filed.
....
....

4. If you had tax-exempt income, have you deducted only that portion of expenses allocable to taxable income? ☐ Yes ☐ No

5. If return is for a trust, enter name and address of grantor:
....
....

6. If return is for an estate, has a United States Estate Tax Return been filed? ☐ Yes ☐ No.

If answer is "No," will such a return be filed?
☐ Yes ☐ No ☐ Uncertain

16—75405-1

Simple trusts not having entries on this page may tear off pages 3 and 4 and file only pages 1 and 2

Schedule D.—GAINS AND LOSSES FROM SALES OR EXCHANGES OF PROPERTY (See Instruction 36)

(I) CAPITAL ASSETS

Short-Term Capital Gains and Losses—Assets Held Not More Than 6 Months

a. Kind of property (if necessary, attach statement of descriptive details not shown below)	b. Date acquired (mo., day, yr.)	c. Date sold (mo., day, yr.)	d. Gross sales price (contract price)	e. Depreciation allowed (or allowable) since acquisition or March 1, 1913 (attach schedule)	f. Cost or other basis and cost of subsequent improvements (if not purchased, attach explanation)	g. Expense of sale	h. Gain or loss (column d plus column e less sum of columns f and g)
1.							$

2. Enter your share of net short-term gain (or loss) from partnerships and other fiduciaries ....
3. Enter unused capital loss carryover from 5 preceding taxable years (Attach statement) ....
4. Net short-term gain (or loss) from lines 1, 2, and 3. Enter here and on line 8 below..........

Long-Term Capital Gains and Losses—Assets Held More Than 6 Months

5.							$

6. Enter the full amount of your share of net long-term gain (or loss) from partnerships and other fiduciaries..........
7. Net long-term gain (or loss) from lines 5 and 6. Enter here and on line 9 below..........

CAPITAL GAINS AND LOSSES

	1. Beneficiaries	2. Fiduciary	3. Total
8. Net short-term gain or loss from line 4, above			
9. Net long-term gain or loss from line 7, above..........			
10. Total net gain or loss			

Enter on line 8 (a), page 1, the net gain shown on line 10, column 3, above. If net loss on line 10, column 3, above, enter as loss on line 8 (a), page 1, whichever of the following is the smallest amount: (i) the amount of the loss, (ii) taxable income computed without regard to capital gains and losses and the deduction for personal exemption, or (iii) $1,000.

COMPUTATION OF FIDUCIARY'S CAPITAL GAINS DEDUCTION

11. (a) Long-term capital gain shown on line 9, column 3, above ....

(b) Short-term capital loss shown on line 8, column 3, above

(c) Excess of line 11 (a) over line 11 (b), above

(d) Long-term capital gains taxable to beneficiaries. (Total of column 9, Schedule C)

(e) Balance (line 11 (c) minus line 11 (d)). (Enter 50% of this amount on line 21, page 1)

COMPUTATION OF ALTERNATIVE TAX

If fiduciary had a net long-term capital gain or an excess of net long-term capital gain over net short-term capital loss shown in column 2, line 10, above, and line 24, page 1, exceeds $18,000, he may find it to his advantage to make the alternative tax computation.

12. Income from line 24, page 1

13. 50% of amount on line 11 (e), above

14. Balance (line 12 minus line 13)

15. Tax on amount on line 14 **(See Tax Rate Schedule in Instruction 25)**

16. 50% of amount on line 13, above

17. Alternative tax (line 15 plus line 16); if less than line 25, page 1, enter this amount on line 26, page 1

(II) PROPERTY OTHER THAN CAPITAL ASSETS

a. Kind of property (if necessary, attach statement of descriptive details not shown below)	b. Date acquired (mo., day, yr.)	c. Date sold (mo., day, yr.)	d. Gross sales price (contract price)	e. Depreciation allowed (or allowable) since acquisition or March 1, 1913 (attach schedule)	f. Cost or other basis and cost of subsequent improvements (if not purchased, attach explanation)	g. Expense of sale	h. Gain or loss (column d plus column e less sum of columns f and g)
18.							$

19. Net gain (or loss). Enter here and on line 8 (b), page 1 $

Schedule E.—FIDUCIARY'S SHARE OF DIVIDEND CREDIT (See Instruction 37)

1. Total domestic corporation dividends qualifying under section 34, before dividend exclusion

2. Beneficiaries' share of dividends from column 5, Schedule C

3. Adjustment of dividend exclusion for 1959 (line 19, page 1)

4. Total (line 2 plus line 3)

5. Fiduciary's share of dividends subject to credit (line 1 minus line 4)

6. Enter: (a) 4% of line 5

(b) Tax shown on line 25 or 26, page 1, less amount on line 27, page 1

(c) 4% of line 24, page 1

7. Enter here and on line 29, page 1, the smallest of the amounts on lines 6 (a), 6 (b), and 6 (c) above

Schedule F.—COMPUTATION OF CHARITABLE DEDUCTION (See Instruction 38)
(Submit statement giving name and address of charitable organization)

1. Amounts paid or permanently set aside for charitable purposes from current year's income ....

2. Tax-exempt interest and foreign income of a foreign trust allocable to charitable distribution.
(Complete lines 3 and 4 below only if gain on line 9, column 2, Schedule D, exceeds loss on line 8, column 2, Schedule D)

3. (a) Long-term capital gain included on line 1 ....
(Do not complete lines (b) and (c) if such amounts are greater than line (a))

(b) Enter gain on line 9, column 2, Schedule D, minus loss on line 8, column 2, Schedule D ....

(c) Enter gain on line 9, column 3, Schedule D, minus loss on line 8, column 3, Schedule D ....

4. Enter 50% of line 3 (a), line 3 (b), or line 3 (c), whichever is smallest ....

5. Enter sum of line 2 and line 4 ....

6. Balance (line 1 minus line 5) ....

7. Enter short-term capital gains and 50% of the long-term capital gains of the current taxable year allocable to corpus, paid or permanently set aside for charitable purposes ....

8. Amounts paid or permanently set aside for charitable purposes other than from income of the current year ....

9. Total (line 6 plus lines 7 and 8). Enter here and on line 14, page 1 ....

Schedule G.—COMPUTATION OF DISTRIBUTABLE NET INCOME (See Instruction 39)

1. Enter amount from line 17, page 1 ....

2. Add: (a) Tax-exempt interest (as adjusted) ....

(b) Foreign income of a foreign trust (as adjusted) ....

(c) Net gain shown on line 10, column 1, Schedule D. If net loss, enter zero ....

(d) Lines 4 and 7, Schedule F ....

(e) Short-term capital gain included on line 1, Schedule F ....

(f) If amount on line 8 (a), page 1, is a loss, enter amount here	
3. Total (line 1 through line 2 (f))	
4. If amount on line 8 (a), page 1, is a gain, enter amount here	
5. Distributable net income (line 3 minus line 4)	

Schedule H.—COMPUTATION OF DISTRIBUTIONS DEDUCTION (See Instruction 40)

1. Total of columns 3 and 4 of Schedule C	
2. Enter the total of column 10, Schedule C	
3. Balance (line 1 minus line 2)	
4. Enter distributable net income (line 5, Schedule G)	
5. Enter the total of lines 2 (a) and 2 (b) of Schedule G	
6. Balance (line 4 minus line 5)	
7. Distributions deduction. (Enter here and on line 18, page 1, the lesser of line 3 or line 6 above)	

During the taxable year did you make an accumulation distribution as defined in Sec. 665(b)? See General Instruction Q.

☐ **Yes** ☐ **No. If "Yes," attach Schedule J (Form 1041).**

☆ U.S. GOVERNMENT PRINTING OFFICE: 1959—O-513529

16—75405-1

FORM **1065**

U.S. Treasury Department
Internal Revenue Service

U.S. PARTNERSHIP RETURN OF INCOME

(To Be Filed Also by Syndicates, Pools, Joint Ventures, Etc.)

FOR CALENDAR YEAR 1959

1959

or other taxable year beginning ...., 1959, and ending ...., 19.....

(PLEASE TYPE OR PRINT PLAINLY)

Name

Number and Street

City, town, postal zone number, State

Employer's Identification Number

Line and Instruction No.	INCOME		
1.	Gross receipts or gross sales .... Less: Returns and allowances		
2.	Less: Cost of Goods Sold (Schedule A)		
3.	Gross profit (line 1 less line 2)		
4.	Income (or loss) from other partnerships, syndicates, etc. **(Attach statement)**		
5.	Nonqualifying dividends (See Instruction 5)		
6.	Interest (fully taxable)		
7.	Rents (Schedule B)		
8.	Royalties **(Attach schedule)**		
9.	Net farm profit (or loss) (Schedule F, Form 1040)		
10.	Net gain (or loss) from sale or exchange of property other than capital assets (from line 12, Separate Schedule D, Form 1065)		
11.	Other income **(Attach schedule)**		
12.	Total income (lines 3 through 11)		

DEDUCTIONS

13. Salaries and wages (other than to partners)		
14. Payments to partners—salaries and interest		
15. Rent		
16. Interest (Explain in Schedule C)		
17. Taxes (Explain in Schedule C)		
18. Losses by fire, storm, shipwreck, or other casualty or theft **(Attach statement)**		
19. Bad debts (Schedule H)		
20. Repairs		
21. Depreciation (Schedule I)		
22. Amortization **(Attach schedule)**		
23. Depletion of mines, oil and gas wells, timber, etc. **(Attach schedule)**		
24. Other deductions authorized by law (Explain in Schedule J)		
25. Total deductions (lines 13 through 24)		
26. Ordinary income (or loss) (line 12 less line 25)		

A. Date business commenced ....

B. County in which located ....

C. Principal business activity (See General Instruction K) ....

D. Is any member of the partnership related by blood or marriage to any other member? ☐ Yes ☐ No

E. Is any member of the partnership a trust for the benefit of any person related by blood or marriage to any other member? ☐ Yes ☐ No

F. Did the partnership, during the taxable year, have any contracts or subcontracts subject to the Renegotiation Act of 1951? ☐ Yes ☐ No

If "Yes," see General Instruction P and enter appropriate amount here ..... $ ....

I declare under the penalties of perjury that this return (including any accompanying schedules and statements) has been examined by me, and to the best of my knowledge and belief is a true, correct, and complete return. If the return is prepared by a person other than a partner or member, his declaration is based on all the information relating to the matters required to be reported in the return of which he has any knowledge.

Sign here ....
(Signature of partner or member) .... (Date)

....
(Signature of preparer other than partner or member) .... (Address) .... (Date)

Form 1065—1959

Schedule A.—COST OF GOODS SOLD

Page 2

1. Opening inventory		
2. Purchases		
3. Cost of labor, supplies, etc.		
4. Total of lines 1, 2, and 3		
5. Less: Closing inventory		
6. Cost of Goods Sold. Enter here and on line 2, page 1		

Note: Any items specially allocated to the partners should be included in the appropriate column of Schedule K, instead of the lines indicated by Schedules B through J. (See General Instruction Q)

Schedule B.—INCOME FROM RENTS

1. Kind and location of property	2. Amount of rent	3. Depreciation (explain in Schedule I)	4. Repairs (explain in Schedule B-1)	5. Other expenses (explain in Sched. B-1)
1. Totals				
2. Net income (or loss) (column 2 less sum of columns 3, 4, and 5). (Enter on line 7, page 1)				

Schedule B-1.—EXPLANATION OF COLUMNS 4 AND 5 OF SCHEDULE B

Column	Explanation	Amount	Column	Explanation	Amount

Schedule C.—EXPLANATION OF LINES 16 and 17, Page 1

Explanation	Amount	Explanation	Amount

Schedule D.—ATTACH SCHEDULE D (Form 1065) TO REPORT SALES OR EXCHANGES OF PROPERTY

Schedule H.—BAD DEBTS. (See Instruction 19)

1. Taxable year	2. Net profit from business	3. Sales on account	4. Bad debts of organization if no reserve is carried on books	If organization carried a reserve	
				5. Gross amount added to reserve	6. Amount charged against reserve
1956...					
1957...					
1958...					
1959...					

NOTE.—Securities which are capital assets and which became worthless within the taxable year should be reported in separate Schedule D, Form 1065.

c59—16—75400-1

Schedule I.—DEPRECIATION. (See Instruction 21)

1. Kind of property (if buildings, state material of which constructed). Exclude land and other nondepreciable property	2. Date acquired	3. Cost or other basis	4. Depreciation allowed (or allowable) in prior years	5. Method of computing depreciation	6. Rate (%) or life (years)	7. Depreciation for this year
Additional first year depreciation (See Instruction 21)						
1. Total						
2. Less: Amount of depreciation claimed in Schedules A and B and elsewhere on return						
3. Balance—Enter here and on line 21, page 1						

Schedule J.—OTHER DEDUCTIONS. (See Instruction 24)

Explanation	Amount	Explanation	Amount

		Total (Enter on line 24, page 1)	

Schedule K.—PARTNERS' SHARES OF INCOME, CREDITS, AND DEDUCTIONS

1. State name and address of each partner. (Designate nonresident aliens, if any.) Where return of partner or member is filed in another internal revenue district, specify district	2. Percentage of time devoted to business	3. Ordinary income (or loss) (line 26, page 1)
(a)		
(b)		
(c)		
(d)		
(e)		
Totals		

Continuation of Schedule K

	4. Payments to partners—salaries and interest (line 14, page 1)	5. Contributions (Attach itemized list)	6. Net short-term gain (or loss) from sale or exchange of capital assets (from line 3, Schedule D)	7. Net long-term gain (or loss) from sale or exchange of capital assets (from line 6, Schedule D)	8. Net gain (or loss) under section 1231 (from line 9, Schedule D)	9. Net earnings from self-employment (from line 10, Schedule N)
(a)						
(b)						
(c)						
(d)						
(e)						
Totals						

NOTE.—See the instructions for other items required to be reported separately.

c59—16—75400—1

Schedule L.—BALANCE SHEETS

ASSETS	Beginning of Taxable Year		End of Taxable Year	
	Amount	Total	Amount	Total
1. Cash				
2. Notes and accounts receivable				
Less: Reserve for bad debts				
3. Inventories:				
(a) Other than last-in, first-out				
(b) Last-in, first-out				
4. Investments in Government obligations				
5. Other current assets—including short term marketable investments **(Attach schedule)**				
6. Other investments **(Attach schedule)**				
7. Buildings and other fixed depreciable assets				
Less: Accumulated amortization and depreciation				
8. Depletable assets				
Less: Accumulated depletion				
9. Land (Net of any amortization)				
10. Intangible assets **(Amortizable only)**				
Less: Accumulated amortization				
11. Other assets **(Attach schedule)**				
12. Total Assets				
LIABILITIES AND CAPITAL				
13. Accounts payable				
14. Mortgages, notes, and loans payable (short term):				
(a) Banks				
(b) Others				
15. Other current liabilities **(Attach schedule)**				

16. Mortgages, notes, and loans payable (long term):

(a) Banks..........

(b) Others..........

17. Other liabilities (**Attach schedule**)..........

18. Partners' capital accounts..........

19. Total Liabilities and Capital..........

Schedule M.—RECONCILIATION OF PARTNERS' CAPITAL ACCOUNTS

	1. Capital account at beginning of year	2. Capital contributed during year	3. Income not included in column 4 plus nontaxable income	4. Ordinary income (or loss) from line 26, page 1	5. Losses not included in column 4, plus unallowable deductions	6. Withdrawals and distributions	7. Capital account at end of year
(a)...							
(b)...							
(c)...							
(d)...							
(e)...							

Schedule N.—COMPUTATION OF NET EARNINGS FROM SELF-EMPLOYMENT. (See Instruction for Schedule N)

1. Ordinary income increased by casualty losses (line 26 plus line 18, page 1). Do not include income received for the performance of services as a doctor of medicine..........

2. Add: Payments to partners—salaries and interest (line 14, page 1)..........

3. Net loss from sale or exchange of property other than capital assets (line 10, page 1)..

4. Total..........

5. Less: Portion of line 4, page 1, which does not constitute net earnings from self-employment....

6. Nonqualifying dividends (from line 5, page 1)..........

7. Interest (See instructions)..........

8. Net rentals from real estate..........

9. Net gain from sale or exchange of property other than capital assets (line 10, page 1)..

10. Net earnings from self-employment. (Enter in column 9, Schedule K)..........

c59—16—75400-1 U.S. GOVERNMENT PRINTING OFFICE

FORM **1120**

U.S. Treasury Department
Internal Revenue Service

U.S. CORPORATION INCOME TAX RETURN—1959

or Other Taxable Year Beginning ______________, 1959, Ending ______________, 19__
(PLEASE TYPE OR PRINT)

A. Check if taxpayer is a sole proprietorship ☐ or partnership ☐ electing under section 1361 to be taxed as a corporation.

B. Is this a consolidated return? ☐ Yes ☐ No (See Instruction I)

C. Are you a personal holding company? ☐ Yes ☐ No (See Instruction H)

Name

Number and street

City or town, postal zone number, State

D. Total assets from line 13 Sch. L (See instruction O)....$

E. County in which located

F. Are you a resident foreign corporation? ☐ Yes ☐ No
If "yes," place incorporated

GROSS INCOME

		Gross Amount of Interest	Less: Amortizable Bond Premium	
1.	Gross Receipts ______ Less: Returns and allowances ______			
2.	**Less:** Cost of goods sold (Schedule A) and/or operations (Attach Schedule)			
3.	Gross Profit			
4.	Dividends (Schedule C)			
5.	Interest on obligations of the United States, etc. issued: (a) Prior to 3-1-41—(1) U.S. savings and Treasury bonds owned in excess of the principal amount of $5,000; and (2) obligations of a U.S. instrumentality			
	(b) On or after 3-1-41, by the U.S. or any agency or any instrumentality thereof			
6.	Other interest			
7.	(a) Rents ______ (b) Royalties ______			
8.	Net gains (losses) (from separate Schedule D)			
9.	Other income (Attach schedule)			
10.	TOTAL income, lines 3 to 9, inclusive			
11.	Compensation of officers (Schedule E)			
12.	Salaries and wages (not deducted elsewhere)			
13.	Repairs (Do not include cost of improvements or capital expenditures)			
14.	(a) Bad debts (Sch. F) ______ (b) Rents ______			

DEDUCTIONS

15. (a) Taxes (Sch. B) ______ (b) Interest ______
16. Contributions or gifts paid (Attach schedule) ......
17. Losses by fire, storm, shipwreck, or other casualty, or theft (Attach sch.) ......
18. (a) Amortization (Attach sch.) ______ (b) Depletion ______
19. Depreciation (Schedule G) ......
20. Advertising ......
21. Amounts contributed under:
    (a) Pension, profit-sharing, stock bonus, annuity plans (Attach sch.) ......
    (b) Other employee benefit plans (Attach sch.) ......
22. Other deductions (Attach schedule) ......
23. TOTAL deductions in lines 11 to 22, inclusive ......
24. Taxable income before net operating loss deduction and special deductions (line 10 less line 23) ......
25. **Less:** Net operating loss deduction ......
26. Taxable income before special deductions ......
27. Special deductions (Schedule I) ......
28. Line 26 less line 27 ......

TAX

29. TOTAL income tax (from line 9, Tax Computation Schedule, page 3) ......
30. Credits for amounts paid on 1959 income tax:
    (a) Tax paid with application for extension of time in which to file ......
    (b) Payments and credits on 1959 Declaration of Estimated Tax ......
31. If tax (line 29) is larger than payments (line 30), the balance is TAX DUE. Enter balance here→
32. If payments (line 30) are larger than tax (line 29) ...... Enter the OVERPAYMENT here→
33. Enter amount of line 32 you want: Credited on 1960 estimated tax ______ Refunded

SIGNATURE AND VERIFICATION (See Instruction E)

I declare under the penalties of perjury that this return (including any accompanying schedules and statements) has been examined by me and to the best of my knowledge and belief is a true, correct, and complete return. If the return is prepared by a person other than the taxpayer, his declaration is based on all the information relating to the matters required to be reported in the return of which he has knowledge.

CORPORATE SEAL

______ (Date) ______ (Signature of officer) ______ (Title)

______ (Date) ______ (Individual or firm signature) ______ (Address)

c59—16—75410—1

Page 2

Schedule A.—COST OF GOODS SOLD. (See Instruction 2)
(Where inventories are an income-determining factor)

1. Inventory at beginning of year	
2. Merchandise bought for manufacture or sale	
3. Salaries and wages	
4. Other costs per books (Attach schedule)	
5. Total	
6. Less: Inventory at end of year	
7. Cost of goods sold (Enter here and on line 2, page 1)	

Schedule B.—TAXES. (See Instruction 15(a))

Explanation	Amount
Total (Enter here and on line 15(a), page 1)	

Schedule C.—INCOME FROM DIVIDENDS

1. Name of Declaring Corporation	2. Domestic Corporations Taxable Under Chapter 1, Internal Revenue Code*	3. Certain Preferred Stock of Public Utilities Taxable Under Chapter 1, Internal Revenue Code	4. Foreign Corporations	5. Other Corporations
Totals				
Total of columns 2, 3, 4, and 5 (Enter here and on line 4, page 1)				

*Except (a) dividends on certain preferred stock of public utilities, which should be entered in column 3; and (b) dividends, which should be entered in column 5, received from China Trade Act corporations, from corporations to which section 931 applies, and from corporations exempt from tax under sections 501 and 521.

Schedule D.—Separate Schedule D (Form 1120) should be used in reporting sales or exchanges of property. (See Instruction 8)

Schedule E.—COMPENSATION OF OFFICERS

1. Name and Address of Officer	2. Official Title	3. Time Devoted to Business	Percentage of Corporation's Stock Owned		6. Amount of Compensation
			4. Common	5. Preferred	

Total compensation of officers (Enter here and on line 11, page 1) ....

Schedule F.—BAD DEBTS. (See Instruction 14(a))

1. Taxable Year	Amount of Notes and Accounts Receivable Outstanding at—		4. Taxable Income Reported	5. Sales on Account	6. Bad Debts of Corporation if No Reserve Is Carried on Books	If Corporation Carries a Reserve	
	2. Beginning of Year	3. End of Year				7. Gross Amount Added to Reserve	8. Amount Charged Against Reserve
1956.							
1957.							
1958.							
1959.							

NOTE: Securities which are capital assets and which became worthless within the taxable year should be reported in separate Schedule D.

Schedule G.—DEPRECIATION. (See Instruction 19 and Schedule H)

1. Kind of Property (if buildings, state material of which constructed). Exclude Land and Other Nondepreciable Property. List Assets in Groups by Depreciation Method	2. Date Acquired	3. Cost or Other Basis	4. Depreciation Allowed (or allowable) in Prior Years	5. Method of Computing Depreciation	6. Rate (%) or Life (years)	7. Depreciation This Year

1. Total ....
2. Less: Amount of depreciation claimed in Schedule A and elsewhere on return....
3. Balance—Enter here and on line 19, page 1....

c59—16—75410-1

Schedule H.—SUMMARY OF AMORTIZATION AND DEPRECIATION SCHEDULES

Part A.—DEPRECIATION		Part B.—AMORTIZATION	
1. Straight line method		8. Emergency facilities	
2. Declining balance method		9. Grain storage facilities	
3. Sum of the years-digits method		10. Research or experimental expenditures	
4. Based on units of production		11. Exploration and development expenditures	
5. Addl. 1st year (Sec. 179)		12. Organizational expenditures	
6. Other methods		13. Trademark and trade name expenditures	
7. Total depreciation claimed		14. Total amortization claimed	

Schedule I.—SPECIAL DEDUCTIONS

1. Deduction for partially tax-exempt interest (See Instruction 5)		
2. Dividends-received deductions:		
(a) 85 percent of column 2, Schedule C		
(b) 62.115 percent of column 3, Schedule C		
(c) 85 percent of dividends received from certain foreign corporations		
3. Total dividends-received deductions (sum of lines 2 (a), (b), and (c) but not to exceed 85 percent of the excess of line 24, page 1 over the sum of lines 1 and 5). (See Instructions in case of net operating loss or if the corporation is a small business investment company.)		
4. Deduction for dividends paid on certain preferred stock of public utilities (See Instructions in case of net operating loss)		
5. Deduction for Western Hemisphere trade corporations (See Instructions in case of net operating loss)		
6. Total special deductions (enter here and on line 27, page 1)		

TAX COMPUTATION FOR CALENDAR YEAR 1959 AND TAXABLE YEARS ENDING ON OR BEFORE JUNE 30, 1960

For other taxable years attach Schedule 1120 FY (See tax computation instructions)

1. (a) Line 28, page 1 ______ (b) plus line 1, Schedule I ______ Enter total here →		
2. If amount of line 1 is:		
(a) **Not over $25,000**—Enter 30 percent of line 1 (32 percent if a consolidated return)		
(b) **Over $25,000**—		
Enter 52 percent of line 1 (54 percent if a consolidated return)		
Subtract $5,500, and enter difference	5,500.00	

3. Adjustment for partially tax-exempt interest. Enter 30 percent of line 1 (b), but not in excess of 30 percent of line 1 . . ______
4. Normal tax and surtax (line 2 less line 3) . . . . ______
5. Income tax (line 4, or line 20 of separate Schedule D) . . . . ______
6. Credit allowed a domestic corporation for income taxes paid to a foreign country or United States possession (submit Form 1118) . . . . ______
7. Balance of income tax (line 5 less line 6) . . . . ______
8. Tax under section 541 of the Internal Revenue Code (from Schedule 1120 PH) . . . . ______
9. Total income tax (line 7 plus line 8). **Enter here and on line 29, page 1** . . . . ______

ADDITIONAL INFORMATION REQUIRED

G. Employer Identification No. ______

H. Date incorporated ______

I. Did the corporation at any time during the taxable year own directly or indirectly 50 percent or more of the voting stock of a domestic corporation? . . . . ☐ Yes ☐ No
Did any corporation, individual, partnership, trust, or association at any time during taxable year own directly or indirectly 50 percent or more of the corporation's voting stock? . ☐ Yes ☐ No
If either answer is "Yes," attach separate schedule showing:
(1) name and address;
(2) percentage of stock owned;
(3) date stock was acquired; and
(4) the District Director's office in which the income tax return of such corporation, individual, partnership, trust, or association for the last taxable year was filed.

J. Did the corporation make a return of information on Forms 1096 and 1099 for the calendar year 1959 in connection with:
Taxable dividends . . . . ☐ Yes ☐ No
Other payments . . . . ☐ Yes ☐ No
(See Instruction G–(1).)

K. Did the corporation, during the taxable year, have any contracts or subcontracts subject to the Renegotiation Act of 1951 . . . . ☐ Yes ☐ No
If answer is "Yes," state the approximate aggregate gross dollar amount billed during the taxable year under all such contracts and/or subcontracts. (See Instruction G–(4)) . . . . . . ______

L. Did the corporation at any time during the taxable year own directly or indirectly any stock of a foreign corporation? . . . . ☐ Yes ☐ No
If answer is "Yes," attach statement as required by Inst. K.

M. Enter amount of income (or deficit) from:
(a) line 32, page 3, Form 1120, 1956 . . ______
(b) line 32, page 3, Form 1120, 1957 . . ______
(c) line 32, page 3, Form 1120, 1958 . . ______

N. If corporation is a cooperative association, check whether:
(1) ☐ farmers' marketing or a farmers' purchasing cooperative association,
(2) ☐ consumers' cooperative association, or
(3) ☐ other cooperative association.

O. Business group code No. and principal business activity (see Page 8, instructions) ______

c59—16—75410-1

Schedule L.—BALANCE SHEETS (See Instructions)

ASSETS	Beginning of Taxable Year — Amount	Beginning of Taxable Year — Total	End of Taxable Year — Amount	End of Taxable Year — Total
1. Cash				
2. Investments in governmental obligations:				
(a) United States and its instrumentalities				
(b) State, Territory, or a possession of the U.S., any political subdivision thereof, or the Dist. of Columbia				
3. Notes and accounts receivable				
(a) Less: Reserve for bad debts				
4. Inventories: (a) Other than last-in, first-out				
(b) Last-in, first-out				
5. Other current assets including short term marketable investments (Attach schedule)				
6. Mortgage and real estate loans				
7. Other investments (Attach schedule)				
8. Buildings and other fixed depreciable assets				
(a) Less: Accumulated amortization and depreciation				
9. Depletable assets				
(a) Less: Accumulated depletion				
10. Land (net of any amortization)				
11. Intangible assets (amortizable only)				
(a) Less: Accumulated amortization				
12. Other assets (Attach schedule)				
13. Total Assets				
LIABILITIES AND CAPITAL				
14. Accounts payable				
15. Deposits and withdrawable shares				

16. Bonds, notes, and mortgages payable (maturing less than one year from date of balance sheet)				
17. Other current liabilities (Attach schedule)				
18. Bonds, notes, and mortgages payable (maturing one year or more from date of balance sheet)				
19. Other liabilities (Attach schedule)				
20. Capital stock: (a) Preferred stock				
(b) Common stock				
21. Paid-in or capital surplus				
22. Surplus reserves (Attach schedule)				
23. Earned surplus and undivided profits				
24. Total Liabilities and Capital				

Schedule M.—RECONCILIATION OF TAXABLE INCOME AND ANALYSIS OF EARNED SURPLUS AND UNDIVIDED PROFITS

1. Earned surplus and undivided profits at end of preceding taxable year (Schedule L)	
2. Taxable income before net operating loss deduction and special deductions (line 24, page 1)	
3. Nontaxable interest on: (a) Obligations of a State, Territory, or a possession of the United States, or any political subdivision of any of the foregoing, or the Dist. of Columbia	
(b) Obligations of the United States issued on or before Sept. 1, 1917; all postal savings bonds	
4. Other nontaxable income (Attach schedule)	
5. Charges against surplus reserves deducted from income in this return (Attach schedule)	
6. Adjustments for tax purposes not recorded on books (Attach sch.)	
7. Sundry credits to earned surplus (Attach schedule)	
8. Total of lines 1 to 7	

9. Total distributions to stockholders charged to earned surplus during the taxable year: (a) Cash	
(b) Stock of the corporation	
(c) Other property (Attach schedule)	
10. Contributions in excess of 5% limitation	
11. Federal income and excess profits taxes	
12. Income taxes of foreign countries or United States possessions if claimed as a credit in whole or in part on line 6, page 3 Tax Computation	
13. Insurance premiums paid on the life of any officer or employee where the corporation is directly or indirectly a beneficiary	
14. Unallowable interest incurred to purchase or carry tax-exempt interest obligations	
15. Excess of capital losses over capital gains	
16. Additions to surplus reserves (Attach schedule)	
17. Other unallowable deductions (Attach schedule)	
18. Adjustments for tax purposes not recorded on books (Attach schedule)	
19. Sundry debits to earned surplus (Attach schedule)	
20. Total of lines 9 to 19	
21. Earned surplus and undivided profits at end of the taxable year (Schedule L) (Line 8 less line 20)	

c59—16—75410-1 GPO

SCHEDULE D (Form 1120)

U. S. TREASURY DEPARTMENT—INTERNAL REVENUE SERVICE

SCHEDULE OF GAINS AND LOSSES FROM SALES OR EXCHANGES OF PROPERTY

1959

FOR CALENDAR YEAR 1959

or other taxable year beginning , 1959, and ending , 19

Name and address

PART I.—CAPITAL ASSETS

a. Description of Property	b. Date Acquired Mo. Day Yr.	c. Date Sold Mo. Day Yr.	d. Gross Sales Price (Contract price)	e. Depreciation Allowed (or allowable) Since Acquisition or March 1, 1913 (Attach schedule)	f. Cost or Other Basis and Cost of Improvements Subsequent to Acquisition or March 1, 1913	g. Expense of Sale	h. Gain or Loss (Column d plus column e less the sum of columns f and g)
Short-Term Capital Gains and Losses—Assets Held for Not More Than 6 Months							
1.							

2. Unused capital loss carryover from five preceding taxable years (attach statement)	
3. Total of short-term capital gains or losses or difference between short-term capital gains and losses	

Long-Term Capital Gains and Losses—Assets Held for More Than 6 Months

4.							
5. Total of long-term capital gains or losses or difference between long-term capital gains and losses							

Summary of Capital Gains and Losses

Classification	Gain or Loss To Be Taken Into Account	
	a. Gain	b. Loss
6. Net short-term capital gain or loss from line 3		
7. Net long-term capital gain or loss from line 5		
8. Net short-term capital gain (line 6, col. a) reduced by any net long-term capital loss (line 7, col. b). Enter here and on line 1, Part III, page 2		x x x x x x x x x
9. Net long-term capital gain (line 7, col. a) reduced by any net short-term capital loss (line 6, col. b). Enter here and on line 2, Part III, page 2		x x x x x x x x x
10. Excess of losses over gains in lines 6 and 7. This excess is not allowable	x x x x x x x x x	

c59—16—75411-1

Alternative Tax Computation for Calendar Year 1959 and Taxable Years Ending on or Before June 30, 1960

For other taxable years attach Schedule 1120FY

11. Line 1, Tax Computation, page 3, Form 1120		
12. Net long-term capital gain reduced by any net short-term capital loss (line 9 of summary, page 1)		
13. Line 11 minus line 12		
14. If amount of line 13 is:		
(a) **Not over $25,000—**		
Enter 30 percent of line 13 (32 percent if a consolidated return)		
(b) **Over $25,000—**		
Enter 52 percent of line 13 (54 percent if a consolidated return)		
Subtract $5,500 and enter difference	5,500.00	
15. Adjustment for partially tax-exempt interest; enter 30 percent of line 1, Schedule I, page 3, Form 1120, but not in excess of 30 percent of line 13 above		
16. Partial tax (line 14 less line 15)		
17. 25 percent of line 12		
18. Alternative tax (line 16 plus line 17)		
19. Normal tax and surtax (line 4, Tax Computation, page 3, Form 1120)		
20. Income tax (line 18 or 19, whichever is lesser). Enter here and on line 5, Tax Computation, page 3, Form 1120.		

PART II.—PROPERTY OTHER THAN CAPITAL ASSETS

a. Description of Property	b. Date Acquired Mo. Day Yr.	c. Date Sold Mo. Day Yr.	d. Gross Sales Price (Contract price)	e. Depreciation Allowed (or allowable) Since Acquisition or March 1, 1913 (Attach schedule)	f. Cost or Other Basis and Cost of Improvements Subsequent to Acquisition or March 1, 1913	g. Expense of Sale	h. Gain or Loss (Column d plus column e less the sum of columns f and g)
1.							

2. Total net gain (or loss). Enter here and on line 3, Part III, below. . . . .

PART III.—TOTAL SCHEDULE D GAINS AND LOSSES

1. Net short-term capital gain from Part I, page 1, line 8 . . . .
2. Net long-term capital gain from Part I, page 1, line 9 . . . .
3. Net gain (loss) other than capital assets from Part II, page 2, line 2 . . . .
4. Total (lines 1–3). Enter here and on Form 1120, page 1, line 8. . . . .

State with respect to each item of property reported in Schedule D (I) and (II): (1) How property was acquired ____________
(2) Whether at time of sale or exchange—(Check appropriate block(s))

☐ (a) purchaser owned directly or indirectly more than 50 percent in value of your outstanding stock,

☐ (b) where purchaser was a corporation, more than 50 percent in value of its capital stock and 50 percent in value of your capital stock was owned directly or indirectly by or for the same individual or his family, and

☐ (c) where purchaser was a corporation, more than 50 percent in value of its capital stock was owned directly or indirectly by you.

State name and address of purchaser ____

FORM **843**
(Rev. Mar. 1959)

U. S. TREASURY DEPARTMENT - INTERNAL REVENUE SERVICE

CLAIM

TO BE FILED WITH THE DISTRICT DIRECTOR WHERE ASSESSMENT WAS MADE OR TAX PAID

District Director's Stamp
(Date received)

The District Director will indicate in the block below the kind of claim filed, and fill in, where required.

☐ Refund of Taxes Illegally, Erroneously, or Excessively Collected.

☐ Refund of Amount Paid for Stamps Unused, or Used in Error or Excess.

☐ Abatement of Tax Assessed (not applicable to estate, gift, or income taxes).

PLEASE TYPE OR PRINT PLAINLY

Name of taxpayer or purchaser of stamps

Number and street | City, town, postal zone, State

Fill in applicable items—Attach letter size sheets if space is not sufficient.

1. District in which return (if any) was filed

2. Name and address shown on return, if different from above

3. Period—*If for tax reported on annual basis, prepare separate form for each taxable year*

From , 19 , to , 19

4. Kind of tax

5. Amount of assessment
$

Dates of payment

6. Date stamps were purchased from the Government

7. Amount to be refunded
$

8. Amount to be abated (not applicable to income, estate, or gift taxes)
$

9. The claimant believes that this claim should be allowed for the following reasons:

I declare under the penalties of perjury that this claim (including any accompanying schedules and statements) has been examined by me and to the best of my knowledge and belief is true and correct.

Signed ....

Dated ...., 19 ....

INSTRUCTIONS

1. The claim must set forth in detail each ground upon which it is made and facts sufficient to apprise the Commissioner of the exact basis thereof.

2. If a joint income tax return was filed for the year for which this claim is filed, both husband and wife must sign this claim even though only one had income.

3. Whenever it is necessary to have the claim executed by an agent on behalf of the taxpayer, an authenticated copy of the document specifically authorizing such agent to sign the claim on behalf of the taxpayer shall accompany the claim.

4. If a return is filed by an individual and a refund claim is thereafter filed by a legal representative of the deceased, certified copies of the letters testamentary, letters of administration, or other similar evidence must be annexed to the claim, to show the authority of the executor, administrator, or other fiduciary by whom the claim is filed. If an executor, administrator, guardian, trustee, receiver, or other fiduciary files a return and thereafter refund claim is filed by the same fiduciary, documentary evidence to establish the legal authority of the fiduciary need not accompany the claim, provided a statement is made on the claim showing that the return was filed by the fiduciary and that the latter is still acting.

5. Where the taxpayer is a corporation, the claim will be signed with the corporate name, followed by the signature and title of the officer having authority to sign for the corporation.

6. If claim is for excess social security (F.I.C.A.) tax withheld as a result of having had more than one employer, include your social security account number, the names and addresses of your employers, and the amount of wages received and taxes withheld by each as part of your explanation in item 9. Do not claim tax withheld if you have claimed the excess withholding on your individual income tax return.

FORM 843 (Rev. 3–59)

GENERAL INDEX